Marketing Channels

The Prentice Hall International Series in Marketing
Philip Kotler, Series Editor

Marketing Channels

Sixth Edition

Anne T. Coughlan
Associate Professor of Marketing
Northwestern University

Erin Anderson
John H. Loudon Chaired Professor of International Management
INSEAD

Louis W. Stern
John D. Gray Distinguished Professor of Marketing
Northwestern University

Adel I. El-Ansary
Professor of Marketing and Research Fellow
University of North Florida

Upper Saddle River, New Jersey

Library of Congress Cataloging-in-Publication Data

Marketing channels/Anne T. Coughlan . . . [et al.]. — 6th ed.
   p. cm.
  Rev. ed. of: Marketing channels/Louis W. Stern, Adel I. El-Ansary, Anne T.
    Coughlan. 5th ed. c1996.
  Includes bibliographical references and index.
  ISBN 0-13-012772-8
   1. Marketing channels. I. Coughlan, Anne T.
  HF5415.129 .S75 2001
  658.8´4—dc21

                                       00-055058

Senior Editor: Whitney Blake
Editorial Director: Jim Boyd
Assistant Editor: Anthony Palmiotto
Editorial Assistant: Melissa Pellerano
Media Coordinator: Joan Waxman
Marketing Manager: Shannon Moore
Marketing Assistant: Kathleen Mulligan
Managing Editor (Production): John Roberts
Production Editor: Keri Jean
Permissions Coordinator: Suzanne Grappi
Associate Director, Manufacturing: Vincent Scelta
Production Manager: Arnold Vila
Manufacturing Buyer: Diane Peirano
Design Manager: Patricia Smythe
Designer: Steven Frim
Interior Design: Lee Goldstein
Cover Design: Steven Frim
Manager, Print Production: Christy Mahon
Page Formatter: Ashley Scattergood
Composition: Rainbow Graphics
Full-Service Project Management: Bennie Sauls, Rainbow Graphics
Printer/Binder: Courier Westford/Coral Graphics

_100228674?_

Credits and acknowledgments borrowed from other sources and reproduced, with permission, in this textbook appear on appropriate pages within text.

10 9 8 7 6 5 4 3 2 1
ISBN 0-13-012772-8

With love to my husband, Charles B. Jameson,
and to our children, C. J. and Catherine
ANNE T. COUGHLAN

Dédié à mes chères filles, Aline et Valérie
ERIN ANDERSON

With love and affection to my wife, Rhona L. Stern
LOUIS W. STERN

With love and affection to my sons, Waleed and Tarik,
and my daughter-in-law, Iman
ADEL I. EL-ANSARY

Brief Contents

Contents

PART THREE

CHANNEL IMPLEMENTATION AND PERFORMANCE MEASUREMENT

PART FOUR
CHANNEL INSTITUTIONS

Preface

This book is intended for an international audience of practicing and future managers. It is written in English, the international language of business. The subject is marketing channels, the companies that come together to bring products and services from their point of origin to the point of consumption. Marketing channels are the downstream part of a value chain. *The originator of goods or services gains access to a market through marketing channels*. Channels of distribution are a critical element of business strategy.

The ideas in this book apply to any channel for any product or service in any market. The generality of the book is shown in its many examples taken from all over the world. These cover a wealth of different products and services, sold to businesses and consumers, selected from the worldwide business press, research, and consulting. Some examples are autopsies; dog and cat food; personal computers; pleasure boats; dolls; stereo speakers; fast food; tires; garden products; fast-moving consumer goods; maternity clothing; uninterruptible power supplies; maintenance, repair, and operating (MRO) goods; furniture; automobiles; airline travel services; and mutual funds. The variety of the list reinforces the generality of the principles. As is appropriate for an international readership, the presentation of each example is as though the reader is unfamiliar with the product or market in question. This book covers the highlights needed to frame the problem, then covers the channel issues in the examples. Channel Sketches provide detailed examples to improve the readability of the main text.

Each chapter is designed to stand on its own. The chapters may be read in any order, and any chapter may be omitted. Each chapter is of a length that can be assigned for a single class or read in one sitting with a single issue in mind. The chapters are designed modularly. Essential definitions are repeated where necessary so that the reader is free to choose one chapter and defer or omit another. Reference is made to other chapters when appropriate for the reader to go further into any topic raised in the chapter at hand. In this way, the reader can select how deeply to delve into all the sections of the book that most closely fit the problem under consideration.

The content of each chapter comes from the best of current research and practice. This book covers a vast and varied literature, bringing in findings, practice, and viewpoints from multiple disciplines (marketing, strategy, economics, sociology, law, political science) and from the best practices of channel managers worldwide. In presenting these works, the focus is on framing the problem and its solution in the language of business rather than on the technical aspects of the research. Yet the book introduces technical vocabulary in the appropriate instances for the manager. The theory, data, and methods that underlie the content of this book are not detailed. Instead, the relevant references are liberally noted and tied to the content, so that the interested reader may delve further into specific points.

The text is organized into four parts. Part One, "Introduction and Analytic Framework for the Book," introduces the basic ideas and concepts underlying channel analysis. It explains why specialized institutions and agencies have emerged to assist in the task of making goods and services available for industrial, institutional, and household consumption. Among the more critical concepts introduced in Chapter 1 are the notions of "service outputs" and marketing "flows" on which the remainder of the book relies heavily. Chapter 2 provides a coherent framework for building, maintaining, and analyzing channel structure and function. It includes demand-side analysis, supply-side analysis of both channel flows and channel structures, the analysis of gaps on the demand and supply sides, and responses by channel managers concerning the creation or modification of channel structures to meet target segments' needs. It also emphasizes the importance of ongoing management and coordination of the channel through the use of channel power sources and the recognition and management of channel conflict. This framework unifies the discussion throughout the rest of the book and forms the basis for the book's approach to channel design and management.

Part Two, "Channel Design: Demand, Supply, and Channel Structure," develops the framework for channel creation or modification. Chapter 3 focuses on the demand side by discussing how to segment a market for the purposes of channel design appropriately, using the core concept of service output demands. Chapter 4 turns to the supply side of the channel, introducing the concept of channel flows to describe the work done by channel members. This chapter emphasizes the importance of distributing flow responsibilities to channel members who can perform them most efficiently. Not only is the allocation of flows important, so is the issue of channel structure. This is the topic of Chapter 5, which discusses the types of firms that can and should be included in the channel, how broadly distributed the channel's products should be, and who specifically should be a member of the channel. Chapter 6 brings together the demand and supply sides through a discussion of gap analysis, whereby gaps can exist on the demand side, the supply side, or both. Sources of gaps, types of gaps, and methods of closing channel gaps are all discussed. Chapter 7 discusses a key issue in channel structure: whether to vertically integrate the channel. This chapter covers the make-or-buy issue in channels, as well as the decision whether to adopt an intermediate solution. These options blend the features of make and of buy. The next part of the book covers how to create such a midrange solution.

Part Three, "Channel Coordination and Implementation," discusses how to get all the members of a channel to work in concert with one another. Concerted or coordinated action does not happen naturally in a marketing channel. This part covers how to overcome this problem by crafting channels that function smoothly in pursuit of common goals. Power is the subject of Chapter 8, which examines how to obtain the potential for influence—and how to use it. Of course, channels are full of conflict, as discussed in Chapter 9. Here, the emphasis is on how to diagnose the true sources of conflict and how to direct conflict to use it as a constructive force for change. A fundamental issue underlying almost every attempt to coordinate a channel is how thoroughly a marketplace is covered (how many places a customer could buy a product or service). The intensity of distribution is related to vertical restraints (such as tying contracts and resale price maintenance) and to how many brands a channel member carries (the degree of exclusivity in dealing). These topics are the subject of Chapter 10. Power, conflict, and intensity of distribution all turn on how to influence channel members. The ultimate form of influence is to forge a strategic alliance in a channel, covered in Chapter 11. Because efforts to coordinate often run afoul of the law, the legal environment (Chapter 12) closes this part.

Part Four, "Channel Institutions," describes and evaluates the predominant institutional forms at each level of a marketing channel. The retailing level has a great variety of forms: The major issues and challenges confronting them are discussed in Chapter 13. This chapter focuses on physical stores, which customers visit. Chapter 14 covers the rapidly growing nonstore alternatives, including electronic channels, catalogs, and direct selling. Further up in the value-added chain is the wholesaling sector, the subject of Chapter 15. A critical element of value added in marketing channels is logistics and supply chain management, the topic of Chapter 16. Finally, Chapter 17 deals with the fascinating, complex, and inherently contradictory channel institution of franchising, discussing how, when, and why franchising works.

The sixth edition differs from the fifth edition in its organization of material, but not in its philosophical underpinning. The framework for analysis is presented first, followed by institutionally oriented chapters, rather than the reverse, as in the fifth edition. The framework is also expanded over more chapters, each of which can be the focus of a single course session. The book is significantly internationalized throughout, reflecting the importance of channel management issues throughout the world. This edition also provides extensive coverage of the impact of electronic commerce on channel design and management, both in examples in each chapter and in the separate treatment of the issue in Chapter 14.

Acknowledgments

Many people have deeply influenced the structure and content of this book. Each author appreciates the contributions of a distinct (but sometimes overlapping) set of people, whereas a fourth set of individuals has influenced us all.

Anne Coughlan thanks Charles B. Jameson, C. J., and Catherine Anne, without whose support and help this work could not have been done. Their patience with a wife and mother who was too often absent deserves high praise. This work is also dedicated to Catherine M. Coughlan and the memory of John M. Coughlan, who have been an inspiration to excellence. Louis W. Stern deserves special thanks for his mentoring and collegiality. Finally, her colleagues and students in the marketing community deserve recognition for their many insights that have shaped this author's thinking over the years.

Erin Anderson expresses her appreciation to marketing doctoral students Frédéric Dalsace and Alberto Sa Vinhas. Their penetrating insights and many ideas have been invaluable. MBA students Harri Cherkoori, Blaise Fiedler, and Bernie Malonson gave helpful feedback.

Louis Stern is indebted to his wife, Rhona, whose encouragement, humor, support, and affection have been sources of inspiration to him. He is also indebted to all of his colleagues at Northwestern who have, over the years, supplied such enormous intellectual leadership to the marketing field. He is especially grateful for the opportunity he has been given to work with so many outstanding doctoral students, both at Northwestern and at Ohio State, where he previously taught.

Adel El-Ansary would like to acknowledge the encouragement and support of a number of marketing scholars. Many thanks to all, particularly those who have been personally supportive and encouraging over the years. A special debt is owed to Louis W. Stern, William R. Davidson, and the late Bert C. McCammon Jr.

Together, we thank Roshawn Blunt, Sanjay Kumar, Alok Maskara, and Laurie Richardson for providing superb research and editorial assistance. The inputs of many colleagues, both in academia and business, have improved the book. We thank in particular Philip Anderson, Reinhard Angelmar, Richard Bartlett, Donald Bielinski, Philip Corse, Rajiv Dant, Adam Fein, Kent Grayson, Ric Hobby, Lois Huff, Patrick Kaufman, Nirmalya Kumar, Janghyuk Lee, Barton A. Weitz, Rick Wilson, Thomas Wotruba, and Enver Yücesan. We especially thank the many MBA students who offered comments and encouragement during the process of writing the book. Thanks for text processing support are due to Françoise Marquis, Laureen Sorreda, and Sylvaine Imbert.

We are also especially indebted to the large number of authors whose work we cite throughout the text. Without their efforts, we could not have written this book.

Anne T. Coughlan
Evanston, Illinois

Erin Anderson
Fontainebleau, France

Louis W. Stern
Evanston, Illinois

Adel I. El-Ansary
Jacksonville, Florida

PART ONE

INTRODUCTION AND ANALYTIC FRAMEWORK FOR THE BOOK

1

Marketing Channels: Structure and Functions

LEARNING OBJECTIVES

After reading this chapter, you will know:

- What a marketing channel is
- Why manufacturers choose to use intermediaries between themselves and end-users
- What marketing flows define the work of the channel
- Who the members of marketing channels are, and in what flows they can specialize
- Why it is important to consider a framework for marketing channel design and analysis

Marketing channels are behind every product and service that consumers and business buyers purchase everywhere. Yet in many cases, these end-users are unaware of the richness and complexity necessary to deliver what might seem like everyday items to them. Usually, combinations of institutions specializing in manufacturing, wholesaling, retailing, and many other areas join forces in marketing channels. These deliver everything from mutual funds to books, from medical equipment to office supplies, to end-users in both businesses and households. This chapter defines the concept of a marketing channel, and then discusses the purpose for using marketing channels to reach the marketplace, the functions and activities that go on in marketing channels; membership in marketing channels; and how a framework for analysis can improve the channel decisions made by an executive acting as a channel manager or designer.

WHAT IS A MARKETING CHANNEL?

The rich array of institutional possibilities in marketing channels is impossible to convey briefly, but consider the following examples:

- *Personal computers.* IBM sold its first personal computers (PCs) in the early 1980s through its employee sales force—direct to business end-users. At that time, there was no consumer market for the products, and PCs seemed expensive enough to merit the high-cost direct sales channel. The personal computer channel quickly changed with value-added resellers (VARs) and retail stores acting as intermediaries to both business and consumer end-users throughout the next several years. Dell Computer, founded in 1984, changed the channel formula once again and has focused its channel strategy on direct sales, first through telephone ordering and today also over the Internet. In 1999 Dell surpassed Compaq Computer to take market share leadership in sales to U.S. businesses, with 30.9 percent of that market and 21.2 percent overall market share in the United States to all buyer segments. Worldwide in 1999, Dell had 9.2 percent market share, second only to Compaq with 13.4 percent market share. The data indicated that the direct sales channel is now an accepted way of buying PCs.[1]

- *Books.* The standard marketing channels for books have always included authors, publishers, book wholesalers, and store-based book retailers selling to end-users. In today's marketplace, however, standard retailers such as Barnes & Noble and Borders find it necessary to operate on-line bookstores to compete with non-store-based Internet booksellers such as Amazon.com and Books.com, and even Internet-based search engines such as BestBookBuys.com. These active competitive moves are being pursued despite the persistent lack of profitability of on-line bookselling due to the high initial cost of setting up the on-line retailing presence. These developments threaten some standard book wholesalers but make new opportunities for shipping and logistics companies that can handle many small shipments, such as UPS and FedEx.

- *Pharmaceutical products.* Pharmaceuticals such as prescription drugs reach the end-user in several different ways. The pharmaceutical manufacturer typically has an employee sales force (but may also use contract salespeople who are not employees) that makes sales calls on physicians, hospitals, distributors, and insurance companies. Most health insurance companies have *formularies*—lists of approved drugs that may be prescribed for particular conditions—and manufacturers use sales effort to convince them to put new drugs on the list (or keep existing ones on it). The drugs may pass through the hands of independent distributors on their way to a retail pharmacy or a hospital pharmacy. Even the physician plays a role in actually prescribing the pharmaceutical that the patient uses. In cases where the patient's health care coverage includes prescription drug coverage, payment may flow not from the patient directly to the pharmacy, but from the insurance company to the pharmacy.

From these examples, we derive our basic definition of a *marketing channel*:

A marketing channel is a set of interdependent organizations involved in the process of making a product or service available for use or consumption.

The definition bears some explication. It first points out that a marketing channel is a "set of interdependent organizations." That is, a marketing channel is not just one firm doing its best in the market—whether that firm is a manufacturer, wholesaler, or retailer. Rather, many entities are typically involved in the business of channel marketing. Each channel member depends on the others to do their jobs.

What are their jobs? The definition makes clear that running a marketing channel is a "process." It is not an event. Distribution frequently takes time to accomplish, and even when a sale is finally made, the relationship with the end-user is usually not over. For example, think about a hospital purchasing a piece of medical equipment and its demands for postsale service to see that this is true.

Finally, what is the purpose of this process? The definition claims that it is "making a product or service available for use or consumption." That is, the purpose of channel marketing is to satisfy the end-users in the market, be they consumers or final business buyers. Their goal is the use or consumption of the product or service being sold. A manufacturer who sells through distributors to retailers, who serve final consumers, may be tempted to think that it has generated "sales" and developed "happy customers" when its sales force successfully places a product in the distributors' warehouses. This definition argues otherwise. It is of critical importance that all channel members focus their attention on the end-user.

The marketing channel is often viewed as a key strategic asset of a manufacturer. This was abundantly apparent in the $70 billion merger in 1998 between Citicorp and Travelers Group (now known jointly as Citigroup). Citicorp was one of the world's biggest banks, whereas Travelers focused on the insurance, mutual funds, and investment banking businesses. One of the merger's major stated goals was the ability of each organization to cross-sell the other's products to its customers and to exploit the two organizations' distribution channels to maximize the penetration of Citigroup's products throughout the world. Citicorp already had a worldwide distribution network of branch banks, which Travelers lacked. Meanwhile, Travelers had 10,300 Salomon Smith Barney brokers, 80,000 Primerica Financial Services insurance agents, and 100,000 Travelers insurance agents, a direct sales force in these markets that Citicorp could neither match nor easily build on its own. In a joint statement to the U.S. House Banking Committee on April 29, 1998, Charles O. Prince, general counsel for Travelers, stated:

> We believe we will be successful because of the quality and breadth of our products and services, and because of each of the company's greatly expanded and innovative distribution channels. Financial products "manufactured" in various parts of our company will be distributed through a broad range of methods, from the Internet and other technology-based methods to branch office locations in one hundred countries around the world to fully individualized, in-home service.[2]

This example makes clear that, whether selling products or services, marketing channel decisions play a role of strategic importance in the overall presence and success a company enjoys in the marketplace.

WHY ARE THERE MARKETING CHANNELS AND WHY DO THEY CHANGE?

The above examples all include intermediaries who play some role in distributing products or services, and some are examples of markets where marketing channel activities or structures have changed over time. This raises the fundamental question of why marketing channels exist and what causes these changes. Why, for example, do not all manufacturers sell all products and services that they make directly to all end-users? And, once in place, why should a marketing channel ever change shape or new marketing channels ever emerge?

We focus on two sources of impetus for channel development and change: demand-side and supply-side factors. Although not classified into these two categories at the time, early work in this area by Wroe Alderson has had a significant influence on thinking on this topic, and the discussion here builds on his original framework.[3]

Demand-Side Factors

Facilitation of Search. Marketing channels containing intermediaries arise partly because they facilitate *searching*. The process of search is characterized by uncertainty on the part of both end-users and sellers. End-users are uncertain about where to find the products or services they want, whereas sellers are uncertain about how to reach target end-users. If intermediaries did not exist, sellers without a known brand name would be unable to generate many sales. End-users would not know whether to believe the claims made by manufacturers about the nature and quality of their products. Conversely, manufacturers would not be certain that they were reaching the right kind of end-user through their promotional efforts.

Instead, intermediaries facilitate searches on both ends of the channel. For example, a manufacturer of many different qualities of paper can sell plain laser-jet paper through a "category killer" discount retailer. For example, Office Depot in the United States sells fine stationery through department stores and specialty stationery stores. An end-user looking for laser-jet paper does not have to worry about searching across all possible paper manufacturers but can be reasonably certain of finding the desired product at a retailer such as Office Depot. This end-user would probably not consider a local specialty stationery store to be an ideal outlet for laser-jet paper. Conversely, the end-user looking for personal stationery would more likely look for it at the stationery store than at Office Depot. These retailers create images for themselves that educate consumers about their positioning and product lines, and thus facilitate the search process on the demand side. It is no longer necessary for each consumer to search the market for manufacturers of these or other goods; the name of the retailer represents availability of the products.

Similarly, a laser-jet paper manufacturer would have a very difficult time searching for and finding the right target market of end-users for its products if office supply retailers did not exist. But gaining shelf space at Office Depot virtually guarantees the manufacturer access to a broad base of potential buyers. Again, search is facilitated, this time from the other end of the channel.

Adjustment of Assortment Discrepancy. Independent intermediaries in a marketing channel perform the valuable function of *sorting goods*. This is valuable because of the natural discrepancy between the assortment of goods and services made by a given manufacturer and the assortment demanded by the end-user. This discrepancy results from the fact that manufacturers typically produce a large quantity of a limited variety of goods, whereas consumers usually demand only a limited quantity of a wide variety of goods.

The sorting function performed by intermediaries includes the following activities:

1. *Sorting out.* This involves breaking down a heterogeneous supply into separate stocks that are relatively homogeneous. (For example, a citrus packinghouse sorts oranges by size and grade.)
2. *Accumulation.* The intermediary brings similar stocks from a number of sources together into a larger homogeneous supply. (Wholesalers accumulate varied goods for retailers, and retailers accumulate goods for consumers.)
3. *Allocation.* This refers to breaking a homogeneous supply down into smaller and smaller lots. Allocating at the wholesale level is referred to as *breaking bulk*. (For example, goods received in carloads are sold in case lots. A buyer of case lots in turn sells individual units.)
4. *Assorting.* This is the building up of an assortment of products for resale in association with each other. (Wholesalers build assortments of goods for retailers, and retailers build assortments for consumers.)

In short, intermediaries help end-users consume a combination of product and channel services that are attractive to them. Intermediaries can thus be viewed as *creating utility* for the end-user. In particular, they can create *possession, place*, and *time* utilities, by having a product in their assortments, in a certain place, and at a certain time that are all valuable to the target end-user.

Supply-Side Factors

Routinization of Transactions. Each purchase transaction involves ordering, valuating, and paying for goods and services. The buyer and seller must agree on the amount, mode, and timing of payment. These costs of distribution can be minimized if the transactions are routinized; otherwise, every transaction is subject to bargaining, with an accompanying loss of efficiency.

Moreover, routinization leads to standardization of goods and services for which performance characteristics can be easily compared and assessed. It encourages production of items that are highly valued. In short, routinization leads to efficiencies in the execution of channel activities, as the following examples demonstrate:

• Metrocall, Inc., is the second-largest paging and wireless messaging company in the United States, with more than four million subscribers. In May 1998, it announced a strategic long-term partnership with Motorola, Inc., a leading worldwide pager manufacturer, to collaborate on a joint distribution strategy. The partners' "Joint Supply Chain Team" included employees of both firms who met on a regular basis to improve distribution to Metrocall's end-users. The routinized cooperation between Metrocall and Motorola was forecast to reduce inventory holding in the channel and increase the frequency of inventory turns, improving profitability for the companies. Stated goals were both to reduce distribution costs and to improve customer service by engaging in electronic data interchange and to have Motorola ship directly to Metrocall's customers, rather than to Metrocall first.[4]

● *Electronic data interchange (EDI)* is a whole system of activities in distribution that standardizes the management of business documents, such as purchase orders, invoices, payments, and the like, between distribution channel members. Although EDI has rather large fixed costs, significant economies of scale mean that large companies that have many repeated transactions with their channel partners reduce their total costs of distribution through using EDI, as well as increasing the accuracy of processing trading documents. For instance, RJR Nabisco claims that processing a paper purchase order costs $70, whereas the EDI version of the same transaction costs less than $1.[5]

● Bergen Brunswig Drug Company, a $16 billion U.S. pharmaceutical supply channel management company, and Longs Drug Stores Corporation of California, agreed in January 1999 to a seven-year exclusive wholesale pharmaceutical distribution contract. Bergen would become the sole supplier of prescription drugs, health and beauty aids, and other medical products to all of Longs's 381 stores in the western United States. Prior to the agreement, Bergen had been one of two distributors supplying Longs. The president of Bergen said, "Our exclusive partnership will no doubt result in streamlined logistics and reduced operating costs for all parties." The president of Longs said, "Streamlining the supply management function by avoiding redundancies that previously existed will have significant benefits for both companies." [6]

● *Continuous replenishment programs (CRP)* are an important trend in inventory management in channels. First used by mass-merchandisers in the United States, manufacturing and retailing partners involved in CRP share inventory and stocking information to ensure that a product is neither understocked nor overstocked on the retail shelf and that the right array of retail products is stocked. Shipments typically increase in frequency but decrease in size per shipment. This leads to lower inventories in the system and higher turnaround, both sources of increased channel profitability. A routinized and mature relationship between channel partners is a must to make CRP a success, and the continuous replenishment program must be customized to each channel relationship to guarantee maximum savings.[7]

Reduction in Number of Contacts. Without channel intermediaries, every producer would have to interact with every potential buyer in order to create all possible market exchanges. As the importance of exchange in a society increases, so does the difficulty of maintaining all of these interactions. For example, a small village of only five specialized households would require ten transactions to carry out decentralized exchanges (i.e., exchanges at each production point). Intermediaries reduce the complexity of this exchange system and thus facilitate transactions. With a central market consisting of one intermediary, only five transactions would be required to carry out centralized exchange in the village example.

Implicit in this example is the notion that a decentralized system of exchange is less efficient than a centralized network using intermediaries. The same rationale can be applied to direct selling from manufacturers to retailers, relative to selling through wholesalers. Consider Figure 1.1. For example, given four manufacturers and ten retailers who buy goods from each manufacturer, the number of contact lines amounts to 40. If the manufacturers sold to these retailers through one wholesaler, the number of necessary contacts would be reduced to 14.

The number of necessary contacts, however, increases dramatically as more wholesalers are added. For instance, if the four manufacturers in our example use two wholesalers instead of one, the number of contacts rises from 14 to 28. If four wholesalers are used, the number of contacts will be 56. Thus, employing more and more intermediaries is subject to diminishing returns simply from the point of view of number and cost of contacts in the market.

It should be noted that in this example we assume the cost and effectiveness of any contact—manufacturer to wholesaler, wholesaler to retailer, or manufacturer to retailer—is the same as any other. This is clearly not true in the real world, where selling through one type of intermediary can carry very different costs from those of selling through another. Supply chain managers in Europe have been changing their distribution models to take advantage of lower necessary numbers of contact points as the European Union progresses. From the usual network that includes a warehouse in each country, channels are evolving into systems with one central European warehouse supported by regional distribution centers. About 75 percent of European firms surveyed by Andersen Consulting in 1998 had moved from nationally based to European management structures, with logistics management following suit. The basic tension in the market requires a balance between buyers' demands for ever-quicker response times (suggesting the need for more direct contacts with higher contact costs in the system) on one hand versus suppliers' cost-minimization desires (leading to the centralization of their distribution networks) on the other hand. Clearly, the tension can be resolved only if the quality of the smaller number of contacts improves proportionately to the decrease in their absolute number.[8]

Further, not all intermediaries are equally skilled at selling or motivated to sell a particular manufacturer's product offering, and this certainly affects the choice of which and how many intermediaries to use. The example also assumes that each retailer contacts each of the wholesalers used by the manufacturers. If a retailer prefers some wholesalers over others, restricting their number can prevent the manufacturer from reaching the market served by that retailer, suggesting the value of using multiple wholesalers.

Nevertheless, judiciously used intermediaries do indeed reduce the number of contacts necessary to cover a market. This principle guides many manufacturers seeking to enter new markets without engaging in high-cost direct distribution with an employee sales force. The trend toward rationalizing supply chains by reducing the number of suppliers used is also consistent with the concept of reducing the number of contacts in the distribution channel. It is interesting in this context, then, to ponder how Internet sellers can efficiently sell their wares because Internet selling implies *disintermediation* (i.e., the shedding of intermediaries rather than their use). Some believe that the individual contact and shipping costs of selling goods such as books over the Internet are high enough to threaten the long-term viability of selling products this way, because a manufacturer that runs its own Internet site must bear the cost of contacts and commerce

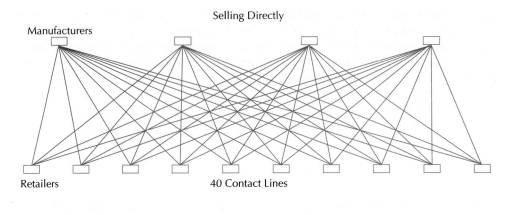

Selling Directly

Manufacturers

Retailers · 40 Contact Lines

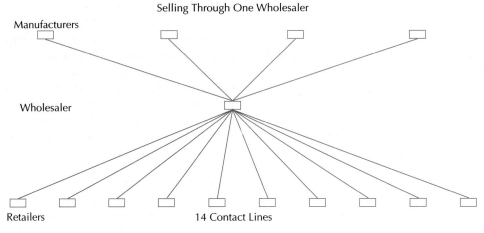

Selling Through One Wholesaler

Manufacturers

Wholesaler

Retailers · 14 Contact Lines

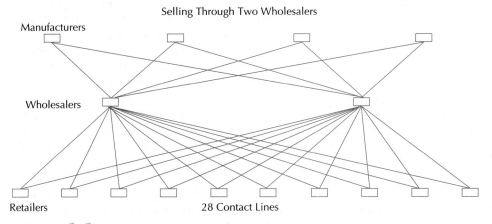

Selling Through Two Wholesalers

Manufacturers

Wholesalers

Retailers · 28 Contact Lines

FIGURE 1.1 **Contact Costs to Reach the Market With and Without Intermediaries**

with each individual buyer, rather than consolidating those transactions in one or a few channel intermediaries.[9] The success of on-line selling, despite this warning, suggests that the cost per contact is much lower over the Internet than it is in a personal selling situation. Hence, individual electronic contacts are not on balance more burdensome than the many costs of interacting with independent intermediaries.

In summary, intermediaries participate in the work of the marketing channel because they both add value and help reduce cost in the channel. This raises the question of what types of work are in fact done in the channel. We turn next to this issue.

WHAT IS THE WORK OF THE MARKETING CHANNEL?

The work of the channel includes the performance of several *marketing flows*. We use the term *flows* rather than *functions* or *activities* to emphasize that these processes often flow through the channel, being done at different points in time by different channel members. In institutional settings, one often hears of the need to carry inventory; to generate demand through selling activities; to physically distribute product; to engage in after-sales service; and to extend credit to other channel members or to end-users. We formalize this list in Figure 1.2, showing eight universal channel flows as they might be performed in a hypothetical channel containing producers, wholesalers, retailers, and consumers. As the figure shows, some flows move forward through the channel (physical possession, ownership, and promotion) whereas others move up the channel from the end-user (ordering and payment). Still other flows can move in either direction or are engaged in by pairs of channel members (negotiation, financing, risking).

We have left out of Figure 1.2 an important flow that permeates all the value-added activities of the channel: the flow of *information*. Information can and does flow between every possible pair of channel members, in both routine and specialized ways. Retailers share information with their manufacturing suppliers about sales trends and patterns through electronic data interchange relationships; when used properly, this information can help better manage the costs of performing many of the eight classic flows (e.g., by improving sales forecasts, the channel can reduce total costs of physical possession through lower inventory holdings). So important is the information content that logistics managers call this the ability to "transform inventory into information." Manufacturers share product and salesmanship information with their distributors, independent sales representatives, and retailers, to improve the performance of the promotion flow by these intermediaries. Consumers can give preference information to the channel, improving the channel's ability to supply valued services. Clearly, producing and managing information well is at the core of developing distribution channel excellence.

Although we discuss channel flows in much more detail in Chapter 4, a few remarks are in order here. First, the flows presented in Figure 1.2 may be done in different ways for different parts of a company's business. Consider, for example, the various ways in which physical possession flows are handled in the automobile channel. In the early to mid-1990s, automobile manufacturing supply chains in Great Britain were managed in a lean, just-in-time manner, but spare-parts supplies were not. The channel for the original product and that for the spare parts were thus not managed jointly. However, mar-

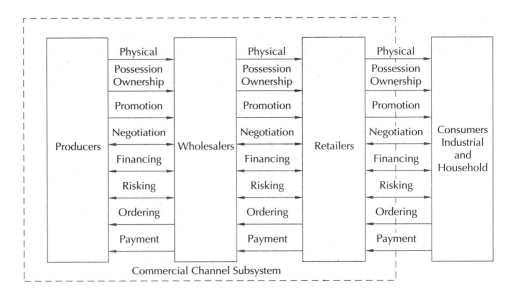

FIGURE 1.2 **Marketing Flows in Channels**

gins on new-car sales started to fall in the mid-1990s, causing manufacturers to pay new attention to the spare-parts channel and to contract with outside logistics company experts to help rationalize the spare-parts system.[10] The different nature of new-car and spare-parts sales now necessitates a custom approach to managing the physical possession of each. As a result, the channel manager may well want to represent these two physical possession activities separately, because they represent important, but different, flows in the movement of products (cars versus spare parts) to the market.

In addition, not every channel member need participate in every flow. Indeed, specialization in the performance of channel flows is the hallmark of an efficiently operating channel. For example, Figure 1.2 depicts a channel in which physical possession of product moves from the manufacturer to wholesalers to retailers and finally to end-users. But an alternate channel might involve not stocking wholesalers, but instead manufacturers' representatives, who generally do not participate in the physical possession or ownership flows because they do not handle physical product. In such a case, the physical possession flow might be performed by the manufacturer and retailer, but not by other intermediaries, on its way to the final end-user.

Similarly, financing may be spun off to a specialist and not be done by other channel members to any great degree. For example, the mission of General Motors Acceptance Corporation (GMAC), a wholly owned subsidiary of U.S. automaker General Motors, is to finance not only ultimate consumers of its automobiles but also the inventories held by dealers. It has worked to cement its key role as financing agent both by introducing innovations such as the 10-minute credit review and by expanding to overseas markets such as Hungary and Greece. As long as GMAC can handle the financing flow at lower cost than other channel members can, others (e.g., dealers) do not need to help consumers finance their automobile purchases. However, recently some superdealers, such as Circuit City's CarMax Used Car Superstore and AutoNation USA, both in the United States, have become large enough to open their own financing arms, challenging GMAC's domination over the financing flow.[11] In general, flows should be shared only among those channel members who can add value or reduce cost by bearing them. However, specialization increases interdependencies in channels, and thus creates the need for close cooperation and coordination in channel operations.

It is also important to note that the performance of certain flows is correlated with that of other flows. For instance, any time inventories are held by one member of the channel system, a financing operation is also underway. Thus, when a wholesaler or retailer takes title and assumes physical possession of a portion of a manufacturer's output, the intermediary is financing the manufacturer. This is consistent with the fact that the largest component of carrying cost is the cost of capital tied up when inventories are held in a dormant state, that is, not moving toward final sale. Other carrying costs are obsolescence, depreciation, pilferage, breakage, storage, insurance, and taxes. If that intermediary did not have to tie up its funds in inventory holding costs, it would instead be able to invest in other profitable opportunities. Capital costs are thus the opportunity costs of holding inventory. Consider the following example of a manufacturer recognizing and responding to this phenomenon:

- Nutmeg Mills is a unit of VF Corporation, a manufacturer of casual clothing and jeans, including the Lee, Wrangler, Rustler, Brittania, Jantzen, Vanity Fair, and Healthtex brands. Nutmeg has used VF's Market Response System 2000 inventory control and replenishment system, designed for use by wholesale buyers, to put interactive kiosks in Sears stores to allow shoppers to preview sports team clothing and then pay by credit card to have items shipped overnight. The system helps Sears minimize stocks of inventory for the dozens of teams whose merchandise Nutmeg sells and offers "Grandma in Seattle" the chance to buy a Cincinnati Bengals football team shirt for her grandson in Ohio. A VF spokesman notes that "it's a terrific service-oriented item because it allows stores to not carry extra inventory and sell items they probably wouldn't carry anyway." Sales through the kiosks are credited to the Sears store where they originated, although at a lower margin.[12]

Of course, cutting such costs out of a channel system must not jeopardize the delivery of product in a timely fashion to end-users. Therefore, such a policy is typically undertaken only in conjunction with quick response manufacturing capabilities such as the overnight shipping noted in the Sears example.

The foregoing discussion suggests that given a set of flows to be undertaken in a channel, a manufacturer must either assume responsibility for all the channel flows itself or else shift some or all of them to the various intermediaries populating its channel. This implies an important truth about channel design and management: One can eliminate or substitute members in the channel, but the flows performed by these members cannot be eliminated. When channel members are eliminated from the channel, their flows are shifted either forward or backward in the channel and therefore assumed by other channel members. The obvious reason to eliminate a channel member is because the flows performed by that channel member can be done as effectively and at least as cheaply by other channel members. Thus, the cost savings from eliminating a channel member should not be expected because that member's profit margin will revert to the rest of the channel, but rather because the flows performed by that channel member will be done more efficiently in another channel design.

WHO BELONGS TO A MARKETING CHANNEL?

The key members of a marketing channel are *manufacturers, intermediaries* (wholesale, retail, and specialized), and *end-users* (business customers or consumers). The presence or absence of a particular type of channel member is dictated by its ability to perform the necessary channel flows to add value to end-users. Often one channel member can be considered the "channel captain." This is an organization that takes the keenest interest in the workings of the channel for this product or service, and that acts as a prime mover in establishing and maintaining channel links. The channel captain is often the manufacturer of the product or service, particularly in the case of branded products. However, this is not universally true, as the following discussion shows.

Manufacturers

By *manufacturer*, we mean the producer or originator of the product or service being sold. The following examples are illustrative:

- Some manufacturers brand their products and thus are known by name to end-users, even if they use intermediaries to reach end-users. Examples include Unilever, the European consumer packaged-goods company; major world automakers such as Mercedes-Benz, Ford, or Toyota; or pharmaceutical manufacturers such as Merck, Pfizer, or Roche.

- Other manufacturers make products but do not invest in a branded name for them. Instead, they do *private-label* production, and the downstream buyer puts its own brand name on the product. For example, the German firm FJM Collections designs fine ladies' handbags, shoes, and other leather goods made from Chinese eel-skin. FJM contracts out production of handbags to manufacturers in Asia and production of shoes to an Italian manufacturer. Neither manufacturer's name is put on the final product, which is branded with the FJM name and sold in fine boutiques throughout Europe.[13]

- Sportswear International (SI) is an Italian manufacturer of casual-wear clothing that makes apparel for various designers, including Moschino, Hamnett, Jean-Paul Gauthier, Strenesse, Krizia, Byblos, and Cavalli. Although these designers' names go on the product, SI is not an invisible manufacturing partner in the channel. It ships product directly to retailers, not through the designers, and hence is not invisible to the retailers. Until recently, the Moschino jeans line was sold through Aeffe, an agent owned by competing Italian manufacturer Aeffe. SI has been recently considering joint venturing with Aeffe USA to comanage the showroom in New York City that presents the lines to the New York fashion market. Such a move would increase SI's visibility in the U.S. market and its importance to the designers who contract out manufacturing to SI.[14]

• A mutual fund company designs combinations of financial instruments (e.g., stocks or bonds) to sell as a bundle to investors. Each is thus itself a diversified portfolio of securities.[15] The mutual fund company can be thought of as a manufacturer because it designs the "product" by choosing what financial instruments will be included in the fund. Figure 1.3 shows the channel members in a mutual fund distribution channel. The investment adviser–management company (i.e., the "manufacturer") is responsible for managing the portfolio of financial instruments in each fund in the mutual fund's family. For example, The Kent Funds is a family of 14 stock, bond, tax-advantaged, and money market mutual funds. One of its funds, The Kent Growth and Income Fund, is made up of a "broadly diversified portfolio of common stocks that appear to be undervalued relative to the market as a whole." Table 1.1 shows the top 10 stocks held by The Kent Funds Growth and Income Fund as of December 31, 1998, and the economic sector diversification of the fund. These are key dimensions of the actual product being sold, that is, the mutual fund share that an investor would choose to purchase. The investment adviser for The Kent Funds, Lyon Street Asset Management Company, actively manages the growth and income fund by investing in and divesting stocks to meet the goal of the fund.

The manufacturer can be the originator of a service as well as the manufacturer of a product, as the mutual fund company example shows. The mutual fund investment adviser's tasks in the channel include the creation of mutual funds and the management of the investments made in companies represented in the funds. No physical product is sold to the end-user (in this case the shareholder). The shareholder instead has bought the right to share in the investment gains (or losses) of the mutual fund's portfolio of holdings. The key channel flow performed by such a manufacturer is the promotion

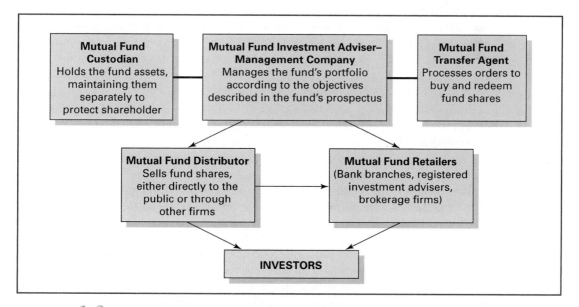

FIGURE 1.3 **The Mutual Fund Marketing Channel**

TABLE 1.1
Characteristics of The Kent Funds Growth and Income Fund

Number of companies in the fund: 256
Number of industries in the fund: 108
Percent of total net assets in top 10 holdings: 23.4%

Top 10 Holdings	Percent of Total Net Assets as of 12/31/98
Microsoft	3.7
General Electric Co.	3.7
Wal-Mart Stores, Inc.	2.6
IBM	2.1
Intel Corporation	2.0
Exxon Corp.	2.0
Merck & Company, Inc.	1.9
Lucent Tech. Corp.	1.9
Pfizer, Inc.	1.8
Cisco Systems	1.7

Economic Sector	Percent of Total Net Assets as of 12/31/98
Oil–energy	6.8
Utilities	10.6
Finance	15.7
Computer and technology	19.4
Other	5.7
Conglomerates	4.9
Basic materials	2.9
Medical	12.5
Retail	7.0
Consumer staples	11.0
Consumer discretionary	3.5

Source: Adapted from information on The Kent Funds Web site (www.kentfunds.com), April 27, 1999.

flow, which is shared by another channel member as well, an intermediary called the fund distributor. Physical possession is not a key flow in the standard sense in service markets, although in the mutual funds industry, a specialized channel member called the fund custodian takes physical possession of the stock and bond certificates of the mutual fund. Ordering functions are handled by yet another specialized intermediary, the fund transfer agent.

The examples also suggest that the manufacturer need not be the channel captain. In the first example, the manufacturer can be viewed as the channel captain. Its ability and desire to proactively manage the channel efforts for its products is intimately tied to its investment in brand equity for its products (e.g., Unilever's Lipton tea or the Mercedes A-class cars). But a private-label manufacturer, such as the supplier of eelskin handbags to FJM Collections, does not own the brand name in the end-user's eyes; another channel member does. Instead it is FJM Collections, which acts as a marketing agent to retailers of fine handbags and leather goods. The brand equity here rests with an intermediary in the channel (FJM), whose interests are to coordinate the actions of all of the channel members to maximize efficiency and effectiveness of the channel effort. The Sportswear International example illustrates that private-label manufacturers sometimes seek a greater role in channel activities. They recognize that a manufacturer that does not play a proactive role in the channel is likely to be pushed into a commodity-supplying position with little visibility or control.

The examples show that the manufacturer's ability to manage a production operation does not always extend to a superior ability to perform other channel flows. This reinforces the insight that intermediaries add value to the channel through their superior performance of certain channel flows, and that manufacturers voluntarily seek out such intermediaries to increase their reach in the end-user market.

All of the product manufacturers are involved in physical possession and ownership flows, until the product leaves their manufacturing sites and travels to the next channel member's site. Manufacturers also engage in negotiation with the buyers of their products to set terms of sale and merchandising of the product. The manufacturer of a branded good also participates significantly in the promotion flow for its product.

Intermediaries

The term *intermediary* refers to any channel member other than the manufacturer or the end-user (individual consumer or business buyer). We differentiate among three types of intermediaries: wholesale, retail, and specialized.

Wholesalers include merchant wholesalers or distributors, manufacturers' representatives, agents, and brokers. A wholesaler sells to other channel intermediaries, such as retailers, or to business end-users, but not to individual consumer end-users. Merchant wholesalers take both title to and physical possession of inventory; store inventory (frequently of many manufacturers); promote the products in their line; and arrange for financing, ordering, and payment with their customers. They make their profit by buying at a wholesale price and selling at a marked-up price to their downstream customers, pocketing the difference between the two prices, net of any distribution costs they bear. Manufacturers' reps, agents, and brokers typically do not take title to or physical possession of the goods they sell. The major flows in which they take part are promotion and negotiation, as they work on selling the products of the manufacturers they represent and negotiating terms of trade for them. Some of these intermediaries, such as trading companies or import–export agents, specialize in international selling, whether or not they take on title and physical possession flows. Chapters 15 and 16 focus in depth on the roles played by these intermediaries in wholesaling and logistics activities.

Retail intermediaries come in many forms today, including department stores, mass-merchandisers, hypermarkets, specialty stores, category killers, convenience stores, franchises, buying clubs, warehouse clubs, catalogers, and on-line retailers. Unlike purely wholesale intermediaries, they sell directly to individual consumer end-users. In the mutual fund industry example (see Figure 1.3), the retail level is represented through branch bank investment services, registered investment advisers, and brokerage firms in the United States. The investment adviser (e.g., Lyon Street Asset Management Company) does not sell directly to end-users but relies on these retail outlets—particularly registered investment advisers—to expand its reach nationwide.[16]

Whereas retailers' role historically has focused on amassing an assortment of goods that is appealing to their consumer end-users, their role today often goes much further. They may contract for private-label (store-label) goods, effectively vertically integrating upstream in the supply chain. Some retailers, such as Office Depot in the United States, actually make more sales to businesses than to consumer end-users, although their storefronts nominally identify them as retailers. Thus, the classic distinction between retailing and wholesaling has shifted, making the distinction between retailers and wholesalers much less meaningful than it once was. Chapters 13 and 14 discuss retailing, direct and network marketing, and electronic retailing channels in depth, and Chapter 17 discusses franchising.

Specialized intermediaries are brought into a channel to perform a specific flow and typically are not heavily involved in the core business represented by the product sold. These intermediaries include insurance companies, finance companies, credit card companies (all involved in the financing flow), advertising agencies (participating in the promotion flow), logistics and shipping firms (participating in the physical possession flow), information technology firms (who may participate in ordering or payment flows), and marketing research firms (generating marketing intelligence that can be useful for the performance of any of the flows). In the mutual fund example (see Figure 1.3), the fund distributor (specializing in promotional activities), the fund custodian (specializing in physical possession activities), and the fund transfer agent (specializing in ordering activities) are all critical channel intermediaries.

End-Users

Finally, it is important to note that end-users (either business customers or individual consumers) are themselves channel members as well. We classify consumers as marketing channel members because they can and frequently do perform channel flows, just as other channel members do. Consumers who shop at a mass-merchandiser such as Wal-Mart or Target and stock up on paper towels are performing physical possession, ownership, and financing flows because they are buying a much larger volume of product than they will use in the near future. They pay for the paper towels before they use them, thus injecting cash into the channel and performing a financing flow. They store the paper towels in their houses, lessening the need for warehouse space at the retailer, thus taking on part of the physical possession flow. They bear all the costs of ownership as well, including pilferage, spoilage, and so forth. Naturally, consumers expect a price cut when they shop at such a store, due to the channel flow costs borne when buying through this channel relative to buying a single package of paper towels at the local grocer.

Channel Formats as Combinations of Channel Members

This variety of channel participants can be combined in many ways to create effective marketing channels. The range and number of channel members is affected by the nature of demand by end-users, and the captaincy of the channel can vary from situation to situation. Appendix 1.1 summarizes different possibilities for channel formats that are manufacturer based, retailer based, service-provider based, and others.

THE IMPORTANCE OF A FRAMEWORK FOR CHANNEL ANALYSIS

Now that we have established what a marketing channel is, how it can be organized and why it includes intermediaries, and who can be the members of a channel, we have to ask how we can use these terms and insights to do a better job of designing and managing marketing channels. A comprehensive framework for analysis is necessary to guide the channel manager through both the initial design of the channel and its ongoing management over time. Without a framework for analysis, important elements of the design or management processes may be ignored, resulting in inappropriately constructed or managed channels. Hence, the concept of interdependence is critical to remember. Because of the extreme interdependence of all channel members and the value of specialization in channels, attention must be paid to all the design and management elements to ensure an effective marketing channel effort. For instance, even the best-designed channel is completely unproductive if the retailer neglects to stock product on the retail shelf. Consumers will not buy what they cannot see in the store!

In Chapter 2, we thus use the terminology introduced in this chapter to discuss a framework for channel design and management that can be followed by sellers of products or services, in one market or across several national markets. This framework is the basis for the succeeding chapters and shapes later discussion of channel institutions such as retailing, wholesaling, and logistics.

Discussion Questions

Consider these examples of marketing channels to answer questions 1, 2, and 3:

- Avon's distribution system delivering cosmetics direct from manufacturer to consumer through a sales force of 400,000 saleswomen.
- MDR, Medical Research Co., sells vitamins and supplements directly to customers at prices considerably higher than national brands available through drugstores and supermarkets. The vitamins are not available through traditional store-type retailers.
- Sara Lee Corporation's consignment marketing channel for its L'eggs pantyhose, wherein retailers take no title for the goods, make no financial investment, and perform no delivery service or display maintenance. But they receive only a certain percentage of the pantyhose sales for their allocation of space to the L'eggs display.

1. Select one of these channels and speculate who the other channel participants are and to what extent each member participates in the eight universal marketing flows.

2. How might these flows be shifted, either among the members now in the channel or to different agencies or institutions not presently included? What do you think would be the implications of such shifts?

3. Within each of these distribution systems, specify what the consumer's role is from a flow-absorption perspective. How, in turn, does this affect the consumer's level of compensation?

4. Should advertising agencies and financial institutions be considered channel members? Why? Why not? Is it more useful, from a managerial perspective, to think of consumers

as members of the channel or as elements of the task environment of the channel? Can consumers be "manipulated" or incorporated by channel management?

5. Started in 1982 by veteran retailer Dave Gold, 99 Cents Only Stores pioneered the deep-discount single-price general merchandise concept. Stocked with 7,000 different items, the stores are clean and bright. The product lineup is dominated by big-name marketers including Procter & Gamble, General Foods, and Colgate-Palmolive. Deep-discount stores are growing fast. For example, by the end of 1998 Family Dollar Stores had 3,000 stores in 38 states. How do you account for the growth of these deep-discount stores alongside Wal-Mart, Sam's Club, and outlet mall stores?

6. According to renowned scholar Wroe Alderson, "the number of intervening marketing agencies tends to go up as distance increases." Distance, in his conception, is measured in terms of "the time and cost involved in communication and transportation." What factors, then, would tend to increase (or decrease) distance? What is the impact of the Web and marketing in cyberspace on distance as discussed by Alderson?

7. Chinese department stores are modeled after American department stores. They carry many designer labels and expensive merchandise. Although many American and European brand names are available, Chinese brands tend to use Westernized names to make products more and more upscale. Most of the mannequins in the stores are white and blond. The stores are overstaffed; sometimes you encounter more employees than customers in the store. Although an increasing number of people shop in these department stores, many small roadside shops that sell clothes, shoes, and household items, compete head-on with the bigger retailers. In smaller stores, unlike in the department stores, bargaining is quite common. How do you account for these channel structures and channel member practices?

Alternate Channel Formats: Definitions and Examples

Alternate channel formats may be based in any of the three sections of the traditional distribution pipeline—manufacturer, distributor, or customer—but they may also have other bases. The following material summarizes in detail a variety of channel formats and the characteristics on which they rely for strategic advantage, and gives examples of specific companies or types of companies or product categories using that channel format. By comparing each of your markets to this information, you can identify opportunities and vulnerabilities.

Manufacturer-Based Channel Formats

1. **Manufacturer Direct.** Product shipped and serviced from manufacturer's warehouse. Sold by company sales force or agents. Many manufacturer-direct companies also sell through wholesaler-distributors.
   Example: Wide variety of products for customers with few service needs and large orders

2. **Manufacturer-Owned Full-Service Wholesaler-Distributor.** An acquired wholesale distribution company serving the parent's and other manufacturers' markets. Typically, these diverse product lines in an industry support synergies between a company's manufacturing and distribution operations. Due to customer demand, some companies also distribute other manufacturers' products.
   Examples: Revlon, Levi-Strauss, Kraft Foodservice, GESCO, clothing and apparel products

3. **Company Store–Manufacturer Outlet.** Retail product outlets in high-density markets; often used to liquidate seconds and excess inventory. They often sell branded consumer products.
   Examples: Athletic footwear, bakery goods

4. **License.** Contracting distribution and marketing functions through licensing agreements, usually granting exclusivity for some period of time. Often used for products in the development stage of the life cycle.
   Examples: Mattel, Walt Disney, importers

5. **Consignment–Locker Stock.** Manufacturing ships product to point of consumption, but title does not pass until consumed. Risk of obsolescence and own-

ership is with manufacturer until used. Concerned with high-priced–high-margin items and emergency items.
Examples: Diamonds, fragrances, tool cribs, and machine repair parts

6. **Broker.** Specialized sales force contracted by manufacturer; the sales force carries other comparable product lines and focuses on a narrow customer segment; product is shipped through another format such as those already listed. Typically used by small manufacturers attempting broad coverage.
Examples: Frozen foods, paper goods, lumber, newer product lines

Retailer-Based Channel Formats

1. **Franchise.** Product and merchandising concept is packaged and formatted. Territory rights are sold to franchisees. Various distribution and other services are provided by contract to franchisees for a fee.
Examples: Blockbuster Video, McDonald's

2. **Dealer Direct.** Franchised retailers carry a limited number of product lines supplied by a limited number of vendors. Often big-ticket items needing high after-sales service support.
Examples: Heavy equipment dealers, auto dealers

3. **Buying Club.** Buying services requiring membership. Good opportunity for vendors to penetrate certain niche markets or experiment with product variations. They also often provide buyers with a variety of consumer services. Today they are largely consumer oriented.
Examples: Compact disk–tape clubs, book clubs

4. **Warehouse Club–Wholesale Club.** Appeal is to price-conscious shopper. Size is 60,000 square feet or more. Product selection is limited and products are usually sold in bulk sizes in no-frills environment.
Examples: Pace, Sam's Club, Price Club, Costco

5. **Mail Order–Catalog.** Nonstore selling through use of literature sent to potential customers. Usually has a central distribution center for receiving and shipping direct to the customer.
Examples: Lands' End, Spiegel, Fingerhut

6. **Food Retailer.** Will buy canned and boxed goods in truckloads to take advantage of pricing and manufacturing rebates. Distribution centers act as consolidators to reduce the number of trucks received at the store. Pricing is not required as manufacturer bar codes are used. Typically includes full line of groceries, health and beauty aids, and general merchandise items. Some food retailers have expanded into additional areas, such as prescription and over-the-counter drugs, delicatessens, bakeries, and so on.
Examples: Publix, Safeway

7. **Department Store.** Offers a wide variety of merchandise with a moderate depth of selection. The typical product mix includes both soft goods (e.g., clothing, food, linens) and hard goods (e.g., appliances, hardware, sporting equipment). Distribution centers act as consolidators of both soft goods and

hard goods. Quick response for apparel goods demands direct link with manufacturer. Having stores on a national basis motivates retailers to handle their own distribution.
Examples: JCPenney, Mervins, R. H. Macy & Company, Dayton Hudson Corporation, Federated Stores

8. **Mass-Merchandiser.** Similar to department store, except product selection is broader and prices are usually lower.
Examples: Wal-Mart, Kmart, Target

9. **Specialty Store.** Offers merchandise in one line (e.g., women's apparel, electronics) with great depth of selection at prices comparable to those of department store. Due to the seasonal nature of fashion goods, partnership with the manufacturer is essential. Manufacturer will ship in predetermined store assortment and usually will price the goods. Retailer in some cases has joint ownership with the manufacturer.
Examples: The Limited, Gap, Kinney Shoes, Musicland, Zale

10. **Specialty Discounter–Category Killer.** Offers merchandise in one line (e.g., sporting goods, office supplies, children's merchandise) with great depth of selection at discounted prices. Stores usually range in size from 50,000 to 75,000 square feet. Buy direct in truckloads. Manufacturer will ship direct to the store. Most products do not need to be priced. National chains have created their own distribution centers to act as consolidators.
Examples: Toys "R" Us, OfficeMax, Drug Emporium, F&M Distributors

11. **Convenience Store.** A small, higher-margin grocery store that offers a limited selection of staple groceries, nonfoods, and other convenience items (e.g., ready-to-heat and ready-to-eat foods). The traditional format includes those stores that started out as strictly convenience stores, but they may also sell gasoline.
Examples: 7-Eleven, White Hen Pantry

12. **Hypermarket.** A very large food and general merchandise store with at least 100,000 square feet of space. Although these stores typically devote as much as 75 percent of the selling area to general merchandise, the food-to-general-merchandise sales ratio typically is 60–40.
Examples: Auchan, Carrefour, Super Kmart Centers, Hypermarket USA

Service-Provider-Based Channel Formats

1. **Contract Warehousing.** Public warehousing services provided for a fee, typically with guaranteed serviced levels.
Examples: Caterpillar Logistics Services, Dry Storage

2. **Subprocessor.** Outsourcing of assembly or subprocessing. Usually performed with labor-intensive process or high fixed-asset investment when small orders are needed for customer. These channel players are also beginning to take on traditional wholesale distribution role in some cases.
Examples: Steel processing, kitting of parts in electronics industry

3. **Cross Docking.** Trucking companies service high-volume inventory needs by warehousing and backhauling product on a routine basis for customer's nar-

rower inventory needs. Driver picks inventory and delivers to customer on picking up customer's shipment.
Examples: Industrial repair parts and tools, various supply industries

4. **Integration of Truck and Rail (Intermodal).** Joint ventures between trucking and rail companies to ship large orders door-to-door from supplier to customer, with one waybill.
Examples: Becomes very economical for large orders, or from manufacturer to customer for a manufacturer with a broad product line

5. **Roller Freight.** Full truckload is sent from manufacturer to high-density customer markets via a transportation company. Product is sold en route, and drivers are directed to customer delivery by satellite communication.
Examples: Lumber products, large moderately priced items with commodity-like characteristics that require routine orders

6. **Stack Train and Road Railer.** Techniques to speed movement and eliminate handling for product to be shipped by multiple formats. For example, importer loads containers directed to specific customers on a truck body in Hong Kong, ships direct, and unloads onto railcars. This can eliminate two to three days' transit time. Large customer orders use multiple transportation techniques.
Examples: Importers

7. **Scheduled Train.** High-speed trains leave daily at prescribed times from high-density areas to high-density destinations. Manufacturer "buys a ticket" and hooks up its railcar, and customer picks up product at the other end.
Examples: High-density recurring orders to large customers with limited after-sales service needs

8. **Outsourcing.** Service providers sign a contract to provide total management of a company's activities in an area in which the provider has particular expertise (computer operations, janitorial services, print shop, cafeteria, repair parts, tool crib). The outsourcer then takes over the channel product flow for products-associated outsourced activity (janitorial supplies). Outsourcing has spread to virtually every area of the business (repair part stockroom, legal and accounting department) and may not use merchant wholesaler-distributors. Wide variety of applications and growing.
Examples: ServiceMaster, ARA, R. R. Donnelly

9. **Direct Mailer.** Direct-mail-advertising companies expanding services in conjunction with market research database services in order to direct-market narrower line products. Product logistics and support either performed by manufacturer or outsourced to a third party.
Examples: Big ticket consumer products; high-margin, low-service-requirement industrial and commercial equipment

10. **Bartering.** Service provider, usually an advertising or media company, signs a barter arrangement with a manufacturer to exchange product for media advertising time or space for product. Bartered product is then rebartered or redistributed through other channels.

Examples: Consumer and commercial products that have been discontinued or for which demand has slowed considerably

11. **Value-Added Reseller (VAR).** Designers, engineers, or consultants for a variety of service industries that joint venture or have arrangements with manufacturers of products that are used in their designs. The VARs often get a commission or discount to service the product later and often carry inventory of high-turn items.
   Examples: Computer software companies that market hardware for turnkey products; security system designers that form joint ventures with electronics manufacturers to sell turnkey products

12. **Influencer–Specifier.** Similar to a VAR, but these firms generally design highly complex, large projects (commercial buildings), do not take title to product, and have a group of suppliers whose products can be specified into the design. Selling effort is focused on both the ultimate customer and the specifier. Distribution of product is handled through other channel formats.
   Examples: Architects, designers, consultants

13. **Financial Service Provider.** These formats have historically been initiated by joint venture with financial service companies to finance margin purchases for customers or dealers (such as floor planning). It has been expanded to allow manufacturers to initiate distribution in new markets and assess these markets (with the help of the financial provider). High-capital, highly controlled distribution channel for one or two suppliers.
   Examples: Branded chemicals, construction equipment

Other Channel Formats

Door-to-Door Formats. To some extent these are variations on the channel formats previously listed. These formats have existed in the United States since pioneer days in situations in which a product has a high personal sales cost and high margins and is sold in relatively small orders (encyclopedias, vacuum cleaners, and so forth). A wide range of variations (e.g., the home-party format) attempt to get many small buyers in one location to minimize the sales cost and provide a unique shopping experience. Variations of the format have also spread to the industrial and commercial markets to capitalize on similar market needs. (For example, Snap-On Tools uses a variation of the home-party system by driving the product and salespeople to the mechanics' garages and selling to the mechanics on their lunch hour.) Each format is different and needs to be analyzed to understand its unique characteristics. A brief summary of the more identifiable formats follows:

1. **Individual On-Site.** Very effective for generating new business for high-margin product requiring a high level of interaction with customers.
   Examples: Fuller Brush, Electrolux, bottled water, newspapers

2. **Route.** Used for servicing routine repetitive purchases that do not need to be resold on each call. Sometimes price is negotiated once and changed only on an exception basis. This concept was historically more prevalent in consumer lines

(e.g., milk deliveries) but has recently spread to a variety of commercial and industrial segments.
Examples: Office deliveries of copier paper and toner

3. **Home Party.** Similar to individual on-site sales, this format takes the product to a group of individuals, as outlined in the introduction.
Examples: Tupperware, Snap-On Tools

4. **Multilevel Marketing.** Salesperson not only sells product but also recruits other salespeople who become a leveraged sales force that gives the original salesperson a commission on sales. Channel can be used for "high-sizzle," high-margin, fast-growth opportunities in branded differentiated products.
Example: Amway, Shaklee, NuSkin, plumbing products, cosmetics, other general merchandise

5. **Service Merchandising–"Rack Jobbing."** Similar to a route but expanded to provide a variety of services with the product. Originally, the rack jobber sold small consumer items to grocery stores, merchandised the product, and owned the inventory, merely paying the retailer a commission for the space. This concept is expanding to the commercial, industrial, and home market in a variety of niches: maintaining a stockroom of office supplies, maintaining repair parts stock, servicing replenishable items in the home such as chemicals, purified water, salt, and so on.
Examples: Specialty items and gadgets or novelties; paperback books, magazines

Buyer-Initiated Formats. These formats have been built on the concept of all buyers joining together to buy in large quantities at better prices. This concept has expanded to give these buyers other securities and leverage that they might not be able to obtain on their own (e.g., private labeling and advertising design). As with the door-to-door concepts, variations of this concept are proliferating to meet individual buyers' needs.

1. **Co-op.** Companies, usually in the same industry, create an organization in which each member becomes a shareholder. The organization uses the combined strength of the shareholders to get economies of scale in any number of areas of its business, such as purchasing, advertising, or private-label manufacturing. This format is generally designed to allow small companies to compete more effectively with large competitors. Although wholesaler-distributors can form or join co-ops, in their use as an alternate channel format co-ops may be direct buyers from non-wholesalers-distributors.
Example: Topco

2. **Dealer-Owned Co-op.** Similar to the co-op format, except the co-op may perform many of the functions rather than contracting them with third-party suppliers (e.g., it may own warehouses). Shareholders–members are generally charged a fee for usage, and all profits in the co-op at year-end are refundable to the shareholders on some prorated basis. In many instances, this format has elements of a franchise.
Example: Distribution America

3. **Buying Group.** Similar to the co-op, except the relationship is usually much less structured. Companies can be members of several buying groups. The loose

affiliation format usually does not continually commit the members to perfor-mance. This format is being used throughout the economy and has taken on a host of roles. A group can buy through the wholesale distribution channel or direct from manufacturers. Often, wholesaler-distributors are members of buy-ing groups for low-volume items.
Examples: AMC, May Merchandising

Point-of-Consumption Merchandising Formats. This concept has grown from the practice of strategically placing vending machines where the demand is predictable and often discretionary and the cost of selling through a full-time salesperson would be too high. This format has spread into commercial, industrial, and home markets for prod-ucts and services never before imagined. The increased use of technology and telecom-munications has opened this channel to even more products and services.

1. **Vending–Kiosk.** Kiosks have historically been very small retail locations that carry a very narrow product line. Through interactive video, on-line ordering technology, and artificial intelligence, this format has been significantly enhanced and can operate unattended. It is also being used for point-of-use dis-pensing of maintenance supplies and tools. Purchases are recorded in a log by the computer to control inventory shrinkage and balance inventory levels.
   Examples: Film processing, candy, tobacco, compact disks, and tapes

2. **Pay-Per-Serving Point of Dispensing.** Product is prepared or dispensed by vending machine at the time of purchase. Vending machines for soup and coffee, soft drinks, and candy or food are usual uses of this format, but it is expanding to include such foods as pizza and pasta.
   Examples: Beverages, food

3. **Computer Access Information.** Many of the computer access information for-mats have not necessarily altered the product flow (products are not available on-line), but they have significantly altered the service and information flow by uncoupling them from the product. This allows the product to pass through cheaper channels.
   Examples: On-line information services, cable movies, news wire services, shop-ping services for groceries

Third-Party Influencer Formats. These formats are designed around the concept that an organization that has a relationship with a large number of people or companies can provide a channel format to these entities for products and services not traditionally associated with the organization (e.g., a school selling candy to the community by using the schoolchildren as a sales force). Here again, the concept has broadened across both the commercial and industrial sectors and deepened in terms of the products and ser-vices offered.

1. **Charity.** This format typically involves sales of goods and services in which the sponsoring charitable organization receives a commission on the sale. All types of products can be included and can be shipped direct or outsourced. Sales force may be nonpaid volunteers.
   Examples: Market Day, World's Finest Chocolate

2. **Company-Sponsored Program.** Employers contract with companies for products and services for their employees or segments of employees on an as-needed basis. The provider has access to the employee base.
   Examples: Health care and drug services, car maintenance

3. **Premium and Gift Market.** Companies buy products customized with company logos or names for sale or distribution
   Examples: Pens, plaques, awards, T-shirts, novelties

4. **Product Promotion Mailing with Normal Correspondence.** Promotion of products is done by mailing to customers with letters and perhaps phone call follow-up. Typically involves promotional inserts with credit card and other billings. Logistics and order fulfillment activities may be handled by others.
   Examples: American Express, VISA, MasterCard

5. **Customer List Cross-Selling.** An unusual format in that the customer list is sold by one company to another. In effect, the marketing function is circumvented. Started in the customer industry but is migrating to the commercial and industrial segments.
   Examples: Catalog companies, credit card companies

Catalog and Technology-Aided Formats. The time-honored catalog marketing channel dates from use by department stores to extend their merchandising ability to the predominantly rural U.S. population of the late 1800s. Catalog use has expanded dramatically to follow the buying habits of consumers and institutions. Although it continues to be a growing threat to the traditional merchant wholesaler-distributor through mail order and linkage to technology, it should be pointed out that catalogs are also a sales tool used by some wholesaler-distributors. Some of the following adaptations illustrate the need to evaluate this format very carefully in all market sectors.

1. **Specialty Catalog.** Uses catalogs to promote a narrow range of special products or services. Mailings are made to potential and repeat customers. Orders come in by mail or phone.
   Examples: Eddie Bauer, Bass Pro Shops, Williams Sonoma

2. **Business-to-Business Catalog.** Similar to specialty catalogs except that the product and customer focus is on business.
   Examples: Moore Business Forms, Global, CompuAdd, Damart

3. **Television Home Shopping and Satellite Networks.** Heavily dependent on technology, these offer shopping in the comfort of your own home. Also have business application. Orders are placed by phone.
   Example: Home Shopping Network

4. **Interactive Merchandising.** Could embody many of the attributes of television home shopping, except that this format allows extensive interactive in-store capabilities, as well as on-line ordering. It may offer inventory checking or physical modeling capabilities and unusually extensive communication linkages.
   Examples: Florsheim, kitchen planning computers in do-it-yourself home centers

5. **Third-Party Catalog Service.** Catalog selling format in which one or more suppliers provide a combined catalog for a group of customers frequenting a certain place.
   Examples: Airline in-flight magazines and catalogs, in-room hotel publications

6. **Trade Show.** A format used in some segments for direct sales order activities. Suppliers sell from booths at major trade shows or conventions. Also used for retail applications.
   Examples: Boats, cars, hardware–software applications

7. **Database Marketing.** Databases of customer buying habits and demographics are analyzed to enable the company to target customers for future mailing. Also used for retail applications.
   Examples: Large grocery–consumer products companies, telephone companies

Notes

1. See, for example, "Dell Takes Significant Lead in U.S. Corporate Marketplace: Ziff-Davis Study Shows Dell Also No. 1 in All U.S. Business Segments," and David P. Hamilton, "PC Shipments Climbed in First Quarter on Strong Demand, but Compaq Slid," *Wall Street Journal*, April 26, 1999, p. A3.

2. Prince's remarks to the U.S. House Banking Committee are printed in PR Newswire, "Benefits of Citigroup Merger Described in Testimony Delivered Before House Banking Committee," April 29, 1998. For other information on the Citicorp–Travelers merger and its distribution implications, see Leah Nathans Spiro et al., "Citigroup: Just the Start?" *BusinessWeek*, April 20, 1998, pp. 34–38; "Finance and Economics: Watch Out for the Egos," *Economist*, April 11, 1998, pp. 55–56; Tracy Corrigan, "Travelers Beats Expectations with $1 BN," *Financial Times*, April 21, 1998, p. 35; "Mega-Bank Impact in Europe," *International Money Marketing*, April 24, 1998, p. 6; Anne Colden, "Insurers Seeking New Niche in Bank Mega-Merger World," *Journal of Commerce*, April 30, 1998, p. 5A; Gregory J. Hoeg, "Merging Sales Operations Is Key; Financial Services," *Best's Review— Life–Health Insurance Edition*, 99, no. 3 (July 1998), p. 92; "Citibank Eyes 11 New Regional Outlets in Japan," *Jiji Press Ticker Service*, July 3, 1998; Brendan Noonan, "Poking Holes in the Umbrella," *Best's Review—Property–Casualty Insurance Edition*, 99, no. 4 (August 1998), pp. 65–67; "Profitable Partners? Don't Bank on It Yet," *Journal of Commerce*, October 5, 1998, p. 8A; "Citigroup to Begin Trading Today, Following Completion of Merger of Citicorp and Travelers Group," *Business Wire*, October 8, 1998; and Rodd Zolkos, "Insurers Starting to Bank on Integration," *Business Insurance*, January 18, 1999, p. 12D.

3. Wroe Alderson, "Factors Governing the Development of Marketing Channels," in Richard M. Clewett (ed.), *Marketing Channels in Manufactured Products* (Homewood, IL: Richard D. Irwin, 1954), pp. 5–22.

4. PR Newswire, "Metrocall Announces Joint Pager Distribution–Fulfillment Partnership with Motorola; Goals Are to Reduce Pager CAPEX and Other Supply Chain Costs," PR Newswire Association, May 26, 1998.

5. The anecdote about RJR Nabisco is drawn from Howard Millman, "A Brief History of EDI," *Infoworld*, 20, no. 14 (April 6, 1998), p. 83.

6. "Bergen Brunswig Drug Company Announces Strategic Partnership with Longs Drug Stores," *Business Wire*, January 28, 1999.

7. See Todd Gordon, "Streamline Inventory Management via Continuous Replenishment Program," Information Access Company (a Thomson Corporation Company), *Automatic I.D. News*, April 1995, p. 62; Elliott Zwiebach, "Reconstruction: Firms in Grocery Industry Streamline Operations for More Efficient Business," Information Access Company (a Thomson Corporation Company), *Supermarket News*, May 8, 1995, p. 32; and Linda Purpura, "Vendor-Run Inventory: Are Its Benefits Exaggerated?" Information Access Company (a Thomson Corporation Company), *Supermarket News*, January 27, 1997, p. 59.

8. Mark Roe, Marc Weinstein, Jon Bumstead, and Heather Charron, "Forging a Strong European Chain," *Transportation & Distribution*, 39, no. 6 (June 1998), pp. 100–1.

9. Chris Clark, "Trying to Sell Books over the Internet? Yeah, Right," *McTechnology Marketing Intelligence*, 18, no. 8 (August 1998), p. 62.

10. Steve McQueen, "Giving Dealers New Cards to Play," *Purchasing & Supply Management*, March 1995, pp. 6–8.

11. See, for example, PR Newswire, "GMAC and Reynolds and Reynolds Team to Provide the World's First Internet Credit Application," PR Newswire Association, July 15, 1996; Alex Taylor III, "This Guy's History!" *Medical Economics*, 73, no. 9 (May 13, 1996), pp. 202–12; PR

Newswire, "GMAC Expands Product Range in Hungary," PR Newswire Association, October 28, 1996; PR Newswire, "GMAC Launches Finance Operations in Greece," PR Newswire Association, September 3, 1996; Earle Eldridge, "Auto Dealers Find Key to Power in Financing," *USA Today*, February 3, 1997, money section, p. 1B; and PR Newswire, "GMAC's 10-Minute Credit Review," PR Newswire Association, March 20, 1997.

12. Andy Bernstein, "Nutmeg, Sears Test Special Order Kiosks," *Sporting Goods Business*, 29, no. 4 (April 1996), p. 20.

13. The FJM Collections example is drawn from a private communication with Franz-Joseph Miller, the president of the company.

14. Information on Sportswear International comes from a private communication with Francesco Dalla Rovere, an executive with the firm, and is based on a project done jointly by Francesco Dalla Rovere, Eric Berg, Read DuPriest, Juan Motta, and Robert Zwiebach in March 1999.

15. General information about mutual funds is available from many sources, one of which is the Web site for the Investment Company Institute (www.ici.org), an industry trade group. Specific information about The Kent Funds is derived from the company's Web site (www.kentfunds.com).

16. "Kent Funds to Expand National Distribution Through Investment Adviser Markets," press release of The Kent Funds, June 1, 1998.

2 An Analytic Framework for Channel Design and Implementation

LEARNING OBJECTIVES

After reading this chapter, you will:

- Be familiar with a comprehensive framework for channel design and management
- Understand the importance of all the steps of analysis to ensuring a well-performing channel
- Understand the end goal of channel management to be the satisfaction of target end-user segments' demands for service outputs
- Recognize the relationship between expressed service output demands and the implied need to perform channel flows at a certain level
- Recognize the mapping from necessary channel flows to most efficient and effective channel structure to perform those flows
- Understand the concept of gap analysis
- Be aware of the role of channel power in aiding in implementation of the optimal channel design
- Be aware of the threat posed by channel conflict to the implementation of the optimal channel design
- Understand the goal of the channel management process to be the coordination of the channel

*W*hat is the best marketing channel for a particular product or service? This question is well worth asking, given the great expense of establishing (or changing) a marketing channel and the high cost of poor decision making in this area. The marketing channel challenge involves two major tasks: (1) to design the right channel and (2) to implement that design. The *design* step involves segmenting the market, identifying optimal positioning responses to segments' demands, targeting the segments on which to focus the channel's efforts, and establishing (in the absence of a preexisting channel) or refining (in the presence of a preexisting channel) the channels to manage in the marketplace. The *implementation* step requires an understanding of each channel member's sources of power and dependence, an understanding of the potential for channel conflict, and a resulting plan for creating an environment where the optimal channel design can be effectively executed on an ongoing basis. This outcome is called channel coordination.

This chapter presents a framework for analysis that defines and discusses the elements of these two tasks and how they interrelate. The rest of the book is organized around this framework. Figure 2.1 depicts the important elements in the channel design and implementation process: segmentation, positioning, targeting, and responsive channel establishment or refinement, which together comprise the channel design process; and channel power and channel conflict issues, which comprise the

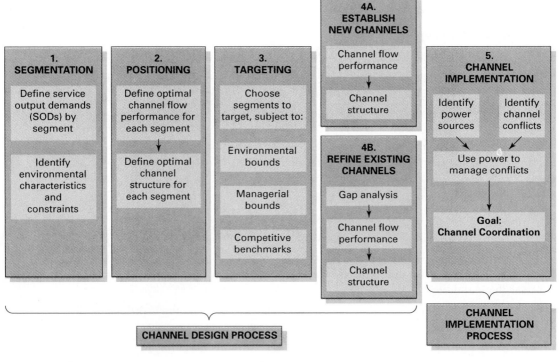

FIGURE 2.1 **Channel Management Schematic**

implementation process. This framework is useful both for creating a new channel in a previously untapped market and for critically analyzing and refining a preexisting channel.

CHANNEL DESIGN: SEGMENTATION

One of the fundamental principles of marketing is the *segmentation* of the market. Segmentation means the splitting of a market into groups of end-users who are (1) maximally similar within each group and (2) maximally different between groups. But maximally similar or maximally different based on what criterion? For the channel manager, segments are best defined *on the basis of demands for the outputs of the marketing channel*. A marketing channel is more than just a conduit for product; it is also a means of adding value to the product marketed through it. In this sense, the marketing channel can be viewed as another "production line" engaged in producing not the product itself that is sold, but the ancillary services that define *how* the product is sold. These value-added services created by channel members and consumed by end-users along with the product purchased are called *service outputs*.[1] Service outputs include (but may not be limited to) *bulk-breaking, spatial convenience, waiting and delivery time*, and *assortment and variety*.

End-users (be they final consumers or business buyers) have varying demands for these service outputs. Consider, for example, two different soft drink buyers: an office employee at work, looking for a soft drink during her afternoon coffee break, and a family buying for at-home consumption. Table 2.1 outlines the differences in service output demands between the two segments of buyers. The office employee has high demands for all service outputs except assortment and variety (for which her demand is moderate, implying willingness to brand switch within reason), whereas the family has the opposite pattern of service output demands. Clearly, a different marketing channel meets the needs of these two segments of shoppers. The office employee cannot travel to a grocery store to buy a can of soda during her break, nor does she want to buy a six-pack or more of cans of soft drinks. She is willing to pay a slightly higher price for the convenience of getting just a single can of soda close to her office. A vending machine would be an ideal retail outlet for her. The family, on the other hand, would not find the vending machine an attractive retail purchase alternative. The family's demand for assortment and variety may not be met by a vending machine, and other service outputs are offered at too high a level, resulting in a higher per-unit price than the family wants (or needs) to pay. A local supermarket does a better job of meeting the family's service output demands for soft drinks. This example shows how the same product can be demanded with a widely varying set of service outputs, resulting in very different demands for the product-plus-service-output bundle by different segments of end-users. An analysis of service output demands by segment is thus an important input into a manufacturer's marketing plan, and can help increase the reach and marketability of a good product to multiple market segments.

Understanding market demands also requires an understanding of the market's *environmental characteristics and constraints*. A market with limited infrastructural

TABLE 2.1

Service Output Demand Differences (an example of segmentation in the soft drink market)

	FAMILY			OFFICE EMPLOYEE	
SERVICE OUTPUT	DESCRIPTOR	SERVICE OUTPUT DEMAND LEVEL		DESCRIPTOR	SERVICE OUTPUT DEMAND LEVEL
Bulk-breaking	"I buy groceries weekly for my family, and all of us like soft drinks."	Low		"I'm on my coffee break and I have time for only one can of soft drink."	High
Spatial convenience	"I drive to the supermarkets in my area to shop."	Low		"I have only 15 minutes for my break, so I need to buy whatever is handy."	High
Waiting and delivery time	"We usually have some extra cans of soft drinks in the house, so I'll just come back the next time if I can't find the soft drinks I want on this trip."	Low		"If I don't get my soft drink right at 3:00 when my break starts, I'll never have a chance to go back later and get one."	High
Assortment and variety	"My husband and I like Coke and Pepsi, but our kids aren't permitted to drink caffeinated soft drinks. They like caffeine-free fruit-flavored soft drinks."	High		"I can't be too particular about which soft drink I pick. It's important to me to get one, as long as it has caffeine."	Moderate

development, for instance, will usually be characterized by consumers with high demands for service outputs such as: 1) *spatial convenience* (because the consumers cannot travel very easily to remote retail locations), 2) *minimal waiting time for goods* (because consumers will not have sufficiently high disposable income to keep "backup stocks" of goods at their homes in case of retail stockouts), and 3) *bulk-breaking* (again because, with low disposable incomes, consumers cannot afford to buy large lot sizes of goods, even if doing so would mean a lower price per unit). An example of the impact of these constraints on consumer purchasing is the market for Wrigley's chewing gum in the People's Republic of China: Individual packs of gum are sold through many small kiosks and stalls in local marketplaces after traveling a circuitous (and high-cost) route through the countryside.[2] If Wrigley's is to sell to Chinese consumers, it must recognize their high service output demands in order to construct a marketing channel to meet those demands.

Consumer analysis for marketing channel design is the topic of Chapter 3.

CHANNEL DESIGN: POSITIONING

When the market has been segmented into groups of end-users, each of which can be described by a set of service output demands, the channel manager should next define the optimal channel to serve each segment. We call this exercise *positioning* or *configuring* the channel (positioning to parallel the segmentation–targeting–positioning paradigm in marketing management). Just as positioning a product means setting its product attributes, price, and promotional mix to best fit the demands of a particular segment, so also positioning refers to the design of the distribution channel to meet the segment's demands. This exercise should be done, even if the channel ends up not selling to some of the segments in the end. The channel analyst may then discover that some segments simply do not make good targets because their demands cannot be adequately met with the channel's current resources. Alternatively, the positioning exercise may reveal some unexpectedly attractive segments to target. Unless the optimal channel is defined for each segment, it is impossible to make a thorough decision about what segments to target.[3]

The optimal channel is defined first and foremost by the *necessary channel flows* that must be performed in order to generate the specific segment's service output demands. Channel flows are all the activities of the channel that add value to the end-user. In enumerating the list of channel flows, we go beyond the concept of the mere handling of the product to include issues of promotion, negotiation, financing, ordering, payment, and the like (see Figure 1.2). For instance, our office employee looking for a soft drink on her coffee break (see Table 2.1) has a high demand for spatial convenience and minimal tolerance for out-of-stock product. This means that the channel flow of physical possession (the physical holding of inventory) takes on great importance for such end-users. Each product or service-selling situation can have its own unique set of service output demands by segment, implying that the differential importance of different sets of channel flows depends on the segment.

Further, the channel analyst must identify the optimal *channel structure* to produce the necessary channel flows, which themselves, of course, result in the generation of the required service outputs that are demanded by a particular segment of end-users in the market. The design of the channel structure involves two main elements. First, the channel designer must decide who are to be the members of the channel. For example, will a consumer packaged-goods manufacturer sell its grocery products through small independent retailers with in-city locations, or through large chain stores that operate discount warehouse stores? Or will it use an outlet such as Indiangrocer.com, an on-line seller of Indian food and household products that operates no retail stores at all?[4] Moving up the channel from the retail level, decisions must be made whether to use independent distributors, independent sales representative companies (called "reps" or "rep firms"), independent trucking companies, financing companies, export management companies, and any of a whole host of other possible independent distribution channel members that could be incorporated into the channel design.

Beyond this decision, the channel manager must also decide the exact identity of the channel partner to use at each level of the channel. For example, if it is deemed advisable to sell a line of fine watches through retail stores, should the outlets chosen be more upscale, such as Tiffany's, or should they be family-owned local jewelers? The choice can have implications both for the efficiency with which the channel is run and the image connoted by distributing through a particular kind of retailer. In a different context, if a company seeks distribution for its products in a foreign market, the key decision may be which distributor is appointed to carry the product line into the overseas market. The right distributor may have much better relationships with local channel partners in the target market and can signficantly affect the success of the foreign market entry.

The other main element of the channel structure is the decision of how many of each type of channel member will be in the channel. This is the *channel intensity* decision. In particular, should the channel for a consumer good include many retail outlets (intensive distribution), just a few (selective distribution), or only one (exclusive distribution) in a given market area? The answer to this question depends both on efficiency and on implementation factors. More intensive distribution may make the product more easily available to all target end-users, but may create conflict among the retailers competing to sell it.

The channel structure decisions of type, identity, and intensity of channel members all should be made with the minimization of channel flow costs in mind. That is, each channel member is allocated a set of channel flows to perform, and ideally the allocation of activities results in the reliable performance of all channel flows at minimum total cost. This is a nontrivial task, particularly because it involves comparing activities across different companies who are members of the channel. Intuitively, an activity-based costing (or ABC) sort of analysis is useful to establish the best allocation of channel flows.[5]

This exercise results in one channel profile for each segment that is identified in the market segmentation stage of the exercise. Each of these channel profiles is called a *zero-based channel*, because it is designed from a zero base of operations—that is, as if no preexisting channel exists in the market. The concept of a zero-based channel means (1) that the segment's service output demands are met and (2) that they are met at minimum total channel cost.

Channel flows are discussed in more detail in Chapter 4, whereas channel structure is the topic of Chapter 5.

CHANNEL DESIGN: TARGETING

At this stage of the analysis, the channel manager is equipped to decide what segments to target. Note carefully that this also means that the channel manager is now equipped to decide what segments not to target! Knowing what segments to ignore in one's channel design and management efforts is very important, because it keeps the channel focused on the key segments from which it plans to reap profitable sales.

Why not target all the segments identified in the segmentation and positioning analyses? The answer requires the channel manager to look at the internal and external environment facing the channel. Internally, *managerial bounds* may constrain the channel manager from implementing the zero-based channel. For example, top management of a manufacturing firm may be unwilling to allocate funds to build a series of regional warehouses that would be necessary to provide spatial convenience in a particular market situation. Externally, both *environmental bounds* and *competitive benchmarks* may suggest some segments as higher priority than others. For example, legal practices can constrain channel design and hence targeting decisions. Many countries restrict the opening of large mass-merchandise stores in urban areas, to protect small shopkeepers whose sales would be threatened by larger retailers.[6] Such legal restrictions can lead to a channel design that does not appropriately meet the target segment's service output demands, and may cause a channel manager to avoid targeting that segment entirely.

Of course, the corollary of this statement is that when superior competitive offerings do not exist to serve a particular segment's demands for service outputs, the channel manager may recognize an unexploited market opportunity and create a new channel to serve that underserved segment. Meeting previously unmet service output demands can be a powerful competitive strategy for building loyal and profitable consumer bases in a marketplace. But these strategies can best be identified with knowledge of what consumers want to buy, and importantly, how they want to buy it, and the necessary response in terms of channel flow performance and channel structure.

We have now identified a subset of the market's segments that the channel plans on targeting, using the segmentation and positioning insights derived earlier.

Chapter 6 discusses the channel manager's targeting decision in the context of environmental and managerial bounds as well as competitive benchmarks.

CHANNEL DESIGN: ESTABLISH NEW CHANNELS OR REFINE EXISTING CHANNELS

Now, the channel manager has identified the optimal way to reach each targeted segment in the market, and has also identified the bounds that might prevent the channel from implementing the zero-based channel design in the market. If no channel exists currently in the market for this segment, the channel manager should now establish the channel design that comes the closest to meeting the target market's demands for service outputs, subject to the environmental and managerial bounds constraining the design.

If there is a preexisting channel in place in the market, however, the channel manager should now perform a *gap analysis*. The differences between the zero-based and actual channels on the demand and supply sides constitute gaps in the channel design. Gaps can exist on the demand side or on the supply side.

On the demand side, gaps mean that at least one of the service output demands is not being appropriately met by the channel. The service output in question may be either undersupplied or oversupplied. The problem is obvious in the case of undersupply: The target segment is likely to be dissatisfied because end-users would prefer more service than they are getting. The problem is more subtle in the case of oversupply. Here, target end-users are getting all the service they desire—and then some. The problem is that service is costly to supply, and therefore, supplying too much of it leads to higher prices than the target end-users are likely to be willing to pay. Clearly, more than one service output may be a problem, in which case several gaps may need attention.

On the supply side, gaps mean that at least one flow in the channel of distribution is carried out at too high a cost. This not only wastes channel profit margins, but can result in higher prices than the target market is willing to pay, leading to reductions in sales and market share. Supply-side gaps can result from a lack of up-to-date expertise in channel flow management or simply from waste in the channel. The challenge in closing a supply-side gap is to reduce cost without dangerously reducing the service outputs being supplied to target end-users.

When gaps are identified on the demand or supply sides, several strategies are available for closing the gaps. But once a channel is already in place, it may be very difficult and costly to close these gaps. This suggests the strategic importance of initial channel design. If the channel is initially designed in a haphazard manner, channel members may have to live with a suboptimal channel later on, even after recognizing channel gaps and making best efforts to close them.

We discuss the gap analysis and mechanisms for closing gaps in more depth in Chapter 6.

CHANNEL IMPLEMENTATION: IDENTIFYING POWER SOURCES

Assuming that a good channel design is in place in the market, the channel manager's job is still not done. The channel members now must *implement* the optimal channel design and indeed must continue to implement an optimal design through time. The value of doing so might seem to be self-evident, but it is important to remember that a channel is made up of multiple interdependent entities (companies, agents, individuals). But they may or may not all have the same incentives to implement the optimal channel design.

Incompatible incentives among channel members would not be a problem if they were not dependent upon each other. But by the very nature of the distribution channel structure and design, specific channel members are likely to *specialize* in particular activities and flows in the channel. If all channel members do not perform appropriately, the entire channel effort suffers. For example, even if everything else is in place, a poorly performing transportation system that results in late deliveries (or no deliveries) of product to retail stores prevents the channel from succeeding in selling the product. The same type of statement could be made about the performance of any channel member doing any of the flows in the channel. Thus, it is apparent that inducing all of the channel members to implement the channel design appropriately is critical.

How, then, can a channel captain implement the optimal channel design, in the face of interdependence among channel partners, not all of whom have the incentive to cooperate in the performance of their designated channel flows? The answer lies in the possession and use of *channel power*. A channel member's power "is its ability to control the decision variables in the marketing strategy of another member in a given channel at a different level of distribution." [7] These sources of channel power can of course be used to further one channel member's individual ends. But if channel power is used instead to influence channel members to do the jobs that the optimal channel design specifies that they do, the result will be a channel that more closely delivers demanded service outputs, at a lower cost.

Chapter 8 develops the concept of power in depth.

CHANNEL IMPLEMENTATION: IDENTIFYING CHANNEL CONFLICTS

Channel conflict is generated when one channel member's actions prevent the channel from achieving its goals. Channel conflict is both common and dangerous to the success of distribution efforts. Given the interdependence of all channel members, any one member's actions have an influence on the total success of the channel effort, and thus can harm total channel performance.[8]

Channel conflict can stem from differences between channel members' goals and objectives (*goal conflict*), from disagreements over the domain of action and responsibility in the channel (*domain conflict*), and from differences in perceptions of the marketplace (*perceptual conflict*). These conflicts directly cause a channel member to fail to perform the flows that the optimal channel design specifies for them, and thus inhibit total channel performance. The management problem is twofold. First, the channel manager needs to be able to identify the sources of channel conflict, and in particular, to differentiate between poor channel design and poor performance due to channel conflict. Second, the channel manager must decide on the action to take (if any) to manage and reduce the channel conflicts that have been identified.

In general, channel conflict reduction is accomplished through the application of one or more sources of channel power. For example, a manufacturer may identify a conflict in its independent-distributor channel: The distributorship is exerting too little sales effort on behalf of the manufacturer's product line and therefore sales of the product are suffering. Analysis might reveal that the effort level is low because the distributorship makes more profit from selling a competitor's product than from selling this manufacturer's product. There is thus a goal conflict. The manufacturer's goal is the maximization of profit over its own product line, but the distributorship's goal is the maximization of profit over all of the products that it sells—only some of which come from this particular manufacturer. To resolve the goal conflict, the manufacturer might use one of the following strategies: (1) It might use some of its power to reward the distributor by increasing the distributor's discount, thus increasing the profit margin it can make on the manufacturer's product line. Or (2), the manufacturer may invest in developing brand equity and thus pull the product through the channel. In that case, its brand power induces the distributor to sell the product more aggressively because the sales potential for the product has risen. In both cases, some sort of leverage or power on the part of the manufacturer is necessary to change the distributor's behavior and thus reduce the channel conflict.

Channel conflict is discussed in detail in Chapter 9.

CHANNEL IMPLEMENTATION: THE GOAL OF CHANNEL COORDINATION

After following all five steps of the channel management schematic in Figure 2.1, the channel will have been designed with target end-user segments' service output demands in mind, and channel power will be appropriately applied to ensure the smooth implementation of the optimal channel design. When the disparate members of the channel are brought together to advance the goals of the channel, rather than their own independent (and likely conflicting) goals, the channel is said to be *coordinated*. This term is used to denote both the coordination of interests and actions among the channel members who produce the outputs of the marketing channel, and the coordination of performance of channel flows with the production of the service outputs demanded by target end-users. This is the end goal of the entire channel management process. As conditions change in the marketplace, the channel's design and implementation may need to respond; thus, channel coordination is not a one-time achievement, but an ongoing process of analysis and response to the market, the competition, and the abilities of the members of the channel.

ORGANIZATION OF THE TEXT

The organization of the text is summarized in Figure 2.2, which restates Figure 2.1 with annotations for chapters dealing with each element of channel management. Chapters 3 through 7 lay out the basic framework for the channel design process; Chapters 8 and 9 discuss channel power and channel conflict. The later chapters build on this basis by adding insights about specific channel institutions and forms, as well as about the environment in which channel decisions are made and how to assess channel performance.

Specifically, segmentation is the topic of Chapter 3. Positioning is covered in Chapter 4 (through a discussion of channel flows) and Chapter 5 (through a discussion of channel structure). The bounds (both environmental and managerial) that circumscribe the targeting decision are the topic of Chapter 6, whereas the legal environment

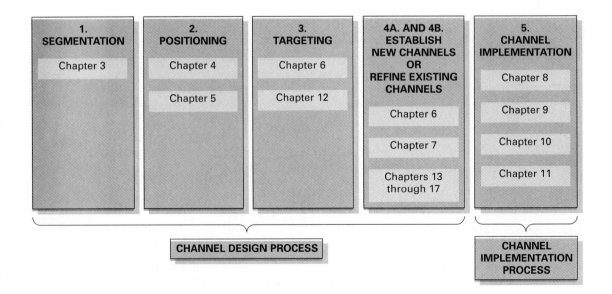

FIGURE 2.2 **Organization of the Text**

and the restrictions it imposes on targeting are covered in Chapter 12. Discussion of topics involving the establishment or refinement of channels occurs in Chapter 6 (on gap analysis), Chapter 7 (on vertical integration as a limit of channel organization), and in Chapters 13 through 17 (which deal with various retail institutions, wholesaling and logistics, and franchising). Channel implementation issues are discussed in Chapters 8 through 12. Chapter 8 covers aspects of channel power and focuses on compensation systems as a specific aspect of reward power. Chapter 9 develops the topic of channel conflict, and Chapter 10 discusses how to deal with channel conflicts raised by issues regarding distribution intensity and vertical restraints. Chapter 11 raises specific implementation issues in distribution alliances, and Chapter 12 covers legal factors that influence implementation of channel designs.

Throughout we provide tools for analysis of the channel, to guide the student or channel manager in the channel management process. After studying the book, the reader will have a firm grasp both of the necessary elements of channel analysis and management, and of the specific institutions that comprise marketing channels in today's worldwide marketplace.

SUMMARY

Figure 2.1 encompasses all of the elements necessary for effective channel management: an analysis of demand factors in the marketplace and their importance for distribution channel design; the responsive design process that characterizes the optimal distribution channel to reach target segments of end-users; the recognition that these decisions are made in the context of environmental and managerial bounds on behavior; the identification and closing of channel gaps wherever possible; and the issues surrounding effective implementation of the optimal channel design.

The discussion suggests that all of these elements of analysis are important in generating a well-designed and well-working marketing channel. None of the elements can be safely ignored. Ignoring the segmented nature of demands for service outputs leaves the channel manager with no guidelines for optimal channel design. Ignorance of the costs of channel flow allocations leads to channels that operate at too high a cost. Failing to close demand-side or supply-side gaps leaves the channel open to competitive challenges. And failure to recognize the threats of channel conflict, or the leverage that channel power confers on the channel manager, can leave a well-designed channel open to poor performance in the marketplace because of improper implementation of the design.

Discussion Questions

1. Why is it that "small, medium, and large" is not as strong a segmentation scheme for service outputs as it might be for product attributes? Use a business-to-business product or market in your answer; for example, steel, semiconductors, fax machines sold to sheet metal fabricators, computer companies, or insurance agents.

2. Explain how the shopping characteristics for the following consumer and industrial goods affect the channels for them:

Consumer Goods	Industrial Goods
Bread	Computer printer ink cartridges
Breakfast cereal	Uranium (for nuclear power plants)
Women's hats	Cement
Refrigerators	Data-processing equipment

3. Describe how the necessary channel flow performance differs when selling and servicing an ultrasound machine (a piece of medical equipment) when targeting two different segments of buyers: (a) a hospital emergency room and (b) an academic medical researcher on a tight government-funded budget, using the machine for laboratory research.

4. Should a channel manager always seek to target the maximum possible number of segments to sell to? Why or why not?

5. The service on high-end automobiles is of very good quality: timely, done by polite and competent professionals, and done at service facilities that give the auto owner access to many amenities (such as free refreshments, free loaner cars, etc.). In what sense can there be a demand-side gap in this service channel?

6. Explain how not keeping up with advances in distribution channel technology (e.g., information technology advances, warehouse management techniques, database management tools, etc.) can cause an otherwise well-working channel to develop a supply-side gap.

7. Why is it important to understand channel power sources and channel conflict sources? Why can we not simply design a zero-based channel and be done with the channel analysis process?

Notes

1. Louis P. Bucklin defines service outputs in *A Theory of Distribution Channel Structure* (Berkeley, CA: IBER Special Publications, 1966) and *Competition and Evolution in the Distributive Trades* (Upper Saddle River, NJ: Prentice Hall, 1972), pp. 18–31. See also Michael Etgar, "An Empirical Analysis of the Motivations for the Development of Centrally Coordinated Vertical Marketing Systems: The Case of the Property and Casualty Insurance Industry," unpublished doctoral dissertation, University of California at Berkeley, 1974, pp. 95–97.

2. Craig S. Smith, "Doublemint in China: Distribution Isn't Double the Fun," *Wall Street Journal*, December 5, 1995, pp. B1, B3.

3. Louis P. Bucklin (*A Theory of Distribution Channel Structure* and *Competition and Evolution*) originally proposed that a knowledge of service output demands leads to the specification of channel flows, and that channel structure should be chosen to minimize flow costs. George J. Stigler, "The Division of Labor Is Limited by the Extent of the Market," *Journal of Political Economy*, June 1951, pp. 185–93, speaks more generally of allocating business activities to their lowest-cost performers. The discussion here is consistent with and based on these ideas.

4. We thank Subjash Bedi and Parry Singh, founders of Indiangrocer.com, for information about this on-line service.

5. For information on activity-based costing, see, for example, Bala Balachandran, "Strategic Activity Based Accounting," *Business Week Executive Briefing Service*, 1994; Ronald E. Yates, "New ABCs for Pinpoint Accounting," *Chicago Tribune*, January 24, 1993; Robin Cooper and Robert S. Kaplan, "Profit Priorities from Activity-Based Costing," *Harvard Business Review*, May–June 1991, pp. 130–35; and William Rotch, "Activity-Based Costing in Service Industries," *Journal of Cost Management*, summer 1990, pp. 4–14.

6. The Large Scale Retail Store Law in Japan requires retailers wanting to open a store larger than 5,000 square meters to follow a complicated bureaucratic process that tends to prevent large stores from opening in-town commercial centers. Other legal constraints exist in some European markets, where "green belts" are sometimes created around cities and inside of which large retailers may not open stores. For a viewpoint on the perceived threat imposed by outlet mall developers in Europe, see Ernest Beck, "Europeans Fear a Mauling by Outlet Malls," *Wall Street Journal Europe*, September 16, 1997, p. 4.

7. Adel I. El-Ansary and Louis W. Stern, "Power Measurement in the Distribution Channel," *Journal of Marketing Research*, 9 (February 1972), p. 47. Other related

definitions and implications of channel power are discussed in depth in Chapter 8.

8. See Louis W. Stern and J. L. Heskett, "Conflict Management in Interorganization Relations: A Conceptual Framework," in Louis W. Stern (ed.), *Distribution Channels: Behavioral Dimensions* (Boston, MA: Houghton Mifflin, 1969), pp. 288–305; Larry J. Rosenberg and Louis W. Stern, "Conflict Measurement in the Distribution Channel," *Journal of Marketing Research*, 8 (November 1971), pp. 437–42; Michael Etgar, "Sources and Types of Intrachannel Conflict," *Journal of Retailing*, 55 (spring 1979), pp. 61–78; Ernest R. Cadotte and Louis W. Stern, "A Process Model of Dyadic Interorganizational Relations in Marketing Channels," in Jagdish N. Sheth (ed.), *Research in Marketing*, 2 (Greenwich, CT: JAI Press, 1979); and Torger Reve and Louis W. Stern, "Interorganizational Relations in Marketing Channels," *Academy of Management Review*, 4 (July 1979), pp. 405–16.

PART TWO

CHANNEL DESIGN: DEMAND, SUPPLY, AND COMPETITION

3 Segmentation for Marketing Channel Design: Service Outputs

LEARNING OBJECTIVES

After reading this chapter, you will:

- Understand the central role played by end-users and their demands in the design of marketing channels
- Know what "service outputs" are and how to identify and analyze them
- Understand how service output demands evolve with changes in consumer demographics and behavior
- Be able to divide a market into channel segments for the purposes of marketing channel design or modification
- Be able to evaluate when and whether to try to meet all expressed service output demands in the short run in a particular market
- Understand the relationship between service output demands and solutions to overall channel design problems

Marketing channel system design and management, like the management of any other marketing activity, requires starting with the end-user. The channel manager must first understand the nature of end-users' demands in order to design a well-working channel that meets or exceeds those demands. The most useful demand-side insights for marketing channel design are not about what end-users want to consume, but about how end-users want to buy and use the products or services being purchased. We will thus take as given a viable product for the market and concern ourselves with the understanding of how to sell it rather than what to sell. This chapter focuses on the demand side of the marketing channel design problem, first by describing end-user behavior and trends in purchase preferences in the marketplace. In all markets, end-users will have differential preferences and demands for service outputs that reduce their search, waiting time, storage, and other costs. Grouping end-users in the market by demands for service outputs (as opposed to preferences for physical product attributes, for example) helps us define potential target market segments for which to design specific marketing channel solutions. We then ask under what marketplace conditions it is most important to meet all service output demands, and how to link together this demand-side analysis with the decisions that must be made on the supply side when designing a channel. Appendix 3.1 presents the service output demands template, a tool for analyzing segmented demands for service outputs.

END-USER CHANNEL PREFERENCES

End-users (both business-to-business buyers and individual consumers) purchase more than a product. The Channel Sketches on Peapod, W. W. Grainger, and Charles Schwab illustrate this idea. In all of these examples, a particular product or service can be bought in multiple different ways. It is not the product that changes, but rather the method of buying and selling the product and its associated services. In the Peapod example, the essential difference to the shopper between a standard grocery store purchasing experience and the Peapod shopping experience lies in the convenience and speed of being able to shop from home and getting delivery directly to one's home, without giving up any product availability or pricing benefits of shopping in the store.

The W. W. Grainger example suggests that this seller believes it can reach some business buyers better by offering them a "one-stop shopping" experience. The alliance among the six companies selling together on the single (OrderZone.com) Web site lets the customer make one purchase decision instead of six and offers consolidated billing as well. This simplifies the business buyer's task and reduces transaction costs, which is of great value in noncore purchasing situations such as these.

The Schwab OneSource example illustrates in a services-buying context that one-stop shopping, comparison shopping, and consolidated statements are all of value to at least some investors who are willing to trade off access to investment advice for the low price and ease of choice offered by the supermarket. But this channel is clearly not for every investor. If it were, standard investment advisers and trust departments of banks would now be out of business.

These examples suggest the need to identify how the end-user wants to buy as well as what the end-user wants to buy. Further, they suggest that different end-users have different demands, and that understanding and responding to those demands can create new business opportunities for manufacturers. We turn next to a discussion of the *how* of distributing products by defining the concept of service outputs in the channel.

CHANNEL SKETCH 3.1

Peapod: Electronic Grocery Shopping[1]

A typical grocery shopping process generally involves several steps, as outlined in Table 3.1.

In this standard grocery shopping experience, the consumer benefits from being able to see and touch the merchandise before buying it. Grocery stores also provide an assortment of products from which to choose and may also offer nongrocery products and services for sale (e.g., pharmacy products, photo finishing, banking services, florist shop, coffee bar, etc.).

Despite the many benefits and great sophistication of today's grocery markets, many consumers are unhappy with the standard grocery store shopping experience. In a survey conducted by Peapod and the M/A/R/C consulting group, only 11 percent of shoppers said grocery shopping is fun; 83 percent said it takes too much time; 50 percent said saving time is more important than saving money; 85 percent were looking for ways to save time; and 93 percent were looking for ways to simplify their lives. In response, a new channel has developed for shopping electronically for groceries. The innovating company in this channel category is called Peapod (www.peapod.com), although it has been followed by other competitors such as HomeGrocer.com and Webvan.com (which raised $100 million in venture capital in 1999 to build a network of warehouses across the United States). Although these other competitors offer variants on a theme, we describe the evolution of the Peapod system as a means of illustrating the service output demands that on-line grocery shopping can meet.

Peapod lets shoppers buy a full array of groceries on-line and have them delivered to the shopper's home. The service lets shoppers use coupons and provides access to many of the ancillary products and services that a bricks-and-mortar grocery store provides.

Founded in 1989 in the Chicago area, Peapod originally took orders on-line through a proprietary software system that allowed the shopper to shop the assort-

TABLE 3.1
Peapod: Grocery Shopping Steps

Shopping Process Step	Who Performs This Step In:	
	A Standard Grocery Store Shopping Trip	A Peapod Shopping Experience
Plan what to buy (prepare shopping list)	Shopper	Shopper
Travel to grocery store	Shopper	Peapod
Walk aisles of store	Shopper	Peapod
Pick grocery items one by one	Shopper	Peapod
Checkout process	Shopper	Peapod
Bag groceries	Shopper	Peapod
Transport groceries home	Shopper	Peapod
Unpack groceries	Shopper	Shopper

ment of the Jewel-Osco Food Store, a major grocery retailer in Chicago, at any hour of the day or night from any computer equipped with the Peapod software. Peapod employees then shopped the aisles of actual Jewel-Osco stores to fill each order, then delivered them to the shopper's home within a prespecified two-hour window (an extra fee entitled the shopper to a half-hour window for delivery). In October 1998, Peapod moved from the proprietary software system to a World Wide Web–based access system, making it accessible from any computer equipped with a Web browser, not just from those equipped with proprietary Peapod software. The new software offers an option for increased checkout speed, nutrition and ingredients lists, and a cumulative list of what has been purchased during an on-line shopping trip. The technology is particularly attractive to dual-career families and to professional women ordering from their workplace. Shoppers familiar with the system can complete an average ($115) order in about 15 to 20 minutes, significantly faster than in-store shopping. Convenience has generated meteoric growth in volume, shown in Table 3.2.

Note that despite the persistent losses that Peapod has generated, the company floated a successful initial public offering (IPO) in 1997 and raised $58 million in capital to fund expansion. Management expects significant software and warehouse investments made over the next few years to generate long-run benefits as the company expands throughout the U.S. market. As of early 1999, Peapod held about 70 percent of the market share in on-line grocery sales in the United States. However, it faces potentially stiff competition from other entrants into the business, including Webvan.com, whose managers have undertaken the building of a nationwide network of electronic grocery shopping operations and warehouses.

Peapod opened its first dedicated distribution center on Long Island, New York, in December 1998, followed by another in suburban Chicago with more to come. The shift from shopping the aisles of actual grocery stores to picking and packing orders from an owned distribution center is expected to decrease the cost of filling orders and lead to reduced delivery costs for shoppers. These facilities are planned to contain an "efficient assortment" of grocery, dairy, and frozen products, and to be replenished on a just-in-time basis by suppliers. Perishable products are planned to be "cross-docked," implying that they will sit in inventory for a minimal amount of

TABLE 3.2
Peapod: Growth Data

YEAR	REVENUES ($ 000)	NUMBER OF MEMBERS	NUMBER OF ORDERS	NET PROFIT (LOSS) ($ 000)
1994	$ 8,346	7,900	70,300	n/a
1995	$15,943	12,500	124,100	($6,592)
1996	$29,173	33,300	201,100	($9,567)
1997	$59,607	71,500	396,600	($12,980)
1998	$69,300	100,000	503,300 (est.)*	($21,565)

Note: * Estimate based on orders in first quarter of 136,600; in second quarter of 128,600; and in third quarter of 112,300. Fourth quarter was estimated as average of first three quarters.

Source: 1997 and 1998 company annual reports.

time. The warehouse is equipped with scanning technologies to automate several warehouse processes, and Peapod has incorporated a new transportation routing system to lower the costs of delivery.

The Peapod shopper pays a delivery charge for using the service, with three delivery charge choices ($9.95 per order with no monthly fee; $5.00 per order plus a flat charge of $4.95 per month; or unlimited deliveries for $19.95 per month with a $60.00 minimum order size). Of the activities described above in a typical bricks-and-mortar grocery shopping trip, only the first (planning what to buy) and last (unpacking) must be done by the Peapod shopper. All others are done by Peapod employees.

Although Peapod was already operating in Chicago; San Francisco–San Jose, California; Columbus, Ohio; Boston, Massachusetts; Houston, Dallas, and Austin, Texas; and Long Island, New York, serving over 100,000 shoppers in 1998. It also rolled out a national service called Peapod Packages in August 1998. This service offers preselected bundles of products to fit niche-buying occasions such as holiday assortments, new baby gifts, and the like. The packages are deliverable across the continental United States. In November 1998, Peapod formed an alliance with a leading on-line specialty food store, GreatFood.com (www.greatfood.com) to offer GreatFood's high-end specialty food products through the Peapod Packages program, adding to the available array of products. Peapod management hopes to tap into a market for special-occasion food purchases as well as bundled meal solutions and specialty food products. By enabling nationwide shipping, Peapod also invests in brand-name recognition for its service in markets that are currently unserved by the full Peapod service.

Peapod has recently ventured beyond its own business boundaries to form alliances with some other Internet-based companies. One of these, the HomeArts Network (www.homearts.com), offers programming from various women's magazines published by the Hearst Corporation. In announcing the alliance, HomeArts' general manager said, "HomeArts' audience, which is 71% female, craves convenience. . . . Peapod offers a very convenient way for time-strapped women—at home or in the office—to access an entire grocery store on their PCs."

Is Peapod a universally desirable channel for shopping for groceries? Not for everyone. Research done by Chicago Strategy Associates found three main segments of grocery shoppers: the "low prices and comparisons" segment (43 percent of respondents), the "efficiency seekers" (39 percent of respondents), and the "branded-products-delivered" segment (18 percent of respondents). Table 3.3 shows the relative importance placed by each segment on the various service outputs of importance in grocery shopping, as found in the research study. The branded-products-delivered segment placed a very high importance on home delivery and on the availability of specific brands desired, in contrast to the other two segments. Further, 44 percent of the respondents in this segment are heavy Internet users, making them prime targets for on-line grocery shopping services. In particular, Table 3.4 details the responses on two dimensions of the valuation of home delivery, showing that only the branded-products-delivered segment places a high value on these offerings. In short, although the on-line grocery channel may be

TABLE 3.3
Peapod: Three Channel Segments for Grocery Shopping

Range of Service Outputs Demanded	Segment's Relative Importance of Service Output		
	Branded Products Delivered	*Low Prices– Comparisons*	*Fast–Efficient Purchase Process*
Purchase process easy to find, select, and buy	**High**	Moderate	**High**
Purchases are delivered to home	**Very high**	Low	Low
Information on product usage–needs planning	Low	**High**	Low
Fast and efficient buying process	**High**	Low	**Very high**
Information on comparing and choosing	Moderate	**Very high**	Low
Ability to see, touch, and inspect products	Moderate	Moderate	**High**
Absolute lowest prices	Moderate	**Very high**	Low
Experience provides social interaction	Low	**Very high**	Low
Place sells specific brands desired	**Very high**	Moderate	**Moderate**
Percent who are heavy Internet users	**44%**	**23%**	**31%**

Source: Reprinted with permission of Rick Wilson, Chicago Strategy Associates, © 2000.

close to perfect for these consumers, they do not constitute the majority of the grocery shopping public at present.

Consistent with these research findings, Peapod had over 100,000 shoppers by 1999, with over one percent household penetration in the cities in which it operates. At the industry level, on-line grocery sales are forecast to reach $33.6 billion bought by 6.9 million U.S. households by the year 2002. However, overall U.S. grocery sales were $401.7 billion in 1997, suggesting that on-line grocery shopping is still not for

TABLE 3.4
Peapod: Three Channel Segments: Value of Home Delivery

On a 10-point scale (1 = lowest importance and 10 = highest importance)		
	Low Price and Efficiency Segments	Home-Delivery Segment
Importance of home delivery in creating ideal grocery shopping experience . . .	**1.8**	**7.4**
Improvement in having groceries delivered to your home would make shopping more ideal . . .	**3.8**	**6.7**

Source: Reprinted with permission of Rick Wilson, Chicago Strategy Associates, © 2000.

everyone. Over 75 percent of Peapod shoppers are female, and most come from dual-income families with children. Seventy-seven percent of Peapod shoppers have a household income of more than $60,000. Shoppers who value the extra service provided by Peapod enough to pay the delivery fee, and who do not mind losing the ability to touch and feel their groceries before buying them, are the most likely targets today. Despite the apparently narrow description of the target market for this channel form, shoppers in the United States are not the only ones who would value the services Peapod provides. A study by Andersen Consulting in the United States and Europe in 1996 found that 42 percent of shoppers wanted home ordering and delivery of groceries, particularly of commodity or staple items. Also a 1996 survey of European food retailers by the *Financial Times* reported that half believe that home delivery of groceries will represent 20 percent of retail grocery volume by the year 2005.

CHANNEL SKETCH 3.2

W. W. Grainger: Industrial Maintenance, Repair, Operating (MRO) Supplies[2]

With 1998 sales of $4.3 billion, Grainger is the leading U.S. distributor of maintenance, repair, and operating (MRO) supplies to commercial, industrial, contractor, and institutional customers. Its products include motors, electrical and lighting supplies, janitorial supplies, tools, HVAC, and many other offerings. Although not glamorous, most business buyers consider these to be necessary purchases because Grainger's products keep buildings and businesses running. Grainger's market share in 1998 of less than 3 percent of the estimated $250 billion to $300 billion (annual sales) U.S. MRO supplies market indicates how fragmented the distribution industry still is in this area.

Historically, Grainger has served its business buyers through catalogs, telephone sales, and direct selling, with products either picked up at the 350 branches scattered throughout the United States or shipped from the six zone distribution centers or the national distribution center. The local presence is critical for many of the items Grainger supplies; when a motor fails on an assembly line, no company can afford to wait while a replacement is sent, even by FedEx. Grainger branch employees have even had customers "deliver" the broken motor and ask for a replacement, unsure what kind is needed.

Grainger's reputation with its 1.5 million customers has been built over 72 years, and employees have extended the layers of goodwill through an emphasis on customer service. Customers who visit the branches or order by phone have a relationship with Grainger employees, which is very important to the company's past success. However, the company recognized early that the Internet would change the way some—eventually perhaps all—customers would buy. Throughout the 1990s, it continuously upgraded its presence on the Internet to communicate with and sell to its customers. The company overview in Figure 3.1 suggests that the company has built its success on effective and responsive customer ser-

- *Employees—more than 11,800, including 1,500 full-time outside sales representatives.*
- *350 local branches, 1 national distribution center, 2 regional distribution centers, 6 zone distribution centers—linked by satellite network to guarantee product availability. Average branch size is 20,000 square feet. Seventy percent of U.S. businesses are within 20 minutes of a Grainger branch.*
- *Serving the needs of diverse markets, including contractors, manufacturers, industrial accounts, commercial accounts (property management, hotels), and institutions (schools, health care facilities, government agencies).*
- *Wide product line—more than 200,000 products available through local branches and on-line through the Grainger.com catalog. Average branch inventory of $2 million allows immediate pickup or same-day shipment or delivery for most products.*
- *Replacement parts—over 220,000 repair and replacement parts from more than 550 suppliers.*
- *Comprehensive electronic databases enable rapid locating of products by description, brand name, manufacturer's model number, and Grainger stock number.*
- *Grainger CD-ROM electronic catalog—free to Grainger customers, it provides account-specific pricing, and users receive regular updates and changes.*
- *Grainger general catalog—more than 2.6 million illustrated catalogs are distributed per year.*
- *Grainger.com—the corporation's Web site providing 24-hour-a-day on-line ordering capability.*

Source: Grainger Web site, www.grainger.com.

FIGURE 3.1 **Grainger: Company Overview**

vice. Service is a multidimensional concept, including convenient and numerous branches and distribution centers, technology to locate and deliver products quickly, up-to-date billing practices, an enormous (in the hundreds of thousands of stockkeeping units) product line, and courteous service. Grainger's challenge is to find ways to integrate the traditional bricks-and-mortar world with the new channel offered by the Internet.

Already offering its customers such a broad variety of products, located close to the customer's site, with the means to find products quickly, it would seem there was little more that Grainger could do to improve its quality of service to the market. Yet throughout 1999, Grainger formed several alliances that have even further increased its breadth of offerings and its electronic presence for its business customers.

Most prominent has been the formation of OrderZone.com (www.orderzone.com), announced in February 1999 and rolled out in May 1999. This specialized business-to-business electronic-commerce Web site offers the products of six companies selling complementary offerings to business buyers: Cintas Corporation of Cincinnati, Ohio (uniforms); Corporate Express Inc. of Broomfield, Colorado (office supplies); Grainger Industrial Supply (MRO supplies); Lab Safety Supply, Inc. of Janesville,

Wisconsin (safety and industrial products); Marshall Industries of El Monte, California (semiconductors and connectors); and VWR Scientific Products of West Chester, Pennsylvania (laboratory supplies). The site offers one-stop shopping for all the products of all six companies, with a single registration process, a single order, and a single invoice. The site uses Web technology developed by Perot Systems that both permits sharing of customer information across the member companies' databases and also prevents the sharing of confidential information across member companies (such as contract pricing terms). Once an order is placed at OrderZone.com, the system distributes the order to all the necessary suppliers for fulfillment. Help is available through either electronic mail or a toll-free customer help line.

The six member companies have a combined sales base of almost $12 billion and 5 million customers. Thus, the potential benefits of cross-selling are very large. Donald Bielinski, Grainger group president, noted that 40 percent of the total cost of supplies results from the processing and management of the order, so OrderZone.com promises savings without compromising product or delivery quality.

But Grainger has not limited its on-line efforts to OrderZone.com. It has signed five other alliance agreements between December 1998 and June 1999, aimed at increasing its on-line presence and availability. Table 3.5 summarizes these agreements.

The value of these agreements becomes clear when one understands the needs of industrial purchasing managers. A study in late 1998 commissioned by Grainger asked 600 purchasing managers of small, medium, and large firms to comment on their use of the Internet for MRO purchases. The Internet was commonly cited (by 64 percent of respondents) for its speed and convenience versus more standard ordering processes. One-fourth of respondents cited the accessibility of the Internet, and one-fifth cited the accuracy of product information available on the Internet, as benefits of using it as an MRO channel. The study showed that Internet ordering was in use by only 8 percent of respondents, but of those using it, the response is very positive. Of those not using the Internet as an outlet for MRO supplies, 49 percent lacked Internet access, and an additional 10 percent lacked computer access, suggesting that as Internet linkages become more common, this channel will increase in importance. By July 1999, Grainger had an annualized rate of on-line sales of $100 million through its company Web site, hardly a dominating percentage of its total sales, but nevertheless the fastest-growing source of sales for the company.

However, the many alliances being formed imply a variety of ways to reach the electronic market. The question is whether all of these venues are needed, and whether the different alliance partners will end up competing with each other for sales rather than reaching different segments of the market. The potential for channel conflict (see Chapter 9) rests at least in part on the ability of these different channels to reach different segments of business buyers with different bundles of non–product service outputs.

TABLE 3.5

Grainger: Summary of Alliances Formed, December 1998–June 1999

DATE	PARTNER	NATURE OF ALLIANCE
December 1998	Requisite Technology	Establishes a new Web site on which Requisite electronically catalogs Grainger's products and facilitates search for them.
April 1999	PDSI	PDSI develops, markets, and supports software to help businesses maintain high-value capital assets such as plants, facilities, and production equipment. Its subsidiary, MRO.com, provides an e-commerce network on which customers can order necessary parts and supplies. In the alliance, Grainger bought a 4 percent equity interest in PDSI and will have its products listed on PDSI's services.
April 1999	SAP AG	SAP™ is the world's largest enterprise software company, helping clients integrate all parts of their organizations to improve supply chain management and improve management decisions. The alliance integrates Grainger's catalog into SAP's Business-to-Business Procurement™ product. This gives SAP customers direct access to Grainger products through one standardized Internet offering. Using this service, the end-user can requisition materials directly from suppliers, while the purchasing department focuses on strategic purchasing decisions.
May 1999	Ariba, Inc.	Ariba is a provider of intranet- and Internet-based business-to-business e-commerce acquisition software. Its Operating Resource Management System™ lets buyers automate buyers' procurement processes. In the alliance, Grainger will make its products available through Ariba's interface, gaining access to Ariba's major national accounts.
May 1999	Commerce One	Commerce One offers an open business-to-business market for electronic procurement. Its site centralizes transaction management functions and automates the indirect goods and services supply chain. Grainger will make its product catalog available through Commerce One and has invested in Commerce One's private funding.

Sources: Grainger Web site, http://www.grainger.com; Susan Avery, "To Manage Catalog Content, Distributors Form Partnerships," *Purchasing*, 125, no. 9 (December 10, 1998), pp. S18–S20; Sharon Machlis, "Supplier Seeks Sales via Web Searches," *Computerworld*, 32, no. 37 (September 14, 1998), p. 20.

CHANNEL SKETCH 3.3

Charles Schwab: Mutual Fund Supermarket versus Standard Mutual Fund Channel[3]

Individuals can choose to invest money in many different ways. Historically, individual investors who chose to invest in stocks or bonds would buy the stocks of individual companies, typically using (and paying for) the services of an intermediary called a stockbroker, who is employed by a brokerage house. Eventually a financial instrument called the *mutual fund* was created. This pool of investments is made up of the shares of many different companies in the case of a stock fund; in the case of a bond fund, the instrument combines many different bonds into one pool. Buying one share of a mutual fund then means buying a tiny fraction of each of the financial instruments in which the mutual fund invests. The mutual fund concept benefits the small investor by providing a way to diversify investment holdings without requiring the purchase of many different individual stocks or bonds. A fee, called a *load*, is often charged as a percent of the amount of money invested in a mutual fund, which is designed to cover the costs of managing and marketing the fund. Each mutual fund focuses on a particular investment strategy; some common variants include high-growth, tax-exempt, emerging markets, and social responsibility funds. Each is characterized by its own trade-off between risk and return, and by a focus on particular sectors of the world economy or certain types of financial instruments in which investments are made. A mutual fund company usually creates and manages a *fund family*, comprised of many funds focusing on many different investment criteria.

Many different types of mutual fund investors exist. We can categorize them into three segments useful for service output demand identification: (1) the do-it-yourself (DIY) investor, (2) the service-demanding investor, and (3) the unsophisticated investor. A DIY investor understands the fees and charges that characterize the buying of mutual funds through different channels, and is interested in minimizing these charges. This investor has a well-founded investment strategy, usually involving investment in many different mutual funds, and is sophisticated enough to be able to execute it without advice. The service-demanding investor is relatively sophisticated in his or her understanding of investment goals and practices, but values investment advice and help more highly, and is less fee-sensitive, than the DIY investor. The unsophisticated investor is the least knowledgeable category of mutual fund buyer, requiring help in both determining an investment strategy and executing it. This segment does not have enough expertise to be able to choose a low-fee investment strategy.

Table 3.6 summarizes the service output demands of these three segments of investors. Note the need to modify the interpretation of specific service outputs to reflect true service demands correctly for this type of purchasing event, as well as the addition of presales service as a fifth service output. DIY investors differ from the other two segments mainly in their high demand for ease of switching among funds (or fund families) and in their low requirement for presales service. The service-demanding and unsophisticated investor segments have similar service output

TABLE 3.6
Schwab: Service Output Demands for Mutual Fund Investors

SOD Defined As:	Bulk-Breaking	Spatial Convenience	Delivery–Waiting Time	Assortment–Variety	Presales Service
	Minimum investment amount	Ease of initiating transactions and transfers between fund families and consequent transfer costs	Initiation–execution time (including between-fund families)	Assortment of funds offered to investors	Amount of investment advice required before sale of mutual fund
DIY sophisticated investor	Varies	High	High	High	Low
Service-demanding sophisticated investor	Varies	Medium	High	High	High
Unsophisticated investor	Varies (likely to be smaller)	Low	Low	High	High

Source: Trent Carmichael, Bill Norris, Rob Rozwat, and Emiko Taguchi, "Charles Schwab OneSource: Channel Audit," 1996. Used with permission of the authors.

demands, except for a higher valuation on quick execution time of trades in the service-demanding investor segment.

Standard distribution channels for mutual funds include (1) direct sales channels, wherein the mutual fund family is sold directly by the fund family's investment adviser, and (2) various indirect channel forms involving the use of brokerage houses or registered investment advisers (RIAs) as intermediaries who help sell the funds and provide investment advice to their clients. Thus, brokerage houses play the same role as do retailers in more standard goods markets. The individual investor (the "consumer" in this case) pays a commission to the broker for the service of acquiring the shares of the mutual funds. These commissions could run as high as 4 or 5 percent of the value of the security purchased; these fees are justified by the investment advice offered and the execution of the purchase of the financial instrument by the broker.

However, over time the DIY segment has grown in size. Many investors now follow financial performance data in the daily newspapers and prefer to manage their own investment portfolios. This segment of investors does not value the investment advice of a broker, particularly at the brokers' fee per trade. These investors could reduce the fees they paid by investing on their own in different mutual funds, purchasing directly from each mutual fund family. Although this channel met their lower demands for presales service, it failed to meet their high demands for ease of transacting and transferring funds from one investment vehicle to another. Further, holding many different mutual funds entailed managing separate financial statements arriving every month from each fund, not always on the same day of the month. This also effectively decreased the investor's flexibility in moving investments from one fund to another. Clearly, these costs were highest for the most active investors.

In response to the emergence of this segment of more knowledgeable and active investors, Charles Schwab (www.schwab.com) opened a "mutual fund supermarket," called Schwab OneSource, in 1992. Built on the foundation of the company's already-successful discount brokerage business, the OneSource concept offered investors a one-stop shopping site at which to choose among hundreds of mutual funds of all sorts, many with no fee charged to the investor for buying them. As of year-end 1998, 1,024 different funds, from 261 different fund families, were offered to investors. Selling and buying was made easy. The investor would get a single account statement monthly, with a report of all of the holdings of every mutual fund in his or her portfolio and their performance. To execute trades, the investor now only had to make a single phone call rather than engage in a complicated swap of shares and money between fund companies. In 1996, Schwab extended its services to the Internet, offering on-line supermarket trading. However, the presence of on-line trading has not diminished the importance of bricks-and-mortar, physical brokerage retail sites.

Schwab's 291 physical branch offices (in place as of year-end 1998) were located so that 70 percent of the U.S. population was within 10 miles of an office. An estimated 60 to 70 percent of its new accounts are opened at one of the physical branches, although over 95 percent of later trades are done over the phone or on-line, rather than through the branches.

Table 3.7 summarizes the service outputs supplied by the three major channels for mutual funds after the advent of the mutual fund supermarket. The match between service outputs demanded and those supplied is very close for the DIY segment and the mutual fund supermarket. The only possible divergence is in minimum investment amount. Typically a minimum investment requirement exists to invest in a mutual fund supermarket. Although DIY investors could have a wide variation in their desired investment amounts, there tends to be a correlation between investment expertise and investment volume. Even on the bulk-breaking dimension, then, the match is quite close.

Consistent with this match between demand for and supply of service outputs, the popularity of the mutual fund supermarket concept has been phenomenal. Figure 3.2 shows the growth in assets handled by OneSource from its founding in 1992 through 1998, along with the amount of other mutual fund assets at Schwab and the number of active investors. Schwab's supermarket has become the dominant mutual fund supermarket, and indeed the dominant seller of mutual funds across the industry. In 1998, Schwab's OneSource controlled fully 18 percent of the cash flow into all mutual funds in the United States, an enormous figure given the low concentration in the industry. In 1998, Schwab's 5.6 million individual investor accounts held $210.6 billion in mutual fund assets, over one-third of which were attributable to OneSource.

Schwab also does business with 5,000 independent financial adviser clients, which is about one-third of the number of such intermediaries. These advisers act as intermediaries as they manage the investment portfolios of their own individual clients but use Schwab OneSource as their agent to handle trades. Through the addition of these advisers to the OneSource channel, the offering of service outputs becomes high enough to appeal to the service-demanding and even the unsophisticated investor segments, who were not the original core targets for the service.

The concept has spawned several nonbank competitors, including Fidelity Investments, Waterhouse Securities, Jack White, Muriel Siebert, Quick & Reilly, Scudder, Dreyfus, and National Discount Brokers, as well as banks running their own supermarkets, such as Bank of America and KeyCorp. Schwab also took its concept of on-line investing overseas in September 1997, launching the Charles Schwab Mutual Fund Trading Center (www.schwabworldwide.com), the first global Web site offering on-line trading of third-party mutual funds to international investors.

It is apparent that the development of the mutual fund supermarket has been a direct response to (1) the changing segmentation in the market and (2) the emergence and growth of the sophisticated DIY investor segment in the marketplace. Meeting the evolving service output demands of such a segment is a highly profitable activity, reinforcing the fact that responding to service output demands through channel design is an important mechanism to increase sales and market share. Schwab clearly views the key benefits of the supermarket as its extensive assortment and variety, leading to one-stop shopping capabilities; the ease with which investors can manage their portfolios, the result of significant technical

TABLE 3.7
Schwab: Service Outputs Supplied by Different Channels for Mutual Funds

SOD Defined As:	Bulk-Breaking Minimum investment amount	Spatial Convenience Ease of initiating transactions and transfers between fund families and consequent transfer costs	Delivery–Waiting Time Initiation– execution time (including between- fund families)	Assortment–Variety Assortment of funds offered to investors	Presales Service Amount of investment advice required before sale of mutual fund
Direct sales by mutual fund family	Medium–high	Low	High (within family) Low (between families)	High (most families offer a variety of funds)	Low
Traditional brokerage and investment advisers	Low	Low	Medium–High	High	High
Mutual fund supermarket	High	High	High (both within and between families)	High	Low

Source: Trent Carmichael, Bill Norris, Rob Rozwat, and Emiko Taguchi, "Charles Schwab OneSource: Channel Audit," 1996. Used with permission of the authors.

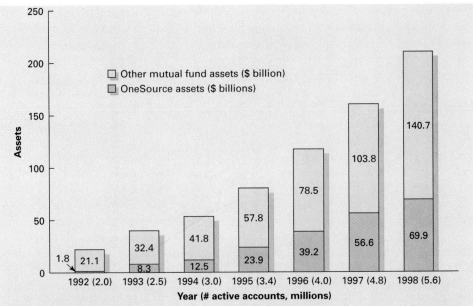

FIGURE 3.2 **Schwab: OneSource and Other Mutual Fund Assets ($ billion)**

investments by Schwab over the years; and in later years, its extensive informational presence on the World Wide Web. Being available to all investors everywhere (i.e., minimizing search costs) appears to be an important recent goal as well. Schwab has begun to create several relationships with banks since 1996, in which the banks (the first two of which were Keycorp and the First Union Corporation) distribute the Schwab OneSource supermarket of funds. Schwab's goal is to have such a relationship with one bank in each of several major markets. The strategy allows Schwab to reach those members of the service-demanding and unsophisticated investor segments who prefer to use banks to buy and sell their mutual fund holdings; prior to this, Schwab had no way of reaching these investors.

SERVICE OUTPUTS

A framework for codifying and generalizing how the end-user wants to buy a particular product was proposed by Louis P. Bucklin as a basis for determining channel structure.[4] We use his original theory here as a foundation to our approach for segmenting the market for marketing channel design purposes. Bucklin argues that channel systems exist and remain viable through time by performing duties that reduce end-users' search, waiting time, storage, and other costs. These benefits are called the *service outputs* of the channel. Other things being equal (in particular, price), end-users will prefer to deal with a marketing channel that provides a higher level of service outputs. As seen in chapter 2, Bucklin specifies four generic service outputs: (1) bulk-breaking, (2) spatial convenience, (3) waiting or delivery time, and (4) product variety. Although this list is generic and can be customized to any particular application, these four service output categories cover the major types of demands end-users make of different channel systems.

Bulk-breaking refers to the end-user's ability to buy its desired (possibly small) number of units of a product or service, even though they may be originally produced in large, batch-production lot sizes. When the marketing channel system allows end-users to buy in small lot sizes, purchases can more easily move directly into consumption, reducing the need for the end-user to carry unnecessary inventory. However, if end-users must purchase in larger lot sizes (i.e., benefit from less bulk-breaking), some disparity between purchasing and consumption patterns will emerge, burdening end-users with product handling and storage costs. Consequently, the more bulk-breaking the channel does, the smaller the lot size end-users can buy and the higher the channel's service output level is to them. This in turn can lead to a higher price for the end-user. The common practice of charging a lower per-unit price for larger package sizes in frequently purchased consumer packaged goods at grocery stores is an example of this pricing phenomenon. Consider selling two small (8-ounce) containers of yogurt versus one large (16-ounce) container of yogurt. The costs of packaging, shelf space, shelf stocking, and labor at the checkout counter are all higher to sell two 8-ounce containers than to sell one 16-ounce container, even though the same total amount of yogurt is sold in both cases. Thus, we would expect the 8-ounce container to carry a higher retail price than one-half the 16-ounce container price, and in general it does.

Spatial convenience provided by market decentralization of wholesale or retail outlets increases consumers' satisfaction by reducing transportation requirements and search costs. Community shopping centers and neighborhood supermarkets, convenience stores, vending machines, and gas stations are but a few examples of channel forms designed to satisfy consumers' demand for spatial convenience. Business buyers value spatial convenience too: Grainger emphasizes in its company information that 70 percent of U.S. businesses are within 20 minutes of a Grainger branch.

Waiting time or delivery time, the third service output identified by Bucklin, is defined as the time period that the end-user must wait between ordering and receiving goods. Grainger offers immediate pickup or same-day shipment or delivery for most products, a signal that quick delivery is highly valued by its targeted industrial customers (no matter whether they buy on-line). The longer the waiting time, the more inconvenient it is for the end-user, who is required to plan or predict consumption far in advance. Usually, the longer end-users are willing to wait, the more compensation (i.e., the lower the prices) they receive. Consider a consumer in Mexico buying some merchandise from Lands' End, a clothing and home goods catalog and on-line retailer based in the United States. An order for $150 in merchandise can be delivered by surface parcel post (8 to 12 weeks) for a $20 delivery charge; air mail (2 to 4 weeks) for a $30 delivery charge; or United Parcel Service (1 to 2 weeks) for a $50 delivery charge. Clearly, the pricing of delivery reflects the value consumers place on getting merchandise sooner rather than later.

Finally, the wider the *breadth of assortment* or the greater the *product variety* available to the end-user, the higher is the output of the marketing channel system and the higher are overall distribution costs, because greater assortment typically entails carrying more inventory. The W. W. Grainger and Schwab examples illustrate a channel offering centered around the benefits of a broader assortment or variety, making it easier for end-users to engage in one-stop shopping. Interestingly, although it may appear that Schwab does not charge a price premium for this service, it in fact charges a fee to mutual fund companies wishing to list their mutual funds on OneSource. This cost is ultimately passed on to individual investors. In general, the greater the level of service outputs demanded by meaningful segments of end-users, the more likely it is that intermediaries will be included in the channel structure. For example, if targeted end-users wish to purchase in small lot sizes, there are likely to be numerous intermediaries performing bulk-breaking operations between mass-producers and the final users. If waiting time is to be reduced, then decentralization of outlets must follow, and, therefore, more intermediaries will be included in the channel structure. Chapter 5 focuses in depth on the reasons for various channel structures.

Service outputs are produced through the costly activities of channel members (i.e., the marketing flows performed by them). For example, Grainger's low waiting time for all of its business customers (whether or not they buy on-line) can be offered only with the help of their significant inventory holdings at each of their bricks-and-mortar branches and distribution centers. Thus, Grainger engages in costly physical possession of inventory in order to produce the service output of low waiting time. As service outputs increase, costs will undoubtedly increase, and these higher costs will tend to be reflected in higher prices to end-users. End-users sometimes have a choice between a low-service output, low-price channel on the one hand (e.g., traveling to the standard grocery store), and a high-service output, high-price channel on the other (e.g., using an on-line grocery service such as Peapod and paying a service fee). The Peapod offering matches the standard grocery store in bulk-breaking; offers greatly increased spatial convenience; minimizes waiting time (because the shopper can specify delivery within either a 90-minute or a 30-minute time window, for different delivery costs); and matches the standard grocery store in assortment and variety offered. Peapod's higher overall level of service outputs results in higher total cost of shopping through it (cost of the groceries plus the delivery charge, which is absent in a standard grocery shopping trip). The less the end-users themselves participate in the marketing flows (in terms of search, physical possession, financing, and the like), the more they should and do pay for the same physical products. The four service outputs discussed here are wide ranging, but may not be exhaustive in all situations. A very commonly added service output is that of *customer education*, referring to the formal or informal provision of information before or after the product sale. *After-sales service*—including configuration, installation, repairs, maintenance, and warranty service—may also be demanded by certain end-users. One should therefore not be inflexible in defining service outputs, as different product and geographic markets may naturally demand different service outputs.[5]

Each of our Channel Sketches illustrates the importance of offering variations in particular service outputs to the marketplace. The W. W. Grainger example focuses mainly on the benefits to the buyer of immediate availability of a broader assortment of products in one shopping venue. Bulk-breaking, spatial convenience, and waiting and delivery time are likely to be the same when buying Grainger's products through standard channels or through the new OrderZone.com channel, but the big gain to the business buyer is the opportunity to indulge in one-stop shopping.

The example of buying mutual funds also exhibits a trade-off among service outputs offered. Schwab OneSource breaks bulk as would a full-service brokerage but beats the full-service brokerage in spatial convenience (it offers on-line trading opportunities rather than the need to telephone or visit one's broker); assortment and variety (hundreds of mutual funds available). But extreme popularity of such services has occasionally led to long waiting times to accomplish specific stock trades, which is costly to the investor wanting to buy a financial instrument at a specific price (delays can mean adverse price swings, making a previously advantageous trade inadvisable). Further, the mutual fund supermarket option may be associated with less investment advice, another valued service output in this market. Thus, the lower cost of using the mutual fund supermarket relative to the full-service broker can be traced at least in part to the lower level of investment advice offered and the slight risk of delay in accomplishing this.

TRENDS IN END-USER PREFERENCES

Changes in both business buyer conditions and individual consumer demographics and psychographics in various countries and markets provide the opportunity for (or the need for) changes in marketing channels to serve them. A summary of some of the most broad-based changes here highlights their implications for changing service output demands.

Trends in Business-to-Business (B2B) Buyer Preferences

Outsourcing. *Outsourcing* refers to the trend toward spinning off particular corporate activities or functions to outside providers. These usually specialize in these areas and therefore offer up-to-date technological know-how as well as lower costs due to economies of scale. Driven by the lure of lowering costs, many activities are now routinely outsourced, including invoicing, shipping, financing, and selling itself.

To appreciate the implications of outsourcing for business buyers' service output demands, consider the Duke University Medical Center in Durham, North Carolina.[6] It has outsourced all of its supplies management functions to Allegiance Corporation (a spinoff from Baxter International, a medical supplies company). A heart bypass operation patient probably checks into the hospital long before the operating room supplies for the operation reach the hospital, thanks to Allegiance's quick, and frequent, delivery of supplies. In fact, the hospital need not even maintain a supply room function and can therefore get rid of the space, personnel, and cost allocated to the receiving and managing of these inventories. But the hospital that does this immediately and drastically increases its demands for bulk-breaking, spatial convenience, low waiting–delivery time, and assortment and variety. Bulk-breaking needs are increased because of the lack of space in which to store extra supplies. Spatial convenience needs remain high because of the necessity of having supplies (e.g., the operating room kit) delivered directly to the operating theater. Quick delivery is a must when the customer carries no backup supplies. And out-of-stocks are not acceptable, making a wide assortment and variety of available products a must.

Downsizing. Another corporate trend that has strong implications for service output demands of the business buyer is *downsizing*, the process of decreasing the number of employees in the company required to do a given set of functions. Downsizing means that each employee, whether a line worker or a manager, is responsible for more (and often a broader variety of) activities. This is likely to increase the demand for service outputs such as customer education when buying business equipment. In some cases, the remaining employees may simply not have enough time or managerial resources to manage the functions that the company used to do itself. In this sense, downsizing can itself lead to outsourcing, that is, the transference of activities from the buyer to the seller.

"Alphabet Soup." Many valuable initiatives have been undertaken in the management of business channels recently. We use the term *alphabet soup* here to describe them, because most have an acronym associated with them. "ECR" (efficient consumer response) refers to the reorganization of the distribution channel to bring groceries more quickly, and at lower cost, from the point of manufacture to the retail store shelf. ECR has spawned imitators, such as "EFR," or efficient food-service response, on the part of the food industry selling to nongrocery outlets (e.g., corporate dining rooms, hospitals, and schools). "JIT" (just in time) and its descendants (such as JIT II) refer to a set of channel activities designed to deliver products to the end-user just when they are needed, thus minimizing inventory holding costs in the channel. JIT methods are widely used in many manufacturing supply chain contexts as well as in the marketing channels for products such as apparel. The adoption of any of these methods increases business buyers' demands for quick delivery (by their very definition), spatial convenience (product cannot be delivered quickly unless it is close), bulk-breaking (to minimize inventory holding), and assortment and variety (to ensure that the right product is always available at the right time).

Trends in Consumer Preferences

Poverty of Time. Consumers are becoming more and more time-constrained, particularly in developed countries. This trend has long been documented in the United States, with its increasing numbers of working women, single-parent households, and homemakers with part-time jobs.[7] However, the trend is now present in many countries of the world, including Japan, Australia, New Zealand, Britain, Italy, Canada, and most other developed nations.[8] With more time spent in the workplace, less time is available for shopping, cooking, do-it-yourself home improvements, and the like. One working homemaker summarized the situation by saying, "We're desperate for a few minutes of rest. If we didn't have help, we would fall down."[9]

The implication for channel managers is that channels offering more service outputs—particularly spatial convenience, broad assortments that permit one-stop shopping, bulk-breaking, and nonproduct services such as home delivery—are likely to find a warm reception with the time-starved consumer. Poverty of time also helps explain the popularity of nonstore retailing options such as catalogs and on-line shopping. And standard retailers respond by offering more services under one roof, to expand the one-stop shopping benefits that consumers crave (e.g., offering bank automatic teller machines in grocery stores).[10]

Increased Knowledge About Products and Availability. Consumers are becoming well-informed about products' characteristics, availability, and pricing. In some cases this knowledge has come with increasing mobility of consumers. For example, as Japanese consumers have traveled more widely outside their country, they have become aware of the sometimes very significant price differences between identical products sold in Japan and elsewhere.[11] In other cases, increased personal computer (PC) literacy drives greater consumer knowledge. One manager from Procter & Gamble predicts that expectations for service and information as well as product performance will increase in the future as a result, making it necessary for the manufacturer and retailer to work with consumers as partners rather than simply selling to them.[12]

The responses by marketing channel managers to increasingly knowledgeable consumers can be many. It is crucial to recognize in what arenas the consumer is becoming more knowledgeable. If knowledge is in the area of product usage or ability to service, then the channel need not provide these educational and postsale service functions, and the channel manager can decrease its prices by deleting these services from the channel. If consumers have greater knowledge of product alternatives, effectively increasing the degree of competitiveness in the marketplace, the appropriate response may be to add relevant services to the channel to differentiate one's offering from those of competitors. If knowledge derives from technological advance, as in the case of increased PC ownership and use, the response may be to add channel forms that capitalize on this knowledge and its implications for preferences in shopping patterns.

Increased Polarity in Incomes. Income distributions in developed nations around the world are experiencing increased disparity from top to bottom. The United States has the greatest disparity between the top and bottom of the income distribution, with the top 10 percent of U.S. men earning almost five times as much as the bottom 10 percent (both figures are for those employed). The disparity is even greater at the extremes of the distribution: A typical U.S. company chief executive officer made hundreds of times as much money as the average worker in the firm in the late 1990s.[13] The top 20 percent of the U.S. population has 42 percent of the country's disposable income, whereas the bottom 40 percent has only 16 percent of it.[14] Although income distributions are more concentrated in other countries, increasing unemployment in some European countries at the end of the 1990s means effectively greater income dispersions: More people are earning basic unemployment benefits, if anything at all.

Such differences translate directly into differences in willingness to pay for the service outputs of a marketing channel. Wealthy consumers, who have a greater opportunity cost of time, will have a higher willingness to pay for service outputs, whereas those further down in the income distribution cannot afford to do so. This does not mean that poorer consumers do not value the service outputs of the channel; rather, they simply do not have the disposable income to pay for them. In economies where these differences become large, opportunities arise for multiple channels to offer different levels of service outputs, at correspondingly different prices, to meet the divergent demands of the marketplace. Marketing channel innovations that reduce the cost of delivering service outputs may also provide an important competitive edge in reaching the more price-sensitive segments of the market.

Increased Numbers of Self-Employed Workers. Outsourcing, layoffs, and downsizing have all become commonplace terms in the marketplaces of many developed nations. In the United States, these developments are part of the corporate landscape, but the trend is not limited to the United States. Even in Japan, a bastion of lifetime employment, many companies have lately been forced to fire employees. Unemployment in Europe has also been high. What do all of these displaced workers do?

In some cases, they start to work for themselves. Self-employed workers have become commonplace in the United States and their businesses even have their own acronym: SOHO (for small office, home office). The growth of independent businesses has increased the demand for bulk-breaking in office supply purchases, computer services, and all the other aspects of running a business. Retail outlets (e.g., category killer Office Depot in the United States) and service providers (e.g., telecommunications services) have sprung up to serve this marketplace, offering competitive prices and service output levels for smaller quantity purchases. The task of promoting to these buyers is also more difficult today, because each one must be reached, but the potential sale per account is smaller than it was in the past. Such changes require innovations in service delivery technologies (e.g., package delivery) to meet the needs of this target group.

The key insight to take away from this discussion of buyer trends is that changes in buyer behavior and shopping patterns create opportunities for channel managers that do not exist in stagnant markets. The clever channel manager uses this information to continuously improve or innovate in the provision of service outputs to target markets. Conversely, if the channel manager does not respond to changes that become pervasive in a marketplace, it risks significant loss of sales and share as rivals respond better to end-users' demands for service outputs in the channel. Finally, many of the trends noted do not imply a universal change in the marketplace, but rather an increase in the diversity of demands by different segments of end-users. A "one size fits all" channel strategy will not be effective in meeting the needs of these diverse groups of buyers. Rather, it may be important either to develop a multiplicity of ways to meet different segments' demands for service outputs or to make a conscious decision about which segments to target most closely.

SEGMENTING THE MARKET BY SERVICE OUTPUT DEMANDS

Service outputs clearly differentiate the offerings of different marketing channels, and the success and persistence of multiple marketing channels at any one time suggests that different groups of end-users value service outputs differently. Thus, to use the concept of service outputs for channel design effectively, we must consider the issue of channel segmentation according to service output demands.

From a marketing research perspective, it is essential to generate a comprehensive understanding of all the relevant service outputs demanded by different end-users. Conducting qualitative focus groups or one-on-one exploratory interviews generate an unbiased list of all the service outputs that apply to the particular product and market in question.[15] This research results in a full set of service outputs that might be demanded by some or all groups of end-users in the market. Once the list of possible service outputs is identified, segmentation of the market can be done in two different ways. The market can be divided into *a priori* segments (such as those often used in product or advertising decisions) and then analyzed in order to see whether those segments share common purchasing preferences.

Research can also be designed and conducted from the start to define channel segments that best describe end-users' service output demands and purchasing patterns. It is much better to follow this latter path, because end-users' preferred shopping and buying habits rarely correlate highly with their preferences for schemes that management and advertising agencies usually employ (product features, media habits, or lifestyles). It is not uncommon for management teams to segment their markets by size of customer: for example, small (say, 1 to 50 employees), medium (51 to 500 employees), and large (over 500 employees) companies in the case of business-to-business sales. This may not be an appropriate channel segmentation dimension for the purposes of channel design, because it is not at all clear that the service outputs desired by all large companies are necessarily different from those desired by all medium and small companies. The channel segmentation process should be carefully designed to produce groups of buyers who (1) are maximally similar within a group, (2) are maximally different between groups, and (3) differ on dimensions that matter for building a distribution system. In any case, appropriately designed channel research seeks to identify linkages between end-user purchasing desires and the defined segments. This matching keeps the focus where it belongs—on segments rather than on markets made up of potential or existing buyers with heterogeneous needs. For example, if one is selling office equipment to the SOHO market, self-employed accountants are likely to be part of a different segment than are start-up scientific research firms. Traditional marketing research techniques such as conjoint analysis, hybrid modeling, or constant-sum scales are useful in quantitative calibration of the importance of various service outputs to different channel segments. It is not enough to ask respondents their preference for various service outputs. Given "free choice," most individuals are always likely to prefer more of all the service outputs. To obtain information that is ultimately useful in designing marketing channels to meet the key needs of target segments, it is essential to understand how end-users are actually likely to behave in the marketplace by making respondents trade off one attribute of the channel for another (e.g., locational convenience versus low price versus extensive product variety versus expert sales assistance). Research tools such as the ones mentioned here can be carefully used to create the necessary trade-off data.[16] Table 3.8 shows how this type of channel analysis, using constant-sum scales, can be used to identify relevant segments for the business marketplace for a new high-technology product. The service outputs (references and credentials, financial stability and longevity, product demonstrations and trials, etc.) are listed down the left-hand side of the table. The columns represent the segments (lowest total cost, responsive support, full-service, and references and credentials) that emerge from a cluster analysis. The names assigned to the segments were derived from the strength of the preferences for specific service outputs. For example, the lowest total cost seg-

TABLE 3.8
Business-to-Business Channel Segments for a New High-Technology Product

Respondents allocated 100 points among the following supplier-provided service outputs according to their importance to their company:

■■■ = Greatest Discriminating   ▒▒▒ = Additional Important

Possible Service Output Priorities	Lowest Total Cost– PreSales Info Segment	Responsive Support– Postsales Segment	Full-Service Relationship Segment	References and Credentials Segment
References and credentials	5	4	6	25
Financial stability and longevity	4	4	5	16
Product demonstrations and trials	11	10	8	20
Proactive advice and consulting	10	9	8	10
Responsive assistance during decision process	14	9	10	6
One-stop solution	4	1	18	3
Lowest price	32	8	8	6
Installation and training support	10	15	12	10
Responsive problem solving after sale	8	29	10	3
Ongoing relationship with a supplier	1	11	15	1
Total	100	100	100	100
% Respondents	16%	13%	61%	10%

Source: Reprinted with permission of Rick Wilson, Chicago Strategy Associates, © 2000.

ment assigned 32 out of 100 points to the service output lowest price but only 8 points to responsive problem solving after sale, whereas the responsive support segment allocated 29 points to responsive problem solving after sale, but only 8 points to lowest price. Finally, the percentage of respondents in each segment is given at the bottom of each column, indicating that the majority of respondents (and thus of the population of customers at large, assuming the sample is representative) are in the full-service segment.

Some interesting insights can be generated from Table 3.8. First, marketing channels serving any of the specific segments will be required to deliver more of some service outputs than others. This means that it is unlikely that any one channel solution will be able to satisfy the needs of all segments. For example, lowest price is highly valued only in one segment (the lowest total cost segment, representing only 16 percent of respondents), suggesting that the majority of the market is not driven primarily by price considerations. This information is invaluable in designing channel solutions that respond to the service output needs of customers, even if doing so implies higher prices than a "no-frills" solution would entail. Further, all segments value installation and training support at least moderately highly; therefore, this support capability must be designed into every channel solution. Similar insights can be gathered by inspecting the rows of Table 3.8 to discern contrasts among segments on other specific service output demands. These insights were then used to propose channel structure solutions to fit each segment's particular needs (for more discussion of the channel structure decision, see Chapter 5). The proposed channel structure is pictured in Figure 3.3. The full-service segment (largest at 61 percent of respondents in Table 3.8) is best served through two possible channels, one including value-added resellers (VARs) and one including dealers as intermediaries. These intermediaries are capable of providing the specific and high levels of service outputs demanded by the full-service segment. At the other end of the spectrum, the lowest total cost segment can be suitably served through a third-party supply channel that outsources most functions. This low-cost, low-service output channel can provide a low price to these customers—precisely the combination they desire. The responsive support segment and the references–credentials segment can be served through similar channels. But the latter segment's desire for validation of the seller makes the additional use of associations, events, and awareness efforts a valuable addition to the channel offering.

This process focuses on service outputs desired rather than on specific channel mechanisms that exist, either currently or potentially. For example, research on mutual fund investing might ask end-users about benefits ("convenient access to many mutual fund families") rather than about specific channels ("mutual fund supermarkets"). Demands for service outputs are likely to persist in time, even while specific

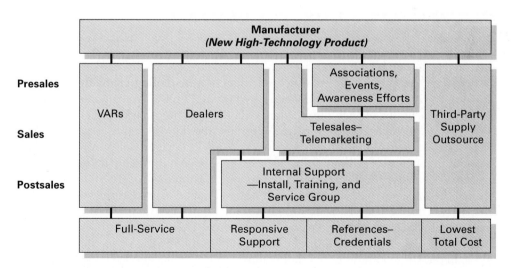

FIGURE 3.3 **Ideal Channel System for Business-to-Business Segments Buying a New High-Technology Product**

Source: Reprinted with permission of Rick Wilson, Chicago Strategy Associates, © 2000.

channel responses change, thus increasing the time horizon over which this information is valuable as well as leading to more creative design of ideal channels. The constant-sum scale approach is typically the most useful in determining which service outputs are relatively most important in driving the ultimate behavior of each unique segment. The technique forces the respondents to trade off one service output versus another, because only 100 points are available to allocate among the service outputs. However, this analysis alone does not tell the full story of the differences between segments of end-users. Also important is the determination of how highly valued the service outputs are overall by various segments of end-users. For example, in Table 3.8, it might be true that the full-service relationship segment values all service outputs more highly than does the lowest total cost segment. Put another way, an end-user in the lowest total cost segment is willing to pay less for a given level of support–maintenance–reliability than is the relationship segment end-user, and this can be true for all service outputs. A constant-sum scale analysis could even produce equal weights for service outputs between two segments, suggesting that the two segments are really just one segment, when in fact end-users in the two segments differ in their overall valuation placed on the channel's service outputs. In short, both relative weights and absolute valuation matter in segmenting a market for the purpose of marketing channel design.

Although it is the most difficult part of the research process, trying to gauge how much end-users are willing to pay for each desired service output is nevertheless important. This knowledge helps in the evaluation of alternative channel approaches to meeting service output demands as the overall system is designed.

MEETING SERVICE OUTPUT DEMANDS

One of the basic precepts in marketing is that the seller should seek to identify and then meet the needs of its end-users in the marketplace. In the marketing channel strategy context, this means creating and running a marketing channel system that produces the service outputs demanded by targeted end-user segments. However, being responsive to service output demands in designing marketing channels can be a very expensive and time-consuming activity. The question arises whether there are market conditions under which a channel manager can profitably serve a segment in the market without fully meeting the service output demands characterizing them. Consider the Peapod grocery shopping example. Grocery shoppers probably had the same service output demands before Peapod existed as they did just after Peapod was introduced. They valued predictable, quick delivery, a full assortment of groceries, bulk-breaking, and spatial convenience. Then why did grocery channels not provide higher service output levels earlier? Similarly, if grocery shoppers elsewhere in the United States or in other countries have similar service output demands, why would grocery channels not immediately seek to meet those service output demands? The answer is multipart in nature. The key factors determining whether and how quickly to respond to knowledge about unmet service output demands include the following:

- *Cost*. Sometimes it is prohibitively expensive from a supply perspective to meet expressed service output demands. The effective price that would have to be charged to end-users to cover the costs of providing these service outputs would be higher than end-users are willing to pay. For instance, even though a Lands' End shopper in Mexico might like to get overnight delivery of a shipment, it is too expensive to offer this service and therefore it is not an option. However, should shipping technologies change, Lands' End would be well advised to update its shipping terms in order to meet this demand.

- *Competitiveness*. The question here is whether existing competitors can beat this channel's current service output provision levels. It may be that no competitor currently in the market exceeds this channel's service output levels. Therefore, the added cost of improving service would not lead to any increase in market share for the channel in question. For example, it routinely takes eight to twelve weeks to get a custom-ordered piece of furniture, because furniture factories typically have not engaged in flexible manufacturing for quick response to product demands. In such a situation, a manufacturer that currently supplies furniture in four to six weeks already beats the competition on the waiting and delivery time service output dimension. If a significant cost is involved in responding even more nimbly to end-user orders, it might not be perceived as worth the investment to do so. However, once competitors do start to invest in flexible manufacturing or other manufacturing methods to decrease response time, the channel in question may quickly need to incorporate its own improvements to its response system to avoid falling behind.

- *Ease of entry*. Competition is not just from firms currently in operation but also from potential competitors, or entrants to the industry. A channel that fails to meet end-user segments' demands for service outputs may find itself surprised by new competition arising with better technologies for meeting those demands. If entry is somehow blockaded, the existing competitors can continue in their current channel strategies. But if entry is easy, it may not be sufficient to provide parity service to the market.

- *Other elements of excellence in the marketing offering*. The marketing channel is one part of the overall marketing mix. A truly superior product or a tremendously low price can lead end-users to buy through a channel that does not quite meet their service output demands. For example, even very time-constrained, wealthy consumers may spend large amounts of time searching for just the right addition to their home décor. Such an end-user finds it necessary to do so because of the lack of a good alternative means of buying the specific product it wants. However, the existence of an unmet service output demand means there is a potential threat to the channel that offers some but not all elements of a marketing mix tailored to the target end-user's demands.

The key insight here is that none of these arguments alone is sufficient to guarantee protected markets and sales, if the channel fails to offer the level of service outputs demanded by target end-users. Where there is a market opportunity, the chances are that rivals (either those currently competing against this channel, or potential entrants) will sooner or later figure out how to exploit that opportunity. Thus, in the short run it is certainly possible to maintain a strong market share, and even loyal end-users, with less than stellar service output demand provision. But over the longer run, the chances of continuing along this course diminish because of the overwhelming incentive to compete for these end-users' sales.

THE ROLE OF SERVICE OUTPUT DEMAND ANALYSIS IN MARKETING CHANNEL DESIGN

After segmenting the market and identifying each channel segment's distinct service output demands, the channel manager can now integrate these insights into the overall marketing channel design and management plan. In particular, this information should be used to *assess segment attractiveness, target a subset of the segments identified,* and *customize the marketing channel system solution used to sell to each targeted segment.*

Assessing the attractiveness of a channel segment is critical. This first step provides a profile of the advantages and drawbacks of each group of potential purchasers.

Targeting a channel segment means choosing to focus on that segment, with the goal of achieving significant sales and profits from selling to that segment. If the channel segmentation exercise has been properly done, targeting multiple channel segments for channel system design purposes implies a need to build different marketing channels for each targeted segment. Because this can be a costly and hard-to-manage activity, channel managers are likely to choose the most attractive subset of all the identified segments to target. This implies a corollary to the targeting concept: *Targeting means choosing which segments* not *to target.* This can be a difficult challenge for a channel management team, because all segments offer the potential for revenue dollars, although not always profits. Segmented service output demand information, however, will help the channel manager choose which segments offer the greatest relative growth and profit opportunities for targeting. Even though other segments may also offer some potential, only the best should be chosen for targeting. "Best" of course has different meanings for different companies and should include the size and sales potential of the targeted segments, the cost to serve them, and the intensity of competition for their business, among other factors.

The information on the targeted segments can then be used to customize the channels: either to design new marketing channels to meet their needs or to modify existing marketing channels to better respond to their demands for service outputs. Service output demand analysis can identify a new market opportunity that leads to the development of novel ways to sell to a particular segment. Innovations in marketing channel design such as Grainger's OrderZone.com or Schwab's OneSource are examples of this response to unmet demands for service outputs. But frequently, a channel is already in place in a specific market, and then service output demand analysis may be used more to indicate how to fine-tune a channel than to suggest radical new channel designs. For example, Lands' End has improved its shipping service to Japan without changing the basic format of catalog or on-line buying that it offers. The company publicizes the service on its Web site (www.landsend.com):

> Our new shipping service from the U.S. to Japan is the best way ever to have your Lands' End order delivered. We call it "Express Mail." It replaces our former Priority Mail and Surface Parcel Post Services. If you relied on these services before, don't worry . . . with Express Mail, the delivery time will be the same or faster and the price will be lower than Priority air rates.

Ideally, the service output demand analysis performed by the channel manager should be used for both positioning (channel design) and targeting purposes. Indeed, pursuing a targeting and channel design policy without this information is tantamount to flying blind:

One cannot be sure of having properly executed a policy without knowing what the marketplace wants in its marketing channel. Given the expense of setting up or modifying a marketing channel, it is prudent to perform the demand-side analysis before proceeding to the supply-side decisions that are also critical to a successful channel policy. With this understanding of the demand side of the marketing channel design problem, we can now turn to the supply side in the next chapter to see how a marketing channel operates to produce service outputs through the concerted efforts of all its members.

Discussion Questions

1. For each of the three scenarios below, categorize the demand for bulk-breaking, spatial convenience, waiting–delivery time, and assortment–variety as high, medium, or low. In each case, explain your answers.

   a. A woman in an emerging-market country of Southeast Asia wishes to buy herself some cosmetics. She has never done so before and is not entirely sure of on what occasions she will wear the cosmetics. She does not live near a big city. She is too poor to own a car, but has a bit of extra money for a small luxury.

   b. A manufacturer uses a particular industrial chemical in one of its large-scale production processes and needs to buy more of this chemical. The rest of the raw materials for its plant operations are delivered in a just-in-time fashion.

   c. Before you visit certain parts of the world, you are required to get a yellow fever vaccine. Many travelers let this slip until the last minute, forgetting that it is advisable (or avoiding an unpleasant shot as long as possible). But, they definitely realize they need the shot, and don't want to have to cancel their trip at the last minute because they didn't get it. They often find themselves making a long trip to a regional medical center because they didn't plan ahead.

2. For the three scenarios in question 1, describe a marketing channel that would meet the target end-user's demands for service outputs.

3. Describe three different buying situations you are familiar with, and the SODs of the buyers in each one. Do you think the service outputs being supplied are close to those being demanded?

4. Give an example of a service output demand that goes beyond the standard ones of bulk-breaking, spatial convenience, waiting–delivery time, and assortment–variety.

5. Your company sells cooking equipment, including pots and pans, cooking utensils, and a line of cookbooks. Describe how you should think about changing your distribution channels in light of the trends in consumer preferences outlined in this chapter.

6. Give an example of an appropriate market segmentation for the purposes of product design that is inappropriate for the purposes of marketing channel design. Conversely, give an example where the product-design segmentation is also useful for marketing channel design purposes. Explain your answers.

7. The typical Peapod shopper fits a demographic profile of relatively high income. Yet many other grocery shoppers value spatial convenience and quick delivery with broad assortment just as much as the current Peapod shopper does, except that their incomes are too low to pay Peapod delivery rates. Should these shoppers be a target segment for Peapod? If Peapod decided to target these shoppers, what would be the implications for its provision of service outputs to the market?

Appendix

3.1 The Service Output Demands Template: A Tool for Analysis

Table 3A.1 shows a completed service output demands analysis in the market for telecommunications equipment and services. This analysis rests on the collection of sophisticated marketing research data. The marketing channel manager is generally well advised to do marketing research to determine what end-users really want in the way of service outputs, because the cost of "guessing" wrong is very high in the channels context.

In this Appendix, we talk about what to do in filling out the service output demands (SOD) template in Table 3A.1. (This is a blank, generic version of that in Table 3.7.) We will not assume here that the channel manager has detailed, quantitative marketing research data, but try instead to give an intuitive idea of how to perform such an analysis and what to do with the information thus codified. The service output demands template is designed to help you (1) segment your market, (2) in ways that *matter* for distribution channel design, and (3) to report on the segments' different demands for service outputs.

Your first task is to identify the segments in the market you are serving. Standard segmentation measures may or may not be appropriate in the channel management context! The key criterion in assessing whether segmentation has been done properly is whether the resulting groups of buyers require different sets of service outputs. For example, we could identify two segments for buyers of laptop computers: men and women. This might be a valid segmentation criterion for some purposes (e.g., choosing advertising media through which to send promotional messages), but it is unlikely to be useful in a channel design and management context, because there is no discernible difference in the service outputs demanded by men and women. A better segmentation might be (1) business buyers, (2) home buyers, and (3) student buyers.

On the SOD template, you then need to fill in information about the service output demands of each of the identified segments. Although more information is always better than less, in the absence of detailed marketing research data it can be useful simply to identify demands as being low, medium, or high, and then to note in what way the service output demands are expressed. Here are a few prototypical examples:

- A business buying laptop computers wants to buy more units than does a home or a student buyer. Because breaking bulk (i.e., providing a smaller lot size) is an effortful process, we would say that the business segment has a low demand for

TABLE 3A.1
The Service Output Demands (SOD) Template

SEGMENT NAME–DESCRIPTOR	SERVICE OUTPUT DEMAND				
	BULK-BREAKING	SPATIAL CONVENIENCE	DELIVERY–WAITING TIME	ASSORTMENT–VARIETY	OTHER SOD(s)
1.					
2.					
3.					
4.					
5.					

INSTRUCTIONS: If quantitative marketing research data are available to enter numerical ratings in each cell, this should be done. If not, an intuitive ranking can be imposed by noting for each segment whether demand for the given service output is *high, medium,* or *low.*

the bulk-breaking service output, whereas the home buyer and the student have a high demand for the bulk-breaking service output because they typically want to buy only one computer at a time.

■ Spatial convenience may be important to all three segments, but for different reasons. Here, it may be important to note that the "sale" of a laptop computer is not over when the unit is initially purchased; postsale service is a critical factor that affects initial purchase decisions and of course also affects subsequent satisfaction of the end-user. With that in mind, one might argue that the home and student buyers have a relatively low demand for spatial convenience at the point of initial purchase, but might have a high demand for spatial convenience when it comes to getting a faulty unit fixed or getting technical service. Conversely, the business buyer may have a high demand for spatial convenience at the initial point of purchase (e.g., may require a salesperson to visit the company rather than having a company representative go to a retail store), but a large enough company may even have in-house computer repair and consulting facilities and hence might have a low demand for spatial convenience for postsale service.

■ The demand for delivery–waiting time is said to be high when the end-user is unwilling to wait to get the product or service. Impulse purchases are a classic product category for which almost all segments of end-users have a high demand for the delivery–waiting time service output. What can we say in the case of our laptop computers? Again, we can differentiate between the delivery–waiting time demands at initial purchase versus at the postsale service step. At initial purchase, the home buyer probably has a low demand for delivery–waiting time, because it is probably not crucial when the machine arrives. However, a student may have a very high demand for quick delivery, particularly if the unit is purchased to match the beginning of the school year! A business buyer may have a very high demand for this service output as well, if the lack of the laptops means lower sales force productivity, for example.

At the postsale service stage, the home buyer may also have a low demand for the delivery–waiting time service output, because this buyer may be willing to put up with a delay in getting technical service or repairs—this buyer's use of the computer may not be a life-or-death matter. The student, however, has a very high demand for the delivery–waiting time service output on the postsale service side, because his or her "cost of downtime" is very high (can't get homework done without the unit). Interestingly, the business buyer may have a low demand for this service output, for two reasons: (1) This end-user may have internal service facilities and hence may not be dependent on the manufacturer's technical service or repair facilities; or (2) this end-user may have excess units in inventory that can be "swapped" for a faulty unit until it is fixed.

■ Assortment–variety demands refer to the segments' preference for a deep assortment in a given category, and for a wide variety of product category choices. In our laptop example, we can rephrase this statement to ask: How intense are our segments' demands for assortment of computer brands, and how intense are their demands for a variety of computers, peripherals, software, and so forth? The business buyer probably has a very *precise* demand for brand of computer, because this end-user typically wants conformity across the units in use in the company. Hence, we would say this end-user has a low demand for assortment. Note, however, that aggregated across the entire population of business buyers, our laptop marketer may observe considerable diversity in brand preference! Thus, we sometimes see a different variety demand when we look at the market in a micro way (customer-specific level) versus a macro way (market-wide perspective). The business buyer may have a moderate to high demand for variety (e.g., software to do word processing, spreadsheets, and database management; printer ports, PC cards, etc. on the demanded list of peripherals), depending on the variety of tasks this buyer wants the laptops to deal with. Among home buyers, the demand for variety is probably the lowest, because they may be the least sophisticated laptop users and may therefore demand only the most basic word-processing and game software. However, their demands for assortment (brand choice) may be high, because an unsophisticated consumer typically wants to see a selection of models and brands before making a purchase decision. The student buyer probably falls in between the other two segments in its demand for assortment–variety: This segment may have more applications or uses for the laptop, necessitating more peripherals and software programs, but may or may not need to see a wide assortment of brands before making the purchase (indeed, the relevant brand set may be quite small if the school has dictated what brands are preferred).

Once filled out, there are several strategic uses of the information codified in the SOD template:

1. It may help you find out why your sales tend to cluster in one segment to the exclusion of others. For example, if you have poor postsale service, you may have a hard time selling to home and student buyers.

2. It may give you an idea for a new channel opportunity to build sales to an underserved segment. Perhaps you can now design a channel structure ideally suited to the needs of student buyers. By so doing, you can lock out competition that otherwise would fight with you on the basis of price alone for these sales.

3. It may alert you to commonalities between and among segments that you previously thought were totally distinct. Home and student buyers may share enough similarities that you can serve both with only minor variations on a single channel theme.

4. You should be able to look at this template and decide what channel form would be best suited to serving each segment. Thus, it provides inputs to match segments to channels.

It is important to remember that this list of four service output demands may not completely characterize demands in a specific market. The whole category of service could have been broken out into a fifth service output demand, for example.

Notes

1. Sources include the Peapod Web site (www.peapod.com); Peapod annual reports, 1997 and 1998; Sharon Machlis, "Filling Up Grocery Carts Online," *Computerworld*, 32, no. 30 (July 27, 1988), p. 4; Joan Holleran, "Partnering with Peapod," *Beverage Industry*, 88, no. 10 (October 1997), pp. 38–41; Subha Narayanan, "Home Shopping: The Way of the Future Is Here," *Retail World*, 50, no. 20 (October 13–17, 1997), p. 6; "A Woman's Place Is on the Net," *Chain Store Age Executive*, June 1997, pp. A16–A18; Tim Dorgan, "Viva la Difference?" *Progressive Grocer*, 76, no. 4 (April 1997), pp. 77–78; Jay A. Scansaroli and Vicky Eng, "Interactive Retailing: Marketing Products," *Chain Store Age Executive*, 73, no. 1 (January 1997), pp. 9A–10A; Laura Liebeck, "Peapod Goes National," *Discount Store News*, 37, no. 16 (August 24, 1998), pp. 4, 63.

2. Sources include personal correspondence with Donald Bielinski of Grainger, October 1999; the Grainger Web site (www.grainger.com); 1998 company annual report; Sharon Machlis, "Supplier Seeks Sales via Web Searches," *Computerworld*, 32, no. 37 (September 14, 1998), p. 20; James C. Anderson and James A. Narus, "Business Marketing: Understand What Customers Value," *Harvard Business Review*, 76, no. 6 (November–December 1998), pp. 53–65; Susan Avery, "To Manage Catalog Content, Distributors Form Partnerships," *Purchasing*, 125, no. 9 (December 10, 1998), pp. S18–S20; PR Newswire, "E-Commerce Gaining Loyalty Among Businesses Buying Operating Supplies Online; Speed and Convenience Cited as Major Advantages of Online Purchasing," PR Newswire Association, December 10, 1998; Andrew Zajac, "Grainger Launches E-commerce Supplies Site," *Chicago Tribune*, February 10, 1999, sec. 3, p. 3; and Larry Riggs, "Entering the Orderzone: W. W. Grainger's Planned Internet Site, Orderzone.com," *Cowles Business Media Inc. Direct*, 11, no. 4 (March 15, 1999), p. 86.

3. Sources include Schwab's Web site (www.schwab.com); Trent Carmichael, Bill Norris, Rob Rozwat, Emiko Taguchi, "Charles Schwab OneSource: Channel Audit," 1996, used with authors' permission; William P. Barrett, "Mutual Fund Supermarkets," *Forbes*, 162, no. 4 (August 24, 1998), pp. 122–23; Associated Press, "Fund Investors Weigh Value of Advice," *Denver Rocky*

Mountain News, July 21, 1998, p. 9B; Rebecca McReynolds, "Doing It the Schwab Way," *United States Banker*, 108, no. 7 (July 1998), pp. 46–56; Carol E. Curtis, "Food Fight in the Supermarket," *U.S. Banker*, May 1998; Sandra Block, "Supermarketing Mutual Funds Competition Increases with One-Stop Shops," *USA Today*, November 7, 1997, p. 1B; Russ Wiles, "Fund 'Supermarkets' Lure Shoppers; Brokerages Tout No Fees, Convenience," *The Arizona Republic*, September 21, 1997, p. D1; PR Newswire, "Schwab Launches World's First Online 'Supermarket' of Mutual Funds for International Investors; Charles Schwab Mutual Fund Center Offers Global Internet Trading of Leading Mutual Funds," PR Newswire Association, September 8, 1997; Peter Van Allen, "Schwab Seeking More Bank Allies for Fund Mart," *The American Banker*, June 6, 1997, p. 1; Christine Williamson, "Schwab Bets on International," Crain Communications *Pensions and Investments*, May 26, 1997, p. 2; Michelle DeBlasi, "Supermarket Wars: No-Load Fund Supermarkets Are All the Rage," *Bank Investment Marketing*, March 1, 1997; Peter Van Allen, "Discounter Schwab Stays Step Ahead of Banks and Other Competitors," *The American Banker*, February 24, 1997, p. 1; Michelle DeBlasi, "More Banks Go to the Supermarket," *Bank Investment Marketing*, January 1, 1997; Reed Abelson, "Charles Schwab Widens Mutual Fund Access," *New York Times*, December 13, 1996, p. D2; PR Newswire, "KeyCorp and First Union Become First Banks to Use Schwab's One-Source Program in Innovative Mutual Fund Offering for Bank Customers," PR Newswire Association, December 12, 1996; Charles Stein, "Fidelity Adds Funds to Its Mutual 'Supermarket' Concept," *Boston Globe*, November 12, 1996; Mary Beth Grover, "Annual Funds Survey: Charles Schwab: The Matchmaker," *Forbes*, 156, no. 5 (August 28, 1995), pp. 160–62.

4. Louis P. Bucklin, *A Theory of Distribution Channel Structure* (Berkeley, CA: IBER Special Publications, 1966); Louis P. Bucklin, *Competition and Evolution in the Distributive Trades* (Upper Saddle River, NJ: Prentice Hall, 1972); and Louis P. Bucklin, *Productivity in Marketing* (Chicago: American Marketing Association, 1978), pp. 90–94.

5. V. Kasturi Rangan, Melvyn A. J. Menezes, and E. P. Maier, in "Channel Selection for New Industrial Products: A Framework, Method, and Application," *Journal of Marketing*, 56 (July 1992), define five service outputs in their study of industrial goods (pp. 72–73). These are product information, product customization, product quality assurance,

after-sales service, and logistics. Some of these are simply specific examples of the generic service outputs defined by Bucklin (e.g., logistics refers to the spatial convenience and waiting–delivery time outputs). However, their work does highlight the value of being aware of the specific application.

6. Mary Connors, "Baxter's Big Makeover in Logistics," *Fortune*, July 8, 1996, pp. 106C–106N.

7. Jan Larson, "The New Face of Homemakers," *American Demographics*, 19, no. 9 (September 1997), pp. 44–50.

8. See, for example, Harriot Lane Fox, "The 1995 British Shoppers Survey (Part 2)," *Marketing* (August 31, 1995), pp. 14–15; Doreen L. Brown, "The Changing Japanese Consumer: New Attitudes, Purchasing Habits on Quality, Value, and Imports," *East Asian Executive Reports*, 18, no. 5 (May 15, 1996), pp. 8, 14; Ang Wan May, "Hypermarkets, Lifestyle Changes Bug Dairy Farm," *Business Times* [Singapore], March 22, 1997, p. 7; Paul Betts, "Big Retail Groups Eye Italian Wallets," *Financial Times*, May 9, 1997, p. 23; "Shop? I'd Rather NAP, Thanks; 6 Hot Consumer Trends," *Profit*, September 1998, p. 48; and "Retailers and Manufacturers Told—Know Your Customer or Die," Canada NewsWire, February 16, 1999.

9. Larson, "The New Face of Homemakers."

10. PR Newswire, "Minnesota Grocers Association Grocers Celebrate 100 Years of Answering 'What's for Dinner?' " PR Newswire Association, August 20, 1997; Beverly Schuch, Cable News Network Financial (CNNFN), "Supermarket as Dining Experience," October 20, 1997, interview on Cable News Network Financial (CNNFN) with Carolyn O'Neil.

11. Brown, "The Changing Japanese Consumer."

12. Larson, "The New Face of Homemakers."

13. "The Best—and the Rest," *The Economist*, Survey of Pay, May 8, 1999.

14. Cambridge International Forecasts Country Report, "United States: Population Trends," April 1999.

15. Such data sometimes already exist. For example, in the computer industry, data on service outputs valued by end-users are collected by firms such as IntelliQuest, Inc. and International Data Group.

16. See Paul E. Green, "Hybrid Models for Conjoint Analysis: An Expository Review," *Journal of Marketing Research*, 21 (May 1984), pp. 155–69. See also Gilbert A. Churchill Jr., *Marketing Research*, 4th ed. (Chicago: Dryden Press, 1987), pp. 364–76.

4

Supply-Side Channel Analysis: Channel Flows and Efficiency Analysis

LEARNING OBJECTIVES

After reading this chapter, you will:

- Be able to define the eight generic channel flows that characterize costly and value-added channel activities
- Understand how the Efficiency Template helps codify channel flow performance by channel and by channel participant
- Understand the role of channel flow allocation in designing a zero-based channel
- Understand how channel flow performance leads to appropriate allocation of channel profits among channel members, using the Equity Principle
- Be able to place the channel flow analysis in the overall channel audit process
- Know how to use the Efficiency Template under conditions of little information

he channel management schematic in Figure 4.1 (which replicates Figure 2.1) specifies that positioning a product offering in the distribution sense requires consideration of how best to organize channel activities on a segment-specific basis. Manufacturers, wholesalers, and retailers participate in marketing channels for the purpose of creating the service outputs (bulk-breaking, quick delivery, spatial convenience, and assortment and variety) demanded by their target end-users. Just as a production plant produces physical products, the members of a marketing channel are also engaged in *productive activity*. This is so even if what they produce may be

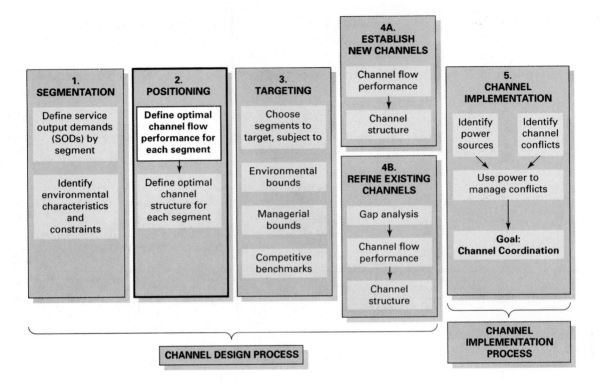

FIGURE 4.1 **Channel Management Schematic**

intangible. The productivity derives from the value end-users place on the service outputs resulting from channel efforts. The activities or functions that produce the service outputs demanded by end-users are the topic of this chapter. We call these activities *channel flows.*

Identifying what channel flows are performed in the marketing channel, by whom, and at what levels is helpful in several aspects of channel management. First, detailed knowledge of the flow performance in the channel helps the channel manager diagnose and remedy shortcomings in the provision of service outputs (discussed in more detail in Chapter 6). Second, the concept of channel flows can be used to design a new channel or revise a currently existing channel to minimize the cost of providing desired service outputs. Third, knowing which channel members have incurred the cost of performing what flows helps in allocating the profits of the channel equitably. This may help channel members preserve a sense of fairness and cooperation and thus avert channel conflicts (the topic of Chapter 9).

We carry over in this chapter our discussion of Peapod, W. W. Grainger, and Charles Schwab, first introduced in Chapter 3 (as Channel Sketches 3.1, 3.2, and 3.3), to illustrate the service outputs concept (see Channel Sketches 4.1, 4.2, and 4.3). This chapter's discussion of these companies focuses on channel flow identification and performance in the channels for groceries, industrial supplies, and mutual funds.

CHANNEL SKETCH 4.1

Peapod: Electronic Grocery Shopping[1]

The Peapod example developed in Channel Sketch 3.1 in Chapter 3 focused on showing how the concept of an electronic grocery shopping service could improve the provision of service outputs to a core segment of end-users: grocery shoppers who valued the same broad assortment and variety available at a standard grocery store, but were also time starved. Such consumers would highly value the spatial convenience and quick delivery that Peapod or its other on-line competitors offered, as it would save valuable time otherwise spent traveling to and shopping in the grocery store itself. In the context of our discussion of channel flow performance in this chapter, we now explore some of the ways in which Peapod's initial channel strategy reshaped the split of channel flow performance relative to that in the standard, bricks-and-mortar grocery shopping experience.[2]

To understand this, note that the inclusion of Peapod in the grocery channel moved both some costs and some performance of channel flows away from the retailer and the final grocery buyer. Figure 4.2 diagrams a typical stream of events when a Peapod customer uses the service, using the original Peapod channel structure in the Chicago market as an example. In the Chicago market, Peapod has partnered with the Jewel-Osco food store chain. The figure shows both what happens in a Peapod shopping event and what the steps imply about flow performance by Jewel, Peapod, and the shopper.

The process starts with the shopper initiating an order by logging on to the Peapod system, shopping, and placing an order along with a desired delivery time (in a 90-minute window).[3] This activity, performed by the shopper, is part of the *ordering* flow, and its cost is the opportunity cost of the shopper's time. To imagine decreasing the cost of the ordering flow even further, and taking that flow cost off the shopper's shoulders, imagine a shopping service that would keep track of the inventories of groceries in the shopper's pantries, refrigerator, and freezer, and automatically place an order when they run low! Such a system might seem unrealistic, but these automatic replenishment systems are already in place in many business-to-business ordering situations. The Peapod software system tries to mimic this minimization of the ordering flow cost by allowing the shopper to store a regular shopping list with Peapod (e.g., one gallon of milk, one box of Cheerios cereal, etc.) that can be evoked every time the shopper connects to the Peapod system to place an order. This saves the shopper time in placing an order made up at least partly of routine replacement purchases. The system also allows for a second choice to be specified when an order is placed. A shopper can thus allow substitutions in the case of out-of-stock merchandise on the store shelf (e.g., substitute Yoplait strawberry yogurt for Dannon strawberry yogurt).

Peapod participates in the ordering flow by receiving the order placed by the shopper; placing it in the shopping queue so that it will be shopped at the appropriate time, given the desired delivery time; and ultimately transmitting the order to Peapod's professional shoppers. At this point, Peapod's actions also perform a *promotion* flow because it stores the order data in a database for future use by

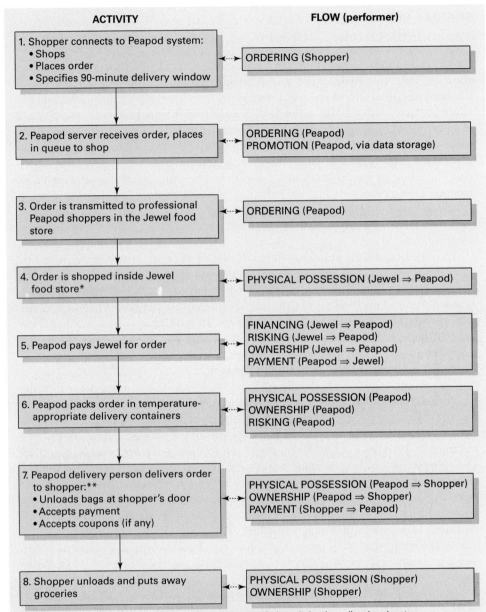

FIGURE 4.2 Peapod Shopping and Fulfillment Process: Original Channel Structure

consumer packaged-goods manufacturers. Peapod sells these data to interested manufacturers who want to investigate a myriad of marketing research questions, including how responsive the consumer is to retail price promotions, what products consumers tend to buy together, and the like. Collecting this ordering data prepares Peapod to better market and promote its database service to its packaged-goods firm customers.

When the time comes, the shopper's order is shopped inside the Jewel food store (note again that this describes the original Peapod shopping channel, which has been modified recently). Peapod employees travel the aisles of the grocery store, picking the shopper's order. Peapod's professional shoppers specialize in certain types of merchandise; for example, one employee focuses on fresh produce, because experience and knowledge in this category greatly improve the quality of the product shopped for the customer. In actually shopping the order, Peapod is taking physical possession of the ordered groceries out of Jewel's hands. Figure 4.2 thus represents this flow as passing from Jewel to Peapod, because Jewel performs physical possession until the time when the order is actually picked in the store. At this point, if an item is not in stock on the shelf, the Peapod shopper substitutes a second choice if the shopper has indicated one.

When the entire order has been shopped, the Peapod shopper originally went through the Jewel checkout line along with all other Jewel shoppers. Peapod soon convinced Jewel to set up a separate checkout lane for the Peapod shoppers, to decrease their time waiting in line to check out. At this time, Peapod also pays for the shopper's order. In so doing, Peapod takes on *financing*, *risking*, and *ownership* flows, as well as participating in the *payment* flow by paying Jewel for the groceries. Financing is done because (although for a very short time) Peapod is financing the shopper's grocery purchases. Ownership devolves to Peapod as it pays for the groceries. Because Peapod owns the groceries until it delivers them to the shopper's home, it therefore also takes on risk: the risk that some items will be spoiled, will melt in transit (e.g., ice cream), or will be rejected by the shopper upon delivery.

To reduce the risk it takes on, Peapod then packs the order in delivery containers that are appropriately temperature-controlled (one shopper's order might be packed in three different containers: one for non-temperature-sensitive goods, one for refrigerated goods, and one for freezer items). A Peapod driver then delivers the order to the destination specified by the shopper (usually the shopper's home). Again, physical possession, ownership, and risking costs are borne as the order is carried in transit from the Jewel store to the shopper's home.

At the shopper's home, the Peapod delivery person unloads the order at the shopper's door, accepts payment, and accepts any coupons the shopper might wish to use. At this step, both physical possession and ownership pass hands from Peapod to the shopper, while payment occurs from the shopper to Peapod. Finally, the shopper him- or herself unloads the groceries, performing physical possession and ownership flows in the channel.

In the absence of Peapod's services, Jewel and the shopper would perform all the flows described in Figure 4.2. Peapod's presence in the channel thus lifts many flow costs off either Jewel's or (more significantly) the shopper's shoulders. In order to make the Peapod system work, Peapod management had to invest very substantial amounts of money in building a computer system, a logistics system, a shopping and delivery system, and personnel training systems. Thus, its ability to take on channel flows did not come costlessly, and the value it thereby created was clearly worth something to the shoppers who use the system.

If the system were completely self-supporting, Jewel and the individual shoppers themselves would pay Peapod for the value it created. The performance of these channel flows and the amount paid would cover the costs to Peapod of creating and maintaining its system. Indeed, Jewel did take an equity stake in Peapod, and shoppers do pay a delivery fee to Peapod for its services. However, the company planned for another revenue source to help defray the costs of delivery to shoppers. This source of revenue was the sale of marketing research and promotional services to consumer packaged-goods manufacturers. Peapod markets its database of shopper purchasing patterns to these manufacturers, and also makes it possible for manufacturers to run on-line marketing research tests or even to offer on-line coupons to shoppers as a means of increasing sales. Peapod of course charges for these services to manufacturers, and the revenue from this side of the business is designed to help defray the costs of running the overall system. For the first ten years of Peapod's existence, it did not make enough money from these marketing research activities plus delivery fees to make positive profits in the business as a whole. However, the concept of on-line grocery shopping has been broadly supported by the venture capital community (e.g., www.webvan.com was able to raise $100 million in 1999 to build a network of warehouses across the United States), because its overall concept of lifting flow costs off busy shoppers' shoulders is an enduringly good idea in a world of increasingly time-starved consumers.

Is the Peapod system as it was initially conceived a zero-based channel? Clearly, the concept meets a target segment's demands for service outputs in a way that previous grocery stores have not been able to do. Although there do exist consumers who actively enjoy grocery shopping and prefer to pick out their own groceries, a segment of consumers exists who welcome help from a third party that would do the shopping for them. This is Peapod's target. Among those who are willing to outsource shopping to an external service, could Peapod increase penetration faster? Some factors work against this. First, some shoppers simply cannot afford the fee for delivery. Second, some shoppers who could afford the fee are not organized enough to put together a big enough shopping list to merit the delivery fee of $5.00 plus 5 percent of the order. Consider a shopper who "plans ahead" and shops once per week for a family of four. The grocery bill might total $100.00, which would generate a Peapod delivery fee of $10.00 (or 10 percent of the bill). By contrast, a consumer who shops three times a week and buys $35.00 of groceries each time, would have to pay $6.75 each time, for a total of $20.25 in delivery fees for $105.00 in groceries (over 19 percent of the total grocery bill). Clearly, this service is more cost-effective the more organized the shopper is and the larger the size of the average order.

CHANNEL SKETCH 4.2

W. W. Grainger: Industrial Maintenance, Repair, Operating (MRO) Supplies[4]

Grainger serves its industrial customers through many different channels, as discussed in Channel Sketch 3.2 in Chapter 3. As an industrial MRO (maintenance, repair, and operating) supplies distributor, it funnels product from its manufacturing suppliers to its industrial customers. As most standard distributors do, Grainger buys product from its suppliers, stores it in its warehouses, takes orders from customers, and arranges for sale, delivery, and payment from them. It therefore performs important physical possession, ownership, financing, risking, ordering, and payment flows. It also of course promotes product through its sales efforts on behalf of its suppliers and negotiates terms and conditions with final industrial buyers (thus lifting the cost of these negotiations from the manufacturer's shoulders). To some extent, then, Grainger participates actively in all the flows in the industrial MRO supplies channel in which it participates, whether it sells through the standard channel or on-line through OrderZone.com.

Given its premier position in the industry, and the still relatively small proportion of its sales that occur on-line, it is worth examining on a disaggregated level how channel flow performance varies from a standard industrial distribution channel to the OrderZone.com channel. Channel flows change (or don't change!) in the following ways:

- *Physical possession*: No change. In particular, each of the six companies participating in OrderZone.com store and warehouse their own product; there is no centralized inventory holding and hence no change in the physical possession flow.

- *Ownership*: No change. Although orders are placed through OrderZone.com, each of the six member companies sells product directly to the ordering customer. OrderZone.com does not act as an ownership intermediary, nor does Grainger take on any ownership flows for either of the other four member companies (Lab Safety Supply is owned by Grainger) or their customers.

- *Promotion*: OrderZone.com itself is a promotional tool, and as such helps to sell the products of all six member companies. A potential buyer of industrial uniforms from Cintas Corporation might go to OrderZone.com and be so impressed by the service that its buying group orders semiconductors from Marshall Industries, another member. This sale might not have accrued to Marshall without the effective promotional efforts represented by the OrderZone.com buying channel. There is no evidence that OrderZone.com replaces the promotional efforts of member companies; rather, it appears to augment them.

- *Negotiation*: No apparent change. Price lists do not change as a result of shopping on OrderZone.com. The customer benefits referred to by member companies focus on convenience, consolidation of ordering practices, and the like—not lower prices.

- *Financing*: No apparent significant change. Financial terms of payment from a member company to a buyer can remain approximately the same as they were before the addition of the OrderZone.com channel, although invoicing is consolidated and thus terms of payment may be consolidated among member companies.

- *Risking*: The risk borne by customers does not change. One of the possible risks of joining together in the OrderZone.com alliance, however, is the potential sharing of confidential information across member companies. This risk is controlled through the proprietary software in the system, which was created by Perot Systems.

- *Ordering*: Major difference between the standard industrial purchasing scenario and the OrderZone.com scenario. A standard purchasing event would involve separate shopping events at each of the six companies, with separate sales calls, separate ordering terms, and duplication of ordering effort. Under OrderZone.com, one-stop shopping means that the customer looks at only one place to buy from all six vendors, thus saving considerably on order costs. Orders received by OrderZone.com are sorted and distributed to all the relevant suppliers for fulfillment by each. OrderZone.com thus participates significantly in the ordering flow, with both upstream member companies and downstream industrial buyers. One Grainger executive noted that: a) 40 percent of the total cost of supplies can be attributed to the processing and management of the order, and b) these costs could be significantly reduced by consolidating the process through one vendor rather than many. Thus, not only are ordering flows transferred from the standard members to OrderZone.com, but the claim is that total cost of ordering can drop as a result.

- *Payment*: OrderZone.com participates significantly in the payment flow, as it issues a consolidated invoice to buyers from all the member suppliers from whom the buyer orders. Using OrderZone.com, MasterCard, Visa, and open-account billing are all available as methods of payment by buyers.

The promotion, ordering, and payment flows are the main ones influenced by the formation of the OrderZone.com alliance. We can again question whether OrderZone.com will replace standard industrial distributor transactions and relationships. The answer is probably no. As of late 1998, shortly before the introduction of OrderZone.com, Grainger had only one percent of its active business accounts registered for a Web account to buy on-line with Grainger and sold less than one percent of its total revenue online. The reason for the slow penetration of usage of the apparently superior channel lies in the relatively lower computer literacy (as well as lack of ownership of state-of-the-art computers with Web browsers) among many of Grainger's core buyers. Until buyers themselves see a channel like OrderZone.com as substitutable for the standard buying process, even the benefit of consolidated billing and one-stop shopping may not be enough for many of its potential customers. The match between flows performed and service outputs supplied must be watched carefully over time to track the relative size of segments of buyers who prefer the usual style of buying to the on-line buying experience.

CHANNEL SKETCH 4.3

Charles Schwab: Mutual Fund Supermarkets versus Standard Mutual Fund Channels[5]

As we saw in Channel Sketch 3.3 concerning mutual fund investors and mutual fund distribution channels in Chapter 3, different distribution channels meet the needs of different segments of mutual fund investors. Here, we look in more depth at the distribution channel itself for mutual funds and how it operates to produce and provide service outputs.

Following the segmentation discussed in Chapter 3, Figures 4.3 and 4.4 depict the various ways in which mutual funds reach different segments of investors. Figure 4.3 shows the various entities that together perform the functions necessary to offer a mutual fund to the marketplace from a "producer" perspective. The mutual fund investment adviser decides what financial investments to make in each mutual fund

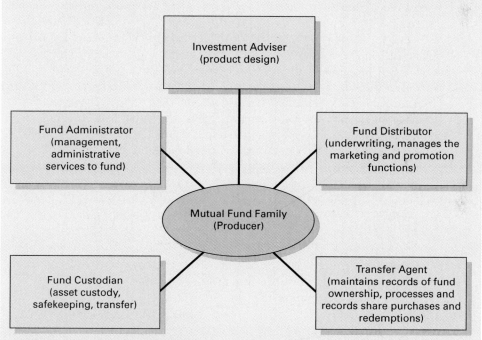

Flows Performed by Various Entities:
Investment Adviser: promotion (through portfolio design)
Fund Administrator: negotiation (through management of administrative processes)
Fund Distributor: promotion (through performance of selling and marketing tasks)
Fund Custodian: physical possession, risking (through responsibility for safekeeping of shares)
Transfer Agent: ordering, payment (through responsibility for processing orders and recording share purchases–redemptions)

FIGURE 4.3 **Schwab: Identities and Roles of Companies Involved in Producing Mutual Funds**

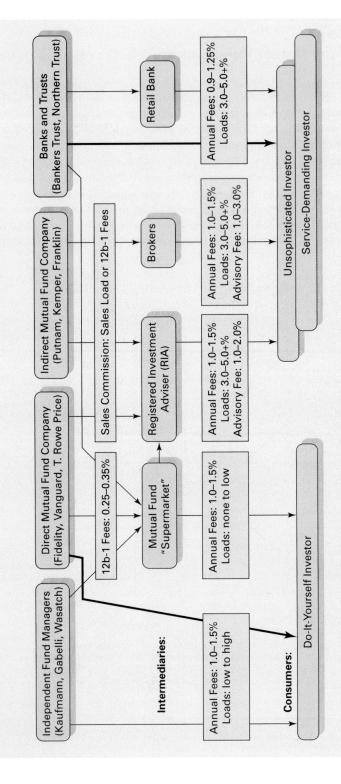

FIGURE 4.4 **Schwab: Structure of Mutual Fund Distribution Channels Producers (including all entities in Figure 4.3)**

Source: Trent Carmichael, Bill Norris, Rob Rozwat, and Emiko Taguchi, "Charles Schwab OneSource: Channel Audit," 1996. Used with permission of the authors.

and thus can be viewed as the product designer. The fund administrator is responsible for coordinating the actions of all the entities at the producer level and provides administrative services to the fund. The fund distributor underwrites the securities in which the fund invests, as well as managing the promotion of the fund to potential and current investors. The fund custodian holds the physical stock or bond certificates in which the fund invests and is responsible for their safekeeping and transfer when the investment adviser decides to acquire new financial instruments or sell off some that are already in the fund. The transfer agent maintains records of the ownership of fund shares and manages the ordering and redemption of shares. The figure notes how these institutional functions map into the performance of important channel flows by each member of the producer group.

Figure 4.4 expands the focus from the producer level to intermediary and final investor levels of the channel. This figure notes the fees or loads charged to investors or to intermediaries. The producers of mutual funds are independent fund managers, direct mutual fund companies (who sell both directly and through intermediaries), indirect mutual fund companies (who sell only through intermediaries), and banks and trusts. All but the indirect mutual fund companies do some direct selling to individual investors. All of the producer types are represented in the line of mutual funds offered by Charles Schwab's OneSource mutual fund supermarket. In this figure, we combine together the various entities that join with the fund's investment adviser in running a mutual fund, including the fund's administrator, distributor, custodian of securities, and transfer agent.

Intermediaries in this set of channels include supermarkets such as OneSource, registered investment advisers (RIAs), brokers, and retail banks (who primarily offer their own bank-proprietary mutual fund families through their own branches). RIAs themselves, acting as a subintermediary, may buy the services of a supermarket such as Schwab's OneSource.

Sophisticated DIY investors buy primarily through the independent fund manager, direct mutual fund company, and mutual fund supermarket channels. Service-demanding and unsophisticated investors buy primarily through RIAs, brokers, and banks.

Figure 4.4 shows that the fees and commissions paid by the investor increase as the length of the channel increases. 12b-1 fees provide marketing money for the mutual fund; annual fees are charged for the management of the fund; and a load is a one-time charge made either at the time shares of the fund are purchased (a "front-end load") or when shares are redeemed (a "back-end load"). All of these fees are charged to the investor directly. Each channel member takes a "cut" of channel profits in return for the costly flows it performs, although in today's world of broad choices, the fees can range from nothing to 5 percent or more of a portfolio's value.

Schwab's OneSource and other supermarkets like it have expanded the role played by a mutual fund intermediary. Brokers and RIAs primarily provide promotional inputs, including investment advice and recommendations of particular financial investments to make. OneSource's presence and product line offering themselves constitute promotional activities, because one particular fund may be able to sell many more shares by being offered in the OneSource line than without that channel placement. Further, Schwab engages in promotions of particular funds at various times, in order to publicize top-performing funds to investors. Schwab also retains control of the promotional relationship with the individual OneSource investor by refraining from sharing the identity of its investors with the mutual fund companies whose shares they buy. Thus, the company can promote directly to the investor, and the mutual fund company has no way of replacing Schwab by selling directly to the investor. Schwab engages in negotiation with mutual fund companies over placement, the fees that will be paid by the mutual fund company to be listed in OneSource (fees range from 15 to 35 basis points, where 100 basis points equals one percent of the share price for the fund). Finally, Schwab also participates significantly in ordering and payment functions; indeed, one could say that these are the most important flows in which it participates. It takes orders from investors, receives payment, handles the transfer of money back to the mutual funds whose shares are bought, and maintains investor records that permit the generation of monthly consolidated investment portfolio statements for its clients. These are all costly but carry a high value added in the channel.

It is important to note that Schwab's OneSource, although originally conceived as a low-cost (but low-service) way for the sophisticated investor to choose from a wide variety of mutual funds, is now also part of a higher-service channel offering more investment advice to a slightly less sophisticated, more service-sensitive segment as well. The trend appears to be to add to the provision of service outputs through the actions both of Schwab itself and of its RIAs, effectively to provide a menu of choices of cost and service to different segments of investors.

CHANNEL FLOWS DEFINED

Eight Generic Channel Flows

Chapter 1 introduced the concept of channel flows (see Figure 4.5, which reproduces Figure 1.2). As that discussion points out, specific channel members may specialize in performing one or more flows and may not participate at all in the performance of other flows. Further, it may be tempting to remove a particular channel member from the channel (i.e., change the channel structure). But it must be remembered that the flows performed by that channel member cannot be eliminated. When a channel member is removed from the channel, its functions need to be shifted to some other channel member to preserve service output provision in the channel. The only exception to this rule would occur if the eliminated channel member were performing flows that were already being performed elsewhere in the channel, so that its contributions to service output provision were redundant and hence unnecessary. For example, a salesperson and an independent distributor sales representative may call on the same customer, resulting in wasted effort and cost. The channel is better off using one or the other, but not both, salespeople in this case.

Every flow not only contributes to the production of valued service outputs but also is associated with a cost. Figure 4.5 gives examples of the channel cost-generating activities associated with each flow. For instance, *physical possession* refers to all channel activities concerned with the storage of goods, including its transportation between two channel members. The costs of running warehouses and of transporting product from one location to another are thus physical possession costs. Peapod bears part of the physical possession flow in the grocery channel by doing the shopping and delivery of groceries. Grainger performs this flow by storing product in its 350 local branches, 6 zone distribution centers, 2 regional distribution centers, and 1 national distribution center.

Note that the costs of physical possession are distinct from the costs of *ownership*, the second flow. When a channel member takes title to goods, it bears the cost of carrying the inventory; capital is tied up in product (the opportunity cost of which is the next highest-valued use of the money). In many distribution systems, such as Peapod's and Grainger's, physical possession and ownership move together through the channel, but this need not be so. In *consignment selling*, for example, product is physically held

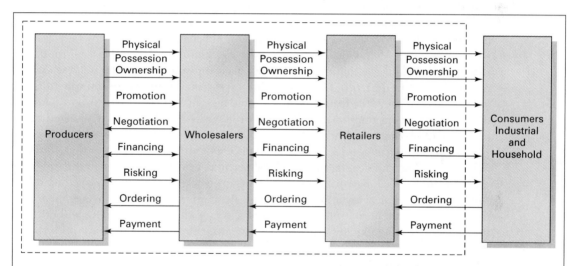

The arrows above show flows of activity in the channel (e.g., physical possession flows from producers to wholesalers to retailers to consumers). Each flow carries a cost. Some examples of costs of various flows are given below:

Marketing Flow	Cost Represented
Physical possession	Storage and delivery costs
Ownership	Inventory carrying costs
Promotion	Personal selling, advertising, sales promotion, publicity, public relations costs
Negotiation	Time and legal costs
Financing	Credit terms, terms and conditions of sale
Risking	Price guarantees, warranties, insurance, repair, and after-sales service costs
Ordering	Order-processing costs
Payment	Collections, bad debt costs

FIGURE **4.5 Marketing Flows in Channels**

by a retailer (e.g., an art gallery owner), but is owned by the manufacturer (e.g., the painter or sculptor). The manufacturer gives up ownership of the product only when it is sold to the final buyer. As Figure 4.3 shows, in the mutual fund marketplace, the custodian maintains physical possession of the actual securities held by the funds, but ownership rests with the fund's investors.

Promotion flows in marketing channels can take many forms, including personal selling by an employee or outside sales force (such as the brokers and registered investment advisers in the mutual fund channel), media advertising, sales promotions (either to the trade or at retail), publicity, and other public relations activities. Promotional activities are designed to: (1) increase awareness of the product being sold, (2) educate potential buyers about the products' features and benefits, and (3) persuade potential buyers to make purchases. They may also have the goal of increasing the overall *brand equity* of the product, which would be productive of sales in the future. Clearly, any channel member can be involved in promotion, not just the retailer or the manufacturer.

The *negotiation* flow occurs whenever terms of sale, or of the maintenance of the ongoing relationships with the market, are discussed and decided upon. The costs of negotiation are mainly measured in the cost of personnel time to do the negotiations and (in the case of legal contractual arrangements) the cost of legal counsel. Sometimes a channel member who specializes in negotiation is brought in.

For instance, one Chicago-area export marketing company was engaged by a manufacturer of dairy equipment. This manufacturer wanted to penetrate new markets outside the United States. The role of the export marketing company was to find a foreign market where the firm's machines could be sold. Eventually, the export marketer discovered that consumption of milk by children was beginning to be encouraged by the government of Thailand. The export marketer negotiated with the Thai government to put its client's machines on a "recommended" list of farm equipment for dairy farmers, as well as finding and negotiating with local partners who would represent the American company in the Thai market. Although the export marketing company played no role in the holding of physical inventory, ownership, standard promotional activities, financing, ordering, or payment, its role as a negotiator was both time-consuming and critically important in making the new marketing effort successful.[6]

Financing costs are inherent in the terms of sale from one level of the channel to another or from the channel to the end-user. Typical financing terms on a business-to-business purchase require payment within 30 days. Sometimes a discount is offered for early payment. If, for example, a 2 percent discount is offered for payment within 10 days, the terms of sale are said to be "2-10 net 30," meaning a 2 percent discount for payment in 10 days, but the net (full) payment amount is due in 30 days. Regardless of the specifics of the payment terms, the key issue is that the seller essentially agrees to finance the buyer's purchase for a period of time (here, 30 days) after the product actually is delivered to the buyer, and thus the seller bears a financial cost—the cost of the foregone income achievable by putting that money to use in an alternative investment activity. Financing flow costs may be borne by the manufacturer or an intermediary, or even by an outside channel member who specializes in these activities, such as a bank or credit card company.

Many sources of *risking* exist in the marketing channel. Long-term contracts between a distributor and a business end-user may specify price guarantees that lock in the distributor to a certain price, for instance. Should the market price for that product rise during the course of the contracting period, the distributor will lose revenue because it will still be forced to sell at the previously agreed-upon lower price. Price guarantees are sometimes offered to intermediaries who hold inventory, in case the product's market price falls before the inventory is sold. Such a practice moves risk from the intermediary's shoulders to those of the manufacturer. Warranties, insurance, repair, and after-sales service activities also represent costs due to risky, unforeseeable future events (such as parts failures or accidents). For example, Peapod bears and manages the cost of risk in its handling of perishable groceries between purchase at the grocery store and delivery to the shopper at home. It controls the risk of spoilage through its ownership and use of temperature-controlled boxes in which groceries are transported from the store to the shopper's home. These boxes guarantee the quality of both frozen and refrigerated goods. In general, either a manufacturer or a reseller may bear the cost of these activities.

Ordering and *payment* flow costs are all the costs incurred in the actual purchase of and payment for the product. Many innovations are occurring today in the performance of these flows, unglamorous though they may seem. For instance, many retailers use *automatic replenishment*, an automated reordering system whereby a computer system tracks levels of inventory in the retailer's system and automatically sends a replenishment order to the manufacturer when stock reaches an agreed-upon low level. This process reduces ordering costs as well as improving in-stock percentages. One of the valuable innovations that Schwab's OneSource brings to the standard mutual fund channel is the consolidation of ordering and payment functions across investors (lowering the cost of dealing with a mutual fund company) and across funds (lowering the investor's cost of portfolio management).

Because of the cost associated with performing channel flows, it is important not to perform unnecessarily high levels of any of the flows. Thus, knowing what service outputs are demanded by target end-users, at what level of intensity, helps the channel manager control the total cost of running the channel through the performance of only those flow levels that create valued service outputs.

Customizing the List of Flows for a Particular Channel

Just as we pointed out in our discussion of service outputs in Chapter 3, it is important to customize the list of flows to the particular channel being analyzed. This can mean clumping together two of the eight generic flows. For example, in some channels, it makes sense to consider the costs of physical possession and of ownership together, if they are always incurred by the same channel members at the same time.

Conversely, it can make sense either to add to the list of eight flows or to expand one of the flows into more than one element. For example, the promotion flow could be considered to be several different flows, each with its own cost: (1) running an employee sales force to engage in personal selling, (2) creating and running advertisements with an outside advertising agency, (3) running a public relations program could all be considered distinct flow processes worthy of separate categorization. Or, the channel manager may wish to categorize physical possession into two flows, one for the storage and delivery costs to sell an original product, and one for the storage and delivery of spare parts.

Finally, the channel manager could conceivably wish to minimize the effort to understand and measure the costs of certain flows that are not very important in the channel. For example, negotiation activities may be negligible in channels of long-standing relationships with long-term contracts, and hence not as worthy of close scrutiny as are other activities and flows.

Why should the channel manager expend so much effort in the categorization of channel activities into specific flows? The key to this process is to generate a list that:

- Has names that channel members can recognize and use
- Matches the ways in which channel costs are incurred and measured by channel members
- Accounts for all the relevant costly flow activities of the channel

Characterizing channel flows in terms of names that are recognizable to channel members is important because it helps the channel manager communicate information about the workings of the distribution operation. If channel members are not comfortable with terms such as *physical possession* but easily recognize the term *storage* or *warehousing* instead, obviously the names in the list of flows should change to represent that familiarity.

Channel flow descriptions also need to match the ways in which channel costs are incurred. If, for example, parts inventorying for postsale service is carried out in a different profit center of a distributor's company than is presale product inventorying, then representing these as two separate flows will best help track the costs of running the channel. These data become useful later on if the channel manager is considering reallocating flows within the channel to minimize channel costs.

Finally, the channel flow description must measure all the costs incurred in running the channel. In the near term, the channel manager needs an accurate accounting of the activities of the channel in order to evaluate the efficiency and effectiveness of flow performance. In the longer term, failure to recognize costly but valuable channel flow performance by any channel member can lead to inappropriate rewarding of channel flow performance and eventually to serious channel conflicts.

DESCRIBING THE CURRENT CHANNEL WITH THE EFFICIENCY TEMPLATE

The first use to which we will put the concepts of channel flows is to describe the productive activities of a currently operating channel. Thus, we introduce here the *Efficiency Template*, to measure the costs borne and value added by each channel member in its performance of channel flows. A detailed description of the application of the Efficiency Template to a real-world channel appears in Appendix 4.1. Here, we discuss its elements and uses.

The Efficiency Template describes (1) the types and amounts of work done by each channel member in the performance of the marketing flows, (2) the importance of each channel flow to the provision of demanded consumer service outputs, and (3) the resulting share of total channel profits that each channel member should reap. Table 4.1 shows a blank Efficiency Template. The rows list the channel flows, and there are two sections of columns: a set of columns determining *importance weights* for the flows and a set of columns to list *proportional performance of each flow* by each channel member.

Consider first the three columns determining the importance weights to be associated with each channel flow. The idea here is to account for both the cost of performance of that flow and the value added through the performance of that flow in the channel. The entries in the Costs column should be percentages adding up to 100 across all the flows. For example, if the costs of promotion accounted for 23 percent of all channel flow costs, the analyst would enter the number 23 in the Cost cell for the Promotion flow. One technique for generating quantitative cost weights is an *activity-based cost (ABC)* analysis of the channel. Activity-based costing is an accounting tool to measure the cost of performing activities within one organization.[7] Here, the task is more comprehensive in nature: To get good quantitative measures of costs, the cost of all the activities of all the channel members must be measured. Of these total costs, the question is then, for example, What proportion of all channel costs is accounted for by promotional activities?

TABLE 4.1
The Efficiency Template

| | Weights for Flows | | | Proportional Flow Performance of Channel Member | | | | |
	Costs*	Benefit Potential (high, medium, or low)	Final Weight*	1	2	3	4 (end-user)	Total
Physical possession**								100
Ownership								100
Promotion								100
Negotiation								100
Financing								100
Risking								100
Ordering								100
Payment								100
Total	**100**	N/A	**100**	N/A	N/A	N/A	N/A	N/A
Normative profit share†	N/A	N/A	N/A					**100**

* Entries in column must add up to 100 points.
** Entries across row (sum of proportional flow performance of channel members 1 through 4) for each channel member must add up to 100 points.
† Normative profit share of channel member *i* is calculated as: (final weight, physical possession) (channel member *i*'s proportional flow performance of physical possession) + . . . + (final weight, payment) (channel member *i*'s proportional flow performance of payment). Entries across row (sum of normative profit shares for channel members 1 through 4) must add up to 100 points.

If strict quantitative measures of cost are not available, the analyst can still use more qualitative techniques to get an estimate of the cost weights to use. A Delphi-type research technique can be applied, for example, with several of the best-informed managers in the channel developing a best estimate of the cost weights to use.[8] Again, the output of such an exercise is a set of weights, adding up to 100, that measure the proportion or percentage of total channel costs accounted for by each flow.

Beyond measuring the cost of performing flows, it is also useful to consider the value created by the performance of each flow. This is a more intuitive process, because it links the performance of flows to the generation of demanded service outputs. Consider the following example. If a new fad product, such as children's Pokemon trading cards and video games, is being introduced to the market, it is crucial to generate awareness and preference for the cards and games. Once awareness has been generated, it is then critical that the products be widely available for children (or their parents) to buy easily. Fad products by definition are not expected to have a long life cycle and therefore the demands for spatial convenience and quick delivery are high. Thus, the promotion and physical possession flows take on great importance, particularly relative to some other flows (e.g., ownership, negotiation, or payment). In such a case, we might rate physical possession and promotion as having a high value addition to the channel, whereas a flow such as payment might rate a low value addition.

The cost and value added of a flow may or may not be positively correlated. For example, if spatial convenience is very important to a consumer wishing to purchase Pokemon children's video games, then the physical possession of those video games at a retailer may add a great deal of value to the channel, even if it is very low cost to do so (due to the small size of the video games). In such a case, the channel analyst might allocate a small cost weight to the physical possession flow, but a high value weight.

The cost weight can then be adjusted to achieve a final set of importance weights for each flow in the channel. The adjustment process is judgmental but generally involves increasing the weight on flows rated as generating high value added in the channel, and demoting the value placed on flows with a low value added. The final weights themselves must add up to 100, so if some flow weights are increased, others must decrease. Again, a Delphi analysis can help channel members arrive at a final set of weights that accurately represent both the cost borne and the value created through the performance of a given channel flow.

The other columns in the Efficiency Template in Table 4A.1 require the channel analyst to allocate the total cost of each flow across all the channel members. Again, the analyst enters figures adding up to 100, to represent the proportion of the total cost of a given flow borne by a particular channel member. That is, if a channel consists of a manufacturer, a distributor, a retailer, and an end-user, the costs of physical possession must be spread across these channel members, and so the cost proportions must add up to 100.

Not all channel members must bear all costs. For example, a manufacturer may use independent sales representatives to aid in selling its product. These sales reps do not inventory any product, nor do they take title to product; they specialize in promotional and sometimes order-taking activities. Hence, the sales rep's cost proportion entry in the physical possession row would be zero, because it does not take physical possession of inventory at all.

The end-user is also a member of the channel for the purposes of channel flow performance. Any time end-users buy a larger lot size than they really need in the short term (i.e., foregoes bulk-breaking), they are performing part of the physical possession flow, as they will have to inventory the as-yet unused product themselves. Similarly, such a consumer bears inventory carrying costs and hence shares in the costs of ownership in the channel. If the end-user pays for the whole lot at the time of purchase, financing is also being borne, because payment is being made early. Thus, end-users can participate in the channel flows in many ways, and as with any other channel member, these costs borne can and should be measured. This is particularly useful when contrasting one segment of end-users versus another, as it helps shed light on such issues as why it costs more to serve some end-users than others (they perform fewer costly channel flows themselves, thrusting this cost back onto other channel members).

With weights assigned to each flow and cost proportions allocated for the performance of each flow across all the channel members, the channel analyst can then calculate a weighted average for each channel member measuring that member's contribution to the cost borne and value created in the channel. This weighted average is calculated as the (weight times cost proportion) for each flow, summed across all the flows. In our example of the building materials company profiled in Appendix 4.1, the manufacturer's weighted average is 28 percent (equal to $[(.35 \times .30) + (.15 \times .3) + (.08 \times .2) + (.04 \times .2) + (.29 \times .3) + (.02 \times .3) + (.03 \times .2) + (.04 \times .2)]$). Similarly, a retailer in the channel contributes 39 percent of the cost–value in the channel, and a customer contributes 33 percent.

These final percentages have a special meaning. Consider the total profit available to the whole channel (i.e., channel contribution), when selling product at full-service list prices. This is equal to the total revenue (were all units sold at list prices), minus all costs of running the channel. Then the data on the cement company in Appendix 4.1 report that the manufacturer's channel flow performance is responsible for generating 28 percent of the channel contribution from selling through the retail channel, the retailer's efforts are responsible for generating 39 percent, and the customer's shouldering of channel flow costs is worth 33 percent. That is, these percentages measure the proportionate value creation of each channel member. We call these percentages the *normative profit shares* of each channel member. Note that being responsible for a large proportion of a low-value flow does not create as much overall value as does performing most of a highly valued flow. Thus, being a busy channel member should not always signal high value creation for the channel. We will return to this meaning later when we discuss the Equity Principle.

What does it mean for an end-user (in this example, a buyer of building materials at retail) to generate channel profits in our building materials company example in Appendix 4.1? These end-users buy reasonably large quantities of these materials and store them for use after the time of purchase. They thus pay in advance for product that they will use only later, and they also are willing to store the cement on their own property, rather than forcing the retailer or manufacturer to warehouse it. Thus, the end-user is in fact performing valued channel flows that are costly to it, just as they would be costly to any other channel member. The performance of these flows merits some reward. In general, the reward given to a segment of end-users who perform valued channel flows is a reduction in price from full-service list price levels. Thus, the end-user should be counted as a channel member for the purpose of measuring performance of channel flows, because different segments of end-users perform different quantities and sorts of channel flow activities and thus lift the cost of performing those flows off the shoulders of other channel members.

It is important to note that a separate Efficiency Template should be created *for each channel used to distribute the product.* One really should create a separate Efficiency Template also for each market segment that buys through each channel, because multiple segments may patronize one channel, but buy in different ways. Thus, in the building materials company's case, there is a separate Efficiency Template for the retailer channel than the one created for the direct channel serving ready-mix concrete companies, precast and construction company buyers. This is necessary because a channel member involved in selling to retail buyers (e.g., the retailer) does not make contributions to the bearing of channel flow costs when selling to direct business buyers in the business channel.

Finally, suppose that full financial data on the costs borne by each channel member are lacking. Thus, precise ratings cannot be entered in the Efficiency Template, because it is not known exactly how much of a given flow's cost is borne by each particular channel member. Must we discard the Efficiency Template in this situation? No—as long as some ranking data are available to calibrate relative intensity of performance of each flow. Appendix 4.1 details how the channel analyst can use even rough ranking data to get a reasonably good approximation of the relative value created by each channel member. As with any approximation system, the rougher the approximations, the rougher the estimates of value created, but as the example in Appendix 4.1 shows, the approximations are often much better than no consideration at all of the relative value added by each channel member.

In sum, the Efficiency Template is a very useful tool for codifying the bearing of cost and adding of value to the channel of each channel member. The Efficiency Template should be channel specific; that is, a separate Efficiency Template must be created for each channel used to sell the product. The Efficiency Template accounts for channel flow costs borne by end-users as well as other channel members. Its uses are many:

- It reveals how the costs of particular flows are shared among channel members.
- It shows how much each channel member contributes to the overall value creation in the channel.
- It reveals how important each of the flows is to total channel performance.
- It can be a powerful tool in explaining current channel performance and justifying changes that channel managers wish to make to currently operating channels.

In cases where the product is sold through multiple channels, the Efficiency Templates can be compared to see differences in costs of running the different channels. This may lead to insights about how to decrease costs without compromising the provision of desired service output levels in the target market.

There are, of course, many situations where a marketing channel does not already exist for a product. Anytime a manufacturer seeks to sell its product in a new market or country, it needs to create a new marketing channel through which to sell the product. The next section describes how to use flow concepts and the Efficiency Template to design a new marketing channel.

USING CHANNEL FLOW CONCEPTS TO DESIGN A ZERO-BASED CHANNEL

What would a channel manager do if given the luxury of being able to design an optimal channel from scratch, without a preexisting channel structure to hamper the design? We call such a channel the *zero-based channel*, and define it as follows:

> *A zero-based channel design is one that (1) meets the target market segment's demands for service outputs, (2) at minimum cost of performing the necessary channel flows that produce those service outputs.*

Notice that there is an unavoidable tension in this concept. On the one hand, the channel manager of course wants to minimize the cost of running the marketing channel, in order to preserve profit margins. On the other hand, enough must be spent on performing channel flows to guarantee the generation of the desired service outputs. Spending too little (or making poor decisions about how to spend money in running the channel) will result in insufficiently low provision of service outputs. Competitors may take advantage of the hole in service output provision by offering a superior combination of product plus service outputs. This can lead to loss of market share and profitability. However, spending too much will produce a higher level of service outputs than is valued by the target market and will unnecessarily increase the cost basis of the channel, again reducing profitability. Achieving the right balance is a continuously demanding task, given the changes occurring in the marketplace.

Even with a preexisting channel, the channel manager should be asking whether the current channel design is zero-based or not. Chapter 6, dealing with gap analysis, tackles this question. The concept of the zero-based channel design can also be applied when designing a new channel where one did not previously exist. For example, Schwab's innovation of the OneSource mutual fund supermarket resulted from a recognition that the preexisting channel for mutual funds did not meet all segments' service output demands. A more economical, but high assortment–variety offering was desired by the sophisticated investor. Grainger and its partners used the concept of aggregating the ordering function to offer a broader assortment and variety to their business customers. And the attractiveness of the Peapod service revolves around the recognition that standard grocery shopping events do not provide as much spatial convenience and delivery time specificity as some consumer segments demanded. Peapod generates higher levels of these service outputs through its performance of the channel flows noted in Figure 4.2.

In short, the establishment of a zero-based channel involves a recognition of *what* level of channel flows must be performed to generate the service outputs demanded—demands that are frequently unmet—in the market.

MATCHING NORMATIVE AND ACTUAL PROFIT SHARES: THE EQUITY PRINCIPLE

The normative profit shares calculated from the Efficiency Template for a currently operating channel give a measure of the share of total channel profits each channel member's efforts are responsible for generating. This share and the actual share of total channel profits garnered by each channel member should be related, as our definition of the *Equity Principle* indicates:

> *Compensation in the channel system should be given on the basis of the degree of participation in the marketing flows and the value created by this participation. That is, compensation should mirror the normative profit shares for each channel member.*

The Equity Principle states that it is appropriate to reward each channel member in accordance with the value that member creates in the channel. Doing so creates the right incentives among channel members to continue to generate that value in the future. Trying to deprive a channel member of its rewards for effort expended and value created, conversely, can result later on in underperformance of necessary channel flows. This creates serious channel conflicts, and sometimes even the dissolution of the channel.

To live by the Equity Principle, channel members must know what costs they have actually incurred and have an agreed-upon estimate of the value created in the channel. Without this, channel members are open to disagreements about the value each one actually adds to channel performance. Worse, these disagreements are likely to be shaped more by each channel member's perception of its own contribution than by the facts of the case. It takes effort to amass the information necessary to complete the efficiency analysis, but the payoffs are worth the effort.

What should be done if actual profit shares do not equal the normative shares suggested by the Efficiency Template? The answer depends on further analysis not only of the channel situation but also of the external competitive environment. There can be competitive situations in which, despite a channel member's contributions to channel performance, that member makes less profit than the Efficiency Template would suggest. This is because the availability of competitors who could easily take this channel member's place limits the profits that can be commanded by the channel member.

As an example, think of a supplier of commodity cookware to mass-merchandiser retailers such as Wal-Mart, Kmart, or Target in the United States. When Wal-Mart began forcing its suppliers to use electronic data interchange (EDI) to transmit orders and financial information, it subsidized the adoption of its proprietary computer system. But the commodity cookware supplier noted that after a period of time, Wal-Mart withdrew the support, forcing the supplier to bear the whole cost of maintaining the EDI system. The value created by use of the EDI system could not have been achieved without the supplier, as well as Wal-Mart, voluntarily using it. Yet apparently, the supplier bore more than its fair share of the cost of the system. Although this is a violation of the Equity Principle, the supplier had little recourse. If it refused to pay the cost of maintaining the EDI system inside its firm, Wal-Mart would simply drop it as a supplier, because in the competitive marketplace, Wal-Mart would be able to replace this supplier. Thus, competitive pressures can cause deviations from the Equity Principle that do not necessarily imply the need to change channel reward systems.

However, in the long run it behooves channel members to adhere to the Equity Principle. Channel partners who do not receive rewards commensurate with their perceived contributions to the channel will not remain highly motivated for long. Should competitive conditions change in the future, they are likely to leave the relationship or at the very least, bargain hard for a more favorable change in terms. In addition, a firm that treats its channel partners poorly develops a bad reputation that hurts its ability to manage other future channel relationships. These problems are a major cause of channel conflict (discussed in more depth in Chapter 9). The astute channel manager carefully balances the risk of such events against the immediate gain to be had by garnering a greater share of channel profits today. And, if competitive conditions do not give one channel member profit leverage over another, we should see rewards at least roughly mirroring the level of flow performance in the channel.

In the Peapod example, this principle is evident if we contrast grocery shopping through Peapod with grocery shopping through a "box store" such as Aldi. Aldi, a European-based grocery retailer, offers products in bulk and in limited variety but at low prices. The company states its philosophy as follows: "we offer the customer a carefully selected range of high quality exclusive own label brands at heavily discounted prices. What's more, these discounted prices are guaranteed week in week out."[9] The chain also chooses retail locations with low rents, which means that they are somewhat remotely located relative to a neighborhood supermarket. Clearly, Aldi is rewarding its shoppers with low prices in return for providing low levels of service outputs to them. Aldi shoppers effectively relieve the Aldi grocery channel of channel flow costs by performing some of these flows themselves. In particular, they perform physical possession flows through their transporting of product from the remote retail locations to their homes, as well as ownership and financing flows through their purchases of large quantities that cannot be consumed quickly.

In contrast, shopping through Peapod, the consumer pays a higher price in two ways: through the payment of regular supermarket prices (which are higher than Aldi prices) and through the payment of delivery fees to Peapod itself. But in return for the higher price for a basket of groceries, the Peapod shopper gets three things: (1) a broader assortment of brands from which to choose; (2) small lot sizes of the products he/she purchases; and (3) home delivery, the ultimate in spatial convenience. Of course, Peapod does not pocket the delivery fees as pure profit, because it incurs costs to provide these service outputs (such as the labor costs of Peapod professional shoppers and of delivery personnel, as well as the capital costs of maintaining a delivery truck fleet). Thus, a correlation exists between the willingness of shoppers to tolerate lower service output levels and perform channel flows themselves, on the one hand, and lower prices on the other hand. The lower prices are the channel's way of endowing the end-user with a portion of the profits of the channel. If Aldi were to charge prices equal to those available through Peapod, it would lose business; consumers (just like any other channel member) demand a fair and equitable share of the channel profits in return for services rendered to the channel.

SUMMARY

Referring back to Figure 4.1, understanding the concept of channel flows is critical to the channel manager's ability to design and maintain a well-working channel. Channel flows are the activities and processes that marketing channel members engage in that both are costly and at the same time add value to the channel. The performance of channel flows results in the generation of service outputs for end-users in the marketplace. With an understanding of the segment(s) of the market that the channel will target, the channel manager can use an analysis of channel flows to evaluate the cost-effectiveness of channel activities.

We introduced the concept of the Efficiency Template to aid in this analysis. The Efficiency Template codifies information about the importance of each channel flow in both cost and value terms, as well as about the proportion of each flow performed by each channel member. An Efficiency Template analysis can be done with a preexisting channel, or it can be the basis for the development of a new channel. In either case, the Efficiency Template produces a metric called the normative profit share for each channel member, a measure of the proportionate value added to the total channel's performance by each channel member.

If there are no intervening adverse competitive conditions, the normative profit shares should mirror at least approximately the actual shares of total channel profits enjoyed by each channel member. This is the Equity Principle. In the short run, it is possible to observe divergences from the Equity Principle, particularly when one channel member is in a very competitive industry. Then, even though the channel member does generate considerable value through its performance of necessary channel flows, it may not be able to reap a proportionate share of channel profits because other possible channel members stand ready to take its place if it demands too high a proportion of total channel profits. But in the long run, reasonable adherence to the Equity Principle helps ensure the continued good efforts of all channel members.

This chapter has focused on the actual channel flows. We turn in the next chapter to a discussion of the overall channel structure—the identity and numbers of various channel members—through which the channel flows are allocated.

Appendix

4.1 The Efficiency Template:
A Tool for Analysis

This Appendix will focus on how to fill out the Efficiency Template for the current channel structure. Filling it out for the zero-based channel follows an analogous process. Contrasts between the two templates will be pointed out. Please refer to Table 4.1, which shows a blank Efficiency Template.

This template is designed to help you understand (1) who is doing what functions and flows in the channel, (2) how much of the combined cost and value each channel member is responsible for, and (3) whether each channel member is being fairly compensated for the performance of these flows. The outputs of understanding these issues are (1) a strengthened ability to defend the allocation of total channel profits among channel members (based on an in-depth analysis rather than on *ad hoc* rationales or inertia); (2) a set of recommendations regarding alteration of the split of channel profits; and (3) a set of recommendations regarding future emphasis to be placed on the performance of particular flows in the channel.

It is important to fill out a separate template for each channel used in the market. For example, IBM uses a direct sales force as well as VARs (value-added resellers) to sell its personal computers. These two distinct channels each require a distinct Efficiency Template.

The first step in filling out the Efficiency Template is deciding what weights to assign each of the channel flows. Your final assessment of weights should take into account (1) the cost of performing this channel flow in the entire channel as a proportion of total channel operation costs, and (2) the value generated by performing this channel flow. If possible, the Costs column of the Efficiency Template should reflect financially sound data collected through a process such as activity-based costing to assess the proportion of total channel costs allocatable to each flow. The Benefit Potential column should reflect the judgmental inputs of managers knowledgeable about the channel concerning the ability of good performance of that flow to create highly valued service outputs. Because these inputs are judgmental, it is suggested that a qualitative input be used such as the ranking low, medium, or high. These rankings should then be used to adjust the purely cost-based weights in the Costs column to arrive at final weights for each flow. Particularly when a flow gets a rating of high in benefit potential, it should receive more weight than its pure cost-based weight would suggest, because it is important not only on the cost side but also on the service output generation side. The sum of the importance weights is 100. Thus, if you wished (for example) to increase the weight put on the promotion flow, it would be necessary to take some points away from some other flow, presumably one or more that received a benefit potential ranking of low.

Once you have come to a decision about weights, you then need to fill in the share of cost of each flow borne by each channel member. Consider the example of promotion on laptop computers in a retail channel. The relevant channel members may include (1) the manufacturer, (2) the retailer, and (3) the consumer. The consumer probably does not do any of the promotional flow, unless word of mouth plays a big role in this market; this implies that the consumer should get a zero in the Promotion row. But both the manufacturer and the retailer perform promotional flows: The manufacturer does national advertising of the laptops, primarily in print media, whereas the retailer uses floor salespeople to promote the product to consumers who walk in the door. Parceling out the costs, suppose that we discover that the manufacturer bears 65 percent of total promotional costs in the channel, and the retailer bears 35 percent. Thus, note that the sum of the three numbers (promotional costs borne by the manufacturer, retailer, and consumer) is 100 percent. You need to replicate this exercise for each of the channel flows in the template.

Can consumers perform channel flows and hence get any entries other than zero in this template? Yes. Consider the example of a consumer shopping for groceries at a hypermarket in France. This consumer buys in large bulk—for example, the consumer buys six weeks' worth of paper goods in one visit to the hypermarket. In so doing, the consumer is bearing physical possession flows (storing inventory in the home instead of going to the store every time he or she needs more paper goods), ownership flows (the consumer purchases the paper goods and hence owns them sooner than needed), financing flows (the consumer pays for the goods when he or she takes ownership, thus improving upstream channel members' cash flow positions), and so on. Contrast this with a shopper who buys only what he or she needs on a daily or biweekly basis. This consumer will typically buy in smaller lot sizes, will not store inventory in the home, and therefore will not perform the abovementioned flows. The consumer who shops at the hypermarket typically gets a lower price than the one who shops at a regular grocery store on a daily basis. Why? Precisely because the hypermarket shopper is bearing the cost of several channel flows. Thus, we can see a direct relationship between the bearing of channel flows and the garnering of channel profits (in the consumer's case, getting a lower price).

This brings us to the bottom line of this template. Once you have filled in both the weights and the proportionate shares of flow performance on the template, you can calculate a weighted average for each channel member, as described at the bottom of Table 4.1. The numbers that result can be written in the bottom row of the Efficiency Template, and they should sum to 100 percent horizontally across the bottom row. What do these numbers mean?

These numbers tell you what proportion of total channel profits each channel member should get, given the current channel structure. We call this the "normative profit share of channel member i in the current channel." It is very important to note that the normative profit share may or may not equal the actual profit share. When these two numbers are not equal, you then need to ask why they are not. Some reasons for a divergence between normative and actual profit shares include the following:

1. Profits are misallocated in the channel and should be reallocated.

2. Competitive conditions force a particular channel member to take a lower profit share than its normative flow performance would indicate; its "economic rents" were essentially competed away in the market.

3. External constraints such as government regulation confer economic rents on a channel member beyond its performance of channel flows. This can be a particularly thorny issue in international channel management.

Finally, it is relevant to ask what these profit shares actually are. Consider total retail sales of your product: that would be retail price times total units sold. Now, subtract from this total revenue the total costs of running the channel, and the cost of goods sold (to net out the part of costs accrued in the manufacturing process). What remains is total channel profits. So, to get a really good handle on the allocation of profits among channel members, you need to do your best to do something like an activity-based costing analysis of the channel.

Now consider some of the contrasts between a template describing the current channel and one describing a zero-based channel:

1. There is no reason why the weights necessarily are the same in the two templates. For instance, you may decide that the current channel under-emphasizes the importance of promotion, and you may therefore decide to increase the proportion of total channel costs spent on promotion in the zero-based channel. That will change the weights allocated to the other flows accordingly.

2. The ratings in the template can be different. You may decide that in the zero-based channel, it makes more sense to have your distributor take care of all inventory-handling functions. Thus, physical possession flow costs will be borne much more heavily by the distributor in the zero-based channel than in the current channel. If this is the case, the Physical possession row will show different percentages in the zero-based versus the current template.

3. The column headings themselves may be different in the two templates. You may decide that the zero-based channel is a vertically integrated channel, so the zero-based template may lack a column heading for the distributor that you now use.

Finally, remember that managers in particular firms may think about this list of flows in a different way than we have enumerated them here. For example, managers may clump physical possession and ownership together into an inventorying function. This is fine, if it is always the case that physical possession and ownership go hand in hand. But if they do not (e.g., if some sales are consignment sales), then the flows need to be separated out.

As an example, consider the efficiency analysis done on a European building materials company. Data were collected from top managers of the company, who were expert in the workings of their channels. Table 4A.1 shows the Efficiency Template for this company's channel used to serve small and medium-size end-users (specifically, contractors) who buy through retailers. Because the building materials are bulky and

TABLE 4A.1

**Building Materials Company Efficiency Template for Channel Serving
End-Users Through Retailers: Undisguised Data**

	Weights for Flows			Proportional Flow Performance of Channel Member			
	Costs	Benefit Potential (high, medium, or low)	Final Weight	Manufacturer	Retailer	End-User	Total
Physical possession	30	High	35	30	30	40	100
Ownership	12	Medium	15	30	40	30	100
Promotion	10	Low	8	20	80	0	100
Negotiation	5	Low–Medium	4	20	60	20	100
Financing	25	Medium	29	30	30	40	100
Risking	5	Low	2	30	50	20	100
Ordering	6	Low	3	20	60	20	100
Payment	7	Low	4	20	60	20	100
Total	**100**	N/A	**100**	N/A	N/A	N/A	N/A
Normative profit share	N/A	N/A	N/A	28%	39%	33%	**100**

expensive to transport, physical possession costs are the largest part of the total channel costs, and hence account for 30 percent of channel costs in total. Financing is also a significant channel cost, with 25 percent of the total. Other flows have smaller costs associated with them. In the Benefit Potential column, physical possession is again listed as the main benefit-conferring channel flow. This is because end-users of these building materials require product to be provided to them in a spatially convenient way (to minimize their own transportation costs) and with minimal time delays. Thus, the final weight allocated to the physical possession flow for this company in this channel was 35 percent, with ownership and financing also increased somewhat in importance. The other flows' final weights are somewhat reduced from their pure cost-based levels.

The channel consists of the manufacturer, who sells direct to retailers, who in turn sell directly to end-users. Small contractors are a major constituency of this segment, and they buy product in advance and hold small inventories themselves; they thus participate in 40 percent of the physical possession flow, with the manufacturer and retailer each taking a 30 percent share. The retailers are very active channel members, particularly in their performance of the promotional, negotiation, ordering, and payment flows, as they buffer the manufacturer by dealing with all the many small customer orders that come in. End-users do none of the promotional flow but participate in a small way in other flows. For their efforts, these end-users deserve one-third of the channel profits, which translates into a price cut for these contractors as compared to the list price that would be charged to an individual buyer (e.g., a do-it-yourself home owner). The retailer earns a normative channel profit share of 39 percent, whereas the manufacturer earns a normative channel profit share of 28 percent. Specifically, one calculates the manufacturer's normative channel profit share as:

$$(.35)(.3) + (.15)(.3) + (.08)(.2) + (.04)(.2) + (.29)(.3) + (.02)(.3) + (.03)(.2) + (.04)(.2)$$

This analysis was done after careful estimation of the total costs of performing all the channel flows in this particular channel. But suppose that the company did not have exact percentage shares for all the flows done by all channel members. Instead, suppose the data were very rough, with ratings of only zero, low, medium, and high available. Further, suppose that if the true rating were zero, a zero is reported; if the true rating is between 1 and 29 percent, a low is reported; if the true rating is between 30 and 69 percent, a medium is reported; and if the true rating is between 70 and 100 percent, a high is reported. Let us code a zero as a 0; a low as a 1; a medium as a 2; and a high as a 3. We would then get an Efficiency Template that looks like Table 4A.2.

In order to translate this into percentages, we then look at these rank-order data for a given flow and ask, "What proportion of the costs of performing this flow is borne by the manufacturer? By the retailer? By the final end-user?" For the case of physical possession, each entry is a 2 (medium). Thus, the point-count total is 6, of which each channel member has one-third of the points. We therefore can allocate 33 percent of the channel flow costs of physical possession to each channel member. In another example, consider the rank-order data for the promotion flow. Here, the manufacturer gets a ranking of 1 (low), the retailer gets a 3 (high), and the end-user gets a ranking of 0. Thus,

TABLE 4A.2

Building Materials Company Efficiency Template for Channel Serving End-Users Through Retailers: Rank-Order Data

	Weights for Flows			Proportional Flow Performance of Channel Member			
	Costs	Benefit Potential (high, medium, or low)	Final Weight	Manufacturer	Retailer	End-User	Total
Physical possession	30	High	35	2	2	2	100
Ownership	12	Medium	15	2	2	2	100
Promotion	10	Low	8	1	3	0	100
Negotiation	5	Low–Medium	4	1	2	1	100
Financing	25	Medium	29	2	2	2	100
Risking	5	Low	2	2	2	1	100
Ordering	6	Low	3	1	2	1	100
Payment	7	Low	4	1	2	1	100
Total	**100**	N/A	**100**	N/A	N/A	N/A	N/A
Normative profit share	N/A	N/A	N/A	?	?	?	**100**

TABLE 4A.3

Building Materials Company Efficiency Template for Channel Serving End-Users Through Retailers: Transformed Rank-Order Data

	Weights for Flows			Proportional Flow Performance of Channel Member			
	Costs	Benefit Potential (high, medium, or low)	Final Weight	Manufacturer	Retailer	End-User	Total
Physical possession	30	High	35	33	33	33	100
Ownership	12	Medium	15	33	33	33	100
Promotion	10	Low	8	25	75	0	100
Negotiation	5	Low–Medium	4	25	50	25	100
Financing	25	Medium	29	33	33	33	100
Risking	5	Low	2	40	40	20	100
Ordering	6	Low	3	25	50	25	100
Payment	7	Low	4	25	50	25	100
Total	**100**	N/A	**100**	N/A	N/A	N/A	N/A
Normative profit share	N/A	N/A	N/A	**32%**	**38%**	**29%**	**100**

of the 4 total points in the promotion flow, 25 percent of them (and hence an estimated 25 percent of the channel flow costs of promotion) are borne by the manufacturer, and 75 percent are borne by the retailer, with 0 percent borne by the end-user.

These transformed data produce percentages like those in the original Efficiency Template, but they are based on rougher data inputs (a 4-point scale rather than a 100-point scale, in effect). The transformed Efficiency Template appears as Table 4A.3.

From this analysis, the manufacturer gets a normative channel profit share of 32 percent, the retailer gets 38 percent, and end-users get 29 percent. These compare rather well with the 28 percent, 39 percent, and 33 percent from the true data in Table 4A.1. Because it is not always easy to do a full activity-based costing analysis of the performance of channel flows, the rank-order data inputs suggested here may provide reasonable estimates instead.

Discussion Questions

1. Give an example where a channel member performs only one flow for the channel, yet is an important member in making the channel work well. Give another example of a channel member who participates in all eight channel flows, and describe how it does so.

2. Many consumer-goods and industrial-goods companies both sell original product and also provide service after the sale. Relative to a system where only product is sold (but no service is necessary), how would you suggest describing the list of channel flows performed by various members of the channel?

3. If a consumer buys an item through a catalog over the phone with a credit card, is the credit card company a channel member? If the product is delivered by FedEx, is FedEx a channel member? If yes, what flows does it perform?

4. Explain how the shopping characteristics for the following consumer and industrial goods affect the channels for them:

Consumer Goods	**Industrial Goods**
Bread	Laser printer toner cartridges
Breakfast cereal	Uranium for nuclear power plants
Women's hosiery	Cement
Refrigerators	Medical machinery (e.g., ultrasound machines)

5. "A channel can be zero-based when targeted at one segment and not zero-based when targeted at another segment." True or false? Explain your answer.

6. Suppose that a set of channel participants decides to spare no expense in meeting all the service output demands of their target market. Assuming they indeed do meet those expressed demands, under what conditions might their channel still not be zero-based?

7. In the Wal-Mart example regarding electronic data interchange, the argument is that in the short run, deviations from the Equity Principle can occur due to competitive reasons. What might make this statement untrue in the long run?

Notes

1. Sources include the Peapod Web site (www.peapod.com); Peapod annual reports for 1997 and 1998; Sharon Machlis, "Filling Up Grocery Carts Online," *Computerworld*, 32, no. 30 (July 27, 1988), p. 4; Joan Holleran, "Partnering with Peapod," *Beverage Industry*, 88, no. 10 (October 1997), pp. 38–41; Subha Narayanan, "Home Shopping: The Way of the Future Is Here," *Retail World*, 50, no. 20 (October 13–17, 1997), p. 6; "A Woman's Place Is on the Net," *Chain Store Age Executive*, June 1997, pp. A16–A18; Tim Dorgan, "Viva la Difference?" *Progressive Grocer*, 76, no. 4 (April 1997), pp. 77–78; Jay A. Scansaroli and Vicky Eng, "Interactive Retailing: Marketing Products," *Chain Store Age Executive*, 73, no. 1 (January 1997), pp. 9A–10A; Laura Liebeck, "Peapod Goes National," *Discount Store News*, 37, no. 16 (August 24, 1998), pp. 4, 63.

2. We leave until Chapter 7 a discussion of more recent modifications of Peapod's strategy to include their own warehouses and take more control of the wholesale-to-retail movement of product. This discussion will focus instead on the basics of flow reallocation and cost bearing in Peapod's initial channel strategy. The sources used to develop this channel sketch are the same as those for the one in Chapter 3.

3. Initially, the Peapod system was a proprietary electronic system accessible by modem. The shopper had to purchase the Peapod software (for a nominal fee), load it on her computer system, and use it whenever she wanted to shop electronically. In 1998, Peapod switched over to an Internet-based software system accessible over the World Wide Web. Now a Peapod shopper can enter the system from any Internet-ready computer, whether at home or work, rather than only through the computer(s) loaded with the proprietary software.

4. Sources include the Grainger Web site (www.grainger.com); 1998 company annual report; Sharon Machlis, "Supplier Seeks Sales via Web Searches," *Computerworld*, 32, no. 37 (September 14, 1998), p. 20; James C. Anderson and James A. Narus, "Business Marketing: Understand What Customers Value," *Harvard Business Review*, 76, no. 6 (November–December 1998), pp. 53–65; Susan Avery, "To Manage Catalog Content, Distributors Form Partnerships," *Purchasing*, 125, no. 9 (December 10, 1998), pp. S18–S20; PR Newswire, "E-Commerce Gaining Loyalty Among Businesses Buying Operating Supplies Online; Speed and Convenience Cited as Major Advantages of Online Purchasing," PR Newswire Association, December 10, 1998; Andrew Zajac, "Grainger Launches e-commerce Supplies Site," *Chicago Tribune*, February 10, 1999, sec. 3, p. 3; and Larry Riggs, "Entering the Orderzone: W. W. Grainger's Planned Internet Site, Orderzone.com," *Cowles Business Media Inc. Direct*, 11, no. 4 (March 15, 1999), p. 86.

5. Sources include Schwab's Web site (www.schwab.com); Trent Carmichael, Bill Norris, Rob

Rozwat, Emiko Taguchi, "Charles Schwab OneSource: Channel Audit," 1996, used with authors' permission; William P. Barrett, "Mutual Fund Supermarkets," *Forbes*, 162, no. 4 (August 24, 1998), pp. 122–23; Associated Press, "Fund Investors Weigh Value of Advice," *Denver Rocky Mountain News*, July 21, 1998, p. 9B; Rebecca McReynolds, "Doing It the Schwab Way," *United States Banker*, 108, no. 7 (July 1998), pp. 46–56; Carol E. Curtis, "Food Fight in the Supermarket," *U.S. Banker*, May 1998; Sandra Block, "Supermarketing Mutual Funds Competition Increases with One-Stop Shops," *USA Today*, November 7, 1997, p. 1B; Russ Wiles, "Fund 'Supermarkets' Lure Shoppers; Brokerages Tout No Fees, Convenience," *The Arizona Republic*, September 21, 1997, p. D1; PR Newswire, "Schwab Launches World's First Online 'Supermarket' of Mutual Funds for International Investors; Charles Schwab Mutual Fund Center Offers Global Internet Trading of Leading Mutual Funds," PR Newswire Association, September 8, 1997; Peter Van Allen, "Schwab Seeking More Bank Allies for Fund Mart," *The American Banker*, June 6, 1997, p. 1; Christine Williamson, "Schwab Bets on International," Crain Communications *Pensions and Investments*, May 26, 1997, p. 2; Michelle DeBlasi, "Supermarket Wars: No-Load Fund Supermarkets Are All the Rage," *Bank Investment Marketing*, March 1, 1997; Peter Van Allen, "Discounter Schwab Stays Step Ahead of Banks and Other Competitors," *The American Banker*, February 24, 1997, p. 1; Michelle DeBlasi, "More Banks Go to the Supermarket," *Bank Investment Marketing*, January 1, 1997; Reed Abelson, "Charles Schwab Widens Mutual Fund Access," *New York Times*, December 13, 1996, p. D2; PR Newswire, "KeyCorp and First Union Become First Banks to Use Schwab's OneSource Program in Innovative Mutual Fund Offering for Bank Customers," PR Newswire Association, December 12, 1996; Charles Stein, "Fidelity Adds Funds to Its Mutual 'Supermarket' Concept," *The Boston Globe*, November 12, 1996; Mary Beth Grover, "Annual Funds Survey: Charles Schwab: The Matchmaker," *Forbes*, 156, no. 5 (August 28, 1995), pp. 160–62.

6. The source is private communication.

7. We will not develop an in-depth discussion of activity-based costing in this text. However, the interested reader is referred to the following sources for information on the activity-based costing paradigm: Robin Cooper and Robert S. Kaplan, "Profit Priorities from Activity-Based Accounting," *Harvard Business Review*, 69, no. 3 (May–June 1991), pp. 130–35; Bala Balachandran, "Strategic Activity Based Accounting," *Business Week Executive Briefing Service,* 5 (1994), p. 1; Michael O'Guin, "Focus the Factory with Activity-Based Costing," *Management Accounting* (1990), pp. 36–41; William Rotch, "Activity-Based Costing in Service Industries," *Journal of Cost Management*, summer 1990, pp. 4–14; and Ronald E. Yates, "New ABCs for Pinpoint Accounting," *Chicago Tribune*, January 24, 1993, pp. 1–2.

8. See, for example, Donelson R. Forsyth, "An Introduction to Group Dynamics," Monterey, CA: Brooks/Cole, 1983. The Rand Corporation is credited with developing the Delphi technique in the 1950s to forecast where the Soviet Union would attack the United States if they were to launch an attack. Rand originally got generals and other Kremlinologists into a room to discuss the issue, and made very little progress. As a result, it developed the Delphi technique to arrive at an orderly consensus.

9. This quote appears on the company Web site at www.aldi.com.

5

Supply-Side Channel Analysis: Channel Structure and Membership Issues

LEARNING OBJECTIVES

After reading this chapter, you will understand:

- The elements of the channel structure decision
- What questions must be asked to make each decision appropriately
- The mapping between the elements of the structure decision and the elements of the channel planning process: the need to meet service output demands, the need to minimize the cost of performing channel flows, and the need to coordinate the actions of channel members

The channel analyst has the necessary information to answer questions about overall *channel structure* once it is known what target segments' service output demands are, and what is the best channel flow performance pattern to generate those service outputs. The channel management schematic in Figure 5.1 (reproducing Figure 2.1) focuses attention on the next issue of import in channel design—deciding on the channel structure. This definition sets the scope of inquiry regarding channel structure decision making:

A description of the channel structure comprises a summary of the types of channel members that are in the channel, the intensity or number of members of each type that coexist in the market, and the number of distinct channels that coexist in the market.

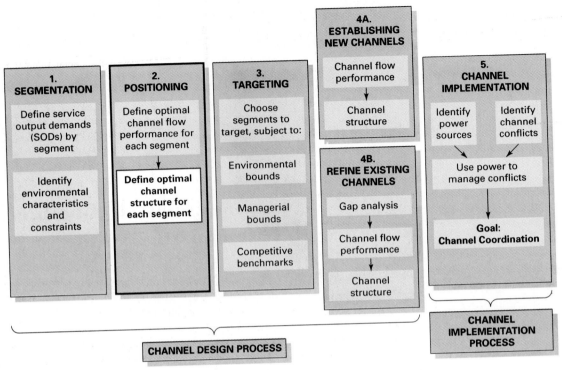

FIGURE 5.1 **Channel Management Schematic**

We next discuss each of these dimensions of channel structure.

WHO SHOULD BE IN THE CHANNEL?

The issue of the identity of the channel's members is the most basic element of channel structure. Figure 5.2 describes the process to decide who should be a member of the marketing channel. The first question is whether to use intermediaries at all (see Chapter 7 on vertical integration). If the answer is "no," the channel is a direct channel with no intermediaries. If the answer is "yes," the next two questions are "what type(s) of nonretail intermediaries (e.g., industrial distributor versus independent sales representative) and retail intermediaries (e.g., catalog versus specialty store versus mass merchandiser) to add to the channel structure?" Finally, once a particular type of intermediary is seen as desirable to add to the channel, its identity must be determined (e.g., which catalog or which industrial distributor to use).

Figure 5.2 includes questions whose answers help make the necessary decision at each level of the decision process. These questions focus on both demand-side and supply-side issues, such as how end-users shop, who is capable of performing necessary flows, and what the costs of performing these flows are. Beyond these efficiency-oriented questions, we also raise questions of cooperation and channel harmony (we defer in-depth discussion of them to Chapters 8–11, on channel coordination).

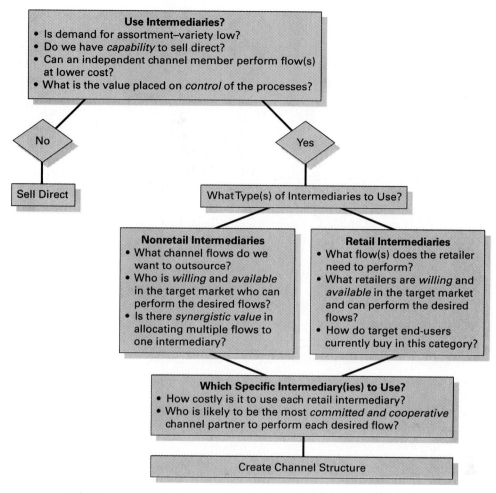

FIGURE 5.2 **Decision Process: Who Should Be a Channel Member?**

Should Intermediaries Be Used at All?

The question of whether to use intermediaries at all (the first step in Figure 5.2) requires us to think about how the channel's end-users prefer to buy the product (or product line) in question. In particular, if the demand for the service output of assortment and variety is low, this implies that end-users are willing to search for the product and to buy it in isolation from other products. To think of two polar opposites, consider a consumer purchasing breakfast cereal versus a consumer purchasing a collectible such as the latest Lladro figurine. In the first case, most consumers have a high demand for assortment and variety; they are unwilling to search for and buy their breakfast cereal at a breakfast cereal store or even from a breakfast cereal catalog. Rather, consumers want to shop for their groceries together, and thus, a cereal company would have a hard time gaining sales if it sold direct without carrying a full line of all groceries. In contrast, the buyer of the Lladro figurine knows precisely what he or she wants, and the array of other products in the retail offering is much less relevant. Lladro could choose to sell direct to the collector, without needing to offer a wide line of collectibles from which to choose. Clearly, a manufacturer could still choose to sell direct even if end-users' demands for assortment and variety are high. However, the manufacturer would then have to make sure that its product line contained all the products desired by end-users in the assortment it offered to the market. Many large industrial manufacturers do precisely this (e.g., Motorola, Boeing, etc.). If the manufacturer does not have a broad enough product line relative to end-users' assortment and variety demands, this need can unduly raise the costs of selling direct and make it an unattractive proposition.

Then, to judge whether to use intermediaries at all, the manufacturer must decide if in fact it has the capabilities necessary to sell direct. To put this in the framework of our channel flows discussion in Chapter 4, this means verifying that the manufacturer can itself perform all the necessary channel flows to produce target end-users' demanded service outputs. This would include, for example:

- Running its own warehousing facilities (if the physical product being sold must be stored between the time of manufacture and the time of purchase)
- Employing its own sales force (if sales force contact is necessary to promote and sell the product)
- Creating its own advertising and other promotional capabilities
- Maintaining its own personnel, programs, and technologies to provide any necessary pre- and postsale service (e.g., educational programs, repair facilities, service engineers, etc.)
- Having sufficient financial strength to finance unsold inventory as well as offer relevant payment terms to end-users buying the manufacturer's products
- Using its own ordering and payment system

The extent of this list suggests that the concept of truly and fully "selling direct" is not likely to be the top choice of many manufacturers. Even those who say they do sell direct may actually be using some intermediaries to help them perform certain selected channel flows, while the manufacturer controls most of the key activities in the marketing channel.

Even if the manufacturer is capable of selling direct, the next question becomes whether any independent channel partners could perform one or more flows at a lower cost than the manufacturer itself could. The latter could, for example, choose to run its own warehouses, but may instead outsource that activity to a third-party logistics company (or 3PL, as they are called) in order to control costs. The examples in Channel Sketch 5.1 illustrate some of the manufacturers using these independent logistics firms as well as some of the benefits of such a change.

Finally, assuming that it has the capability to sell direct and its end-users are willing to buy direct, the manufacturer choosing whether to use intermediaries must decide how important *control* of the channel is. Frequently an independent channel intermediary could help reduce the cost of performing one or more flows in the channel. But cost is not the only criterion for using an intermediary. It is also critical to ask whether there

CHANNEL SKETCH 5.1
Third-Party Logistics Firms Take on Flow Performance

- In 1992, National Semiconductor, a worldwide manufacturer of semiconductor and electronics equipment, employed almost 800 people to perform logistics functions alone. Each manufacturing plant had a warehouse, along with several distribution centers around the world. When the market moved toward supplier-owned inventory, National hired FedEx to reengineer its logistics functions. FedEx created, and now runs for National, a centralized warehouse in Singapore, implemented direct-to-customer shipping, and permitted National to reduce its logistics force to just 60 people. The average customer delivery cycle time has dropped from four weeks to seven days, and National's distribution costs have dropped from 2.9 percent of sales to 1.2 percent of sales. Outsourcing warehousing and logistics functions to FedEx saved National $27 million in the first five years the new system has been in operation.[1]

- Until the mid-1990s, AlliedSignal Inc., a $14 billion aerospace, automotive, and engineered materials manufacturer, ran its own logistics operations in a decentralized manner, leading to the use of more than 700 U.S. carriers alone. Shipments outside the United States were similarly uncoordinated. This not only reduced the company's negotiation power with shippers but also prevented a clear view of what was going on in the channel. AlliedSignal has now contracted with two logistics providers: D. F. Young in the United States and HRT in Europe. The logistics firms coordinate all order processing and shipping arrangements to reduce shipping delays and increase bargaining power with shippers.[2]

- Raytheon Aircraft Company's Hawker business jet manufacturing operation hired Emery Worldwide to perform international transportation and supply chain management functions for it. Motorola uses another logistics firm, BAX Global, to manage both assembly and distribution of cellular phones in the Asia-Pacific market.[3]

is a chance of poor performance on the part of an independent channel partner, and if so, what its impact would be on end-user satisfaction.

One illustration of the risks of outsourcing important functions to an intermediary occurred at Gibson Greeting Cards in 1998.[4] In that year, the company (the third-largest greeting card company in the United States) outsourced production and packaging of its greeting cards to outside companies in a move to cut costs, forecasting savings of several million dollars over the next two years. However, one of the company's vendors in charge of final packaging of cards delivered Thanksgiving and Christmas cards to retailers a month later than scheduled. Primarily due to this event, the company sustained a loss in the third quarter of 1998. Thus, failing to perform on just one part of the channel process (here, the delivery of physical product to retailers) can lead to disastrous consequences for a company. A company in a less constrained financial position than Gibson might decide to avoid such risks by maintaining control of key functions itself.

The choice to sell direct or use intermediaries is both a fundamental and a complex business decision, involving insights into demand-side factors, supply-side factors, and coordination and conflict factors. Chapter 7 discusses all of these issues in depth. The key insight is that using an intermediary to perform one or more channel flows in the chosen channel structure is a fairly likely event, because so many conditions have to be met in order for pure direct selling to be optimal. If the manufacturer therefore chooses to use one or more intermediaries, the question then becomes what types of intermediaries to use.

What Types of Intermediaries Should Be Used?

Given that the decision has been made to use intermediaries, the manufacturer needs to decide what sorts of intermediaries to use. Nonretail or retail intermediaries can be used. Some questions are common to the decision to add either a non-retail intermediary or a retail intermediary. One is what channel flow or flows must be performed by that intermediary to meet target end-users' service output demands. For example, if it is important to have product stocked throughout a market area in the warehouses of an intermediary (i.e., the intermediary must perform the physical possession flow in order to meet demands for spatial convenience), an independent sales representative is not a good choice, because usually they do not hold stock. On the other hand, suppose end-users value customer education more than spatial convenience. Then the promotion flow, as represented by sales effort, is the crucial input and not physical possession and stocking. The manufacturer can then choose an independent sales rep agency rather than an employee sales force and be able to meet service output demands very well. Table 5.1 lists other possibilities for types of intermediaries capable of performing particular flows.

Another key question is what nonretail or retail channel partners are both willing and available to participate in the manufacturer's channel efforts. Gibson Greeting Cards, for example, lost some key retail accounts in 1998 including Wal-Mart and Kmart due to those retailers' decisions to consolidate their supplier lists (i.e., the retailers became unwilling to carry the line), but signed on others such as Goody's and Card and Party Giant Stores. In other cases, a manufacturer may find a desirable intermediary who is unfortunately unavailable because of other exclusive distribution relationships it has signed. This can be a particular problem when entering foreign markets, where there may be a limited number of potential intermediaries to choose from, and those who are present may already be committed to other distribution contracts. The example of Pepsi losing its Venezuelan distributor to Coca-Cola in August 1996, profiled in Channel Sketch 5.2, illustrates the key importance of having access to distribution before sales can be sustained.

Beyond these common questions, one particularly appropriate to the decision to use nonretail intermediaries is whether synergies exist in allocating more than one flow to a single intermediary. Consider the issue of transporting product by truck from the manufacturer's plant to the site of the consignee (the buyer). Manufacturers frequently use independent trucking companies to transport the product, thus outsourcing the physical possession of the product to the trucker. However, increasingly shippers want their transportation firms to perform a whole array of integrated logistics functions, not just

TABLE 5.1

Mapping from Flows to Be Performed to Appropriate Intermediary Choices

Flow to Be Performed	Examples of Intermediaries That Can Perform Flow
Physical Possession	Contract warehouse Shipping company (e.g., FedEx, UPS, air freight) Distributor Retailers (including bricks and mortar, catalog, on-line)
Ownership	Contract warehouse Distributor Retailers (including bricks and mortar, catalog, on-line)
Promotion	Distributor Independent sales representative Broker Retailers (including bricks and mortar, catalog, on-line) Franchisees
Negotiation	Distributor Export marketing company Independent sales representative
Financing	Distributor Broker Retailers (including bricks and mortar, catalog, on-line) Credit card company Banks Franchisees
Risking	Distributor Retailers (including bricks and mortar, catalog, on-line) Credit card company Franchisees
Ordering	Distributor Independent sales representative Retailers (including bricks and mortar, catalog, on-line) Franchisees
Payment	Distributor Shipping company (e.g., Schneider) Retailers (including bricks and mortar, catalog, on-line) Franchisees

CHANNEL SKETCH 5.2

Pepsi Loses Its Bottler in Venezuela[5]

Venezuela was one of Pepsi's top 10 global markets for soft drinks, holding a 40 percent share of the $1 billion market in 1996. The Cisneros Group of Venezuela became Pepsi's first independent bottler outside North America in 1940 and had been a loyal partner ever since. PepsiCo's CEO, Roger Enrico, and Cisneros's CEO, Oswaldo Cisneros, were close friends. Cisneros also bottled Hit brand beverages, which commanded another 45 percent share of the Venezuelan soft drink market. Coca-Cola was left with just over 10 percent of the soft drink market in Venezuela. Venezuela was held up as a model market for Pepsi, which trailed Coke significantly in total world market share with Coke holding a 49.2 percent market share in 1995 and Pepsi holding a 15.7 percent market share internationally.

It came as a shock, therefore, when the Cisneros Group announced on August 16, 1996, that it was switching allegiance and becoming a Coca-Cola bottler in a joint venture agreement worth $500 million. Coke agreed to take a 50 percent stake in the Cisneros bottling business, including the Hit soda brand, a 45 percent market share product. In a day, Pepsi's distribution network in Venezuela was wiped out, including 4,000 delivery trucks and 18 bottling plants, and Coke's potential market share rose accordingly. Prior to this event, Pepsi's annual sales in Venezuela had been $400 million, with profits estimated at $10 million per year. It stood to lose all of this with the loss of its bottling partner. The development was all the more unusual because of the extreme rarity of bottlers switching in the global soft drink industry. Cisneros had aspirations to become an "anchor bottler" for Coke, which would position the company to expand throughout Latin America and increase its soft drink business significantly.

Pepsi immediately tried to have the joint venture declared illegal, as its contract with Cisneros did not expire until 2003. Pepsi also alleged that Coke's joint venture would lead to monopolization of the Venezuelan soft drink market. On August 23, 1996, the Venezuelan government's antitrust agency, Procompetencia, began an investigation into the joint venture contract to determine if in fact it would illegally monopolize the market. In a preliminary ruling on September 9, 1996, the government ruled that Cisneros could continue to bottle Coke and refuse to bottle Pepsi for the time being, although it prevented Cisneros from removing Pepsi that was already on retail store shelves. The final ruling on the antitrust suit was deferred until December 1996, when the joint venture was formally approved, with the constraint that Coca-Cola place in trust Cisneros's regional soft drink brands in order to prevent undue market domination. Procompetencia also fined Coca-Cola $1.9 million for violating antimonopoly regulations.

With no access to bottling or distribution, Pepsi was forced to find a new partner in Venezuela. On November 13, 1996, it announced a joint venture, to be called Sopresa, with Empresas Polar, the country's dominant beer brewer and a bottler of a small-share soft drink brand, with Polar holding 70 percent equity and Pepsi holding 30 percent. The new partners acknowledged it would take at least two years to regain Pepsi's lost level of distribution throughout the country.

Pepsi continued to pursue its antitrust claim against Cisneros, and the International Court of Arbitration in Paris ruled in September 1997 in favor of Pepsi. The Cisneros Group was directed to pay $94 million to Pepsi for early cancellation of its bottling and distribution contract. All parties were quoted as saying that the ruling and the amount were expected.

What went wrong for Pepsi? Roberto Goizueta, CEO of Coca-Cola, said, "You let me have the bottling plants and the trucks and the highly efficient systems, and I'll let you have the TV commercials. I'll beat you to a pulp over time." This statement highlights the crucial importance of a physical distribution presence in each market to the maintenance of healthy market share.

the transportation portion of the physical possession flow. Channel Sketch 5.3 shows some examples of services these logistics companies now offer. Shippers can now pass on to their logistics partners such functions as transportation, warehouse management, invoicing, and inventory tracking. The examples show how allocating multiple flows to one intermediary can further reduce cost. For instance, using an integrated third-party logistics company to handle hazardous chemicals minimizes the number of times the product has to change hands, lessening the risk of dangerous spillage or leakage.

CHANNEL SKETCH 5.3

Integrated Third-Party Logistics Firms: Providing Synergy Through Performing Multiple Flows[6]

Managing the supply chain through integrated logistics practices has become one of the foremost ways to build and maintain a competitive advantage in many industries today. Some studies suggest that companies can reduce inventory levels by as much as 40 percent by using advanced systems. From 1995 to 1998, the supply chain management business grew in volume from $744 million to $2.9 billion, suggesting the widespread recognition of the issue. This has partly been driven by the general trend toward downsizing in corporations, forcing the outsourcing of functions that formerly resided in-house. As a result, companies increasingly are looking for one logistics provider who can meet all their needs, including warehousing, data management, shipping, and invoicing. Here are a few examples of the trend:

- Trucking companies such as JB Hunt, TNT, and US Freightways now handle warehousing as well as transportation.

- Arrow Electronics, a distributor of electronics components, has some clients who want it to handle purchasing as well as materials handling.

- Ocean Spray, a $1.45 billion agricultural cooperative of cranberry and citrus growers in North America, hired Schneider Logistics to manage all freight-related responsibilities among its plants, warehouses, and distribution centers in the United States and Canada. Schneider uses its SUMIT® system to provide logistics services for this and other clients. SUMIT manages data about shipments; optimizes the choice of carriers for each shipment; uses paperless order management technologies to reduce paperwork throughout the delivery system; and offers invoiceless carrier payment.

- More and more chemicals companies are choosing to outsource their supply chain management functions, leading to an upsurge in the number of qualified third-party logistics providers to this industry. A key issue is the safe handling of shipments of hazardous product, which has caused the industry to lag behind others in the adoption of third-party logistics services. Logistics firms such as Chemical Leaman, Exel Logistics, Mark VII, and Schneider now provide these services. Some also now offer environmental services. For example, Chemical Leaman's subsidiary EnviroPower is a consulting group that advises clients on issues surrounding the packaging and shipment of hazardous chemicals, and Return Logistics offers recycling and disposal programs along with centralized database controls.

- Intermodal shipping involves the use of more than one kind of transportation company to move goods from the seller to the consignee (e.g., rail and truck, or rail, ship, and truck). Mark VII, an integrated third-party logistics firm, has plans to add inventory ownership to the array of logistics services the company already offers to shippers using intermodal shipping. Under the proposed system, the buyer would not have to take title to the inventory shipped until the time of actual delivery to the customer, rather than at the time the product leaves the seller's warehouse. Mark VII would bear ownership costs while the shipment is in transit. The company forecasts savings in cash flow requirements as a result of consolidating the multiple charges paid in intermodal shipping.

When considering using a retail intermediary, the particular question that must be asked is how end-users actually buy the product. It is possible to educate end-users to buy through new retail outlets, given sufficient promotional and educational efforts, but it can be easier to match the product to the type of outlet end-users are familiar with. Further, certain types of retail outlets carry particular connotations, which may or may not match the overall market positioning the manufacturer seeks for the product. For example, when the West Bend Company first sought to enter the Japanese market, it decided to sell popcorn poppers or electric coffeemakers. A Japanese catalog company wanted to carry West Bend's Stir Crazy popper, priced at the equivalent of US $285 (the Stir Crazy popper sold in the United States for about US $30 at the time). West Bend decided that although this retail outlet was open, it was not an appropriate place to sell its product, particularly as a first market entry strategy. The pricing of the product would be so inconsistent with the positioning of the line that West Bend feared its ability to roll out other products later. As well, catalogs did not carry the high-quality image it sought to build in the market.[7]

The key from the end-user side is therefore to seek a retail intermediary that (1) matches consumers' desired shopping patterns and (2) connotes the overall quality and positioning level that the manufacturer seeks for its product.

Which Specific Intermediaries Should Be Used?

The last, and most specific, issue to deal with in answering the question of who should be in the marketing channel is which specific intermediary or intermediaries to choose, from among the choices available, given the choice to use a particular intermediary type.

As in the consideration of the type of intermediary to use, the specific identity of the intermediary chosen should rest on a combination of efficiency and coordination factors. Among available intermediaries, for example, a manufacturer may choose the one that is the least costly to incorporate into the channel. Sometimes this even means using another manufacturer's own sales force and distribution abilities, a relationship called *piggybacking*. In a piggybacking channel, the *rider* is the firm making the product that needs distribution; the *carrier* is the other manufacturer who has excess capacity in its distribution system to accommodate the rider's product. The benefit to the rider is the avoidance of the cost of hiring a large employee sales force. The benefit to the carrier is the fee earned by carrying the rider's product, along with any synergies that result from adding a complementary product to its line.[8] The total channel costs are thus lower than they would be, were the manufacturer to sell direct. This arrangement is found among pharmaceutical companies, consumer packaged-goods companies, and financial services companies.

The issue of coordination is just as important as that of efficiency, however. Consider a specific piggybacking example. Dove International, a maker of super-premium ice cream products in the United States, is a part of the M&M/Mars Company, which also makes a wide variety of candy products. The M&M/Mars distribution channel did not specialize in freezer trucks for transporting ice cream, so Dove signed on an ice cream company, Edy's (also a superpremium ice cream maker), to physically distribute Dove products to grocery stores.[9] The match was clearly a good one from the perspective of availability of the right distribution channel resources. Because the arrangement appeared to be working so well, Dove signed a permanent contract with Edy's for distribution of its products. At this point, effort by Edy's began to erode, and without reliable physical distribution, Dove's sales and profits dropped. The moral of the story is that it is difficult to expect a piggybacking partner to maintain effort when the extra product carried is a direct competitor to the carrier's own line, particularly without retaining any leverage through the contracting process.

If the possibility for a negative outcome is so great, who would be a good piggybacking partner? One way to pick a partner who is likely to exert good-faith efforts on behalf of the rider is to find a firm making complementary, rather than directly competitive, products. Such a partner is more likely to want to do a good job representing the rider's product, because sales of its own products may actually increase as a result.

Another common technique is to engage in *reciprocal piggybacking*, where each firm sells both its own products and those of the partner. Mattel, an American toy manufacturer, and Bandai, a Japanese toy maker, signed a reciprocal piggybacking agreement in 1999 in which Bandai pledged to sell Mattel toys in Japan (where Mattel had previously had trouble selling on its own), and Mattel pledged to sell Bandai toys in Latin America (where Bandai has no presence). As part of the agreement, Mattel will buy 5 percent of Bandai's stock. This is part of a potentially much more extensive relationship between the two companies.[10] The deal is Mattel's third try at setting up a distribution system in Japan, after a partnership with a British marketing firm failed as did an attempt to set up its own employee sales network. In a reciprocal arrangement like the Mattel–Bandai one, neither partner would want to exert weak selling effort, for fear that its own product would suffer the same fate at the hands of its partner.

In sum, all of the levels of decision making about membership in the channel revolve around three key factors: demand-side issues, supply-side or efficiency issues, and coordination issues. These same sorts of factors also come into play in answering the other channel structure questions of optimal number of channel members at a given level in the channel, and of whether to use dual distribution.

HOW MANY CHANNEL MEMBERS SHOULD THERE BE AT A GIVEN LEVEL OF THE CHANNEL?

Part of the channel structure decision is the choice of *distribution channel intensity*. Because this topic is covered in depth in Chapter 10, we discuss it only briefly here, in order to place it in the array of decisions encompassing channel structure determination.

The choice of channel intensity is a decision about how many of a certain type of channel partner to engage in one market. In our Lladro figurine example, relatively limited distribution intensity is chosen, because end-users are willing to search for the figurine. There is no need to offer it for sale in many retail locations, and indeed, if the manufacturer did so, this might create fierce price competition among the retailers. As retail margins drop, the incentive to exert retail effort on behalf of the brand would lessen. This would clearly be undesirable for a brand such as Lladro.

In contrast, breakfast cereal can be found for sale in every supermarket, hypermarket, local grocery store, convenience store, and even in some vending machines, as well as at every restaurant and food service outlet. Clearly, a much higher level of intensity holds for breakfast cereal than for collectible figurines. Similar comparisons can be made for common industrial supplies (distributed as intensively as possible) versus customized, specialty products such as hazardous chemicals, engines, and the like (distributed in a much less intensive way).

The continuum of possibilities for intensity of distribution is often described as ranging from *exclusive* (only one outlet per market) through *selective* (a few outlets in each market) to *intensive* (available as widely as possible in the market). In choosing the appropriate level of intensity of distribution, the manufacturer must balance potentially conflicting factors. End-users' willingness to search is one important criterion; if willingness to search is very low, then a higher level of channel intensity is appropriate.

From the channel efficiency point of view, it is important to appoint enough intermediaries to cover the market, but not so many that none can make money selling the product. Saturating the market with retailers, for example, can simply increase the intensity of price competition among them. This has the benefit of reducing retail prices, but may harm sales if the retailers find the line unattractive to promote. The problem can be particularly difficult if a manufacturer seeks to sell a relatively new, unknown product for which retail promotion will be necessary, but for which end-user awareness (and hence willingness to search) is low. The need for significant channel effort by the downstream channel partner suggests the value of more selective distribution, but end-user factors suggest that intensive distribution would increase sales more quickly. The manufacturer must then decide between these competing suggestions to find the best short- and long-run intensity of distribution for its product.

One example of dealing with this trade-off concerns an information company, selling access to published academic and business information, choosing the level of distribution intensity in an Asian country. It had been using just one distributor, which had a steady stream of sales but never increased them past a certain level. The manager of international sales knew from his experience in other analogous world markets that the sales potential in this market was considerably higher than the achieved sales levels of its exclusive distributor. He therefore appointed two other distributors to sell in the same market along with the original distributor. Predictable complaints came from the original distributor, who argued that his market was being taken from him, his livelihood would suffer, and so on. The sales manager had been careful, however. The other two distributors had expertise in reaching different end-users in the market, so that domain conflict would be lessened (although not eliminated completely). In addition, he appointed an employee to aid all three distributors in growing the market and selling to end-users. This employee was not paid on the basis of commission, and thus had no reason to sell on his own. The original distributor now felt some competitive pressure, because his performance would be compared directly with those of the other two distributors. The two new distributors were anxious to do well with this new account. The result was a sextupling of sales in the first year after the move, with a significant increase in the original distributors' sales contributing part of the overall increase.[11]

In short, the competitive urges to intensify distribution intensity overcame the potential for channel conflict to increase overall sales very significantly in the market. The appointment of an employee to aid in selling was also viewed as an important good-faith gesture by the manufacturer, and helped deflect negative feelings among the distributors. The moral of the story is that competition in the channel is not bad, but distribution intensity without some investment in differentiating the channels created thereby is not a wise management decision.

A SINGLE CHANNEL OR DUAL DISTRIBUTION?

In addition to choosing which type of intermediary to use and how many of them to use, the channel manager must also decide whether to operate one overall marketing channel or multiple channels side by side in a single market. Whenever more than one channel coexists in a market, we say that this market is characterized by *dual distribution*.[12] Computer manufacturers including IBM, Hewlett-Packard, and Compaq have added direct selling via the Internet to their portfolio of channels (e.g., distributors, value-added resellers) to reach the market. An increasingly large proportion of both business buyers and individual consumers find distributors and value-added resellers of relatively little value. Hewlett-Packard includes on its Web site a list of approved systems integrators that buyers can contact when their needs go beyond simple purchases. These manufacturers clearly recognize the need for segmented distribution offerings to meet the needs of different classes of buyers.[13]

The choice of whether to engage in dual distribution should be made based on demand–segmentation factors, supply–cost factors, and coordination factors. On the demand side, dual distribution is a natural response to a recognition of segments of end-users who demand different service outputs. Each such segment's ideal channel is unique, and the responsive channel manager creates a customized channel for each defined segment. A soft drink maker such as Coca-Cola or Pepsi sees the importance of distributing its products not only through grocery stores but also through food service outlets (restaurants, bars) and through vending machines. The grocery store buyer is looking for less bulk-breaking, less spatial convenience, and less speedy delivery than is the vending machine or food service consumer. Failing to sell through all three sorts of channels would mean missing these very important segments of the market.

Dual distribution can also be a means of controlling total distribution costs. A sales call by a salesperson can cost $200, whereas a direct-mail piece may cost only $1 and a telemarketing call may cost $20. When selling to a segment of buyers whose individual purchases are small, direct selling is fundamentally uneconomical. These insights drive manufacturers not only to allocate individual flows to intermediaries (as discussed in Chapter 4), but sometimes to set up completely different channels to sell to lower-volume end-users. The example of Canada Life's strategy to use direct marketing to sell casualty insurance, profiled in Channel Sketch 5.4, is illustrative here.

CHANNEL SKETCH 5.4

The Dual Distribution Decision: Two Companies' Experiences[14]

General Electric Capital Information Technology Solutions (GECITS)

GECITS, a General Electric (GE) company, sells products (notebook PCs up to UNIX computer servers) and services (PC installation up to information technology consulting) to information systems buyers around the world. It has been acquiring some of its distributors and integrating forward to sell directly to end-users, while simultaneously keeping its network of independent value-added resellers (VARs). GECITS management argues that the new channel helps the company provide a wider array of channel choices to its customers, with a focus on high value-added, niche products coming from the in-house channel.

VARs fear that the addition of the direct channel will make GECITS directly competitive with them. Even worse is the threat of access to lower-cost financing from General Electric Capital Services, another GE company, combined with the possibility of using its buying power to get deep discounts from its suppliers. GECITS argues the risk of such problems is low. GE requires each of its businesses to stand on its own, minimizing the possibilities for cross-subsidization across businesses through (for example) low-cost financing. Further, GECITS management claims its focus is not to build a broad range of business, but to focus on the niche products and service combinations at the higher end of the business. However, management does not deny the possibility of competition between its own and an independent channel in cases where the total product–service offerings are comparable.

Canada Life

Canada Life Assurance is a major Canadian life insurance company that has recently rethought its distribution structure. Historically life insurance was sold through a set of exclusive agents, but as competition has increased, barriers to entry have fallen, and consumers have become more sophisticated and demanding, it has seen the need to follow what it calls a "multidistributional" approach. Canadian law has changed to allow banks, mutual fund companies, broker–dealers, and direct marketers to compete with standard insurance companies, often with much lower cost structures than characterize the standard agent structure. The company cites four reasons for following a multiple-channel strategy: (1) segmentation in consumer preferences; (2) the company's capacity to sell more broadly than a pure agent channel permits; (3) the cost of doing business through the agency channel; and (4) the resulting lack of service to certain segments of consumers. In response, Canada Life uses a core of 900 career agents, but augments this with a network of partnerships with stock brokerage houses and other distributors; private brand channels; direct marketing, which is extremely effective in selling casualty insurance; and on-line selling.

Canada Life recognizes the potential for interchannel conflict, particularly from agents who feel disenfranchised by the use of so many new channels. Efforts are made to support agents, particularly those who commit to representing Canada Life exclusively, through expense allowances, fringe benefits, and other perquisites not offered to other intermediaries. Although management is not sure what the right number of channels is, it believes that "Ultimately, by covering all the channels effectively, we are enhancing our ability to keep outside competitors from moving in."

However, on the coordination dimension, dual distribution can lead to conflict (discussed in more detail in Chapter 9). Here we can highlight a few of the key issues, which are echoed in both the GECITS and Canada Life examples in Channel Sketch 5.4. One major problem is the potential for conflict over customer accounts. We call this *domain conflict*, that is, a conflict over the permitted activities for each channel member.

Consider the following general, but very common, problem. A manufacturing company selling industrial equipment uses a combination of independent distributors to sell to small and medium-size accounts, and an employee sales force to handle large or "house" accounts. The account sales level defining "large" is not precisely set, but distributors have a sense for how large an account can get before it merits house account status. What are the distributor's incentives in this case? It does want to grow and develop new accounts, because the sales efforts exerted are rewarded with profits to the distributorship. However, past a certain point, the distributor is likely to manage the size of its larger accounts in order to prevent them from growing too big! If it continues to exert best efforts and is successful in growing an account, its "reward" may be to have that account taken away by the manufacturer. The existence of dual distribution thus generates conflict, as the distributor finds that an account it perceives to be its own, that it has grown through its own sales efforts, is simply taken away.

One solution to this problem is to establish exclusive distribution as the channel structure. Then all conflicts over domain are automatically solved, because neither dual distribution nor intensive distribution is present to create competition among intermediaries. But this is not a demand-sensitive solution, because not all customers want to be served in the same way. A clever competitor that differentiates its channel offerings will tend to steal away customers who are not served well by a "one size fits all" channel strategy.

Thus, managing the potential for domain conflict in the context of a dual distribution channel structure becomes a more attractive solution. Some companies reimburse distributors in one way or another when they take an account in-house; for example, by offering a declining commission over a period of a few years after the account is moved in-house. Canada Life gives its core agent channel special incentives to reward them as it expands its channel structure. Such actions recognize the productivity of sales efforts in one time period on actual sales in later time periods; an account relationship once established generates sales in the future as a result of earlier efforts. Ethan Allen set up a revenue-sharing formula to compensate its licensed exclusive store owners for sales made by Ethan Allen directly over its new Web site. Any store providing delivery and service on an item sold over the Web site receives 25 percent of the sale price, and when Ethan Allen ships an item direct from its factory to the consumer, the store owner in the buyer's territory gets 10 percent of the purchase price.[15] This compensation is designed to reduce conflict by rewarding store owners for continuing to participate in channel flows. Store owners react positively to such overtures, because they signify commitment by the manufacturer to the retail network, even while recognizing the emerging importance of selling on the Internet.

Another tactic manufacturers use to manage this type of conflict is to invest separately in the development of new accounts (so-called *prospects*) for its distributors. It thus creates a pool of new sales accounts to replace the few that are taken away from time to time. Any of these efforts fundamentally seeks to reward the distributor for the honest effort it has exerted on behalf of the manufacturer's product, and is a demonstration of the Equity Principle in action (see Chapter 4).

SUMMARY: OPTIMAL CHANNEL STRUCTURE AS AN ELEMENT OF THE ZERO-BASED CHANNEL STRATEGY

The decision on channel structure has many levels, including whether or not to use intermediaries at all, what types of intermediaries to use, and which specific intermediaries to use within the chosen type. Beyond this, issues of channel intensity and dual distribution shape the overall structure decision. Our discussion of these decision levels consistently raises three sets of factors to consider: demand-side factors, supply-side factors, and channel coordination factors.

Channel Structure as a Response to Demand-Side Factors

In the end, the chosen channel structure must help to meet targeted segments' expressed demands for service outputs. Certain channel structures, including certain types of intermediaries, are typically well suited to supplying particular service outputs. When the demand for bulk-breaking is high, an intermediary that can benefit from economies of scope (in offering many different product lines) and scale (in serving many consumers) lowers the total cost of selling in small lot sizes to the market. When demands for spatial convenience or quick delivery are high, more intensive distribution is indicated, again frequently leading to the use of intermediaries in order to control the cost of setting up multiple selling sites. When end-users' demands for assortment and variety are high, putting one's product into the hands of a distributor or retailer is usually superior to selling direct. The only exception would be when the manufacturer itself makes such a wide array of products that it provides the required assortment and variety itself.

End-user demands can also affect the identity of the specific intermediary chosen. In one industrial company considering consolidating its distributor list, customers were polled first to see how strong their preferences for their current distributor were. If preferences were strong enough, the distributor was kept. This practice is primarily focused on meeting end-user demands, but can lead to inefficiencies in channel management or even to channel conflict. The manufacturer or channel manager must carefully weigh these factors in choosing or altering the list of actual intermediaries included in the channel.

In most markets, there is some variation in the demands for these service outputs, of course, and this leads to a potentially difficult decision regarding the establishment of dual distribution in the marketing channel. Although dual distribution is a positive response to segmentation in service output demands, it can also lead to difficulties in channel coordination that require clever management to control.

Channel Structure as a Response to Supply-Side Factors

On the supply side, the key issues determining membership of an intermediary in the channel structure are availability and cost-effectiveness. On occasion, an intermediary is found that would perform well in a manufacturer's marketing channel, but is already committed in an exclusive distribution arrangement with another supplier, thus effectively blocking access to that specific intermediary.

Even if available, an intermediary must pass the test of cost-effectiveness. As discussed, a main reason for using an intermediary is its ability to perform flows at lower cost than the manufacturer could do if selling direct. Indeed, some intermediaries are added to a channel structure to improve the performance of individual flows, such as warehouse management, payment functions, negotiation, or promotion. It can be important to bundle the performance of multiple flows for one channel intermediary to perform, in order to create synergies across flows.

Done correctly, the addition of channel intermediaries should therefore lower the total cost of channel management. Clearly, each intermediary must be compensated for performing flows. But if they are more efficient than the manufacturer is, the manufacturer can also benefit from a net increase in unit profits as well as an increase in sales volume due to more efficient provision of the desired service outputs.

THE IMPACT OF STRUCTURAL DECISIONS ON CHANNEL COORDINATION

An efficient zero-based channel is no more than a dream unless the intermediaries brought into the channel actually are motivated to do a good job. Using an intermediary because of the promise of lower channel costs, without verifying that the intermediary's compensation is sufficient to motivate high-quality performance, can lead to a worse outcome than if the manufacturer were to sell direct. Failing to follow the Equity Principle can ruin the effectiveness of an otherwise well-designed channel structure.

Channel intermediaries may not perform their jobs adequately because their compensation is not as high as the compensation available from other activities or selling other products. Manufacturers who use independent sales representatives, compensated through commission, need to be aware of how their commissions compare to those available from other suppliers. Alternatively, a decision to sell intensively rather than selectively or exclusively in a market area may be perceived by the original intermediary to diminish the potential for the manufacturer's product and therefore reduce the incentive to sell. Meanwhile, the decision to sell exclusively can also lead to problems of insufficient effort exertion as the exclusive intermediary has no pressure to maximize channel effort. As discussed above, management techniques exist to control the possibility of these sorts of problems in the channel.

In sum, the right channel structure has to meet several important criteria:

- Does it meet target segments' demands for service outputs?
- While meeting service output demands, does it also allocate channel flows as closely as possible to the lowest-cost performers of those flows, thus leading to a minimization of total channel cost?
- Does the channel manager choose intermediaries who are able and willing to perform their assigned flows in a high-quality and timely manner?
- Does the reward system in the channel reflect adherence to the Equity Principle, leading to continued incentives of all parties to exert best efforts in the channel?

This is a significant business challenge. But the framework provides a set of goals to aim for and a means of identifying how an existing channel might fall short of those goals. This issue, identifying and closing channel gaps, is the topic of the next chapter.

Discussion Questions

1. Why does a discussion of channel structure follow the discussions of service outputs and of channel flows? Describe how insights about service outputs, channel flows, and channel structure together help determine the zero-based channel design.

2. Describe a distribution channel situation where the casual observer would argue that the manufacturer sells direct, but in fact at least one intermediary is used. Identify the intermediary and the flow or flows performed by that intermediary.

3. Many manufacturers who sell direct in their home markets choose to use intermediaries to perform many flows in foreign markets. Some of them then choose to change the channel structure in the foreign market after a period of time and institute direct selling, meaning the use of an employee sales force, sales office, and warehouse. Why is this choice about channel structure such a common pattern? Appeal to the factors discussed in this chapter.

4. Give an example of a situation where a new method of distribution was introduced to sell a particular product and end-users were educated in adopting the new method of shopping. Give another example where the attempt was made to switch end-users to a new method of shopping, but it failed.

5. It is not uncommon to hear a manufacturer complain about an independent distributor, saying that the distributor gets a certain percentage off list price when it buys product from the manufacturer as a wholesaler, then marks up the price and pockets the margin

as profits. The disgruntled manufacturer then wants to get rid of the distributor and pocket that margin itself. What is the fallacy in this line of thinking?

6. Some time ago, the Toro company (an American manufacturer of lawn mowers, snow-blowers, and related equipment) sold only through a selective network of authorized dealers. These dealers provided significant amounts of pre- and postsale service to end-users, as well as holding and owning inventory, promoting, and the like. Toro decided to expand its intensity of distribution and began selling lawn mowers and snowblowers through mass-merchandisers such as Kmart. The authorized Toro dealers reacted extremely negatively and threatened to drop the Toro line completely. Explain what the problem was, using terms discussed in this chapter, and suggest solutions Toro could use to deflect the problem it created.

Notes

1. Beth M. Schwartz, "Electronics Supply Chains: Still Standing Tall," *Business and Management Practices, Transportation and Distribution*, 39, no. 10, pp. 29–33; Ronald Henkoff, "Delivering the Goods," *Fortune*, November 28, 1994, p. 64; Janah Monua and Clinton Wilder, "FedEx Special Delivery," *Informationweek*, October 27, 1997, pp. 42–60; Magnier, Mark, "Federal Express Logistics Service to Expand in Asia," *Journal of Commerce*, October 26, 1994, p. 2B.

2. "'One-Stop' Logistics Plan Helps AlliedSignal Control Supply Channels," *Purchasing*, 123, no. 9 (December 11, 1997), pp. 79–80.

3. Michael D. White, "Air Cargo Takes Wing," *World Trade*, 12, no. 6 (June 1999), pp. 60–62.

4. James P. Miller, "Gibson Expects to Report Loss in 3rd Quarter," *Wall Street Journal*, October 9, 1998, pp. A3, A6; "Gibson Greetings Will Outsource Manufacturing of All Its Cards," *Wall Street Journal*, April 1, 1998; "Gibson: Is Success in the Cards?" *BusinessWeek*, June 22, 1998; and "Gibson Greetings Expects Loss for 1998 Third Quarter," Gibson Greetings press release from www.gibsongreetings.com.

5. See Roderick Oram, "Cola War Defection Hits Pepsi in Vital Market," *Financial Times*, August 17, 1996, p. 1; Chris Roush, "Coca-Cola Pulls Rug from Under Pepsi with Deal in Venezuela," *Atlanta Journal and Constitution*, August 17, 1996, business section, p. 1G; Glenn Collins, "A Coke Coup in Venezuela Leaves Pepsi High and Dry," *New York Times*, August 17, 1996, sec. 1, p. 35; Glenn Collins, "International Business: How Venezuela Is Becoming Coca-Cola Country," *New York Times*, August 21, 1996, p. D1; Leslie Hillman, "A Huge Defection Leaves Pepsi Flat in Venezuela," *The Houston Chronicle*, August 25, 1996, business section, p. 3; Bill Saporito, "Parched for Growth," *Time*, 148, no. 11 (September 2, 1996), p. 48; Chris Roush, "Venezuela Refuses to Halt Coca-Cola's New Bottling Deal," *Atlanta Journal and Constitution*, September 10, 1996, business section, p. 2F; Chris Roush, "The 'Anchors' of Coca-Cola's Empire," *Atlanta Journal and Constitution*, October 13, 1996, business section p. 1D; Patricia Sellers, "How Coke Is Kicking Pepsi's Can," *Fortune*, 134, no. 8, (October 28, 1996), pp. 70–84; "PepsiCo Is Preparing to Return to Venezuela," *New York Times*, November 14, 1996, p. D3; Raymond Colitt, "Pepsi Launches Attack on Venezuela Market," *Financial Times*, November 14, 1996, p. 27; Chris Roush, "Pepsi Finds Bottler in Venezuela," *Atlanta Journal and Constitution*, November 14, 1996, business section, p. 2F; Chris Roush, "Venezuela OKs Coca-Cola Venture," *Atlanta Journal and Constitution*, December 11, 1996, business section, p. 2F; "PepsiCo Begins South American Marathon; Joint Venture with Empresas Polar Aims to Win Back Lost 80% Share of Venezuela Cola Market," *Financial Times*, December 13, 1996, p. 29; Glenn Collins, "PepsiCo Wins $94 Million for Defection by Bottler," *New York Times*, September 4, 1997, p. D5.

6. See Jennifer Ouellette, "Keeping an Eye on Logistics," *Chemical Marketing Reporter*, 249, no. 24, (June 10, 1996), p. SR11; Jennifer Ouellette, "Riding Logistics' Wave," *Chemical Marketing Reporter*, 250, no. 23 (December 2, 1996), pp. SR15–SR16; Ken Mark, "Still Hot: Outsourcing Remains Solid Option for Many Companies," *Materials Management & Distribution*, 43, no. 9 (1998), pp. 28, 30; PR Newswire, "Schneider Logistics Reaches Goal for Ocean Spray," PR Newswire Association, October 9, 1998; Edward Alden, "Complexity Prompts Calls for Third Party," *Financial Times*, December 1, 1998, Survey—Supply Chain Logistics, p. 2; John Gallagher, "Brave New IMC World," *Traffic World*, 257, no. 8 (February 22, 1999), pp. 34–35; Schneider Web site at www.schneider.com.

7. Jonathan Hibbard, Kent Grayson, and Anne T. Coughlan, *The West Bend Case*, 1992. Used with permission of the author.

8. We are depicting piggybacking relationships as completely positive and beneficial. There are also risks of engaging in this type of distribution alliance, also known as a *horizontal distribution alliance*. The risks and benefits are discussed in greater depth in Chapter 13. For a discussion of

these alliances in particular in the airline and pharmaceutical industries, see also Alvarado, Ursula Y., "Horizontal Distribution Alliances: Their Formation and Success," Ph.D. Dissertation, Northwestern University, Evanston, IL, June 1999.

9. Edy's ice cream is marketed by Dreyer's (www.dreyers.com). The same ice cream is sold in the United States as Dreyer's west of the Rocky Mountains and as Edy's east of the Rocky Mountains.

10. "Mattel Forms Toy Alliance with Bandai of Japan," *Wall Street Journal*, July 22, 1999, p. A20; "Execution of a Letter of Intent Regarding an Alliance Between Bandai Co., Ltd. and Mattel, Inc.," Bandai Web site at www.bandai.co.jp; "Mattel, Inc. and Bandai Co., Ltd. Establish Global Marketing Alliance," Mattel Web site at www.mattel.com.

11. Private communication with Paul Tucci.

12. Other useful sources with insights on dual distribution channel management include Rowland T. Moriarty and Ursula Moran, "Managing Hybrid Marketing Systems," *Harvard Business Review*, November–December 1990, pp. 146–55; Al Magrath, "Managing Distribution Channels," *Ivey Business Quarterly*, 60, no. 3 (spring 1996), p. 56; and Gary L. Frazier, "Organizing and Managing Channels of Distribution," *Journal of the Academy of Marketing Science*, 27, no. 2 (Spring 1999), pp. 226–40.

13. Ephraim Schwartz and Dan Briody, "IBM, HP Go to Direct-Sales Model," *Infoworld*, May 10, 1999, p. 8; Peter Burrows, "Can Compaq Catch Up?" *Business Week*, May 3, 1999, pp. 162–66; Gary McWilliams, "PC Problems May Snag Compaq Crusade," *Wall Street Journal*, April 15, 1999, p. B7.

14. The GECITS example is based on Robert L. Scheier, "GE's Jerry Poch: Big Bucks, Big Plans," *VARBusiness*, March 16, 1998, pp. 54–63. The Canada Life example is based on David A. Nield, "The Evolving State of Distribution," *LIMRA's MarketFacts*, 17, no. 2 (March–April 1998), pp. 30–34.

15. James R. Hagerty, "Online: Ethan Allen's Revolutionary Path to Web," *Wall Street Journal*, July 29, 1999, p. B1; "Ethan Allen Announces Plans for E-Commerce Initiative," *Business Wire*, July 29, 1999; C. Gopinath, "E-Commerce Stirs the Retail Pot," *Businessline*, August 16, 1999, p. 1; Anne Watson, "E-Commerce Is Terrific—Until the Delivery Goes Awry," *Wall Street Journal Interactive Edition*, October 12, 1999.

6

Gap Analysis

LEARNING OBJECTIVES

After reading this chapter, you will:

- Be able to define a channel gap either as a shortfall or an oversupply of service outputs demanded (a demand-side channel gap), or as an overly high total cost of running the channel (a supply-side channel gap)
- Understand the sources of channel gaps
- Be familiar with the different types of channel gaps, on both the demand side and the supply side
- Be able to identify strategies for closing the various types of channel gaps
- Be able to use the Gap Analysis Template to summarize the knowledge about channel gaps in a given channel situation and suggest means of closing the gaps

sing the analysis of service output demands, marketing channel flows, and channel structure described in Chapters 3, 4, and 5, the channel planner has a good idea of the ideal channel structure to meet target segments' needs. The obvious next step is to build the channel that both meets service output demands and does so at minimum cost of performing the necessary channel flows. We call such a channel the *zero-based channel*.

However, the zero-based channel may not exist or may seem difficult to build. Consider the following questions that should be answered when structuring the ideal channel system:

- What nonvalued functions (e.g., excessive sales calls) can be eliminated without damaging customer or channel satisfaction?
- Are there to be any redundant activities? Which of them could be eliminated to result in the lowest cost for the entire system?
- Is there a way to eliminate, redefine, or combine certain tasks in order to minimize the steps in a sale or reduce its cycle time?
- Is it possible to automate certain activities in a way that reduces the unit cost of getting products to market, even though it will lead to increased fixed costs?
- Are there opportunities to modify information systems to reduce the costs of prospecting, order entry, or quote generation activities?[1]

In cases of new channel design, where there is no previous channel presence in the market, the planner may face environmental or managerial bounds that seem to prevent the establishment of the zero-based channel. In cases where a channel already exists in the marketplace, it may not be the zero-based channel. In either situation, we say that one or more *channel gaps* exist.[2] The purpose of this chapter is to discuss the sources of channel gaps and the types of channel gaps that exist, along with techniques for closing channel gaps.

SOURCES AND TYPES OF CHANNEL GAPS

Sources of Gaps

Gaps in channel design can come about simply because management has not thought carefully about target end-users' demands for service outputs or about managing the cost of running their channel. The advice in this situation is simple: Channel managers must pay attention to both the demand and the supply side in designing their channel to avoid these gaps.

But gaps can also arise because of bounds placed on the best-intentioned channel manager. That is, the manager seeking to design a zero-based channel for the company's product may face certain constraints on his or her actions that prevent the establishment of the best channel design. Before diagnosing the types of gaps, then, it is useful to discuss the bounds that create these gaps. We concentrate on two such sources: environmental bounds and managerial bounds. (Figure 6.1, the Gap Analysis Framework)

Environmental Bounds. Characteristics of the marketplace environment in which the channel operates can constrain the establishment of a zero-based channel.[3] These *environmental bounds* in turn create channel gaps. Two key instances of environmental bounds are local legal constraints and the sophistication of the local physical and retailing infrastructure.

Legal conditions in the marketplace can prevent the establishment of a vertically integrated channel structure by a company entering from abroad.[4] For example, a for-

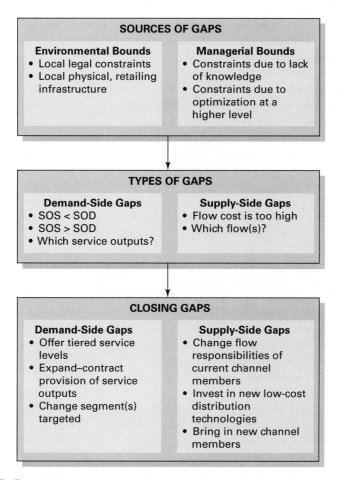

FIGURE 6.1 **The Gap Analysis Framework**

eign company may own no more than 25 percent of the equity of a U.S. airline, and Australia has a similar percentage constraint. Country governments also restrict *cabotage*, the practice of carrying passengers on further legs of an air trip after they have landed at a port of entry to a country. Such constraints make it essentially impossible to set up vertically integrated sales channels and operations inside foreign countries. One alternative channel arrangement is a *horizontal distribution alliance (HDA)*, also called a *code-sharing arrangement*, with an airline native to the country of entry. Through a code-sharing agreement, the entrant airline gains the right to market seats on intracountry flights of the host airline. The host airline carries the entrant airline's passengers within the country of entry. Although it might be both more profitable and a higher service practice to set up a vertically integrated channel in the host country, the environmental bound of government regulation prevents it from occurring.[5]

Legally based environmental bounds can be more subtle and indirect as well. Until 1992, the Japanese Large Scale Retail Store Law prevented stores of more than 1,500 square meters of floor space from opening without a complicated set of paperwork and the permission of their neighbors. The application process supposedly took between 12 and 18 months, but reputedly took as long as 10 years to complete in some cases. Failure was a common outcome, because incumbent retailers in a market area were unlikely to welcome a large store. It could threaten either their sales or those of their friends and neighbors in the local retail community. This was a particular problem for foreign retailers seeking to set up large stores, such as Toys "R" Us. In 1992, and again in 1994, the law was relaxed somewhat, although not repealed, so that the application process was constrained to take no more than 12 months. Nevertheless, over the years this law has influenced the average size of Japanese retail establishments, and the resulting small size of the typical store has led to many inefficiencies and high costs in the retail structure overall. An analysis by Isao Nakauchi, chairman of Daiei, Japan's largest supermarket chain (and an advocate of retail deregulation), showed that each of the company's new store openings required 20 different permits and more than 200 pages of documentation. He estimated the cost at ¥60 million annually.[6]

Governmental regulations and practices can also indirectly result in difficulties in distribution. For example, state franchise laws in the United States prohibit the sale of automobiles to consumers by any agents who are not car dealers. This means that on-line services such as www.Autobytel.com or www.Autoweb.com act more as a middleman to identify potential customers to dealers than as deal-closing channel members. Even Microsoft's www.CarPoint.com, which formed a venture with Ford to allow buyers to order cars over the Internet, requires buyers to negotiate a price with a standard dealer. Were the state franchise laws overthrown, traditional dealers would face much greater competition from both on-line sellers and manufacturers seeking to sell direct.[7]

Beyond environmental bounds due to governmental dictates, the physical and infrastructural environment may prevent the establishment of certain types of distribution channel structures.[8] In many emerging-market countries, there is not a complete infrastructure of roads, warehouses, and retail establishments to accommodate the sale of mass-market consumer goods. As a result, a distribution channel model based on developed-country experiences needs to be modified in order to be successful, and even with modification, may not be as profitable or as satisfactory as desired. Wrigley's chewing gum, an American brand manufactured in China, travels through a complex physical distribution structure. It includes trucks, ships, more trucks, and the small-scale distribution carried out by single distributors on bicycles and carts. It can take months for the product to reach the final retail location where it is sold. Instead of being able to negotiate contracts at a national level with broad-based retail chains, Wrigley salespeople visit individual kiosk owners in cities like Shanghai to encourage the stocking and sale of the gum. Not surprisingly, profit margins are lower than in the United States, although companies like Wrigley persist in their channel efforts in countries like China because of the extremely large commercial opportunity.[9]

Environmental bounds may exist not because of a lack of economic power in a market, but simply because of the lifestyle and population density in the market. Hong Kong is an island of 1,034 square kilometers with a population of over six million people. The residents are fairly wealthy by world standards. But because of the very high population density (almost 6,000 people per square kilometer, compared with 170 people per square kilometer in Los Angeles), few but the very most wealthy residents own cars.

Using a car in the streets of Hong Kong is frequently an exercise in frustration, given the road congestion. The city's excellent public transportation system includes a fine subway, which is the preferred method of transport for many. In this environment, consider trying to import a retail model like that of Sam's Club, the warehouse-style hypermarket owned by Wal-Mart. Sam's Club operates on a very low cost basis, stocking a relatively small variety of stockkeeping units (SKUs), selling large lot sizes of each product (thus avoiding the cost of bulk-breaking), and locating in low-rent remote shopping areas to control the cost base further. This permits Sam's Club to offer very low prices for its products. The formula works very well in a society where consumers are relatively wealthy, own cars, have houses with ample storage space (freezer, refrigerated, and non-refrigerated), and have a large enough family to make large-scale buying attractive. Sam's Club has therefore been a success in the U.S. market. But when Wal-Mart entered into a joint venture with the C. P. Pokphand group of Thailand to open an analogous store, called Value Club, in Hong Kong, the concept was a failure. Hong Kong residents could not travel to and from the store on the subway, carrying back large lot sizes of dry goods, paper products, and the like, even if they were offered at extremely attractive prices per unit. Nor could the typical Hong Kong resident store such purchases in their small apartments. Their lifestyle was more suited to daily grocery shopping in a neighborhood store that could commit to stocking small quantities of all the groceries the family would want to buy. Even though the experience of other hypermarket retailers in other countries suggests that local shoppers like lower prices and are frequently willing to make the trade-off of traveling somewhat farther to get lower prices, this sort of improvement in retailing concept cannot work in an environment that naturally prevents it.

In sum, environmental bounds occur outside the group of companies directly involved in the channel. They constrain channel members from establishing a zero-based channel either because of an inability to offer an appropriate level of service outputs or because the constraints impose unduly high costs on channel members. In contrast, managerial bounds may also limit channel design, but emanate from within the channel structure itself or from the orientation or culture of specific channel members. We turn to this issue next.

Managerial Bounds. *Managerial bounds* refer to constraints on distribution structure arising from rules within a company. The most typical managerial bounds exist inside the company manufacturing the product to be sold through a channel. Sometimes a desire to control the customer, or simply a lack of trust among channel members, prevents management from implementing a less bounded channel design.

The bound imposed by management may be due to a lack of knowledge of appropriate levels of investment or activity in channel flow performance. For example, one U.S. telecommunications company managed its promotional effort at the corporate sales level with an employee sales force. Salespeople responsible for large corporate accounts had the job title "national account managers." On a separate basis, the company was trying to penetrate foreign markets for telecommunications services and built a separate international sales force to do so. But top management did not take into account the fact that most of the largest American companies operate in many countries outside the United States, and would like to have one corporate-level contact for telecommunications services worldwide. Meanwhile, in a bid to cut costs, the company stopped allowing international travel on company funds for any manager whose job title did not include the word *international*. In effect, by issuing this rule, it guaranteed that its promotional sales force would be unable to meet key customers' demands for one-stop shopping for telecommunications services in the worldwide market. It was a serious (but clearly correctable) managerial bound.

The telecommunications example is one of miscalculation on the part of management. But this is not always the reason for a managerial bound. In many cases, a conscious choice not to optimize the distribution activities at one level of the organization is made, in favor of a greater common good. In one well-known case, an international electronics firm chose to decrease the effectiveness of its distribution operation in Switzerland by forcing the centralization of all European inventory in Spain. This decreased channel-wide inventory holding costs and improved order fill rates, but made it more difficult for consumer electronics retailers in Switzerland to import the products.[10] Some distribution intensity was therefore likely to be lost as certain retailers became unwilling to do the customs paperwork necessary to stock the products. However, from a channel-wide perspective this channel gap was justified, suggesting the importance of considering the level of aggregation over which to assess channel performance.

Whether channel gaps arise because of environmental bounds, managerial bounds, or simply due to a lack of attention to the well-being of the channel, they can profoundly affect either side of a zero-based channel: the demand or the supply side. We turn to a taxonomy of channel gaps from a demand- and supply-side perspective next.

Types of Gaps: Demand-Side Gaps

If gaps exist on the demand side, they create what we call a *service–value gap*. These gaps can arise in two ways. Let us think about a single service output. A demand-side gap can exist either when the amount of a service output supplied is less than the amount demanded (we can say SOS<SOD), or when the amount supplied is greater than the amount demanded (SOS>SOD).

In the first case, too low a level of the service output is produced for the target market (SOS<SOD). Consider Channel Sketch 6.1, concerning Tupperware. In this case, a demographic change—increasing participation by women in the workforce in the United States—leads to a higher cost of time. These working women now find a party-plan selling system too time-consuming. In essence, this method of selling does not meet their demand for quick delivery through a quick shopping experience when time is short. Meanwhile, Tupperware products are premium priced, so that the high prices do not counter-balance diminution in service output. Perhaps in conjunction with generally expanding sales among party-plan and multilevel companies, the end result has been a reduction in the ratio of Tupperware's U.S. sales to worldwide sales over the last 15 years.

Channel Sketch 6.2, detailing gaps in National Semiconductor's distribution channels, shows how they can exist in the provision of multiple service outputs simultaneously. Prior to its partnership with FedEx, National was unable to meet customers' demands for timely delivery of semiconductor chips. Partial out-of-stocks on orders meant that National was unable to provide demanded assortment and variety. This in

CHANNEL SKETCH 6.1
Tupperware Expands Its Channels[11]

Tupperware Corporation is a worldwide seller of high-quality consumer products for the home. The company's product line centers on plastic storage containers with the special seals that the Tupperware brand is known for. In addition to food storage containers, Tupperware makes microwave cookware, tableware, canisters, children's toys, and cooking products. All products come with a lifetime guarantee, and the company focuses on new-product design to keep its product line appealing.

Beyond the Tupperware seal on its containers, the company is known best for its party-plan direct-selling channel design. Tupperware uses intermediaries called consultants to sell its products directly to final consumers. They may sell on a one-to-one basis, but more commonly hosts Tupperware parties—gatherings of friends where Tupperware is exhibited and sold. The Tupperware consultant makes 35 percent commission on the sales of Tupperware products. Personal testimonials visible on the company's Web site indicate that a consultant can make $100 in just two hours of selling. The Tupperware consultant can also recruit other consultants; if sales volumes are high enough, she earns commissions on the sales of her recruits as well.

This channel system has the great benefit of being very low cost to run. The consultants are not company employees and thus are not paid salaries or benefits. Corporate promotional expenditures need not be high, because the core channel strategy revolves around promotional efforts made through the direct-selling process. Further, sales are made to friends and acquaintances, permitting a grassroots expansion of market sales. Through this strategy, Tupperware built up its worldwide network to one million consultants in over 100 countries, and about $1.25 billion in sales in 1997.

However, sales in 1998 dropped by 11.9 percent to $1.1 billion. There were several reasons for the decline, including economic woes in Asia. But lagging sales in the United States over the last 15 years (by the end of 1998, less than one-fifth of the company's sales came from the United States) were also attributed to a change in lifestyle (and hence in service output demands!) in the core female target market. As more and more women returned to work, fewer had time for socializing with friends, including having Tupperware parties. The issue was not product quality, but ability to provide the target market with a quick and easy way of buying Tupperware. One Web search for the word *Tupperware* turned up a link to a consultant's Web site that was clearly positioned for the time-constrained shopper, reading, "We offer Tupperware at the guaranteed lowest price anywhere, direct to your home, without the hassle of having a Tupperware party."

As a result, in the Christmas season of 1998, the company began to sell through kiosks located in shopping malls in Chicago; San Diego, California; Orlando, Florida; and Durham, North Carolina. Although specific financial results for the kiosks were not reported, they were cited as "successful." In 1999, the company augmented these efforts with two other channel expansion tactics. The first, in May 1999, was the airing of a series of shows on Home Shopping Network (HSN).

Tupperware products were sold on the shows, and special promotions tied the broadcasts to actual Tupperware parties underway across America. The company cited the need to increase awareness of its core party-plan selling system, along with expanding product sales to new customers, as reasons for the HSN shows.

The second channel initiative was the launching of an interactive Web site in August 1999, which provided not only information about the company and contact information for consultants and distributors but also a means of buying Tupperware on-line, directly from the company. Company management emphasized that the goal of the Web site was not to bypass its consultants or undermine the party-plan selling method, but to reach new consumers who would not otherwise have access to Tupperware products. Indeed, the company prohibits its consultants from selling Tupperware directly over the Internet, although consultants with Web sites can receive e-mail requesting a catalog and send a catalog to the interested buyer. Tupperware chairman Rick Goings said, "There are people who go to Tupperware parties, and there are people who don't. We want to reach the people who don't want to go to Tupperware parties."

To reinforce the complementary, rather than competitive, nature of the Web site, Tupperware did not offer its full product line for sale on-line. Consumers wanting to see more than the most popular items were given easy access to information on finding the consultant closest to them, providing a means of feeding sales leads to their direct selling force. The Web site also effectively increased the assortment and variety available to the Tupperware shopper by offering a personal recipe database, capabilities to exchange recipes by e-mail, family fun tips, and the ability to create customized invitations to a Tupperware party. The Web site was also designed to be appealing to the consultants themselves, with inspirational stories about successful consultants, ideas for organizing parties, and information on joining the Tupperware direct sales force.

Tupperware's channel structure changes can be seen as a response to the recognition of a growing demand-side gap in its U.S. channel. As more and more women have become increasingly time impoverished, the party plan as a sales tool has fallen into disfavor, because it fails to meet a core service output demand: for quick delivery in the sense of minimal shopping time. Meanwhile, women are flocking to the Internet in increasing numbers, making the Web site a productive channel for reaching consumers who might not otherwise buy Tupperware. It remains to be seen what relative importance alternative channels will play in the future, compared to the direct-selling consultant channel.

CHANNEL SKETCH 6.2

Gaps in National Semiconductor's Channel System[12]

The lowering of worldwide trade barriers has created a global marketplace for the exchange of goods and services. Companies source their supplies, manufacture, and sell all on a transnational basis. This development has created gaps for companies that do not keep up with the integrated logistics business.

Conversely, those companies that excel at the logistics of moving supplies to manufacturing and finished goods to customers can significantly decrease their costs of doing business in the new global marketplace. Some have called logistics improvements the ability to *replace inventory with information*, highlighting the importance of managing information well in order to reduce inventory holding costs. The story of National Semiconductor's partnership with FedEx typifies the trend.

National Semiconductor began the search for an external supplier of logistics services in 1991. At the time, its internal logistics force numbered 780 employees. The process of producing and delivering electronic chips to customers was very complex. National produced its semiconductors in six "wafer fabrication" plants: four in the United States, one in Great Britain, and one in Israel. The semiconductors were then shipped to seven assembly plants, located mainly in Southeast Asia. The finished products then had to be shipped to buyers such as IBM, Toshiba, Ford, and Siemens, each with its own scattered network of plants around the world. National found inventory stockpiled everywhere along this channel, including at assembly plants, customer warehouses, consolidators, forwarders, customs clearers, and distributors. Chips could travel any one of 20,000 different routes to market, on any one of 12 different airlines, stopping at as many as 10 different warehouses. There was, in short, a clear supply-side gap in the system, centered around the physical possession and ordering flows.

This poor performance on the supply side in turn created demand-side gaps. National at this time had a fill rate of 95 percent of product ordered within 45 days of the time of order. The delivery time itself could clearly be improved, but in addition, customers never knew *which 5 percent* of their orders would not be delivered, even within 45 days. This remaining portion of the order could take as long as 90 days to deliver! As a result, customers were forced to order 90 days' worth of inventory of everything they would need, so as not to run out of stock of anything. In effect, National was failing to provide not only quick delivery but also the assortment and variety desired by customers. As a result, customers ordered larger total lot sizes than they wished, thus failing to achieve the desired level of bulk-breaking as well. Further adding to the problems, National discovered (after a large activity-based costing exercise) that most of the products it sold did not generate positive net profits.

National decided to partner with FedEx to provide integrated logistics services, reduce total inventories in the system, decrease delivery times, and increase in-stock percentages throughout its channel. FedEx took over the running of National's warehousing operation and all functions relating to order fulfillment. It took responsibility for designating what carriers would move National product around the globe. It significantly simplified the company's delivery system, consolidating all finished product in one central facility in Singapore. There, product was sorted and delivered by airfreight to customers around the world. It would no longer be necessary to coordinate deliveries from multiple assembly plants, and information was instantly available on what products were in stock in the centralized distribution facility.

What were the results of these changes? First of all, it is important to note that implementing these changes took months: Revamping an entire physical delivery system just doesn't happen overnight (although package delivery can!). In 1991, before signing on FedEx, National's logistics costs equaled 3 percent of its $2 billion in annual revenues, or $60 million. By 1994, National's logistics costs had dropped to 1.9 percent of revenues, and by 1997, to 1.2 percent of revenues. In the first two years after partnering with FedEx, National's revenues rose by half a billion dollars, even while it was cutting the costs of doing business—evidence that both supply-side and demand-side gaps were being closed. Delivery times shrank by 1994 to four days or fewer, and by 1997, to 24 hours. National's computers and those of FedEx are linked, so that when an order comes in to National, it is also automatically routed to FedEx, maximizing the speed of fulfillment. Other benefits to this system include faster payment (if product is delivered faster, it is paid for faster), reduced pilferage of product out of warehouses (because average inventory holding quantities have fallen), and more generally, an increased ability to engage in *postponement* in meeting orders.

Finally, the key to success in this sort of integrated logistics system is *information management*. FedEx invests about $1 billion annually in information technology, making it just as important a part of its strategic offering to the market as are its 600 airplanes and 40,000 ground vehicles. Information technology investments such as those permitting the linkage of National's and FedEx's computers naturally tie the two partners more closely together, so that the information exchanged not only improves service levels but also increases the loyalty of National to FedEx as a logistics partner.

turn resulted in the purchase and holding by customers of high volumes of "safety stocks" to try to ensure that they would not run out of key components due to poor delivery performance by National. It is no wonder that in the early 1990s, National was only the thirteenth largest semiconductor manufacturer in the world in sales volume!

Note that, in contrast to the Tupperware and National Semiconductor examples, a demand-side gap may exhibit a low service output offering accompanied by a low price. But in this demand-gap case, even though the price may be low, target end-users may not perceive there to be sufficient *value* (i.e., utility for the price paid). As a result, the bundle consisting of the product plus its service outputs will likely not be purchased. In short, the service–value gap can arise on the demand side because the level of service is too low, even controlling for a possibly lower price, to generate a reasonable amount of value for the end-user.

In the second case, too high a level of the service output is produced for the target market (SOS>SOD). Byerly's, a very upscale supermarket in the Midwest, tried to succeed by offering superior service in its markets, including an extensive, varied, and expensive array of take-out and eat-in foods, custom-designed bakery goods, an upscale coffee bar, the finest in produce and other goods, and guaranteed short lines at the checkout counter. All of this was of course accompanied by very premium pricing of the groceries. In this case, target consumers were offered all the service output they wanted—and more. This may seem like a good idea, but in fact is not. Because service outputs are costly to produce in the channel, overproducing them either results in too high a price for the bundle of product plus accompanying service (which was the case for Byerly's), or causes profit margins to suffer because the channel has to bear the cost of producing nonvalued service. Again, a service–value gap is created, but this time because the surfeit of service (which is not valued by the consumer) is accompanied by a price that the consumer perceives as too high for the bundle. Byerly's eventually went out of business in the northern Chicago suburbs.

The key insight here is of course that erring on either side is a mistake for the channel manager. Providing too high a level of a service output is just as bad as providing too low a level. On the one hand, channel costs (and hence prices) rise too high for the value created, whereas on the other hand, the channel "skimps" on providing service outputs for which the target market would be willing to pay a premium. Profit opportunities are lost on both sides.

Note that there can be a demand-side gap in more than one service output. Indeed, it is possible for the level of one service output to be too low while the level of another is too high. In the Tupperware example, although the provision of quick delivery is insufficient to meet the needs of the busy working woman, the level of customer service and education is excellent. It is delivered through the Tupperware parties where the consultant demonstrates uses of the products. The channel manager might actually believe that in some sense the "extra" amount of one service output can compensate for a shortfall of another. But service outputs may not be good substitutes for each other, and when they are not, no excess of one service output compensates for too little of another. For example, a small neighborhood variety store offers extremely high spatial convenience, but may not offer as much assortment and variety as a hypermarket, and may charge higher prices. The decline of these small variety stores in many urban and suburban areas in the United States suggests that consumers are not willing to trade off a poor assortment and variety offering for extreme spatial convenience. It is important to get the combination of service outputs "just right."

It is also important to note that ideally one should check for demand gaps both *service output by service output* and *segment by segment*. Our Tupperware example shows a shortfall in one service output demand (quick delivery) along with a surfeit of another (customer service and education). But further, a demand-side service gap for one target segment may be an exactly right amount of that service output for another target segment. Again using Tupperware as an example, not all American women are too time impoverished to enjoy shopping in a party atmosphere for Tupperware; after all, Tupperware's U.S. sales in 1998 were about $150 million.

Alternatively, consider the Herman Miller story in Channel Sketch 6.3. Here, the existing channel, with contract office furniture dealers, served the medium to large business market very well. But the market changed over time, with the emergence of the SOHO (small office–home office) market. These end-users did not want to buy large volumes of office furniture, sold in a high-cost, made-to-order purchase environment. Instead, they wanted affordability and the ability to buy high-quality office furniture in a convenient, quick way. What had been a suitable channel for one segment was unsuitable for a newly emerging segment of end-users.

CHANNEL SKETCH 6.3
Office Furniture Channel Gaps at Herman Miller Inc.[13]

Purchases of office furniture have traditionally been made by company office managers. Thus, the office furniture market has traditionally worked through a business-to-business selling process. One of the largest office furniture manufacturers in the world, Herman Miller Inc. of Michigan, focused almost exclusively on this market in its product and channel design until the mid-1990s. This meant selling through a network of 200 contract office furniture dealers. Their revenue derived from large business-to-business sales and doing service and repairs on the large volumes of office furniture in corporate offices.

By the mid-1990s, however, a new market for office furnishings had arisen: the so-called SOHO (small office–home office) market. The Business and Institutional Furniture Manufacturers' Association estimates that there are about 40 million home offices in the United States alone. Because neither Herman Miller nor its major competitors focused on this market, these buyers bought office furniture from office supply stores such as Office Depot (which were emerging simultaneously with the growth of the SOHO market) or general-purpose furniture stores. These outlets frequently did not offer the quality available from the industry leaders.

We can view this situation as a gap on the demand side of the channel. An appropriate channel for the SOHO buyer would first sell in small quantities; would be spatially convenient; would offer prompt delivery (unlike the industry norm of six to eight weeks); and would offer a variety of furniture in sizes and types to fit the home office. In short, a new channel was needed, because the existing dealer channel was not interested in serving this market.

Herman Miller responded to this challenge in two ways. In 1994 it formed a division called "Herman Miller for the Home" to develop a new network of retailers who could sell in small quantities to individual buyers. Its products, such as the Herman Miller Home Office line, were distributed initially through such outlets as Chicago's Crate & Barrel, an upscale retailer of furniture and housewares, and through specialty stores offering such products as ergonomic furniture. Because the end-user was typically not well-versed in office furniture design, Herman Miller arranged to train retail sales staffs to find out exactly what furniture the buyer would really need. Salespeople were given planning kits with tracing paper and scale models of the Herman Miller items so that end-users could plot out their office designs. Crate & Barrel enhanced the promotional effort by mailing out fliers to current customers and to those likely to have home offices. This addition to the Herman Miller channel structure understandably was not cheered by the existing dealers, who felt threatened by the creation of a new channel that could conceivably compete with them. Herman Miller management maintained, however, that the move was market expanding rather than cannibalizing of the existing dealers' business. The company had heard complaints from architects and other customers wanting to buy one or a few specialty products, such as the famous Eames chair, who found the dealers reluctant to serve them. And because many of the contract office furniture dealers relied on Herman Miller for a significant proportion of their sales, the manufacturer held a position of power.

In a second channel structure modification, Herman Miller created an on-line presence in 1997 that not only publicizes the Herman Miller line but also offers its office furniture products for sale to the end-user. The site provides interactive floor-planning software called Room Planner that lets the potential buyer custom-design a room, with furniture drawn to scale so that the buyer can verify how the room will look and that the planned furniture will fit in the room. Design ideas are provided, with combinations of furniture to meet various home office design needs. When the buyer is satisfied with the design, the furniture can be purchased on-line and, in many cases, delivered within two weeks, much faster than is usually possible. The on-line shopping facility provides the ultimate in spatial convenience (shopping in the comfort of one's own home), a full assortment of three different lines of Herman Miller furniture (as well as other products, such as non–home office furnishings), bulk-breaking, and relatively quick delivery.

To support these service outputs, Herman Miller has had to innovate on the supply chain side as well. It has partnered with Menlo Logistics, a company specializing in inventory management software and systems, to better control its production processes and implement "quick response manufacturing" (QRM). And it created a new division, called SQA ("simple, quick, and affordable"), focusing on producing lower-cost, quickly deliverable office furniture designs. SQA sales are aimed at companies with fewer than 250 employees, which includes the SOHO market. The products were initially sold through independent sales representatives, but because some reps were trying to sell to larger-volume customers (traditionally the domain of the dealers), Herman Miller has phased out independent reps and is focusing on having its dealers develop separate SQA dealerships within their traditional dealer locations. However, dealers who choose to sell to SQA accounts must commit separate floor space to it as well as committing to special training to serve this segment of buyers.

The result is furniture orders deliverable in five to six days (rather than six to eight *weeks*). After forming the partnership in 1997, production efficiencies were so great that Herman Miller was able to move its Northeast United States distribution facility into an 80 percent smaller warehouse than it originally had, yet handle more product than before the agreement. This translated into an immediate savings of about $6,000 per month on warehouse space rental. The company's cost of goods sold dropped by $56 million over a four-year period (1995 to 1999), and sales volumes have increased by four times the industry average. By seeking to better close the demand-side gaps in the SOHO market, Herman Miller has discovered methods of reducing channel management costs as well.

Segmentation helps identify for which clusters of potential buyers demand-side gaps exist, rather than suggesting a need for global changes in channel strategy. We will see that knowing for what segment one's service output offering is correct can be a useful piece of information when deciding how to close demand-side gaps.

Types of Gaps: Supply-Side Gaps

A supply-side gap exists when the total cost of performing all channel flows jointly is too high. This can occur only when one or more channel flows are performed at too high a cost: holding the level of service outputs constant when there exists a lower-cost way of performing the channel flow in question. Note that it is meaningless to say that flows are performed at too low a cost—as long as demanded service outputs are being produced! A supply-side gap can result from high-cost performance of any of the relevant channel flows, from physical possession to payment.

Channel Sketch 6.2, concerning National Semiconductor's channel gaps, illustrates supply-side gaps in the performance of the physical possession and ordering flows. Whenever a channel system is audited and inventories are found in large amounts everywhere in the channel, it is a sign that physical possession costs may be too high. In National's case, partnering with FedEx showed that the costs of physical possession were millions of dollars too high. One manager for National at the time it began their partnership with FedEx noted that National did not even know exactly how much logistics was costing before it set out to improve the system. This is not an uncommon situation and suggests that the first step in closing a supply-side gap is to understand the actual costs of running the channel.

In the National Semiconductor example, the gaps on the supply side spawn gaps on the demand side as well. But a supply-side gap need not imply that insufficient levels of service outputs are being offered to target end-users. Bulk may be broken appropriately, assortment and variety may appear adequate, and product may be delivered sufficiently, quickly, and in a spatially convenient way. But the cost of achieving these service output levels may simply be higher than currently available distribution technologies allow. When this is the case, there is a pure supply-side gap even though there is no demand-side gap. Channel Sketch 6.4, describing changes in the roles and compensation for travel agents in the United States and Europe, illustrates such a gap. There, travelers were very happy with the extensive service they received from travel agents. However, airlines believed they were paying too much for travel agents' services—and that in many cases, the commissions they were paying these agents were cross-subsidizing lower-revenue-producing activities in the travel agencies. Further, after about 1996, alternative, lower-cost channels for issuing tickets (such as electronic, paperless ticketing directly by the airlines) were becoming easily available, so that it was not necessary or optimal to grant such high commissions to travel agents. The resulting drop in commissions has caused travel agents to increase fees to travelers themselves, so that those who are enjoying the services (the travelers) bear the costs of them more directly.

CHANNEL SKETCH 6.4

Gaps in the Travel Services Channel[14]

It used to be that a traveler wanting to fly from one city to another would call the travel agent, describe his or her travel needs, and wait for the travel agent to check available routings, fares, and conditions. The traveler would then choose the most attractive routing, and the agent would book the ticket, print it out, and provide other ancillary services, such as keeping track of whether fares dropped between the time of ticketing and the time of travel. In such a case, the agent would alert the traveler to the fare change and rewrite the ticket. Agents could also arrange hotel rooms, car rentals, tour packages, and other modes of transportation such as cruises, trains, or buses.

The traveler never paid the agent any direct fee for these services. Instead, the airline paid a commission to the travel agent equal to 10 percent of the value of the ticket. A $500 ticket would result in a $50 commission payment, a $200 ticket generated a $20 commission payment, and so on. Other transportation companies paid similar commissions to the travel agents. Airlines also offered bonuses, called overrides, to travel agents who surpassed certain volumes of tickets written on their airline, in an attempt to influence the agent to concentrate his or her business on their airline. This system worked fairly well for many years, even though it resulted in some inequities. For example, it does not take twice as much work to write up a $500 ticket than to write up a $250 ticket, yet the commission is twice as high. In effect, expensive travel itineraries subsidized the services of the travel agent serving travelers buying lower-fare tickets.

In February 1995, this system changed. Figure 6.2 shows a time line of events that have significantly changed compensation to travel agents, the relationships they have with airline companies, and the relationships and compensation arrangements they have with corporate clients as well as individual travelers. On February 10, 1995, Delta Airlines announced that it would limit the commissions paid to travel agents on domestic (within the United States) flights, citing a need to cut costs, as well as a desire to stop the cross-subsidization of low-fare ticketing. Round-trip tick-

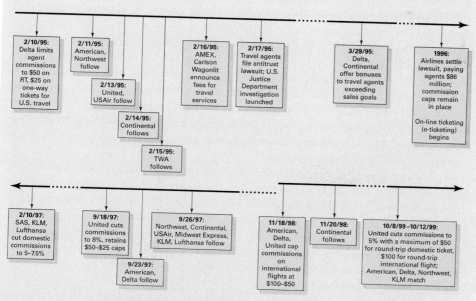

FIGURE 6.2 **Time Line of Changes in the Airline Travel Channel**

ets would earn a commission of 10 percent up to a maximum of $50 per ticket, and one-way tickets would earn a commission of 10 percent up to a maximum of $25 per ticket. Thus, whether a round-trip ticket cost $500 or $1,500, the commission would be capped at $50. The industry estimated that it cost the average travel agent $29 to process and print an airline ticket. The other major U.S. airlines quickly followed, as the time line shows. Although there is evidence that Delta and Continental subsequently (in March 1995) offered larger travel agents bonuses for achieving sales goals, by and large the new commission structure stuck.

The response by travel agents was immediate and extremely negative. They argued that the airlines were squeezing the travel agents' profits, that the travel agents provided valuable services to both the airlines (in marketing their flights) and travelers (in searching for good fares and itineraries). Some travel agents initially boycotted ticketing flights on Delta, but this strategy failed when all the major airlines joined in the commission decrease. Almost immediately, major national travel agent networks such as American Express Travel Services and Carlson Wagonlit extended their nascent practices of charging fees directly to travelers for service rendered. An antitrust lawsuit was also filed against the airlines, alleging that they had colluded to fix prices through these commission changes. This lawsuit was subsequently settled; the airlines paid some $86 million to travel agents, without admitting any wrongdoing or rescinding the commission cuts.

By 1997, electronic ticketing and other selling methods (such as direct relationships between airlines and some large corporate customers) were emerging as viable channel alternatives to using travel agents to book travel. Nevertheless, during this whole period, travel agents continued to write approximately 80 percent of all airline tickets in the United States, and a similar percentage in Europe. Despite the airlines' dependence on this channel for sales, major European carriers also slashed their commissions in early 1997. And in September 1997, the major U.S. carriers, as well as KLM and Lufthansa, further capped commissions at 8 percent, down from the previous level of 10 percent. In late 1998, commissions on international flights were cut as well, and in 1999 commissions were reduced further to 5 percent of ticket values. The trend is clear: a downward spiral in the commissions travel agents have been able to command, despite the maintenance of their skills in hunting for appropriate routings and fares for their consumers, and despite the continuing heavy dependence of airlines on travel agents for ticketing services. How can these developments be explained?

The evidence does not suggest a demand-side gap in the provision of service outputs to travelers. Indeed, travel agents were the lowest cost way a traveler could get the varied information about flight schedules, restrictions, and fares from an array of different airlines. The alternative of telephoning each airline directly and then comparing all the options would be far too burdensome for most individual or corporate travelers. Travel agents by this time had sophisticated computerized reservation systems to help them search for and book tickets, which gave them a real edge in providing these services to travelers.

Instead, the evidence suggests that a supply-side gap caused the shift in commissions to travel agents. One Lufthansa executive remarked that commission changes were driven by an audit of the actual work necessary to write a ticket, and that this audit revealed that the travel agents simply did not merit the pay they were getting for the services provided, and in addition, that overpayments on high-priced tickets were being used to subsidize other facets of the travel agent's business that did not benefit the airlines directly. In a world where very low-cost alternatives such as electronic, paperless ticketing exist, the costly process of hand issuing a ticket is hard to justify.

The response by the travel agents over this time period has progressed past the initial responses of anger and lawsuit filing, to a recasting of their businesses. Some travel agents in fact did go out of business, unable to cover their costs. Others refocused their businesses away from a heavy dependence on airline ticketing, toward the more lucrative leisure travel (cruises, tour packages) businesses. Some began to sell merchandise such as luggage and travel books in addition to providing travel services. And the accepted way of doing business changed. Before the commission cuts, the standard practice was for travel agencies to give rebates to corporate customers for certain volumes of travel booked. But after the commission cuts, the system shifted to one where the remaining commissions were passed through completely to the corporate customer, and in return the travel agency charged for services provided to these customers. One survey conducted by ASTA, the trade association for travel agents, found in 1998 that more than 68 percent of travel agencies now charge fees of one sort or another to their travelers (both corporate and individual travelers). Table 6.1 summarizes the popularity of various fees. This change likely increases the total efficiency of the system. In particular, those who consume the services (the corporate customers) now have to pay directly for those services. This reduces the incentive to overconsume travel agency services, which tends to happen when the customer perceives that they are costless.

TABLE 6.1
Service Fees Charged by Travel Agents, 1998

TYPE OF FEE	% OF AGENTS CHARGING FEE
Special coupons and promotions	87.9
Refunds or exchanges	86.1
Issuing at least some airline tickets	85.5
Cancellations	80.8
Trip planning and research	76.8
Communications costs (long distance, fax, telex)	71.8
Special services (e.g., theater tickets)	70.6
Issuing all airline tickets	70.0
Hotel-only reservations	65.6
Visa–passport services	64.1
Railway tickets	57.6
Lost ticket applications	53.6
Car-only reservations	53.6
Accounting and reporting	39.0

Source: Adapted from Melanie Payne, "Many Travel Agencies Begin Service Fees in Wake of Airline Commission Cuts," *Akron Beacon Journal*, July 29, 1998, citing ASTA survey data.

It is also possible to generate a supply-side gap by simply doing too little of one or more channel flows. For example, insufficient investment in the payment flow could cause a channel to be hobbled by outdated payment and invoice tracking methods, increasing the costs of doing business relative to competitors who might have already adopted a more up-to-date payments system. Even when this does not produce a demand-side gap, it inflicts higher costs than necessary on channel members to generate the desired level of service outputs pertaining to payment services.

The criterion defining a supply-side gap carefully states that the total cost of performing all flows jointly is higher than need be. This means that a supply-side gap may not exist, even if one flow is performed at an unusually high cost, as long as this minimizes the total cost of performing all flows jointly.[15] For example, one electrical wire and cable distributor expanded across the United States and internationally, acquiring many other independent distributors and eventually building an international network of warehouses. Some of the products it stocked and sold were specialty items, rarely demanded but important to include in a full-line inventory (i.e., end-users demanded a broad assortment and variety). But it was very costly to stock these specialty items in every warehouse around the world. Thus, the distributor chose to stock such an item in just one or two warehouses. This minimized the cost of physical possession of inventory in the warehousing sense. However, sometimes an end-user located far from the warehouse, but valuing quick delivery very highly, demanded the specialty product. To meet that service output demand, the distributor chose to airfreight the required product to the end-user, incurring what seems like an inefficiently high transportation cost to ship the product. However, the key here is that this high transportation cost is still lower than the cost of stocking the specialty product in all possible warehouses, waiting for the rare order for that product. In such a situation, there is not a true supply-side gap, because the total cost of performing channel flows is minimized.

In this electrical wire and cable distributor example, it makes abundant economic sense to incur high shipping costs, because much lower inventory holding costs result. Further, both of those costs are borne by the same channel member: the distributor itself. The optimal allocation of channel flow activities and costs is not so easy when different channel members perform the two flows. Imagine in the distributor case that it bears the inventory holding cost, but another intermediary (say, a broker) were to bear the shipping costs to the end-user. Without close coordination and cooperation between the channel members, it is likely that the distributor would benefit from lower warehousing costs, at the expense of the broker, who would have to bear higher shipping costs. Even though the entire channel system might benefit from this method of inventory holding and shipping, the optimal solution (involving high shipping costs but low inventory holding costs) is unlikely to occur unless the distributor and broker make an explicit arrangement to share the total costs and benefits fairly.

In sum, a supply-side gap occurs whenever channel flows are performed in a jointly inefficient (high-cost) way. Sometimes, one or more flows may appear to be performed inefficiently, but channel members purposefully trade off inefficiency in one flow for superefficiency in another flow, resulting in overall lower costs. But high costs of performing flows are usually a strong signal of supply-side gaps. Further, a supply-side gap can occur even when there is no evidence from the demand side of any problem in channel performance. End-users may be delighted with the level of service they get along with the products they buy. The price for the product-plus-service-outputs bundle may even be perceived as reasonable. However, if a supply-side gap is accompanied by a price that is reasonable in the end-user's eyes, it is a good bet that at least some channel members are not receiving the level of profit that adequately compensates them for the flows they are performing. This is because a supply-side gap inflicts costs on channel members that are higher than they have to be. Either end-users pay for that increased cost through higher prices, or channel members pay for it through decreased profit margins. A true zero-based channel both offers the right level of service outputs and does so at minimum total cost to run the channel.[16]

Combined Channel Gaps

Our study of demand-side and supply-side gaps produces six possible situations, depicted in Table 6.2, *only one of which is a no-gap situation*. The table shows several things. First, it is important to identify the source of the gap. If the gap arises from the cost side but the right amount of service outputs are being produced, for example, then it is important *not to reduce or increase service output provision* while reducing cost. Alternatively, there may be both a demand-side gap with too high a level of a particular service output produced and a supply-side gap (flows are performed inefficiently). Then reducing the level of service outputs offered without also increasing efficiency will not fully close the gap. Even worse, if there is a demand-side gap with too low a level of service outputs provided, combined with a high-cost supply-side gap, the temptation may be to cut service provision in an attempt to reduce channel costs. The result would be doubly disastrous: Not only would service levels suffer even more, but efficiency on a flow-by-flow basis would not improve. Thus, if proper identification of the source of the gap is not done, the solution may be worse than the original problem.

To use Table 6.2 completely in a typology of channel gaps, the channel manager must specify whether there exist demand gaps (and of which type) for each particular service output valued in the marketplace. This explicitly permits the manager to identify both overavailability and underavailability of each service output in a single framework. Further, Table 6.2 is target segment–specific. That is, the table should be analyzed separately for each segment targeted in the market, because a demand gap with one segment may not be a gap at all in another (or the gap may go in the opposite direction).

TABLE **6.2**
Types of Gaps

Cost Performance Level	Demand-Side Gap (SOD>SOS)	**No Demand-Side Gap (SOD = SOS)**	Demand-Side Gap (SOS>SOD)
No supply-side gap (efficient flow cost)	Price–value proposition = right for a less demanding segment!	**No Gaps**	Price–value proposition = right for a more demanding segment!
Supply-side gap (inefficiently high flow cost)	Insufficient SO provision, at high costs: price or cost too high, value too low	High cost, but SOs are right: value is good, but price or cost is high	High costs *and* SOs = too high: no extra value created, but price or cost is high

Combinations of supply-side and demand-side gaps are also possible because of the interlinking between supply-side (allocation of channel flows) decisions and the provision of service outputs on the demand side. The principle of postponement and speculation, developed by Louis P. Bucklin, is a good example of this phenomenon.[17] Postponement refers to the desire of both firms and end-users to put off incurring costs as long as possible. For a manufacturing firm, postponement often means delaying production until orders are received, thereby avoiding differentiation of inputs such as raw materials into finished goods (e.g., iron ore into carbon steel). Postponement minimizes the manufacturer's risk of selling what is produced as well as eliminating the cost associated with holding relatively expensive inventory, thus helping to control total channel costs. But suppose that end-users have a high demand for quick delivery; in other words, they too want to postpone (i.e., they want to buy at the last minute). In this situation, manufacturers engaging in postponement cannot meet the service output demands of the target end-users, and although they may not face a supply-side gap, they most certainly will face a demand-side gap.

End-users with high demands for quick delivery thus cause the successful channel to lessen its reliance on postponement in favor of an increased level of speculation. Under speculation, goods would be produced in anticipation of orders, rather than in response to them. Frequently, the lowest-total-cost channel that employs speculation is one that uses a channel intermediary. Intermediaries specialize in the holding of finished inventories for the manufacturer (such as a retailer holding finished goods for consumers), in anticipation of sales to end-users. Although speculation is risky and creates costs associated with holding finished goods inventory, it also permits economies of scale in production, because the manufacturer can make product in large batch lot sizes. This is something that postponement does not do. Nevertheless, as demand for quick delivery increases, eventually total channel costs rise. This generally results in a higher total price paid for a product supplied speculatively. Note that in the Channel Sketch of National Semiconductor, even though National Semiconductor did speculate in its production of chips, its failure on the logistics side failed to produce the demand-side benefits of speculation, thus producing the worst of both worlds: a high-cost inventory holding system that still did not provide quick delivery for its customers. We can also interpret the subsequent logistics alliance between National and FedEx as follows: It helps National to better implement a strategy of postponement, while not just maintaining but even improving delivery times to customers—a winning strategy on both the supply and demand sides.

Certain conditions also exist under which end-users are willing to speculate, for example, when offered a particularly good price or "deal" on a product (i.e., bananas go on sale at the grocery store). But when end-users speculate, they also tie up their capital in household inventory and run the risk of obsolescence (e.g., they may not be able to eat all the bananas they buy before the bananas start to spoil).

Clearly, the "right" amount of speculation in inventory holding in the channel depends jointly on the costs of speculation and the intensity of demand for quick delivery by end-users (measured by their willingness to pay a price premium for ever quicker delivery). One solution that Bucklin suggests is to minimize the total cost of offering a particular delivery time to the end-user. This total cost sums up the most efficient level of channel costs and the cost to the end-user of waiting that long for the inventory. Figure 6.3 depicts this solution. The curve *ABC* depicts the lowest possible cost of delivering product to end-users as a function of the required delivery time. The longer the delivery time is permitted to be, the lower cost the methods are that the manufacturer can use. In particular, postponement, possible only with long delivery times, is a lower-cost method of delivering product than is speculation. The curve *ABC* might encompass not only the move along the speculation–postponement continuum but also the switch to different technologies and channel structures that provide the particular delivery time in the lowest cost way.

Meanwhile, curve *DE* in Figure 6.3 depicts the end-user's cost of holding goods as a function of the delivery time offered. For very short delivery times (i.e., very quick delivery), there is no cost of inventory holding. As delivery times increase, however, the end-user must speculate and buy "safety stocks" of product in advance of their usage, and hence the end-user's inventory holding costs increase. Finally, curve *AFG* is the sum of the channel's and the end-user's costs of acquiring product offered with a particular delivery time. Under the idea that the end-user must pay for all channel costs (plus some profit margin for the channel members!) in the end, it is desirable to seek the lowest-total-cost method of inventory holding. Thus, a cost-minimization orientation would direct the channel to seek the combination of postponement and speculation that corre-

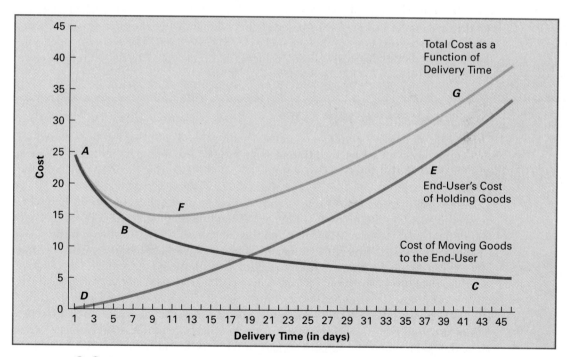

FIGURE **6.3** **Channel Costs and the Principle of Postponement–Speculation**
Source: Adapted from Louis P. Bucklin, *A Theory of Distribution Channel Structure* (Berkeley, CA: IBER Publications, University of California, 1966), pp. 22–25.

sponds with point *F* in Figure 6.3, as this minimizes total channel costs of providing a particular delivery time.

The same type of analysis could be applied to the marketing flow costs associated with providing other service outputs, for example, availability, bulk-breaking, product variety, and information provision. A more complete set of criteria not only would include total cost minimization but also would appropriately factor in the utility or benefit accrued by the end-user in providing these service outputs. Clearly, focusing on efficiency—that is, cost minimization—inside the channel itself will not provide a channel solution that minimizes gaps for the channel; and attention to the relative value placed on postponement and speculation by both channel members and end-users helps highlight the sources of some channel gaps.

Given the multidimensional nature of our gap analysis, it may be no wonder that there are persistent gaps in channel design in many selling situations. Careful identification of the type of gap, and which segment is affected, prevents mistakes in gap resolution. The next section discusses more precisely the tools available to the channel manager to close the gaps that have been identified in the channel design.

CLOSING CHANNEL GAPS

Identifying the types of gaps that inhibit channel performance is an important step, but not the final one in seeking a zero-based channel design. Once the gaps are identified, it is then up to the managers of the channel to try to close them. The recommended solution depends on the diagnosis of the problem; different types of gaps require different solutions.

Closing Demand-Side Gaps

Three main methods of closing demand-side gaps exist: (1) offering multiple, tiered service output levels to appeal to different segments; (2) expanding or retracting the level of service outputs provided to the target market; and (3) altering the list of segments targeted.

First, offering more than one service output level simultaneously can help close demand gaps when the product is targeted at multiple segments with differing service output demands. Herman Miller pursued this solution in selling its office furniture (see Channel Sketch 6.3). Two different channels have been added to the standard contract office furniture dealer channel used to sell to larger business customers. One addition was the series of retailers such as Crate & Barrel, added specifically to target the SOHO market. The other channel added to target the SOHO market was Herman Miller's Internet channel. Each of these exhibits special characteristics designed to appeal particularly to the customer buying for a single home office or a small business office. Note that even when the targets appear to be as different as in the Herman Miller example, there is still some degree of conflict expressed by the preexisting channel members (see Chapter 9 for an in-depth discussion of channel conflict). Ideally, these separate channels would be completely self-contained so that no customer sets overlap between them, but in the real world, some mixing of segments and channels is likely.

Second, service output provision can be changed in an upward or downward direction, depending on whether the gap arises from a lack or an excess of service output provision. Remembering that service outputs are produced directly through the performance of channel flows, this means that either the intensity of flow performance will change (without changing the identity of channel members performing the flows), or there will be some change in the responsibility for flow performance. This change in responsibility can be accomplished by shifting flow responsibility within the current set of channel members or by actually changing the structure of the channel itself. Our Channel Sketch of National Semiconductor shows an increase in the level of service outputs offered to the market, achieved by an alteration of the channel structure to add FedEx as a channel member.

Third, channel managers may simply decide that it would be easier and more profitable to change the actual segment targeted, rather than try to change the level of service output provision. A good example is the response of some South American grocery retailers when faced with the incursion of foreign hypermarkets into their home markets. The competition became very rough, because the foreign entrants could typically underprice the local, smaller retailers on similar goods. Retailers such as Pao de Azucar and Disco, both of Brazil, have responded by not trying to compete with the hypermarkets to serve the mass-market customer (formerly their bread and butter). Instead, they capitalize on their assets that the foreign entrants lack: favorable locations and their ability to provide high-margin local services such as delivery. They have successfully refocused their channel strategies to target the upscale, quality- and service-sensitive shopper that the foreign hypermarkets such as Carrefour cannot target and are not as interested in targeting.[18]

Closing Supply-Side Gaps

Channel gaps arising from high-cost channel flow performance on the supply side can also be managed through multiple means: (1) changing the roles of current channel members; (2) investing in new distribution technologies to reduce cost; and (3) bringing in new distribution function specialists to improve the functioning of the channel.

The channel manager may not find it necessary to take extremely drastic action and may therefore follow the first route. It involves keeping the current roster of channel members, but changing their roles and channel flow responsibilities to improve cost efficiency. However, simply shuffling flow responsibilities among the current channel members may not be sufficient to achieve flow cost efficiencies. The second avenue for action provides for the channel members to invest in new technologies that reduce the cost of flow performance. Channel Sketch 6.4, on the travel services industry, illustrates this tactic. The advent of electronic technologies permitting paperless ticketing directly by the airlines, as well as the more well-established computerized reservation systems, have both decreased the cost of searching for and issuing airline tickets significantly. When these costs were decreased, the 10 percent commissions prevailing in the airline ticketing process became too high. The readjustment of the entire commissioning system not only realigned the rewards for ticket issuance but also reduced inefficient cross-subsidization of low-fare ticketing with commissions from high-fare tickets.

A third option to reduce supply-side gaps is to alter the channel structure to bring in members who specialize in state-of-the-art performance of one or more flows. This solution is the cornerstone of National Semiconductor's strategy; its partnership with FedEx inserts FedEx directly into National Semiconductor's marketing channel to increase the efficiency of performance of the whole channel. Even though FedEx takes a portion of channel profits, it increases the size of the channel profit "pie" sufficiently to more than pay its way.

Challenging Gaps Produced by Environmental or Managerial Bounds

The discussion of closing gaps implicitly assumes it is in the channel manager's power to identify these gaps and to take the necessary actions to close the gaps. This is certainly true when their source is managerial oversight, errors in judgment, or if there is willingness to change in the face of a changing marketplace. But what if the source of gaps is a set of environmental or managerial bounds that remain after other channel improvements have been made?

Some bounds simply cannot be relaxed completely, making it impossible to achieve a true first-best channel design outcome. Consider our example of National Semiconductor, partnering with FedEx. Despite all its gains, the company still sees barriers to efficiency caused by national laws and regulations. For instance, Japan requires an original purchase order with every shipment, making it impossible to consolidate orders and minimize the paperwork costs of the ordering and payment flows. National has achieved only a partial solution to this problem, involving its customers handling the necessary paperwork. With environmental bounds such as these, the best that a channel manager can do is to optimize around them, knowing that competitors face the same constraints to doing business effectively.

However, many bounds can be and routinely are challenged. Robert Galvin, former head of Motorola Corporation, speaks of having helped to write the standards and trade rules by which business is done in the countries in which Motorola sells. His attitude suggests that the "rules of the game" can be influenced by the companies doing business in these markets.[19] Some, faced with what seem like intractable rules of foreign market entry, enlist the aid of their home governments to help in lobbying the host country to relax the regulations restricting entry. Toys "R" Us used this technique to speed up the process of getting permission to open stores in Japan. Other suggestions for challenging bounds include the following:

- "Buy-in" should be achieved across the organization. Participation and voice in the channel design process must be given to all relevant functions and levels.
- An energetic champion should be found to manage the change process. The champion must have power, credibility, political skills, and most important, tenacity.

- It should be made clear who or which group in the organization is responsible for channels, as soon as possible in the process. Task forces comprised of key individuals from various interest groups help buy-in if they are involved with the process from the outset.

- The approach must be truly customer driven, because then the results are very difficult to argue against. Opposing the suggested design identifies the critic as opposed to delivering customer satisfaction. Nevertheless, patience and persistence are required, because movement toward the optimal system will not be immediate, given the tradition-bound ideas that generally surround channel decisions.

- There must be a mechanism built into the design that permits the organization to stay in touch with the end-users of its products or services.[20]

The point is that *where you invest your marketing dollars matters*. You can invest them in changing the ground rules of engagement in the market in such a way that permits you to put together a channel structure that is closer to the zero-based model.

PULLING IT TOGETHER: THE GAP ANALYSIS TEMPLATE

We have described what channel gaps are, where they come from, and what types of gaps exist on both the demand and supply sides. We have also suggested means of closing these gaps in various situations. Table 6.3, the Gap Analysis Template, is a means of pulling together all of the disparate analyses that are done in evaluating gaps and seeking to close them.

The Gap Analysis Template leads the analyst to identify whether there are demand gaps (first line) or supply gaps (second line) for each service output (the four columns). Note that the template is target segment–specific, because (as we saw in the Channel Sketch on Herman Miller) what is a well-working channel for one target segment may be totally inappropriate for another. The template next asks the analyst to summarize the source of the channel gap problem (if a gap exists), as well as any environmental or managerial bounds constraining the final solution to the problem. The desired outcome must also be specified, so that the analyst makes explicit the goal of the gap analysis. Next, the tactics to close the gap should be decided upon. Finally, and very importantly, the analyst should specify the predicted change in channel performance (e.g., profit, market share, sales, etc.). This last step is crucial because it is vital to do more than simply catalog the problems in the current channel. The analyst needs to provide a concrete set of goals to aim for in closing channel gaps. Ideally, after a suitable period of time, the analyst should check to see whether the predicted results have in fact been achieved—that is, the analyst should be held accountable for the suggested changes to the channel.

Table 6.4 shows an analysis of the Channel Sketch of National Semiconductor using the Gap Analysis Template. This information suggests that the gaps are approximately similar for all customers, so only one template is filled out (i.e., we treat the market as if it were one segment for the purposes of the gap analysis). The analysis makes clear that

TABLE 6.3

Gap Analysis Template (target segment–specific)

	BULK-BREAKING	SPATIAL CONVENIENCE	WAITING AND DELIVERY TIME	ASSORTMENT AND VARIETY
Level provided (low–OK–high)				
Efficiency (OK–high cost)				
Source of problem				
Environmental– managerial bounds				
Outcome desired				
Tactics to close gap				
Predicted change in channel performance				

gaps in several (but not all) service outputs exist on both the demand and supply sides; suggests methods of closing the gaps; and documents the expected (as well as achieved) goals of the gap reduction exercise.

When all is said and done, the final channel structure may be close to the zero-based design, but not actually zero based. That is, because some environmental or managerial bounds may have not been lessened, the final channel solution is constrained. The end product is the best that the channel manager can produce, but still deviates from the first-best or zero-based channel. We can thus call it a "second-best" channel design, with the understanding that the first-best design is not always attainable.

Finally, we should point out that the process of gap analysis is never done. Not only ironmental bounds change over time, but end-users' demands for service outputs, as the available distribution technology, also change over time. This propensity nge creates a never-ending opportunity for channel design innovation to pursue ving target of the zero-based channel for each targeted segment in the market.[21]

TABLE 6.4

Gap Analysis Template (National Semiconductor)

	BULK-BREAKING	SPATIAL CONVENIENCE	WAITING AND DELIVERY TIME	ASSORTMENT AND VARIETY
Level provided (low–OK–high)	Low: customer forced to buy large lot sizes	OK	Very low: 5% of product ordered takes up to 90 days to deliver	Very low: out-of-stocks (OOS) not predictable
Efficiency (OK–high cost)	Low: scattered production and distribution facilities	Low: scattered facilities	Very low: multiple shipments necessary with OOS	Low: OOS
Sou⋯	Scattered facilities, ⋯redictable	Scattered facilities	Scattered facilities, poor communication	Scattered facilities, poor communication
E⋯			Lack of information in-house, but willingness to improve	Lack of information initially; discover majority of products don't generate profit, hence plan to drop many
			72-hour delivery	No OOS

⋯g, shipping) to FedEx. Consolidate to one ⋯. Adopt airfreight to ship to customers.

⋯MM in 2 years).

⋯f revenue to 1.2%).

⋯ost reduction in-house, plus value of sales increases,

⋯vas achieved).

⋯ved 24-hour delivery in 1997).

1. Are managerial b⋯? Under what conditions can a managerial bound on a channel design be ju⋯

2. Give an example of a purchase occasion when you chose not to buy a product at a particular outlet because the service output levels were not appropriate. Identify whether the demand gap was in the provision of *too low a level* or *too high a level* of service outputs. What did you do instead? Buy at another outlet with better service output provision? Do you know people who would be happy to buy from the outlet that you rejected? Why would they be happy to do so?

3. Use the concept of demand-side gaps to explain why it is frequently a bad idea to transplant a channel design from one country directly to another without any modification.

4. A manufacturer is in the habit of offering liberal payment terms to his distributors: They can pay anytime within 45 days of receipt of his merchandise. The manufacturer currently has a line of credit with his bank to cover accounts receivable, and he pays an interest rate of prime = 1 percent on the balance on loan from the bank. One of his key distributors approaches him and offers to pay for shipments by immediate bank funds transfer upon receipt of merchandise, if the manufacturer will reduce the price by 1 percent. Does this offer close a gap? If so, what sort? Demand side? Supply side? What flow?

5. A retailer forms long-term supply relationships with several of its key manufacturers who supply it with product to sell in its stores. Part of the long-term agreement involves setting prices annually instead of on a transaction-by-transaction basis. Has a supply-side gap been closed here? What flow or flows have been involved in this change? Are there instances where this can increase (rather than decrease) the cost of running the channel?

6. When does a supply-side gap directly imply a demand-side gap, and when are they independent?

7. What are the disadvantages of closing channel gaps by incorporating a new channel member into the channel who is expert in performing one or more flows?

8. We have discussed how the increase in the percentage of working women in the United States has created a demand-side channel gap for Tupperware. Give an example of how an aging population could create demand-side gaps in a different channel situation, and suggest a means of closing the emerging gap.

Notes

1. Adapted from Gary Gebhardt, "Achieving Maximum Marketing Efficiency," *Frank Lynn Associates, Inc. Client Communique*, 4 (January 1992), p. 3.

2. Louis W. Stern and Frederick D. Sturdivant, "Customer-Driven Distribution Systems," *Harvard Business Review*, 65 (July–August 1987), pp. 34–41, originally discussed a process for confronting gaps in distribution systems as a part of the overall channel design process.

3. See, for example, Ravi S. Achrol, Torger Reve, and Louis W. Stern, "The Environment of Marketing Channel Dyads: A Framework for Comparative Analysis," *Journal of Marketing*, 47 (fall 1983), pp. 55–67; Ravi S. Achrol and Louis W. Stern, "Environmental Determinants of Decision-Making Uncertainty in Marketing Channels," *Journal of Marketing Research*, 25 (February 1988), pp. 36–50; Michael Etgar, "Channel Environment and Channel Leadership," *Journal of Marketing Research,* 15 (February 1977), pp. 69–76; F. Robert Dwyer and Sejo Oh, "Output Sector Munificence Effects on the Internal Political Economy of Marketing Channels," *Journal of Marketing Research*, 24 (November 1987), pp. 347–58; and F. Robert Dwyer and M. Ann Walsh, "Environmental Relationships of the Internal Political Economy of Marketing Channels," *Journal of Marketing Research*, 22 (November 1985), pp. 397–414.

4. For example, Achrol and Stern, "Environmental Determinants of Decision-Making Uncertainty in Marketing

Channels," refers to macroeconomic indicators, the extent of regulation–deregulation, and entry barriers as potential inhibitors of optimal channel design, all of which are affected by local legal practice and stricture.

5. See, for example, Gellman Research Associates, Incorporated, "A Study of International Airline Code Sharing," prepared for Office of Aviation and International Economics, Office of the Secretary of Transportation, U.S. Department of Transportation, 1994; "Airline Alliances," *Airline Business*, 12, no. 6 (1996), pp. 27–55; "Strategic Alliances: How to Choose the Right Partner," *Aviation Strategy*, September 1998, pp. 17–19; and Ursula Y. Alvarado and Anne T. Coughlan, "Alliance Structure and Success in the Global Airline Industry; An Empirical Investigation," working paper, August 1999.

6. See a description of the Large Scale Retail Store Law at the Japan External Trade Organization Web site at http://222.jetro.go.jp/it/e/pub/changing1995.

7. Alex Taylor III, "Would You Buy a Car from This Man?" *Fortune*, October 25, 1999, pp. 165–70.

8. Achrol and Stern, "Environmental Determinants of Decision-Making Uncertainty in Marketing Channels," refers to the present and projected state of technology, the geographic dispersion of end-users, and the extent of turbulence and diversity in the marketplace as factors that can inhibit optimal channel design. All of these are examples of infrastructural dimensions of the market. Achrol and Stern

also consider a set of competitive factors, such as industry concentration and competitors' behavior, which can be thought of as different dimensions of the "infrastructure" facing a firm seeking to manage its channel structure appropriately.

9. Craig S. Smith, "Doublemint in China: Distribution Isn't Double the Fun," *Wall Street Journal*, December 5, 1995, p. B1.

10. This note is based on the Belmont Electronics Case, Harvard Business School, underdevelopment.

11. This passage builds on material available through the following sources: the Tupperware corporate Web site at (www.tupperware.com); Kristen Bryceland, "Storage and Organization: Tupperware to Sell on the Web," *Business and Industry, Responsive Database Services*, 73, no. 6 (1999), p. 44; Brad Liston, "Tupperware's Net Parties," *San Francisco Chronicle*, March 13, 1999, p. B2; Mike Schneider, "The Party's Pooped," *Chicago Tribune*, April 14, 1999, sec. 8, p. 10; "Tupperware Launches New Web Site with E-Commerce Feature," *Business Wire*, August 10, 1999; Andrea Isabel Flores, "Tupperware to Launch Online Sales, Creating Rival to Own Representatives," *Wall Street Journal*, August 10, 1999, p. B8; and "Tupperware Goes Online," *The Gazette* [Montreal], August 11, 1999, p. D3.

12. Information for this section came from Mel Mandell, "Assessing Outsourcing," *World Trade*, November 1993, p. 58; Ronald Henkoff, "Delivering the Goods," *Fortune*, November 28, 1994, p. 64; Giles Large, "Exclusive World of Distribution," *Asian Business*, February 1995, p. 43; Pedro Pereira, "FedEx Opens Doors to World," *Computer Reseller News*, February 17, 1997, p. 248; Scott Woolley, "Replacing Inventory with Information," *Forbes*, March 24, 1997, pp. 54–58; Heidi Elliott, "Delivering Competition," *Electronic Business Today*, May 1997, pp. 34–36; Monua Janah and Clinton Wilder, "FedEx Special Delivery," *Informationweek*, October 27, 1997, pp. 42–60; Beth M. Schwartz, "Electronics Supply Chains: Still Standing Tall," *Transportation & Distribution*, 39, no. 10 (October 1998), pp. 29–33; and Michelle Sheares, "FedEx Customises Supply Chain Solutions to Give Firms an Edge," *Business Times* [Malaysia], December 14, 1998 p. 1.

13. Information for this section came from Joanne Cleaver, "Crate & Barrel Furniture Adds Line Targeting Home Offices," *Crain's Chicago Business*, June 20, 1994, p. 45; "Miller SQA Selects Synquest Manufacturing Solution," *Business Wire*, August 12, 1996; Michael J. Pachuta, "Herman Miller Designer Look Spreading to Smaller Offices," *Investor's Business Daily*, January 30, 1997, p. B14; "Menlo Logistics Pioneers Production Metering Model," *Business Wire*, November 5, 1997; Gregory S. Johnson, "New Logistics Plan Sits Well with Furniture Maker," *Journal of Commerce*, November 17, 1997, p. 13A; Libby Estell, "A Streamlined Supply Chain Could Be Your Link to Increased Sales," *Sales & Marketing Management*, February

1999, pp. 63–67; Scott Kirsner, "Furniture Movers," *The Industry Standard*, February 15, 1999, pp. 30–36; and Helen Atkinson, "Enter the Digital Warehouse," *Journal of Commerce*, April 29, 1999, p. 6A.

14. References for this passage include Edwin McDowell, "Delta Limits Commissions, Stirring Outrage of Agents," *New York Times*, February 10, 1995, p. D1; PR Newswire, "Airline Pilots Encourage Travel Agent Reductions," PR Newswire Association, February 10, 1995; James F. Peltz, "Delta to Be First Airline to Cap Agent Commissions," *Los Angeles Times*, February 10, 1995, p. D2; Anthony Faiola, "Delta Cuts Travel Agent Commissions," *Washington Post*, February 10, 1995, p. D3; James F. Peltz and Stuart Silverstein, "Sky Caps; Travel Agents Incensed at Moves to Cut Commissions," *Los Angeles Times*, February 11, 1995, p. D1; "More Airlines to Cut Travel-Agent Fees—Move Could Force Layoffs, Put Some Agencies Out of Business," *Seattle Times*, February 11, 1995, p. D1; John Rebchook, "United Joins Pack in Cutting Agents' Fees," *Denver Rocky Mountain News*, February 14, 1995, business section, p. 32A; Charles Boisseau, "United, USAir Cap Agent Fees; Speculation High on Other Carriers," *The Houston Chronicle*, February 14, 1995, business section, p. 3; "UAL, USAir Join Move to Cap Commissions," *Financial Post Daily*, February 14, 1995, p. 5; Babette Morgan, "Airline Fee Cap Steams Agents," *St. Louis Post-Dispatch*, February 15, 1995, business section, p. 1C; Kim Norris, "Jilted Agents Consider Fees for Ticketing Services," *St. Petersburg Times*, February 15, 1995, business section, p. 1E; Chris Woodyard, "Travel Agencies Look to Courts for Satisfaction," *Los Angeles Times*, February 16, 1995, p. D1; "Feds 'Watching' Airlines' Cuts in Agent Commissions," *Atlanta Journal and Constitution*, February 17, 1995, p. G9; "Travel Agents Resist Cuts in Commissions from Airlines," *Los Angeles Times*, February 18, 1995, p. D2; Dina Bunn, "Travel Agents Fight Commission Cuts," *Denver Rocky Mountain News*, February 18, 1995, p. 61A; PR Newswire, "ASTA Launches Aggressive Legal, Legislative Actions to Seek Relief for Agents from Airline Commission Caps," PR Newswire Association, February 21, 1995; Richard Tomkins, "U.S. Travel Agents Sue Airlines over Commissions," *Financial Times*, February 22, 1995, p. 8; Del Jones, "Agents Strike Back," *USA Today*, February 22, 1995, p. 1B; Bob Dart, "Booking Fee Cap Defended," *The Phoenix Gazette*, March 2, 1995, p. D1; Roland Gribben, "BA to Cut Travel Agent Rates," *The Daily Telegraph*, March 4, 1995, p. 3; Adam Bryant, "Some Airlines Break Ranks Over Fees Paid Travel Agents," *New York Times*, March 29, 1995, p. D1; Erika Gonzalez, "Commission Caps, On-Line Alternatives Hurt Nation's Travel Agencies," *Daily Camera*, April 2, 1996; Amon Cohen, "All Change for Agents," *Financial Times*, February 10, 1997, p. 14; Terry Maxon, "United Airlines Slashes Travel Agents' Sales Commissions," *The Dallas Morning News*, September 19, 1997; Alexis Ariano, "Local

Agents Join United Boycott," *Daily Record* [Baltimore, MD], September 23, 1997, p. 1; Judith Evans, "Travel Agents Vow to Escalate Fight," *Washington Post*, September 24, 1997, p. C9; Eric Fisher and Peter Kaplan, "American, Delta Trim Fees to Agents," *Washington Times*, September 24, 1997; Donna Rosato, "Travel Agents Map Survival Strategy; Airline Cuts Could End Era of Free Service," *USA Today*, September 26, 1997, p. 1B; Randolph Heaster, "Caught in the Squeeze; Fliers Face Higher Ticket Prices as Airlines, Travel Agents Fight Over Business," *Kansas City Star*, October 5, 1997, p. F1; Lesley Clark, "Will Fuss Over Travel Agent Fees Hit Flyers in the Wallet?" *The Times-Picayune*, December 28, 1997, p. D3; Melanie Payne, "Many Travel Agencies Begin Service Fees in Wake of Airline Commission Cuts," *Akron Beacon Journal*, July 29, 1998; Jeffrey Leib, "Delta, American Airlines Cap Commissions for Travel Agents," *Denver Post*, November 18, 1998; Lee Hawkins, "Delta, American Airlines Join United to Cap Travel Agent Commissions," *Milwaukee Journal Sentinel*, November 20, 1998; Dan Reed, "Continental Airlines Joins Cap on Travel Agent Commissions," *News-Sentinel*, November 21, 1998; John Schmeltzer, "United Cuts Agent Commissions," *Chicago Tribune*, October 8, 1999, sec. 3, pp. 1, 2; Scott McCartney, "Most Big Airlines Match Price Hikes of Late Last Week," *Wall Street Journal*, October 11, 1999, p. B15; Scott McCartney, "Northwest and KLM Reduce Commissions, Matching UAL Move," *Wall Street Journal*, October 12, 1999, p. B20; and John Schmeltzer, "American, Delta Lower Agent Fees," *Chicago Tribune*, October 12, 1999, sec. 3, p. 6.

15. Louis P. Bucklin calls this phenomenon "functional substitutability," *A Theory of Distribution Channel Structure* Berkeley, CA: IBER Publications, University of California, 1966.

16. In ibid., Bucklin calls the zero-based channel the "normative channel."

17. Louis P. Bucklin, "Postponement, Speculation and the Structure of Distribution Channels," in Bruce E. Mallen (ed.), *The Marketing Channel: A Conceptual Viewpoint* (New York: John Wiley, 1967), pp. 67–74.

18. "Retailing in South America: Survival Skills," *The Economist*, July 12, 1997, pp. 57–58.

19. David P. Baron, *Business and Its Environment* (Upper Saddle River, NJ: Prentice Hall, 1996), p. 6.

20. See Louis W. Stern, Frederick D. Sturdivant, and Gary A. Getz, "Accomplishing Marketing Channel Change: Paths and Pitfalls," *European Management Journal*, 11 (March 1993), pp. 1–8.

21. Milind Lele, "Matching Your Channels to Your Product's Life Cycle," *Business Marketing*, December 1986, pp. 61–69, discusses at an aggregate level how the optimal channel form might change as a product moves from introduction through maturity to decline in its life cycle. Although these insights are useful in the aggregate, each segment and each market's bounds and gaps may vary at different paces over time, with the need to respond individually to these different changes.

7

Vertical Integration: Owning the Channel

LEARNING OBJECTIVES

After reading this chapter, you will:

- Understand vertical integration as a continuum from make to buy, rather than a binary choice
- Match observable distribution institutions to positions on the continuum
- Frame the decision in terms of how owning the channel, or some of its flows, influences long-term efficiency
- Explain six reasons why outsourcing ordinarily enhances long-term efficiency
- Define and explain six categories of company-specific capabilities
- Trace how these categories become general purpose over time
- Show how these categories tip the balance toward vertical integration downstream
- Trace the impact of a volatile environment on the returns from forward integration
- Relate integration to markets that are thin due to rarity, not specificity
- Explain the sources of performance ambiguity and relate them to the returns from forward integration
- Recognize the role of vertical integration in learning and in creating strategic options

his chapter concerns the most fundamental question to ask when structuring a delivery system: *Should only one organization do all the work*, thereby vertically integrating into the distribution stage? In other words, for each flow that the customer is willing to pay to have performed, who should perform it? Should it be a single organization (e.g., manufacturer, agent, distributor, retailer—all rolled into one company)? Or should distribution be outsourced (upstream looking down), or should production be outsourced (downstream looking up), thereby keeping separate the identity of manufacturers and downstream channel members?

Nine Puzzles

•   When retailers accept delivery of merchandise from Whirlpool, a large multinational producer of electrical appliances, the driver pulls up in a Whirlpool truck. When the appliance is unloaded, it sometimes has a blemish. The driver ("delivery agent") immediately becomes a claims adjustor and commits Whirlpool to offer a markdown as an inducement to the retailer to keep the goods and repair it. It is invisible to the customer (and to Whirlpool's own sales force) that the negotiator actually works for a third-party logistics provider, Kenco, which manages every aspect of Whirlpool's inventory and owns all the trucks. Whirlpool appears to be vertically integrated into logistics, but it is not nor has it been for decades.[1] Yet, Whirlpool can afford to do its own logistics in-house and certainly has the scale of business to do so. Why let another company perform such a large and critical function?

•   Luxottica is a little-known Italian company specializing in eyewear.[2] Its many brands, however, are famous: Giorgio Armani, Chanel, Yves St. Laurent, Ray-Ban, and a host of others. Luxottica, the world's largest maker of branded eyewear, is highly profitable. This producer also owns the world's largest optical chain, Lens Crafters, a U.S. firm, which it bought in 1995 from a company (U.S. Shoe) eager to recoup its capital and reclaim its management attention from a highly competitive business. At the time, Lens Crafters was bigger than Luxottica. Luxottica's brands have enormous power. Why take such a risk to purchase a retailer when there are plenty of other ways to take these brands to market? What is the reason to vertically integrate forward? And why only in the United States?

•   Best Power makes uninterruptible power systems. To compete against larger producers in the U.S. market, Best Power owned its own distribution channel. Even though the company was gaining market share, it has virtually dismantled its in-house operation and has turned to independent value-added resellers. This is a painful decision: Why take down a company-owned channel?[3]

•   In the North American automobile industry, the normal pattern for decades has been for suppliers to use dealers to reach their markets. Why, now, are suppliers purchasing their channels or setting up wholly owned new channels?[4]

•   Why do conglomerates that are vertically integrated forward into distribution prosper in Brazil and Chile but not elsewhere?[5]

- Why are some specialty coffeemakers in the United States investing in vertically integrating forward to the retail level—but generally sticking to narrow installations, such as supermarket kiosks and service contracts for large office buildings?[6]

- Jean Delatour is a large chain of discount jewelry retail stores in France. The chain has an unusual strategy: It locates large, warehouse-like stores near formidable competitors—hypermarkets—yet aims to compete not only with these enormous stores but also with smaller, focused jewelers offering a luxurious atmosphere in convenient urban locations. Jean Delatour is vertically integrated backward into the production of everything but clocks and watches. Why that exception? And what role does integration backward into production play in the retailer's strategy?[7]

- The U.S. pork industry is dominated by 20 meatpackers accounting for over 85 percent of production. These packers supply branded and unbranded pork to wholesalers and retailers to serve the institutional and retail customer. Certainly, with this scale, the packers can afford to vertically integrate backward. Yet, only one percent of their production comes from their own sources of hogs. For that little—why bother to keep any facilities at all? Why not outsource 100 percent to independent hog producers?[8] This is a question of production upstream: How does the packers' rationale relate to their channel strategies downstream?

- The supermarket industry in North America is brutally competitive. Some retailers are investing heavily in creating their own private-label brands. Yet, the limited distribution of these brands makes it uneconomical to match the national brands' massive promotional campaigns, and these national brands have built formidable brand equity over the decades. It would seem a folly to enter their markets, not to mention the negative effect on trade relations of competing with one's own suppliers. Why integrate backward so late in the product life cycle?[9]

To integrate is to become one, or singular. When the manufacturer integrates a distribution function (making sales, fulfilling orders, offering credit, and so forth), its employees do the work and it has integrated forward or downstream from the point of production. Of course, vertical integration also occurs from the downstream direction: It is not unusual for a downstream channel member, such as a distributor or retailer, to assume its own branded source of product, thereby integrating backward. Whether the manufacturer integrates forward or the downstream channel member integrates backward, the result is that one organization does all the work and the channel is said to be vertically integrated. In this chapter, we will cover the circumstances that make such a move economically viable and some economically debatable, albeit common, rationales.

Make or Buy: A Critical Determinant of Company Competencies

In marketing channels, make-or-buy decisions (vertically integrate or outsource) are critical strategic choices. This is because the firm's decision to own some or all of its marketing channel has an enduring influence on its ability not only to distribute but also to produce. The manufacturer becomes identified with its marketing channels, influencing its base of end customers and forming their image of the manufacturer. In addition, the manufacturer gains much of its *market intelligence* from its channels: What the manufacturer knows or can learn about its markets is heavily conditioned by how it goes to market.

Hence the decision whether to vertically integrate forward helps to determine what the manufacturer currently does and what it could learn to do. This decision, once made, is difficult to reverse: It involves making commitments that are not always easy to redeploy. Thus, a firm's vertical integration choices in distribution are enduring and important: These structural decisions should be made carefully, with emphasis on how they influence the firm's future performance path.[10]

It is surprising, therefore, how little consideration many manufacturers give to their vertical integration decisions downstream. Indeed, many do not decide how to structure their channels: They merely react to opportunities or to problems, one by one, as they arise and try to create an appealing *post hoc* rationale. The eventual outcome is an ill-assorted collection of distribution choices made at different times by different managers facing different pressures. The marketing channel that emerges (in reality, the channel that merely happens) is incoherent and functions far below what the manufacturer should expect from its channel. Unfortunately, past choices tend to lock it into these regrettable channels.

Vertical integration of distribution involves many complex issues. Because the consequences are so great and the decisions so difficult to change, a company's internal discussions of vertical integration are heated, often dysfunctional. Too many constituents enter the discussion to present obstacles and demands. And once the firm makes a decision, it is usually difficult to implement.

Abstract presentations of the issue (e.g., some speeches at trade conventions) often come in the form of long lists of pros, cons, examples, and admonitions. Major and minor issues are freely mingled without prioritization. The same fundamental argument comes up many times under different labels. Some ideas are double and triple counted. More important arguments may be underweighted.

A structured way is needed to work through the issues; frame a coherent, comprehensive rationale; and reach a decision that can be communicated convincingly. It is always useful to compare the rationale against the prevailing patterns of managerial practice. To do so, this chapter presents a framework for deciding whether the manufacturer should integrate a given flow or a subset of flows in going to market.[11] The premise is that more often than not, the manufacturer should not vertically integrate a downstream flow, because it is typically inefficient to do so. However, it should own the channel to a market if it has the resources to own and would increase its efficiency in the long run by so doing.

This chapter covers how to decide when the firm (any firm) should perform a distribution flow itself. For ease of presentation, we start with the manufacturer going forward, then extend the arguments to downstream going backward. Before the end of this chapter, we will revisit each of the nine puzzles presented.

This chapter presents the vertical integration issue *in distribution*. The chapter focuses only on the principal points of consideration and only when integrating channel flows. The next section considers what vertical integration entails, in terms of benefits and costs, long and short term. Next comes a framework for thinking through, from an economic standpoint, when a channel (or set of channel flows) should be owned by one party only. Finally, we leave aside what firms should do and consider why they integrate when the economic rationale for so doing is not overriding. Here, the chapter goes beyond the strictly normative financial viewpoint to bring in some of the complexities, constraints, errors, and organizational politics that have considerable influence on whether a firm will make or buy a given distribution flow.[12] In particular, we focus on vertical integration for purposes of learning or of creating a strategic option.

THE COSTS AND BENEFITS OF VERTICAL INTEGRATION IN MARKETING CHANNELS

To appreciate the hidden costs and benefits of vertical integration, imagine that you are a manufacturer looking downstream at the set of flows that your customer is willing to pay to have performed. Figure 7.1 presents your options in the abstract in terms of make versus buy, with relational governance as a midrange option.

Degrees of Vertical Integration

Under classical market contracts (the epitome of the buy mode), manufacturers and downstream channel members:

- Are interchangeable
- Deal with each other in a completely independent and impersonal fashion (arm's-length contracting)

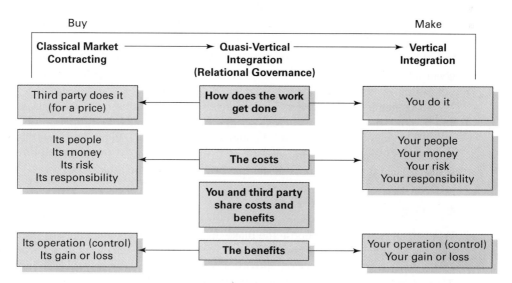

FIGURE 7.1 **The Continuum of Degrees of Vertical Integration**

- Negotiate each transaction as though it were the only one
- Begin and end their transactions based solely on the merits of the current set of offerings

At the extreme of buy, manufacturer–distributor arrangements involve no sharing (of risk, of expertise, of image, etc.), no distinction, and no continuity. This buy model is a useful baseline in thinking about distribution. However, many, if not most, arrangements with third parties exhibit some degree of relationalism, meaning that the manufacturer has a greater share of the costs and benefits than is the case under strict delegation to a third party (classical market contracting).[13]

Relational governance means compromising between the make–buy extremes by creating channels that have some properties of both owned and independent channels.[14] Relational governance can be created in many ways.[15] Building and maintaining close, committed relationships is covered in Chapter 11. One of the principal methods of building commitment is *selective distribution*, covered in Chapter 10. Another method, whereby two organizations attempt to coordinate as though they were only one, is franchising, covered in Chapter 17. Franchising and close relationships are channel strategies to simulate vertical integration (this is *quasi-vertical integration*, another term for relational governance).[16] Making these systems work requires power, the subject of Chapter 8.

Along the continuum of degree of integration, the fundamental issue is how the work of the channel is done. When your employees carry out the flow, you have vertically integrated (the buy option).

In short, vertical integration is not a binary choice but a matter of degree. Degrees of integration form a continuum, anchored by the extremes of classical marketing contracting and vertical integration. *Buy* is a large zone of relationships with third parties, and some of these relationships operate in a manner that resembles a single firm. Indeed, customers often believe they are dealing with the manufacturer when they are actually dealing with a committed third party in the marketing channel (such as Kenco in the Whirlpool puzzle).

Where the argument for integration is strong, *but not entirely compelling*, relational governance should be considered instead as a way to simulate vertical integration without assuming its burdens.

In principle, every distribution arrangement is unique and can be placed somewhere along the degree-of-vertical-integration continuum. It is a function of the relationship's operating methods and the nature of the contract, if any, between the parties. In practice, certain common institutional arrangements tend to correspond to regions within the continuum. Common examples are presented in Table 7.1.

Costs and Benefits

What changes when you choose the make option? If you are a manufacturer, your organization assumes all the accounting costs of distribution, which include all personnel costs. It also bears the risk of the distribution operation and is responsible for all actions. These costs (e.g., warehousing) are substantial and are frequently underestimated, particularly by firms that are accustomed to production but not to distribution.

TABLE 7.1

Examples of Institutions Performing Some Channel Functions

Function	Classical Market Contracting	Quasi-Vertical Integration	Vertical Integration
1. Selling (only)	Manufacturers' representatives	"Captive" or exclusive sales agency[*]	Producer sales force (direct sales force)
2. Wholesale distribution	Independent wholesaler	Distribution joint venture	Distribution arm of producer
3. Retail distribution	Independent (third party)	Franchise store	Company store

[*] Operationally, a sales agency deriving more than 50 percent of its revenues from one principal.

Many manufacturers find the heaviest of these costs to be the opportunity cost of the personnel. Manufacturers often have no one available to be diverted from the core activity of manufacturing. And because they do not know the market for expertise in distribution, they find it difficult to hire qualified personnel to meet service output demands economically. The top management of the vertically integrated firm is responsible for ensuring distribution, and often finds that it does not have sufficient managerial resources to give attention to the distribution responsibility. (Of course, this and every other argument can be reversed for downstream channel members integrating upstream—this is a useful mental exercise.)

Substantial benefits are required to justify these costs. The fundamental reason given for firms to integrate forward into distribution is to control the operation. But from an economic standpoint, control per se has no value whatsoever. It is valuable only as a means to improve the firm's overall economic results.[17] Manufacturers integrate forward (and resellers integrate backward) when they believe they will gain from it in profit terms. Without that profit gain, control is psychologically appealing to managers (they direct a larger empire) but goes against the interests of shareholders.[18]

Sometimes this means merely appropriating the returns from the performance of marketing channel flows themselves, to add to the returns from production. In this sense, vertical integration is a business opportunity like any other. A firm seeking to grow might consider taking on more of its current value chain if these other elements are attractive as a business proposition in and of themselves. This is part of the reason for pork packers to integrate backward. In the United States, raising hogs is a growth business that has attracted capital from many sources—why not from parties already in the value chain?

Similarly, a major reason automakers move into their downstream operations is because auto manufacturing is losing appeal as a business proposition. Competition, flat demand, and overcapacity have obliged producers to become efficient in the factory and more effective in their marketing. They are reaching the limits of improvement in their profits. Much of the price of an automobile is due to channel costs. The next logical place to find revenues and cut costs is the channel, not the factory. Further, much of an automobile's profit is not in its sale but in its maintenance. By integrating downstream, automakers tap into a steady flow of maintenance contracts for the products they manufacture.[19]

From this perspective, it is actually surprising that vertical integration is not even more common in channels than it really is. It is appealing to think that know-how from one part of the value chain could be amortized by applying it upstream or downstream. Yet, downstream and upstream activities are very different, and conform to different financial models, a theme that will be expanded in the next section. These fundamental differences drive firms to grow and diversify into other (perhaps related) businesses, but often at the same level of the value chain (e.g., production, wholesaling, logistics, retailing—wherever their expertise and expectations lie).

More often, appropriating returns from channel functions means directing the performance of channel flows for the purpose of improving sales and margins obtained at the integrator's level of the channel. The retailer is interested in improving returns from retailing. The manufacturer is interested in using the channel to improve production results, rather than in running a profitable marketing channel operation in and of itself. Of course, if the integrator mismanages the acquired part of the channel, the result will be an unexpected loss.

The manufacturer who wishes to focus solely on production, will turn to the marketplace for distribution services. Here, it will seek a third party—an outside organization—and will contract with that organization to perform channel flows in return for some economic consideration, normally a price.

The Terms of Payment to Third Parties

The price is usually expressed as a *margin* (the difference between the price paid the manufacturer and the price obtained by the reseller), as a *commission* (a fraction of the resale price), or as a percentage of the reseller's business (a royalty).

These are the most common ways to price the performance of channel flows. However, many variations are possible, such as paying the third party a flat fee or a lump sum, or reimbursing some of the reseller's expenses. The third party may also agree to work in return for some future consideration, such as the rights to future business, or a percentage of equity in the manufacturer. Such arrangements are particularly common for entrepreneurial start-ups, new firms that are often poorly capitalized.

For example, *fulfillment houses* (which take orders generated by a seller, compose a package from warehoused goods, and ship the package) may agree to process the orders of a new mail-order firm without charge for a limited time in return for the rights to that firm's paying business after it becomes established. Here, the fulfillment house not only is carrying out the ordering flow for the manufacturer but also is providing a backward flow of the risking and financing flows (see Chapter 4).

Arrangements—other than a commission or a gross margin, paid as the business is done—are not unusual. However, they are not the norm because they are risky. Paying a reseller a fee or reimbursing expenses subjects the manufacturer to the risk of *moral hazard* (i.e., being cheated after the arrangement has been put into place), because it is difficult to verify that the paid-for activities have been performed or that the expenses are not inflated. Hence, the manufacturer will hesitate to pay in this manner.

If the manufacturer agrees to pay in future business or in equity stakes, the downstream channel member assumes risk and will hesitate to accept being paid in this manner. The future business may never materialize, or the equity stakes may turn out to be without value—or even a liability, if the channel member cannot cover its obligations. For every success story (a supplier, getting in "on the ground floor" of what turns out to be a successful channel, or a downstream channel member getting in on the creation of the next successful producer), there are plenty of failures. Of course, everyone involved trumpets the successes and hides the failures, creating the impression that this deferred payment strategy is less risky than it really is.

This is not to say that channel members do not operate on deferred payment. For example, French *boulangers* (artisan bakers), having finished their apprenticeships, often start operations in a small town. As these artisans typically bring only their skills to the task, and as start-up capital is limited in Europe, the tiny new bakeries are frequently financed by producers of flour. Millers supply flour on extremely generous credit terms, on the understanding that they will be preferred suppliers if and when the *boulangerie* builds a clientele. There is no legal obligation to do so: The understanding is based on the norm of reciprocity in the industry.

Outsourcing shifts all the costs—accounting costs, including personnel, plus the risk of failure and the responsibility for action—to the third party. In return for assuming costs, the third party benefits by controlling the operation. This in itself is of no benefit in economic terms unless the third party can use that control to generate profits over and above the costs of distribution (both accounting and opportunity costs).

DECIDING WHEN TO VERTICALLY INTEGRATE FORWARD: AN ECONOMIC FRAMEWORK

It may seem that vertical integration is always desirable, for who would wish to be without control? Obviously, the decision must be more complex than this. Control has more hidden costs than benefits. This section presents a decision framework for determining when a greater degree of forward vertical integration is *economically* (as opposed to psychologically or politically) *justifiable*, as a function of the characteristics of the manufacturer and its choices. This framework is designed to cut through the confusion in systematic fashion by prioritizing the issues. Not every consideration is covered: The last section of this chapter covers justifications that are harder to justify economically but may be just as legitimate.

In this section, we examine the decision of not to vertically integrate forward. First, all the supporting arguments are marshaled. Then the preliminary outsource decision is challenged to see if the logic of outsourcing holds under the manufacturer's circumstances. If not, we consider whether vertical integration can replace it. The decision maker first reasons as an advocate of the presumption of the superiority of outsourcing; then as the critic who attacks the outsourcing argument; and finally as the arbitrator, who determines whether the advocate of outsourcing has been compellingly overturned. *If not, the outsourcing decision carries the day.*

The reader may find this exercise arbitrary, as the line of argument goes first all the way to one side, then all the way to the other. However, at the last (judging) phase, balance is finally achieved.

Efficiency: The Traditional Criterion

The premise of this section is that the organization's goal is *to maximize its overall effi-ciency in the long run*. This is the overall efficiency of the firm. It does not refer to any single flow or product; indeed, the long run may be longer than the life cycle of a given product. In deciding whether to integrate forward into distribution (or, for the down-stream channel member, backward into production), the appropriate question is whether taking on this flow increases efficiency, and does so more than some other use of the resources needed to provide the flow.

Why select this criterion? It is not always appropriate: Other criteria sometimes carry the day. (These will be discussed in the last section of this chapter.) But efficiency matters, and matters a very great deal. Why? *Efficiency* is the ratio of results obtained (roughly, operating performance) to the resources used to calculate them (roughly, over-head, reflecting the amortization of fixed investments). In the short term, the firm may be able to sustain losses or tolerate mediocre results (the numerator). Or the firm may be able to justify dedicating inordinate resources (the denominator) for the results achieved. But providers of resources will not permit this situation to last indefinitely. There comes a day of reckoning when the returns to resources will matter.

For our purposes, the relevant terms are the revenues, direct costs, and overhead incurred under vertical integration forward, compared to those incurred under out-sourcing. We use these terms in a conceptual sense only. It is unlikely that the decision maker could create proper and precise accounting estimates for his or her situation. Fortunately, for purposes of channel decision making, this is not necessary. *It is enough to focus on factors that drive revenue up and costs or overhead down.*

Conceptually,

$$\frac{\text{Revenues} - \text{Direct Costs}}{\text{Overhead}} = \frac{\text{Net Effectiveness}}{\text{Overhead}} = \text{Efficiency}$$

Efficiency is the ratio of net effectiveness to overhead (*results to resources*). And net effectiveness is the revenues that accrue under vertical integration minus the direct (variable) costs incurred after integrating. For vertical integration to be efficient, it must somehow increase revenues more than it increases variable costs, in order to improve net effectiveness. But it is not enough merely to improve net effectiveness. Vertical inte-gration is certain to encumber resources, thereby increasing overhead. *The use of these resources must be justified by the increase in net effectiveness.*

Obviously, two circumstances could preclude vertical integration forward, even if it would add to efficiency. One is that the firm does not have and cannot obtain the resources to integrate forward. The other is that the firm has other priorities that con-tribute even more to efficiency and that exhaust the firm's capacities. The manufacturer should pursue these other actions instead, even if vertical integration has a positive pay-off with a return on overhead that exceeds the firm's hurdle rate returns on resources employed (e.g., capital).

Outsourcing as the Starting Point

A very substantial body of research suggests that any manufacturer should begin with the seemingly artificial premise that the distribution flow should be outsourced.[20] Why should outsourcing, that is, market contracting, be the default option for the distribution flow? The fundamental rationale is that, under normal circumstances in a developed economy, *markets for distribution services are efficient*.

This does not mean that markets for distribution services function perfectly, or even that they function well! It means that given current environmental conditions, technology, and know-how, it is difficult for a given manufacturer to get better operating results than can be delivered by the level of third-party services available to the manufacturer. It is noteworthy that the argument is strictly comparative, not absolute. And it does not mean that there is no room for improvement. However, improvement would require the manufacturer to introduce new technology or know-how that would change prevailing methods. Thus, the manufacturer would need to take on substantial risk.

Here lies an explanation for the profitability of conglomerates in Chile and Brazil. In the rest of the world, the producer loses because it is an overstretched generalist. Conglomerates make a range of unrelated products. Their lack of synergy means that specialists can beat conglomerates one product category at a time. But in Chile and Brazil, conglomerates have built their own roads, bridges, railroads, and airports to compensate for poor transportation infrastructure. This massive investment in distribution logistics is then amortized over the conglomerate's range of products. The distribution advantage overcomes the production disadvantage, and can do so because of the inadequate provision of basic distribution services.

The efficient markets argument does not mean that all manufacturers will receive the same downstream services. Superior manufacturers offering superior rewards will attract better providers of marketing channel flows, or will obtain the best level of service a given provider can offer. Other manufacturers will obtain what is left.

In sum, efficient markets for third-party marketing channel services means the manufacturer will be hard pressed to improve on the results it can obtain in the marketplace for marketing channel flows. Why should this be so?

Six Reasons to Outsource Distribution

An outside party has six advantages in performing a channel function. Focusing on downstream functions for the moment, these are:

1. Motivation
2. Specialization
3. Survival of the economically fittest
4. Economies of scale
5. Heavier market coverage
6. Independence from any single manufacturer

Let us examine these one by one.

Motivation. Outside parties have *high-powered incentives* to do their jobs well because they are independent companies, accepting risk in return for the prospect of rewards. Both positive motivation (profit) and negative motivation (fear of loss) spur the third party to perform. Sales agents, for example, are often more willing to prospect for customers. They are more persistent and more inclined to offer a trial close to a negotiation than are company salespeople. This is one reason why financial services, such as insurance, are often sold by third parties.[21] An outsider is attracted by entrepreneurial rewards and driven by fear of losses.

Part of motivation is the willingness to operate within a certain financial model. Downstream operations are frequently detail-oriented businesses that operate on narrow margins and focus on inventory turnover and cost management. For a producer, this mode of thinking is often alien, and the risk-adjusted returns may not appeal.

Key to the motivation advantage is that outside parties are *replaceable*, hence subject to *market discipline* by their principals. For example, if a distributor is underperforming, the manufacturer moves to another distributor. Because the mere threat of such a move is credible, it provides an incentive for the distributor to attempt to meet the manufacturer's demands or to find an acceptable compromise. These demands include sharing distribution cost savings with the manufacturer, placing sales efforts on particular products, presenting products in a certain way, advertising, carrying more inventory—there is no limit to the possible requests to make of a third party.

Distributors are thus under constant pressure to improve operating results, which includes both increasing sales and decreasing costs. In contrast, a company distribution organization cannot be so readily terminated or restructured, and precedent makes it difficult to make substantial changes to incentive systems. Internal politics shields employees, making it more likely that an integrated distribution operation will become an unresponsive, inefficient bureaucracy. This is particularly the case where labor law makes it difficult to terminate employees, as is true in much of Europe. However, even in countries such as the United States, where employment is traditionally at the will of the employer, firing a single employee, let alone an entire division, is administratively difficult. *Replaceability is the key to making the buy option work.*

Specialization.   Outsiders have this advantage. For wholesalers, distribution is all they do—they have no distractions. The reverse is true for manufacturers. Specialization engenders and deepens competence. This is why Whirlpool has been a pioneer for decades in the outsourcing of logistics. Kenco is a large logistics provider, deeply versed in the intricacies of storage, shipping, and delivery. Outsourcing allows each party (Whirlpool and Kenco) to stick to its specialty. This advantage has always existed. Increasing competition has made firms appreciate it more. A generalized move to identify and strip down to core competencies—only—is behind many decisions to outsource channel flows.

Survival of the Economically Fittest.   If specialists fail to do their functions better than their competitors do, they do not survive. Distribution in most sectors has low mobility barriers: The business is easy to enter and easy to exit. Such businesses attract many entrants and readily eliminate the lesser performers among them, because they can exit swiftly. This argument is connected with specialization, because an incompetent marketing channel member cannot stay in business by subsidizing its distribution losses with gains in other sectors, such as production. This is one reason why Whirlpool entrusts all its logistics to Kenco, a long-established, large specialist in logistics only.

Economies of Scale.   Outside parties *pool the demands* of multiple manufacturers for marketing channel flows. This allows them to achieve *economies of scale* by doing a great deal of one thing (a set of distribution flows) for multiple parties. In turn, these economies of scale enable the outsider to perform flows that would otherwise be uneconomical to do at all. By offering many brands in a product category, a distributor can do enough business to amortize the fixed costs of distribution facilities, logistical software, and the like. Similarly, a retailer that specializes in a single category of merchandise (such as appliances) pools the demand of many manufacturers for retailing services. The retailer's deep brand assortment, albeit in a narrow category of products, attracts customers. The customer base in turn justifies the existence of the specialty store or the category killer, which would otherwise be uneconomical.

This is a major reason why specialty coffee producers in North America generally confine their forward integration activities to supermarket kiosks and large office building contracts. The scale needed to make these operations work is small. An office building under contract is a captive audience with stable demand. A delivery truck can handle it readily. A supermarket kiosk is less predictable, but the supermarket covers the costs of the site and will lease space in kiosks at advantageous rates because specialty coffee is a traffic builder for the store. In contrast, running a freestanding coffee shop is a substantial endeavor: It is difficult to reach the scale of business needed to make it pay. Starbucks does so, but requires hundreds of stores to justify the necessary investment in brand building and retailing expertise. Starbucks is a retailer that later integrated backward, not a wholesaler that integrated forward.

Heavier Market Coverage. Heavy coverage of a market stems from the independent's ability to call on many customers, including small customers, to call on them often, and to call on them concerning a broad range of their needs. For example, a manufacturers' representative ("rep," or independent sales agent) can create a portfolio of products and services meeting related needs. Via this portfolio, the rep can justify the activity of making a call on a prospect that is a small account—for any single brand of any single product. By meeting multiple needs for that customer, the rep can sell multiple brands and products on a single call, converting a small prospect (for a brand) into a large prospect (for the salesperson). Further, by being able to meet many needs at once, the rep can induce time-pressed purchasers, who value one-stop shopping, to meet with them and to spend enough time so that the salesperson can learn a good deal about the customers. The rep can then parlay this deep customer knowledge into more compelling sales presentations of a greater range of offerings. The sale of one product "leads into" the sale of another; that is, the rep creates selling synergy within the portfolio of offerings.

Similarly, by meeting multiple needs, distributors are able to draw customers to their locations. Once there, customers spend time making purchases, and one purchase often encourages another. For example, in office supplies, the prospect orders standard white paper for a printer, then remembers to order toner, then thinks of the need for nonstandard paper or colors, and so forth. The astute salesperson uses this interchange to learn about the customer's installation, information that is useful when it is time to replace the printer itself.

In short, sales mount in a pyramid if the intermediary has composed an appealing assortment of goods that represent related purchase occasions to the buyer. It is difficult for most manufacturers to duplicate the thorough coverage afforded by third parties, because few manufacturers can match the breadth of related products and services the third party can assemble. Some manufacturers do have very broad product lines, as broad as a distributor's. However, the distributor is free to select only the best products from a variety of manufacturers, bypassing the "weak links" in any manufacturer's offerings. Few broad-line manufacturers are uniformly strong in all elements of their product line.

Key here is that the independent can realize potential synergies that a vertically integrated manufacturer cannot reproduce. Why? Because the vertically integrated manufacturer may offer to carry the lines of its competitors, in order to duplicate the independent's assortment. However, competitors and sellers of complementary goods and services will hesitate to sell their products through the manufacturer's distribution arm. They fear the sales force will favor its own products at their expense.[22] This is why a manufacturer's acquisition of a distributor often provokes the distributor's other principals to terminate their contracts and seek representation elsewhere. It is also a reason why downstream channel members do not integrate backward into production more often.

The ability to amortize the cost of a call, then, creates a powerful advantage by allowing the independent to *cover a market much more thoroughly and much more economically* than can most vertically integrated manufacturers. The importance of this fundamental point is often understated. The sheer arithmetical advantage afforded by superiority of coverage cannot be overlooked when reasonable estimates are incorporated in a spreadsheet analysis of the make-or-buy choice. This is much of why Best Power dismantled its direct sales force. Although the salespeople were effective, its narrow product line prevented them from calling on any but the largest customers. The value-added resellers who replaced them call on a huge range of customers and know how uninterruptible power supplies fit into the larger picture of the customer's needs.

Independence from Any Single Manufacturer. For their customers, diversified outside providers of channel flows can serve as a sort of independent counsel, an impartial source of advice that does not come from a single manufacturer. (Some channel members give this up: For a discussion, see Chapter 10.) Further, many outside specialists are local entities. Therefore, they are stable with the same personnel serving the same customer set year after year. They have the opportunity to know their customers well, and strong customer loyalties often result.

Many manufacturers disagree: They consider independence ("obstinacy" or "conflict of interest") as one of the biggest drawbacks of outsourcing. They desire vertical integration so that they can resolve their differences of opinion by giving orders to subordinates. But this represents a rather optimistic view of how things actually get done inside vertically integrated firms. The manufacturer's distribution arm, just like a third party, will seek to avoid carrying out orders it considers misguided.

It is worth considering *why* an independent would resist doing what the manufacturer desires. An independent acquires substantial information about the marketplace. If the independent has reservations about the manufacturer's ideas, it behooves the manufacturer to listen and to engage the channel member in a dialogue. The downstream channel member is analogous to a test market for a new product. If the test-market results are poor, the appropriate reaction is to make modifications and test it again.

VERTICAL INTEGRATION FORWARD WHEN COMPETITION IS LOW

At this point, you may be thinking that this sketch of independents is idealized and overly favorable. You are right. It is time to change orientation and to become the critic of one's preliminary "decision" to outsource. But it is not enough merely to offer criticisms of third-party distribution. The critic must also make the case that a vertically integrated firm would do the job better. It would contribute enough to revenue or reduce direct cost enough to offset any other increases in direct cost, and to justify the necessary increase in overhead. This goes back to a foundation of marketing channels: You can eliminate the channel intermediary, but you cannot eliminate the functions it performs.

Two caveats open the discussion. First, vertical integration always involves substantial setup costs and overhead. Therefore, it is worth considering only if a substantial amount of business is potentially at stake. Second, it is worth considering only if the firm is prosperous enough to be able to muster the necessary resources.

The economic advantages of outsourcing distribution are variations on a familiar theme: Competitive markets of any kind are efficient. Finding situations that do not favor outsourcing distribution means finding situations in which markets for distribution services are not competitive.

Company-Specific Capabilities

The first and most frequent noncompetitive scenario is that of *small-numbers bargaining* arising from *company-specific capabilities*. Here is a hypothetical example that is prototypical.

> Atlas Electronics is a distributor of electronic components. Atlas is one of many distributors in its market area, because electronic components is a fiercely competitive industry. Atlas's salespeople are electrical engineers, well versed in their industry, its products, its customers, and the applications they make of the products.
>
> Jupiter Semiconductors is one of the many manufacturers that Atlas represents. It is a differentiated manufacturer whose products are unique.
>
> Over the years, Atlas salespeople have learned the myriad idiosyncrasies of the Jupiter product line, including how it functions in conjunction with other brands of electronic and electrical components. They have learned how their customer base makes application of Jupiter products. Atlas management estimates that, even though Jupiter provides training at its factory, Atlas salespeople still require two years of on-the-job experience selling Jupiter to master this knowledge. These two years are necessary *even though the salespeople are skilled and knowledgeable about the industry in general*.

The key word here is *idiosyncrasies*. Because Jupiter products are quite different from competing semiconductors, even a salesperson who knows the industry requires substantial training and on-the-job experience to master them. That mastery, in turn, is an asset: It is of considerable value in selling Jupiter products—*only*. This knowledge is a company-specific capability, the company being Jupiter.

The greater the value of company-specific capabilities, the greater the economic rationale for the manufacturer to vertically integrate forward into distribution. The holders of the capabilities (here, the salespeople, and by extension, their employer, Atlas) become so valuable that they are irreplaceable. If it takes two years to bring a salesperson to the mastery level, salespeople with at least two years of Jupiter experience are very expensive to replace. Not only must the replacement be trained but there is an opportunity cost of less effective sales effort during the recruiting and training period. Thus, Jupiter is in small-numbers bargaining with Atlas. Jupiter cannot replace its sales quickly, even if it spends enough to hire very competent salespeople with generalized industry experience.

Small-numbers bargaining destroys the fundamental premise of competitive markets. It does so by destroying the presumption of market discipline. Because only small numbers of people possess company-specific capabilities, only small numbers of organizations are truly qualified to bid to perform the function (in this case, selling). And if the firm cannot readily find qualified bidders, it cannot credibly threaten to move its business (terminate the contract with Atlas) when it is dissatisfied.

Thus, the firm (Jupiter) cannot count on competitive markets to ensure efficient outcomes. Atlas salespeople may now engage in such behaviors as shirking, misrepresenting the product, unethical behavior, falsifying expense accounts, and demanding more compensation to do the same work. This is *opportunism*, which is self-interest seeking in a deceitful or dishonest manner.[23]

In these circumstances, Jupiter needs to step in and replace the market mechanism in order to prevent opportunism.[24] The visible hand of Jupiter management can replace the invisible hand of the market. By vertically integrating forward, the manufacturer creates an administrative mechanism, thereby increasing overhead. It can use that mechanism to direct activities *for which the market would not otherwise provide incentives*.

How does this solve the problem? After all, it is really the salespeople who are irreplaceable. Whether they are employed by Atlas (outsourcing) or by Jupiter (vertical integration), they can still do great damage by leaving their jobs or by shirking or failing to cooperate.

The answer is that Jupiter gains more control over the salespeople directly. As Jupiter employees, salespeople have only Jupiter products to sell. They draw their income from a single principal, rather than from a third party gathering revenue from multiple principals. Salespeople report to a Jupiter manager whose sole concern is their performance on behalf of Jupiter—not any other principal or organization. Thus, salespeople are now highly dependent on Jupiter. The company has the ability to employ negative sanctions against them directly, as well as to offer positive incentives, such as a salary, bonus, or commission. It controls not only monetary compensation but also nonmonetary compensation. Thus, it can build employee loyalty via its personnel practices. Finally, Jupiter has the right to demand detailed information on what the salespeople do (the right of "audit" or monitoring). In contrast, Atlas management would act as a buffer, refusing to allow a single principal to direct its personnel.

In short, Jupiter gains much more power over the salespeople by eliminating a third party and employing the holders of the critical resources directly. This is not to say these irreplaceable salespeople will be easy to manage. *They can still practice opportunism against Jupiter*. Vertical integration will never eliminate shirking, dishonesty, and the like. However, opportunism will be lessened. In *comparative efficiency terms*, the manufacturer is better off. With less opportunism, revenues should increase—because salespeople are working more, and more effectively—and direct costs should decline (e.g., lower costs due to lower expense account claims). Thus, net effectiveness should increase somewhat.

However, the value of company-specific capabilities must be very high to justify vertical integration. Only when these idiosyncratic assets are very valuable is there much room for opportunism. By integrating, the firm greatly increases its overhead. Further, the manufacturer gives up some of the third party's coverage and economies of scale, which decreases net effectiveness. Therefore, vertical integration may actually *decrease* efficiency unless the potential for opportunism is so substantial as to constitute a greater threat than the cost of overhead and the lost benefits of dealing with an outsider.

You may wonder why Jupiter needs to intervene at all. If the problem is opportunism by salespeople, why not charge Atlas (their employer) with controlling opportunism, rather than employing Atlas's salespeople directly? Jupiter cannot credibly threaten to terminate Atlas as its distributor. But does not Atlas have an interest in satisfying Jupiter, therefore in controlling salesperson opportunism itself?

After all, if Jupiter, the manufacturer, really does vertically integrate, Atlas, the distributor, will lose *its own investment*. The know-how Atlas has acquired about Jupiter products and customer applications cannot be redeployed to the service of another principal. This know-how has zero salvage value; there is no alternative use for it. Thus, Atlas loses its investment in knowledge, as well as in the customer relationships it has built up serving Jupiter customers. Because Jupiter products are unique, it will be difficult to convert these customers to another principal's products. Should not Atlas, contemplating the long-run prospect of losing Jupiter, undertake voluntarily to use its own influence as an employer to control the opportunism of its salespeople?

In rational terms, it would appear that the mere threat of vertical integration should allow Jupiter to pressure Atlas in such a way as to simulate the outcome of market forces. However, there are two counterarguments. One is that it is not just the salespeople who can practice opportunism but Atlas itself. The irreplaceable nature of its salespeople puts Jupiter in small-numbers bargaining with Atlas itself. The distributor may then use the vulnerability of Jupiter to demand more (e.g., better margins) while doing less to earn it (e.g., holding lower inventories). The second argument is that Jupiter cannot justify vertical integration until Atlas's opportunism becomes very substantial. If Atlas stays within a certain latitude of abuse, Jupiter will find it cheaper to be the victim of opportunism than to vertically integrate. The same rationale explains why insurance companies tolerate a certain degree of claims fraud: To a point, it is cheaper to pay false claims than to pay the costs of detecting and fighting false claims.[25]

Let us alter the scenario, taking it back in time. Jupiter is contemplating selling in Atlas's territory and has no representation. Should it sign up Atlas as its distributor, or should it vertically integrate, setting up a distribution branch to serve Atlas's market? Knowing that its products are idiosyncratic, Jupiter may foresee the scenario of getting into small-numbers bargaining with Atlas or any other distributor that sells its products.

If the idiosyncratic assets involved are sufficiently valuable, Jupiter is better off, in efficiency terms, by vertically integrating *to begin with*. And a good deal of field research demonstrates that it is highly likely that this is what Jupiter will indeed do.

This is not to say that a manufacturer cannot work efficiently with a third party where idiosyncratic assets are at stake. But to do so is very difficult and requires careful structuring of the arrangement to achieve relational governance.

In short, *the accumulation of company-specific assets creates an economic rationale to vertically integrate*. These assets go by many labels.[26] Economists call them "transaction-specific assets" because they are customized ("specific") to a business relationship ("transaction"). They are also called transaction-specific "investments" because effort, time, know-how, and other resources must be expended to create them.

Typically in marketing channels, these capabilities grow slowly over time, often without the realization of either party, until a crisis or an opportunity forces the parties to take stock of the assets they have accumulated. The key concepts here are (1) assets: tangible or intangible, they can be used to create economic value; (2) specific: that is, made to specifications, customized, tailored, particular to, or idiosyncratic. Specific assets cannot be redeployed to another application without significant loss in value.

Company-Specific Capabilities in Distribution

In distribution, most of the important company-specific capabilities are intangible. (In contrast, vertical integration upstream from production turns on physical assets, such as customized parts and assemblies.) Below is a description of the six major forms of company-specific capabilities that accrue in the distribution arena.

The Most Important Forms. Idiosyncratic knowledge, form 1, is not merely knowledge of the manufacturer, its products, its operating methods, and the applications its customers make of these products. It is that *part* of this knowledge base that *cannot be readily redeployed to another principal*. There is a great deal to know about a company that makes standard products, uses industry-generic operating procedures, and whose customers use its products as they would use those of a competitor. Downstream channel members make investments to acquire this knowledge, which is indeed an asset. But it is *not an idiosyncratic asset*. It is a *general-purpose asset*, meaning it can be put to the service of another principal without loss of productive value. It is only when a principal makes unusual products or has its own unique methods of operation or has customers who make customized uses of the products that the downstream channel member acquires idiosyncratic information, hence a company-specific capability. *Ordinary principals do not need to vertically integrate downstream*: They can generate efficient distribution outcomes if they use the market for distribution services.[27] A principal that requires company-specific capabilities is at least moderately exotic. See Channel Sketch 7.1 for an example.

Relationships, form 2, are connections between distributor personnel and the personnel of the manufacturer or the manufacturer's customers. The existence of a relationship implies the ability to get things done quickly and correctly and to make oneself understood swiftly.

CHANNEL SKETCH 7.1

Jean Delatour

Idiosyncratic knowledge is behind Jean Delatour's integration into the production of jewelry. The chain aims directly at hypermarkets, which have made great inroads into jewelry by using bulk purchase power to offer lower prices than most jewelers can match. Superficially, Jean Delatour mimics this strategy. Like hypermarkets, the stores are huge, unappealing boxlike structures made of corrugated metal and located on the peripheries of urban areas—indeed, near the hypermarkets themselves. Shoppers come expecting a price appeal, which they do find.

But they also find unique merchandise, because the chain manufactures the jewelry it sells. Backward integration also permits Jean Delatour to renew its collection twice a year, catering to the increasing fashion orientation of jewelry. And the chain practices the dying art of custom production on site. Every store has a workshop, permitting a customer not only to design a piece of jewelry but also to see it realized within a week—at prices reflective of Delatour's expertise and presence in production.

To complete its uniqueness, the chain uses its production expertise to create a novel shopping experience. A computerized kiosk shows customers minute-by-minute activity on the Antwerp diamond exchange, creating merchandising excitement. Next to the kiosk, loose diamonds rated and certified by the chain are sold (under blister packs!). Customers often select them to fit into their own design of jewelry (aided by a lavishly staffed sales operation). This is not typical behavior: By projecting its production expertise, the retail chain creates an idiosyncratic experience that alters buyer behavior.

The only category Jean Delatour does not make is watches and clocks. This requires a different expertise, which the chain does not possess. Powerful brand names dominate this category, and few customers are interested in designing their own. Thus, Jean Delatour outsources production. Why carry the category at all? The reason is consumer expectation of assortment: A "real" jewelry store must carry fine watches and clocks.

For some transactions, relationships are essential. For example, just-in-time supply arrangements involve exquisite coordination. For a manufacturer to supply a downstream channel member on a just-in-time basis (i.e., to replenish supplies just at the time it becomes necessary) requires very close cooperation between the manufacturer and the channel member. This demands relationships, and the cost (accounting cost and opportunity cost) of a failed supply arrangement makes these relationships essential.[28]

Brand equity, form 3, is a critical idiosyncratic investment in the manufacturer's brand name. Here we can distinguish two cases. In one case, the brand name enjoys substantial brand equity with consumers *independent of the downstream channel member's actions*. In this case, vertical downstream is not only unnecessary but wasteful. The manufacturer can use brand equity as a source of power over channel members (Chapter 8). Here, the manufacturer does not need to integrate forward in order to exert considerable influence over the channel.

But in the second case, *downstream channel members have a critical impact on the firm's brand equity*. Brand equity is not created in a manner largely independent of their actions. For example, channel members have a great influence on brand equity when

- A sales force is required to explain the brand. This is often the case for industrial products.
- The brand's strategy demands it be stocked, displayed, and presented in a particular manner, but to permit too low a downstream margin to invite the channel member to provide the support itself. This is why perfume makers sometimes rent dedicated space from department stores and pay the salespeople.[29]
- A support service, before or after sales, is required to make sure the branded product is properly installed and used, so that the customer is satisfied and positive word of mouth is created.

In all these cases, brand equity is created and maintained via customer experiences, which are driven by marketing channel activities. If the brand name can be made truly valuable, it can be a substantial asset, one that is, of course, specific to the manufacturer. To protect that asset, the firm may vertically integrate. Failing this step, the firm may attempt to protect the investment by forging close relationships downstream; by franchising, or vertical restraints; or by seeking other means of influencing its channel members.

This is behind much of the increase in private-label activity by North American supermarkets. They are not simply putting their name on what a manufacturer would be making anyway. The new style of private label is to use one's knowledge of the product category to design a new product and to work with manufacturers to figure out how to make it. A leader here is the Canadian chain, Loblaws, which keeps an R&D facility for this purpose. Loblaws conducted a market research to identify a demand for a much richer cookie than was currently available. The chain worked with a producer to devise a way to overcome substantial technical obstacles to manufacture. Then Loblaws branded the product (Decadent cookies) and invested heavily to promote it. The brand was so successful that even though Loblaws holds only 20 percent of the Canadian market, Decadent became the market share leader. Loblaws' investment backward (into product design and development) paid off handsomely. The chain has repeated this success in many categories.[30]

At a high enough level of value, the manufacturer is justified in trading influence for more control by vertically integrating forward. An example of this phenomenon is the ongoing rivalry between Coca-Cola and Pepsi Cola (see Channel Sketch 7.2).

Know-how, relationships, and brand equity (when driven by downstream activities): These major categories of company-specific capabilities justify vertical integration forward. These are all intangibles. However, several categories of tangible assets also play a role.

Dedicated capacity, form 4, is distribution capability (warehousing, transportation, selling, billing, and so forth) that has been created for a manufacturer *and which, by itself, represents overcapacity*. Thus, if the manufacturer terminates the business, the downstream channel member has excess capacity, which it cannot redeploy without sac-

CHANNEL SKETCH 7.2

Decades of Rivalry Between Coke and Pepsi in the United States

Both Coca-Cola and PepsiCo began U.S. operations in the early twentieth century by outsourcing distribution to third parties, one per market area. The producers also outsourced the assembly of the product to their channel members. These latter are known as "bottlers" because they formulate the product from ingredients supplied by the producer, according to the producer's instructions. They package the output in an operation called "bottling," even though many containers other than bottles are now used. Initially, this decision was justified because transportation costs dominated the economics of the soft drink business. Weight was the driver: The product itself is heavy, and the empty glass bottles were returned to the store, where the bottler picked them up and transported them back to the plant to be cleaned and refilled. By producing and distributing locally, the independent bottler held down transportation costs. Brand building was a minor activity achieved largely by the producers via limited national advertising. The business was stable, simple, and small.

By the 1960s the business had changed dramatically. Coke and Pepsi were so well diffused in the United States that they had displaced conventional drinks on many purchase occasions (even for breakfast!). Transportation became a lesser cost, in part because disposable containers replaced returnable bottles. Producers ran enormous national advertising campaigns requiring complex promotional tie-ins by all of their many regional bottlers, simultaneously. The products and their packaging became more complex and volatile, while the product line expanded greatly. Building brand equity replaced holding down transportation costs as the most important aspect of the business. *And the bottlers were necessary to do it.* Brand equity rested on their cooperation with the producer on terms of trade, delivery, promotions, advertisements, new products and packages, new-product testing, custom promotion for key accounts, selling methods for key accounts, and the like. These activities were all tightly synchronized with the producer, who in turn ensured that brand-equity building was consistent across market areas. The result was incessant and fruitless negotiation ("haggling") between the producers (Coke, Pepsi) and their bottlers. Transaction costs were getting out of control.

Coca-Cola ultimately vertically integrated forward into distribution, market by market, and is now largely the owner of its U.S. channels, a strategy it continues to repeat in Europe and expand in the United States. Pepsi is now following the same route. Both producers have done so by purchasing most of their bottlers (an acquisition strategy, versus a "greenfield" strategy, which is creating new operations). The economic value of this strategy is illustrated by one difference between the two producers. One segment of the business is "fountain sales," in which institutions (such as restaurants) perform the final mixing step to create the product and dispense it in single servings without bottling it (serving "from the fountain"). For contractual reasons, Pepsi is unable to integrate distribution to the fountain segment. Coke has, however, integrated to serve this segment and has much lower transaction costs than does Pepsi, due to eliminating haggling and poor coordination with bottlers. This transaction cost advantage has helped Coke achieve dominance in the segment. Coke is not the only beneficiary: The consumer has also benefited from lower fountain prices, made possible by passing on transaction cost savings.[31]

In this case, vertical integration into distribution has been highly successful. However, it is notable that even these producers have had difficulty reconciling the differences, both financial and operating, between manufacturing and distribution. By 1986, Coca-Cola had decided to spin off its distribution arm as a separate company, motivated in part by the desire to separate bottling (which requires substantial cash and operates on high volumes at low margins) from the production of concentrate (which exhibits the opposite properties). This is a classic difference between production and distribution: Management felt that mixing these businesses discouraged investors and lowered the company's stock price. Initial results for the newly independent bottler, Coca-Cola Enterprises (CCE), were disappointing. Coca-Cola now considers that it used its large equity stake in CCE to overcontrol its bottling subsidiary from its corporate headquarters in Atlanta, Georgia. The result was that management had lost touch with the considerable differences between markets that occurs at the field level. After five years of deceiving results, Coca-Cola turned CCE over to management recruited from an acquired bottler, then granted autonomy to CCE to enable it to respond locally to each unique marketplace and to focus on the myriad details that are usually more critical in distribution than in production. Seeing CCE's autonomy has reassured independent bottlers that Coca-Cola is sincere when it assures bottlers that it respects their acumen and independence. The results of decentralization in terms of growth and profits have been exceptional, so much so that CCE's share price has actually grown faster than that of Coca-Cola itself. One result is that Pepsi has imitated Coke's strategy of spinning off bottling as a separate company.[32]

rifice of productive value (i.e., losses). The key is that this capacity, dedicated to a manufacturer, could be put to use in serving another manufacturer—if there were demand for it, which there is not.

A forward-looking channel member will hesitate to incur these obligations, fearing the opportunism of the manufacturer once the capacity has been put in place. Channel members may refuse to add the capacity or may require very high compensation to do so. It may be worthwhile in efficiency terms for the manufacturer to integrate forward. Conversely, once the capacity is in place, the downstream channel member is vulnerable, and may be economically justified in protecting its investment in dedicated capacity. It can do so by vertically integrating backward—acquiring the manufacturer—in order to hold the business.

Site specificity, form 5, is when a manufacturer may need marketing channel flows performed in a location that is well suited to the manufacturer but ill suited to other manufacturers. A channel member that creates a facility (e.g., a warehouse) near the manufacturer has created a general-purpose asset if it is near other manufacturers, whom the warehouse could serve. But if the manufacturer is in a location remote from other suppliers, the warehouse will be difficult to redeploy. Its value is specific to the manufacturer; it is worth little or nothing to other ones.

For example, in the nineteenth century, there was great demand for explosives in the United States for purposes of clearing land and building infrastructure. To minimize the handling risk, explosives manufacturers produced the ingredients in their factories, mixed them partially, and shipped the mixture to their distributors. Even the mixture was volatile, hence dangerous to ship. Distributors then assembled and shipped the final product to customers. Some explosives manufacturers, notably DuPont, sited their own plants in remote locations. Rather than assume the risk of shipping its mixtures to distant distributors (who were sited nearer to customers), DuPont induced distributors to build warehouses close to its remote locations (a site-specific asset). Of course, this shifted the risk of explosion in transit from the manufacturer to the distributor, who now had to transport the final product considerable distances to the final customer. Thus, distribution warehouse locations near an isolated manufacturer were an asset to the manufacturer—only. For some markets, manufacturers could not find an entrepreneur willing to create such a site-specific asset for them. They were forced either to do business with a more distant distributor (give up the value of the site) or to build and staff their own nearby warehouses. Both solutions are costly to the manufacturer.

Another example occurs in maritime shipping of cargo.[33] For many products, raw materials are mined in remote parts of the world and shipped from one obscure port to another obscure port. They are processed in a refinery that is special-built to handle the output of the originating mine. Cargo carriers may refuse to offer service on such routes, because few other customers desire to ship in either direction. Thus, manufacturers are sometimes obliged to integrate forward into shipping. Alternatively, they may form alliances with shippers.

Customized physical facilities, form 6, is when the actual physical facilities themselves can be another important transaction-specific asset. For example, a distributor may, for a particular manufacturer, stack the merchandise onto nonstandard pallets, which in turn require nonstandard forklifts to lift them, and nonstandard shelf sizes to hold them.

In distribution, physical adaptations of this sort are frequently not critical. What is of greater value is proprietary hardware and software that binds an upstream and downstream channel member together. For example, some U.S. insurance companies in the 1980s offered their independent insurance agencies assistance in automating their offices. Agents who accepted did not always realize that they were converting their paper systems or prior computer systems to the underwriter's proprietary software system, which was incompatible with that of other insurance providers.

The same scenario occurs in maritime shipping when the shipping vessel is specific to a narrow use, for which there are very few users (such as shipping liquefied nitrogen). A ship may even be specific to a single user (some vessels are fitted to handle a particular brand of car). Redeploying these ships to appeal to a broader group of users requires extensive retrofitting (the brand of car) or may be impossible (liquefied nitrogen). The key factor is that the assets needed (the ships) to carry out the function (shipping cargo) are difficult to redeploy to the service of multiple users, thereby creating contracting hazards. The carrier hesitates in fear of the manufacturer's opportunism, while the manufacturer also fears the carrier's opportunism. Although rationally it may appear that there is a "balance of fear" that should make all parties be reasonable, the reality is that neither side is eager to enter into small-numbers bargaining with the other. Vertical integration is a viable solution.

Specific Assets Can Change to General-Purpose Assets. In the long term, many specific assets gradually lose their customized nature and become general purpose. This usually happens when the reason for specificity is innovation. Whenever a manufacturer brings an innovative product, process, or practice to a market, that innovation is, by definition, unique. There will be no bidders qualified to distribute the new product or capable of carrying out the new process or practice. The manufacturer will have to train an organization. Assuming the manufacturer can find an organization willing to make the investment, the manufacturer will of necessity enter into small-numbers bargaining. Foreseeing this situation, the manufacturer may choose to vertically integrate. For example, when entering foreign markets with unusual products, manufacturers tend to set up their own distribution arms to sell them, in spite of the expense and uncertainty involved.

But the novelty of the arrangement often disappears over time. Practices diffuse, products and processes are copied, and competitors enter with similar methods. And the market for providing these once-specific services expands, as more providers acquire the requisite know-how, relationships, sites, and physical facilities. The day may come when the manufacturer no longer needs to be vertically integrated. An example occurs in the nineteenth-century United States (see Channel Sketch 7.3).

CHANNEL SKETCH 7.3
Gustavus Swift Revolutionizes Meatpacking[34]

In the 1870s, cattle were raised in the West and shipped live to the East by rail car. Many animals died on the trip and survivors arrived in an emaciated state. Upon arrival, they were slaughtered, and 60 percent of the animal was discarded. The remaining meat was dressed locally and sold fresh. Gustavus Swift saw the production economies of gathering the animals, slaughtering them, and dressing the meat in western cities in massive slaughterhouses, then shipping the meat by refrigerated rail car to the East. This was a novel way to distribute fresh meat. The critical aspect was a refrigerated rail car whose invention Swift commissioned in 1878.

Three years later, the designs were ready. Swift then discovered that the railroads, fearing the loss of the lucrative business of shipping live cattle, refused to build his refrigerated rail cars. So Swift integrated into railroad car construction. Then the main railroad association refused to carry his cars. Fortunately, Swift did not have to build his own railroad, as a competitor existed and agreed to use his (highly idiosyncratic) refrigerated cars. To meet the cars upon arrival, Swift built an elaborate network of branch houses and delivery routes. Swift's vision was correct: He was able to offer high quality at low prices, thereby overcoming opposition to the idea of eating fresh meat slaughtered many days before in a distant location. It was not only the idiosyncratic rail car that made this possible but also the entire idiosyncratic system of wholesaling the meat. As demand expanded, Swift continually refined his model, keeping it idiosyncratic.

The speed with which Swift's model was imitated is instructive. Within a year, Philip Armour was imitating Swift (even today, Swift and Armour are valuable brand names in packaged meats, demonstrating the enduring value of their pioneering advantage). By the mid-1880s, several other meatpacking firms had imitated Swift. The local, fragmented meatpacking industry was soon dominated by a handful of giants, all imitating Swift's distribution. By the 1890s, his model had been imitated in other industries, notably beer, and later, dairy products and bananas, spreading finally to frozen foods. Eventually, Swift's model was no longer Swift's model, but simply the know-how of transporting chilled perishables. A highly idiosyncratic asset passed into rare but general know-how, then passed into simply know-how.

What was once specific becomes general. Small-numbers bargaining then gives way to large-numbers bargaining, and the competitiveness of the marketplace is restored. A manufacturer entering the market at that point would do well to outsource. But it may not follow that the vertically integrated manufacturer would do well to dismantle its vertically integrated distribution operation.

Switching Costs. Such a move involves *switching costs*. Switching costs are the *one-time losses* incurred in taking down the current operation and setting up a new operation (here, from vertical integration to outsourcing, although switching costs are incurred in either direction of the switch). These include accounting costs, opportunity costs, and psychological costs associated with terminating or displacing the operation that is being dismantled, as well as recruiting, relocating, training, and setup of infrastructure associated with the new operation. Note that these are *one-time costs of setup and takedown*. Switching costs should not be confused with the operating costs of the new system once it is in place.

The switching costs of going from a company operation to a third party are particularly painful because this involves terminating the positions of employees. But terminating their positions need not mean terminating their employment or their relationships. Some manufacturers shift these employees to other positions in their firm. Indeed, innovative firms often have pressing needs for experienced personnel and welcome the opportunity to free them up from distributing what have become standardized products through standardized processes. Failing transfer of personnel, progressive employers realize that former personnel possess company-specific knowledge and relationships of value and, if handled correctly, retain a loyalty to them. Thus, manufacturers often arrange for their new third party to hire their former staff. This is particularly the case under European labor laws, which frequently encourage, even demand, this practice.

A creative solution involves actually setting up former employees in business as third-party providers of distribution services (sales agencies, franchisees, dealers, distributors, export agents, etc.). For many manufacturers, this ensures exclusive representation of their products and services. For example, Rank Xerox sets up exclusive office-equipment dealers on high streets (urban commercial districts) owned by former employees in Europe. However, exclusivity is not essential. Some firms set up truly independent agencies, supporting them by training, secured bank loans, and promises of representation for a guaranteed number of years. Indeed, rather than viewing this practice in altruistic terms as a humane way to dispose of excess personnel, some firms view it as a proactive solution to the problem of finding good representation in markets where the "good" third parties are "locked into" their competitors.

These are means of minimizing switching costs. The switching-costs concept itself is easy to discuss in theory but difficult to estimate in practice. Research shows that firms contemplating switching are often conscious of those costs that accountants can track (such as recruiting costs). This is particularly the case in the United States where surveys of such costs as incurred by firms are regularly conducted and easily available. Other costs—such as the opportunity cost of lost business during the disruption of the transition, or the psychological cost of the change—are often overlooked or misstated.

Indeed, the nature of switching costs is so fluid that managers manipulate their estimates, often unconsciously, to justify decisions they have made on other grounds. For example, it has been demonstrated that manufacturers who are satisfied with the performance of their manufacturers' representatives become desirous of retaining them. They estimate the one-time costs of switching to a company sales force to be very high.[35] Yet, in otherwise similar circumstances, if they have reasons to wish to "go direct" (including dissatisfaction with performance), they will estimate the switching cost to be low.

The presence of switching costs in distribution is a major reason why late movers in a market or industry often have an advantage over established firms. Late movers can enter directly with outsourced distribution in industries or markets that have lost their specificity (have become ordinary). Incumbents are left to struggle with the obstacles to switching and may find these so great that they must either carry excessive overhead (by staying vertically integrated) or exit the business, due to inability to distribute effectively and efficiently.

Rarity versus Specificity: The Effects of Thin Markets

The key to asset specificity is that a resource, tangible or intangible, not only creates substantial value (making it an important asset) but that this asset loses value if redeployed to a different usage or user. These assets are customized, making them highly unusual. Some assets are *rare* (in short supply), but are *not specific*. For example, the conjunction of selling ability and technical knowledge that makes a good salesperson for semiconductors is uncommon, whereas demand for their services is enormous: These salespeople are rare. Hence, they are expensive. A semiconductor manufacturer may be tempted to reduce selling costs by employing salespeople directly, rather than going through a manufacturers' representative. Unless the manufacturer's products are unlike other semiconductors, or its methods are highly unusual, this strategy will not work. The manufacturer will discover that in lieu of paying high commissions to the manufacturers' representative, it is meeting a high payroll. Indeed, the manufacturer's costs will actually increase, as it is giving up the rep's economies.

Another case of rarity (not due to specificity) is due to *industry consolidation—the concentration of market share in the hands of a few players*.[36] Consolidation among manufacturers due to mergers and acquisitions command headlines. But it is also a substantial phenomenon downstream. For example, wholesale distribution was the second most active industry for mergers and acquisitions in the United States in 1997. The effect of consolidation is to prune markets so much that they become thin. Hence, suppliers can't find resellers or agents, and downstream channel members can't find suppliers. In fear of having little real choice, organizations scramble to form alliances with those players they estimate will be left standing as a level of an industry consolidates. Because alliances often serve to exclude other parties, this thins the market even further. To foreclose the prospect of dealing with a monopolist, many firms elect to integrate backward or forward as consolidation occurs.

Turning the Lens Around: Should the Channel Member Integrate Backward?

For purposes of exposition, the principles here have been presented from the standpoint of the manufacturer looking downstream. However, the principles are perfectly general and can be applied to the downstream channel member contemplating backward integration into production. Several of the issues already discussed have been presented in this fashion, because if the manufacturer is at risk of being held up by the channel member who owns a unique asset, the channel member is also at risk of being held up by the manufacturer. The manufacturer that is willing to abandon the channel member inflicts a loss on that party, who is left with an asset that is suddenly worthless. This prospect tempts the channel member to integrate backward, just as it tempts the manufacturer to integrate forward.

The symmetry of this situation is often overlooked. Many readers will find it more "natural" to consider the prospect of a manufacturer integrating forward than the prospect of, say, a distributor integrating backward. And yet, backward integration is not at all unusual. Indeed, it is often invited by manufacturers themselves, who welcome the infusion of capital and know-how, particularly market knowledge.

How, then, should a downstream channel member consider the issue? It should consider it in the same fashion. In general, vertical integration is a poor idea. In making an exception, the key issue is this: Does the ongoing transaction involve specificities in assets that are of great value? These may be in any form: know-how, relationships, the creation of brand equity, dedicated capacity, site, and physical facilities. Where these specificities are of value, a contracting hazard exists. The higher the value of these company-specific capabilities, the more worthwhile it is to take out protection, first in the form of relational contracting and eventually in the form of vertical integration (backward). This can be done by acquisition of a supplier (this is how Starbucks entered wholesaling) or by greenfield investment (launching a new operation, as did Loblaws in setting up an R&D unit).

VERTICAL INTEGRATION TO COPE WITH ENVIRONMENTAL UNCERTAINTY

An uncertain environment is one that is *difficult to forecast*. This may be because the environment is very dynamic (fast changing) or very complex (therefore, difficult to grasp). Such volatile environments pose special challenges.[37] Should the manufacturer integrate forward in order to meet them?

This very controversial issue has generated mixed evidence. One school of thought holds that a manufacturer needs to take control in order to cope with this environment. It can then learn more about the context and carry out a coherent strategy for dealing with it. Accordingly, it is argued that uncertainty demands integration.

An opposing school of thought likens managing under uncertainty to betting on the winner of a race among many comparable horses: One bet is as good as another, and most bets will lose anyway. By this viewpoint, the firm is urged not to bet until the race is far enough along that it is possible to improve one's odds by guessing who is winning (or at least avoiding those who are losing). Accordingly, the manufacturer is advised not to commit to any distribution system, including its own system, unless and until the uncertainty is reduced to a level that makes it easier to ascertain what is the best way to distribute in this environment. This means outsourcing. The argument is that uncertainty demands distributing through third parties, changing third parties as the situation demands (committing to no one).

Proponents of vertical integration retort that it is defeatist to wait until the race is well along to place a bet. By integrating, the firm can alter the course of the race! Critics respond that it is arrogant of the manufacturer to imagine that it possesses such wisdom. Better to switch from one third party to another, and finally settle on the best option (the best third party, or one's own means of going to market) when it can be ascertained what *is* the best option.

The proponents retort that the best option may be closed by the time the manufacturer is ready to settle on it. A key feature of this argument has to do with how easy it is to change the marketing channel as the environment changes. Proponents of vertical integration often underestimate the difficulty of making real organizational change happen once in-house distribution is in place.

Both sides of the debate have valid arguments. How to incorporate them into one approach? A useful frame to resolve this issue is to complicate it slightly (see Figure 7.2).

One begins by asking whether there are (or will be) substantial company-specific capabilities involved in distribution. If not, the firm can easily change third parties and can find new third parties. This flexibility is of great value in volatile environments. *Absent significant specificity, uncertainty favors outsourcing.*

But if specificities are substantial, flexibility is already lost. The firm will become locked into its third parties, and the manufacturer faces the worst of all worlds: Small-numbers bargaining in an environment that requires constant adaptation. The result will be endless bargaining, high levels of opportunism, and high transaction costs. *In the presence of significant specificity, uncertainty favors vertical integration forward.*

There is, of course, a third argument: In the presence of significant specificities, don't go into the business at all! To justify the overhead of vertically integrating, the business must be very promising, and yet, the nature of uncertainty is such that it is difficult to tell how promising the business really is. This conundrum can be solved by avoiding it altogether. Perhaps the most common approach to distributing in uncertain environments when specificities are high is not to enter the market at all. Because it is difficult to observe that which firms decided *not* to do, it is not known how often such business activities are never undertaken. Yet, non–market entry, although difficult to notice, is always present—and is frequently attributed to other factors.

For example, multinational business activity occurs at very low levels in sub-Saharan Africa, even though rich potential markets exist in a region of more than 700 million peo-

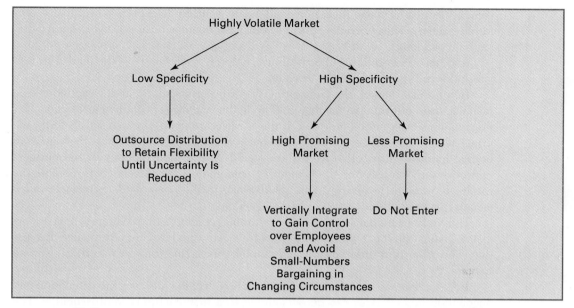

FIGURE 7.2 **How Environmental Uncertainty Impacts Vertical Integration**

ple. This is often attributed to high political risk and lack of economic development. Yet multinationals operate in other risky, underdeveloped markets, many of which were largely ignored only a decade earlier. Why continue to overlook this region? One explanation is that (1) many African markets are little known and potentially highly volatile and (2) the lack of distribution infrastructure implies that much of what the manufacturer does to distribute will be idiosyncratic in that market. The combination of uncertainty and specificity, as opposed to uncertainty alone, may help explain low investment in Africa (of course, many other factors contribute to the phenomenon). In contrast, some politically risky Asian countries have better distribution infrastructure, permitting multinationals to find qualified third parties already operating in the market. With specificity removed, uncertainty can be handled by outsourcing, encouraging more market entry.

It is noteworthy that market entry by some firms encourages more entry, and that it does so by reducing specificity. Once a number of multinational corporations (MNCs) have entered a market, they create a pool of local personnel who know their procedures. This makes it easier to find qualified third parties, qualified to work in a manner that is nonstandard in the market but standard in MNCs. India, for example, has seen growth in the number of qualified joint venture partners and distributors as a cumulative result of decades of multinational investment.

VERTICAL INTEGRATION TO REDUCE PERFORMANCE AMBIGUITY

Thus far we have covered scenarios (specificity, rarity, specificity and uncertainty) in which competition in the market for distribution services fails to yield efficient outcomes. They turn on one idea: Few bidders are available to replace a firm that is performing poorly. This, of course, presumes that the manufacturer can tell that outsourcing is not working.

Another scenario favoring vertical integration is not a failure of the market to provide bidders. It is a failure of information.

In a normal market, the contracting firm (the principal, or, in our exposition, the manufacturer) offers to pay an organization (in the language of contracting, an agent) for distribution services to be provided. If the services are not performed satisfactorily, the principal either negotiates for better outcomes with the agent or finds another agent. In normal markets, many other agents are qualified, and their bidding for the business improves the efficiency of the principal's outcomes. This process (bid, monitor the results, reconsider the arrangement, rebid) works well—*assuming the principal can tell what it is getting.*

Herein lies a fundamental problem with market contracting. When there is *performance ambiguity*, the manufacturer cannot discern what level of performance it is getting. Therefore, the process by which market contracting improves outcomes cannot function.[38]

For example, let us take the selling function, which combines the promotion and negotiation flows.[39] This can be outsourced to a manufacturers' representative. The manufacturer knows the rep's performance in terms of sales. If sales levels are a good indicator of performance, the manufacturer has little performance ambiguity. And this is the case most of the time because most sales forces are charged primarily with selling, and the manufacturer usually has some idea what level of sales is reasonable to expect.

But if the product is radically new, say, a discontinuous innovation—unlike anything that currently exists—current sales may not be a good indicator of performance. This is because radically new products diffuse slowly. In addition, no one knows what is a reasonable sales level for such a product. The result is that if the manufacturers' representative goes for long periods with low or no sales, the manufacturer does not know whether it should be dissatisfied and search for a new rep. *Fundamentally, it is impossible to tell how well the rep is doing. There are no baselines and many excuses for failure. Hence, performance ambiguity is high.*

In general, one class of circumstances creating performance ambiguity occurs when the sorts of measures that *would* indicate performance are unknown, as is the case for the discontinuous innovation. In this case, the principal may vertically integrate forward not to circumvent small-numbers bargaining but to *gain information and control.*

By monitoring what salespeople are doing in detail, the principal can discern excuses from genuine reasons for low sales. The principal can also acquire, via its salespeople, market research that helps establish the accurate baseline of performance. Further, and this is perhaps the most powerful advantage, the principal can control the salespeople's behavior. Failing good indicators of achievement, the principal can fall back on the ability to direct salespeople to do what it considers best to develop the market. Instead of rewarding for outputs (achievements), the principal can reward for inputs (activities). In the absence of good information about what outputs are and what they should be, inputs are the next best substitute.

In general, market contracting yields indicators of current results. Where current results are not good indicators of performance, there is ambiguity. The principal may raise long-term efficiency by vertically integrating forward *to gain information* and *to gain the ability to direct behavior*.

When are current results poor indicators of performance? First, when performance indicators do not exist. Second, when measures of performance output do exist, but the measures themselves are of poor quality. For example, pharmaceutical firms are unable to tell how much their salespeople are selling in many markets. Salespeople ("detailers") call on specifiers (such as doctors) and describe ("detail") the drugs, hopefully in a persuasive fashion. Specifiers in turn prescribe the drugs, which leads the patient to ask the pharmacist for the drug, which leads the pharmacist to purchase the drug, often from a wholesaler.

Pharmaceutical firms do have measures of performance (sales): They know how much they sell and ship to wholesalers and pharmacy chains. But to bring this information down to the selling level involves (1) approximating the movement of stock over time from wholesalers and chains to the individual pharmacy, and (2) at the pharmacy level, matching up the drug to the person who was the specifier. These approximations can be done, but they are so arbitrary that it is difficult to consider them accurate and timely indicators of the relationship between detailing and sales. Thus, the path from sales activity to orders is so convoluted that drug companies could not tell if their salespeople were effective. How, then, to compensate a contract sales force?

In general, measures are poor when they are untimely or inaccurate. Late or inaccurate information, or no information, creates performance ambiguity. This performance ambiguity induces pharmaceutical firms to employ a sales force, and to use the power of the employer to monitor and direct activity (calling on defined specifiers at a certain frequency, detailing particular drugs on a call, reporting back to the firm the reaction of the specifier). In this way, the firm satisfies itself that salespeople are doing the right thing (detailing "correctly" and providing market research). Of course, these activities are thought to create performance (sales). If this belief is incorrect, the pharmaceutical firm will be unknowingly wasting resources. This is the risk and responsibility cost of vertically integrating. (*Note*: In some markets, specialty research firms have arisen that purchase detailed prescription information from pharmacists, consolidate it into reports at the level of the specifier, and sell the information to pharmaceutical firms. This reduces performance ambiguity in this sector in many markets.)

The fundamental issue is that the outputs, or achievements, of a third party would not serve as good indicators of performance, either because there is no real baseline against which to compare results or because the data that are obtainable are of poor quality. The solution, in either case, is to vertically integrate in order to direct employees to perform what are believed to be appropriate behaviors, in lieu of tallying their results and compensating them for results obtained.

If the solution to performance ambiguity is to monitor and direct activities, rather than to tally achieved results, one might ask how vertical integration really solves the problem. Would it not be adequate to write a contract with another organization specifying what activities are desired, and then let that organization do the monitoring and directing? After all, the essence of outsourcing is delegating to another organization. Why not delegate the *execution of activities*, as opposed to the achievement of results?

Technically, this is indeed possible. The problem is that it is impossible to verify that the activities are actually being performed. To verify the claim, it is necessary to monitor or audit activity, and this violates the independent status of the third party.

Why not bypass auditing, instead placing one's trust in the third party's promise that it will execute the desired activities? This, too, is possible, and it is sometimes done. However, it is very difficult to know when a party can be trusted. Many a firm has come to regret having placed its trust in a third party. Although trustworthy parties exist, it is exceedingly difficult to know whom they are. It is also difficult, though not impossible, to create incentive structures such that the agent has no desire to betray the principal's trust—and the principal has no desire to take advantage of the agent's promise, once given. The solution of mutual trust is covered in Chapter 11.

SUMMARY OF THE DECISION FRAMEWORK

The logic of the economic argument for greater degrees of vertical integration is summarized in Figure 7.3. This shows the nature and direction of the effects of noncompetitive markets on the elements of efficiency.

What about the normal case, in which markets are not thin? Under these circumstances, the critic of the initial outsourcing decision has made a good case for vertical integration (see Figure 7.4), given that substantial business is at stake and the firm has the resources, if these circumstances prevail.

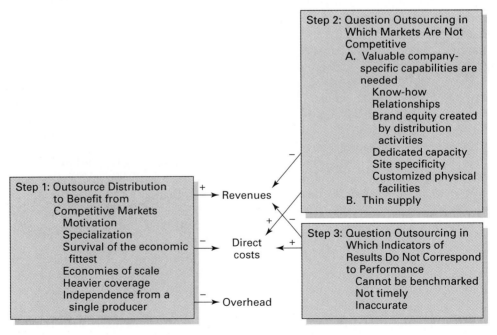

FIGURE 7.3 **The Effects of Outsourcing**

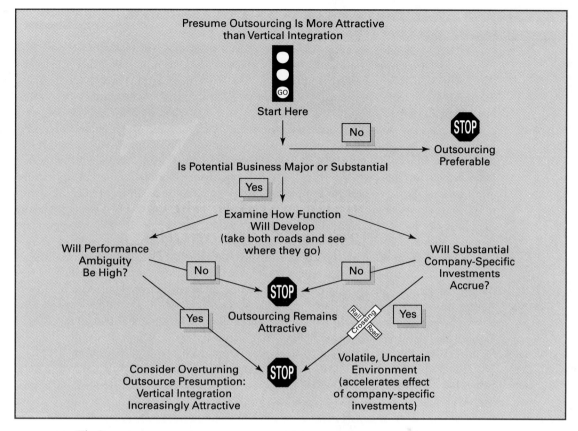

FIGURE 7.4 **Road Map to the Vertical Integration Decision**

1. Company-specific capabilities are likely to become substantial. These can be intangible (know-how, relationships, downstream activities creating brand equity) or tangible (dedicated capacity, site specificity, physical customization). The effect of idiosyncratic assets is magnified by environmental uncertainty.

2. Performance ambiguity, due to no measures of results or poor measures of results, forces the firm to monitor and direct activity rather than tally up and pay for performance.

Where the prosecution can make the case that markets work poorly, but vertical integration is too drastic a solution, relational contracting is an efficient solution.

Thus far, the argument has been strictly normative: What should the firm do to maximize long-term efficiency? Although the firm can never calculate the numbers—at least, to an accountant's satisfaction—the direction of the arguments is clear, given the premise that, when in doubt, outsourcing is best. But do managers really follow these guidelines? In competitive industries, the evidence indicates that they do, eventually and roughly. We now turn to the evidence as to what firms really do and when they deviate from efficiency-maximizing normative prescriptions.

VERTICAL INTEGRATION AS A CLASSROOM OR AS AN OPTION

According to economic theory, efficiency is a paramount criterion. Firms that overlook it should be swiftly eliminated by the relentless workings of the market mechanism. Assuming the normative theory is correct, there should be no divergence between theory and practice.[40]

Of course, some divergence exists for a variety of reasons. Markets are never perfectly competitive. Firms can subsidize shortcomings in one domain with successes in another domain, keeping the erring firm in the market. Barriers to exit keep the market from swiftly forcing the departure of inefficient firms. Noneconomic considerations enter in, such as a government, employee group, or investor desirous of keeping a firm in business or of encouraging business practices for multiple reasons. Decision makers may be more focused on the short run than on the long run. Above all, managers are human and not machines at the service of an efficiency-maximizing investor.

Many of them, if given the opportunity, would choose vertical integration, reasoning that more control is always better than less. This leads to optimism: Managers frequently underestimate the direct costs and overhead of vertical integration, while overstating the increase in revenues that is likely. This is particularly the case when they have little experience with the functions they propose to integrate. Taken all together, it is inevitable that the long-run efficiency of performing a single function is not the only factor at work when firms make vertical integration decisions in distribution.

When a firm makes a vertical integration choice with no clear efficiency rationale, two other effectiveness rationales are frequently offered. Vertical integration is presented as a classroom or as an option.

Vertical integration as a classroom is when having operations in another part of the value chain may be justified as a window of observation, therefore a way to learn. An example is Luxottica, the eyeglass maker. The firm is majority owned by Leonardo Del Vecchio, whose rags-to-riches story turns on becoming a worker in an eyeglass factory, as a way to leave an orphanage. Del Vecchio became a highly skilled artisan, founding Luxottica in 1961. Today, his self-description anchors him firmly in production: "I am a technician, a producer. It is thanks to our products, our quality, and our productivity that we have made our way."[41] Luxottica's Italian factory is noted for extreme productivity, which enables the firm to compete with lower-cost Asian production.

Lens Crafters offers an enormous selection of frames, offers eye examinations, and manufactures prescription glasses on the premises in one hour. It has a substantial presence in the U.S. market, which is the largest and most representative in the world. Del Vecchio justifies his purchase of Lens Crafters by saying, "It's an ideal observatory to know what the market wants."[42] He has other "observatories" as well in a web of exclusive wholesalers serving the European channel of individual opticians. Thus, Del Vecchio uses both intermediate and extreme degrees of vertical integration as a way to understand end-user demand for eyeglasses.

Luxottica uses this market knowledge in its dealings with designers. Even such powerful names as Sergio Tacchini are obliged to submit their designs for consideration, modification, and approval by Luxottica's house technicians. Designers tolerate this control because Luxottica is a proven performer and the world's largest eyeglass producer.

The producer also uses its market knowledge to forecast eyewear fashions 18 months in advance of making 500 new models a year. In short, relational governance and vertical integration give Luxottica expertise power (Chapter 8) upstream. The knowledge also drives the firm's growth strategy. Luxottica paid a high price in 1999 to purchase Ray-Ban (sunglasses). Del Vecchio justifies the price by citing a need to diversify out of prescription eyewear. He fears that corneal surgery to correct vision will reduce the size of the market dramatically in coming years.

Learning is a rationale often given for some vertical integration, forward or backward. For example:

- Pork packers justify their miniscule 1 percent vertical integration backward into raising hogs, saying this is a way for them to learn about their suppliers so as to stay capable of exercising quality control. They cite a pressing need to demonstrate their reliability (in quality) to downstream channel members and to control their risk, due to their investments in branded products. Why no more than 1 percent? Close relations with hog suppliers supplement the packers' closeness to the market, raising their share outside of independent market contracting to 7 percent. This is an enormous business in units, offering an adequate classroom. And because there is little that is company specific or uncertain, and the market for supplying pigs is not thin, there is no need to integrate on a larger scale.
- Automakers justify forward integration as a way to understand how buyers will react to the prospect of Internet sales.
- Specialty coffee drinkers seek variety and stimulation. Specialty coffee producers use their limited retail presence to experiment with new beans and roasting methods and to monitor changes in preferences.
- Jean Delatour learns about customer tastes by making jewelry to the buyer's design.
- Private-label efforts focus supermarkets on making sense out of the enormous databases they generate by scanning transactions.

In short, integration forward or backward is often justified as a way to learn, a sort of classroom–laboratory–observation post. The decision to integrate is not made on the basis of the stand-alone efficiency gains of the flow being integrated. It is made on grounds that integration increases effectiveness (profits) for the operation as a whole.

Is this a sensible economic rationale, or is it a rationalization? It is difficult to know. Certainly, learning is a lofty objective, easy to invoke to explain any act of vertical integration, no matter how ill advised it might be on operating grounds. In a world of omniscient accountants, the inefficiencies that accrue would be calculated and charged to budgets for R&D or market research. This would throw a spotlight on this resource allocation decision and spark debate as to its merits.

This is not to say that learning is not a worthwhile investment. It is no accident that the most large-scale integration in our examples (Jean Delatour and Luxottica) occurs in fashion-sensitive industries, where massive and frequent change is certain but its direction is unknown. But in many cases it is difficult to know whether learning is an economically justifiable reason to vertically integrate.

Vertical integration as an option is a somewhat related argument. In finance, purchasing an option means paying for the right to write a contact now, to be exercised (or not exercised, at the buyer's option) at a specified future date. If not exercised, the option expires. Options are justified as a form of insurance: You pay a relatively small amount now in case of catastrophe later. But in this theory, the catastrophe is often of the opportunity cost variety (I could have made a profit if I could buy now at yesterday's price).

The idea has been generalized to marketing strategy.[43] A strategic option is a relatively limited investment now, made to hold open the door to making a greater investment later, should developments prove this to be a good idea. Many joint ventures are justified on this basis. Like a financial option, a strategic option can be exercised (converted to a substantial investment) or allowed to expire (dismantled or downsized). The key is not to hold an option indefinitely; this is mere indecisiveness, rather than purposeful hedging against risk. An options strategist makes the decision whether to exercise or dispose of its opportunity as soon as it becomes clear which way to go.

Superficially, this looks like the learning rationale. The difference is that an investment in learning is constant: Jean Delatour and Luxottica know fashions change constantly, so they keep a permanent classroom on a large scale. An investment in an option is meant to be temporary. It is a wedge, designed to preserve an opportunity until management can figure out whether to pursue it.

This means that using vertical integration as an option is sensible when sea shifts occur in an unpredictable manner. This occurs in high-velocity environments, such as sectors of the information technology industry.[44] It is one reason why firms such as Sun Microsystems, IBM, and Hewlett-Packard regularly keep a large staff on payroll to handle some channel flows in some sectors.

Options can turn out to be useful even in more stable environments. For example, Woolworth's is an old U.S.-based retailer, which became preeminent in the early 1900s by a strategy of selling a large assortment of mundane items at very low prices. Over time, other formats made its strategy obsolete. Management invested heavily in trying to save the old format and lost huge sums in so doing. Ultimately, an experiment in specialty retailing that it launched in 1974 kept Woolworth's going. The experiment—Foot Locker—gave Woolworth's (now the Venator Group) an option, which it exercised to reinvent itself as a chain of athletic specialty stores (including Lady Foot Locker and Kids Foot Locker).[45]

These options are something like paying for insurance coverage: They drain resources steadily, but can pay off handsomely when you most need the protection. Like learning, option thinking is a rationale that can be invoked to justify any vertical integration decision in channels. Also like learning, it is a rationale that sometimes makes sense—and often masks a rationalization.

SUMMARY

Who should do the work of distribution, in whole or in part? Should it be the same party doing manufacturing and distribution? Should two parties split the work? If so, how? Splitting the work means sharing the costs (resources, risk, responsibility) and the benefits (or lack of them!). The fundamental idea behind this analysis is that any player should respect that the work of any other player requires competencies. Therefore no party should merely assume that it can take over another party's functions and perform them better or more cheaply. In short, arrogance has no place in a vertical integration decision, which should be undertaken with respect for the competence of another type of organization.

Being committed to a system (such as outsourcing) is not the same thing as being committed to a given member of the system. Vertical integration is too often used as a way to go around unsatisfactory results from or relationships with another organization. If this is the rationale, the firm should first ask whether the current relationship can be made to work better (using the techniques in this book, for example), or whether another third party would be more effective. Vertical integration is a drastic step that invariably raises overhead, and that often fails to reduce direct costs or increase revenue. The step should not be undertaken lightly.

Many readers will be surprised at the assertion that markets for distribution services are frequently efficient. This does not mean that a firm cannot do better by vertically integrating. But it does mean that, to get better results, the firm must be prepared to make a very substantial commitment and often to operate in a manner that is unusual for its industry or market. For vertical integration to improve on outsourcing, the firm must take large risks and make substantial commitments.

It is never possible to estimate transaction costs, production costs, and efficiency precisely under any scenario, vertically integrated or otherwise. However, the framework presented here allows the decision maker to forecast the direction in which these costs will go and to arrive at a rough approximation of which system works best in the longer term.

A decision path is suggested, beginning with the assumption that outsourcing distribution is superior, to profit from six advantages of the outsider: motivation, specialization, survival of the fittest, economies of scale, coverage, and independence. The next step involves questioning this assumption under these circumstances: company-specific capabilities (especially when combined with environmental uncertainty), thin markets (rare, rather than idiosyncratic), and performance ambiguity.

Some readers find themselves uncomfortable with opportunism, one of the fundamental ideas underlying this analysis. They find self-interest seeking in a deceitful or dishonest manner to be a concept that is negative, discouraging, perhaps unrepresentative of human nature (or perhaps representative of the worst of human nature). However, it is important not to personalize the discussion. Opportunistic behavior is a characteristic of organizations interacting with each other in conducting business. This is not to say that it is the nature of two people interacting with each other in their private lives. Further, to focus on opportunism does not mean that all organizations are opportunistic at all times. Some are, and it is difficult to forecast in advance who will be.

An important reason to undertake vertical integration is to gain market research or to create an option, to be evaluated in the future. Thus, in certain circumstances it is justified to integrate distribution not to do a better job of distributing but to do a better job of learning or to hold open a door to a future investment. Integration forward or backward is often a means of improving overall performance, not improving the performance per se.

The vertical integration decision is fundamental, because it drives the firm's capabilities for the long term and is difficult to reverse. Other chapters that follow cover other methods of improving the performance of marketing channel flows. "Owning it all" is a solution of last resort to the problems of distributing effectively and efficiently.

Discussion Questions

1. Assume you are the manufacturer of a broad line of moderately priced furniture. When would you seriously consider owning your own retail outlets? What factors would you take into account in making your decision?

2. Is it likely that vertical disintegration is typical of growing industries whereas vertical integration is typical of declining industries? Explain.

3. Debate the pros and cons of forward vertical integration of wholesaling functions by manufacturers and by retailers.

4. According to Bucklin (see Chapter 2, note 1), the issue of channel performance focuses on the conflict that exists between two major dimensions of channel performance. On the one hand, consumers and users are concerned primarily with lowering the costs of the goods and services sold and therefore with reducing the costs of distribution. On the other hand, buyers want to benefit from and receive some marketing services in conjunction with the good or service they purchase. However, provision of these services increases the cost of distribution. Compare and contrast vertical integration and outsourcing relative to the performance dimensions mentioned by Bucklin. Which would tend to be superior overall?

5. A theme that appears in advertisements for stores owned by manufacturers is "Buy factory direct at our store. You'll save money. We can offer you low prices because we cut out the middleman." Evaluate this argument. Is it valid? Would you expect a factory store to offer lower prices? Why or why not? Are there other differences you would expect to find between a manufacturer-owned store and an independent retailer?

Notes

1. "A First-Party Perspective," *Material Handling Engineering*, 52 (June 1997), pp. 51–52.

2. Nathalie Villard, "Cet Italien Fabrique Toutes les Lunettes du Monde," *Capital*, 10 (June 1999), pp. 63–64.

3. Daniel Lyons, "Turning to the Channel to Stay Afloat," *Computer Reseller News*, December 15, 1997, pp. 117, 124.

4. Richard Wise and Peter Baumgartner, "Go Downstream: The New Profit Imperative in Manufacturing," *Harvard Business Review*, 50 (September–October 1999), pp. 133–41.

5. "When Eight Arms Are Better Than One," *The Economist*, 350 (1998), pp. 71–72.

6. Jacqueline Kochak, "A Hill of Beans," *Restaurant Business*, 97 (July 1998), pp. 52–53.

7. Raphael Sellerin, "Jean Delatour: Le Category Killer," *LSA*, 10 (September 9, 1999), pp. 62–63.

8. John D. Lawrence, V. James Rhodes, Glenn A. Grimes, et al., "Vertical Coordination in the U.S. Pork Industry: Status, Motivation, and Expectations," *Agribusiness*, 13, no. 1 (1997), pp. 21–31.

9. David Dunne and Chakravarthi Narasimhan, "The New Appeal of Private Labels," *Harvard Business Review*, 53 (May–June, 1999), pp. 41–52.

10. E. Raymond Corey, Frank V. Cespedes, and V. Kasturi Rangan, *Going to Market: Distribution Systems for Industrial Products* (Boston: Harvard Business School Press, 1989).

√ 11. Erin Anderson and Barton A. Weitz, "Make or Buy Decisions: Vertical Integration and Marketing Productivity," *Sloan Management Review*, 27 (spring 1986), pp. 3–20.

12. Louis W. Stern and Torger Reve, "Distribution Channels as Political Economies: A Framework for Comparative Analysis," *Journal of Marketing*, 44 (summer 1980), pp. 52–64.

13. Jean-Francois Hennart, "Explaining the Swollen Middle: Why Most Transactions Are a Mix of 'Market' and 'Hierarchy'," *Organization Science*, 4, no. 4, pp. 529–47.

14. Jan B. Heide, "Interorganizational Governance in Marketing Channels," *Journal of Marketing*, 58 (1994), pp. 71–85.

15. Oliver E. Williamson, "Comparative Economic Organization: The Analysis of Discrete Structural Alternatives," *Administrative Science Quarterly*, 36 (June 1991), pp. 269–96.

16. F. Robert Dwyer and Sejo Oh, "A Transaction Cost Perspective on Vertical Contractual Structure and Interchannel Competitive Strategies," *Journal of Marketing*, 52, no. 2 (April 1988), pp. 21–34.

17. Oliver E. Williamson, *The Mechanisms of Governance* (New York: Oxford University Press, 1996).

18. Mark Bergen, Shantanu Dutta, and Orville C. Walker Jr., "Agency Relationships in Marketing: A Review of the Implications and Applications of Agency and Related Theories," *Journal of Marketing*, 56, no. 3 (1992), pp. 1–24.

19. This is part of the general migration of consumption away from products and towards services. This theme is developed in Wise and Baumgartner, "Go Downstream."

20. Aric Rindfleisch and Jan B. Heide, "Transaction Cost Analysis: Present, Past, and Future," *Journal of Marketing*, 41 (October 1997), pp. 30–54.

21. Erin Anderson and Richard L. Oliver, "Perspectives on Behavior Based versus Outcome-Based Sales Force Control Systems," *Journal of Marketing*, 51 (October 1987), pp. 76–88.

22. Vern Terpstra and Bernard L. Simonin, "Strategic Alliances in the Triad: An Exploratory Study," *Journal of International Marketing*, 5, no. 1 (1993), pp. 4–26.

23. George John, "An Empirical Investigation of Some Antecedents of Opportunism in a Marketing Channel," *Journal of Marketing Research*, 21 (August 1984), pp. 278–89.

24. Erin Anderson, "Determinants of Opportunistic Behavior: An Empirical Comparison of Integrated and Independent Channels," *Journal of Economic Behavior and Organization*, 9 (May 1988), pp. 247–64.

25. Benjamin Klein, "Why Hold-Ups Occur: The Self-Enforcing Range of Contractual Relationships," *Economic Inquiry*, 34 (July 1996), pp. 444–63.

26. Scott E. Masten, James W. Meehan Jr., and Edward A. Snyder, "The Costs of Organization," *Journal of Law, Economics, and Organization*, 7, no. 1 (1991), pp. 1–25.

27. Anne T. Coughlan, "Competition and Cooperation in Marketing Channel Choice: Theory and Application," *Marketing Science*, 4, no. 2 (spring 1985), pp. 110–29; Timothy W. McGuire and Richard Staelin, "An Industry Equilibrium Analysis of Downstream Vertical Integration," *Marketing Science*, 2, no. 2 (1983), pp. 161–91.

28. Gary L. Frazier, Robert E. Spekman, and Charles R. O'Neal, "Just-in-Time Exchange Relationships in Industrial Markets," *Journal of Marketing*, 52, no. 4 (October 1988), pp. 52–67.

29. Benjamin Klein and Kevin M. Murphy, "Vertical Restraints as Contract Enforcement Mechanisms," *Journal of Law and Economics*, 31 (October 1988), pp. 265–97.

30. Dunne and Narasimhan, "The New Appeal of Private Labels."

31. Timothy J. Muris, David T. Schefman, and Pablo T. Spiller, "Strategy and Transaction Costs: The Organization of Distribution in the Carbonated Soft Drink Industry," *Journal of Economics and Management Strategy*, 1 (spring 1992), pp. 83–128.

32. Joan Holleran, "Strength Through Sense: 1999 Company of the Year: Coca-Cola Enterprises, Inc.," *Beverage Industry*, 90 (January 1999), pp. 16–20; Dyan Machan, "There's Something About Henry," *Forbes*, 162 (October 5, 1998), pp. 82–84; Lauren R. Rublin, "Offerings in the Offing: Pepsi Play," *Barron's*, 79 (March 1, 1999), pp. 34–35.

33. Stephen Craig Pirrong, "Contracting Practices in Bulk Shipping Markets: A Transactions Cost Explanation," *Journal of Law, Economics, and Organization*, 36 (October 1993), pp. 937–76.

34. This example is from Alfred D. Chandler, *The Visible Hand: The Managerial Revolution in American Business* (Cambridge, MA: Belknap Press, 1977).

35. Allen Weiss and Erin Anderson, "Converting from Independent to Employee Sales Forces: The Role of Perceived Switching Costs," *Journal of Marketing Research*, 24 (February 1992), pp. 101–15.

36. This discussion is based on Adam J. Fein and Sandy D. Jap, "Manage Consolidation in the Distribution Channel," *Sloan Management Review*, 41 (fall 1999), pp. 61–72.

37. F. Robert Dwyer and M. Ann Walsh, "Environmental Relationships of the Internal Political Economy of Marketing Channels," *Journal of Marketing Research*, 22, no. 4 (November 1985), pp. 397–414.

38. Bergen, Dutta, and Walker, "Agency Relationships in Marketing."

39. Erin Anderson, "The Salesperson as Outside Agent or Employee: A Transaction-Cost Analysis," *Marketing Science*, 4 (summer 1985), pp. 234–54.

40. Erin Anderson, "Selling Efficiency and Choice of Integrated or Independent Sales Forces: A Test of Darwinian Economics," *Management Science*, 34 (May 1988), pp. 599–618.

41. Patrick Bonazza, "Le 'Signore' des Lunettes," *Le Point*, May 14, 1999, pp. 107–11. Quotation from p. 109.

42. Ibid., p. 111.

43. Bruce Kogut and Nalin Kulatilaka, "Options Thinking and Platform Investments: Investing in Opportunity," *California Management Review*, 36, no. 2 (1994), pp. 52–71.

44. Jay B. Barney, "How a Firm's Capabilities Affect Boundary Decisions," *Sloan Management Review*, 40 (spring 1999), pp. 137–45.

45. Peter J. Williamson, "Strategy as Options on the Future," *Sloan Management Review*, 40 (spring 1999), pp. 117–26.

8

Channel Power: Getting It, Using It, Keeping It

LEARNING OBJECTIVES

After reading this chapter, you will:

- View power as a tool, without value connotations, and explain why it is critical to marketing channels
- Explain the consequences of using power to appropriate the rewards earned by other channel members
- Understand the relation between power and dependence and explain when dependence exists
- Distinguish five sources of power and explain when each is effective and why
- Describe how to build power
- Explain how to use power as a tool to manage conflict and increase cooperation
- Understand the importance of the balance of dependence, and whether the weaker party should exit the relationship or take countermeasures
- Distinguish six strategies for converting power into influence, and project a channel member's reaction to each influence strategy
- Describe how the framing of an influence attempt drives the target's reaction

A good way to start an argument is to ask a roomful of people to define *power*. Several will offer definitions with confidence, only to discover their ideas generate controversy. Others will concede they are not sure how to define power, but will insist that a definition is not really necessary because they can recognize power in any case ("I know it when I see it"). Experience shows, however, that many of us possess a false confidence: We really don't know how to recognize power, although we are quite sure we do. We see power when it doesn't exist. Conversely, we overlook power when it does exist. And we know that it has far-reaching consequences, whether we can define power neatly. Power is a subject of endless fascination, and rightly so.

In marketing channels, getting power, using it correctly, and keeping it are subjects of paramount importance. Virtually every element of marketing channels is permeated by considerations of power. These channels are systems made up of players who depend on each other. Interdependence must be managed, and power is the way to do it. The organizations who are players in a marketing channel must acquire power and use it wisely, first for the channel to work together to generate value, and second for each player to claim its fair share of that value.

How the players gain and use their power today drives whether they can keep it tomorrow. Many different sources and uses of power exist: They are not equivalent. Some are efficacious in the short term but disastrous in the long term. While for others, it is the opposite. Therefore, it behooves each member of a channel to understand where the power lies and weigh the best way to use it—and to react to the power of the others.

This chapter begins by considering the fundamental questions: What is the nature of power? Is it good or bad? and Why is it so important in marketing channels? We then turn to how to index power in a channel relationship. We cover two ways to estimate how much power is in a relationship. One way is to inventory five types of power. The other is to estimate how dependent each organization is on the other. We discuss how to deal with imbalances in power, and what the consequences are of using one kind of power rather than another. Finally, we cover how to convert power (which is a latent ability) into influence.

Over the last three decades, very substantial resources have gone into studying the dynamics of power in actual distribution channels. This chapter focuses on presenting the *major conclusions of this enormous body of research* and examining their *implications for the practicing manager*. The generalizations presented here are field tested. Readers interested more in how these conclusions were developed and tested should consult the references contained in this chapter's endnotes.

THE NATURE OF POWER

Power Defined

Power is the ability of one channel member (A) to get another channel member (B) to do something it *otherwise would not have done*. Simply put, power is a potential for influence.

Power is rather difficult to diagnose, because false positives are common. That is, power seems to exist when one firm (the *target* of influence) follows the path that another firm (the *influencer*) desires. This is cooperation—but it isn't power if the target would have done it anyway, regardless of the other firm.

For example, a manufacturer would like to see a distributor cut its prices on the manufacturer's brands. Next month, the distributor lowers those prices. Was the manufacturer's power at work? Perhaps not. The power could lie elsewhere: Customers could have provoked the price cut, or the distributor's competitors, or even the manufacturer's competitors. These are outside forces. Perhaps the initiative came from inside the distributor organization. The distributor may be moving to a strategy of higher volume at lower margins, for example, or may be clearing out old inventory. What looks like the manufacturer exercise of power over the distributor may in fact be an act of free will, or a response to the power of the environment or of other players. *Influence* means altering *what would have been* the course of events. Exercising power means exerting influence.

Seeming acts of compliance are common in channels. This sort of misdiagnosis of power (a "false positive") is hazardous. False positives lead A to overestimate its ability to exert influence, and therefore to make change happen. This optimism leads A to undertake channel initiatives that are doomed to fail. It is important to understand how a channel member has power in order to tell whether it has the potential for influence.

Power is hypothetical, speculative, impossible to verify precisely. Any ability that is unused is easy to overlook. And no one can be sure what would have happened in the normal course of events anyway. This means *"false negatives" are also common in channels*. Channel member B can be acting under A's influence without knowing it, indeed, while denying it. For example, B may believe it is freely pursuing its economic self-interest—without realizing how much A has framed the cost–benefit trade-offs (exercising reward power) so that B's self-interest nicely coincides with A's desires.

Is Power Good or Bad?

Power is an emotionally charged term. It is laden with negative connotations: abuse, oppression, exploitation, inequity, brutality. And properly so: Power can be used to do great damage. In channels, it can be used to force a member to help generate value but not to receive compensation for it. Used in this way, power is (and should be) condemned.

But this critical view of power is one sided. Because power is the potential for influence, great benefits can be achieved by the judicious use of power to drive a channel to operate in a coordinated way.

For example, Hewlett-Packard is a pioneer in using the principle of postponement to achieve mass-customization at low prices.[1] H-P designs printers that consist of standardized independent modules that can be combined and assembled easily to make many variations of the core product. H-P once made a complete printer in a factory, then shipped it to the channel. Because customers demanded many versions of each printer, this policy resulted in high inventories, but of what turned out to be the wrong products.

In response, H-P used its considerable power to push light manufacturing and assembly out of the factory and down into the channel, a move that generated conflict. But the result is lower inventories and fewer stockouts, an ideal combination that is very difficult to achieve (Chapter 16). The end-customer gains by having greater choice, even while paying a lower price. The downstream channel member gains by being able to offer its customers greater choice while holding lower inventory. H-P gains by expanding the market and taking a greater share, all the while building brand equity for the future. And H-P, desirous of preserving its sterling reputation for fair play, does not attempt to appropriate the downstream channel members' share of the wealth the channel has generated.

It is tempting to believe that H-P could have achieved this win–win result without wielding power, or pressuring its reluctant channel members. Indeed, H-P is also an exemplar of building strategic alliances with distributors (Chapter 11): Why, then, did it need to exercise power? Had the channel seen how well it would work to assume some of the factory's functions, channel members would surely have adopted postponement of manufacturing of their own free will. But this clarity, this certainty, exists only with the benefit of hindsight. Mass-customization via postponement of stages of assembly was a radical idea, and even now is not widely used in most industries. Embracing the idea at that time would have required an act of faith. Absent faith, it actually required H-P's usage of power.

So is power good or bad? Like a hammer, *power is a tool*. A tool is neutral. We can judge how someone uses the tool, but then we are deciding whether the *usage* is good or bad. Power is merely an implement. It is value neutral. *Throughout this book, power is treated as a term with no connotations, either positive or negative.*

Why Marketing Channels Require Power

Marketing channel members must work with each other to serve end-users. But this interdependence does not mean that what is good for one is good for all. Each channel member is seeking its own profit. *Maximizing the system's profits is not the same as maximizing each member's profits.* All else constant, each member of the system is better off to the extent that it can avoid costs (or push them onto someone else), while garnering revenues (perhaps by taking them from someone else). And one party's cost may generate disproportionate benefit to another party.

For example, consider the scenario of a manufacturer who would like to set a high price at wholesale, to gain more revenue from its one and only (exclusive) retailer. The retailer, to preserve its margin, then will set a higher retail price (exclusivity will permit the retailer to uphold this price). As a result, retail demand will be lower than the level that would maximize the total channel's profits. This is called the problem of "double marginalization," because it involves an inefficiency resulting from the taking of two margins rather than one in the channel. If the manufacturer (or the retailer) were vertically integrated forward (or backward), this single organization, generating one income statement, would set a lower retail price, following a strategy of lower overall margins but higher volumes.[2] Both the channel (higher profits) and the final customer (lower prices) would be better off. But because the retailer has one income statement and the manufacturer has another, retail prices will stay higher and unit sales lower.

Similarly, the amount of inventory to hold in a supply chain is a source of conflict. A common scenario is when downstream channel members would like to order at the last minute and hold minimal stock, thereby transferring inventory holding costs upstream. Upstream channel members would like to see high inventory in the pipeline to (1) gain economies of scale (due to long production runs), (2) make sure customers have large selection and short waits, and (3) motivate downstream channel members to make every effort to sell off the merchandise (so as to reduce their inventory holding costs). Chapter 9 (conflict and cooperation) develops these ideas further.

In general, there is usually a "better way" to operate a marketing channel, a way that increases overall system profits. But the organizations comprising the channel are unwilling to adopt this approach. What is best for the system is not necessarily best for its members. And organizations are fearful—with good reason—that their sacrifices will be to someone else's gain.

Left alone, most channel members will not fully cooperate to achieve some system-level goal. Enter power, as a way for one player to convince another player to change what it is inclined to do. This change can be for the good of the system or for the good of a single member. The tools of power can be used to create value or to destroy it, to appropriate value or to redistribute it. What usage to make of power is up to the decision maker. But whether the intent is malevolent or benevolent, channel members *must* be engaged in the exercise of building, using, and keeping power at all times. They must employ power, both to defend themselves and to promote better ways for the channel to generate value.

Let us examine how this is done. We will begin with an elegantly simple conceptualization: Power is really the mirror image of dependence. Unfortunately, diagnosing how much power each channel member has can be difficult. To remedy this problem, we turn to the idea that there are five sources of power, and that firms can invest in creating each one.

POWER AS THE MIRROR IMAGE OF DEPENDENCE

How can we index how much power a channel member has?

One way of conceptualizing power, drawn from sociology, is strikingly simple. A's power over B increases with B's dependence on A.[3] If dependent on party A, party B is more likely to change its normal behavior to fit A's desires. Party B's dependence gives party A the potential for influence.

Specifying Dependence

But what is dependence? B depends more heavily on A:

1. The greater the *utility* (value, benefits, satisfaction) B gets from A and
2. The fewer *alternative* sources of that utility B can find

Dependence is the utility provided, multiplied by the scarcity of alternatives. *Both elements are essential for dependence to occur.* If B doesn't derive much value from what A provides (low benefits, or low utility), then it is irrelevant whether there are alternative providers: B's dependence is low. Conversely, if A provides great value, but B can readily find other sources to provide just as much value, then it is irrelevant that A benefits B: Dependence is still low. Either low utility or low scarcity of alternatives (i.e., many alternatives) is like multiplying by zero: The product (dependence) is always zero.

Thinking of my power as your dependence is useful because it focuses the analyst on *scarcity*, which is the question of how readily B can replace A. This point is easy to overlook. Channel members often consider themselves powerful because they deliver value to their counterparts. But their counterparts don't need them if they are easy to replace, and this reduces their power.

It's easy to overestimate one's own scarcity. For example, distributors of maintenance, repair, and operating supplies (MRO items) systematically overestimate how readily their customers would shift orders away from them. Yet, large industrial plants in North America tend to use a single distributor for no more than 20 percent of their requirements. By keeping a portfolio of distributors, these plants can and do redirect their MRO business easily.[4]

A common channel scenario is that a manufacturer tries to change a downstream channel member's behavior, only to be surprised to see the downstream organization refocus on competing brands. Also common is the scenario wherein a reseller thinks a manufacturer is dependent because end-customers are loyal to the reseller. Manufacturers sometimes do change resellers without share loss, demonstrating their brands have equity that allows them to keep end-customers. Both these scenarios occur when a party generates benefits but underestimates how easily it can be replaced, and therefore overestimates its power.

Measuring Dependence Directly

How can you form a reasonable estimate of how much a channel member depends on you? A direct method is to assess both utility and scarcity separately and then combine them.

To assess utility, you could tally up the benefits you offer. It is then important to understand the channel partner's goals, and how its organization values what you provide. You might estimate the utility you provide by inventorying five bases of power, to be discussed. Or you might estimate roughly the profits you generate, directly and indirectly, as a summary indicator of the benefits you offer. Because you want to assess the worth *it attaches* to what *you provide*, focus on what is important to it (it may be volume rather than profits, for example).

To assess how easily you could be replaced, consider two factors. First, who could be or become your competitors? What other organizations exist or might enter the market that could supply what you provide, *or an acceptable equivalent*? If there are none, you can stop here.

But if there are alternatives, a second question arises: How easily can the channel member switch from your organization to one of these competitors? If switching is easy, your power is nil (in which case, it doesn't matter if you misestimated the utility you offer!). But switching away from your organization may be impractical or prohibitively expensive. In this case, you are scarce (even though alternatives to you do exist on paper). If you provide benefits, the other side needs you, and this makes you powerful.

Consider a manufacturer, P, of specialty steel, supplying distributors X and Y. How much power does P have over each of its distributors? For both X and Y, the manufacturer's brand opens the customer's door for the distributor's salespeople, who then sell other products in their portfolio. Benefits, therefore, are substantial. But manufacturer P has three competitors making equivalent products, so P looks to be easily replaceable. Therefore, Y doesn't depend on P, and P has little power over Y.

The situation is different for X, a small distributor, struggling to establish itself in its marketplace. The other three manufacturers won't supply X on the same terms as will P. So X has no real alternative to P (the other three manufacturers don't give the same benefits): X is therefore dependent on P.

Manufacturer P would also have power if X or Y has made investments in P that are difficult to transfer to another manufacturer. This could include adopting P's proprietary ordering software, taking training in the unique features of P's products, joint advertising with P, and forging close relationships with P's personnel. Even though there are three other suppliers, a distributor would be reluctant to sacrifice these investments by switching suppliers (covered in depth in Chapter 11). The high costs of switching make P a *de facto* monopolist, as the distributor has no ready alternative to P. Thus, the dependence of the distributor, in the face of apparent competition in supply, confers power on manufacturer P.

You now have assessed separately the benefits you provide and the difficulty a channel member would have in replacing you. You can combine these to get a sense of the dependence of your channel member upon you. The conclusion is often sobering. Many parties come to realize through this exercise that they are replaceable, in spite of the value of their offerings.

Measuring Dependence via Proxy Indicators

Several other more direct and simpler ways are often used to approximate dependence. The idea is to develop a rough proxy indicator in lieu of a thorough and detailed (i.e., slow and costly) assessment of utility and scarcity. Although each proxy indicator has its drawbacks, these methods are easier to implement and frequently offer a reasonable approximation.

One quick method of approximating the other party's dependence is to estimate what *percentage* you provide *of its sales or its profits*.[5] The assumption here is that the higher it is, the more important you are, and therefore the more dependent it is. The premise of this approach is that, to be important, you must be providing benefits, and switching costs are likely to exist whenever those benefits are a large fraction of business. Therefore, importance is thought to be a proxy for dependence. This argument has considerable merit. However, the sales-and-profit method is an approximation. It does not capture all the benefits you provide, nor does it directly assess your scarcity. For some situations, the method works poorly. For example, most franchisees derive 100 percent of their sales and profits from the franchisor, even though some franchisees are more dependent than others.[6]

Another method of approximating the other party's dependence is to ask how well you perform your role in the channel *compared to your competitors*. The greater your superiority over them (your *role performance*), the fewer alternatives exist at your level of performance, and therefore the greater their dependence on your organization.[7]

This direct method comes closer to assessing scarcity. However, it does not address the importance of your role: Even if you perform it better than do competitors, your counterpart may not derive great utility from your organization. Further, if only one other organization performs the role as well as you do, the other party still has a meaningful alternative, and has even more alternatives if it is willing to accept some decline in role performance.

Role performance does not index dependence well in certain circumstances. For example, many emerging economies have sectors that are sellers' markets: Demand far outstrips supply, barriers to entry keep supply restricted, and there are many candidates to be resellers. In these sectors, every channel member is dependent on every supplier, regardless of its role performance.[8]

In spite of these potential shortcomings, role performance does appear to be a reasonable proxy for dependence in most circumstances outside of sellers' markets. Excellence in service provision confers uniqueness (scarcity), even if the product being sold is a commodity. Superb role performance creates dependence (hence power) because excellence is scarce *and* valuable.

We now turn to another approach to indexing power, based on a different philosophy about how power grows. This bottom-up approach focuses on taking an inventory of five ways to amass the potential to change a channel member's behavior. We will change the terminology of firms A and B, to focus on the firm that wants to make change happen (the *influencer*) and the firm whose behavior it wants to alter (the *target*).

FIVE SOURCES OF POWER

Power (the potential for influence) is an ability, and abilities are not easy to assess. An enormous body of research attempts to catalog all the facets and manifestations of power and to ascertain who has power and what happens when they use it. Here, we will highlight how power is gathered, used, and maintained in marketing channels.

How do you take inventory of the extent of an organization's ability to change the behavior of another organization?[9] There are numerous ways to do it, and a considerable debate rages as to what is the best approach. Quite a number of methods work fairly well.[10] One way of thinking about indexing power has proven to be particularly fruitful in marketing channels. The French and Raven approach, borrowed from psychology, holds that the best way to index power is to *count up to it from five power sources:* rewards, coercion, expertise, legitimacy, and reference.[11] Each of these is reasonably observable and some can be subdivided. So even though power is hidden, it can be approximated by compiling estimates of its sources. The most important of these is the ability to bestow rewards.

Reward Power

A reward is a *benefit* (or *return*) given in recompense to a channel member for altering its behavior. In distribution channels, there is, of course, great emphasis on the financial aspect of rewards. Financial returns need not always be immediate, nor precisely estimable, but the expectation of eventual payoffs, even indirectly, do pervade channel negotiations. *Reward power* is based on the belief held by B that A has the ability to grant rewards to B. The effective use of reward power rests on A's possession of some resource that B values and believes it can obtain by conforming to A's request.

Of course, the ability to grant rewards is not enough: B must also perceive that A will grant rewards. This means convincing B that (1) what A desires really will create benefits and (2) B will get a fair share of those benefits. An example is Decathlon, a French chain of sporting goods stores that has risen from one store in 1976 to a preeminent position in 1999. The chain (181 stores in France, over 30 in other markets) sells 30 percent of all the sporting goods purchased in France and is credited with fueling an enormous primary demand effect in its category. Decathlon enjoys a long run of growth in sales and profits. Much of its spectacular performance is due to excellence in marketing to the French consumer.

Decathlon has parlayed its huge consumer appeal into reward power, which it uses to influence its suppliers. The chain wields great power, even over such household names as Reebok and Nike. These suppliers object vigorously to Decathlon's policies of discounting, aggressive development of house brands, side-by-side display of competing brands, and—some suppliers charge—reverse engineering of its suppliers' branded products to develop "knock offs" under the house brand names. But suppliers not only tolerate these policies, they also supply Decathlon at very low prices. One supplier explains the Decathlon negotiating tactic this way:

> "Rather than demand a discount of 20 or 25%, they segment their demands—5% because they sell your goods in high volume, 5% because they put your goods on the buyer's reference list in their foreign stores . . . one is often trapped, because each one of these discounts is justified separately."

Each one of these demands is justified—that is reward power! Adding to these specific financial rewards is another, more psychological reward whose profit implications are difficult to estimate. Supplier salespeople reluctantly accept a great deal from Decathlon, in part because its buyers are considered the most professional and easiest to deal with in the business. Supplier salespeople praise their expertise and politeness ("always courteous, keep their appointments, don't make you wait"), comparing them favorably to buyers from hypermarkets (these are notoriously tough negotiators in all departments: Hypermarket sporting goods buyers are said to terrorize their suppliers). Outside the salesperson–buyer level, other boundary-spanning personnel reap rewards from Decathlon. For example, a supplier of winter sport products says, "They're the only ones to furnish us a serious sales forecast during the season. That helps us anticipate our own purchases."[12]

In short, Decathlon has cultivated a reputation for being able and willing to generate enough payoff to suppliers, year after year, that they will tolerate a very great deal. It is impossible to put a price on some elements of the rewards the chain offers. But suppliers value these rewards so much that they have tolerated Decathlon's ever-increasing investments in house brands (which today account for 60 percent of store sales). Of course, these brands compete directly with their suppliers. But Decathlon's reliable promise of rewards permits this sort of cooperation–competition to continue, even with the world's best-known names in sports. And it is not due to monopoly: Much of the remaining 70 percent of sporting goods in France goes through large, capable, and somewhat comparable chains (e.g., Go Sport and Intersport).

Coercive Power

Coercive power stems from B's expectation of *punishment* by A if B fails to conform to A's influence attempt. Coercion involves any negative sanction or punishment of which a firm is perceived to be capable. Examples are reductions in margins, the withdrawal of rewards previously granted (e.g., an exclusive territorial right), and the slowing down of shipments. Coercion is synonymous with the potential to threaten the other organization, implicitly and explicitly.

Coercive power is the reverse of reward power. Technically, it can be considered negative reward power—a reward that is withheld, that doesn't materialize. Why treat it as a separate category? Why not consider "negative rewards" as being just a step below giving a low level of rewards?

The reason is because channel members don't see it this way. They do not view negative sanctions as being the absence of rewards, or fewer rewards. They view coercion as an attack on themselves and their business. Coercion is synonymous with aggression and provokes self-defense. The threat and use of negative sanctions is often viewed as "pathological." When channel members perceive low rewards, they react by indifference or withdrawal. But when they perceive coercion, they react by considering a counterattack. This defensive reaction means that using coercive power is usually less functional over the long run than are other power bases, because these usually produce more positive side effects.[13] Therefore, coercion should be employed only when all other avenues to evoke change have been traveled. Perceived aggression provokes retaliation (see Chapter 9 on conflict).

The user of coercive power may be surprised at the intensity of the target's reaction. This reaction may be delayed, because the target marshals its forces and composes its counterattack. But often the reaction is itself an act of coercion. For example, some department store chains, such as Saks Fifth Avenue and Bloomingdale's, see the opening of factory outlet stores as a manufacturer's efforts to coerce them into greater cooperation.[14] Rather than cooperate, they have retaliated against these suppliers, both in the short run—by canceling orders—and in the long run—by opening their own factory outlet stores, which they use to underprice their own suppliers' stores.

There are various ways to fight back. Many of them are not dramatic and may even pass unremarked. In general, when the target perceives that the influencer uses threats, the target will downgrade its estimation of the value of the influencer's business.[15] In the short term, the relationship will be damaged in three ways. The target will be less satisfied with: first, the financial returns it derives from the influencer; this reaction is part perception and part reality. Second, the nonfinancial side of the relationship. It will view its partner as being less concerned, respectful, willing to exchange ideas, fulfilling, gratifying, and easy to work with. Third, the target will sense the relationship has become more conflictual.

Why should the influencer care about the target's disillusionment? The answer comes in the short run (target is less cooperative), in the medium run (target is less trusting), and in the long run (target feels less committed to its relationship).[16] What the influencer gains from its coercion may be lost later. There is an opportunity cost to alienating a channel member. Coercion erodes the relationship, sometimes so slowly that the influencer doesn't realize what it is losing.

This does not mean that channel members should never employ coercion. Sometimes the benefit is worth the cost. For example, electronic data interchange (EDI) is a way of sharing information across firms. Its potential to reduce costs has led many firms to adopt it in recent years. But that potential is more evident in hindsight than in foresight. Some evidence indicates that at least half of the early users of EDI were forced to do so by other members of the supply chain, who imposed deadlines for adoption by threatening to stop their orders.[17] If it soon becomes clear that EDI is beneficial, a channel member may forgive its partner for using coercion. Indeed, surviving the crisis that these threats provoke often strengthens channel relationships. But if the coerced channel member does not benefit or perceives a benefit, the relationship will be seriously damaged.[18]

It is important to steer how a channel member perceives the use of power. Even reward power can be perceived as coercion if not presented correctly. From a channel-management perspective, the use of reward power generally produces better results in helping forge long-term working relationships than does the use of coercive power. Rewards can be suspect, however, because they are so closely related to coercive measures. Withdrawing a reward is perceived as a coercive act. And both reward and coercive power demand that the influence agent monitor the actions of the party whose behavior is supposed to change, so that the appropriate rewards or punishments can be administered in case of compliance or noncompliance. In other words, reward power has many of the attributes of coercive power and therefore is a double-edged base of power.

Rather than focusing solely on reward and coercion, the manager should also invest in and use the remaining three power bases. Let us turn to these.

Expert Power

Expert power is based on the target's perception that the influencer has special knowledge, useful expertise that the target doesn't possess. Cases of channel members assuming expert roles are widespread; indeed, such expertise is at the heart of the division of labor, specialization, and comparative advantage in channel function organization. This is why it has become very common for small retailers to rely heavily on their wholesale suppliers for expert advice. Even large retailers can benefit.

For example, VF Corporation is a major manufacturer of clothing and lingerie, selling 17 brands (including Lee and Wrangler jeans, Vanity Fair lingerie, Healthtex children's clothes, and Jantzen bathing suits). These products pose a horrendous stocking problem: thousands of size, fabric, style, and color combinations. Sales are fashion sensitive and markets have significant local variations. The cost of a stockout is high: Inventory holding costs are enormous. VF has invested over $100 million to develop a supply chain information system. The core of the system is the analysis of market data (consumer information, point-of-sale data, and so forth) *at the level of a retail store in a given location*. This complex system allows VF to develop a recommended stocking plan for a store, one that minimizes overstocks and understocks. Pilot tests of the system with cooperating retailers suggest the system can make substantial reductions in inventory, while increasing the turn rate of the inventory in stock. With this system, VF hopes to gain expert power over its customers.[19]

The value of expertise is so great that it underpins an important channel form: franchising (Chapter 17). One of the major reasons why franchisees pay fees is to rent the expertise of franchisors in setting up their business. Once operations are running, franchisors must keep demonstrating their expertise in order to keep earning their royalties and holding the loyalty of the network.

The durability of expert power presents a problem in channel management, however. If expert advice, once given, provides the recipient with the ability to operate without such assistance in the future, then the expertise has been transferred. The power of the original expert in the relationship is reduced considerably. A firm that wishes to *retain expert power* over the long run in a given channel has three options. First, it can dole out its expertise in small portions, always retaining enough vital data so that other channel members will remain dependent on it. But this would mean it would have to keep other channel members uninformed about some critical aspect of channel performance. Such a strategy can be self-defeating, because it is important that all channel members work up to their capacities if the channel as a whole is to function successfully.

Second, the firm can continually invest in learning and thereby always have new and important information to offer its channel partners. The firm must accumulate knowledge about market trends, threats, and opportunities that other channel members would find difficult to generate on their own. The cost of this option is not trivial, but the benefits, in terms of achieving channel goals, are likely to be high.

A third option is to transmit only customized information. This means encouraging channel partners to invest in transaction-specific expertise, because it is so specialized that they could not easily transfer it to other products or services. In other words, the specific nature of the expertise, along with the costs involved in acquiring it, would impede exit from the channel.

Some writers subdivide this power source, referring to expertise as the provision of good judgments (forecasts, analyses) and information as the provision of data (such as the news that a competitor has just dropped prices).[20] A good illustration that information isn't identical to expertise comes from the supermarket industry in North America where these stores receive huge amounts of consumer purchase data from their checkout scanners. To turn this information into insight, they give the data for each product category to selected suppliers ("category captains"), who use their knowledge of the type of product to see the patterns in millions of transactions. Supermarkets have information power over suppliers, who then invest in converting this into expertise power over supermarkets. This exercise is so important that both sides view it as an investment in building a strategic alliance.[21]

Crucial to the retention of expert power is the ability of a channel member to position itself well in the flow of communication and information within a channel system. For example, manufacturers may be highly dependent on other channel members for information on consumer demand. Retailers and industrial distributors occupy preferred positions in this respect because of their close contacts with consumers of the manufacturers' products. By gathering, interpreting, and transmitting valuable market information, one channel member can absorb uncertainty for others. Through this process of uncertainty absorption, channel members come to rely on the information gatherer and processor for inferences about market developments.

For example, several decades ago General Foods (now called Kraft Foods) conducted a massive study of materials handling in distribution warehouses. It then made its results and recommendations available to wholesalers through a group of specialists carefully trained to help implement the recommendations. The company also undertook a major study of retail space profitability and then offered supermarket owners the opportunity to learn a new approach to space-productivity accounting called direct product profit (DPP). The approach (Chapter 17) has since received widespread attention by mass-merchandisers.

Using expert power is not as easy as it may sound, even for an organization that holds considerable knowledge that would be useful to the channel. There are three difficulties:

1. To be able to exercise expert power, a channel member must be trusted. Otherwise, others perceive the expert advice as an attempt at manipulation and discount it.

2. Experts are usually accorded very high status; therefore, it is difficult to identify with them. This impedes building the necessary trust.

3. Independent-minded, entrepreneurial businesspeople don't like to be told what to do. They believe that they are the experts, and are often right!

If the influencer is to employ expert power over the target, the latter must be willing to accept the influencer's information and judgments. This is easier if there is a good working relationship in which the target believes in the basic competence and trustworthiness of the influencer's personnel.[22] It is also easier when the target needs the influencer is dependent.[23]

Legitimate Power

To be legitimate is to be seen as right and proper, as being in accordance with what is seen as normal or established standards. *Legitimate power* stems from the target company's sense that it is in some way obligated to comply with the requests of the influencer: The target thinks compliance is right and proper by normal or established standards. Thus, the influencer has legitimate power whenever the target feels a sense of duty, of being bound to carry out the influencer's request. The key feature of legitimate power is that the decision makers feel constrained morally, socially, or legally to go along with the influencer. This sense of responsibility or duty comes from two sources: the law (*legal legitimate power*) and norms or values (*traditional legitimate power*).

Legal legitimate power is conferred by governments, coming from the nation's law of contracts and the laws of commerce. For example, in many countries, patent and trademark laws give owners a certain amount of freedom and justification in supervising the distribution of their products. Commercial laws allow firms to maintain agreements, such as franchises and other contracts that confer legitimate power to demand behavior that is not required in conventional channel arrangements. (See Chapter 12 for more on this topic.)

In some cases, legal intervention in the functioning of channels is so great that legitimate authority is the principal source of channel power. For an example, see Channel

Sketch 8.1, which describes how downstream channel members selling liquor in Illinois invested to acquire legal legitimate power—which they dissipated in a short period of time.

CHANNEL SKETCH 8.1
Investing in Legitimate Power

In the U.S. state of Illinois, the distribution of liquor is strictly regulated. Retailers are required to deal with wholesalers, rather than directly with producers. This, of course, obliges producers to deal with wholesalers. A state law adopted in 1999 made it virtually impossible for liquor producers to change from one wholesaler to another. This legal lock-in gives the wholesalers an unusual degree of legitimate power over their suppliers. The law was passed after pressure from up to 19 professional lobbyists at one time—a serious investment by the wholesalers in building their legitimate power.[24] Ironically, the purpose of the law (as stated by its supporters) is to create a source of countervailing power against the potential reward and coercive power of large liquor producers, which control dozens of brands. The new law limiting the producers' right to terminate a wholesaler is intended to promote "stability" in liquor distribution, in the belief that stability will work in the public interest by creating lower retail prices.

Legal legitimate authority is not immutable. Liquor wholesalers in Illinois dissipated their newfound and hard-won legitimate power with astonishing speed. These wholesalers lost little time after the new law's passage in sharply raising their prices to retailers. This created a public outcry. Subsequent lawsuits by several producers kept the issue in the public eye. Allegations surfaced in the press that the owner of one distributor, a prominent political fund-raiser and contributor, had used his influence with the governor and state legislators to secure passage of the bill.

Just a few months after the law took effect, a higher court ruled it unconstitutional and blocked the state of Illinois from enforcing it. The state's governor decided not to appeal the decision—and even switched his support to the repeal of the law he had backed just months before. Governor Ryan explained his position:

> After the bill was passed and I signed it and it became law, there was, I guess, a certain set of arrogance that came into being, and they [the distributors] raised their prices. . . . I sat down with my people and said, "Look, I see no reason for us to be involved in this." There isn't any sense in going through with the expense and effort.

In principle, a major source of legitimate power is the contract channel members write with each other. In practice, contracts frequently do not carry the force one would expect them to have. In many cultures, particularly outside the Anglo-Saxon sphere of influence, contracts are difficult to enforce. Channel members often don't bother to write them (indeed, merely asking for a contract will signal distrust, which is self-perpetuating). Even in such litigious nations as the United States, channels frequently operate with sketchy, incomplete contracts—or no contract at all! And many channel members are unaware of the terms of their contracts ("the lawyer will look it up if we need it") or pay little attention to clauses. Instead, they go by norms developed in the context of their relationship.[25] This is not peculiar to channels: Reliance on working understandings rather than norms is typical, *even in societies with a strong tradition of legal structuring of commercial relationships.*[26] This does not mean channel members don't invest in crafting thorough contracts; often they do, particularly in franchise arrangements. But it should not be assumed that a well-considered contract is all the power a channel member needs.

Legal legitimate authority exists objectively: The influencer can remind the target of its presence. In contrast, traditional legitimate authority is more ephemeral because it does not exist without the consent of the target. This authority is based on values internalized by the target: The target feels the influencer "should" or "has a right to" exert influence and the target has an obligation to accept it.

The appearance of legitimate power is obvious inside a firm. When a supervisor gives a directive to a subordinate, the latter feels that the former has a right to direct him or her in a certain manner and therefore will generally conform to the superior's desires. Such legitimized power is synonymous with authority and is a major reason to vertically integrate forward or backward in a channel (see Chapter 7). *But no such hierarchical authority exists in most marketing channels.*

Channel members sometimes forget this. A major source of friction between them is when one company is seen as trying to invoke authority, treating another like a subsidiary. This is often the case when those who interface, such as a district sales manager, with independent channel members, such as a sales agency, come from a background of dealing with employee channel members, such as a direct sales force. These boundary spanners often exhibit behavior patterns conditioned on the days when they really did have authority. Their normal, unconscious behavior can seem imperious and arrogant. Unintentionally, they threaten the channel member's autonomy as an independent business, creating needless resistance.

Legitimate power does exist in dealings between organizations, as in a marketing channel, but it doesn't stem from hierarchical authority. It stems from *norms, values,* and *beliefs.* One firm may believe that a channel member deserves to be accorded a certain deference, perhaps because of its successful track record or exemplary management. For example, the largest firm could be considered the leader (channel captain) by others. If this is the case, then legitimate power is available to that firm.

Norms of behavior arise in a channel, norms that define roles and effectively confer legitimate power on certain channel members. For example, distributors in the information technology (IT) industry have a different norm than that of many other industries: They are far more likely to honor a supplier's request to name their customers and detail their shipments. Norms—expectations of "normal" behavior—exist not only within industries but also within certain channels, some of which manage to build such norms as:[27]

- *Solidarity.* Each side expects the other to focus on the relationship on the whole, rather than thinking transaction by transaction.

- *Role integrity*. Each side expects the other to perform complex roles that not only cover individual transactions but also cover a multitude of issues not related to any single transaction.
- *Mutuality*. Each side expects the other to divide up its joint returns in a way that assures adequate returns to each side.

These norms, once created, give one channel member the ability to exert legitimate power over the other, by appealing to the norms as a reason to comply with a request.

Ultimately, the degree of traditional legitimate power is subjective. *It exists in the eye of the beholder*. Channel members build their legitimate power base by investing in partnership building to increase a sense of common norms and values (see Chapter 11 on strategic alliances). Traditional legitimate power can also be built by selecting channel partners on compatibility in their attitudes, values, and operating methods. Hence, some franchisors screen prospective franchisees on the basis of their attitudes toward legitimate authority. They favor candidates who express respect for the franchisor as an authority figure and for the franchise contract as a binding document. They screen out candidates who view a contract as "just a piece of paper," who take a skeptical approach to the franchisor ("try and convince me"), and who are "too" independent minded ("I'll do it my way, and if you don't like it, sue me"). Franchisors fear these candidates would become troublemakers if they joined the franchise system because they won't attribute legitimate authority to the franchisor.

Referent Power

Referent power exists when B views A as a standard of reference and therefore wishes to identify publicly with A. Between individuals, there are many personal, psychological reasons why person B would feel a oneness with person A and would wish to be associated (identified) with A. In a marketing channel, a prominent reason why one organization would want to be publicly identified with another is prestige. Downstream channel members would like to carry high-status brands to benefit their own image. Upstream channel members "rent the reputation" of prestigious downstream firms.[28]

The existence of referent power within many channels is undeniable. It is especially visible when wholesalers or retailers pride themselves on carrying certain brands (e.g., Harley-Davidson motorcycles, Ralph Lauren clothing, Estée Lauder perfumes), and when manufacturers pride themselves on having their brands carried in certain outlets (e.g., Neiman-Marcus, Nordstrom, and Saks Fifth Avenue). Creating and preserving referent power (the ability to confer prestige) is a major reason for manufacturers to restrict distribution coverage to selected outlets, as well as for downstream organizations to restrict representation to selected brands (Chapter 10).

Separating the Five Power Sources

When taking stock of the extent of power in a channel relationship, the five sources of power are a useful framework for generating ideas. But it is important not to double count a power source when taking a power inventory. The separation between one source of power and another is not always clear. *Many ways to change what a channel member would have done exhibit several sources of power.*

An example is Quiksilver, an Australian maker of sports clothing and accessories targeted at adolescents.[29] In Europe, the traditionally preferred brand in this category is Nike. In a mere two years, Quiksilver not only has, as of 1999, entered the top 20 preferred brands in this category but also has become number six in stated preference among the 11 to 17 age group. By astute market research, innovative product design, narrow targeting, and creative advertising, Quiksilver has come to enjoy an image as the cutting-edge, preferred brand of "boarders" (surfboards and snowboards). This is an image (defiant, outdoors, athletic, risk-taking, and nonconformist) that many European adolescents would like to project. Quiksilver has high prestige in the youth market generally and, although expensive, is *the* reference brand for many consumers. The manufacturer tightly restricts its distribution at retail by selling directly to selected outlets.

Quiksilver exercises referent power over some of these stores, which would like to be associated with the brand. It has used its power to convince nearly 300 stores in Europe to hold large inventories in Quiksilver "corners" or even to sell only this brand. The manufacturer's competitors call this employing the technique of "teasing." A merchant gives the brand a trial, say by ordering 100 items. The manufacturer deliberately fills only part of the order, say 70 of the items. These sell quickly. The store realizes it has stocked out but, given the trial is incomplete, is not sure what demand might have been in total units and in which items. So the store goes to the manufacturer to start another trial to resolve its uncertainty. This time, it meets with a demand to open a "corner."

This example employs every power base, not just referent power. Reward power comes from the brand's customer preference; indeed, it is difficult to separate completely the benefit of Quiksilver's prestige and the value of the sales the brand name generates. Expertise power comes from Quiksilver's exceptional understanding of one segment of the adolescent market. Teasing involves both coercion (the implied threat of withdrawing the brand unless the store devotes a corner) and expertise (the manufacturer has a good idea of demand but ensures the store is uncertain what the demand curve is like at higher stock levels). Legitimate power may come from industry norms, which make tactics such as teasing acceptable, and by agreements governing minimum inventory levels and the design of the corners.

Of course, the power in not all on Quiksilver's side. As the brand's appeal has grown, the producer has been able to convince prestigious retailers in prime locations (such as Covent Garden in London) to open Quiksilver corners. Here, the referent power goes in both directions but is greater in the case of many of the outlets. Quiksilver rents the retailers' reputation, as well as loaning its own.

It is so difficult to categorize the five sources of power neatly (without being arbitrary) that many users of the framework don't even try. They mainly rely on three *broader groupings.*

One method is to separate out *coercive* power and lump all the others together into *noncoercive* power. This saves categorizing expert, legitimate, and referent power explicitly because they just go into the broad noncoercive inventory. Even this is a bit arbitrary: Is withholding a reward coercive or is it reward power? To circumvent the problem, this approach treats as coercion the removal of something a channel member already has. Everything else is noncoercive (no further distinction). For example, a sales agent has coercive power over a supplier if it can credibly threaten to reduce coverage or to drop some of the line. Offering to increase coverage or take on more of the line would be classed as noncoercive power. Similarly, an auto supplier's power base is coercive if it could slow down auto deliveries and noncoercive if it could speed them up. A variation on coercion that has been practiced is to slow down the delivery of popular cars and speed up the delivery of cars that turn slowly. This is coercive because it worsens the dealer's situation with more stockouts and more inventory.

Another way to minimize distinctions is to consider only *mediated* and *unmediated* (no further categorization) power. Power is mediated by the influencer when it can be demonstrated to the target: The influencer can oblige the target to acknowledge these power bases. They are reward, coercion, and legal legitimate power bases. Bases unmediated by the influencer would not exist without the perception of the target: These are expert, referent, and traditional legitimate power.

It is much easier for the influencer to create and wield mediated power. Unmediated power is more subtle and builds more slowly, through a process that is not easy to decipher. Because unmediated power rests on the target's implicit consent, the management of the influencer cannot simply put a program in place to guarantee an increase in unmediated power. This means it is very difficult for a competitor to duplicate unmediated power, once acquired, because even the influencer isn't entirely sure how it acquired its unmediated power. The uncertain imitability of unmediated power makes it a potent competitive advantage.[30] *Channel members that have expert, referent, and legitimate power, however they acquired it, should consider carefully before endangering this strategic intangible asset.* This sort of asset cannot enter a balance sheet, yet is so valuable that it motivates mergers and acquisitions in marketing channels.

Combining the Five Power Sources

Thus far, the five power bases and their subdivisions have been presented separately. In marketing channels, they are used in combination, which can create *synergistic effects.*[31] On the one hand, legitimacy may enhance expertise and vice versa, identification may increase with the use of appropriate rewards, and coercion may sometimes be necessary to reinforce legitimacy. Expert, referent, or legitimate power may also be accompanied by reward power that contributes to a channel member's willingness to change its behavior. For example, Toys "R" Us allowed McDonald's to open McDonald's restaurants inside of Toys "R" Us stores in Japan because of the following:

- McDonald's legitimate power through an equity stake McDonald's held in the Japanese Toys "R" Us operations.
- McDonald's expertise power because it knew how to do business in Japan and where to locate stores.
- McDonald's reward power because Toys "R" Us expected to make more money by doing this than through some other process.

On the other hand, there may be conflict between certain bases. For example, the use of coercion by a channel member may destroy any referent power that member might have been able to accumulate. Coercion may have a similar effect on expert power, for which trust is a prerequisite.

In addition, there are economic, social, and political costs associated with the use of the various power bases. These costs (in particular, endangering one's reputation in the channel) must be taken into account prior to the implementation of programs in which they are incorporated. Influence attempts are also constrained by norms that exist within channel systems. These norms, which are, in fact, "rules" of the channel's "game," aid in defining appropriate industrial behavior and can be even more restrictive than public laws in certain situations. For example, during periods of short supply in the steel industry, many buyers are willing to pay above-"normal" prices for steel. This alternative is less expensive than shutting down production. Because of short supply, steel distributors in the established marketing channels can command higher prices. But they frequently refrain from doing so, because they feel that their customers expect a certain level of restraint from them, even though some of their customers go outside the established channel structure and purchase higher-priced steel from gray market sources. The established distributors also refrain from using coercive power, such as boycotts, against their customers who buy from these sources, because the norms of market behavior among them do not sanction such actions.

Putting It Together: What Is Power and How Do You Index It?

We have come full circle in our discussion of power. Figure 8.1 shows how the nature and sources of channel power are related. Reading right to left, this figure shows that

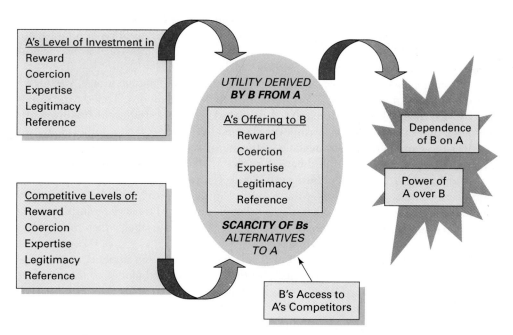

FIGURE 8.1 **The Nature and Sources of Channel Power**

thinking of power as dependence harks back to asking how much utility one party gets from the other, and how easy it would be to find this utility elsewhere. In turn, how much one party offers to another can be framed as the five power bases (reward, coercion, expertise, legitimacy, and reference). The more a channel member invests over time to be able to provide these five sources, the greater its utility. Of course, its competitors' power bases determine just how scarce that utility is—as long as a channel member really has access to those competitors.

THE BALANCE OF POWER

The reader may have noticed that the discussion so far is partial and one sided. It is time to point out that *power is a property of the relationship*. In stating a power relationship, it is not sufficient to say "A is powerful." A is powerful *in relation to B* but may be weak in relation to some other party. And in the A and B relationship, A has some sources of power of its own, but so does B. B has *countervailing power*, its own power bases, which it can use to offset the power sources of A. When taking an inventory of A's reward power, it is important to (1) focus on only one relationship at a time, rather than making general statements about power, and (2) count up not only A's ability to reward B but B's countervailing power, its ability to bestow rewards upon A. Channel outcomes rest on the *balance* of power *in a given relationship*.

Net Dependence

Thus far, we have focused on A's power over B, conceptualizing it as B's dependence on A. Of course, *dependence is never entirely one way*. Just as B depends on A to provide utility, it is also the case that A depends on B for utility of a different type. A and B are interdependent. A's dependence on B creates countervailing power for B to use against A. This blunts A's ability to pressure B to alter its behavior.

An example is Agfa, a European maker of premium photographic film.[32] Although a household name in Europe, Agfa is little known in North America. To fight the dominance of Kodak and Fuji in this market, Agfa Canada crafted a strategy of supplying private-label film to retailers such as supermarkets and drugstores. These outlets had captured a large share of the photofinishing business. Agfa management reasoned that such an important product line merited having a private label, which Fuji and Kodak refuse to provide. So Agfa approached these outlets and offered to help them expand their photographic business. Using its extensive expertise in the industry, Agfa helped retailers segment the market, set up a stock plan, and open or expand their photofinishing outlets. Then it supplied them premium-quality film under private label, which the retailers have priced and marketed as high quality.

The business has done well. Agfa Canada has become very dependent on these retailers: They generate great benefits, and the brand equity belongs to the retailer's label, not to Agfa. To change accounts, Agfa's switching costs would be high. In the short term, at least, *Agfa has few alternatives*.

But *neither do the retailers*. Premium-quality film is not an easy-to-find commodity. The few other premium manufacturers refuse to supply private label, in order to protect their own brands. Because their private-label film is positioned as high quality, retailers have few alternatives to Agfa: Were they to downgrade the film, their brand equity would suffer. And the business is desirable for them as well, for both its own profits and its ability to generate store traffic.

In short, *dependence is mutual* between Agfa and its retailers. Each side's dependence is high, so each side holds power over the other. But in the relationship, power is balanced. *To get a complete picture of power, net dependence should be assessed*, in addition to each side's dependence. Chapter 11 offers a complete discussion of how to balance off net dependence to build strategic alliances.

High mutual dependence is synonymous with high mutual power. This situation gives channel members the ability to create very high levels of value added.[33] Each party has leverage over the other. This can be used to drive coordination, to enhance cooperation.[34] High mutual dependence is conducive to creating and maintaining strategic channel alliances. More generally, *high and balanced power is an effective way to achieve coordination* for two reasons. First, the two sides can drive each other to craft and implement creative, win–win solutions. One of the greatest drawbacks of imbalanced relations is that the weaker party cannot oblige the stronger party to invest enough in relationship-specific assets.[35] Absent pressure, the less dependent party minimizes investments unless they can be transferred easily to another relationship. This hurts its ability to generate value added.

A second way that high and balanced (symmetric) dependence encourages cooperation is by blocking exploitation. There is no weaker party in the relationship: Both are giants. Each can force the other to share gains equitably. This fosters norms of fairness and solidarity, which makes coordination easier to achieve. Symmetric dependence promotes bilateral functioning by increasing each side's willingness to adapt in dealing with the other.[36]

Symmetry in dependence means that each side has countervailing power, which it can use for self-protection. Of course, symmetry also occurs when mutual dependence is low—neither side has much need of the other. This low–low combination is very common in marketing channels, so common that it is the baseline for channel management. Channels with low–low dependence (each side is dispensable) tend to operate closely along the lines of classic economic relationships.[37]

Imbalanced Dependence: Is Exploitation Inevitable?

What happens when channel member A is much more dependent than channel member B? The balance of power favors B when A is open to exploitation.[38] All too often, that potential is realized. The more dependent party suffers, in economic terms as well as in the noneconomic benefits it draws.[39] This occurs even when the more powerful, less dependent channel member is not attempting to appropriate the rewards due to A.

An example is Marks and Spencer, Britain's largest and most profitable retailer.[40] In most countries, textile and clothing manufacturers market their own brands. Many have their own retail outlets, such as Hugo Boss in Germany, Stefanel in Italy, and Tommy Hilfiger in the United States. In Britain, however, clothing retailers have their own house brands, which are higher in status than many manufacturer brands. Marks and Spencer (M&S) is the leader, with its St. Michael clothing line. Over the years, M&S has cultivated preferred suppliers among British textile and clothing firms. As the retailer's success has grown, so has its suppliers' success. A number of them have gradually come to devote up to 90 percent of their production to M&S, and have built factories in Britain rather than elsewhere to serve the company's demand for private-label clothing. This fits the M&S "Buy British" policy.

However, clothing sales in Britain have gone flat, particularly at M&S. This has provoked a crisis in the textile and clothing industries. The company has cut back its private-label orders as its sales have fallen. Its suppliers are discovering that it is difficult to replace this business. They have not cultivated their own brand equity, so they find it difficult to place their goods in retail shops. By supplying to M&S specification, their design capabilities have withered. Growth markets exist outside of Britain, but local factories have no advantage in serving them. Even M&S is expanding outside the country, but does not extend its Buy British policy outside its home-market stores.

The result of the decline in the fortunes of M&S in clothing is that its dependent private-label suppliers are suffering heavily. One indicator is mass layoffs. Another is stock prices, which are more depressed for M&S suppliers than for the clothing industry in general. Even absent exploitation, appropriation, or bad faith, the many suppliers of the M&S channel are paying a price for having become dependent on a single retailer.

Of course, the specter of exploitation is always present. The weaker, more dependent party often feels its vulnerability and is quick to suspect the stronger party of bad faith. Asymmetric relationships are more conflictual, less trusting, and less committed than relations of interdependence.[41] What can channel members do when they are drawn into imbalanced relationships and find themselves the weaker party?

Imbalanced Dependence: Countermeasures for the Weaker Party

The weaker party can take three countermeasures. When B is dependent on A, but A is not dependent on B, then B can cope with its hazardous situation by reducing its dependence on A. These three routes are:

1. Developing alternatives to A
2. Organizing a coalition to attack A
3. Exiting the situation, removing itself from danger by no longer seeking the benefits A provides

In channels, the first reaction is the most common of these three countermeasures. Fear of exploitation drives channel members to develop countervailing power as their dependence increases. For example, some sales agents (manufacturers' representatives, or reps) tailor their operations to some of the principals they represent. This creates potentially dangerous imbalances in dependence. To balance dependence, and therefore power, some reps go to great lengths to cultivate the customers of these principals, building loyalty directly to the rep agency. This means the rep can induce the customer to change to another brand if necessary. The rep ensures it could replace the principal by taking its customers elsewhere. Rep agencies that pursue this strategy fare better in profit terms than do the agencies that neglect to balance their dependence after tailoring their operations to a principal.[42]

This example preserves the ability to add a supplier if necessary. Many channel members deliberately keep a diversified portfolio of counterparts to allow them to react immediately if any one organization exploits the imbalance of power. For example, U.S. automobile dealers once represented only one brand of car. They were not legally obliged to do so (unlike Europe—see Chapter 10 about distribution intensity), but followed an industry norm of one dealer–one brand. This made them highly dependent on the manufacturer. The oil crisis of the early 1970s encouraged dealers to add other lines to be able to offer fuel-efficient cars. From there, it was a short step to diversification. Now many auto dealers have multiple locations, each representing a different brand, or even a single location selling multiple brands. Having a diversified portfolio of brands reduces the dealer's dependence on any single make of car. This enables them to resist a given automaker's pressure. Diversification reduces the risk of being exploited.

Another countermeasure for B is to organize a coalition to counter A's power. More generally, this strategy brings in third parties.[43] There are a number of ways to do this. A common method in Europe is to write contracts calling for mandatory arbitration of disputes. Arbitrators are usually private, but the third party could also be a government body. An example is shown in Channel Sketch 8.2.

CHANNEL SKETCH 8.2

French Produce Suppliers Court Allies

French producers of fresh produce have long complained that distribution is too highly concentrated in the hands of a few giant wholesalers. Having few alternatives makes the growers dependent: They charge that wholesalers exploit that dependence to pay the growers very little. The wholesalers, in turn, complain that they themselves are exploited by a few powerful retailers. And the retailers explain that the public obliges them to keep their own prices down.

Frustrated at their inability to obtain "fair" prices for their goods, produce growers have turned to a third party: the Ministry of Agriculture.[44] Growers' associations have convinced it to issue, during a trial period, an edict directing retailers to post a double price for nine fruits and vegetables. One is the retail price. The other is the price the grower received. It is up to retailers to ascertain what this price is, to post it, and to update it daily.

The objective is to make the consumer aware of the substantial markup being taken from one end of the channel to the other. The government hopes consumers will experience a "crisis of conscience" that will oblige channel members to work together to find a way to offer better compensation to growers. Is it working? This edict has created an uproar, which has sparked a public debate. Channel members are protesting vigorously. As a practical matter, it is an administrative nightmare to ascertain the price the grower received. Wholesalers naturally do not wish to reveal this information to retailers. Cost accounting issues to ascertain the price are surprisingly complex. Most of all, each player wants to be sure the public realizes that

> the entire markup doesn't go to any single player. And that is precisely the growers' and the government's objective: To educate consumers and bring them into the dispute on the side of the growers. Whether the edict is modified or withdrawn, growers have increased their power by involving parties outside their distribution channel.

In this example, growers achieved the effect by banding together into trade associations. Automobile dealers in the United States have been successful using the same tactic. By organizing, then lobbying state legislatures, dealers have pushed through "Dealers' Day in Court" laws in many states. These laws limit automakers' ability to coerce or pressure their dealers by creating new grounds for lawsuits and new penalties for heavy-handed suppliers.

Developing alternatives to A is one strategy, whereas organizing a coalition to attack A is another. A third countermeasure is to withdraw from the business and therefore from the relationship. This is the strategy of ceasing to value what A can give. Exiting the business and putting the resources elsewhere (e.g., selling off one's auto dealership) is a strategy many channel members consider unthinkable. But it is not. This is certainly the most conclusive way to escape dependence on A!

The weaker party can rectify imbalanced dependence by reducing its own dependence in these three ways. A more creative strategy is to *raise the other party's dependence*. This can be done by offering greater utility and by making oneself more unusual, hence more scarce. Chapters 10 (channel intensity) and 11 (channel alliances) go into detail on these alternatives.

Tolerating Imbalanced Dependence: The Most Common Scenario

The most common reaction to being the weaker party in an imbalanced relationship is no reaction. More often than not, the more dependent party accepts the situation and tries to make the best of it. What happens next? Are stronger parties always exploitative? Do weaker parties always suffer? Should imbalanced relationships be avoided at any cost?

This question has become more pressing due to the global phenomenon of consolidation. In many industries and markets, mergers and acquisitions are leaving only a few giant players in the channels.[45] Channel Sketch 8.3 shows some examples of their effects.

CHANNEL SKETCH 8.3

Tales of Consolidation

As of early 2000, Carrefour and Promodès are working furiously to complete one of the world's largest mergers. These two giants of retailing will become the world's second-largest retailer. Their abrupt merger is widely believed to be a reaction to Wal-Mart's entry into Europe in the late 1990s. Hundreds of executives from both companies are working in joint task forces to "harmonize" their purchasing plans. Their suppliers are preparing for anything but harmony.

One of the merger's stated objectives is to increase net profits by 26 percent a year, which would double the returns of two already profitable giants, and in only three years. Suppliers fear they will be the source of these economies. Even though the merger has been approved in late 1999 by Brussels (the European Commission's headquarters) and by the French authorities, Carrefour and Promodès each postponed their annual buying season from autumn 1999 to the new year, announcing a program called "Negotiations 2000." Task forces are working around the clock to compare each chain's terms of trade and decide on a common negotiation strategy. Big losers are expected to be private-label suppliers, who have tailored their products and processes to brands that will be eliminated.

Particularly fearful are the smaller and medium-size suppliers, which include many of the private-label producers. The postponement of the negotiating season leaves them worried. Says one, "Carrefour wants to multiply its profits by two. If this translates into cutting off their suppliers, one can fear the worst. I hope the group is aware that it needs to have challengers to create a counterweight to the multinationals." Says another specialized supplier, in an expression of pessimism, "The end point of this merger is to gain productivity." Their fears do not stop at being cut off or negotiated into an untenable position. Some suppliers fear the retail giant will, for example, slow down payments for merchandise received.

In the short run, smaller suppliers may be protected by the glare of government scrutiny. Both Brussels and Paris have made it clear they expect the firms to honor promises not to abuse smaller suppliers. Brussels, in particular, is concerned that several dozen markets will be vulnerable to exploitation, because the merger could create dominant positions in some areas. Nonetheless, the merger has been approved, management is working punishing hours to speed the merger to completion, dramatic decisions are being made rapidly, and the opposition (mainly consumer activists and supplier associations) is moderating its public criticism of the merger. Industry observers are betting they see the inevitable and do not wish to anger the soon-to-emerge retailing colossus.[46]

Once consolidation occurs, changes follow rapidly. The U.S. magazine publishing industry is a case in point. By 1995, smaller or independent newsstands and bookstores had lost share in the business of retailing magazines (news, sports, lifestyle, and so forth). A few very large retail chains had become major players. Abruptly and simultaneously, several of these huge retailers announced a paring of their wholesalers by two-thirds, and invited bids for their business. In 18 months, the number of magazine wholesalers declined from over 300 to under 100, victims of plunging profit margins. The survivors of the shakeout of 1996, many of which bought out their competitors at low prices, turned to magazine publishers with a long list of demands. Confronted with a few large wholesalers, the suppliers are being obliged to alter their methods. In this way, consolidated retailers have pushed their agenda in front of the suppliers, even though they are not the suppliers' customers.

What do these retail chains want? They are focusing on the ratio of sales to display space, swiftly eliminating the less profitable titles, location by location. They are also pressing their wholesalers to solve their problem of which stock to send to which stores, as magazine demand varies considerably by locality. Retailers are asking wholesalers to work out a chain's allocation levels store by store and to deliver more frequently, to avoid stockouts. And the wholesalers' most profitable retailers are asking for highly preferential terms of trade.

Wholesalers, struggling to meet these new demands, press their suppliers for assistance. The result is a new willingness to reconsider every norm in the magazine publishing industry. For example, a practice that is normal in this industry but unusual in most others is to print massive production runs of a magazine, load the stores with a huge inventory, then take back and shred all the unsold copies. Apparently, this practice exists because the product—an issue of a magazine—is highly variable in quality and is quickly obsolete. Further, local demand is difficult to forecast. Hence, publishers eschew forecasting and stuff the channel instead. Retailers tolerate overstocks because the wholesalers take back stock (which they, in turn, send to the publisher). This bedrock practice is now under scrutiny: Players are debating whether to adopt the nonreturnable practices of other industries.

Another idea being reexamined is the industry wisdom that says demand isn't forecastable locally. Several wholesalers are pooling their data through an organization they have created. This investment in expertise power allows them to learn how to forecast demand right down to the level of one issue of one title in one store— during any hour of operation. If they succeed, they will be in position to influence the behavior of their suppliers (the publishers) and their customers (the retailers). This is a considerable improvement in outcomes for the survivors of the shakeout of 1996.

Will all this consolidation drive out smaller publishers, smaller retailers, and new or alternative magazine titles? Already, a new set of secondary wholesalers has sprung up to distribute these products and represent these channel members, many of which were cut off by the large wholesalers that survived the shakeout. The viability of these wholesalers is demonstrated by the primary demand effect they have created by opening up new markets—stores that had never sold magazines before.[47]

Many relationships of imbalanced dependence actually do work well. For example, department stores employ buyers to pick merchandise for each department. Some manufacturers come to dominate these buyers: The buyers depend on them to supply appealing merchandise with a strong brand name, but the suppliers don't depend on the store as a major outlet. The store might be a family-owned regional chain or a single store in one city, or it might be weak in some departments, while being strong in others. In spite of this imbalance of power, department stores in the United States have been demonstrated to benefit from a dominant-supplier relationship when the market environment is stable (*predictable*). Department stores are able to minimize price reductions by working closely with a dominant supplier when demand is predictable. This outcome is common because suppliers usually refrain from exploiting their department stores' buyers' vulnerability.

But in unpredictable settings, dominant suppliers become a liability. The store doesn't have the power to oblige a dominant supplier to be flexible in reaction to fluctuating demand. In highly *uncertain* market environments, high mutual dependence is preferable: Both suppliers and buyers are motivated to find common solutions to the complex stocking problem. In general, in a diverse and unpredictable market, one-sided dependence is dangerous. Stores are better off with either high balanced dependence to oblige accommodation or low dependence to enable switching suppliers.

In short, imbalanced dependence is not always detrimental. It can work well, particularly in stable environments, which do not put much strain on the channel. In general, imbalanced power relationships work well when the less dependent party voluntarily refrains from abusing its position of power. The channel can function very effectively when the stronger party is careful to treat the more vulnerable one equitably.[48] It then improves the quality of the relationship, hence, the functioning of the channel. Further, every channel member has a reputation at stake. Unfair treatment of one channel member reduces that reputation, making it difficult to attract, retain, and motivate other channel members in the future.

When does the more vulnerable, more dependent channel member consider it is being treated fairly? Equitable treatment comes in two forms. One form of fairness is *distributive justice*, which refers to how the rewards of the relationship are divided up among the channel members. For example, many automobile dealers are dependent on manufacturers with strong brand names, brands in which the dealer invests heavily in ways that are difficult to salvage if the dealership switches brands or goes out of business. The dealer is dependent on the maker. But the maker often can find multiple candidates to become dealerships: The maker is less dependent on the dealer. The latter, being the more vulnerable party, is quick to suspect manufacturer exploitation, which hurts the relationship. This deterioration can be avoided if the manufacturer shares profits with dealers in ways these consider fair.

In weighing distributive fairness, dealers do not merely consider absolute rewards. They compare the benefits they derive from the relationship against four baselines:

1. Their own inputs (what they put into the relationship)
2. The benefits derived by their own colleagues (comparable dealers)
3. The benefits they think they can get from their next best alternative, which may be selling another make of car or even investing their capital elsewhere[49]
4. The other party's inputs (what the car maker puts into the relationship)

Low rewards (in the absolute) seem fair if:

- The dealer invests little
- Other dealers don't gain much either
- The dealer sees no better use for the resources
- The car maker is investing heavily in the relationship, in which case, it is "fair" that the dealer wouldn't earn much, even if the maker is highly profitable

Conversely, dealers may not be satisfied with high rewards because their baseline of comparison can make them think they deserve even more. Even high absolute rewards will be perceived as inequitable (not high enough) by the dealer if:

- The dealer invests heavily
- The maker invests little
- Other dealers are very profitable
- Other opportunities are appealing

The other facet of fairness is *procedural justice*, which is equity in the way the stronger party treats the weaker one on a day-to-day basis in its normal operating procedures. This issue is separate from the fairness of the rewards the weaker party derives. For example, auto dealers consider their supplier to be fairer in a procedural way when the automaker:

1. Communicates both ways (listens as well as talks)
2. Appears to be impartial
3. Is open to argument and debate

The supplier's "boundary personnel," those who interact with the dealer, play an important role here. When they

1. Explain themselves
2. Are courteous
3. Are knowledgeable about channel members' situations

Then dealers develop a strong sense that the supplier is procedurally fair.

This does a great deal to make the relationship work smoothly, in spite of the inherent imbalance in dependence. Indeed, field evidence shows that procedural justice actually has more impact than distributive justice on the vulnerable party's sense that the relationship is equitable. One reason is that the latter is not readily observable (who really knows all the factors that influence it?), whereas the former is readily and regularly observable.[50]

EXERCISING POWER: INFLUENCE STRATEGIES

To this point, we have described circumstances in which power ought to be present (dependence, the five bases) and the consequences of the balance of dependence. Fundamentally, power is invisible: We can never be sure how much power one party has in a channel relationship. This leads to an intriguing question: What happens if a firm has power but doesn't exercise it? Will the other party realize that there is unused, or latent, power? And what happens to power if no one uses it? Do the players alter their behavior anyway? Does unused power wither away? Can power be "banked," or stored, to be used when needed?

These questions are fascinating, but evidence from the field suggests that they are moot. *The more that parties have power, the more they tend to use it.* They don't leave it in a power bank or act in the same way they would if they were powerless. Latent power is rapidly converted to exercised power.[51]

Six Influence Strategies

But how? Converting the potential for influence into real changes in the other party's behavior requires communication.[52] The nature of that communication affects channel relationships.[53] Boundary personnel (those who represent their company to other channel members, e.g., salespeople, purchasing agents, and district managers) use strategies to influence their channel counterparts. Extensive study of field interactions reveals that most of their channel communications can be grouped into the following six categories, or *influence strategies*:

1. *Promise strategy.* If you do what we wish, we will reward you.
2. *Threat strategy.* If you don't do what we wish, we will punish you.
3. *Legalistic strategy.* You should do what we wish, because in some way you agreed to do it. (The agreement could be a contract, or it could be the informal working understanding of how the parties do business.)
4. *Request strategy.* Please do what we wish (no further specification).
5. *Information exchange strategy. Without mentioning what we wish,* pursuing a general discussion about the most profitable way for the counterpart to run *its* business. This strategy is oblique. The objective is to change the counterpart's perceptions of what is effective in a way that favors the objectives of the influencer. It is a subtle form of persuasion: The counterpart is left to draw the conclusion as to what it should do.
6. *Recommendation strategy.* It is the same as information exchange, but states the conclusion this time. "You will be more profitable if you do what we wish." Compared to information exchange, the recommendation strategy is more overt, making it more likely to generate skepticism and counterargument.

Each of these influence strategies rests on having certain sources of power. Figure 8.2 maps influence strategies to their corresponding power bases.

Channel members that have not invested in building the corresponding bases find their usage of influence attempts futile. Of course, how much of each base a channel member has depends on the influencer and on the target. For example, Nestlé has far more reward power and will use the promise strategy more effectively with a small retailer rather than with a hypermarket.

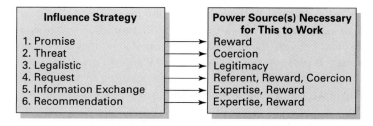

Influence Strategy	Power Source(s) Necessary for This to Work
1. Promise	Reward
2. Threat	Coercion
3. Legalistic	Legitimacy
4. Request	Referent, Reward, Coercion
5. Information Exchange	Expertise, Reward
6. Recommendation	Expertise, Reward

FIGURE 8.2 **Using Power to Exert Influence**

As a general rule, boundary personnel eventually come to use all six strategies in each of their relationships. But each relationship has a style, depending on which strategies are used most often. The predominant style, the influence strategy used more often, influences how well the firm converts its power into actual behavior changes. This is because channel members interpret the six strategies differently.

The Consequences of Each Strategy

The first three styles (promise, threat, legalistic) often provoke a backlash because they are perceived as heavy-handed, high-pressure techniques. Counterparts resent them and tend to respond by using the same strategies themselves. In particular, the use of threats provokes conflict and damages the counterpart's sense of satisfaction, both economically and psychologically. In the short term, high-pressure techniques are effective. But they have damaging longer-term effects on the counterpart's trust and commitment.[54]

What about a promise strategy? Logically, it should be seen as a reward, which is altogether positive. But the object of this influence attempt often doesn't see a promise in such a cold-eyed manner. A promise can be perceived as a bribe, as insulting and unprofessional, something of a forcing technique. Or the promise may be seen as a veiled criticism of the counterpart's performance ("If they really thought I was doing a good job, they would have given me this already"). Promises beget more promises: Using this strategy encourages the counterpart to respond with its own promises. Using such a strategy sets off a spiral of haggling.

Over the longer term, it has mixed effects. From a process standpoint—psychological satisfaction based on interpersonal processes—channel members dislike the promise strategy. But from a strictly economic standpoint, channel members welcome promises. The counterpart usually delivers on these promises, and the channel member's financial indicators improve. This in turn does a great deal to dampen conflict.

The conclusion? The promise strategy, while self-perpetuating, is an effective way to change a channel member's behavior, even though it raises interpersonal tension.

The last three influence strategies (request, information exchange, recommendation) are more subtle, more nuanced than the first three. Channel counterparts welcome these efforts and do not take offense at their usage. These three strategies increase all facets of a counterpart's satisfaction, economically and interpersonally. Information exchange and recommendation do not provoke the impression of high pressure, of heavy-handedness, even when the influencer's objective is the same as under promises, threats, or legalism. Indeed, information exchange is so subtle that it is somewhat risky: It won't work if the counterpart doesn't even think of the behavior that is desired.

This risk doesn't occur with the recommendation strategy. Recommendation, although more overt because the desired behavior is stated, does not threaten the counterpart's autonomy. It presents the desired action as being in the counterpart's own overall business interests. And it is difficult to imagine reacting to a pure request as being heavy-handed. Such a request, no reason given, is so low pressure that it is almost surprising that this strategy is common! Some evidence indicates that these two light-handed strategies, request and recommendation, are used most often. The most heavy-handed strategies, threats and legalisms, are used least often.[55]

This pattern is somewhat different in close, long-term relationships. Here, information exchange, recommendations, and promises are the dominant influence strategies.[56] In these more committed relationships, the parties refrain from threatening each other and spend little time making requests without stating a reason. They are candid in their efforts to influence each other. Offering a reward for desired behavior is a frequently used strategy, along with leaving the other party to draw conclusions (information exchange) and arguing that the desired behavior benefits the counterpart (recommendations). In long-term relationships, the importance of win–win solutions is accepted by both parties. This may be why the promises strategy is normal and does not appear to generate resentment, backlash, or pressure, as it often does in more conventional channel relationships.

A caveat is in order here. Most of the available systematic evidence suggests that more subtle influence strategies improve the interpersonal quality of a relationship, whereas more overt influence strategies risk provoking resentment. However, most of this evidence is from Western business cultures. We should exercise caution in extrapolating to other settings. For example, overt efforts to influence distributors by employing threats and citing one's contract will damage relationships in North America. In Japan, these techniques may actually improve the interpersonal quality of working relationships between distributors and suppliers. This is not to say Japanese distributors welcome threats! Yet what may be perceived as menacing in a Western context may be perceived as an appropriate exercise of authority, based on a supplier's prestige in the channel. This status may confer an inherent right to exact some degree of obedience.[57]

In other words, what is considered coercive power in one culture may be considered legitimate power in another. It is likely that how a power base is perceived is to some degree culture specific. Unfortunately, evidence of these differences is sparse at the present time.

How to Frame an Influence Attempt

It is a truism that what you present is less important than how you frame it. Considerable evidence indicates that framing effects are powerful in channels.[58]

For example, let us take a distributor that is already carrying a supplier's line. The supplier is launching a major, risky, unproven new product and wants to influence the distributor to agree to carry it as well. How should the influencer frame the message to the target?

The *valence* of the frame is whether it is presented as a positive or a negative.

- *Positive frame.* If you *do* take on our new product, you *will* get substantial additional marketing support.
- *Negative frame.* If you *don't* take on our new product, you *won't* get substantial additional marketing support.

Both statements say the same thing: The new product is accompanied by its own support. But the positive frame is more effective because the negative frame focuses the target on what sounds like a loss of something. Human beings feel threatened by losses; indeed, they dread loss more than they value gains. Negative framing makes decision makers feel pressured. It damages their satisfaction and trust and threatens their auton-omy.

Valence is a matter of sheer presentation. In contrast, a more substantial issue is whether to frame an influence attempt as *contingent*.

- A contingent appeal hinges on compliance: *If you* take on our new product, *we will* give you the distributor-of-the-year award.
- A noncontingent appeal is *unilaterally* bestowed whether compliance is forth-coming: "Congratulations, you've been named our distributor of the year! Oh, and we have a new product to propose to you. . . ."

It is no surprise that targets are more satisfied, more trusting, and feel their auton-omy is more respected when the influencer uses contingent appeals. What is surprising is the way in which contingent framing undermines the force of the appeal. Often, the target can be persuaded without the contingency. If a contingency is presented and the target complies, the side effect is that the target believes it complied because of the con-tingency. At the limit, targets feel bribed, pressured, purchased. Their intrinsic motiva-tion (sense that they complied for their own reasons) declines. In contrast, minus the contingency, the target has to explain compliance and is likely do so by deciding "This is what we wanted to do. This makes sense for us." This reasoning solidifies the relation-ship.

The implications are these: Train boundary spanners to use positive frames, and don't offer a contingent argument where a noncontingent argument will do.

It is worth noting that these framing effects work when the influencer initially approaches the target. *Once the performance outcomes are known, they override the ini-tial framing effects.* For example, if, five years later, the distributor finds the new line performs well, negative frames and contingent appeals will be forgiven and forgotten. But if the line performs poorly, positive frames and noncontingent appeals won't stop the recrimination.

SUMMARY

Channel power is the ability to alter another organization's behavior. It is a tool, neither good nor bad. And it is a necessary tool. What is good for a marketing channel is not necessarily in the interests of every channel member. Power is needed to make channels realize their potential to add value. Like any tool, judicious use of power is wise. In chan-nels, this means sharing rewards equitably with channel members, even those in weak positions.

One way to think about power is to conceptualize the power of A as being equal to the dependence of B. The dependence of B on A is high when B derives great utility from dealing with A and can't find that utility easily in one of A's competitors. Real alter-natives to A are few when there are few competitors, or when B faces very high switch-ing costs if it leaves A. Thinking of power as dependence focuses the analyst on the issue of replaceability, an important aspect of power.

Power can also be conceptualized as coming from five sources. Reward power is the ability to deliver benefits in return for altering behavior. This is the most natural, and generally most effective, means of exerting power. One reason it works so well is that it is frequently unobtrusive. The players, in responding to economic incentives, are often unaware that they are altering their behavior to fit another's preferences.

Coercive power is the ability to impose punishment. It works well in the short run and is therefore addictive. It also escalates: Coercion tends to be reciprocated by the channel counterpart. In the long run, in Western business cultures, coercion is a corrosive influence. It either destroys relationships quickly or erodes them slowly. Occasionally, coercion is justified in the short term to make major change happen, change that benefits all parties. But unless this benefit is apparent, coercive tactics will damage even successful relationships.

Expert power comes from holding valuable information (including expert judgment) the channel member could use and doesn't have. It is an extremely effective mechanism in channels, although it is often difficult to implement. Legitimate power comes from laws, contracts, and agreements, as well as from industry norms and from norms and values specific to a channel relationship. Referent power comes from a channel member's desire to identify with another organization, often for reasons of borrowing prestige. These five bases of power can have synergistic effects when used together in a skillful manner.

Of course, power is a two-sided affair. In particular, dependence operates in both directions. When B is dependent on A, it is often the case that the dependence is mutual: A depends on B as well. These mutually dependent relationships often generate exceptional value added. Each side has leverage to drive the other to develop win–win solutions.

When dependence is imbalanced, the weaker party is the more dependent of the two. This is an uncomfortable position, because the stronger party can readily exploit or ignore the weaker one. The more dependent party can take countermeasures, including diversifying (building in alternative suppliers of the channel member's services), forming a coalition to bring pressure on the powerful member, and exiting the business.

Nonetheless, imbalanced relationships are very common and can function quite well. The key is restraint on the part of the stronger party. It is important not only to act equitably but also to be perceived as a fair player. The stronger party can take steps to ensure it is seen as just, in both the distribution of rewards and the daily procedures it follows in its channel relationships.

Translating power, a latent ability, into influence involves communication with six common influence strategies. Three of them—promise, threat, and legalistic—are fairly obtrusive. In Western cultures, they often provoke resentment and conflict. These strategies may not be out of place in other business environments. Of these three obtrusive methods, the strategy of making promises (offering rewards for desired behavior) is quite effective, on the whole, and is a staple of strong, long-term relationships. Three other common influence strategies are making requests for no stated reason, exchanging information (failing to draw a conclusion while discussing the other party's business), and making recommendations (the explicit form of exchanging information). These strategies are more subtle (in some cases, too subtle). They do not explicitly invoke the influencer's desires and interests; hence, they are perceived as low-pressure strategies. Their effectiveness is heightened by their unobtrusive nature.

In the short term, a negative or contingent framing is usually inferior to a positive or noncontingent framing. In the long run, performance outcomes substantially override these effects.

Power permeates all aspects of marketing channels. The interdependence of channel members makes power a critical feature of their functioning. Channel members must invest over time to build power. They must assess power accurately and use it wisely, both to carry out their initiatives and to protect themselves. To ignore considerations of power is to sacrifice opportunities and to expose vulnerabilities.

Discussion Questions

1. What is the relationship between coercive and reward power? Between reward power and referent, expert, and legitimate power? Give three examples to support your arguments.

2. Why is it unlikely that a marketing channel will be coordinated naturally? Why is power necessary to achieve coordination?

3. "Suppliers should not deal with intermediaries who are more powerful than they are." Debate this statement, which is often heard at trade association meetings.

4. "We should not deal with powerful suppliers. They are sure to abuse us—after they use us." Debate this statement, often heard in the meeting rooms of distributors and sales agents.

5. DuPont Agricultural Chemicals is an extremely large and diversified supplier of herbicides and pesticides to farmers. Several of its competitors are also large and diversified, such as Monsanto and Dow. Imagine a dealer, selling a full line of whatever a corporate or individual farmer would use, including agricultural chemicals. Is it possible to imagine a scenario in which the dealer is more powerful than DuPont is? What factors might make this possible?

6. You are the owner–manager of an auto dealership in Germany, selling the Audi line. Your dealership is exclusive to Audi, you have invested heavily to build the dealership, and your contract is such that, if you decide to sell your dealership, Audi has the right to approve or disapprove any buyer you might find. What is the balance of power in your relationship? What sort of working relationship are you likely to have with your supplier? What could your supplier do to ensure you do not become alienated?

7. Consider the Audi scenario in question 6, and put yourself in the role of the Audi liaison—the factory rep. What influence strategies would you use, and why? Now put yourself in the position of the factory rep's supervisor. What kind of person would you hire for this position? How would you supervise and compensate your rep?

8. "We give this supplier a lot of sales and a pretty good level of profit. We hold up its brand name, and we tend to follow its advice. This means we have very high leverage over it. We've got a lot of power, and we should use it." Debate this statement. Is it correct? What else do you need to know to assess whether it is true?

9. When is a channel member likely to overestimate its power? When will it underestimate its power?

10. What is the relationship between thinking of power as dependence and thinking of power as five sources? Which one is simpler? Which approach is more useful to a manager?

11. "Coercion is just a negative reward. It's all reward power. Power all comes down to one question: Where's the money?" Debate this statement.

Notes

1. Edward Feitzinger and Hau L. Lee, "Mass Customization at Hewlett-Packard: The Power of Postponement," *Harvard Business Review*, 75 (January–February 1997), pp. 116–21.

2. Abel P. Jeuland and Steven M. Shugan, "Managing Channel Profits," *Marketing Science*, 2, no. 3 (1983), pp. 239–72.

3. Richard M. Emerson, "Power–Dependence Relations," *American Sociological Review*, 27 (February 1962), pp. 31–41.

4. Arch G. Woodside, "Measuring Customer Awareness and Share-of-Requirements Awarded to Competing Industrial Distributors," *Industrial Marketing and Purchasing*, 2, no. 2 (1987), pp. 47–68.

5. Adel El-Ansary and Louis W. Stern, "Power Measurement in the Distribution Channel," *Journal of Marketing Research*, 9 (February 1972), pp. 47–52.

6. Sudhir H. Kale, "Dealer Perceptions of Manufacturer Power and Influence Strategies in a Developing Country," *Journal of Marketing Research*, 23 (November 1986), pp. 387–93.

7. Gary L. Frazier, "On the Measurement of Interfirm Power in Channels of Distribution," *Journal of Marketing Research*, 20 (May 1983), pp. 158–66.

8. Gary L. Frazier, James D. Gill, and Sudhir H. Kale, "Dealer Dependence Levels and Reciprocal Actions in a Channel of Distribution in a Developing Country," *Journal of Marketing*, 53 (January 1989), pp. 50–69.

9. El-Ansary, Adel and Louis W. Stern, "Power Measurement in the Distribution Channel," *Journal of Marketing Research*, 9 (February 1972), pp. 47–52.

10. James R. Brown, Jean L. Johnson, and Harold F. Koenig, "Measuring the Sources of Marketing Channel Power: A Comparison of Alternative Approaches," *International Journal of Research in Marketing*, 12, no. 2 (1995), pp. 333–54.

11. John R. French Jr. and Bertram Raven, "The Bases of Social Power" in Dorwin Cartwright (ed.), *Studies in Social Power* (Ann Arbor, MI: University of Michigan, 1959) pp. 150–67.

12. Jean-Yves Guerin, "Decathlon: Les Secrets d'un Champion," *L'Essential du Management*, April 1999, pp. 12–16. Quotations from p. 15.

13. John F. Gaski and John R. Nevin, "The Differential Effects of Exercised and Unexercised Power Sources in a Marketing Channel," *Journal of Marketing Research*, 22, no. 2 (May 1985), pp. 130–42.

14. Charles L. Munson, Meir J. Rosenblatt, and Zehava Rosenblatt, "The Use and Abuse of Power in Supply Chains," *Business Horizons*, 30 (January–February 1999), pp. 55–65. This article gives many examples of channel power in operation.

15. Inge Geyskens, Jan-Benedict E. M. Steenkamp, and Nirmalya Kumar, "A Meta-Analysis of Satisfaction in Marketing Channel Relationships," *Journal of Marketing Research*, 36 (May 1999), pp. 223–38.

16. Inge Geyskens, Jan-Benedict E. M. Steenkamp, and Nirmalya Kumar, "Generalizations About Trust in Marketing Channel Relationships Using Meta Analysis," *International Journal of Research in Marketing*, 15, no. 1 (1998), pp. 223–48.

17. Munson, Charles L., Meir J. Rosenblatt, and Zehava Rosenblatt, "The Use and Abuse of Power in Supply Chains," *Business Horizons*, 30 (January–February 1999), pp. 55–65.

18. Paul Hart and Carol Saunders, "Power and Trust: Critical Factors in the Adoption and Use of Electronic Data Interchange," *Organization Science*, 8 (January–February 1997), pp. 23–42.

19. Eryn Brown, "VF CORP. Changes Its Underware," *Fortune*, December 7, 1998, pp. 79–82.

20. Bertram H. Raven and Arie W. Kruglanski, "Conflict and Power" in P. Swingle (ed.), *The Structure of Conflict* (New York: Academic Press, 1970), pp. 69–99.

21. David Dunne and Chakravarthi Narasimhan, "The New Appeal of Private Labels," *Harvard Business Review*, 53 (May–June 1999), pp. 41–52.

22. Erin Anderson and Barton Weitz, "Determinants of Continuity in Conventional Channel Dyads," *Marketing Science*, 8 (fall 1989), pp. 310–23.

23. Janet E. Keith, Donald W. Jackson Jr., and Lawrence A. Crosby, "Effects of Alternative Types of Influence Strategies Under Different Channel Dependence Structures," *Journal of Marketing*, 54, no. 3 (July 1990), pp. 30–41.

24. Douglas Holt, "Liquor Distributors Test New Law," *Chicago Tribune*, June 29, 1999, pp. 1, 20; Editorial, "Gov. Ryan Gets Message in a Bottle," *Chicago Tribune*, January 25, 2000, p. 20; Douglas Holt and Joseph T. Hallinan, "Ryan Backs Move to Repeal Liquor Law," *Chicago Tribune*, January 25, 2000, pp. 1–2. Quotation from p. 1; Ray Long and Joseph T. Hallinan, "Philip Wants to Let Courts Sort Out Liquor Law," *Chicago Tribune*, January 26, 2000, pp. 1–2.

25. Erin Anderson and Barton Weitz, "The Use of Pledges to Build and Sustain Commitment in Distribution Channels," *Journal of Marketing Research*, 24 (February 1992), pp. 18–34.

26. Ian R. Macneil, *The New Social Contract: An Inquiry into Modern Contractual Relations* (New Haven, Connecticut: Yale University Press, 1980); Patrick J. Kaufmann and Louis W. Stern, "Relational Exchange Norms, Perceptions of Unfairness, and Retained Hostility in Com-

mercial Litigation," *Journal of Conflict Resolution*, 32 (September 1988), pp. 534–52.

27. Jan B. Heide and George John, "Do Norms Matter in Marketing Relationships?" *Journal of Marketing*, 56 (April 1992), pp. 32–44.

28. Wujin Chu and Woosik Chu, "Signaling Quality by Selling Through a Reputable Retailer: An Example of Renting the Reputation of Another Agent," *Marketing Science*, 13 (spring 1994), pp. 177–89.

29. Vincent Giolito, "Quiksilver Surfe sur la Mode Ado," *L'Essentiel du Management*, March 1999, pp. 18–19.

30. Steven Lippman and Richard R. Rumelt, "Uncertain Imitability: An Analysis of Interfirm Differences in Efficiency Under Competition," *Bell Journal of Economics*, 13, no. 1 (1982), pp. 418–38.

31. John F. Gaski, "Interrelations Among a Channel Entity's Power Sources: Impact of the Exercise of Reward and Coercion on Expert, Referent, and Legitimate Power Sources," *Journal of Marketing Research*, 23 (February 1985), pp. 62–77.

32. Dunne, David and Chakravarthi Narasimhan, "The New Appeal of Private Labels," *Harvard Business Review*, 53 (May–June 1999), pp. 41–52.

33. Robert F. Lusch and James R. Brown, "Interdependency, Contracting, and Relational Behavior in Marketing Channels," *Journal of Marketing*, 60 (October 1996), pp. 19–38.

34. Lars Hallén, Jan Johanson, and Nazeem Seyed-Mohamed, "Interfirm Adaptation in Business Relationships," *Journal of Marketing*, 55 (April 1991), pp. 29–37.

35. Lauranne Buchanan, "Vertical Trade Relationships: The Role of Dependence and Symmetry in Attaining Organizational Goals," *Journal of Marketing Research*, 29 (February 1992), pp. 65–75.

36. Jan B. Heide, "Interorganizational Governance in Marketing Channels," *Journal of Marketing*, 58 (January 1994), pp. 71–85.

37. Robert F. Dwyer, Paul H. Schurr, and Sejo Oh, "Developing Buyer–Seller Relationships," *Journal of Marketing*, 51 (April 1987), pp. 11–27.

38. Keith G. Provan and Steven J. Skinner, "Interorganizational Dependence and Control as Predictors of Opportunism in Dealer–Supplier Relations," *Academy of Management Journal*, 32, no. 1 (March 1989), pp. 202–12.

39. William T. Ross, Erin Anderson, and Barton Weitz, "Performance in Principal–Agent Dyads: The Causes and Consequences of Perceived Asymmetry of Commitment to the Relationship," *Management Science*, 43 (May 1997), pp. 680–704.

40. "Unravelling," *The Economist*, 351 (January 2, 1999), p. 63.

41. Nirmalya Kumar, Lisa K. Scheer, and Jan-Benedict E. M. Steenkamp, "The Effects of Perceived Interdependence on Dealer Attitudes," *Journal of Marketing Research*, 32 (August 1994), pp. 348–56.

42. Jan B. Heide and George John, "The Role of Dependence Balancing in Safeguarding Transaction-Specific Assets in Conventional Channels," *Journal of Marketing*, 52, no. 1 (January 1988), pp. 20–35.

43. Steven J. Skinner and Joseph P. Guiltinan, "Perceptions of Channel Control," *Journal of Retailing*, 61 (winter 1985), pp. 65–88.

44. Jerome Parigi and Daniel Bicard, "Double Affichage: Un Engrenage Dangereux," *LSA*, August 1999, pp. 16–18.

45. An excellent discussion of this trend and its implications is Adam J. Fein and Sandy D. Jap, "Manage Consolidation in the Distribution Channel," *Sloan Management Review*, 41 (fall 1999), pp. 61–72.

46. Régine Eveno, "Fusion: Le Nouveau Carrefour Prend Corps," *LSA*, February 3, 2000, pp. 24–27. Quotation from p. 25.

47. Cris Beam, "Retailers Rule," *Folio: The Magazine for Magazine Management*, 26 (March 15, 1997), pp. 24–26.

48. Nirmalya Kumar, Lisa K. Scheer, and Jan-Benedict E. M. Steenkamp, "The Effects of Supplier Fairness on Vulnerable Resellers," *Journal of Marketing Research*, 32 (February 1995), pp. 54–65.

49. James C. Anderson and James A. Narus, "A Model of the Distributor's Perspective of Distributor–Manufacturer Working Relationships," *Journal of Marketing*, 48 (fall 1984), pp. 62–74.

50. Nirmalya Kumar, "The Power of Trust in Manufacturer–Retailer Relationships," *Harvard Business Review*, 76 (November–December 1996), pp. 92–106.

51. Gaski, John F. and John R. Nevin, "The Differential Effects of Exercised and Unexercised Power Sources in a Marketing Channel," *Journal of Marketing Research*, 22 (May 1985), pp. 130–42.

52. Reinhard Angelmar and Louis W. Stern, "Development of a Content Analytic System for Analysis of Bargaining Communication in Marketing," *Journal of Marketing Research*, 15 (February 1978), pp. 93–102.

53. This discussion is based on Gary L. Frazier and John O. Summers, "Perceptions of Interfirm Power and Its Use Within a Franchise Channel of Distribution," *Journal of Marketing Research*, 23, no. 2 (May 1986), pp. 169–76.

54. Geyskens, Inge, Jan-Benedict E. M. Steenkamp, and Nirmalya Kumar, "A Meta-Analysis of Satisfaction in Marketing Channel Relationships," *Journal of Marketing Research*, 36 (May 1999), pp. 223–38.

55. Gary L. Frazier and John O. Summers, "Interfirm Influence Strategies and Their Application Within Distribu-

tion Channels," *Journal of Marketing*, 48 (summer 1984), pp. 43–55.

56. Brett F. Boyle, Robert Dwyer, Robert A. Robicheaux, et al., "Influence Strategies in Marketing Channels: Measures and Use in Different Relationship Structures," *Journal of Marketing Research*, 29 (November 1992), pp. 462–73.

57. Jean L. Johnson, Tomoaki Sakano, Joseph A. Cote, and Naoto Onzo, "The Exercise of Interfirm Power and Its Repercussions in U.S.-Japanese Channel Relationships," *Journal of Marketing*, 57 (April 1993), pp. 1–10.

58. This discussion is based on Lisa K. Scheer and Louis W. Stern, "The Effect of Influence Type and Performance Outcomes on Attitude Toward the Influencer," *Journal of Marketing Research*, 29 (February 1992), pp. 128–42.

9
Managing Conflict to Increase Channel Coordination

LEARNING OBJECTIVES

After reading this chapter, you will:

- Distinguish circumstances where conflict is not negative and is neutral or even positive
- Understand how to diagnose conflict in terms of issues, frequency, intensity, and importance
- Trace the negative effects of high conflict on channel performance
- Sketch the inherent sources of conflict in channel relationships
- Separate conflict into three main causes: goals, perceptions, and domains
- Understand why multiple channels have become the norm and describe ways to address the conflict they create
- Understand why many suppliers actually like gray markets while protesting to the contrary
- Trace the spiral of coercion and reciprocation
- Describe the workings of institutionalized mechanisms that management can use to dampen conflict, and distinguish between those that management can decree and those that arise in a relationship (norms)
- Categorize conflict resolution styles and describe their effect on how well a channel functions
- Sketch the effect of economic incentives (especially hidden ones) on conflict

hannel conflict is a state of opposition, or discord, among the organizations comprising a marketing channel. It may seem curious that *conflict is a normal state in a channel*. Indeed, a *certain amount of conflict is even a desirable state*: For purposes of maximizing performance, a channel can be too harmonious. How can managers direct conflict to create functional channel outcomes?

This chapter examines how to recognize the many forms of conflict, including latent conflict (of which channel members may be unaware), perceived conflict, functional conflict, and overt conflict. The parties to a conflicting channel often diagnose their disagreements inaccurately. This chapter presents methods to help a third party discern the true nature and level of conflict in a channel relationship.

The chapter also covers questions such as:

- What are the effects of conflict, long and short term, on the functioning of the channel, its coordination, its ultimate performance, and its future?
- How does conflict arise, and how can it be managed?
- What are the best strategies for containing destructive, excessive conflict, and redirecting the antagonists to achieve higher levels of channel coordination and performance?

Fortunately, a very substantial body of field research exists to offer answers to these questions, based on the combined experience (much of it negative) of a variety of channels. This chapter covers the lessons to be drawn from the mistakes of existing channels—and from their successes. Background on how these lessons were drawn from field research is in the references cited in the endnotes.

ASSESSING THE DEGREE AND NATURE OF CHANNEL CONFLICT

What Is Channel Conflict?

The word *conflict* is derived from the Latin *confligere*, to collide. By the everyday meaning of the word, there is little that could be constructive in a conflict. Conflict, like collision, has negative connotations: contention, disunity, disharmony, argument, friction, hostility, antagonism, struggle, battle . . . the many synonyms are emotionally laden. In individual personal relationships, conflict is almost invariably viewed as something to avoid, a sign of trouble.

For purposes of managing marketing channels, these everyday interpretations of *conflict* should be set aside because they are one sided. Conflict between and among organizations comprising a channel should be considered in a more neutral light. Conflict per se is not negative in distribution channels. Rather than keeping channel members apart and damaging their relationship, *some conflict (and in some forms) actually strengthens and improves a channel*. To see why, let us reexamine what *conflict* means.

Channel conflict arises when the behavior of a channel member is in opposition to its channel counterpart. It is opponent centered and direct, in which the goal or object sought is controlled by the counterpart.

Channel conflict occurs when one member of a channel views its upstream or downstream partner as an adversary or opponent. The key is that interdependent parties at different levels of the same channel (upstream and downstream) attempt to block each other. In contrast, competition is behavior in which a channel member is working for a goal or object controlled by a third party (such as customers, regulators, or competitors). Competing parties struggle against obstacles in their environment. Conflicting parties struggle against each other.[1]

Conflict implies an incompatibility at some level. Conflict frequently exists at such a low level that channel members do not fully sense it. This *latent conflict* is due to conditions that set the interests of the parties at odds. Latent conflict is the norm in marketing channels. Inevitably, the interests of channel members collide as all parties pursue their separate goals, strive to retain their autonomy, and compete for limited resources. If each player could ignore the others, latent conflict would be nil. But companies linked as a channel are fundamentally interdependent.[2] Every member needs all the other members in order to meet the end-user's service output demands and to do so economically.

This fundamental interdependence is a given, taken for granted as a fact of life in marketing channels. Organizations, unlike most people, face more conflicts than they can deal with, given the time and capacities available. To cope, organizations focus attention on only a few of their latent conflicts at a time.[3] Frequently, the ones they overlook involve their channel partners. Therefore, they fail to factor in latent conflict when they develop new channel initiatives and are surprised to meet active opposition to their suggestions for improvement.

Latent conflict exists when the conditions are right for contention, but the organization is unaware of it. Perception is missing. In contrast, *perceived conflict* occurs when a channel member senses that some sort of opposition exists: opposition of viewpoints, of perceptions, of sentiments, of interests, or of intentions. Perceived conflict is cognitive, that is, emotionless and mental. It is a situation of contention.

Two organizations can perceive they are in disagreement, but their individual members experience little emotion as a result. They describe themselves as "businesslike" or "professional" and consider their differences to be "all in a day's work." This, too, is a normal state in marketing channels and gives little cause for alarm. Indeed, the members would not describe their dealings as conflictual, even though they oppose each other, perhaps even on important issues.

But when emotions (affect) do enter, the channel experiences *felt conflict*, or affective conflict. At this stage, the players describe their channel as conflictual because organization members experience negative emotions: tension, anxiety, anger, frustration, hostility. When conflict reaches this level, organization members begin to personalize their differences. Their descriptions of the interactions between their organizations begin to sound like disputes between people (i.e., they personify and then vilify the companies). Economic considerations fade into the background as the antagonists impute human features and personal motives to channel organizations. Often, emotions of outrage and unfairness reach a point that managers refuse economically sensible choices and hurt their own organizations in order to "punish" their channel counterparts.[4]

If not managed, felt conflict can escalate quickly into *manifest conflict*. This opposition is visible because it is expressed in behavior. Between two organizations, manifest conflict usually appears as blocking each other's initiatives and withdrawing support. In the worst cases, one side tries to sabotage the other or take revenge. Fundamentally, one side tries to block the other from achieving its goals.

Conflict is often considered as a state: The level of conflict in a channel relationship is assessed, something like taking a photograph. But conflict is also a process, something like filming a movie: It consists of episodes or incidents. How each episode is interpreted by the parties depends on the history of their relationship. When substantial felt and manifest conflict occur frequently in a channel relationship, each new conflict incident will be seen in the worst light. Malevolent motives will be attributed to the channel counterpart, great weight will be attached to a single incident, and a channel member will become convinced its counterpart is incompetent, operates in bad faith, and so forth. Conversely, a positive history creates a positive future: A new conflict incident will be downplayed or charitably interpreted.

Measuring Conflict

How should the observer go about diagnosing the true level of conflict that an organization faces in a channel relationship? The best way is to gather four kinds of information. The following example is from an assessment of how much conflict automobile dealers experience in their relationships with car manufacturers.[5]

Step 1: Counting Up the Issues. What are major issues of relevance to two parties in their channel relationship? For car dealers, *one study* uncovers 15 issues of relevance to dealers in their relationships with the manufacturer, including inventories (vehicles and parts), allocation and delivery of cars, the size of the dealer's staff, advertising, allowances for preparation of the car, and reimbursement for warranty work. It does not matter whether the issues are in dispute at the moment. What matters is that they are major aspects of the channel relationship.

Step 2: Importance. For each issue, ascertain how important this issue is to the dealer. This could be done judgmentally or by asking dealers directly. For example, they may indicate on a scale of zero to ten (very unimportant to very important) how important each issue is to the dealership's profitability.

Step 3: Frequency of Disagreement. For each issue, ascertain judgmentally or by collecting data how often the two parties disagree over this issue. For example, dealers may be asked to recall discussion with the manufacturer over the issue during the last year and to indicate on a scale of zero to ten (never to always) how frequently those discussions involved disagreement.

Step 4: Intensity of Dispute. For each issue, ascertain judgmentally or by collecting data how intensely the two parties differ on the issue (how far apart the two parties' positions are). For example, dealers may indicate on a scale of zero to ten (not very intense to very intense) how strongly they disagree during a typical discussion they have of the issue.

These four kinds of information should be combined to form an index of manifest conflict for each issue:

$$\text{Conflict} = \sum_{i=1}^{N} \text{Importance}_i \times \text{Frequency}_i \times \text{Intensity}_i$$

Adding their products over all the N issues (for the car dealers, $N = 15$) forms an index of conflict. These estimates can be compared across dealers to see where the most serious conflict occurs and why.

Behind this simple formula is an insight that channel combatants, overtaken by emotion, can easily overlook. There is no real argument over any issue if

- The difference of opinion rarely occurs (low frequency).
- The issue is petty (low importance).
- The two parties are not very far apart on the issue (low intensity).

If any of these elements is low, the issue is not a genuine source of conflict. This principle is expressed by the fact that multiplying by zero creates a product of zero. So if an allowance for prepping a car is a minor issue, it is of no real import that disagreements over it are intense or frequent. Likewise, if the dealer and supplier are not far apart in their positions about car prep allowances, it is of little relevance if the issue is important or comes up regularly. Finally, if preparation allowances seldom present themselves as a topic of discussion, there is little need for concern, even if it is an important issue on which the parties hold quite different opinions.

When a relationship is complex, many issues arise. The 15 issues ($N = 15$) for car dealers occur because selling cars is no simple affair. In general, the more roles a channel member assumes, the greater the scope for disagreements, and therefore the greater the potential for conflict. For example, franchising is a complex channel form in which each side (franchisor and franchisee) has elaborate role descriptions (see Chapter 17). Accordingly, one study inventories 20 major issues in a franchising relationship.[6]

This conflict formula is efficient in capturing the overall sense of frustration in a channel relationship. The usefulness of the formula is that it allows the diagnostician to be specific, to pinpoint exactly where and why the parties are in opposition. The combatants themselves are frequently unable to disentangle the sources of their friction. Particularly in highly conflictual channels, the personalities involved become polarized and come to believe that they disagree more than they really do. Inflamed relationships lead people to double count issues; to overlook issues on which they do agree; and to exaggerate the importance, intensity, and frequency of their differences. A third party can help them see the true sources of their disagreements. This is the first step to finding a solution.

THE CONSEQUENCES OF CONFLICT

When Conflict Is Desirable

Conflict is usually thought to be dysfunctional, to hurt a relationship's coordination and performance. Although this is generally true, opposition actually makes a relationship better on certain occasions. This is functional (useful) conflict. *Functional conflict* is common when channel members recognize each other's contribution and understand that each party's success depends on the other(s). In these channels, the parties are able to oppose each other without damaging their arrangement. Their opposition leads them to:

1. Communicate more frequently and effectively
2. Establish outlets for expressing their grievances
3. Critically review their past actions
4. Devise and implement a more equitable split of system resources
5. Develop a more balanced distribution of power in their relationship
6. Develop standardized ways to deal with future conflict and keep it within bounds[7]

Conflict can be functional because channel members drive each other to improve their performance. By raising and working through their differences, they incite each other to do better and challenge each other to break old habits and assumptions. See Channel Sketch 9.1 for examples.

CHANNEL SKETCH 9.1
Examples of Functional Conflict

Procter & Gamble Challenges French Wholesale Pricing Practices[8]

National norms in pricing are the subject of a long conflict between Procter & Gamble and several French hypermarket chains. The hypermarket concept originated in the late 1950s. Its format is the combination of food and nonfood consumer goods under one huge roof, usually on the outskirts of cities. Several hypermarket chains have been able to use their market power and popularity to impose a unique pricing arrangement on their suppliers. Ordinarily, retailers negotiate their margins up front, when they purchase the merchandise. In addition, hypermarkets have been able to negotiate a second round of margins that vary with the brand's success and that are determined and paid after the merchandise has been sold. Called "delayed margins," suppliers make these end-of-year payments to hypermarkets only, in order to assure good store and advertising placement for the coming year. These payments (sometimes called "the French exception," as they are unknown elsewhere in Europe) are substantial: Some sources put them at between 8 percent and 30 percent of a brand's annual revenue in the chain! Critics charge that delayed margins inflate consumer prices and increase the hypermarkets' already considerable power over suppliers and over alternative retail formats in the marketplace.

Procter & Gamble has chosen to jeopardize billions of French francs of revenue to fight the hypermarkets to end delayed margins. As of 1999, P&G's refusal to pay has provoked a boycott by the hypermarket parent corporations. Thus, such French brands as Pantène shampoo, Oil of Olay hand cream, and Pampers diapers couldn't be found in many stores, including nonhypermarket subsidiary chains. Hypermarket resistance so encumbered P&G's new brand introductions that P&G has been forced to advertise a toll-free telephone number to tell consumers where to find the products.

After six months of this "guerilla warfare," P&G France, sustained by its U.S. parent's revenues, refused to disclose its losses. It has held firm, betting that the distributors cannot continue to boycott dozens of brands, many of them with high market shares and strong brand equity. As of this writing, cracks are appearing in the distributors' united front. Early signs are that P&G may be able to do what has seemed impossible: to convince powerful hypermarket chains to eliminate the French exception and calculate margins in a more conventional fashion. This is likely to lower margins for the suppliers and higher margins for the hypermarkets. But these margins will be negotiated in one step beforehand, without reference to how sales turn out over the course of the year.

Is this conflict functional? Certainly, it is likely to produce functional results for French consumers, suppliers, and retailers. It may even be functional for hypermarkets themselves. It is not clear whether delayed margins are preferable to lower prices negotiated beforehand. And by ending this unique practice voluntarily, these highly visible large chains, often accused of exercising monopolistic power, may escape the scrutiny of regulators and the ire of consumer groups.

Conflict over Co-op Advertising Improves Coordination in the Plumbing and Heating Supplies Industry[9]

The plumbing and heating supplies industry in the United States has a long history of conflict between suppliers and wholesalers over the use of co-op (cooperative) advertising money. Co-op advertising is a program whereby suppliers share the cost of local advertising done by downstream channel members, advertising that features the supplier's products. In principle, co-op advertising is in the interest of both parties. It can be a powerful way to build supplier–wholesaler partnerships by bonding them in a presentation to the market. In practice, co-op advertising in most industries is the source of much conflict. Resellers accuse suppliers of exercising too many bureaucratic controls over the ads, delaying payment of co-op funds once the campaign is over, and finding pretexts to refuse to pay at all. In turn, suppliers accuse downstream channel members of diverting co-op money to other purposes, running poor ad campaigns, and featuring their products with those of competitors.

Conflict over co-op in the plumbing and heating supplies industry has led some channel partners to devise creative new ways to do a better job of joint advertising. Some wholesalers have created their own internal advertising staff, greatly increasing their promotion competence. Some suppliers have revisited their own procedures and have devised streamlined approval and reimbursement policies, as well as upgrading their own co-op staffs. They have removed hurdles to reimbursement, eliminated bureaucratic rules, and shown a willingness to trust their channel partners and work with them to run joint ad campaigns.

Some suppliers have copied techniques from other industries. For example, some suppliers build a predefined co-op allowance into the wholesale price of some items. This sum (say, $2, as part of a $122 faucet) is tracked and set aside as co-op money. If the distributor runs a large-enough campaign by a fixed date, it collects the fund, which otherwise reverts to the manufacturer. This is a technique copied from Procter & Gamble in selling fast-moving consumer goods. The existence of the fund puts pressure on the channel member to advertise (so as not to "lose" the money it has "advanced") and on the supplier to be flexible (so as not to be seen as appropriating money for which it is the custodian).

Personal Computer Resellers Assume New Functions[10]

The personal computer market has become increasingly difficult for most PC makers and their distributors because of the competition of build-to-order manufacturers selling direct (Dell, Gateway, and others). Over the years, as purchasers have become more sophisticated, demanding, and price conscious, direct selling has taken increasing shares of the market. This has put strains on the relationships between suppliers and their traditional reseller channels.

Compaq has been particularly hard hit. The brand built its market leadership by forging excellent channel relations with third parties. It has been reluctant to alienate channel members by doing what some of its competitors are doing: pressuring channel members to accept lower margins and setting up a substantial direct channel to compete head-on with Dell and Gateway. Instead, Compaq had continued to cultivate relationships with its 100,000 points of sale worldwide. In 1997, the computer maker set up a system of guaranteed prices and merchandise take back in order to convince resellers to hold more inventory. The result has been bloated inventories, in an era when inventory becomes obsolete very quickly.

Compaq's troubles are typical of the PC industry today. As the firm's troubles have mounted, Compaq has cut dramatically the number of its resellers and warehouses. It has held its small direct-sales arm to 15 percent of sales to avoid channel conflict with its remaining resellers. The firm has revisited its marketing strategy and is refocusing its business, putting a new emphasis on product innovation and on Internet-related products.

All of this is a functional adaptation to the progression of the personal computer's product life cycle. But can this sort of competitive pressure, which exists throughout the PC industry, be functional for traditional PC channels? In some ways, channel conflict over direct selling has been a positive force. How? Direct selling has obliged all parties to reexamine the patterns and habits they have adopted over time with the result that all parties are refining their roles. For example, a number of PC distributors have allowed suppliers to shift the function of final assembly and customization from the factory to the distributor. This allows traditional PC makers and their channels to mimic direct sellers, taking costs out of the total channel system and allowing more flexibility in response to end-user demand. Some observers claim that a distributor-assembly system allows even greater customization than can be purchased from the build-to-order PC makers.

If so, why wasn't this change in functions made earlier? The answer is that channel assembly is an enormous change; politics and inertia have kept it from happening earlier. One manufacturer puts it: "There are so many mechanics involved in this and so many egos to go with it. You have to change cultures before this will work." Channel conflict has been the impetus to make the change happen.

In principle, all channel conflict should be of this functional variety. In practice, it is not: Much conflict is destructive, not constructive. When is conflict functional?[11]

From the downstream channel member's viewpoint, functional conflict is a *natural outcome of close cooperation* with a supplier. Working together to coordinate tightly inevitably generates disputes in ample measure. But when channel members are committed, these disputes serve to raise performance in the short term and do not damage the level of trust in the relationship.

Cooperative relationships are inevitably noisy and contentious. The resulting conflict should be tolerated, even welcomed as normal. This functional conflict is even more likely if the downstream channel member has considerable influence over the supplier. *An influential channel member is a disputatious one*—and is willing to give and take to push the channel to outperform its competitors. This should serve as a warning to suppliers that like to work with weaker channel members that they can dominate. The resulting relationship will appear harmonious—but will not realize its full potential to perform.

Are peaceful channels better channels? Much depends on the reason why conflict is low. Often, when channel members are not in opposition (low conflict), their relationship is not one of peace and harmony. It can be one of *indifference*. The two parties then do not bother to disagree about anything. There is no issue between them about which they have an opinion, no issue that is important to them or over which they care to invest the effort to argue.

This is readily observed when a distributor, sales agent, or downstream channel member has too many principals to pay attention to all of them. Similarly, many suppliers don't have the capacity to attend to all their channel members. Under these circumstances, one side neglects the other.

Frequently, neglect is mutual. These relationships exist on paper and may even transact some business. Their lack of conflict disguises a lack of engagement. Thus, conflict is quite low—and so is the performance of the channel. *These channels need to increase their activity levels and communication levels—steps that will increase conflict.* This increase should be welcomed, not avoided.

To improve the performance of such a channel, its members need to care enough to communicate, cooperate—and to discover, inevitably, their points of opposition. Their perception of conflict will grow, of course. Managed properly, their *emerging disagreements can be channeled into constructive conflict*. Even as perceived conflict becomes felt (emotions are aroused), channel members may prod each other into better results. This is functional conflict.

Eventually, however, conflict escalates into substantial manifest conflict, accompanied by tension and frustration. If not kept within bounds, manifest conflict becomes damaging, and ultimately destructive.

How Intense Conflict Damages Channel Performance and Coordination

Given that some channel friction is mundane, should it be accepted as inevitable, dismissed as normal? No, because high channel friction creates costs. These are summarized in Figure 9.1. Behind this figure is a very substantial amount of field research documenting the outcomes of literally thousands of channel relationships in developed, mostly Western, economies.[12] The distillation of that experience is that high levels of manifest conflict affect an organization's satisfaction in a manner that damages the channel's long-term ability to function as a close partnership.

Consider a focal firm in a channel—the organization whose viewpoint we wish to understand. Figure 9.1 takes the viewpoint of any organization in the channel, either the supplier or a downstream channel member, and sketches what that organization will experience as it senses higher and higher levels of tension, frustration, and disagreement in a channel relationship. Perceived conflict will increase, as will felt (affective) conflict and manifest conflict (blocking behaviors).

As conflict increases, the focal firm will derive less from the channel. It will be less satisfied with the business rewards (financial and strategic) the relationship gen-

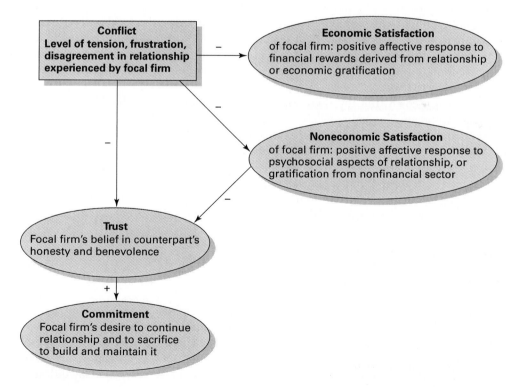

FIGURE 9.1 **How High Levels of Conflict Erode Channel Relationship**

Source: Based on Inge Geyskens, Jan-Benedict E. M. Steenkamp, and Nirmalya Kumar, "A Meta-Analysis of Satisfaction in Marketing Channel Relationships," *Journal of Marketing Research*, 36 (May 1999), pp. 223–38.

erates. This decrease in satisfaction is of mixed origin. Undoubtedly, accountants can document one element. Profit indicators really do decline when conflict rises. Moreover is that in judging satisfaction, the focal firm weighs in its assessment of what it could expect to gain from alternative uses of its resources. Conflict may increase a sense of disappointment by inflating the focal firm's sense that better alternatives exist.

Disappointing, unsatisfactory economic payoffs are bad enough in themselves. But the consequences of conflict do not end there. For the focal firm, the effects of conflict are not confined to financial aspects. Its satisfaction with the psychological and social side of the relationship declines as well.

It is tempting to disregard this unpleasant side effect of conflict, simply because it does not translate easily into profit terms. But to the focal firm, interpersonal dissatisfaction is a serious affair. It not only makes a workday less gratifying to the individuals involved (which is an important negative outcome in itself) but also damages the solidarity of the relationship. Unsatisfactory social relationships impede building or maintaining trust in a channel counterpart. Trust is a critical foundation for durable, well-coordinated relationships (see Chapter 11 on strategic alliances for more on developing trust). Trust—the belief that the other party will act with fairness, honesty, and concern for your well-being—is essential to build committed relationships, in which the parties make sacrifices in order to build and maintain their channel.

Conflict undermines channel commitment by damaging the focal party's trust in its counterpart. This powerful effect occurs in two ways. First, conflict directly and rapidly hurts the focal party's confidence in the counterpart's benevolence and honesty. Second, conflict reduces interpersonal satisfaction, which, in turn, delivers another blow to trust.

Conflict is costly. But this does not mean that an organization should always avoid conflict. Any channel member will encounter conflict when it changes course or undertakes a new initiative. *The benefits of change may be worth the costs of conflict.* Figure 9.1 does not suggest that conflict should be minimized on all occasions. But it does suggest that conflict carries costs, some of which take time to materialize. Therefore, conflict should be managed, and organizations should choose to enter a conflict, rather than discovering that their initiatives are not worth the consequences of the opposition they create. Next we consider some of the principal causes of conflict in channels.

MAJOR SOURCES OF CONFLICT IN MARKETING CHANNELS

Most conflict is rooted in differences in (1) channel members' goals; (2) their perceptions of reality; and (3) what they consider to be their domains, or areas where they should operate with autonomy. The most complex of these three sources of conflict is the last, because domain conflict has many subdimensions. A critical one is product–markets: It is now ordinary for manufacturers to go to market by so many different routes that their channel members are bound to compete for some of the same business. Where channels are redundant, competition for the customer will turn into conflict with the supplier. Other subdimensions of domain conflict include clashes over what is each party's role and sphere of influence. Let us begin with one of the most intractable problems: clashing goals.

Competing Goals

Each channel member's set of goals and objectives is very different from those of other members. This built-in difference in what the firms are seeking to achieve is fundamental to all businesses, not just channels. A substantial literature on the theory of principals and their agents has been built around the clash between the desires of the principal—who creates work—and the agent—to whom the principal delegates the work. This inherent difference in what they are trying to achieve and what they value leads principals to devise ways to monitor and motivate their agents. *Agency theory* underscores how competing goals create conflict in any principal–agent relationship, regardless of the personalities and players involved and regardless of the history of their relationship. Too often, channel members personalize their conflicts and believe that a change of partner or of personnel will solve their problems. Yet fundamental goal conflict remains.[13]

Goal divergence, and subsequent conflict, is extremely common. A prototypical example occurs in the dealer channel for personal computers. For instance, Compaq pursues goals of high growth and high market share. These goals are crucial to survive in industries, such as personal computers, that experience standards races and substantial economies of scale. Thus, Compaq has sought to expand its reach beyond its traditional dealer channel into newer channels such as mail-order sales and superstores. In periods of short supply and heavy demand, it has been obliged to ration supplies of computers to its traditional dealers. It aimed to serve all of its channels fairly and to reach consumers with different service output demands. But the goal of the traditional dealers does not include supplying other channels with Compaq computers. Indeed, that serves only to increase intrachannel competition as far as dealers are concerned, and therefore frustrates the dealers' profit goals. The dealers have expressed their dissatisfaction with Compaq by steering their customers to competitors' brands rather than lose the customer to a rival retailer.[14]

This is a good example of a generic and perennial goal conflict between suppliers and resellers. Resellers carry a supplier's line in order to maximize their own profits. They can do so by several routes: (1) achieving higher gross margins per unit (pay the supplier less while charging the customer more), (2) increasing unit sales, decreasing inventory, (3) holding down expenses, and (4) receiving higher allowances from the manufacturer. Of course, the manufacturer wishes to maximize its own profits. To this effect, the supplier prefers to see the reseller do almost exactly the reverse: Accept lower gross margins (pay the supplier more while charging the customer less), hold more inventory (avoid stockouts, maximize selection), spend more to support the product line, and get by without allowances. The two parties' overall profit goals lead them to collide on every objective but one: Raise unit sales.[15]

Table 9.1 lists frequent reasons for conflict that are inherent in the division of labor between upstream and downstream in a marketing channel.[16]

Surprisingly, a great deal of tension, anxiety, and frustration in a channel is due not so much to actual goal clashes as to the players' *perceptions* that their goals diverge.[17] It

TABLE 9.1
**Natural Sources of Conflict: Inherent Differences in Viewpoints
of Suppliers and Resellers**

	Supplier Viewpoint	Reseller Viewpoint	Expression of Clash
Financial goals	Maximize own profit by: • Higher prices to reseller • Higher sales by reseller • Higher reseller expenses • Higher reseller inventory • Lower allowances to reseller	Maximize own profit by: • Higher own-level margins (lower prices from our supplier and higher prices to our customer) • Lower expenses (less support) • Faster inventory turnover (lower reseller stocks) • Higher allowances from manufacturers	**Supplier:** You don't put enough effort behind my brand. Your prices are too high. **Reseller:** You don't support me enough. With your wholesale prices, we can't make money.
	Focus on:	Focus on:	
Desired target accounts	• Multiple segments • Multiple markets • Many accounts (raise volume and share)	• Segment corresponding to resellers' positioning (e.g., discounter) • Our markets only • Selected accounts (those that are profitable to serve)	**Supplier:** We need more coverage and more effort. Our reseller doesn't do enough for us. **Reseller:** You don't respect our marketing strategy. We need to make money too.
Desired product and accounts policy	• Concentrate on our product category and our brand • Carry out full line (a variation for every conceivable need, plus our efforts to expand our line outside our traditional strengths)	• Achieve economies of scope over product categories • Serve customers by offering brand assortment • Do not carry inferior or slow-moving items (every supplier has some of these)	**Supplier:** You carry too many lines. You don't give us enough attention. You're disloyal. **Reseller:** Our customers come first. If we satisfy our customers, you will benefit. By the way, shouldn't you consider pruning your product line?

Source: Based on Allan J. Magrath and Kenneth G. Hardy, "A Strategic Paradigm for Predicting Manufacturer–Reseller Conflict," *European Journal of Marketing*, 23, no. 2 (1989), pp. 94–108.

is quite common in channels for the players to believe that the incongruity in their goals is higher than it actually is. This misperception fuels conflict.

Differing Perceptions of Reality

Differing perceptions of reality are important sources of conflict, because they indicate that there will be differing bases of action in response to the same situation. As a general rule, channel members are often confident that they know "the facts of the situation." Yet, when their perceptions are compared, they are frequently so different that it is difficult to believe they are members of the same channel. Perceptions differ markedly, even on such basic topics as:[18]

- What the attributes of the product or service are
- What applications it serves and for which segments
- What the competition is

Given such a basic divergence of ideas about the situation, it is not surprising that channel members also disagree about more subjective, judgment-laden subjects, such as how readily the product or service is sold, what the value added of each channel member is, or how each side behaves. Indeed, channel members often hold very inaccurate expectations of what each other will do; these lead them to choose suboptimal strategies, which heightens conflict. Inaccurate expectations also lead to surprise, and frequently opposition, when the parties "fail" to act as expected.[19]

Why are misperceptions so common and so serious? A major reason is *focus*. The supplier is focused on its product and its processes, and is typically removed from customers. A downstream channel member, in contrast, is focused on its functions and its customers, and is typically removed from manufacturing. These differences expose channel members to varying information and influences, giving them different pieces of the overall picture.

Seldom do channel members cooperate fully enough to assemble the entire picture from their separate pieces. When they do share information, they uncover dramatic differences in perception. A lack of communication exacerbates conflict due to different perceptions of reality. Frequent, timely, and relevant communication assists in aligning perceptions and expectations.[20] This is an excellent investment in the prevention of conflict.

Even in domestic markets, channel members conflict over their different views of the situation. This problem is exacerbated when channel members come from different national business cultures. For example, a study of channels composed of U.S. suppliers and Mexican distributors demonstrates how cultures clash, which creates differences in perception and interpretation of the channel environment.[21] Regardless of the product or service sold, the channel members experience greater-than-usual friction, due in part to *culturally divergent ideas of what is appropriate behavior*. This, in turn, damages channel performance.

The solution to this problem is twofold. One is communication, which is made more difficult by cultural divergence. It is tempting to skimp on communication with a channel member from another culture. Nonetheless, more frequent, thorough, candid, and detailed communication involving more people in both organizations goes a long way toward rectifying the performance problems of cross-cultural channels.

The other solution is for each organization to develop greater sensitivity to the business culture of the other channel member. Greater cultural sensitivity, in turn, is built on the foundations of respect for and understanding of the channel counterpart's language, customs, values, attitudes, and beliefs. Channel members that slight the importance of national culture or that economize on communication pay a price: excessive conflict, with a negative impact on channel performance.

Clashes over Domains

Each channel member has its own domains, or spheres of function. Much conflict in channels occurs when one channel member perceives that the other is not taking proper care of its responsibilities in its appropriate domain. This can mean doing the job wrong, not doing the job at all, or trying to do the other channel member's job!

A classic example is market research. In many channels, each side (upstream, downstream) considers this the domain of the other. Another common case is pre- and post-sales support: Suppliers and resellers clash regularly over who should do it, how it should be done, and how it should be compensated. Still another is inventory: Often, suppliers consider it the reseller's duty to carry quite a bit of it, whereas resellers consider it the supplier's duty to make sure they can be restocked quickly from a central location. Obviously these sorts of who-should-do-what and how-should-it-be-done disputes can carry into many domains.

An example of resolving such disputes effectively is J. E. Ekornes, a Norwegian home furniture manufacturer.[22] Domain conflict was one of many reasons for the firm's declining European sales in the 1990s. Ekornes's salespeople were paid entirely on commission, with the result that they signed up too many retailers and then failed to support them. Rather than competing with other furniture retailers for the customer, retailers turned to conflicting with Ekornes. The supplier ended up with hundreds of adversarial relationships and disappointing results in the marketplace. Conflicts took place over three key issues:

- *Domain.* Each side thought the other should be providing more support. Ekornes thought the retailers should give the brand more marketing and service support. The retailers thought the supplier's salespeople should be giving them more support.
- *Perceptions of reality.* Ekornes believed its retailers were not committed to the brand's success, whereas retailers believed Ekornes was not trustworthy.
- *Goals.* Ekornes wanted higher European sales, whereas retailers wanted higher gross contribution in their own markets.

To its credit, Ekornes took drastic measures, controversial internally, to turn its channel adversaries into allies. Effectively, the supplier internalized the conflict, forcing its personnel to change methods radically.

Realizing that the fundamental problem was low profits for channel members, Ekornes dropped two-thirds of its retailers, removing intrabrand competition. Once given exclusivity, retailers began to make profits by competing with other furniture makers for the buyers' business, rather than conflicting with Ekornes over concessions. Ekornes took on a new domain: heavy support, including training, for its channel. It converted salespeople from commission pay to salary plus bonus, conditional on how well they served the retailers. Retailers reciprocated by taking on a new domain—local advertising—and by dropping competing lines. The results are spectacular, for both Ekornes and its retailers.

Conflict is usually due to multiple causes. A fundamental issue in this example is clashing over markets, developed in the next section.

CLASH OF MARKET DOMAINS

One of the most serious sources of conflict occurs when channel members are potentially competing with each other for the same business. One solution to this problem—giving some degree of exclusivity to a channel partner—is covered in detail in Chapter 10 on distribution intensity and vertical restraints.

Intrachannel Competition

From the upstream viewpoint, the problem of domain clash occurs when a supplier sees its downstream partners represent its competitors. Of course, much of the time, they do so—downstream partners frequently position themselves as providers of an assortment, and seek economies of scale by pooling demand for a class of products. Indeed, in this way many agents and resellers are able to provide high coverage and keep their prices down. This doesn't prevent channel members from disputing with each other about it. But representing competitors is usually an accepted fact of life, as long as the downstream is not thought to be too eager about meeting its responsibilities in the competitors' domains.

The more acrimonious disputes occur when the upstream party believes it has an understanding or agreement to limit competition, and the downstream is reneging. Often, the "understanding" cannot be proven, but when it can be documented, the conflict can become quite expensive. For example, a California medical supply firm won almost $5 million in damages from a distributor for breach of contract. An arbitration panel found that its downstream channel partner, in violation of contract, promoted a competitor's products. Also at issue was the supplier's claim that the downstream channel member divulged its trade secrets to competition, allowing them to copy the products. This is a common allegation in disputes over channel domains.[23]

From the downstream viewpoint, domain clash occurs when a supplier sells through many of the firm's direct competitors in a market. This is intensive distribution, covered in Chapter 10.

Another source of domain conflict occurs when multiple types of channels represent the supplier's products to the same geographical market. There are many labels for this, including dual distribution (using both integrated and independent channels), plural distribution (using multiple types of channel members, such as discounters, sales ages, company salespeople, and value-added resellers—which may or may not be owned by the supplier), and hybrid distribution. Perhaps the best label is *multiple channels:* using more than one route (type of channel member, whether integrated or independent) to get to the same market.[24] For example, General Electric serves small and medium-size electrical contractors in the same geography via two channel types, both independently owned: category killers (huge specialty stores, such as Home Depot) and the traditional channel type, electrical distributors. Note that using multiple channels is not the same as distributing intensively—intensive distribution can be achieved by going through many channel entities, but all of the same type. Ekornes, for example, had many redundant channel members, but they were all traditional furniture dealers.

Multiple Channels: No Longer Unusual

Multiple channels have always been common. But at one time, many companies used primarily one route to market: Their other routes were secondary and were often downplayed, even disguised, in order to avert channel conflict and avoid confusing customers. This was especially the case when suppliers owned sales–distribution organizations, thereby competing directly with their own channel customers for the end-user.

An explosion in the use of multiple channels has taken place, to the point that it is now the norm rather than the exception. Why? Among other reasons, heightened competition drives suppliers to change their channels, whereas fragmented markets make it harder to serve customers efficiently through only one channel type. Channels were once kept simple to facilitate their administration. However, technological advance has made it feasible to manage a far more complex channel structure.

Suppliers like multiple channels because they may increase market penetration and raise entry barriers to potential competitors. Many different channel types afford the supplier a window on many markets. In addition, many channel types are bound to compete with each other. Suppliers are prone to consider this competition "healthy," and sometimes they are right.

Of course, customers like multiple channels when it means they can find a channel that meets their service output demands. Multiple channel types make it easier for the customer to pit one channel against another in a search for more services at lower prices. Thus, multiple channels make markets: Suppliers and customers can more easily find each other and match their needs to channel types.[25]

The danger of multiple channels is the same as the danger of intensive distribution: Downstream channel members may lose motivation and can withhold support (a passive response), retaliate, or exit the supplier's channel structure (active responses). See Channel Sketch 9.2 for examples. This is particularly the case when the customer can free ride, gaining services from one channel while placing its business with another. The ironic result is that, by adding channel types, the supplier may come to reduce, rather than increase, the breadth and vigor of its market representation.

CHANNEL SKETCH 9.2

Examples of Domain Clash and Reseller Response

Revlon Cosmetics[26]

Revlon, founded in 1932, was once the market share leader in cosmetics in the United States. It has lost share of market and, in 1998 and 1999, has gone into the red, losing millions of dollars.

Revlon's decline is primarily a story of management missteps, particularly in marketing. The firm was prosperous in 1985, when it was purchased by Ron Perelman, essentially using borrowed funds. To meet interest payments and draw down debt, Perelman focused Revlon on short-term profits. As a result, Revlon slowed its pace of new-product development and took greater risks in new-product introduction.

Troubles began when a new product turned out to be defective. Recovery was costly. Gradually, failure to introduce successful new products eroded the firm's market position. Revlon responded by lavish ad campaigns featuring top models, and by holding prices high to create an image of exclusivity (and keep profits up to meet its debt schedule). But nothing reversed steady market share gains by competitors.

Under cash flow pressure, Revlon abruptly changed its channel strategy to try to increase volume. In the 1990s, the firm jeopardized its prestigious image by expanding distribution to popular outlets, such as discount and drugstores—while maintaining high prices. Then it broke its understanding that it would confine department store distribution to high-end chains. When Revlon decided to distribute through a popular-price chain, JCPenney, competitors finally retaliated. Prestigious chains (Bloomingdale's, Macy's, May Department Stores) terminated Revlon as a supplier.

Revlon tried to compensate by using promotions to load supermarkets (yet another channel form) with high inventories of Revlon products. But when customers failed to purchase, supermarkets simply returned their unsold goods. In a further search for volume, Revlon vertically integrated forward by purchasing a perfume chain (The Cosmetic Center) and then funneled the returned inventory through the stores, priced at deep discount. The strategy failed. An industry observer suggests, "What do you want? A customer won't buy makeup in outdated colors, even at 30% cheaper." The Cosmetic Center chain went bankrupt, costing Revlon millions of dollars.

Revlon's decline is fundamentally one of marketing errors. By alienating its channels, Revlon hastened its decline, but channels did not create Revlon's troubles. Revlon's traditional channels withdrew support, sometimes visibly (termination), sometimes less visibly (lower stocks, lesser displays and sales effort) as Revlon expanded distribution to their direct competitors, as well as to competing channel formats (e.g., discount stores). The new channels were unwilling to do Revlon's bidding (the supermarkets) or unable to do so (The Cosmetic Center). Fundamentally, Revlon tried to have it all: high volume and high margins, in spite of low investment in product development. The resulting channel conflict should have been taken as market feedback, a verdict on the supplier's marketing strategy. Instead, Revlon brushed channel resistance aside and resorted to pressuring its channels by selling aggressively to their competitors, both within and across retail formats. Revlon indeed got the higher coverage it sought, but not the higher support it needed. The results have been stagnant sales and mounting losses.

As of this writing, Revlon is in the process of closing some of its European operations, and the company, still heavily indebted and now deeply in the red, is for sale.

Toy Channels Retaliate Against Meccano[27]

Meccano is an old and well-known brand of toys in Europe. Generations of children remember hours spent assembling intricate and elaborate metal constructions (buildings, vehicles, shapes) using the distinctive screws, disks, and bright pre-punched metal strips that Meccano sells in kits. Founded in France in 1898, Meccano dominated the European market for construction toys, a market it had essentially created. Meccano enjoyed the approval of parents, who saw its products as educational toys that occupied children for long periods and taught them mechanics—as well as patience and precision. The kit, once assembled, could become an object of display, but the point of the exercise was to build the kit more than to play with the completed construction.

Meccano's troubles began in the 1960s with the entry of the Danish firm Lego. In France, Lego's colorful plastic snap-together blocks were potent competition to Meccano's screw-and-bolt metal pieces. As sales stagnated, Meccano was sold, first to General Mills, then to a French capitalist, and finally to a set of its own managers financed by a leveraged buyout.

What did these owners do? Facing mounting competition from video game consoles and computer games, Meccano responded with new products. Intending to leverage its brand equity, the firm enlarged its product line and engaged in expensive product launches. As part of this strategy, in the 1990s, one of the series of owners decided to purchase the U.S. equivalent product, the brand Erector. Meccano relaunched Erector sets by an ad campaign and by signing up traditional toy merchants, who offered sales and display support and who paid high wholesale prices. The strategy worked. Meccano saw its fortunes soar. The firm's turnaround appeared complete.

Then came the promise of an enormous order from the Toys "R" Us chain, the giant discount toy specialist. Meccano accepted the order, failing to anticipate retaliation by the traditional toy merchants that had resuscitated Erector sets. Furious, these stores boycotted the brand. Meccano had the possibility of signing on other accounts (massive discount stores, such as Wal-Mart, Target, and Kmart), but was unable to do so. Why? To get the Toys "R" Us order, Meccano had granted the chain exclusivity in the mass-merchant channel. Rebuffed, these chains instead took on Steeltech, a less expensive Chinese-made copy of Meccano.

Thus weakened, Meccano experienced a series of other problems, some brought about by the failure of several new products. As of this writing, Meccano has been purchased for the sum of one franc by a Franco-American venture capitalist. The new owner plans a capital injection to enable Meccano to see the results of an extensive rework of its products, designed to adapt the line to the changing tastes of children. Meccano has made kits that break its own unspoken rules (e.g., no material but metal, no nontraditional colors, no human figures). In particular, management believes that children want to assemble the kits more quickly and easily (no more hours twisting screws and consulting blueprints) and to play with the kits once assembled. The new product line is thus a considerable departure from the company's past. To launch it, Meccano is counting on the support of newly recruited distribution channels, support which looks to be forthcoming. Signs of channel support for the new line is a major reason why Meccano was able to find a buyer—even for one franc.

A major reason why suppliers fail to anticipate that multiple channels will actually reduce their channels' motivation is that suppliers tend to think of their markets as distinct and well-behaved segments. They reason that one type of customer would like to buy in one manner (say, convenient and cheap, with few services), whereas another type prefers another manner (say, full support, with willingness to spend time negotiating and to pay a higher price). Each segment calls for different service outputs, hence different channel types (say, a discount catalog and a value-added reseller, VAR). Thus, suppliers expect that by offering multiple channels, they can serve multiple segments. They genuinely believe their channels will not compete and dismiss their channels' complaints, warnings, even threats.

On paper, a multiple-channel strategy is always appealing: Buyers are neatly categorized, and each customer segment is served by one type of channel. The strategy collapses when customers refuse to stick to their assigned categories, which happens quite often. Of course, customers free ride (getting advice from the VAR, then placing the order with the discount catalog). This is especially true for business-to-business customers, whose purchasing agents are paid to extract maximum value at the lowest delivered price. And, increasingly, the same customers behave differently on different occasions when purchasing the same item. Wright Line learned this to its great cost: Segmentation schemes must consider the nature of the purchase, not just the nature of the buyer (Channel Sketch 9.3).

CHANNEL SKETCH 9.3
Wright Line[28]

Wright Line was a profitable supplier of products to help computer centers organize and file electronic information. The brand's marketing strategy was to sell at premium prices through its own sales force to large computer centers, offering high service and support for its large product line.

As the mainframe computer market waned, Wright Line sought to cover smaller customers. In an ambitious reorganization plan, Wright Line set up three internal divisions, corresponding to different channels, each intended to serve a different customer segment. One division, direct sales, continued to seek and serve large customers. Another division sold via telemarketing, meant for medium-size customers. In addition, Wright Line built a third division to seek representation by furniture dealers and in catalogs offered by computer makers and office supply houses. This was intended to serve small customers.

The idea was a good one: to increase the variety and intensity of coverage in order to increase sales, while matching service levels (therefore cost) to order sizes. This is prototypical reasoning in going to multiple channels. Unfortunately, nobody did what management thought it would do.

Large and medium-size customers shopped all the channels, sometimes pitting channel members against each other in price wars. Large accounts, in particular, proved to be willing to behave like small accounts on some occasions (e.g., for fill-in orders). To make matters worse, Wright Line made a classic marketing error: It had segmented its accounts by their current business with Wright Line, rather than by their potential business in the product category. Consequently, in any given year, small customers would become large and large customers would become small, necessitating their reassignment. This disruption of the relationship was damaging to Wright Line morale and to customer loyalty.

Third parties freely competed with Wright Line's own divisions, often beating them on price. Management had not anticipated that they could do so because it viewed them as middlemen and did not understand the services they rendered, nor the economies of scale they could reap by selling multiple lines.

Wright Line's own channels fought vigorously to protect their "turf," even manipulating orders to prevent customer reassignment. Morale plummeted, causing turnover, which led to a spiral of declining sales performance and escalating sales cost.

Did all these new channels increase sales? Yes. Unfortunately, they increased costs even faster. Profits fell along with morale. Distracted by channel infighting, management failed to invest enough in new-product development. Eventually, Wright Line refocused on something closer to its original channel strategy. The supplier used a field sales force as its primary channel, treating a small in-house telemarketing and catalog unit as a supplement. The sales force received credit for all catalog sales and closed all sales generated by telemarketing, which served only to create leads.

Nonetheless, Wright Line was so weakened by the channel conflict that it fell to a hostile takeover in 1989.

Is It Really a Problem?

The manufacturer's essential trade-off is between more market coverage—the benefit—and higher levels of channel support and channel conflict—the cost. When should multiple channels be used and how much? In particular, what percentage of a supplier's potential transactions should be in conflict (wherein the customer is called up by multiple channels)? The answers are not well understood at this time.

Of course, *multiple channels don't always compete*. Often, channel members think they serve the same customer on the same occasion, when they really don't. For example, Coca-Cola in Japan faced strong opposition from its retailers when it installed vending machines. Eventually, Coke was able, by market research, to show that it was correct in its claims that vending machines were used for different occasions and offered a different value to the same customer.[29]

Multiple channels can even help each other by building primary demand for the product category or by building demand for each other. The classic example is the combination of a store and a direct-marketing operation (such as a catalog or Web site). Potential customers are exposed to a brand both ways and can then purchase as they wish. Some retailers use this synergy to explore markets: Once catalog sales from an area reach a certain level, they take it as a sign that it's time to open a store.

Of course, the accounting for these combinations is approximate: The supplier cannot really know, for example, how many customers tried on clothing in the store, went home to think about it, then ordered from the Web site or catalog. Small wonder that many of these combinations have the same owner (such as Victoria's Secret for lingerie, Lands' End and Ann Taylor for clothing, and now Gateway for computers). Conflict can be handled by a corporate accountant (to allocate costs and revenues) and a human resources manager to administer compensation.

When channels are independent, it is not so easy to settle disputes. To date, suppliers have not paid enough attention to mechanisms to compensate potential victims of excessive channel conflict. The growth of electronic commerce will make this a more pressing problem by elevating free riding to epidemic levels. To cope, suppliers and downstream channel members will be obliged to devise new ways of doing business, such as adding in flat payments (the equivalent of salary); fees for services (the equivalent of an expense account); or overrides, whereby one channel member is automatically compensated for sales made by another (the equivalent of a group bonus).

The most obvious benefit to a supplier of multiple channels is better coverage. Other motives, usually unspoken, are based on the idea that *one channel can help a supplier to manage another.* For example, many suppliers serve industrial customers by a manufacturers' representative (independent sales agency, or rep). In the same market, they may also reserve some customers (house accounts), serving them via company employees. This is dual distribution (vertically integrated and outsourced). This practice is so common that it is often grudgingly accepted, in which case it will not create enough conflict to harm a channel relationship. Suppliers use more house accounts:

1. When the nature of the selling task is ambiguous, making it difficult to tell how well a rep is really doing (the performance ambiguity problem)
2. When the selling task is complex, and the salesperson is in position to learn so much about a sales task that he or she effectively becomes too valuable to replace (the lock-in problem)

These circumstances create a dependence of the supplier upon the rep and make it difficult to identify underperforming reps. The integrated channel partially solves both problems (see Chapter 7 on vertical integration). By keeping a small sales force, the supplier learns more about the task, thereby gaining a performance benchmark. Further, the supplier can more credibly threaten to terminate a rep if it already has a sales presence in a market. In short, the second channel is useful for learning and for keeping options open.[30]

This theme reappears in Chapter 17 on franchising: Having company outlets *and* franchised outlets helps the franchisor to run its entire distribution program, indeed, the entire business, better.

What Suppliers Can Do

An important issue is *what responsibility suppliers have to protect* their multiple channels from each other. Some suppliers, of course, often feel no regret, assume no responsibility, and take no action. Many suppliers question what action they *could* take even if they do want to protect their channels. Actively trying to prevent one channel from competing with another (e.g., by terminating discounters) can provoke legal action (see

Chapter 12) and is often futile anyway. Suppliers can try to manage the problem by devising different pricing schemes for different channels, which is also legally dubious. This creates an opportunity for arbitrage. The next section on gray markets shows how this can get out of control.

Suppliers can offer more support, more service, more product, and even different product to different channel types in order to *help them differentiate themselves* (see Chapter 10 on distribution intensity and Chapter 11 on strategic alliances). In general, suppliers will gain more cooperation from multiple channels in terms of pricing, stocking, and display if they can supply what the buyer considers to be differentiated product lines to different groups of retailers.[31] For example, Xerox in the United States announced the rollout of a line of network printers available only through outside resellers, not through its own direct sales force.[32]

A variation on this theme is to offer different brand names to different channels. For example, many individual investors wish to purchase mutual funds without paying sales charges (loads) to brokers. Providers of these investment vehicles often have their own employee brokers and do not wish to appear to compete with them. This has led to multiple brand names under different pricing schemes in different channels. Citigroup sells some mutual funds to third parties under the Salomon Brothers brand. It sells other funds under the Smith Barney name through its own Smith Barney brokers. In this case, the funds are different; Citigroup won't risk alienating its brokers by selling the same thing under two names in two places. Other firms do try to sell the same product under different names, and this can work.[33] But even if customers don't know, the channels do and will often let the customer know.

Taken to the extreme, creating differentiation via different brands or products in various channels is a strategy of not really selling the same thing through multiple channels, that is, not using multiple channels. A common variation on this theme is to sell the "primary" or "flagship" part of the product line through one channel, usually an independent channel, and to sell secondary or peripheral products through another, usually a captive channel. For example, in the IT industry, Pioneer Electronics sells its major products through distributors and everything else over the Internet. Customers can access anything the supplier makes in this fashion, while the major business goes to independents. The supplier contents itself with product sales that might not interest the channel in any event.[34]

An example of active intervention occurs in the marketing of durables, which are distinctive in that often they can be rented or sold, and then resold. Automakers practice a strategy of keeping factories running and battling for market share by selling huge volumes at ridiculously low prices to auto rental agencies. In the U.S. market in the 1990s, this virtual dumping of new cars was facilitated because many automakers owned large shares of rental companies.

The result was that some rental agencies began reselling their fleet cars almost as soon as they purchased them. Suddenly, the sales lots of rental agencies were full of barely used cars—at very attractive retail prices. Invariably, this newly important channel hurt auto dealers, creating enough conflict to bring the issue to court. Several automakers then intervened by buying used cars back from the rental agencies (thereby starving the agencies' car lots) and reselling them to dealers (thereby feeding the dealer's used car lots). This policy of intervention has allowed automakers to have it both ways: to keep volume up, while keeping two important channels from going to war, to the detriment of the channels . . . and eventually the suppliers.[35]

Conflict over domains is one of the most visible and least tractable forms of opposition in marketing channels. Over the long term, it is an almost inevitable step as companies adjust to the advancing life cycle of the products and services they sell. *Domain conflict often leads to a new channel strategy and a new equilibrium* in which different channel forms come to coexist and to do business in new ways.

For example, salespeople selling financial services fiercely resist on-line trading, seeing it as a way for their clients to free ride on their advice and to learn to invest without them. But it is likely that Internet investing will create a primary demand effect (diverting customer money to brokerages) and will accelerate the demand for advice on the part of many customers. Accordingly, investment brokerage houses, such as Paine Webber, are experimenting with new ways to price services to their customers and new ways to compensate their brokers.[36] Ultimately, the channel clash should create a new equilibrium in the industry, as summed up by an angry Merrill Lynch broker who has tried to dissuade his clients from using the firm's new Internet trading service. Turning philosophical, he shrugs and says, "The Internet? I may as well get to like it and figure out how to make money out of it."[37]

This adjustment comes about when all parties can be made to realize that the environment has changed and that markets have split into new segments, each demanding a different level of service outputs. Thus, sellers of insurance in Canada have been forced to diversify their channels beyond the traditional insurance agency, adding stockbrokers, investment dealers, bank, direct mail and direct telemarketing, and the Internet. This change is due to several factors: regulatory changes, market saturation, more sophisticated customers, and fierce competition. Canada Life puts it thus: "The raw reality is that as a company, we need to protect ourselves by having others sell our product as well. And so, the move to go multichannel is as much defensive as it is aggressive."[38]

Conflict that is seemingly about overlapping domains is frequently rooted in different perceptions. For example:

- Canada Life perceives that many investors will no longer purchase through brokers, whereas brokers think that other channels are taking business they could write.
- Merrill Lynch brokers perceive the company's Internet site steals business from them. The brokerage house believes that Internet investors won't deal with brokers, either because they are a different type of buyer or because they use the Internet to do those transactions they would refuse to place through a broker.
- As noted earlier, Coca-Cola's supermarkets in Japan perceive that vending machines take their business. Coke thinks the machines sell to the same people, but not on the same purchase occasions.

Coke is an example of the best way to deal with perceptual differences masquerading as domain conflict: Find a way to prove your point, and spend the time and money to do so.

Unwanted Channels: Gray Markets

One of the most pressing issues for channel managers, especially global marketers, is the existence and persistence of gray markets.[39] *Gray marketing* is the sale of authorized, branded product through unauthorized distribution channels—usually bargain or discount outlets that provide less customer service than the authorized channels do. A great variety of products is sold through gray markets, including Swatch watches, designer clothing, and other chic apparel items. Gray marketing can be contrasted with black marketing, or counterfeiting, which involves selling fake goods as branded ones. Counterfeiting remains illegal in almost all world markets; in contrast, gray marketing is in many cases completely legal.[40]

Who is supplying these unauthorized outlets? The usual suppliers are[41]

- Authorized distributors and dealers, often in other markets
- Professional arbitragers, which include
  - Import–export houses
  - Individuals, professional traders, who buy huge amounts at retail where prices are low, then transport them to where the prices are high. Often, these people live near borders.
- The ultimate source—the protesting "victim"; that is, the supplier itself, through either the home office or its foreign divisions

What motivates these more-or-less clandestine sources of supply, and their customers, the gray marketers? Several factors create an environment ripe for the development of gray markets. One is *differential pricing to different channel members:* One channel often overorders to get a discount, then sells off the excess to unauthorized channels. Another factor is the practice of pricing differently to *different geographic markets*, whether because of taxation or exchange-rate differences or simply because of differences in price sensitivity across regions. For example, foreign companies producing and selling in the People's Republic of China (PRC) sometimes must compete for sales with smugglers who sell branded product that has been exported out of China and then reimported into China to avoid local taxes. In this case, although the product is authorized branded product, it is categorized as illegally "smuggled" product because of the avoidance of import taxes upon its reentry into the PRC.

Alternatively, domestic products sometimes are sold through high-service, high-price channels at home, opening up an *opportunity* to introduce gray-marketed goods through discount retailers. As an example, the Japanese discount chain Jonan Denki has been known to cover all the expenses of taking employees on post-Christmas shopping sprees to Europe, where they shop the sales at designer outlets such as Louis Vuitton and Chanel; legally bring the goods back to Japan; and then put them on sale in Jonan Denki stores at a price lower than the prevailing retail prices at authorized outlets in Japan.[42]

The development of emerging markets and the worldwide liberalization of trade also favor the growth of gray markets. These *economic fundamentals* create incentives for firms to capitalize on brand equity and volume potential by offering similar products across different countries. The problem with this strategy, however, is that optimal prices vary substantially across countries due to differences in exchange rates, purchasing power, and supply-side factors (e.g., distribution, servicing, and taxes).

Of course, the minute that price differences exist across boundaries or territories, substantial gains are available through arbitrage. This, in large part, explains the growth of gray markets. Gray markets need not involve cross-border trade: They are also common in domestic markets in which suppliers want to keep their products out of certain channels (e.g., discount chains).

Although purchasers frequently gain from the availability of gray goods (due to their lower prices), other *members of the channel are often negative* toward them. Manufacturers complain that gray goods impair their ability to charge different prices in various markets. In addition, if service levels provided by gray market retailers are lower than those of authorized dealers, brand equity may suffer. Gray goods may be a concern for manufacturers but frequently the strongest critics of the escalation in gray marketing are authorized dealers. Gray markets unequivocally erode potential volume for authorized dealers and may place severe pressure on after-sales service functions. All in all, this suggests that gray markets are generally bad: When it is feasible to intercept and monitor gray goods, it seems always to be in a producer's interest to do so.

Despite the many arguments against gray markets, it is curious that they not only continue to exist but are estimated to be growing quickly. Further, gray markets seem particularly active in countries such as the United States, Canada, and the European Union, where manufacturers have both the means and in some cases the legal framework to stop them.

Despite the evidence that some manufacturers do have legal recourse to limit the proliferation of gray goods, in most cases, there is limited proof of their doing so. It is not easy to block gray markets.[43] Evidence exists that suppliers make less effort to stop them (are *more tolerant* of gray markets) under several circumstances:[44]

- When violations are difficult to detect or document (especially in distant markets or when customers are geographically dispersed)
- When the potential for one channel to free ride on another channel member is low anyway (e.g., when resellers don't provide much service or are able to charge separately for services rendered)
- When the product is more mature
- When the violator (the distributor that is supplying the gray market) doesn't carry competing brands in the supplier's product category

The last item listed is the most surprising: Such dealers are more vulnerable to the supplier's pressure. Suppliers may be more indulgent of these distributors because they are likely to be high performers and because they exhibit more loyalty than does a distributor that, in the supplier's product category, is diversified. Further, suppliers often grant a distributor some degree of market protection in return for the distributor's pledge of exclusive dealing in the category. The supplier may hesitate to alienate an important distributor in a relationship of mutual dependence.

Putting the evidence together, it appears that manufacturers weigh the costs (often high) and the benefits (sometimes low) of taking enforcement action and very frequently decide to look the other way. They are particularly forgiving of channel members that have made a powerful pledge to them (exclusive dealing), and they are philosophical about gray markets for maturing products, which are subject to greater price competition.

Many manufacturers not only do little to stop gray markets but are actually *positively disposed* toward them! This suggests that other incentives may be at work. The manufacturer increases its market coverage. Further, gray markets serve two purposes the supplier may favor when the product is more mature: They put pressure on authorized channels to compete harder, and they make the product available to a price-sensitive segment. The supplier may be better off in profit terms by tolerating gray markets, all the while claiming publicly to object—as long as authorized channels don't cut back purchases or support in protest.

An intriguing possibility is that gray markets allow a supplier to serve two segments, while appearing to serve only one. One segment cares a great deal about the shopping experience (including displays, atmosphere, sales help, the seller's reputation, and the like) and is less concerned about price. Another is the reverse and will buy anywhere, in any way, from anyone to get a low price. The price-*in*sensitive segment is likely to be the supplier's target segment for profit reasons. Gray markets allow a supplier to serve the price-sensitive segment surreptitiously, while maintaining a more highbrow image.

In short, gray markets are a major cause of channel conflict, in part because *both upstream and downstream channel members are of two minds about them.* Suppliers have reason to bemoan them in public and encourage them in private. Downstream channel members protest about "unfair" competition even though they themselves are often the source of the goods. And even if channel members really do want to stop gray marketing, the many economic incentives to sell through unauthorized outlets mean that sought-after products will always be subject to some level of gray market activity. Enforcement is not so easy and carries its own cost. It is little wonder that gray markets are such a common cause of channel conflict.

FUELING CONFLICT

A recurring theme of this chapter is that channel conflict should be managed to make sure it is not excessive and is primarily of the functional form. Channel players need to know what circumstances fuel conflict and what they can do to stay out of the high-conflict zone.

Conflict Begets More Conflict

An excellent predictor of how much channel members will dispute in the future is how much conflict they have experienced in the past. *Conflict creates more conflict.* A major reason why it proliferates is that once a relationship has experienced high levels of tension and frustration, the players find it very difficult to set their acrimonious history aside and move on. Each party questions whether the other is capable of becoming committed to the relationship.[45] Each discounts positive behaviors and accentuates negative behaviors by the other side. The foundations of trust are thoroughly eroded by high levels of conflict.

Field experience indicates that high and sustained conflict, once experienced, is extremely difficult to overcome. Even when the individuals involved move on to other positions, the organization retains a memory of acrimony and withholds its full support from the channel. Withholding support in anticipation that the other party will not commit is a self-fulfilling prophecy: The other side reciprocates.

Threats

Abundant field research demonstrates that a highly effective and reliable way to increase channel conflict is to threaten a channel member.[46] To threaten means to imply that punishments, or negative sanctions, will be applied if desired behavior or performance is not provided (i.e., if compliance is not forthcoming). The evidence is powerful that a strategy of repeated threats raises the temperature of a relationship by increasing conflict and by reducing the channel member's satisfaction with every aspect of the channel relationship. Threats are perceived as coercion that eventually moves the threatened firm's sense of conflict into the zone of tension, frustration, and collision.

Coercive power is discussed in Chapter 8. It is worth repeating here that coercive power is a tool, like a hammer. It can be put to positive purpose if used properly. For example, channel members can and do pressure each other into taking actions that improve each party's performance. The coercion is mightily resented at the time, but, if handled well, will be overlooked in the short term, forgiven in the medium term, and actually appreciated in the long term.

But any tool can be overused. In general, heavy reliance on coercive tactics is dangerous to the functioning of a distribution channel. A major reason is that these tactics escalate rapidly. Punishment and the threat of it provoke retaliation in kind. For example, in relationships between automobile suppliers and their dealers, the single best predictor of a dealer's punitive actions against a supplier is . . . the supplier's punitive actions against the dealer![47] Car dealers and automakers can find many ways to punish each other, including becoming difficult to work with, cutting service, and withholding information. This reciprocity of aggression rapidly comes to damage the channel's performance.

Contributing to the escalation of channel warfare is another factor: *The better the weapon, the greater the likelihood of using it.* The greater a party's punitive capability—ability to hurt the other channel member—the more coercive that party will be. When a supplier threatens a dealer that is capable of doing real damage, the supplier risks provoking coercion in kind. And as coercion begets coercion, channel members rapidly begin to sanction each other. For example, automakers punish dealers by failing to deliver cars on time. Auto dealers retaliate by withholding information from the manufacturer. Each reaction escalates their conflict—which encourages each side to try to contain the deteriorating situation by . . . more coercion.

In short, *using coercion is like striking a match.* One match lights another. Under the right circumstances, a fire breaks out and will damage the channel.

Where the players have a short time horizon, conflict is often handled by the use of aggressive or coercive strategies.[48] These strategies, in turn, accentuate conflict. Channel members also tend to employ punitive tactics when they have a power advantage over their counterpart (see Chapter 8).[49] This means that in one-sided channels, the dominant party is more likely to threaten the dominated party. Therefore, it is not surprising that channel members count on a shorter time horizon in these imbalanced relationships. When power is lopsided, each channel member suspects the relationship will end sooner than when power is balanced.[50] (For further discussion of imbalanced relationships, see Chapter 8.)

Industrial Marketing Channels in Developed Economies. Industrial marketing channels in developed economies are a good example of balanced power.[51] Frequently, each side is differentiated and each side has many alternatives to the current channel partner. Thus, upstream and downstream channel members are powerful within their relationships. In these circumstances, both supplier and distributor tend to be intolerant of coercive tactics.

The dynamics of such balanced business-to-business relationships are revealing: They are anything but indifferent. Disagreements abound over a variety of issues, including inventory policies, new-account development, participation in training and sales promotion programs, and representation of competing suppliers. Much of this difference of opinion is latent: It exists, but doesn't manifest itself in action.

Each side uses influence strategies in the relationship (see Chapter 8). Sometimes the influencer is seen as coercive, employing threats and high pressure. Otherwise, the influencer is seen as noncoercive: Discussion revolves around exchanging information, sharing points of view, discussing strategies, asking for cooperation (without threatening), and discussing possible payoffs. In business-to-business channels, both sides do use coercive influence strategies to some degree. (Field evidence suggests that suppliers are somewhat more fond of coercion than are distributors.) But how much?

As a general rule, both sides rely more heavily on noncoercive strategies, particularly when dealing with powerful counterparts. *Important relationships encourage noncoercive influence attempts*: Channel members hesitate to jeopardize these relationships and realize that coercion can create a spiral of aggression and retaliation. In addition, powerful parties in balanced business-to-business relationships tend to refrain from coercion, even though they may be in the best position to use it!

This self-restraint is revealing. One of the best ways for a channel member to gain power is to perform its channel role exceptionally well. For example, suppliers gain power over distributors by doing a superior job of developing end-user preferences, ensuring product availability, providing quality products, offering superior technical support, and so forth. These suppliers are powerful because they offer benefits that are difficult for distributors to find elsewhere. Yet, in spite of their power, they rely most heavily on noncoercive means of influencing their distributors. In turn, these are less likely to use coercion in dealing with such suppliers. *Powerful parties rely on persuasion and communication, rather than resorting easily to heavy-handed strategies*.

Does this mean that channel members should never coerce each other? No—the message is not that coercion should be ruled out. On occasion, organizations do need to raise the temperature of their relationships to improve channel performance. And coercion in a channel is not comparable to coercion in a personal relationship: A place exists in business relationships for negotiating via withholding benefits or applying sanctions.

The message is not that threats should be disallowed but that they are an extremely potent way to raise conflict. Therefore, threats should be used with caution, in the realization that coercion can easily be taken too far. This will provoke the other side to retaliate in kind, will reduce satisfaction, and will make the channel counterpart question whether it is worth discussing the issues to devise a solution. Coercion is particularly risky when used with a powerful channel member. In sum, in marketing channels, the use of coercion rapidly escapes the user's control.

CONFLICT RESOLUTION STRATEGIES: HOW THEY DRIVE CONFLICT AND SHAPE CHANNEL PERFORMANCE

How do channel members cope with conflict? We can distinguish two approaches. One is to try to keep conflict from escalating into the dysfunctional zone in the first place. This is done by developing institutionalized mechanisms, such as arbitration boards or norms of behavior in a channel, so as to diffuse disputes before they harden into hostile attitudes. The other is to use patterns of behavior to try to resolve conflict after it becomes manifest. These are discussed in the following sections.

Resolving Conflict: Institutionalized Mechanisms Designed to Contain Conflict Early

Channel members sometimes develop policies to address conflict in its early stages, even before it arises. These policies become institutionalized—part of the environment of the relationship, unquestioned and taken for granted. They serve many functions: Their conflict-management function is often overlooked by the participants themselves. These mechanisms include joint memberships in trade associations, distributor councils, and exchange-of-personnel programs. Some channels build in appeal to third parties, such as referral to boards of arbitration or mediation, a mechanism particularly popular in Europe.

Information-Intensive Mechanisms. Many of these mechanisms are designed to head off conflict by creating a way to share information. An *information-intensive mechanism* is risky and expensive: Each side risks divulging sensitive information and must devote resources to communication. Trust and cooperation are helpful conditions because they keep conflict manageable.

Armstrong World Industries, Inc., a tile maker, uses a *channel diplomat* approach to preventing and resolving channel conflict. It has centralized customer service for many of its distributors and retailers at its headquarters in Lancaster, Pennsylvania, assigning each of them a single contact person who is supposed to be fully versed in all of Armstrong's products and authorized to make adjustments of as much as $1,000 on the spot.[52] This shows the kind of concessionary behavior characteristic of information-intensive mechanisms for blocking the escalation of conflict. It is an example of using expertise power (Chapter 8) to reduce conflict.

Joint membership in trade associations (e.g., the committee jointly founded by the Grocery Manufacturers of America, GMA, and the Food Marketing Institute that was responsible for developing the Universal Product Code) is another example of devising and institutionalizing a mechanism to contain conflict. More recent efforts of this group include efforts to resolve conflict issues that arise while ordering and billing, as well as furthering progress on the efficient consumer response (ECR) efforts discussed in Chapter 16 on logistics.[53]

Some channels use an *exchange of persons* as an institutional vehicle to turn channel members to devising solutions rather than engaging in conflict. This may involve a unilateral or bilateral trade of personnel for a specified period. For example, once a year, each of the top 60 executives of franchisor Hardee's Food Systems has to spend a week behind the counter of one of the company's restaurants.[54]

Another example is the close connection between Wal-Mart and Procter & Gamble personnel. Although such exchanges require clear guidelines because of the possible disclosure of proprietary information, the participants take back to their home organizations a view of their job in an interorganizational context and a personal and professional involvement in the channel network, as well as added training. Participants in such programs also have the opportunity to meet with channel counterparts who have the same specific tasks, professions, and interests. These shared tasks form the basis of continuing relationships that are extraorganizational in content and interorganizational in commitment.

Co-optation is a mechanism designed to absorb new elements into the leadership or policy-determining structure of an organization as a means of averting threats to its stability or existence. Effective co-optation may bring about ready accessibility among channel members because it requires the establishment of routine and reliable channels through which information, aid, and requests may be brought.

For example, August Busch, chairman of Anheuser-Busch Company, a beer brewer, meets with a 15-member wholesaler panel four times a year to hear its complaints and suggestions.[55] And in the automobile industry, manufacturers are involving dealers in functions that formerly were carried out only by manufacturers. For example, Oldsmobile dealers sat on a committee to review the advertising agency contract the company had with Leo Burnett; and Mercedes includes seven dealer members on its marketing committee, which previews new models and offers marketing advice to the company. One advertising agency spokesperson responsible for the General Motors Saturn account says, "You can't fully eliminate conflict and disagreement. But if you work together you can resolve it in a way that everybody buys into it."[56]

Co-optation thus permits the sharing of responsibility so that a variety of channel members may become identified with and committed to the programs developed for a particular product or service. However, as with any information-intensive method of forestalling conflict, co-optation carries the risk of having one's perspective or decision-making process changed. It places an "outsider" in a position to participate in analyzing an existing situation, to suggest alternatives, and to take part in the deliberation of consequences.

The best working relationships will institutionalize a number of these mechanisms, not just one. For instance, 3M, a company noted for its marketing skills, uses 11 different ways of staying in close contact with and managing conflict in its office products distribution system: (1) association involvement, (2) a dealer advisory council, (3) a program called Business Planning Partners, (4) fieldwork, (5) personal letters, (6) a market needs conference, (7) a branch coordinators' conference, (8) a national office study, (9) market needs research, (10) individual distributor conferences, and (11) informal minicouncils.[57] These mechanisms reinforce each other and are part of the operating channel environment. As such, they serve to prevent conflict from escalating out of the functional zone. They also serve to *increase* manifest conflict by bringing latent conflict to the fore and forcing an examination of channel practices. The examination is mutual: It is not 3M's one-sided effort to convince channel members to comply with its desires and agree with its perceptions.

Third-Party Mechanisms. Co-optation brings together representatives of channel members. In contrast, mediation and arbitration are ways to bring in third parties that are uninvolved with the channel. This mechanism prevents conflict from arising or keeps manifest conflict within bounds. *Mediation* is the process whereby a third party attempts to secure settlement of a dispute by persuading the parties either to continue their negotiations or to consider procedural or substantive recommendations that the mediator may make. The mediator typically has a fresh view of the situation and may perceive opportunities that "insiders" cannot. He can gain acceptance on some solutions by suggesting them.

Effective mediation succeeds in clarifying facts and issues, in keeping parties in contact with each other, in exploring possible bases of agreement, in encouraging parties to agree to specific proposals, and in supervising the implementation of agreements.[58] For example, mediation by a former Businessland executive was instrumental in resolving an extremely dysfunctional conflict between Businessland, at one time the largest company-owned chain of personal computer stores, and Compaq Computer Corporation, one of its largest suppliers.[59]

Mediation and arbitration are supported by their own institutional framework in many markets. For example, the Centre for Dispute Resolution (CEDR) was launched in 1990, backed by the Confederation of British Industry. It uses a variety of techniques, including mediation, to resolve channel and other business conflicts.[60] Since its launch, CEDR has handled hundreds of cases, worth hundreds of millions of pounds, with a very high success rate.[61]

The mere presence of the mediation mechanism serves to contain conflict. For example, 11 large franchisors (Pizza Hut, McDonald's, Burger King, Dunkin' Donuts, Hardee's, Holiday Inn Worldwide, Jiffy Lube International, Southland Corporation, Wendy's, Kentucky Fried Chicken, and Taco Bell) launched a mediation program in February 1993 to prevent disputes with franchisees from progressing to the litigation stage. The franchisors have signed a pledge that they will seek mediation before going to court to settle disputes. Although franchisees have not been asked to sign the pledges, they see it as a positive sign that disputes may be settled amicably so that the franchise relationship is preserved.[62]

Mediation can also encourage channel members to increase their communication with each other regarding their objectives and goals. In fact, a mediator may combine channel members' often conflicting utility functions to arrive at an appropriate utility function for the group (the channel). This channel utility function, which also can take into account the power of the individual channel members, can be used to predict outcomes in bargaining situations.[63] In this way, mediators can help channel members find an implementable solution that reflects more than one party's concerns.

Mediators help the parties devise their own decision. An alternative to mediation is *arbitration*, wherein a third party actually makes a decision. Arbitration can be compulsory or voluntary. In the compulsory arbitration process, the parties are required by law to submit their dispute to a third party whose decision is final and binding. In the voluntary arbitration process, parties voluntarily submit their dispute to a third party whose decision is final and binding. Like mediation, arbitration is a well-structured industry in many market environments. For example, in the United States the American Arbitration Association offers commercial arbitration rules, which are so well accepted that government agencies sometimes oblige channel members to use them.[64]

Institutionalizing the practice of taking disputes to third parties, such as arbitrators, can serve to forestall conflict. This is because parties, facing the prospect of outside intervention, often will settle their differences internally rather than let them get to a point that a third party would be called. Of course, third parties are also a means to deal with conflict after it reaches high levels. There is some indication that using third parties once conflict is underway contributes to the success of channel relationships. Third-party intervention to settle open conflicts is associated with channel members' greater satisfaction with the financial rewards they derive from their relationship.[65]

Building Relational Norms.   The mechanisms discussed so far are policies, which can be devised, put into place, and maintained by management. Their use represents a conscious choice of resources. These policies serve as a way for management to forestall conflict, as well as to manage it once it occurs.

But there is an important class of factors that serves to forestall or direct conflict and that management cannot simply decide to create. These are *norms* that govern how channel members manage their relationship. They grow up over time as a relationship functions. A channel's norms are its expectations about behavior, expectations the channel's members at least partially share. In channels that are alliances, it is common to observe norms such as:

- *Flexibility*. Channel members expect each other to adapt readily to changing circumstances, with a minimum of obstruction and negotiation.
- *Information exchange*. Channel members expect each other to share any and all pertinent information—no matter how sensitive—freely, frequently, quickly, and thoroughly.
- *Solidarity*. Channel members expect each other to work for mutual benefit, not merely one-sided benefit.

These *relational norms* tend to come in a package: A relationship has a high level of all these norms if it has a high level of any of them.[66] A channel with strong relational norms is particularly effective at forestalling conflict. It discourages the parties from pursuing their own interests at the expense of the channel. These norms also encourage the players to refrain from coercion and to make the effort work through their differences, thus keeping conflict in the functional zone.[67]

Of course, management cannot decide to create relational norms and then "just do it." They are created daily by the interactions of the people who constitute a marketing channel. These norms can be positive or negative. For example, a channel can have a norm of cutthroat competition or of pure self-interest seeking. Unlike policies, managements do not decree norms. And unlike policies, norms are not easy to observe, announce, or publicize.

To this point, we have considered strategies that are intended to forestall excessive conflict. These mechanisms also keep conflict functional if it does occur. Next we turn to the behaviors and processes that organizations employ on a daily basis with the intention of coping with conflict once it is underway.

Styles of Conflict Resolution

Some conflict is a normal, even desirable, property of channels. How do channel members cope with manifest conflict? As a general rule, they seek not to eliminate it but to use it as a force for change. Sometimes these efforts are functional, but frequently they only make the situation worse. This section considers the conflict resolution strategies channel members use and examines the consequences in terms of how satisfied channel members are with their relationship. Note that the discussion is not about how channel members handle a particular issue or incident: It is about the *general conflict resolution style* they employ in their relationship.[68]

Figure 9.2 shows one way to conceptualize how channel members deal with conflicts. This framework focuses on a channel member's approach to bargaining. For example, a retailer, in its dealings with a supplier, brings to the bargaining table a certain level of *assertiveness* (strength of emphasis on achieving its own goals, such as building store traffic, increasing the uniqueness of its assortment, or increasing margins) and a level of *cooperativeness* (concern for the other party's goals, such as the supplier's goals of building volume, creating a distinctive image, or taking share from a competitor).

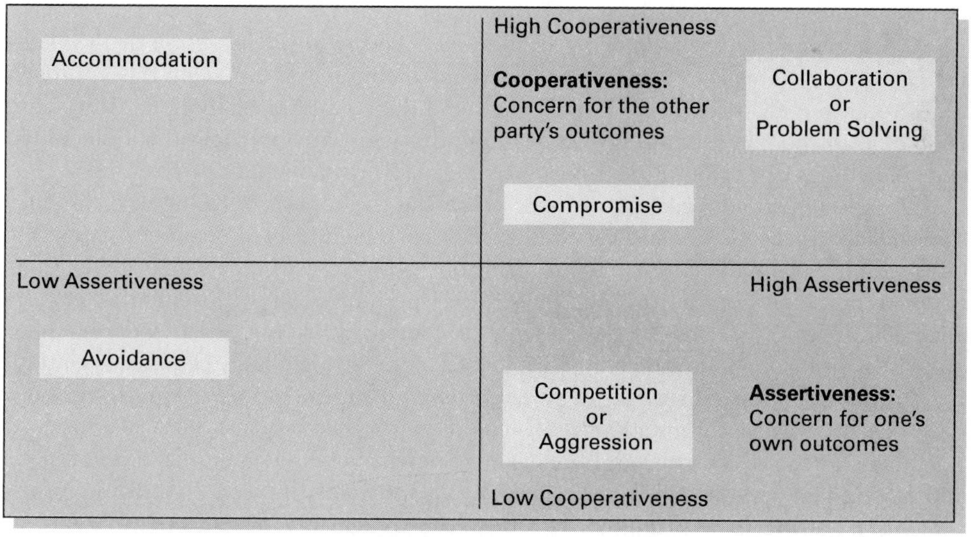

FIGURE 9.2 **Conflict Resolution Styles**

Source: Based on Kenneth W. Thomas, "Conflict and Conflict Management," in M. D. Dunnette (ed.), *Handbook of Industrial and Organizational Psychology* (Palo Alto, CA: Consulting Psychologists Press, 1976), pp. 889–935.

A relatively passive channel member (perhaps one in a weak position or represented by a poor negotiator) has an *avoidance* style of dealing with conflict. It attempts to prevent conflict from occurring by . . . failing to press for much of anything! Typically, the avoider wants to save time and head off unpleasantness. They often do this by minimizing information exchange, thereby circumventing discussion. In most channels, avoidance is associated with relationships of convenience, wherein neither side feels much commitment to the other.

Another style of dealing with conflict is to be accommodating to the other party, meaning to be more focused on its goals than on one's own. Unlike avoidance (a passive strategy), this is more than just another way of keeping the peace. *Accommodation* is a proactive means of strengthening the relationship by cultivating the *other* channel member. It signals a genuine willingness to cooperate, encourages reciprocation, which in turn should build trust and commitment over the longer term. But it exposes the accommodator to being repeatedly exploited, unless the other side reciprocates.

A strategy of *competition* (or aggression) involves playing a zero-sum game by pursuing one's own goals while ignoring the other party's goals. This approach focuses on pushing one's own position while conceding very little. Not surprisingly, this style aggravates conflict, fosters distrusts, and shortens the time horizon of the channel members vis-à-vis their relationship. Channel members tend to limit their usage of the aggressive style, especially in long-term relationships.

A very different style is to *compromise* repeatedly, pressing for solutions that let each side achieve its goals, but only to an intermediate degree. This is a centrist approach that gives something to everyone, the compromise strategy seems to be fair. It is used often to handle minor conflicts, wherein it is easiest to get both sides to concede, thereby speeding the search for a resolution.

Close, committed relationships are better served by a *collaboration* or *problem-solving* strategy. This is an ambitious style. The channel member taking this approach wants to have it all—to achieve its own goals and the counterpart's, both to a very high degree! Many people claim to be interested in this win–win approach: It is fashionable and contributes to a favorable self-image, as well as a favorable public presentation.

Our discussion here is about actually practicing the approach. Doing so is difficult. The collaboration style of handling conflict requires a high level of resources, especially information, time, and energy. The problem solver tries to get both sides to get all their concerns and issues out in the open quickly, to work immediately through their differences, to discuss issues directly, and to share problems with an eye toward working them out. Problem solving requires creativity in trying to devise a mutually beneficial solution. It is an information-intensive strategy. In pursuing it, negotiators are sure to reveal a good deal of sensitive information, which could then be used against them.

This approach is popular in franchising. Franchising creates mutual commitment and a long-term horizon. The issues involved are major. In any given franchisor–franchisee pairing, at least one party (often, the franchisor) has considerable power, which enables it to promote a collaboration style. Of course, the franchisee can be and often is the more powerful party; franchisees often bring a problem-solving style to the relationship.[69] However, some disputes strain the parties' ability to deal with them internally. Thus, third-party intervention is used frequently in franchised channels. This is particularly the case when a franchisee is very highly dependent on the franchisor. Franchise systems also resort to third parties for the most difficult disputes, those where the issue is complex, involves high stakes, or has policy implications.[70]

Resolving Conflict and Achieving Coordination via Incentives

To this point in our discussion of conflict resolution styles, we have focused on the negotiator's style. What are the best arguments to use to persuade the channel member? Considerable field evidence indicates that economic incentives work extremely well, regardless of the personalities, the players, and the history of their relationship. This is not surprising: Just as reward power is a highly effective way to influence a channel member (Chapter 8), appealing to economic self-interest is a highly effective way to settle a dispute. Thus, good negotiators pursuing a collaboration style of resolving conflict find ingenious ways to tie their arguments into economics. Further, *economic arguments work extremely well when combined with a strong program of communications in a good interpersonal working relationship*.

A good example occurs with manufacturer-sponsored promotion programs aimed at retailers. In fast-moving consumer goods (FMCG) industries, suppliers spend enormous sums to create point-of-purchase (POP) advertising and displays for in-store use. These programs are a major issue of dispute. Manufacturers charge retailers with taking the promotion money without mounting the promised promotion. In turn, retailers charge manufacturers with not giving them their fair share of promotion allowances and with promising more than they actually deliver. The acrimony generated over this issue alone consumes pages of the grocery trade press.

Evidence shows that much of the acrimony can be dissolved by combining appealing economic incentives to participate with a pay-for-performance system, and presenting the proposal through a salesperson who has a good working relationship with the retailer. Economic incentives (such as a premium for participation) have an obvious appeal. The salesperson's good relationship helps him or her to direct the retailer's attention to the incentives. And the pay-for-performance system (e.g., paying for items sold on promotion rather than merely items ordered) screens out retailers who are fundamentally uninterested in cooperating with the supplier.[71]

Economic incentives are not merely a matter of offering a better price or a higher allowance. These are quite visible and are easy for competitors to match in any case. Persuasive economic arguments are usually based on the *package* of factors that collectively create financial returns for a channel member.[72] For example, independent sales agencies have been shown to be highly sensitive to a product's ability to generate profits by:

- Compensating for lower volume by higher commission rate, and vice versa
- Compensating for lower commission rates by being easier to sell, thereby requiring less sales time (cutting costs)
- Establishing the sales agent in a growing product category (contributing to future profits)
- Increasing overall sales synergy, thereby spurring sales of other products in the agent's portfolio

In addition, independent agencies respond to indirect arguments about risk. A principal can settle disputes if it can convince the agent that sales are not unpredictable but instead can be accurately forecasted. And all of these arguments can be conveyed more effectively by principals that invest in vigorous programs of two-way communication within the channel.[73]

SUMMARY

Conflict, a negative in most human relationships is also a negative in many channel relationships. But it is not uniformly undesirable. Indeed, a channel can be too peaceful; indifference and passivity often pass for harmony, masking great differences in motivation and intention. And a contentious channel is often one engaged in functional conflict: The parties are raising and working through their differences, in search of a better understanding and a higher plane of performance. Channel conflict is often a necessary stage on the way to adapting to environmental changes. Thus, conflict in channels should not be judged automatically as a defect, as a state to be eliminated. Instead, conflict should be monitored, then managed. This can mean trying to increase conflict, as well as trying to reduce or redirect it.

Managing conflict first means assessing it. A good way to do so is to index, for each issue that is relevant to a channel, the level of frequency of disagreement, the intensity of disagreement (how far apart are the parties), and the importance of the issue. If any of these is low, the issue is not a great source of conflict, the participants' opinions notwithstanding. The product of intensity, frequency, and importance of dispute over each issue, summed over the issues, gives a good rough approximation of actual conflict and suggests to the arbitrator how to convince parties to resolve their differences. This implies that more complex relationships are likely to experience more conflict.

Conflict is a staple in marketing channels because of built-in differences in viewpoint and goals. Goal differences are real enough: Curiously, perceived differences can actually outweigh them as causes of opposition. Different perceptions also spark much dispute, in part because channel members see different pieces of the channel environment. A perennial source of conflict is clash over domains, wherein suppliers perceive their channels represent competitors, and downstream channel members perceive their suppliers pit them against other channel members and other channel forms. The latter situation (multiple channels) has become quite normal as industries mature and customers become more demanding. Solutions involve communication, concession, creative compensation, compensating multiple parties, working together to devise win–win approaches, and selling differentiated products through different channels. Solutions also involve accepting conflict for the sake of serving customers better or more economically.

A major source of friction is gray markets, which are growing rapidly. These exist because both parties, and especially suppliers, have reasons to permit them privately while bemoaning them publicly. For suppliers, reasons include higher sales, as well as the ability to prod authorized channels and to reach a different segment. Objectives aside, gray markets are not easy to eliminate, leading firms to tolerate them under certain circumstances.

Conflict is self-perpetuating, self-fueling. Once it is underway, parties develop long memories and interpret events in a negative light. And the cycle is easily started by threats, which beget reaction in kind, especially the more capable the other party is of actually doing harm. Reciprocation of coercion can easily send the channel into a self-destructive spiral of aggression.

A number of ways to resolve disputes are effective. Institutionalized mechanisms to contain conflict early exist in abundance, including information-intensive strategies and the use of third parties. Once conflict is underway, the styles of the parties influence the course of their dispute. The most effective style is driving toward achieving the goals of both parties (collaboration, or problem solving). For this to work requires the commitment of both parties, and works well when both parties are powerful in the relationship.

Of course, conflict can also be resolved via the use of economic incentives, which are quite effective when coupled with good communication. Particularly good incentives are less visible (therefore harder for competition to match) and encourage channel members to make an effort or investment and assume some risk in order to collect them.

Discussion Questions

1. A marketing channel is an interdependent set of entities: They need each other. Why, then, is conflict a normal state in channels? And why does vertical integration fail to eliminate conflict completely?

2. When do suppliers tolerate gray marketing, and why?

3. "As markets mature, it is essential to set up multiple channels (different types), and to let them compete head on." Debate this statement. What responsibility, if any, do suppliers have to manage conflict between multiple channels? How can they go about doing so?

4. Refer to the Channel Sketch of Meccano. If you had been part of the management team when the Toys "R" Us deal was being negotiated, would you have opposed it? Was there a way to avert the catastrophic outcome? Was this outcome just bad luck? What would you have suggested doing instead? What channels would you approach today to launch the new product line, and how would you try to manage conflict as these channels grow?

5. Wherehouse Entertainment Inc., a 339-store retailer based in Torrance, California, sells used compacts disks (CDs) of music in its stores, showing them alongside new CDs. Immediate responses by music companies included withdrawal of co-op advertising support by Sony, Warner Music, Capitol-EMI, and MCA. They argue that it may be legal to resell a used music CD, but doing so cuts into the profits from new CDs and deprives artists of royalties. Garth Brooks, a best-selling artist, has refused to release his CDs to stores selling used disks. Another retail chain that sells used CDs retorts that the major record label companies should look to their own distribution channels as culprits, and should stop selling CDs at very low prices through record clubs offering deep-discount promotions to members. Categorize the emergence of channel conflict that this move by Wherehouse has produced, and make some suggestions about how to control or manage the conflicts.

6. When is coercion a good idea, and why? When is it most likely to be used, and by which channel members?

7. What can channel members do to prevent conflict from becoming dangerous? To what extent can management control conflict in its early stages?

8. "If you don't negotiate aggressively, you won't get anything. You have to push for what you want with channel members, and you have to negotiate hard." Debate this statement. What are the best conflict resolution styles, and when is each style likely to be used?

9. If economic incentives are effective ways to resolve conflict, why not simply offer better terms to the trade? What are the best ways to resolve conflict by making a resolution economically appealing? Why is it effective to couple incentives with communication?

Notes

1. Louis W. Stern, "Relationships, Networks, and the Three Cs," in D. Iacobucci (eds.), *Networks in Marketing* (Thousand Oaks, CA: Sage Publications, 1996), pp. 3–7.

2. Louis W. Stern and James L. Heskett, "Conflict Management in Interorganizational Relations: A Conceptual Framework," in Louis W. Stern (ed.), *Distribution Channels: Behavioral Dimensions* (Boston: Houghton-Mifflin, 1969), pp. 156–75.

3. Louis R. Pondy, "Organizational Conflict: Concepts and Models," *Administrative Science Quarterly*, 14, no. 1 (1967), pp. 296–320.

4. Rami Zwick and Xiao-Ping Chen, "What Price Fairness? A Bargaining Study," *Management Science*, 45 (June 1999), pp. 804–23.

5. James R. Brown and Ralph L. Day, "Measures of Manifest Conflict in Distribution Channels," *Journal of Marketing Research*, 18 (August 1981), pp. 263–74. This article is the basis for the discussion and example of measuring channel conflict.

6. Jehoshua Eliashberg and Donald A. Michie, "Multiple Business Goals Sets as Determinants of Marketing Channel Conflict: An Empirical Study," *Journal of Marketing Research*, 21 (February 1984), pp. 75–88.

7. F. Robert Dwyer, Paul H. Schurr, and Sejo Oh, "Developing Buyer–Seller Relationships," *Journal of Marketing*, 51 (April 1987), pp. 11–27.

8. Sylvain Courage, "Monsieur Propre Defie les Geants de la Distribution," *Capital*, 10 (December 1999), p. 20.

9. Bruce Webster, "Uses and Abuses of Co-op Advertising," *Supply House Times*, 15 (March 1998), pp. 57–64.

10. Sylvain Courage, "Compaq Tombe de Haut," *Capital*, 15 (November 1999), p. 46. Hassan Fatah, "The Channel Fights Back," *MC Technology Marketing Intelligence*, 18 (January 1998), pp. 22–23.

11. James C. Anderson and James A. Narus, "A Model of the Distributor's Perspective of Distributor–Manufacturer Working Relationships," *Journal of Marketing*, 48 (fall 1984), pp. 62–74.

12. Inge Geyskens, Jan-Benedict E. M. Steenkamp, and Nirmalya Kumar, "A Meta-Analysis of Satisfaction in Marketing Channel Relationships," *Journal of Marketing Research*, 36 (May 1999), pp. 223–38.

13. Mark Bergen, Shantanu Dutta, and Orville C. Walker Jr., "Agency Relationships in Marketing: A Review of the Implications and Applications of Agency and Related Theories," *Journal of Marketing*, 56, no. 3 (1992), pp. 1–24.

14. Kyle Pope, "Dealers Accuse Compaq of Jilting Them," *Wall Street Journal*, April 7, 1993, p. B1.

15. Allan J. Magrath and Kenneth G. Hardy, "A Strategic Paradigm for Predicting Manufacturer–Reseller Conflict," *European Journal of Marketing*, 23, no. 2 (1989), pp. 94–108.

16. Ibid.

17. Eliashberg, Jehoshua and Donald A. Michie, "Multiple Business Goals Sets as Determinants of Marketing Channel Conflict: An Empirical Study," *Journal of Marketing Research*, 21 (February 1984), pp. 75–88.

18. George John and Torger Reve, "The Reliability and Validity of Key Informant Data from Dyadic Relationships in Marketing Channels," *Journal of Marketing Research*, 19 (November 1982), pp. 517–24.

19. James R. Brown, Robert F. Lusch, and Laurie P. Smith, "Conflict and Satisfaction in an Industrial Channel of Distribution," *International Journal of Physical Distribution & Logistics Management*, 21, no. 6 (1991), pp. 15–26.

20. Robert M. Morgan and Shelby D. Hunt, "The Commitment-Trust Theory of Relationship Marketing," *Journal of Marketing*, 58 (July 1994), pp. 20–38.

21. Douglas W. LaBahn and Katrin R. Harich, "Sensitivity to National Business Culture: Effects on U.S.-Mexican Channel Relationship Performance," *Journal of International Marketing*, 5 (December 1997), pp. 29–51.

22. Nirmalya Kumar, "The Power of Trust in Manufacturer–Retailer Relationships," *Harvard Business Review*, 60 (November–December 1996), pp. 92–106.

23. "Newsmakers: Acacia Inc.," *Sales and Marketing Management*, 148 (April 1996), p. 20.

24. The discussion in this section is based on communications with Alberto Sa Vinhas and Gary L. F., "Organizing and Managing Channels of Distribution," *Journal of the Academy of Marketing Sciences*, 27, no. 2 (1999), pp. 226–40.

25. Frank V. Cespedes and Raymond Corey, "Managing Multiple Channels," *Business Horizons*, 10, no. 1 (1990), pp.

67–77; Rowland T. Moriarty and Ursula Moran, "Managing Hybrid Marketing Systems," *Harvard Business Review*, November–December 1990, pp. 146–50.

26. Sophie Chapdelaine, "Revlon Prend des Rides," *Capital*, 10 (October 1999), pp. 44–45.

27. Chantal Bialobos, "Meccano en Pieces," *Capital*, 10 (December 1999), pp. 53–54.

28. Rowland T. Moriarty and Ursula Moran, "Managing Hybrid Marketing Systems," *Harvard Business Review*, 44 (November–December 1990), pp. 146–50.

29. Christine B. Bucklin, Pamela A. Thomas-Graham, and Elizabeth A. Webster, "Channel Conflict: When Is It Dangerous?" *McKinsey Quarterly*, 7, no. 3 (1997), pp. 36–43.

30. Shantanu Dutta, Mark Bergen, Jan B. Heide, et al., "Understanding Dual Distribution: The Case of Reps and House Accounts," *Journal of Law, Economics, and Organization*, 11, no. 1 (1995), pp. 189–204.

31. Miguel Villas-Boas, "Product Line Design for a Distribution Channel," *Marketing Science*, 17, no. 2 (1997), pp. 156–69.

32. Jerry Rosa, "Xerox Connect Puts Pieces in Place for Channel Strategy," *Computer Reseller News*, 10 (October 26, 1998), p. 64.

33. Patrick McGeehan and David Franecki, "Loads, No-Loads Invade Each Other's Territory," *Wall Street Journal*, August 2, 1999, pp. R1, R7.

34. David Jastrow, "Vendors Air Concerns over EDI Sites," *Computer Reseller News*, 10 (May 11, 1998), p. 45.

35. Devavrat Purohit, "Dual Distribution Channels: The Competition Between Rental Agencies and Dealers," *Marketing Science*, 16, no. 3 (1997), pp. 228–45; Devavrat Purohit and Richard Staelin, "Rentals, Sales, and Buybacks: Managing Secondary Distribution Channels," *Journal of Marketing Research*, 31 (August 1994), pp. 325–38.

36. Bethany McLean, "Paine Webber Is Alive and Kicking," *Fortune*, 40 (July 5, 1999), pp. 124–28.

37. Katrina Brooker, "Cold Calling in a Cold World," *Fortune*, 40 (July 5, 1999), pp. 34–38.

38. David A. Nield, "The Evolving State of Distribution," *Life Insurance Marketing and Research Association's MarketFacts*, 17 (March–April 1998), pp. 30–34. Quotation from p. 33.

39. This section is adapted from David A. Soberman and Anne T. Coughlan, "When Is the Best Ship a Leaky One? Segmentation, Competition, and Gray Markets," INSEAD working paper 98/60/MKT, summarized in David Champion, "Marketing: The Bright Side of Gray Markets," *Harvard Business Review*, 76 (September–October 1998), pp. 19–22.

40. Robert E. Weigand, "Parallel Import Channels—Options for Preserving Territorial Integrity," *Columbia Journal of World Business*, 26 (Spring 1991), pp. 53–60; Gert Assmus and Carsten Wiese, "How to Address the Gray Market Threat Using Price Coordination," *Sloan Management Review*, 36 (Spring 1995), pp. 31–41.

41. Mark Henricks, "Harmful Diversions," *Apparel Industry Magazine*, 58 (September 1997), pp. 72–78.

42. "Shop Tactics in Tokyo," *The Economist*, February 5, 1994, p. 69.

43. Frank V. Cespedes, E. Raymond Corey, and V. Kasturi Rangan, "Gray Markets: Causes and Cures," *Harvard Business Review*, 88 (July–August 1988), pp. 75–82; Matthew B. Myers and David A. Griffith, "Strategies for Combating Gray Market Activity," *Business Horizons*, 42 (November–December 1999), pp. 2–8.

44. Mark Bergen, Jan B. Heide, and Shantanu Dutta, "Managing Gray Markets Through Tolerance of Violations: A Transaction Cost Perspective," *Managerial and Decision Economics*, 19, no. 1 (1998), pp. 157–65.

45. Erin Anderson and Barton Weitz, "The Use of Pledges to Build and Sustain Commitment in Distribution Channels," *Journal of Marketing Research*, 24 (February 1992), pp. 18–34.

46. Geyskens, Steenkamp, and Kumar, "A Meta-Analysis of Satisfaction."

47. Nirmalya Kumar, Lisa K. Scheer, and Jan-Benedict E. M. Steenkamp, "Interdependence, Punitive Capability, and the Reciprocation of Punitive Actions in Channel Relationships," *Journal of Marketing Research*, 35 (May 1998), pp. 225–35.

48. Shankar Ganesan, "Negotiation Strategies and the Nature of Channel Relationships," *Journal of Marketing Research*, 30 (May 1993), pp. 183–203.

49. Kumar, Scheer, and Steenkamp, "Interdependence, Punitive Capability, and Reciprocation."

50. Erin Anderson and Barton Weitz, "Determinants of Continuity in Conventional Channel Dyads," *Marketing Science*, 8 (fall 1989), pp. 310–23.

51. This discussion is based on Gary L. Frazier and Raymond C. Rody, "The Use of Influence Strategies in Interfirm Relationships in Industrial Product Channels," *Journal of Marketing*, 55 (January 1991), pp. 52–69.

52. Vindu P. Goel, "Armstrong Sharpens Its Focus in Shadow of Belzbergs," *Wall Street Journal*, November 25, 1989, p. A5.

53. Louis W. Stern and Patrick J. Kaufman, "Electronic Data Interchange in Selected Consumer Goods Industries," in Robert D. Buzzell (ed.), *Marketing in an Electronic Age* (Boston: Harvard Business School Press, 1985), pp. 52–73.

54. "Hardee's: The Bigger It Grows, the Hungrier It Gets," *BusinessWeek*, May 4, 1987, p. 106.

55. "Even August Busch Can Only Handle So Much Beer," *BusinessWeek*, September 25, 1989, p. 187.

56. Mary Connelly, "Auto Dealers Flex Their Muscles," *Advertising Age*, March 22, 1993.

57. Presentation by J. P. Wilkins, Marketing Director, Office Products, 3M Company, St. Paul, Minnesota, 1984.

58. Todd B. Carver and Albert A. Vondra, "Alternative Dispute Resolution: Why It Doesn't Work and Why It Does," *Harvard Business Review*, 72 (May–June 1994), pp. 120–30.

59. G. Pascal Zachary and Andy Zipser, "Businessland Is Compaq's Land Yet Again," *Wall Street Journal*, March 8, 1990, p. B1; G. Pascal Zachary, "Businessland Founder Struggles to Pull Firm Out of a Deep Slide," *Wall Street Journal*, March 18, 1991, p. A1.

60. Simon Carne, "Alternative Ways to Solve Disputes," *Financial Times*, March 21, 1991, p. 14.

61. Ellen John Pollack, "Mediation Firms After the Legal Landscape," *Wall Street Journal*, March 22, 1993, p. B1.

62. Michele Galen, Laurel Touby, Lori Bongiorno, and Wendy Zeller, "Franchise Fracas," *BusinessWeek*, March 22, 1993, pp. 68–73.

63. Jehoshua Eliashberg, Stephen A. LaTour, Arvind Rangaswamy, and Louis W. Stern, "Assessing the Predictive Accuracy of Two Utility-Based Theories in a Marketing Channel Negotiation Context," *Journal of Marketing Research*, 23 (May 1986), pp. 101–10.

64. "Airco Agrees to Settle Disputes with Distributors Through Arbitration," *FTC News Summary*, April 13, 1979, p. 3.

65. Jakki Mohr and Robert Spekman, "Characteristics of Partnership Success: Partnership Attributes, Communication Behavior, and Conflict Resolution Techniques," *Strategic Management Journal*, 15, no. 1 (1994), pp. 135–52; Jakki Mohr and Robert Spekman, "Perfecting Partnerships," *Marketing Management*, 4 (winter–spring 1996), pp. 34–43.

66. Jan B. Heide and George John, "Do Norms Matter in Marketing Relationships?" *Journal of Marketing*, 56 (April 1992), pp. 32–44.

67. Jan B. Heide, "Interorganizational Governance in Marketing Channels," *Journal of Marketing*, 58 (April 1994), pp. 71–85.

68. This material is based on Kenneth W. Thomas, "Conflict and Conflict Management" in M. D. Dunnette (ed.), *Handbook of Industrial and Organizational Psychology* (Palo Alto, CA: Consulting Psychologists Press, 1976), pp. 889–935; Shankar Ganesan, "Negotiation Strategies and the Nature of Channel Relationships," *Journal of Marketing Research*, 30 (May 1993), pp. 183–203; Sandy D. Jap, Stijn M. J. van Ossalaer, and Barton A. Weitz, "Conflict Management Approaches and the Moderating Role of Perceived Mutual Commitment in Principal–Agent Relationships," Working Paper, Sloan School of Management, 1999.

69. Jeffrey L. Bradach, "Using the Plural Form in the Management of Restaurant Chains," *Administrative Science Quarterly*, 42 (June 1997), pp. 276–303.

70. Rajiv P. Dant and Patrick L. Schul, "Conflict Resolution Processes in Contractual Channels of Distribution," *Journal of Marketing*, 56 (January 1992), pp. 38–54.

71. John P. Murray Jr. and Jan B. Heide, "Managing Promotion Program Participation Within Manufacturer–Retailer Relationships," *Journal of Marketing*, 62 (January 1998), pp. 58–68.

72. Erin Anderson, Leonard M. Lodish, and Barton Weitz, "Resource Allocation Behavior in Conventional Channels," *Journal of Marketing Research*, 24 (February 1987), pp. 85–97.

73. Jakki Mohr and John R. Nevin, "Communication Strategies in Marketing Channels: A Theoretical Perspective," *Journal of Marketing*, October 1990, pp. 36–51.

10

Channel Implementation Issues Regarding Distribution Intensity and Vertical Restraints

LEARNING OBJECTIVES

After reading this chapter, you will:

- Describe the idea of selectivity as the negotiated and often reciprocal limitation of the number of trading partners in a market area
- Explain why manufacturers prefer more coverage, especially in fast-moving consumer goods, while preferring the downstream channel member to limit its assortment in their product category
- Explain why downstream channel members prefer less coverage, while preferring more assortment in the manufacturer's product category
- Explain why limited distribution is preferable for brands with a high-end positioning or a narrow target market
- Explain the mechanism by which limiting the number of trading partners raises motivation and increases power
- Describe selectivity as a way to reassure trading partners against the threat of opportunism
- Forecast when either side (upstream, downstream) will concede to a limitation of the number of its trading partners
- Describe means of maintaining intensive coverage while containing its destructive effects on the channel
- Connect selectivity to other forms of vertical restraints.

The legal implications of these topics are covered in depth in Chapter 12.

*I*ntensive distribution means that a brand can be purchased through many of the possible outlets in a trading area (at saturation, *every* possible outlet). The opposite is exclusive distribution, whereby a brand can be purchased only through one vendor in a trading area, so that the vendor has a "local monopoly" on the brand. Both saturation and exclusivity are out of the ordinary. Typically, a brand is distributed with some degree of intensity, achieving partial coverage of available outlets in a market area. How thoroughly to cover a given trading area is a critical channel decision for a manufacturer: the way a product or service is presented to the market depends in great measure on how readily it is available. Degree of channel intensity (alternatively, degree of selectivity) is a major factor driving the *manufacturer's ability to implement its channel programs*.[1]

The more intensively a manufacturer distributes its brand in a market, the less the manufacturer can influence how channel members perform marketing channel flows. To control the performance of flows, a manufacturer must refrain from blanketing or saturating a trading area's distribution outlets. Yet, by limiting coverage, the manufacturer may be giving up sales and profits to its competitors. Naturally, manufacturers prefer to maximize coverage and actively resist the idea of deliberately restricting the availability of their brands. *When and why should a manufacturer limit coverage?* This chapter focuses on this complex trade-off between easy buyer access, which comes with intensity, and influence over channel members, which comes with selectivity.

It turns out that this decision is linked to a more general issue: To what degree should a manufacturer seek to impose unusual contractual restraints on the downstream channel member's conduct of its own business? These *vertical restraints* constitute interference in another business. There is a great variety of such mechanisms, including restricting the channel member's ability to seek out whatever business it pleases, to resell the product, to set the price, and to carry competing brands. These contractual means of interfering with the autonomy of another business raise legal issues, covered in Chapter 12. There are also ways to write a contract so as to simulate vertical integration, where two companies become one, with a common goal.[2] Vertical restraints are designed to oblige the downstream channel member to set aside its own goals and to act as if it were a unit of the manufacturer. Put simply, vertical restraints are a sweeping contractual means of increasing the manufacturer's power over the downstream channel member.

Most of this chapter considers the choice of *degree of selectivity*. This is considered from both viewpoints: the upstream (manufacturer) considering how many outlets to pursue and the downstream (e.g., the reseller) considering how many competing brands to carry in a product category. Limiting the number of channel partners is a complex decision. It is frequently presented as the imposition of unwanted restrictions by a strong player on a weak one. This is a limited and often misleading viewpoint. A more useful way to frame the issue is as the outcome of a negotiation, which reflects patterns of trade-offs and reciprocity. This chapter presents selectivity as a negotiated settlement and covers how selectivity influences a channel member's ability to implement its channel strategy. Other forms of vertical restraints are briefly considered as parallel mechanisms, which complement the intention of selectivity.

COVERAGE VERSUS ASSORTMENT: FRAMING THE DECISIONS OF UPSTREAM AND DOWNSTREAM CHANNEL MEMBERS

Why More Coverage Is Better for Manufacturers of Convenience Goods

When it comes to availability of a brand in a trading area, more is better—or so it would seem. It appears almost a truism to say that the more outlets carry a brand, the more it will sell. This should happen because better coverage makes it easier for a buyer to find the brand. This matters particularly for those brands that do not command strong loyalty. In addition, if prospective purchasers encounter a vigorous sales effort for the brand in every outlet they visit, and if many outlets carry the brand, the prospect must surely surrender to the combined persuasion of all these outlets! How could it not be true that more coverage is better?

The answer hinges on the nature of the product category. Many categories of product or service are routine, low-involvement purchases, which the buyer considers minor and low risk (so that making a significant error is unlikely). Fast-moving consumer goods (FMCG) such as coffee or facial tissues fall into this category, as do many products such as office supplies purchased by businesses. Buyers are unwilling to search across outlets for these items. Easy availability is paramount. These convenience goods are for everyday life.[3] Given an acceptable brand choice, buyers will tend to take what is on offer, rather than search for their favorite brand.

One indication of this phenomenon is that FMCG brand market share is disproportionately related to distribution coverage (see Figure 10.1 for examples of such relationships).

After a certain threshold of coverage has been reached, securing a few more points of distribution coverage is frequently associated with a sharp upturn in market share. One reason this occurs is that, for many mundane products, most consumers will not leave a store to visit another one if they cannot find their preferred brands. They tend to buy from the set of brands they find if at least some brands are acceptable to them. Small retailers, constrained by space, stock only the top one or two brands, knowing that will suffice for most of their customers on most of the purchase occasions a small store serves. Collectively, they move large amounts of merchandise, and in these stores, consumers have very little brand choice. Hence, coverage over a threshold level boosts coverage in small outlets, which rapidly boosts a brand's market share disproportionately. This creates a spiral: The higher the brand's market share, the greater the likelihood that other small stores will adopt that brand, which increases share, and so on ("the rich get richer").[4]

For convenience goods, from the buyer's perspective, more coverage means easy availability, a factor of considerable importance. *All else constant, higher degrees of distribution intensity will always boost sales.* For anything other than convenience goods, this statement does not hold.

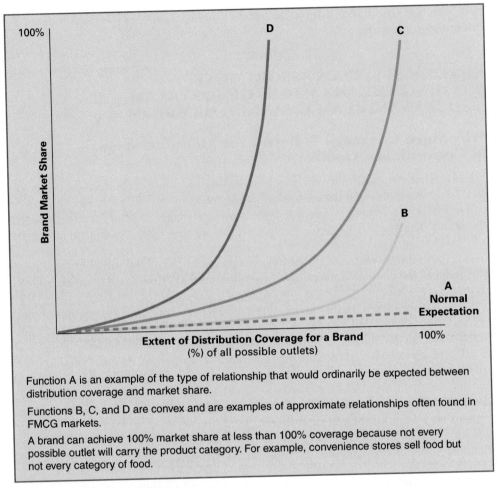

Function A is an example of the type of relationship that would ordinarily be expected between distribution coverage and market share.

Functions B, C, and D are convex and are examples of approximate relationships often found in FMCG markets.

A brand can achieve 100% market share at less than 100% coverage because not every possible outlet will carry the product category. For example, convenience stores sell food but not every category of food.

FIGURE 10.1 **Sample Representations of the Coverage–Market Share Relationship for Fast-Moving Consumer Goods**

Why Downstream Channel Members Dislike Intensive Distribution

From the downstream channel member's perspective, however, more coverage for a given brand is a negative, not a positive. Among other factors, channel members differentiate themselves by offering unique assortments. Intensive distribution means that a channel member's competitors have the same brand, thereby eroding the outlet's uniqueness. *Each channel member would prefer exclusivity.* This clash of interests between manufacturers (brand owners) and downstream players builds a permanent source of conflict into the channel.

When a market is saturated, that is, all possible outlets carry a brand, a channel member cannot present the brand as a reason why a buyer should visit that outlet rather than a competing outlet. And, once the buyer does appear, the outlet must give the buyer a reason to purchase on the spot. Inertia is one reason: A prospect will buy to avoid the nuisance of shopping elsewhere, particularly for a minor purchase such as toothpaste or pasta sauce. But for a more important purchase such as a digital camera, the buyer will delay a decision and continue to shop, unless the channel member can present some reason—usually a price cut—to buy now. This sets channel members up directly against each other, thereby driving ferocious intrabrand price competition. To avoid this scenario, computer maker Nexar Technologies allows resellers to put their own private logos on a Nexar box. In this way, resellers achieve the appearance of exclusivity. Nexar's chairman explains it thus: "We are conscious to establish relations so we don't get resellers to bang heads against each other."[5]

From the manufacturer's perspective, intrabrand price competition at the retail level (but not, of course, at the wholesale level!) is desirable—in the short term. Channel members will move more product by charging lower prices and are likely to fund it by slashing their own margins. The manufacturer realizes higher volume at the same wholesale price. For example, Coca-Cola soft drinks are offered as promotions by many retailers. The larger super and hypermarkets often carry a large product (size, multipaks, flavors) variety, which can take up a large amount of shelf space. In order to induce shoppers to buy the products, the stores offer low promotional prices.

But this situation cannot go on indefinitely. Channel members, realizing the brand is unprofitable for them, will press for relief in the form of lower wholesale prices. If wholesale prices are not cut, the problem of low margins persists. If wholesale prices are cut, the problem may still persist. Resellers will be obliged to compete the higher margin away at resale, thereby failing to resolve their profitability problem.[6] In the example of Coca-Cola products, the stores may not incur accounting losses on the drinks, but they may incur significant opportunity costs that come with end-of-aisle displays and advertising to accompany the promotions. This will make channel members reconsider their brand support.

Except for the most powerful brands, the likely outcome is that some channel members drop the brand. If enough of them do so, the brand declines to a lower degree of distribution intensity and the problem of intrabrand competition is resolved. Of course, it is the channel members, not the manufacturer, deciding who will constitute the marketing channel in this scenario. It is likely that the manufacturer will lose many of its preferred outlets and keep many inferior outlets instead. This is because the best outlets have the most alternatives.

Channel members drop a brand in three ways.

1. They may do so overtly, by discontinuing the saturated brand and substituting another that is less intensively distributed in their trading areas. Of course, for very strong brands, the clientele will not accept the substitution, but for more typical brands, the substitution strategy is likely.
2. Channel members may discontinue the entire product category if they cannot find a satisfactory substitute brand and the category is not essential.
3. A channel member may appear to carry a brand by offering nominal stock and display, but attempt to convert prospective customers to a different brand once they are on site.

The most flagrant form of this behavior is to advertise one brand to bring customers to the site ("bait"), then persuade them to buy another brand ("switch"). *Bait-and-switch tactics* are most common for brands with high buyer recognition, because such brands are attractive bait. For example, an electronics store may run advertisements promoting a Whirlpool washing machine, but upon arrival at the store the sales assistant may guide the buyer to a different, lesser-known brand on which the store earns higher margins.

In general, manufacturers expect that downstream channel members will support their brands vigorously and are indignant when they discover the actual support is often tepid. Manufacturers are given to criticizing such "disloyal" downstream channel members and to questioning their professionalism. Uncountable angry discussions ensue over the manufacturer's opinion that channel members fail to do enough for its brand.

All too often, manufacturers fail to ask themselves *whether it is in the channel member's interest to do more* for their brands. Frequently, it is not. Channel Sketch 10.1 covers how Royal Canin makes itself appealing to retailers by limiting availability. This sketch is striking because it is about what should be a convenience good—dog and cat food.

Another factor at work is more subtle than incentives. It is the problem of *free riding*. Imagine you are a retailer selling audio products and pursuing a high-quality strategy. To implement this strategy, you invest heavily. Your store is well located and appealing. You stock any type of audio product, including stereo speakers. In the speaker category, you stock the full product line of a hypothetical speaker brand called Johanson. To support this brand, you carry substantial inventory (even of slow-moving items), devote showroom space, advertise on behalf of Johanson, maintain a well-stocked repair facility, offer extended warranties, and so forth. You retain a large and well-trained sales staff to explain each category of audio product (speakers, amplifiers, and so forth), to point out the myriad features of each brand and model, to explain how features translate into benefits, to help prospects discover what trade-offs they prefer, and to help prospects match their preferences to their options.

Your strategy is to attract an appreciative clientele, which will compensate you for your expenses by paying higher prices and becoming loyal clients. This strategy has worked well for you. Your store has a reputation, which it "lends" to every brand it carries.[7] Your clientele views you as their purchasing agent and trusts you to screen products for them.

Recently, Johanson hired a new distribution manager, who has aggressively pursued competing outlets and has gained a considerable increase in coverage. Now your salespeople are complaining that they are spending their time on "browsers," who end lengthy interactions about Johanson speakers with "I'm going to think about it." They leave the store with an informed decision about what they want. Then they visit other stores and bargain for a better price on the precise model they have selected—as a function of your assistance to them. Other stores can offer a better price because they do not offer your level of support. Nor do they need to, thanks to your assistance to their customers. These stores are free riding on you. You bear the costs. They gain the benefits.

As the store manager, your inclination is to discontinue the Johanson brand. This may, however, be costly. Your parts and merchandise inventory may not be returnable for full credit. The knowledge your personnel have gained about Johanson will be rendered worthless. Your advertising on behalf of Johanson not only will be wasted but also

CHANNEL SKETCH 10.1

Royal Canin[8]

Royal Canin is an independent company that holds the leading position in Europe for dog and cat food, with an 18 percent market share. This leads the multinationals brands, such as Nestlé (Friskies, Fido), Mars (Pal, Whiskas), and Colgate (Hills). Royal Canin began in 1966, when a French veterinarian, Henri Lagarde, noticed that many of his canine patients had dull fur and eczema. The cause was poor nutrition. Lagarde began making dog food in a biscuit form, cooking the biscuits in an oven in his garage. When his patients recovered glossy coats and healthy skin, Lagarde decided to close his practice and go into the pet food business.

Lagarde's first customers were dog breeders and other veterinarians. His first salespeople were the owners whose dogs he had cured; then Lagarde cultivated breeders. From breeder endorsements, Lagarde built a strong business; people who buy puppies from a breeder don't dare to change the recommended brand. Over the years, Royal Canin invested heavily in R&D and built up a very sophisticated and complete product line. The product range is enormous, offering food for every type and age of dog or cat and every level of activity. A color-coding system and a strict store planogram (outlining how the shelf should be filled) helps the owner find the right product quickly. A key to the brand's success is loyalty: Owners begin with puppy or kitten food, then follow the Royal Canin color-coded line through all the stages of their pet's life.

A key to the brand's excellent results (13 percent margins and a very successful entry into the stock market) is distribution. Initially, the brand sold only to breeders. Then Lagarde switched to hypermarkets. But the brand was displayed in the middle of inexpensive competitors, and the line was not properly presented.

Early in the 1990s, Royal Canin switched to selling through specialty outlets: garden stores with pet departments, as well as pet stores. These outlets account for the bulk of the brand's sales today. These specialists, as opposed to (people) food stores, are more welcoming to salespeople. They will take time to talk with Royal Canin "counselors," generally student veterinarians, who explain the line and offer advice about animal health. These stores send their floor salespeople to Royal Canin seminars. And they stock the full line, displayed as suggested by the supplier. These stores reach a buyer willing to pay a substantial premium over the ordinary pet food available in food stores. Why? Lagarde explains it thus: "People feel guilty if they don't give the best to their animals."

The result for Royal Canin is high market share, high margins, fast growth, and a high valuation on the Paris stock exchange. These results are due to astute marketing of a superior product. Limiting distribution has proven to be a key element. That pet owners are willing to go to pet and garden stores to buy Royal Canin (rather than buying another brand where they buy their own food) is an indication that, even for a convenience good, the right presentation and sales assistance makes a difference.

will raise embarrassing questions about why you no longer carry the brand. Your Johanson-specific investments are not readily redeployable to another brand.

Hence, you may continue to sell Johanson, but an acrimonious relationship with the manufacturer is now a certainty. Hence, even though you are an ethical retailer, you will not feel it dishonorable to engage in a certain degree of bait and switch, as long as you can switch to a brand you feel comfortable endorsing. This will not pose an obstacle, because there are multiple excellent brands of audio speakers. One day, you *will* become irritated enough to contact the sales representatives of some of Johanson's competitors! *As a retailer, you will not tolerate free riding indefinitely.*

Can the Manufacturer Sustain Intensive Distribution?

Intensive distribution often creates a situation of lackluster sales support, defection of downstream channel members, and even bait-and switch tactics. How can the manufacturer remedy this situation?

One solution is contractual: The manufacturer can attempt to *impose a contract on the channel member* demanding certain standards of conduct (e.g., barring bait and switch), then bring legal action against offenders. This expensive route requires documentation (e.g., of recurring bait-and-switch tactics), as well as legal resources. This muscular method of implementation is likely to alienate other channel members and to generate unfavorable publicity for the brand.

Another solution is to invest in a *pull strategy to build brand equity*. Customer preference may then oblige the channel member to carry the brand, pay a high wholesale price, charge a low retail price, and make up the low gross margin elsewhere. This strategy is used frequently, and to great effect, in FMCG.[9] The consumer demand for either Coca-Cola or Pepsi forces most channel members to carry one if not both of these brands. As noted earlier, one reason it works so well is because these are convenience goods: Service is not required, and many customers buy their preferred brands routinely, without thoroughly investigating alternatives on each shopping occasion. If they do not find their preferred brands in more than a few product categories, they will be dissatisfied with the outlet, and the outlet cannot convince them to change their preferences. Hence, channel members surrender and carry those intensively distributed brands that have high brand equity. However, this extremely costly strategy requires the manufacturer to make continuing, massive investments in advertising and promotion.

Even this strategy has its limits. Mattel, a large toy company, discovered this with its Barbie doll, the company's cash cow. Barbie has phenomenal brand equity, prompting Mattel to expand its 90 Barbie models to 450 in 15 years. This avalanche of new products, produced in high volumes, provoked market saturation. The price of Barbies dropped steadily. Nonetheless, the supplier kept pumping out volume. In 1998, huge retailers such as Wal-Mart and Toys "R" Us warned of huge overstocks. Barbies, once a sought-after gift item, began to appear on the shelves of supermarkets, displayed across from jams and other inexpensive foodstuffs. Mattel started dumping goods by promotions on cable television. In reaction to the degradation of the brand's image and the gross surplus of stocks in the channels, resellers began to cut prices by as much as 75 percent. As the brand's price tumbled, so did Mattel's stock price. In 2000, Mattel's president, the architect of the policy, was forced to resign.[10]

A third solution for the manufacturer with low sales support is to bow to the inevitable and *limit its market coverage*, that is, elect some degree of selectivity in its distribution. One advantage of this approach is that the manufacturer has the opportunity to target desired channel members, rather than merely settling for those who do not eliminate themselves when intrabrand competition becomes too intense for channel members to realize adequate profits on a brand. Another advantage is better working relationships.

For example, Bang & Olufsen (B&O) is an expensive, stylish, high-end maker of electronic products. In the 1990s, B&O was well distributed in France with 170 outlets but was losing millions of francs. In 1996, a new manager, Elisabeth Sandager, negotiated a deal: She would leave her career with a prestigious cosmetics manufacturer and take on the troubled B&O division, on condition that she have complete freedom to change strategy. She put zero budget into advertising, instead focusing on distribution. Borrowing from cosmetics the idea that display and presentation are more important than coverage, Sandager terminated representation to 100 outlets. These outlets handled the glamorous, avant-garde brand poorly and displayed it among products such as dishwashers. The remaining 70 outlets conformed to personalized marketing plans developed by Sandager. They accepted training at B&O University in marketing, management, and communication. And they lifted the brand's sales by 100 percent. Cutting coverage by nearly 60 percent, yet raising sales by 100 percent, has made B&O France highly profitable.[11]

In some trading areas, a fourth solution is possible—the imposition of *resale price maintenance (RPM)*. RPM is a vertical restraint; that is, an interdiction by the manufacturer of normal behavior for channel members. Resale price maintenance means the manufacturer can legally set a price floor below which channel members cannot charge their own customers to resell the product or service. RPM permits the manufacturer to limit the normal pricing behavior of its resellers.[12] The legality of RPM varies widely in world markets: It has been illegal in the United States since the late 1970s.[13]

Where RPM is allowed, manufacturers can use it to set minimum resale prices high enough so that all channel members have an acceptable margin, even at high levels of distribution intensity. Thus, RPM enables artificially high levels of coverage. For the purchaser, the good news is that the brand is easy to find and resellers will compete on a nonprice basis (selling services, amenities, and so forth). The bad news is that it is difficult to get a discount: Resellers are obliged to disguise discounts and are subject to legal action for so doing, even if they do not have a formal contract with the manufacturer. In the United Kingdom, RPM is applied to over-the-counter (OTC) medications, thereby preventing large discount retailers from lowering prices. The local chemists support RPM because they claim that without it many of the individually owned pharmacies would be driven out by the large retailers. However, at the time of writing, the British government is reviewing this practice and may overturn it.

Barring artificial solutions, such as resale price maintenance, how much coverage should a manufacturer aim to achieve? Curiously, the answer to this question hinges on a seemingly unrelated question: *In a given product category, how many brands should a downstream channel member carry?* Let us turn to this issue, and then return to the manufacturer's coverage problem.

Degree of Category Exclusivity: The Downstream Channel Member's Decision

For simplicity, let us consider a distributor and take the example of an industrial supply house. The supply house sells consumables and some durables to manufacturing plants of all kinds and to some offices in a trading area. Due to the generality of the demand, the distributor must carry thousands of stockkeeping units in hundreds of product categories. For any given product category, say, metalworking fluids, the industrial supply house must decide *how many brands to carry*.

For simplicity, the distributor might prefer to carry one. However, it is likely to carry many more, partly to benefit from competition, even if limited, but largely to meet the assortment demands of its customer base.[14] Part of the appeal of an industrial supply house is that whatever the buyer might want is there, in stock. Keeping a broad assortment satisfies customers even though it drives up inventory-related costs.

For each product category, the distributor must decide how large its brand assortment will be: very broad (all brands), or narrower, even a single brand (i.e., giving a brand *category exclusivity*, otherwise known as *exclusive dealing*).[15] A priori, the importance of assortment leads the distributor (more generally, a downstream channel member) to resist giving a manufacturer category exclusivity. Of course, manufacturers generally prefer not to be presented alongside their competitors, creating another built-in source of permanent channel conflict.

Thus, we have two conflicts. Manufacturers wish to blanket a trading area with outlets; the outlets prefer the reverse. Downstream channel members prefer to have multiple brands to offer in a category, whereas manufacturers prefer the reverse. *Here are the makings of a negotiated settlement.*

We have another conflict: Manufacturers wish downstream channel members to support their brands vigorously and take low margins, whereas channel members prefer lower costs and higher margins. Here again is an *opportunity to trade one's way to a mutually satisfactory arrangement*.

The rest of this chapter concerns how, when, and why a trade of competing interests comes about.[16]

STRIKING A DEAL: HOW MUCH SELECTIVITY TO TRADE AWAY

The Threat of Complacency

To this point, we have focused on one reason to cover a market intensively: to make it easy for a prospect to find the brand. Another reason to seek higher degrees of distribution coverage is driven not by customer behavior but by channel member behavior. Whenever coverage of a brand is highly selective, the manufacturer faces a difficult circumstance. When a small set of channel members carries the brand, intrabrand competition is low. *This is a dangerous situation.* When there is insufficient competition, even channel members with the very best intentions will be inclined not to give their most vigorous efforts to the brand. *Quasi-monopoly in distribution*, as in any other activity, *encourages complacency*, hence inadequate performance.

A certain degree of intrabrand competition in a market area is beneficial to the manufacturer. It brings forth each channel member's best efforts, without going so far as to put the channel member in a losing situation. Yet, attaining enough coverage to create the optimal degree of intrabrand competition can clash with other objectives, as described later.

One of the greatest drawbacks of selective distribution is the danger that selectivity fosters lackluster representation. The rest of this chapter will cover how to balance this risk, which inevitably accompanies selective distribution, by creating other methods of motivating channel members when coverage has been limited. Channel Sketch 10.2 details how a boat builder, Bénéteau, skillfully avoided this risk after acquiring a rival, Jeanneau.

CHANNEL SKETCH 10.2

Bénéteau Acquires Jeanneau[17]

A fierce rivalry existed for decades between two French builders of pleasure boats, Bénéteau and Jeanneau, the "enemy brothers of the coast." In 1995, Jeanneau was in serious financial trouble. Management reluctantly accepted an offer of acquisition by rival Bénéteau. Observers criticized the move, arguing that Jeanneau's situation was desperate and that Bénéteau, which had its own problems, was not strong enough to salvage its acquisition. Today, the critics retract their judgments. Bénéteau-Jeanneau is prosperous, growing, and making an impression with its new products at boat shows.

But shortly after the acquisition, such an outcome seemed unlikely. The rivalry was so strong that the head of Bénéteau, Annette Roux, hesitated to visit Jeanneau. Roux is the granddaughter of Bénéteau's founder and was concerned that her presence would only inflame the old feud. How did the fusion succeed?

The key was achieving economies of scale while preserving the identities of the two brands. Bénéteau's image is one of risk, innovation, sportiness, and stylishness. The brand is avant garde, and its customers are elitist, even for the boating industry. In contrast, Jeanneau is conservative, comfortable, classic, and reassuring. This said, there is some overlap in their clientele, leading the two to compete fiercely. Boat owners used this rivalry, and the fact that towns that contained a Jeanneau dealer also had a Bénéteau dealer, to play the two brands against each other and drive down prices.

Annette Roux astutely found selected economies of scale in production, personnel management, financing, accounting, and purchasing. She ensured that the two brands did not become similar in any way the customer could detect. A small point is typical and telling: Teak, a traditional wood for boats, is reserved exclusively for Jeanneau, whereas mahogany, a more daring and unusual wood for boats, is reserved exclusively for Bénéteau. Yet, in her drive for economies of scale, for sharing operations, Roux surprised and angered many observers by refusing to alter each brand's channels.

Why this contradiction? Why preserve two channels, generally competing in exactly the same markets? Observers, managers, and dealers all expected Bénéteau dealers to acquire the Jeanneau line. This is the practice of automakers in Europe, such as Group Volkswagen, which allows a single dealer to sell all of the group's brands—Audi, Volkswagen, Seat, and Skoda. Roux rejected this example, arguing that each brand needed to pursue its own strategy, and that fusing the dealerships would lessen interbrand competition too much. The managing director of Bénéteau puts it like this:

> First, I'm convinced that people defend their own flag better than an ensemble imposed by headquarters. Second, if the dealers for Bénéteau and Jeanneau had merged, we would have left an empty site in every port—for the competition!

Time has proved the wisdom of keeping two distribution channels and letting them compete with each other. Each brand is prosperous. Customers are unable to use one dealer to drive down the prices of the other because the brands are well differentiated, much better than they were as independent companies. Headquarters steers the marketing of each brand in different directions to lessen cannibalization, and each dealer network then drives each brand hard, aiming at potentially the same customer without making any effort to steer the customer to one brand or the other.

The Nature of the Product Category

In deciding how much selectivity to grant to channel members in a market area, the manufacturer should begin with features common to the product class. As noted earlier, buyers will not expend much effort to purchase *convenience goods* such as milk or copier–printer paper. To fit buyer behavior, these should be distributed as intensively as possible. For *shopping goods* such as an electric kettle or a fax machine, buyers will do some comparison of brands and prices across outlets, suggesting an intermediate degree of selectivity is desirable. For *specialty goods* such as a stereo or production machinery, buyers will expend considerable effort to make the "right choice." For this, they will make an effort to find outlets they can trust, suggesting that highly selective, even exclusive distribution is acceptable, even desirable, to the buyer. This generalization applies to both industrial and consumer products and services.[18]

Although a useful starting point, these ideas are somewhat difficult to operationalize, because it is not evident when buyers are willing to search and to what degree. One indication of a search good is that a category is new; for both industrial and consumer products, new categories often require considerable channel member support to induce prospects to become customers.[19] New-to-the-world categories do not even start out as search goods, because no one is searching for them yet.

To distribute specialty goods, and to a lesser degree, shopping goods, *it is less important to have many outlets than it is to have the right outlets*. Manufacturers should carefully select, cultivate, and support the correct outlets in a trading area, which is a policy of selective distribution.

It is important to *separate selective distribution from poor coverage*. A brand has poor coverage when few outlets will take it, or when the right outlets will not carry it. Merely examining the percentage of outlets carrying the brand in a trading area does not indicate whether a manufacturer's coverage is selective or mediocre.

Brand Strategy: Quality Positioning and Premium Pricing

Thus far, in determining what degree of selectivity a manufacturer should grant in a market area, we have covered *product class factors*, as well as cost factors that apply to distributing any good or service. We now turn to a class of factors that apply to a given *brand and its marketing strategy*. The first consideration is the brand's positioning on the quality dimension.

In any product category, the strategy of a given brand may be to attempt to position as high quality. Mercedes-Benz automobiles and Bang & Olufsen audio equipment are examples of brands positioned as high quality. Operationally, this means conveying an image that the brand has superior ability to perform its functions, or, more simply, that it is superior as to be excellent. This position, typically accompanied by a premium price, is difficult to achieve. To do so, the manufacturer must pay particular attention to the image or reputation of the channel member representing the brand, because this image will be imparted to everything the channel member sells. Therefore, the manufacturer should prefer channel members that themselves excel in handling high-end brands.

By definition, excellence is scarce. Manufacturers will be obliged to focus on the subset of channel members that matches the brand's intended image. *Selective distribution is called for to support the high-quality positioning*. This is particularly the case when premium pricing is part of the positioning: Higher-priced products are usually limited in their distribution availability.[20] Broadening coverage to other outlets will dilute the brand's positioning of superior quality.

Of course, these high-end-image channel members will be in great demand and have their choice of brands to represent. It can be difficult to induce them to carry any given brand, even one positioned as premium. Even though the manufacturer will not seek intensive coverage, it will need a capable sales force to convince the target channel members to carry and support the brand. And, of course, there must be a segment of buyers interested in high quality, convinced the brand is high quality, and willing to exert effort to make a high-quality purchase. Put differently, the high-quality brand's marketing strategy must be correct if the channel is to succeed in implementing it.

Of course, brands not positioned as high quality are not presented as low quality. They are instead positioned as adequate, but not superior, in quality. Often the brand will be featured on other attributes, frequently convenience or low price. Either of these is consistent with a more intensive distribution policy.

A variation on the theme of high quality is a theme of *scarcity*. Some manufacturers deliberately create product shortages. The idea is that scarcity can be appealing (if not everyone can get the product, it may be psychologically more desirable). Artificial scarcity is a marketing strategy that is coupled with selective distribution in order to increase the illusiveness, hence the allure, of the product. Harley-Davidson pursues this strategy, underproducing its motorcycles and limiting distribution to a few outlets, many of them company owned. This creates long waiting lists and holds up a Harley's mystique and resale value. Similarly, Beanie Babies are small plush toys stuffed to feel like bean-bags. Ty Inc., the supplier, deliberately supplies restricted quantities and furthers the hard-to-find feature of the toys by distributing them only through small, specialist toy shops.[21]

The producer of a brand positioned as high quality faces a difficult circumstance. Coverage has been restricted. Now that only a restricted set of channel members carries the brand, intrabrand competition is low and the threat of channel complacency is high. Yet, attaining enough coverage to motivate channel members can put the brand into outlets that clash with its intended high-quality positioning. *How can the manufacturer balance off selectivity in distribution with its need for channel members to exert extra effort to support the brand?*

One method used effectively in North America is to ask channel members to sign unusually demanding contracts in order to represent the brand. This is common practice in the selling of stereo speakers, for example. These restrictive contracts curtail the channel member's freedom of choice in managing the brand. For example, they may contain clauses detailing channel member obligations with respect to displays, promotions, and sales goals. Or they may specify conditions under which the manufacturer may terminate the arrangement without further obligation. In contrast, it is common for contracts to reflect only a broad and general understanding—if indeed there is even a contract at all.

Another form of restrictive contract is to agree to meet demanding goals. For example, J. E. Ekornes, a Norwegian manufacturer of home furniture, profiled in Chapter 9 on conflict. Ekornes saturated the French market with 450 furniture dealers, making it difficult for any of them to make money on the brand. It completely redesigned its channel, pulling back to 150 dealers and asking them to help redraw territories so as to guarantee exclusive distribution to each one. In return for this concession, Ekornes's surviving dealers signed contracts committing them to ambitious sales goals. Indeed, the 150 dealers committed to figures that significantly improved on the actual results achieved by the original 450 dealers. They have more than met these goals. In three years, the company's sales tripled.[22]

Why are restrictive contracts effective? Manufacturers can use restrictive contracts as a way of *screening out* resellers who are reluctant to support the brand. This is because channel members inclined to dishonor promises of brand support will be reluctant to sign a restrictive contract. Knowing this, some managers of high-end brands couple a policy of selective distribution with a policy of insisting on restrictive contracts for all downstream channel members. These manufacturers broaden their distribution coverage somewhat beyond the level they would choose if they employed lenient contracts, or no contracts. They do so because they can be confident that the additional resellers will hold up the brand's image.

Ekornes, for example, might have gone to 120 dealers of which it was confident of their willingness to uphold the image of its Stressless brand. The company would have relied on its own judgment in culling from 450 to 120. But the 150 dealers willing to commit in a legal document to very ambitious goals were a self-selected group. Each of these dealers sent Ekornes a credible signal that it was the right dealer in which to invest. The contract provided a way for dealers to signal to Ekornes and provided it with an effective way to screen them.

In short, high-end brands per se tend to use selective distribution; some high-end brands use selective distribution *and* restrictive contracts. In this latter case, brands tend to achieve somewhat broader coverage than do other high-end brands. This may seem odd, because many channel members will not sign restrictive contracts. The reason this works is because many well-known and easy-to-identify high-end resellers are somewhat more willing to sign restrictive contracts: They know they will meet the requirements.

The manufacturer's problem arises with other resellers who wish to carry the brand: Should any of these be added to the channel? High-end brands count on the screening property of a tight contract. The reasoning behind this policy is that those resellers whose internal operations and ability to handle premium brands are uncertain will not bind themselves by legally allowing a producer to circumscribe their managerial freedom of choice. Once the contract is signed, the channel member has an incentive to observe it. Therefore, the high-end manufacturer can take on more channel members with less risk of diluting the brand image *if* it insists on restrictive contracts *and* stays within a fundamentally selective range of coverage.

Brand Strategy: Target Market

Some brands target a niche market, that is, a narrow and specialized band of buyers. One might expect that manufacturers would seek broad coverage in this case, to maximize the probability that these customers can be found. In practice, the reverse occurs. Producers of brands targeting a narrow spectrum of the market will target a narrow spectrum of outlets. *The more restricted the target market, the more selective the distribution.*

To some extent, this policy is not by choice: Channel members are less interested in niche brands than in those with broader appeal. In addition, niche markets are not necessarily difficult to access. Often, the target buyers are a homogenous group with common shopping patterns. Only a select band of resellers is necessary, or perhaps even appropriate, to reach them.

Having a narrow target focus and pursuing a high-quality position are two different marketing strategies. A brand may not position as superior quality, yet may be aimed at a specialty group. Or, it can position itself as superior quality while pursuing multiple segments. Liz Claiborne, Inc., the clothing company bearing its founder's name, sells high-end clothing for women. However, this company has lines targeting various segments such as casual and sportswear; suits and dresses; petites for shorter women; Elisabeth for larger-sized women; and even Lizgolf for golf and active attire.

A good example of a specialty group is pregnant women who are searching for maternity clothing. Often women are interested in making minimal investments in a wardrobe that they will wear for only a limited time. They may sacrifice better-quality fabrics and designer labels that they would typically choose for clothing purchases. Dan Howard's Maternity Factory Outlets offer a selection of maternity clothes at reasonable prices. Women can either visit one of the company stores in many U.S. cities or shop online.

Of course, one can pursue a niche strategy, providing a superior-quality brand to a specialty group, such as A Pea in the Pod, a maternity clothing company. Through its 50 boutiques in the United States, the company sells high-end maternity clothes that cater to professional women desiring business attire, as well as fashion-conscious women who want maternity clothes that follow the current fashion trend. The generalization that a restricted target segment implies selective distribution applies to any narrowly focused brand, regardless of its quality positioning.

To summarize to this point, we have focused on the marketing strategy of the brand, given the nature of the product category. For brands that appeal to channel members and therefore could achieve more intensive coverage, the great danger of offering more selective coverage is that channel members will lose motivation and become complacent. Mindful of this danger, strong manufacturers hesitate to limit coverage. In theory, this cost is worthwhile for some product categories, for which consumers will exert effort to shop. In practice, these categories are difficult to identify. It is sensible to key selectivity more to the brand strategy than to the nature of the product category. Selectivity makes sense to support a premium positioning, to pursue a narrow target market, and to pursue a niche strategy (premium positioning in a narrow target market). One effective technique in high-end markets is to expand coverage slightly more than is typical by using restrictive contracts to screen out potentially dubious resellers.

Many manufacturers seek more influence over channel members, regardless of their brand strategy. We now turn to another motivation, apart from strategy, for selectivity. This motive is simply to gain influence downstream.

BARGAINING FOR INFLUENCE OVER CHANNEL MEMBERS

Many manufacturers desire to have inordinate influence over their downstream channel members. Rather than accepting the premise that market outcomes are efficient and channel members know best, these manufacturers have strong views about how channel members should handle their brands. They are unwilling to take a hands-off approach, to let the invisible hand of competition guide the actions of their marketing channels. They do not believe that market incentives will lead the channel member to perform channel flows appropriately for their brands. These "interventionist" manufacturers would like to manage their channels as they manage their subsidiaries.

Market selectivity is one of the best tools they have for so doing. Higher degrees of selectivity function as a sort of currency that can be used to purchase higher degrees of influence over channel members. A manufacturer wishing to direct a channel member can "purchase" a certain amount of cooperation (really, acquiescence) by the skillful use of selective distribution.

The reason is that such distribution allows a downstream channel member to achieve higher margins *and* higher volume on a given brand. Further, selectivity allows a channel member, such as a reseller, to differentiate its assortment, creating strategic advantage. Hence, a higher degree of selectivity is an extremely powerful incentive. *Manufacturers can use selective distribution to "buy" considerable influence over a downstream channel member.* And indeed, those who grant exclusivity do make more efforts (of any kind) to influence their channel members' behavior.[23] They do not give up coverage only to sit back and let market forces operate freely. Their influence is an expensive purchase, as low coverage carries a considerable opportunity cost. Which manufacturers find the purchase worthwhile? *When is influence over a channel member's behavior worth the opportunity cost of limited market coverage?*

One answer that has already been noted is that the investment is worthwhile when the brand has a premium-quality position. To maintain the premium, manufacturers must be sure the brand is presented and supported in an appropriate fashion, which limits the set of resellers. The next section goes into other producer rationales for effectively trying to direct channel member behavior. The principle is that the more direction the manufacturer needs to exert, the more it must restrict its distribution in order to gain the channel member's acquiescence.

Desired Coordination

Some producers wish to influence reseller decisions and activities in great detail. Inevitably, this drive to control the downstream will lead the manufacturer into conflict, because it will pressure the channel member to do something that it would not have done otherwise. For example, the producer may wish to dictate prices, promotional activities, displays, how the brand is presented by salespeople, and stocking levels, or may wish to limit the channel member's ability to resell to a customer of its own choosing. This is outright interference in the management of the reseller's business. The reseller will resist, and the manufacturer will need power to overcome that resistance. By offering protection from intrabrand competition, the manufacturer exerts reward power. In general, all else constant, *the more the manufacturer wishes to coordinate activities* with the channel member (i.e., to direct the channel member's activities to align them with the manufacturer's preferences), *the more selectively the manufacturer should distribute.*

This is effective not only because it increases the manufacturer's reward power over a given player. It also reduces the number and variety of players. With a large and heterogeneous group of players, it is difficult for the producer to exert influence over them all. A major reason is that managers have limited resources. The manufacturer's ability to give the proper time, attention, and support is strained when there are many channel members. One person can handle only so much. And hiring more people creates coordination problems internally. A smaller channel is a simpler channel to manage because simplicity enhances control.

Nonetheless, many arguments for selectivity are elaborations of the fundamental idea that *selectivity creates reward power, which in turn creates influence.* Below is a list of such arguments for the manufacturer's side.

- Because exclusive or limited market coverage means higher average reseller margins, the manufacturer should be able to attract better resellers.
- Paradoxically, the manufacturer may attract more resellers under a selective regime! This is because under an intensive regime, each reseller may estimate that margins will be too low to be worthwhile; hence, no reseller bids for the business.
- With a small but dedicated group of resellers, the manufacturer may enjoy more vigorous overall market efforts, albeit from a smaller group of channel partners.

- And if each reseller competes vigorously, the manufacturer may actually reach a greater range of customers and reach them more effectively.

- This is particularly important when the manufacturer needs a more motivated selling effort; for example, for a new market or when selling a new product.[24] Motivated resellers may be willing to take a greater risk on behalf of the manufacturer; for example, by carrying more stock or investing in building a new brand name.[25]

- This in turn encourages market entry (entrants trade some degree of exclusivity for strong representation) . . .

- And raises the overall level of competition across brands at the product category level.

Channel Sketch 10.3 shows how Linn Products applied this reasoning to boost sales and margins.

The reasoning here may seem rather perverse, because it reduces to the dubious argument that local monopolies are desirable. Clearly, an opportunity cost offsets all this purported benefit. A local monopoly can be desirable only under delimited circumstances.

CHANNEL SKETCH 10.3

Reducing Coverage to *Increase* Sales and Margins[26]

Linn Products Ltd., based in Waterfoot, Scotland, produces top-quality high-fidelity equipment. Linn's products command 10 to 20 times the prices of the comparable cheapest stereo components on the market.

In 1991, Linn's management introduced a new selling and service strategy that placed heavy demands on its resellers. Under the new plan Linn required each reseller to demonstrate products before each sale and to stock a minimum level of inventory. Linn's dealers were outraged. As a result, 82 retailers in the United Kingdom alone refused to continue selling the brand, leaving the company with only 55 local resellers. At the time of the change in policy, Linn's annual sales dropped from £11 million to £9 million. However, management remained confident that by establishing a selective distribution network, sales would eventually grow through increased market share and through propagation by loyal customers, either from upgrades or referrals of new customers. Linn also wanted to expand into different geographic markets and believed its selectivity strategy would position the company to do so.

Five to six years after the shift in its distribution policy, Linn's sales were approaching £20 million. Indeed, with the product demonstrations and personalized service, an average sale to a single customer increased, and previous customers were coming back to upgrade a single component at a time. Clearly, Linn will remain a niche player in the stereo market, but by adopting a selective distribution strategy, the company boosted its sales and has maintained control over the presentation of its products to the marketplace.

Fundamentally, the argument can be made that intensive distribution creates a large but ineffective army; that is, a huge number of indifferent channel members, each of which represents the brand, but only in a desultory fashion. By limiting coverage, the manufacturer creates only a small strike force, yet composed of elite soldiers. When is a large army preferable to an elite strike force? The coordination rationale is, at root, a family of arguments for an elite strike force; that is, limiting the number of trading partners *in order to gain more influence over each one.*

Of course, these arguments may be employed in reverse for the downstream channel member. If the organization represents only a handful of suppliers, it can offer greater rewards to each supplier, thereby gaining influence. This influence can be used to induce the manufacturer to do a better job of supporting the downstream channel member; for example, by offering lower prices or promotional materials or better credit terms. The downstream channel member weighs the advantages of an army of potentially indifferent suppliers versus an elite strike force of more motivated suppliers.

Manufacturer-Specific Investments by Downstream Channel Members

Earlier, we introduced a retailer of Johanson stereo speakers and described the investments the retailer had made. These assets are not readily redeployable to the service of another brand. They become sunk costs if the relationship ends. Most of the investments a downstream channel member would make in a manufacturer are *not* specialized: They can be reused, transferred to another brand. But some brands do demand that a reseller or agent acquire capabilities and commit resources that have no alternative use; in particular, for industrial goods and services. Several major categories of these specific investments exist.

- To the extent that a brand's applications and features are unique, the sales staff must learn about them to sell effectively. This is *idiosyncratic knowledge.*
- A brand may require *unusual handling or storage* (e.g., a brand shipped on nonstandard pallets requires custom shelving and may even require specialty forklifts).
- *Servicing* the brand postsale may involve brand-specific *parts and know-how.*
- *Customer training* that is brand specific may be required.
- Joint promotions that *mingle the identity of buyer and seller* may have occurred, making it difficult to disentangle the downstream channel member and the brand.

In consumer goods channels, these kinds of investments are particularly heavy when the end user buys from a contractor–dealer. These dealers assemble and install technical products or those requiring substantial customization. The dealer incorporates the supplier's product into systems to meet each buyer's needs. These dealers specify, assemble, and install to a degree that makes them look (to the consumer) more like a manufacturer than a reseller. Contractor–dealers handle such products as swimming pools, climate control (heating and cooling), fireplaces, metal buildings, greenhouses, security systems, garage doors, solar energy, and custom doors and windows.[27]

In short, for some brands or product categories, manufacturer-specific assets are necessary to distribute the brand effectively. Naturally, however, downstream channel members prefer not to make them. These investments are expensive in themselves. More importantly, they raise the reseller's dependence on the manufacturer.[28] Hence, they make the reseller vulnerable to manufacturer opportunism (deceptive seeking of one's self-interest). A rational reseller would hesitate to make these investments and incur the subsequent dependence on the producer.

Therefore, the producer needs to induce the reseller to make these investments. Offering a degree of selectivity is an effective means to do so, because it increases the rewards the reseller can gain from the brand. However, what is to prevent the manufacturer from reneging on its agreements once the reseller has made brand-specific investments? The manufacturer must assure the reseller that its vulnerability will not be exploited once the investments are in place.

An effective way to reassure the reseller is to limit distribution. The fewer channel partners the manufacturer has in a market area, the more difficult it is to shift resources away from a given reseller. An exclusive agent, distributor, or retailer is extremely difficult to replace. Manufacturers that limit distribution thereby increase their own dependence on their downstream channel members. They have counterbalanced the dependence resellers incur by making manufacturer-specific investments.

In short, a policy of *selective distribution in a market area can be understood as a means of balancing dependence in a distribution channel.* By limiting its coverage, the manufacturer accepts being dependent on the downstream channel. Because this is not to be done lightly, the manufacturer will do it in exchange for the reseller's acquisition of brand-specific assets. The manufacturer negotiates, exchanging limited distribution coverage for the reseller's acquisition of brand-specific assets. *One vulnerability is offset by another.*

> *Selective distribution is currency that the manufacturer can use to induce the reseller to make brand-specific investments.*

Dependence Balancing: Trading Territory Exclusivity for Category Exclusivity

The idea of *balancing dependence* is instrumental to understanding how upstream and downstream channel members use selectivity as a strategic tool to enhance their business interests.[29] The principle is that no one wishes to be dependent on another channel member, because this gives the other party power and therefore creates vulnerability (covered in detail in Chapter 8). However, to distribute effectively often requires one side (e.g., the reseller) to create a source of dependence on the other side (the manufacturer). This dependence is unlikely to be incurred: The reseller will resist. One way to overcome their resistance is for the manufacturer to create an *offsetting dependence* of its own upon the reseller. This *calculated mutual dependence*, or mutual vulnerability—which has been likened to a sort of balance of terror in international politics—is designed to bring stability to a relationship by making it unprofitable for either side to exploit the other. This reasoning is explored in more depth in Chapter 11 on strategic alliances.

Selective distribution has been presented as a currency with which the manufacturer purchases reseller investments in brand-specific assets. This section highlights an even more direct exchange: Some degree of territory exclusivity for some degree of category exclusivity. *In general, the more the manufacturer limits its coverage of a market area, the more a reseller limits its coverage of the associated product category.*

At the extreme, each side trades exclusivity for exclusivity. Resellers offer the manufacturer exclusivity in its product category. In return, manufacturers offer the reseller exclusivity in its market area. This is a swap of category exclusivity for territory exclusivity. Of course, this is the extreme case. It is more common to exchange some degree of selectivity, without going so far as to eliminate other brands for the reseller or other resellers for the manufacturer. Returning to the example of the industrial supply house, management might agree to reduce its line to four instead of six of the ten brands offered by metalworking fluids manufacturers. In exchange, the manufacturer who requested this reduction authorizes ten instead of twenty distributors in the supply house's territory. Exchanging (market) selectivity for (category) selectivity is frequent, particularly in business-to-business marketing. Each side voluntarily limits the number of its trading partners.

Failing to balance up dependence due to exclusivity is quite dangerous. For an example of the abuses and waste this can create, see Channel Sketch 10.4 on marketing channels for the European automobile market.

CHANNEL SKETCH 10.4
European Marketing Channels for Automobiles

In the 1980s, the European Economic Community granted a block exemption to the automobile industry. It permitted automakers to ignore EU rules against vertical restrictions until 1995. In particular, automakers were given the right to give exclusive markets to their dealers, at the suppliers' discretion, *and to oblige dealers not to carry competing brands*. Thus, the EU legislated a bargaining issue, making it impossible for dealers to negotiate a swap of exclusive dealing for exclusive territories. This built-in imbalance in the automakers' favor was intended to benefit the consumer. The rationale was to enable automakers to ensure their cars were "properly" sold and serviced, in part to promote customer service, particularly postsale. This is thought to promote automobile safety.

Automakers wasted little time in forbidding their dealers to carry competing brands and in exercising discretion in how much exclusivity to give in defining markets. At the same time, European and North American automakers complained that Japanese car makers impose anticompetitive nontariff barriers to foreign entry into the Japanese market—by tacitly blocking their domestic dealers from stocking foreign cars! The business press was quick to note the contradiction.

In the ensuing public debate, European car makers claimed that the difference, rather than being hypocrisy, was somehow due to the market and that making comparisons of distribution policies would be "superficial." Critics replied that the real reasons foreign cars have trouble getting distribution in Japan is because consumers don't like the cars—and foreign automakers have been *too* selective in screening offers of representation by existing Japanese dealerships.

In Europe, car makers used their power to create networks of dealers representing only their brands. Multibranding was forbidden, even if the dealer operated in different locations under different names.

How did the car makers use this legislated power? They created many dealerships in markets they saw as being an adequate size to support a dealer. The makers also supplemented the system as they saw fit. For example, in France, cars are sold not only by 5,000 regular dealers but also by an army of 18,000 agents, such as garages, operating on commission and doing very little to sell or support the brand. This makes 23,000 points of sale, as many as in the United States (which has five times the population and many times the geographical size of France).

The result: By the mid-1990s, the average outlet in the United States was selling six times more cars than the average French outlet. The situation was similar throughout Western Europe. This is a curious outcome. Why create so many points of sale, quite a few of them offering only nominal representation? Whose interest does this serve? Let us examine the state of European auto distribution channels for the largest brands.

Automakers in Europe find it relatively easy to dominate these atomized dealers and agencies. But the channels are grossly inefficient because they have few economies of scale. Critics charge that customers can't bargain with dealers readily enough for the brand of their choice, because the dealers are kept separated to some degree by the automakers. Yet, some car dealers argue that the car makers use their power to create missize territories, some of them so small that the intrabrand competition makes it easy for a buyer to drive a dealer's margins too low to survive.

A major consulting firm concluded that the result of the automakers' practices is that, in Europe, an automobile is a high-technology product, targeted at a mass-market, yet distributed through essentially a network of small businesses. This is an unusual outcome: Compare this situation to other high-tech products, such as computers. It is hardly a natural market outcome that car channels would not contain large businesses.

In 1995, the EU suppressed a harshly critical internal report on the effects of its block exemption. The report, that was leaked to the press, attributed price differences of up to 40 percent for a given model to the exclusive distribution system. After debate, the EU renewed the block exemption for another seven years. But in deference to critics, the EU gave some bargaining power back to the dealers, allowing them the right to represent multiple brands if they are sold in different locations.

In response, car makers have put great pressure on their dealers not to represent competing brands. Defending this policy publicly, a spokesman for Citroën argues that exclusivity benefits the customer: "The customer can better negotiate his price if he can put several suppliers into competition than if he finds himself faced with one single vendor distributing several brands." It is certainly true that more brand choice empowers consumers. And as the EU has gradually reduced barriers to entry, Asian car makers have given consumers more choice. The dealers are finding it ever harder to make money. Says one observer, "A lot of dealers are former garagists, undercapitalized and not very solid." Falling margins make it impossible for them to meet their expenses, let alone renovate their aging facilities and cope with increasing supplier-level competition. Yet, automakers continue to pressure dealers not to take on other brands—with mixed success.[30]

Some dealers have decided to accept conflict with their supplier over this issue. This is how Daewoo, a Korean supplier, was able to enter the French market. Initially, Daewoo tried to sell through a hypermarket chain. The government blocked this (said to have been influenced by the head of Peugeot-Citroën, Jacques Calvet, who is a powerful lobbyist and a well-known public figure). So Daewoo turned to dealers as soon as the 1995 renewal of the block exemption permitted multiple branding. Daewoo launched its dealer network in March 1995 with 50 dealers, and built to having more dealers than BMW in less than two years! About half were existing dealers for other brands, typically sports cars, 4 × 4s, luxury cars, and other cars that complement Daewoo's economical, functional positioning. These businesses have met the EU's rules by opening a new location for Daewoo and dedicating personnel to that location. Daewoo is betting that these multibrand dealers will achieve substantial operating economies, particularly in terms of getting better credit terms from banks.

As the 1995 seven-year block exemption is moving toward expiration, automakers have wrung substantial production costs out of their systems and are now searching for ways to cut distribution costs. Volkswagen, for example, estimates that 40 percent of its car's retail price is due to costs of distribution. Very high retail prices choke volume growth, and EU barriers to foreign entry are declining steadily. Thus, experiments are under way to cut distribution costs, and it is widely recognized that the dealer network is badly sized and organized (how badly depending on the supplier). Volkswagen, for example, has been terminating dealerships with the aim of having fewer but larger, more efficient, better-located dealers. One observer suggests that massive restructuring will result in large, multibrand dealers serving customers who are typically willing to travel 50 kilometers to buy a car. Those same customers will travel only 10 kilometers for service: The dealer will serve them with service satellites, all supported by its centralized scale economies.

It is noteworthy that during the past two decades, automakers in Europe have enjoyed inordinate power over their dealers. They have not abused that power to the point that dealer outcries have provoked the EU to withdraw its block exemption of the industry or otherwise regulate distribution. Instead, they have tended to practice procedural justice, as detailed in Chapter 8 on power.[31] This is why the force for reform of auto distribution channels is not a political force on the part of the dealers. It is the drive for economic efficiency brought on by increasing competition at the supplier level.[32]

For the manufacturer, trading selectivity for selectivity is a means to influence the composition of the downstream channel member's brand portfolio. This is important for manufacturers that wish to influence the competitive set in which their brands are presented.[33] For the downstream channel member, bargaining selectivity for selectivity is a means of influencing the set of carriers in its market area, hence the set with which it can be compared readily.

Secondary Effects of Manufacturer-Specific Investments

To this point, we have discussed two direct effects of manufacturer-specific (i.e., difficult to redeploy) investment. One is that the reseller becomes a more potent channel member, increasing its performance on behalf of the brand. The other is that the reseller becomes more dependent, hence more vulnerable to manufacturer opportunism.

Reassurance: Using Selectivity to Stabilize Fragile Relationships

As discussed in Chapter 8, considerations of power pervade marketing channel decisions and often destabilize channel relationships. In the complex negotiation between upstream and downstream channel members, both sides are preoccupied with concerns about what will happen once an agreement has been struck. The more vulnerable party fears misuse by the other side of its power. In particular, the former fears the other side will renege on their working understanding of rights and responsibilities, a common form of opportunism. These fears destabilize the relationship, thereby reducing channel effectiveness. Therefore, the stronger party may be motivated to reassure the vulnerable party of its good faith. In general, limiting the number of trading partners is an effective way to do so. *A stronger party that offers selectivity to a weaker party is balancing the other side's dependence.*

Dependence balancing has been discussed in the case of specific assets, which are put in place as the relationship grows. But even before the assets arise, a channel member may be concerned about the other side's power. A frequent example in business-to-business markets occurs when a brand has a favorable position, or pull, with the customer base. This could be due to product uniqueness, favorable image, or other sources of brand equity. Naturally, a distributor may be concerned that the manufacturer will use its brand-name pull first to create distributor dependence, then to supplant or exploit the distributor.

To reassure him, strong manufacturers frequently limit their coverage, thereby increasing their downstream dependence (dependence balancing). On the face of it, this behavior is puzzling. The stronger the brand, the easier it is to increase coverage. Yet, many manufacturers voluntarily refrain from maximizing coverage.

In the same vein, many sell some fraction of their products direct (i.e., bypass their channels for selected orders, selling directly to the channel's customer base). Sometimes *direct selling* is explicitly negotiated with downstream channel members, in which case, it is not opportunism, because there is no deception or bad faith. More often, the practice is simply carried out, often with attempts to disguise it (which *is* opportunism).

Manufacturers usually refuse to disclose the extent of their direct selling. If and when distributors or other downstream channel members discover a direct sale, the manufacturer typically claims the customer insisted on bypassing the channel. As this is often true, most channel members tolerate direct selling to a point. At some point, however, the channel member is certain to suspect manufacturer opportunism. This, of course, destabilizes the relationship.

To restore confidence, industrial suppliers tend to offset direct selling. In a given trading area, *the more direct selling they do, the more they are likely to limit the number of channel members in the area*. This can be interpreted as if it were a tacit understanding: "I reserve the right to go to your customers, but in return, I will not sell through as many of your competitors as I would otherwise." Limiting coverage may be seen as a sort of payment of damages. The manufacturer that will do so encourages channel members to set aside their concerns and represent the brand vigorously, in spite of direct selling.

The logic of offsetting sources of relationship instability also applies to the downstream channel member. Some distributors, for example, have *a loyal customer base*, so loyal that the distributor heavily influences brand choice.[34] Here, the distributor is powerful, and the manufacturer may reasonably fear its opportunism. To allay this concern, distributors with loyal customers often limit brand assortment in a product category, even though these distributors are attractive to any manufacturer. Although they can represent anyone, they limit their number of trading partners, which serves to balance the manufacturer's dependence on them.

The Price of the Concession: Factoring in Opportunity Cost

In bargaining away the right to have an unlimited number of trading partners, the manufacturer is making a concession to the downstream channel member. Of course, when the concession is substantial, the manufacturer will be less willing to make it. Two circumstances are crucial to assess the price of the concession: the *importance* of the market area and the *competitive intensity* of the product category.

For a minor market area, the manufacturer will concede selectivity more readily than for a major market area. For major markets the opportunity cost of lower coverage is substantial. Hence, the manufacturer will bargain harder before agreeing to limit coverage.

This leads to a growing source of conflict. It is not unusual for a manufacturer to agree to limit its coverage, even to the point of exclusive representation, for a market it perceives to be minor. Over time, the manufacturer may reassess and conclude the market is actually a major one—especially if the downstream channel member appears to be doing very well with its products. Hence, the manufacturer may try to renege eventually on its implicit or explicit agreement to practice selectivity.[35]

For intensely competitive product categories, manufacturers are more reluctant to limit the number of their downstream trading partners. Here again, the reason is the opportunity cost of this concession to downstream channel members. Manufacturers fear that prospective buyers will not be motivated to make the effort to seek out a limited set of points of purchase when the competition at the category level is fierce. Hence, lower coverage appears to be a very risky proposition.

A source of conflict arises in these circumstances due to differing perceptions. It is easy for the manufacturer in an intensely competitive product category to be doing poorly *because of the competition*, but to misattribute its disappointing performance to insufficient coverage. This sometimes leads to a spiral of marketing-channel mediocrity. Rather than addressing the reasons for competitive disadvantage in the first place, a manufacturer may instead seek a quick remedy: higher sales via more coverage. To get this, it may lower its standards, distributing through inferior downstream channel members. This in turn may provoke the original channel members to withdraw support for the brand, leaving the manufacturer even worse off, in spite of being available through more outlets.

The idea that some degree of selectivity is a bargaining chip for the manufacturer is summarized in Figure 10.2.

Turning to examine the other side of the relationship, a downstream channel member will hesitate to limit its number of brands in a product category when the category is a major one in the channel member's assortment. Thus, an industrial supply house that does little business in metalworking fluids will agree more readily to limit its brand selection than will a competitor to whom metalworking fluids are an important category. To that latter business, the opportunity cost of limiting assortment is too great.

Downstream channel members also hesitate to grant selectivity in intensely competitive categories. This is an expensive concession: Prospective buyers may lose interest when they realize that many brands are missing from the assortment. Competitive intensity makes it more likely that buyers will be aware of alternative brands, will have strong preferences, and will insist on presentation of a more complete assortment.

For the Manufacturer
Limiting coverage is currency
More selectivity = more money
Exclusive distribution =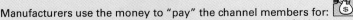

Manufacturers use the money to "pay" the channel members for:
- Limiting its own coverage of brand in product category (gaining exclusive dealing is *very* expensive)
- Supporting premium positioning of the brand
- Finding a narrow target market
- Coordinating more closely with the manufacturer
- Making supplier-specific investments
  - New products
  - New markets
    - Differentiated marketing strategy requiring downstream implementation
- Accepting limited direct selling by manufacturer
- Accepting the risk of becoming dependent on a strong brand

Manufacturers need to "pay more" when:
- The product category is important to the channel member
- The product category is intensely competitive

FIGURE 10.2

For the Downstream Channel Member
Limiting brand assortment is currency
Fever brand = more money
Exclusive dealing =

Downstream channel members use the money to "pay" the supplier for:
- Limiting the number of competitors who can carry the brand in the channel member's trading area
- Providing desired brands that fit the channel member's strategy
- Working closely to help the channel member achieve competitive advantage
- Making channel-member-specific investments
  - New products
  - New markets
  - Differentiated channel member strategy requiring supplier cooperation
- Accepting the risk of becoming dependent on a strong channel member

Downstream channel members need to "pay more" when:
- The trading area is important to the supplier
- The trading area is intensely competitive

FIGURE 10.3

In short, for either side, *selectivity is an expensive concession when the object of negotiation is important* (for the manufacturer, a market area, and for the reseller, the product category). Selectivity is also expensive *when the object of negotiation (market area or product category) is intensely competitive*. These concessions are expensive because the *opportunity cost* of limiting the number of trading partners is great.

The idea that some degree of limitation of brand assortment is a bargaining chip for the downstream channel member is summarized in Figure 10.3.

Here, as in all analyses of selectivity, it is important to distinguish between *choosing* to limit the number of trading partners and being *unable to attract or unwilling to support* many trading partners. It is hardly a concession for a manufacturer to promise exclusivity to the only reseller willing to represent the brand, or to the only reseller the manufacturer is willing to supply. Similarly, it is a cheap concession for a reseller to carry one brand in a minor category, perhaps the only brand it cares to represent or the only manufacturer with which it is able to make a supply agreement.

BACK TO THE BASICS: CUTTING COSTS AND RAISING SALES

To this point, we have focused on strategic reasons why upstream and downstream channel members might limit the number of trading partners. We close our treatment of this issue by addressing two basic questions: All else constant, does selectivity in representation cut costs in any significant way, and does intensity of representation really increase sales? These issues have been saved for last in order to disentangle them from more strategic reasons for selectivity, whose cost and revenue implications are indirect and difficult for an accountant to estimate.

Saving Money by Limiting the Number of Trading Partners

Earlier, we noted that many manufacturers consider that more coverage is always better because it creates higher sales. Of course, there are associated costs. For a manufacturer, each outlet is an account, and each requires sales attention and support. Fulfilling each account's orders entails costs of ordering, shipping, financing, and so forth. Many manufacturers carry accounts whose orders do not justify even the accounting and opportunity costs of serving them. At some point, many accounts cost more to serve than the coverage-based benefits they offer.

One way around this obstacle to achieving greater distribution intensity is to serve outlets via master distributors, which achieve economies of scope and scale in serving their clientele. Of course, the manufacturer loses control and information in going this route, but the additional coverage is often worthwhile.

What is at issue here is a simple and fundamental reason for some degree of selectivity, which is that it costs money to secure representation per se. Note that the rationale here is *not* to gain more influence by increasing one's reward power. It is simply to *cut costs by dealing with fewer entities*. For example, Michelin in Italy used master distributors simply because there are so many small tire dealers in Italy. Here is a list of savings manufacturers may realize by dealing with fewer downstream channel members.

- Manufacturers limit the number of trading partners to keep their selling expenses down. By not serving marginal resellers, they reduce the number of salespeople or the expenses (travel, entertainment, samples, etc.) associated with a large account base.
- Manufacturers that, as a matter of policy, offer high levels of support to each channel member tend to distribute more selectively in order to limit the total costs of channel support.
- To the extent that fewer resellers means lower turnover, there is less opening, training, and servicing of new resellers.
- Fewer channel partners often means fewer but larger transactions, reducing inventory holding costs and other processing costs.
- Fewer but larger orders imply more accurate forecasting of demand, which in turn enables better production planning and lower inventories.

From the reseller's standpoint, dealing with a smaller number of brands can also offer important economies. Consolidating demand into a smaller number of brands may facilitate forecasting and improve inventory practices. Dealing with few suppliers may economize on the expenses of running the reseller's purchasing function.

Do More Trading Partners Really Mean More Revenue?

Many managers believe that it goes without saying that brands will sell more when they are carried by more downstream channel members. What evidence exists concerning the coverage–sales relationship indeed fits prevailing beliefs. Although the evidence is not conclusive, it does appear that, in general, brands that are more widely available do indeed have higher sales, hence higher market share.

But *why* is this so? It is tempting to conclude that more outlets cause more sales. If so, seeking wider coverage would appear to be always a desirable policy. Yet, it is not at all clear why we see more sales accompanying more intensive distribution. The relationship may be spurious (i.e., caused by a third factor driving both sales and coverage).[36] For example, a brand backed by excellent marketing will sell more, due to the marketing plan. Well-marketed brands also appeal to the trade. Hence, good marketing will create *both* higher sales and greater coverage. Revenue and coverage may both be results of superior marketing.

Perhaps more importantly, most of the rationales for limiting coverage have to do with increasing profit. Increasing revenue may not increase total profit.

This said, it would be simplistic to argue that limited coverage always raises a brand's image, therefore always increases unit margins. It may not increase per-unit margins. A good counterexample is "twin" automobiles. Car twins are essentially identical physically, often made in the same factory, but are marketed under different brand names. Rational, well-informed consumers should refuse to pay more for one brand than another, and yet, frequently they do.[37] In particular, consumers pay more for one brand of a pair of twins when that brand has greater coverage (more dealers). It is not clear why this is so. Consumers may infer that a brand with more dealers is more reputable. Or they may pay a premium to be closer to a service facility. Or they may reason that a somewhat more widely distributed brand will be easier to resell. Whatever the reasons, coverage actually increases margins for car twins. (Note that most car twins do *not* appear in the luxury segment, where it is essential to limit the number of dealerships in order to cultivate an upscale image.)

In short, it does appear that more coverage tends to accompany more sales. However, this does not mean a manufacturer should always seek the broadest coverage. It may not be the actual cause of more sales. Further, there is a limit to how much coverage a market will support, and this limit depends on the nature of the product category and of the brand.

What of the reseller's side of the issue? Do more brands mean more sales? Here, evidence is sparse. And again, the causality of any relationship can be questioned. If a dealer carrying more brands has higher revenue, is it because the dealer carries more brands, or because a superior dealer, who would sell more under any circumstances, can attract more brands?

Concluding the Issue of Limiting the Number of Trading Partners

We caution the reader not to simplify the issue down to cutting costs and raising revenues. Fewer trading partners do mean lower accounting costs per head, on the whole. But the opportunity cost of fewer partners often dwarfs their accounting costs. And although more trading partners are often associated with greater sales, it is not clear whether this is cause and effect, or whether other factors are at work. Fundamentally, the choice of how many trading partners turns not only on accounting costs and benefits but also on strategic costs and benefits. These are usually more important, although more difficult to estimate.

STIMULATING THE BENEFITS OF SELECTIVITY WHILE MAINTAINING INTENSIVE COVERAGE

Selective distribution has the benefit of increasing the manufacturer's ability to motivate and to control downstream channel members, at the cost of reducing healthy intrabrand competition and making it more difficult for the prospective purchaser to find the brand. Covering a market intensively makes the opposite trade-off. Some manufacturers experiment in search of ways to gain most of the benefits of selective distribution, while retaining intrabrand competition and making it easy for the prospect to become a buyer. There is little systematic evidence about how successful these experiments are. What exists is anecdotal and is probably skewed to the positive side, because manufacturers do not publicize their failures. Here are some methods that may or may not be effective or efficient means of gaining the best of both worlds (intensive *and* limited coverage).

One method, noted earlier, is to invest in *brand building*, so as to generate so much brand equity that downstream channel members will tolerate high intrabrand competition and not destroy the brand by such tactics as bait and switch. This highly expensive method appears particularly effective for fast-moving consumer goods (think of Coca-Cola, for example), because the channel member's ability to change a strong brand preference is already limited by the low-involvement nature of the product category.

Another method is to couple information sharing with *frequent introduction of new products* that have a low failure rate. Perhaps the best-known exemplar of this approach is 3M, famous for its competence in new-product development.[38] Channel members are willing to maintain ties unusually close with 3M, considering how intensively the company distributes. The steady stream of well-marketed new products, coupled with information, is a welcomed and rather scarce combination, which appears to overcome channel members' reluctance to coordinate activities with 3M.

A popular variation of information sharing is *lead generation*. A lead is a request from a prospective purchaser to be contacted by a manufacturer. Leads are usually generated via marketing efforts (advertisements soliciting names and coordinates, trade shows, and so forth). Manufacturers can invest in generating leads, then turn them over to a downstream channel member to contact the prospect. A good manufacturer lead generation program (one that yields accurate coordinates of prospects with a high probability of purchasing) can induce channel members to accept having more intrabrand competition than they would otherwise tolerate (see Channel Sketch 10.5).

An intriguing and lesser known approach is to offer *"branded variants,"* variations of models of a branded product.[39] The key feature is that some of the variations (i.e., combinations of levels of attributes) are made available only to certain resellers, not to the entire channel. For example, watches carrying the Seiko brand vary in terms of the color of the watchband, whether the watch is digital or analog, and what type of hand the watch possesses (size and luminosity). The key to the branded variant strategy is that certain combinations are made available only to selected channel members, thereby giving them a sort of exclusivity.

CHANNEL SKETCH 10.5

Using Lead Generation Programs to Keep Downstream Channel Members in the Network[40]

In early 1999, Compaq Canada began introducing changes in its sales model that impacted its third-party distribution network, which had traditionally been responsible for sales of Compaq's computers. As part of the new model, Compaq created a telemarketing center whose employees began to target the small to medium-size business segment. This segment comprises companies with 20 to 200 computer users.

Compaq's telemarketing group aims to generate interest in this segment. The group will collect customer leads that Compaq in turn will pass on to a local dealer. Compaq claims that the dealers will continue to sell equipment and to provide support service to the targeted businesses. However, Compaq's resellers have raised concerns that the manufacturer's larger objectives are to shift to its own direct sales force. Thus, going forward Compaq will need to remain cognizant of its distributors' concerns and to provide them with evidence of commitment (i.e., a steady stream of productive leads) to show that they are an essential part of Compaq's distribution network in Canada.

Evidence to date suggests this strategy is effective for strong brand names of shopping goods, for which the consumer feels some involvement in the product category. Durables and semidurables fit this description well if they are not yet commodities. The customer feels a certain level of risk, due to the importance of the category and the sense that products are not interchangeable. The purchase of a mattress and box springs fits this situation. In these categories, strong brand names can attract a retailer, and differentiating by creating a variant builds some level of retailer commitment to the brand. Sealy manufactures mattresses that are sold in bedding, furniture, and department stores through the United States. For its various resellers, Sealy takes a particular product having the same characteristics (durability, firmness, padding, and number of springs) and makes variants (differing by color, covering style, and the "made for" label) for each set of resellers. Evidence to date, although not definitive, suggests that manufacturers that pursue a branded variants strategy induce more stores to carry the brand and induce the stores holding the variant to put more service (such as stocking and displaying many models of the brand, and offering sales assistance) behind the brand.

Why does the strategy work? Because busy consumers invest time to develop a preference within the store's considerable selection of the brand name's models. The power of the brand name assures them that it is worthwhile to examine alternatives within the brand's line. Warned by salespeople that other stores don't have an identical selection (a credible statement, given the store's large offering in the brand), many consumers are unwilling to take the time to visit another store and to take the risk that the variant they favor is not there. Hence, they conclude their purchase without shopping further.

The methods listed so far are power-based efforts to increase influence when there are many downstream channel members. Building pull increases the manufacturer's coercive power: The threat is that customers will be dissatisfied if they do not find the brand. In contrast, other methods are ways to exert reward power. Coupling information with frequent new-product introduction offers an unusual combination to help downstream channel members build their sales base. Generating leads and offering branded variants are also a form of reward power.

A different approach is to focus on *mitigating the buyers' costs of selective distribution*. For example, many durable goods require manufacturer-specific service. Traditionally, this is offered at the point of sale. To induce resellers to invest in service facilities, manufacturers are obliged to be more selective in coverage, which in turn inconveniences the customer. One solution is to decouple sales and service by establishing separate service-only facilities. Relieved of the service burden, more stores would be qualified to offer sales.

When General Electric decided to adopt more intensive distribution for its small electrical ("traffic") appliances some years ago, it found that it could not obtain adequate service from its expanded retail network. The company had to institute a nationwide, company-owned chain of service centers in order to solve this significant marketing problem. Eventually, it sold off its entire traffic appliance business to Black & Decker. To some extent, the widespread availability of consumer electronics in superstores and discounters, such as Circuit City, Best Buy, and Wal-Mart, is a major reason why these retailers offer virtually limitless return policies to customers. Rather than investing in repair facilities, they merely ship the returned merchandise (defective or not) back to the manufacturer for credit against future purchases.[41]

In short, there are ways to distribute more intensively while retaining at least some of the benefits of distributing selectively. These methods are expensive and not easy to duplicate, which may explain why they are not commonly practiced. Whether and when the costs outweigh the benefits is an open question.

VERTICAL RESTRAINTS: IS THIS ANTICOMPETITIVE BEHAVIOR?

A vertical restraint is a contractual interdiction by the manufacturer of normal behavior for channel members. These restraints constitute interference in the running of the channel member's own business. The policy issue arises when a vertical restraint is legal: In that case, when it is a good idea to employ them?

The most common type of restraints falls into three categories:

1. *Customer coverage policies* limit the reseller's right to do business freely with any customer of its choosing. Any attempt to confine wholesalers' or retailers' selling activities to one segment (geographical or otherwise) is such a policy, often referred to as a territorial restriction. There are many variations of this idea, including absolute confinement and profit pass-over arrangements. Absolute confinement involves a promise by a channel member that it will not sell outside its assigned territory. Often combined with such a promise is a pledge by the supplier not to sell to anyone else in that territory. Profit pass-over arrangements, in contrast, permit selling outside one's assigned customer base but require that a channel member who sells to a customer located outside its assigned territory compensate the distributor in whose territory the customer is located.

2. *Pricing policies* are designed to oblige the downstream channel member to observe prices dictated by the manufacturer. Resale price maintenance is an example of such a policy.

3. *Product line policies* are intended to oblige the channel member to carry some products and not others. Exclusive dealing falls here when it is forced upon the channel member by the manufacturer. Other such policies include tying. Tying exists when a seller, having a product or service that buyers want (the tying product), refuses to sell it unless a second (tied) product or service is also purchased. Thus, a manufacturer of motion picture projectors (the tying product) might insist that only its film (the tied product) be used with the projectors. Similarly, a manufacturer of shoe machinery (the tying product) might insist that lessees of the machinery purchase service contracts (tied service) from it for the proper maintenance of the machinery.[42]

Three points are important concerning these restraints:

1. They are all means of attempting to structure a marketing channel contractually so as to steer a channel member's behavior. As such, these policies are often used as a package together with some degree of selectivity in distribution and are often employed for the same reasons.[43] *Vertical restraints are a way to induce each side to carry out its commitments.*[44]

2. Although legally controversial in many countries, *these restraints are not necessarily anticompetitive*. Many of these are designed to dampen intrabrand competition *for the purposes of enhancing interbrand competition.*[45] In addition, they increase manufacturer control. It may be desired for positive reasons, such as ensuring the proper handling of the product for safety or performance concerns. Indeed, the potential benefits of vertical restraints are so great that the European Commission in 1997 concludes, "Anti-competitive effects of vertical restraints are likely to be insignificant in competitive markets." The Commission considers most markets to be competitive, on grounds that supplier or distributor market power is usually both contested (many competitors) and contestable (low barriers to entry).[46] For the European Commission to make such a sweeping statement is significant, because the Commission has two objectives: to foster competition and to promote the integration of the economies of the member states into a single internal market. Because these objectives are ambitious, one would expect the Commission to be suspicious of vertical restraints.

3. Much of what we know about vertical restraints comes from legal disputes over them. As a result, it is easy to think of these policies as being imposed on weaker downstream channel members by powerful manufacturers, to be used (and abused) as a means of coercion. For example, exclusive dealing is often presented as being forced upon distributors, as though they would never limit their assortment voluntarily. Yet, exclusive dealers often accept these arrangements willingly, report that they function quite well, and derive substantial benefits from them.[47] This is in stark contrast to the image of powerful manufacturers exploiting weak resellers to the point of driving them into court to defend themselves. The more normal, everyday workings of channel members do not become

court cases. And in these private arrangements, vertical restraints are bargaining issues, over which each side negotiates (accepting, modifying, or rejecting proposed restraints) as part of an overall calibration of the domains and roles of each player in the marketing channel. Power does enter, as it enters into any negotiation. However, we should not assume the manufacturer is powerful and the distributor is powerless. For example, powerful distributors can and do oblige manufacturers, even *Fortune* 500 firms and renowned multinationals, to offer them such concessions as limited use, even no use, of other distributors in their trading areas. It is more useful to think of vertical restraints as *reciprocal patterns of concession as part of a bargaining process*.

SUMMARY

The decision of how thoroughly to cover a market area is, for the manufacturer, a critical policy choice, because it substantially influences how well the manufacturer can implement its channel plans. This is because the intensity of coverage drives how much reward power the manufacturer has over downstream channel members, and how much it depends on its downstream counterparts.

At first glance, the issue is deceptively simple from the manufacturer's viewpoint. Its sales force would like freedom to open as many accounts (sign up as many channel members) as possible. The customer would like to find an outlet nearby, especially for convenience goods. And channel members will be pressured by market forces to sell more (e.g., by cutting prices) if at least some of their competitors carry the brand. All these factors suggest that more coverage is better. The corporate lawyer, concerned about incurring allegations of restricting competition, is likely to approve. On the manufacturer's side, only the corporate accountant, adding up the costs of servicing many outlets placing small orders, is likely to object.

But the issue is far more complex. Channel members will object vigorously. Unable to differentiate themselves and to maintain margins in the face of withering intrabrand competition, channel entities will ask the manufacturer for relief. If their competition is not reduced, they will withdraw their efforts, perhaps even use the brand to bring in traffic—to be diverted to another brand. Other entities will refuse to join the manufacturer's channel. And they will refuse to undertake actions to support the brand unless those efforts can be readily redeployed to another brand. In general, the manufacturer will experience a lack of cooperation. Implementation problems rise exponentially when coverage is too high for downstream channel members to earn a reasonable return on the brand.

A multitude of ways exists to cope with the implementation problems created by intensive distribution. All of them are expensive and some are difficult to implement. These include creating so much brand equity as to exercise pull over the channel's customers (effectively obliging the channel to carry the brand), sharing valuable information and feeding low-risk new products to channel members, offering branded variants, and decoupling service and sales.

A more direct, and often cheaper and more effective way to influence the channel is to limit one's coverage. This move raises the manufacturer's dependence on its resellers, as each becomes more important and would require more effort to replace. But in return, the manufacturer can reassure channel members that it will not be opportunistic. For example, the manufacturer can allay fears that resellers making brand-specific investments will be exploited once the investments are in place. The manufacturer can allay fears that it will abuse a strong brand position, or that it will undercut channel members by unreasonable levels of direct selling.

Apart from allaying fears of opportunism, the manufacturer can use limited distribution to induce the channel member to make concessions of its own. Prime among these is limiting brand assortment by offering some degree of category selectivity, even so far as offering category exclusivity, or exclusive dealing. More generally, by limiting coverage, the manufacturer is able to offer greater rewards to each channel member. Manufacturers can use this influence to attract only the best resellers (important for a high-quality positioning), and those matching a particular customer profile (important when the target segment is very focused). Manufacturers may also use reward power to exercise greater influence over how channel members market their brands (important for manufacturers that, for whatever reason, are reluctant to let market forces dictate outcomes).

In short, the manufacturer can increase its influence over channel members, and its ability to motivate them, by limiting coverage. In the process, the corporate accountant can be appeased by the cost savings due to serving a smaller but more active account base. The same argument applies in reverse to a downstream channel member: Representing fewer brands can increase leverage over a manufacturer while reducing costs.

Will the customer be better off? Yes, if the manufacturer's choice of channel members and ideas of how to control them lead to outcomes that meet the customer's needs (e.g., needs for product safety, repair services, sales efforts, and so forth). And the customer may not necessarily pay a higher price: To the extent that limited intrabrand competition fosters vigorous interbrand competition, the customer may actually pay a lower price. The customer will be inconvenienced by lesser availability, which will be a minor factor for specialty goods in any case.

Fundamentally, this chapter is about limiting intrabrand competition for the purpose of increasing interbrand competition. This can be achieved by attracting the right channel partners, motivating them highly, and gaining their cooperation with the manufacturer's initiatives. If these initiatives are well considered or if the manufacturer skillfully uses channel feedback to improve its ideas, the result will be a well-executed marketing plan, one that facilitates the manufacturer's competitive efforts vis-à-vis other brands.

Viewed from the standpoint of the downstream channel member, inducing the supplier to accept restrictions or accepting restrictions on one's own actions (such as the right to carry competing brands) are points of negotiation. The channel member can enhance its ability to serve customers and can build its own competitive advantage by judicious negotiation over vertical restraints, including demanding reciprocity in making concessions.

Other forms of restraining intrabrand competition (such as restrictions on the reseller's customer base) are in the same spirit as limiting coverage, and are often used in conjunction with limited distribution. These are considered in more depth in Chapter 12 on the legal environment.

Discussion Questions

1. Which is preferable—intrabrand or interbrand competition? Can there be one without the other? Where do you stand on the issue of intrabrand competition: Is it necessary in order for there to be viable general competition from a macro perspective? Discuss these questions in the context of resale restrictions and the granting of exclusive territories.

2. An industrial supply house carries only a single brand of a grease-cutting compound used to clean the concrete floors of factories. That brand is prominent and well viewed by the clientele. What are all the possible reasons why the distributor would carry only one brand? Is this normal behavior? What do you expect the relationship with the manufacturer of this brand to be like? What would you expect is this manufacturer's degree of intensity of coverage in this distributor's market area?

3. Why do greater sales and greater coverage go together? Should manufacturers always seek greater coverage? Conversely, should resellers always seek to carry more brands in their assortment for a given product category? Why or why not?

4. "A brand can never be available in too many places." Debate this statement.

5. "A distributor should stock as many brands as possible for each product category demanded by its clients." Debate this statement.

6. If you were a new brand entering the market for a consumer durable, how much coverage would you seek? What arguments would you give to channel entities as to why they should carry your brand? What questions and objections are they likely to have? To convince them to stock your product, would you pursue a branded variants strategy?

Notes

1. Gary L. Frazier, Kirti Sawhney, and Tasadduq Shervani, "Intensity, Functions, and Integration in Channels of Distribution" in V. A. Zeithaml (ed.), *Review of Marketing 1990* (Chicago: American Marketing Association, 1990), pp. 263–300.

2. Patrick Bolton and Giacomo Bonanno, "Vertical Restraints in a Model of Vertical Differentiation," *Quarterly Journal of Economics*, 103 (August 1988), pp. 555–70.

3. The terminology of convenience, shopping, and specialty goods refers to consumer markets and was developed in Mervin Copeland, "Relation of Consumers' Buying Habits to Marketing Methods," *Harvard Business Review*, 1 (March–April 1923), pp. 282–89.

4. David J. Reibstein and Paul W. Farris, "Market Share and Distribution: A Generalization, A Speculation, and Some Implications," *Marketing Science*, 14, no. 3 (1995), pp. G190–G202.

5. Kelly Spang, "Nexar Broadens Channel Reach with Two Deals," *Computer Reseller News*, December 15, 1997, pp. 81–82. Quotation from p. 82.

6. James A. Narus and James C. Anderson, "Rethinking Distribution," *Harvard Business Review*, 96 (July–August 1996), pp. 112–20.

7. Wujin Chu and Woosik Chu, "Signaling Quality by Selling Through a Reputable Retailer: An Example of Renting the Reputation of Another Agent," *Marketing Science*, 13 (spring 1994), pp. 177–89.

8. Chantal Bialobos, "Le Sacre de Royal Canin," *Capital*, 10 (December 1999), pp. 50–51. Quotation from p. 51.

9. Robert L. Steiner, "The Inverse Association Between the Margins of Manufacturers and Retailers," in *Review of Industrial Organization*, vol. 8 (Boston: Kluwer Academic Publishers, 1993), pp. 717–40.

10. Sophie Chapdelaine, "Les Malheurs de la Famille Barbie," *Capital*, 11 (March 2000), pp. 38–40.

11. Chantal Bialobos, "La Francaise Qui Remet Bang & Olufsen Au Diapason," *Capital*, 10 (November 1999), p. 34.

12. William Breit, "Resale Price Maintenance: What Do Economists Know and When Did They Know It?" *Journal of Institutional and Theoretical Economics*, 147 (1991), pp. 72–90; Ross A. Fabricant, "Special Retail Services and Resale Price Maintenance: The California Wine Industry," *Journal of Retailing*, 66, no. 1 (1990), pp. 101–18.

13. Mary Jane Sheffet and Debra L. Scammon, "Resale Price Maintenance: Is It Safe to Suggest Retail Prices?" *Journal of Marketing*, 49, no. 4 (fall 1985), pp. 82–91.

14. Sharmila C. Chatterjee, Saara Hyvönen, and Erin Anderson, "Concentrated vs. Balanced Sourcing: An Examination of Retailer Sourcing Decisions in Closed Markets," *Journal of Retailing*, 71 (spring 1995), pp. 23–46; E. Raymond Corey, Frank V. Cespedes, and V. Kasturi Rangan, *Going to Market: Distribution Systems for Industrial Products* (Boston: Harvard Business School Press, 1989.

15. Howard P. Marvel, "Exclusive Dealing," *Journal of Law and Economics*, 25 (April 1982), pp. 1–25. Exclusive dealing is also sometimes referred to as "exclusive purchasing."

16. Comprehensive references for this material are Adam J. Fein and Erin Anderson, "Patterns of Credible Commitments: Territory and Category Selectivity in Industrial Distribution Channels," *Journal of Marketing*, 61 (April 1997), pp. 19–34; and Gary L. Frazier and Walfried M. Lassar, "Determinants of Distribution Intensity," *Journal of Marketing*, 60 (October 1996), pp. 39–51.

17. Anne Cantin, "Bénéteau-Jeanneau, Fusion Modele," *Management*, 10 (November 1999), pp. 32–34. Quotation from p. 33.

18. Gordon E. Miracle, "Product Characteristics and Marketing Strategy," *Journal of Marketing*, 29 (January 1965), pp. 18–24; Patrick E. Murphy and Ben M. Enis, "Classifying Products Strategically," *Journal of Marketing*, 50, no. 3 (July 1986), pp. 24–42.

19. V. Kasturi Rangan, Melvyn A. J. Menezes, and E. P. Maier, "Channel Selection for New Industrial Products: A Framework, Method, and Application," *Journal of Marketing*, 56 (July 1992), pp. 69–82.

20. Gerard J. Tellis, "The Price Elasticity of Selective Demand: A Meta-Analysis of Econometric Models of Sales," *Journal of Marketing Research*, 25 (November 1988), pp. 331–41.

21. "You've Beanie Had," *The Economist*, September 4, 1999, p. 66.

22. Nirmalya Kumar, "The Power of Trust in Manufacturer–Retailer Relationships," *Harvard Business Review*, 60 (November–December 1996), pp. 92–106.

23. Kirti Sawhney Celly and Gary L. Frazier, "Outcome-Based and Behavior-Based Coordination Efforts in Channel Relationships," *Journal of Marketing Research*, 33 (May 1996), pp. 200–210.

24. Rangan, V. Kasturi, Melvyn A. J. Menezes, and E. P. Maier, "Channel Selection for New Industrial Products: A Framwork, Method, and Application," *Journal of Marketing*, 56 (July 1992), pp. 69–82.

25. European Commission, *Green Paper on Vertical Restraints in EU Competition Policy* (Brussels: Directorate General for Competition, 1997). Available at http://europa.eu.int/en/comm/dg04/dg04home.htm.

26. Hazel Southam, "Turning the Tables at Linn," *Marketing*, May 20, pp. 20–21; Adrian Murdoch, "Music Man,"

Chief Executive, 130 (December 1997), p. 24; The Linn Products Ltd. Web site (www.linn.co.uk).

27. Allan J. Magrath and Kenneth G. Hardy, "Working with a Unique Distribution Channel: Contractor-Dealers," *Industrial Marketing Management*, 17, no. 1 (1988), pp. 325–28.

28. Lauranne Buchanan, "Vertical Trade Relationships: The Role of Dependence and Symmetry in Attaining Organizational Goals," *Journal of Marketing Research*, 29 (February 1992), pp. 65–75.

29. Jan B. Heide and George John, "The Role of Dependence Balancing in Safeguarding Transaction-Specific Assets in Conventional Channels," *Journal of Marketing*, 52 (January 1988), pp. 20–35.

30. Jean-Pierre Gaudard, "Distribution: Une Remise in Cause Nécessaire Mais Délicate," *L'Usine Nouvelle*, September 1996, pp. 79–81.

31. Nirmalya Kumar, Lisa K. Scheer, and Jan-Benedict E. M. Steenkamp, "The Effects of Supplier Fairness on Vulnerable Resellers," *Journal of Marketing Research*, 32 (February 1995), pp. 54–65.

32. Julie Wolf, "EC Commission Unveils Blueprint for Car Industry," *Asian Wall Street Journal*, April 30, 1992, p. 5; Valerie Reitman, Nichole M. Christian, and Audrey Choi, "Trade Tensions: U.S. Big Three Auto Makers Use Different Tactics in Japan, Europe," *Asian Wall Street Journal*, May 22, 1995, p. 20; "Système de Distribution Exclusive Reconduit," *L'Usine Nouvelle*, June 29, 1995, p. 4.

33. Jan B. Heide, Shantanu Dutta, and Mark Bergen, "Exclusive Dealing and Business Efficiency: Evidence from Industry Practice," *Journal of Law and Economics*, 41 (October 1998), pp. 387–407.

34. Gul Butaney and Lawrence H. Wortzel, "Distributor Power versus Manufacturer Power: The Customer Role," *Journal of Marketing*, 52, no. 1 (January 1988), pp. 52–63.

35. R. Preston McAfee and Marius Schwartz, "Opportunism in Multilateral Vertical Contracting: Nondiscrimination, Exclusivity, and Uniformity," *American Economic Review*, 84, no. 1 (1994), pp. 210–30.

36. John U. Farley and Harold J. Leavitt, "A Model of the Distribution of Branded Personal Products in Jamaica," *Journal of Marketing Research*, 5 (November 1968), pp. 362–68.

37. Mary W. Sullivan, "How Brand Names Affect the Demand for Twin Automobiles," *Journal of Marketing Research*, 35 (May 1998), pp. 154–65.

38. Frazier, Gary L. and Walfried M. Lassar, "Determinants of Distribution Intensity," *Journal of Marketing*, 60 (October 1996), pp. 39–51.

39. Mark Bergen, Shantanu Dutta, and Steven M. Shugan, "Branded Variants: A Retail Perspective," *Journal of Marketing Research*, 33 (February 1996), pp. 9–19.

40. Kevin Restivo, "Compaq Call Centre to Take Corporate Calls," *Computer Dealer News*, 14, no. 48 (December 21, 1998), p. 12.

41. Timothy L. O'Brien, "Unjustified Returns Plague Electronics Makers," *Wall Street Journal*, September 26, 1994, p. B1.

42. Scott E. Masten and Edward A. Snyder, "United States v. United Shoe Machinery Corporation: On the Merits," *Journal of Law and Economics*, 36 (April 1993), pp. 33–70.

43. Thomas R. Overstreet, *Resale Price Maintenance: Economic Theories and Empirical Evidence* (Washington DC: Federal Trade Commission Bureau of Economics, 1983).

44. Benjamin Klein and Kevin M. Murphy, "Vertical Restraints as Contract Enforcement Mechanisms," *Journal of Law and Economics*, 31 (October 1988), pp. 265–97.

45. Shantanu Dutta, Jan B. Heide, and Mark Bergen, "Vertical Territorial Restrictions and Public Policy: Theories and Industry Evidence," *Journal of Marketing*, 63 (October 1999), pp. 121–34.

46. European Commission, *Green Paper on Vertical Restraints*, Quotation from p. 27.

47. Zhan G. Li and Rajiv P. Dant, "Effects of Manufacturers' Strategies on Channel Relationships," *Industrial Marketing Management*, 28, no. 1 (1999), pp. 131–43.

11

Strategic Alliances in Distribution

LEARNING OBJECTIVES

After reading this chapter, you will:

- Define and describe the hallmarks of committed relationships in marketing channels
- Distinguish upstream and downstream motivations to form an alliance
- Describe why many channel members don't want and don't have committed relationships
- Sketch the performance implications of channel alliances
- Explain the role of a long time horizon and describe how to lengthen it
- Forecast and explain the prevalence of asymmetric commitment
- Explain why channel members deliberately increase their vulnerability and how they manage this exposure
- Detail the role of idiosyncratic investments and give example for any channel member
- Sketch the bases of trust
- Describe how trust is built over time in a marketing channel
- Differentiate the five phases of a close marketing channel relationship

Marketing channels typically are composed of multiple companies, each pursuing its own interests. Because these interests are competing, channel members often fail to cooperate with each other, and even work at cross-purposes.

Strategic alliances in distribution are forged to solve this problem. *In a well-functioning alliance, two parties in a marketing channel function as if they were one*. They may make end-customers believe they are dealing with a single organization that is fully vertically integrated.

Achieving such close coordination in a marketing channel is an almost utopian ideal. Yet, it can and does happen. Some strategic alliances perform marketing channel flows so well that the members cooperate even better than do the divisions of a firm that really is a single vertically integrated market channel. This extraordinary achievement brings obvious benefits to the channel. But the costs are high and many of them are hidden. And although the channel as a whole functions effectively, to the buyer's benefit, it is not always the case that each member of a distribution alliance shares equitably in the rewards of their coordinated efforts.

What is the difference between a strategic alliance and any other well-functioning marketing channel? What do the members of the alliance hope to get out of it? Do they actually gain the benefits they seek? At what cost? What characterizes an alliance in distribution? How can these alliances be built? In the end, is a distribution alliance worth its cost? A great deal of progress has been made in recent years to answer these questions, and to illuminate the nature and value of strategic alliances in distribution. This chapter takes an inventory of the answers that have been developed to date.

STRATEGIC ALLIANCES: THEIR NATURE AND THE MOTIVES FOR CREATING THEM

What Is a Strategic Distribution Alliance?

In a *strategic alliance*, two or more organizations have connections (legal, economic, or interpersonal) that cause them to *function according to a perception of a single interest*, shared by all the parties. An alliance is strategic when the connections that bind organizations are enduring and substantial, cutting across numerous aspects of each business. Membership causes each party to alter its behavior to fit the alliance's objectives. Alliances go under many labels, including close relationships, partnerships, relational governance, hybrid governance, vertical quasi-integration, and committed relationships.

Strategic alliances are a subject of fascination and not just in marketing channels. They have been called a "fad of the 1990s."[1] Ironically, in the 1970s, close, committed business partnerships were widely considered unnatural, unusual, and inferior forms of governance in Western business. There has been an overcorrection, such that alliances are now touted in some circles as a universal cure for any deficiency. Other ways of managing channels, such as the creative and equitable use of power (Chapter 8), have been inaccurately dismissed as ineffective or passé. This chapter presents a balanced view of what alliances can do, when they are appropriate, and how they are built and maintained.

The term *alliance* has become so popular that it is overused. Many so-called strategic alliances are really just tactical arrangements of convenience, or are merely normal business relationships that run with little conflict. Sometimes an alliance is really a relationship of imbalanced power, in which the more powerful organization exerts control over the weaker ones. The result is that the organizations do function as one, but not because their enduring connections give them a single overriding interest. In an alliance, power is balanced and it is high: Each side exerts considerable influence over the other.[2]

A distribution alliance exhibits genuine commitment. Commitment exists when an organization desires the relationship to continue indefinitely. However, this in itself is not enough to make an alliance. The organization must also be willing to sacrifice to maintain and to grow the relationship. These sacrifices may take the form of giving up short-term profits or of not pursing other opportunities, preferring instead to devote the organization's resources to the alliance. Sacrifices also are made, for example, to accommodate the other side's needs, more so than would be done for an ordinary business transaction. In general, a committed party works hard to maintain and to grow the relationship, even though growth demands resources and puts a strain on the organization.

Growing the relationship means the organization risks becoming dependent on its partner. The committed organization accepts to bear or takes steps to manage this risk. For example, a sales agency may add salespeople to accommodate the needs of a principal with which it has an alliance. Consequently, the agency has more at risk, including a greater share of its business coming from one source. The committed agency either will bear that risk or will cultivate other businesses (thereby growing even more) to diversify its portfolio. This keeps the allied principal's share of the agency's revenue within bounds.

Commitment is difficult to observe. It is an attitude, an intention, and an expectation, all wrapped into one. *True alliances encumber the parties involved, imposing on them obligations that may be very costly.* Many organizations profess commitment to each and every one of their business relations. This encourages pleasant interactions among people in upstream and downstream organizations, but is seldom an accurate description of how their organizations really deal with each other. True commitment is often revealed rather than professed. In contrast, superficial commitment is disguised, presented as though it were real. Usually, the disguise is not effective. Figure 11.1 lists a cluster of behaviors and attitudes that have been demonstrated to accompany genuine commitment. Although no single indicator is particularly informative, the set taken together gives a good index of the strength of commitment an organization has toward a member of a marketing channel.

Commitment, then, means a long time horizon, plus an active desire to keep the relationship going, plus a willingness to make sacrifices to maintain and grow the relationship. A committed distribution relationship is often likened to a marriage.

Of course, one spouse may be committed when the other is not. This is a situation of asymmetric commitment. It is not common in strategic alliances in distribution. Upstream and downstream channel members tend to commit in a symmetric way: Both are committed or neither is committed. The reasons for this symmetry are discussed later in this chapter.

The marriage analogy is misleading in one important respect: Channel organizations can and do have multiple alliances simultaneously. A better analogy is to a deep friendship. These are difficult to build and costly to maintain, putting a natural limit on their number.

A committed party to a relationship (a manufacturer, a distributor, or another channel member) views its arrangement as a long-term alliance. Some manifestations of this outlook show up in statements such as these, made by the committed party about its channel partner:

- We expect to be doing business with them for a long time.
- We defend them when others criticize them.
- We spend enough time with their people to work out problems and misunderstandings.
- We have a strong sense of loyalty to them.
- We are willing to grow the relationship.
- We are patient with their mistakes, even those that cause us trouble.
- We are willing to make long-term investments in them, and to wait for the payoff to come.
- We will dedicate whatever people and resources it takes to grow the business we do with them.
- We are not continually looking for another organization as a business partner to replace or add to this one.
- If another organization offered us something better, we would not drop this organization, and we would hesitate to take on the new organization.

Clearly, this is not normal operating procedure for two organizations. Commitment is more than having an ongoing cordial relationship. It involves confidence in the future, and a willingness to invest in the partner, at the expense of other opportunities, in order to maintain and grow the business relationship.

FIGURE 11.1 **Symptoms of Commitment in Marketing Channels**
Source: Adapted from Erin Anderson and Barton Weitz, "The Use of Pledges to Build and Sustain Commitment in Distribution Channels," *Journal of Marketing Research*, 24 (February 1992), pp. 18–34.

Why Forge a Strategic Distribution Alliance? Upstream Motives

Why would an upstream channel member, such as a producer, desire to build a committed relationship with a downstream channel member, such as a distributor? Distribution alliances begin with the producer's recognition that it can profit from the many advantages a downstream channel member can offer, at least in principle. Chief among these, manufacturers tend to appreciate the ability to achieve better coverage and to do so at lower cost (including lower overhead).

At minimum, *manufacturers must respect downstream channel members* before building an alliance with them. Yet, it is surprising how often producers fail to appreciate the value that channel members provide them, and how often they overestimate their own ability to duplicate effectively and efficiently the third party's performance of these flows. It has been observed that "some manufacturers have a 'do it in house–technical' culture that prevents them from understanding, respecting, and trusting intermediaries to any degree."[3]

Given respect as a building block, manufacturers desire an alliance in order to motivate distributors to represent them better, in their current or in new markets, or with new products. Of course, there are ways to improve representation without going so far as to build an alliance. These include exerting power, particularly reward power, and encouraging functional conflict—disputes that move the parties to aligning their viewpoints or agreeing on a course of action. Building commitment is, however, an effective and durable way to motivate downstream channel members. This is particularly true when the organization is being asked to assume the significant risks involved in performing channel flows for new products or in new markets.

A producer may seek an alliance in order to coordinate marketing efforts with distributors more tightly, and thereby to do a better job of reaching the ultimate customer. Along these lines, the manufacturer may seek greater cooperation, in particular, in the exchange of information. Via alliances, it hopes to gain information about the marketplace. Yet downstream channel members have economic motives to withhold this information. Distributors, for example, may withhold market information to prevent the manufacturer from using the information against them in negotiations (e.g., overpricing). Or they may withhold information for a simpler reason: It takes time to brief a principal, and that time has other uses. Downstream channel members are often compared to a wall standing between the manufacturer and the final buyer, blocking the manufacturer's view and reducing its understanding of the final buyer. By gaining distributor commitment, the manufacturer hopes to increase information sharing, to look over the wall.

An emerging motive to forge an alliance downstream is a wave of consolidation in wholesaling. Mergers and acquisitions in many industries are transforming the wholesaling level from many smaller players (fragmentation) to a handful of giant players (consolidation). Manufacturers seek alliances because they see the pool of potential partners drying up. They fear losing distribution, not only due to the small number of players left standing, but because the survivors are themselves powerful organizations that often enter into more or less privileged relations with selected manufacturers. An alliance is a way to rebalance the power arrangement, as well as to retain access to markets.[4]

In the longer term, the manufacturer seeks to erect barriers to entry by future competitors. One of the best possible barriers is a good distribution network. The reason a channel is so valuable a barrier is that, unlike a price cut or a product feature, it is so hard to duplicate. A committed channel may refuse to carry or to actively promote an entrant's brands. Finding another that works as well as a distribution alliance is a challenging task for many manufacturers.

An example is the justly celebrated alliance between two old adversaries, Procter & Gamble (P&G) and Wal-Mart.[5] Both are noted for using their considerable power to sway the trade. P&G's brand appeal and market expertise in hundreds of fast-moving consumer goods is so dominant it has been described as a "self-aggrandizing bully." Wal-Mart, the massive retailer, uses its volume and growth to oblige its suppliers to do business as it dictates: no intermediaries, extraordinarily low prices, extra service, preferred credit terms, investments in customized EDI (electronic data interchange) technology, and so forth.

These upstream and downstream giants built an alliance using the techniques described in this chapter, particularly making investments tailored to each other. For P&G, the payoffs have come in several forms. The supplier receives continuous data by satellite from individual, denoted Wal-Mart stores (*not* pooled). This microlevel data covers sales, inventory, and prices for each stockkeeping unit of each brand P&G sells. P&G is responsible for reordering from itself and automatically shipping, often directly to the stores. The cycle is completed by electronic invoicing and electronic funds transfer.

This paperless system allows P&G to produce to demand, to cut inventories, and to reduce stockouts. Overall logistics costs have been reduced. P&G does an enormous business with Wal-Mart, protected from competition by the investments it has made and its intimate knowledge of Wal-Mart's needs. And P&G has an excellent source of market research in the store-level data it garners from Wal-Mart.

Why Forge a Strategic Distribution Alliance? Downstream Motives

The motives of downstream channel members to build alliances revolve around having an assured and stable supply of desirable products. Consolidation is a motive here: As mergers and acquisitions concentrate market share among a few manufacturers in many industries, downstream channel members commit to the survivors to maintain product supply. Channel members also build alliances to make their own marketing efforts more successful. By coordinating their efforts with a supplier, channel members hope to work better together. This is not an objective in itself; it matters because it *helps the channel member to serve its customer better*. This in turn translates into higher volume and higher margins.

Channel members seek to cut costs via alliances. For example, by coordinating logistics, they can increase inventory turnover, keep lower levels of stocks, and take fewer write-downs of obsolete stock. The best of all worlds is achieved when stock costs are cut and the channel member suffers fewer out-of-stock situations.

Downstream channel members, such as distributors, also build alliances to differentiate themselves from other distributors. By positioning themselves as the manufacturer's preferred outlets for desirable brands, distributors differentiate their assortment and related service. And by differentiating themselves, downstream channel members discourage new competitive entry into their markets.

Distributor differentiation is often based on a strategy of offering value-added services, such as preventive or corrective maintenance, application assistance, on-site product training, engineering and design, technical expertise on call, special packaging and handling, and offering expedited, free telephone assistance. Distributors pursuing this strategy are more likely to work closely together with their suppliers, which helps the distributor set itself apart from fierce competition, even while it helps the manufacturer build the market for its products.[6]

Returning to the alliance between P&G and Wal-Mart, what benefits does the retailer gain? Inventories are lower, and the chain can offer its customers lower prices and greater availability of well-known brands. Wal-Mart is no longer responsible for managing its inventory (of course, this is only a benefit if the function is done well, which it is). And the paperless transaction system permits Wal-Mart to enjoy float: The retailer doesn't pay its supplier until after the consumer pays for the merchandise. This system, difficult to build and to duplicate, gives Wal-Mart a formidable competitive advantage in the saturated retail arena.

Upstream and downstream channel members fundamentally pursue alliances for their same reasons: *enduring competitive advantage, leading to profit*. Both parties seek to improve their coordination within the channel, in order to serve customers better and hold down accounting costs and opportunity costs. They seek to build stable relationships that are difficult to duplicate. In this way, they aim to discourage entry into their respective businesses. Fundamentally, distribution alliances may resemble marriages, but the motives of both players are calculated strategically and economically.

Do Alliances Outperform Ordinary Channels?

Do the parties to an alliance do their calculations correctly? Do alliances really outperform ordinary channel relationships?

At first glance, the answer seems to be "yes." Committed parties trust each other, and trust today enhances performance tomorrow.[7] Trusting parties will do more for each other, going so far out of their way to help each other that their actions resemble altruism rather than economic profit maximization. (As will be discussed, this appearance is deceiving.) Trusting parties find it easier to come to agreements, to work out conflicts, to work with each other. In particular, trust helps the parties cope with unfavorable outcomes and turn them around.[8] Trust is social capital: Just like financial capital, organizations use it to increase their effectiveness.

Differentiation and commitment go together. Manufacturers whose marketing strategy is to differentiate their offerings (as opposed to a solely cost leadership strategy) are more likely to build closer relationships with channel members. These relationships enable producers to implement their strategy successfully in the marketplace. This is particularly important in many industrial markets, where the channel, rather than advertising, has a huge impact on the brand's image.[9]

And it is not just manufacturers that benefit. Evidence indicates that some distributors have a pronounced market orientation. More than other distributors, they focus their organizations on collecting, spreading, and using information about customer needs to differentiate themselves. These distributors often ally with suppliers who are also market oriented. Together, the market-oriented pair tends to build an alliance, and from it, the market-oriented distributors gain a notable improvement in their financial performance.[10]

In general, commitment today means cooperation tomorrow. The long-time horizon that is part of an alliance creates better strategic and economic outcomes.[11] Concrete evidence shows that channel partnerships generate higher profits together. Evidence also suggests that typically each side of a channel partnership collects more profit from its alliance.[12] Channel partnerships are frequently able to generate higher profits and share them, rather than degenerating into a situation whereby one side gets the lion's share of the benefits the partnership generates. In contrast, although upstream buyer–supplier alliances (industrial procurement) do create wealth jointly and split it to the benefit of both sides, it is also quite common for one side to profit from their mutual efforts at the expense of the other.[13] Channel members may be able to achieve profit sharing because each member contributes to a value package for a customer. The customer may penalize partnerships when the value package changes, which gives each partner leverage when it comes time to divide the gains from their alliance.

If alliances perform better, should every manager make it a priority to build only mutually committed channels? The answer is "no" because alliances are very difficult and very costly to create. And there is no guarantee that spending enough time and money will make commitment happen. Many circumstances do not lend themselves to vertical quasi-integration.[14] Even in the right circumstances, building commitment is not easily done. Worst of all, we know how to recognize committed relationships when we see them, but it is very difficult to specify how to create some of the critical properties of an alliance.

The rest of this chapter inventories what we know to date about the properties marketing channel alliances exhibit and about how to build them. (Further information on the research that is the source of these lessons from the field is contained in the articles cited in the chapter endnotes.) We conclude by returning to and closing the issue of when alliances are worth building.

BUILDING COMMITMENT BY CREATING MUTUAL VULNERABILITY

The Minimum Necessary: Expectations of Continuity

A channel member who wants to build commitment into a relationship must begin by enhancing the expectation that the prospective partners will be doing business with each other for a long time. The *expectation of continuity is essential* before any organization will cooperate and invest to build a future.[15] And continuity is not taken for granted. Channel members know that they will be replaced if their performance doesn't satisfy.

Worse yet, in environments where legal barriers to termination are low (such as the United States), channel members fear they will be replaced even if their performance does satisfy! For example, principals often engage agents or resellers to represent products that are secondary or to penetrate markets that are considered peripheral. If the downstream channel member makes a success of the business, it should (and does) fear that the producer will take the business away or will renegotiate the terms of the arrangement to appropriate some of the unexpected gains.[16]

What inspires a channel member's confidence that a business relationship will last?[17] Several key factors have been identified for downstream channel members. Their expectation of doing future business on behalf of a principal strengthens for:

- Producers whom they trust
- Producers with whom they enjoy two-way communication, including active give and take of ideas
- Producers who enjoy a reputation for treating other channel members fairly
- Producers with whom they have been doing business for some time already

Communication plays a particularly powerful role. Trust and communication operate in a reinforcing cycle: the more trust, the more communication, which leads to more trust, which strengthens communication even more, and so forth. *Frequent, candid, detailed mutual communication is a must for a healthy channel partnership.*[18] This said, more than a few members of would-be channel alliances think they enjoy better communication and higher trust levels than they really do.

This is a hidden problem in old, seemingly stable channel relationships. Communication is often rather low in these older relationships, as though the two parties think they know each other so well that communication is superfluous. Older channel relationships frequently look stronger than they really are, because both sides take them for granted and permit communication to decline. Eventually, lack of communication will damage the trust that resides in old, stable relationships. Old relationships, whose continuity is assumed by both sides, can disintegrate suddenly. The catalyst is frequently a change in management in either organization—typically, executive succession for the agent or distributor, manager rotation for the producer. But the underlying reason is not so much the change in management as it is the decline of communication and the subsequent hollowing out of trust in old relationships.

Continuity expectations are higher when power is balanced in a relationship. When power is imbalanced, the weaker party fears being exploited and is more likely to defect. Knowing this, the stronger party discounts the future of the relationship because it expects the weaker party to withdraw or to go out of business. Thus, even when one party has the upper hand, it has less confidence that its relationship will last, compared to a balanced-power scenario—in developed economies. Chapter 9 on conflict discusses why imbalanced relationships are more stable in emerging economies. But, as noted earlier, these relationships are not alliances, even though they have continuity.

The combined stakes of the two parties also plays a role: The more the two sides get from the relationship, they more they expect it to continue. At least one party has too much to lose to let the relationship end without fighting to preserve it. Ideally, both parties have stakes (e.g., both derive substantial revenues from the arrangement), so both parties have an interest in not capriciously letting the relationship end.

That the relationship has a future in the eyes of the players is a minimal condition for building commitment. To erect a true alliance, the next step is crucial: Each side must believe that the other is committed.

Why Commitment Is Nil Unless It's Mutual

Given some expectation of continuity, the next step in alliance building is to earn the other party's commitment.[19] To do so, it is essential to be committed to the relationship. Seriously asymmetric commitment is rare because partners to an alliance do their calculations. They do not accept the obligations of being committed unless they believe their counterpart is also committed, also ready to assume obligations. Channel members who doubt the commitment of another organization may proclaim themselves partners, in the interest of preserving appearances, but they do not believe in, nor do they practice, commitment.

But can't a channel member be deceived? Isn't it possible to convince a channel partner that one's commitment is genuine when it is not? The evidence suggests this strategy does not work in most circumstances. Both upstream and downstream channel members are usually well informed about each other's true state of commitment. And they carefully condition their own attitude on what they believe (reasonably accurately) the other's commitment is.

How do they know each other's true states? In part, they are aware because organizations, unlike some people, are not very good actors. Even if all points of contact are instructed to put up a façade, the counterpart sees through and discerns reality. This works both ways: Truly committed firms may project they are not so committed, because they want to conceal what they see as their dependence, their vulnerability. But the projection fails: Their partners are not misled.

Wisely, organizations do not gauge each other's intentions so much by what the organization says as by what it does—and by what it has done. The past lingers in relationships. For example, although a certain level of conflict is to be expected in marketing channels, some parties have experienced an unusually high level of conflict. These relationships are very difficult to salvage. Sustained conflict operates like a feud, making it extremely difficult to move on to build commitment. Both upstream and downstream channel members discount the commitment of old adversaries, even if new management appears and assures its channel partners that "everything will be different now." The assurance is not taken to be convincing. Managements that permit conflict to go out of control for an extended period incur an opportunity cost: The relationship is unlikely ever to become a true partnership, even if peace is finally achieved.

The past lingers on in a positive sense as well. For example, once trust is established between two organizations, it persists, even as individuals move on.[20] This surprises many people, who believe that intangible relational states (such as trust, conflict, and agreement on goals) belong only to people and change when individuals leave their positions. However, relational states also belong to organizations and outlive personnel turnover. This organizational memory plays a large role in conditioning what each party thinks is the commitment level of its channel counterpart.

What happens when the players come to suspect that commitment is *not* aligned?[21] There is a stage one, in which one party suspects—usually rightly—that it is more committed to the relationship than is the other party. This is an uncomfortable position, and the party that feels "overcommitted" does not like it. This party feels vulnerable, fears being exploited, perceives more conflict in the relationship, and derives lower profits than it would if the commitment levels were seen (and correctly so) to be more balanced. Conversely, the "undercommitted" party *does* like its position of feeling less tied to the relationship than does its counterpart. This party is more satisfied with what it gets from its partnership.

But this situation cannot go on indefinitely. Sooner or later, there is a stage two, in which the overcommitted party scales back to bring the relationship into alignment. See Chapter 8 on power and Chapter 9 on conflict for more on the balance of commitment in relationships.

What is going on here is a circle of perception followed by adjustment (Figure 11.2). Two parties, such as a supplier and a distributor, reveal their level of commitment to each other deliberately, and to a great extent inadvertently. Thus, most perceptions of commitment are at least reasonably accurate. From these perceptions, organizations calibrate their own commitment as an act of reciprocation. This is how commitment tends

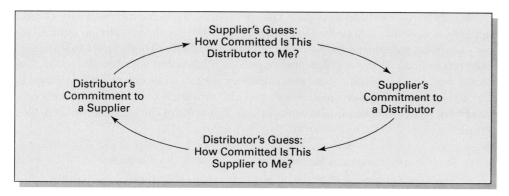

FIGURE 11.2 **The Circle of Commitment**

to reach alignment, often at mutually low levels. *To ratchet commitment up, one party must convince the other that its true commitment is higher, so that reciprocity will raise mutual commitment.*

How the Other Side Gauges Your Commitment

Consider that you are a distributor dealing with a supplier. You will gauge the supplier's commitment to you based on its past behavior. You focus on two critical aspects: (1) Have you had an acrimonious past with this supplier? and (2) What actions do you see the supplier taking to tie itself to doing business with you? Such actions convince you of the supplier's genuine commitment.

These actions take two forms. One is to give you some degree of protection from your competitors selling the supplier's brand. The greater the degree of selectivity you see the supplier exercising in its coverage of your market, the more you believe the supplier is truly committed to a business partnership with you. At the limit, if you believe the supplier gives you territory exclusivity, you gauge this to be a highly committed supplier. Conversely, the more you see your competitors selling the same brand, the less commitment you believe your supplier feels toward you.

What if your supplier practices direct selling? This is the practice of keeping house accounts, which the supplier serves directly, thereby competing with its own downstream channel members. Shouldn't this destroy your confidence in their commitment? It appears that a manufacturer can practice direct selling to a rather substantial degree, yet still inspire confidence in its resellers. How does this happen?

To some extent, many manufacturers camouflage the full extent of their direct selling. But this is not the major factor. Downstream channel members have some private tolerance for direct selling, although many deny it publicly. They believe that some customers will only deal directly. If so, the business is already lost to downstream channel members. And they believe that some customers have needs the supplier is better able to fill. The key issue here is the perception that the manufacturer is handling direct business fairly, as opposed to "being greedy" (taking business capriciously or unnecessarily from the channel member).

As a distributor judging a supplier, selectivity is one indicator you would use to infer supplier commitment to you. Another major factor is the supplier's efforts to build assets that cannot be redeployed from you to another distributor. These assets are *idiosyncratic* (specialized, customized) to your supplier's relationship with you. *Were the supplier to replace you, it would need to write off (or greatly write down) its investment in you.* To duplicate the value created with you, the supplier would need to make a new investment in the competitor who replaces you. Examples of these difficult-to-redeploy investments are:

- Supplier personnel and facilities dedicated to you, the distributor
- The supplier's stock of learning about you—your methods, your people, your strengths and weaknesses
- Compatible reporting systems, geared to the peculiarities of your system (especially if your system is proprietary)
- Investments designed to identify your business and its business in the mind of the customer
- General training programs, that help you run your business better
- A location near you, at a remove from your competitors

These investments vary in how easy they are to redeploy, but all of them are costly to move. Dedicated personnel can be reassigned, if there is other work for them, but their relationships with you become worthless. Facilities may be retrofitted, if they are still needed, but with effort. Learning about you can be discarded, unless your competitors are essentially interchangeable, which is unlikely. The supplier could put on training programs for your replacement, but can't recoup the training invested in you. The supplier could serve your competitor from a location especially suited to you—but will incur extra cost. Worst of all for the supplier will be explaining to customers that representation has changed. Channel Sketch 11.1 details an example of idiosyncratic investments made by manufacturers in supplying supermarkets.

CHANNEL SKETCH 11.1
How Manufacturers Bind Themselves to Supermarkets[22]

Distributor's brands, house brands, private labels—these are all terms for products sold under a brand name that is proprietary to a distributor or to a retailer. Increasingly, private labels are being employed as a way for downstream channel members to differentiate themselves and to offset the power of their suppliers (see Chapters 8 and 9 on power and conflict, respectively).

In France, the private-label strategy is so well implanted that several retailers have multiple private labels. They apply to different positioning (such as gourmet food, biological products, or country-style preparation) across multiple product categories (such as frozen foods, canned goods, and pasta). Typically, the brand names do not connote the chain at all: Nothing signals the consumer that this is a house brand. But none of the big chains manufactures any of these products.

The suppliers of private-label products are obliged to make a range of adaptations. Typically, they are already suppliers of other products under their own brands. Approached by the retailer, they agree to modify their methods and supply under the retailer's chosen brand name. As part of the package, they cut 10 to 20 percent off their prices. Then comes the product modification, all at the supplier's expense. They may be asked to alter the recipe or to change their production process or to change ingredients. Chains often employ famous chefs to make up recipes, then ask the suppliers to surmount the problems of making them. For example, Promodès, a giant retailing chain, asked one producer of canned goods to use only French-grown ingredients, in keeping with the French-countryside position of its brand. The producer had to strike a deal with growers in an obscure region to raise the proper beans. Another supplier of baked goods paid 40,000 francs for a specialty mold. Such adaptations are typical.

Could these investments be put to another use? Perhaps, although the lengths producers go to in creating these assets are likely to yield no premium elsewhere. And the most idiosyncratic aspect of these investments is the brand name, which belongs to the supplier.

Suppliers favor these goods for their uniqueness and their superior margins relative to the brands supplied by multinationals, such as Unilever. But it is necessary to build brand equity for them. Retailers cannot match Unilever's advertising, because the expenditure can be amortized only over the store's clientele, not over the entire population. Instead, retailers play their unique card: shelf space. Over the years, they have steadily increased the quality and quantity of space given over to house brands, at the expense of suppliers' brands. They also engage in lavish periodic in-store promotions.

The dependence of house-brand suppliers on their downstream channel members is considerable, due to the customized, nonredeployable nature of these investments. To some extent, the dependence is mutual, because no other supplier has made the investments either, and because the products are of great importance to the chains. To the extent that consumers would notice any change the chains might make if they switched suppliers, the small to medium-size firms that create these brands are protected. One indication of their confidence in the strength of their alliance is their willingness to add personnel to keep up with the brand's growth. Strict French labor laws make it difficult to downsize, making the addition of labor capacity a very credible commitment by suppliers to their retailers.

These idiosyncratic (to you) investments are otherwise known as *credible commitments, pledges,* or *company-specific investments.* When you see manufacturers invest in you in this fashion, your confidence in their commitment soars, because they are erecting a barrier to their own exit from their relationship with you.

Consider the other side of the situation. You are now the supplier, gauging how committed the distributor is to its relationship with you. You, too, will discount the commitment of a formerly acrimonious relationship. And you will believe in the commitment of a distributor that gives you some degree of selectivity in your product category.

At the limit, you will be inspired by the apparent commitment of a distributor that gives you category exclusivity (in your category, carries only your brand).

You will believe in the commitment of a distributor that invests in you in an idiosyncratic manner, one that would be difficult to transplant whole to a competing supplier. You would welcome the distributor's

- Dedication of people and facilities to your line
- Investment in upgrading and training the personnel serving your line
- Efforts to learn about you and build relations with your people
- Training of its customers on the use of your line
- Efforts to ally its name and yours in customers' eyes
- Investment in a reporting system particularly compatible with yours (especially if yours is proprietary)
- Location of a facility near you and far from your competitors

If your relationship with this distributor ends, and if the distributor has another use for these assets (another supplier to take on), what happens to these assets? Some of them can be adapted, but at substantial cost. Others must be re-created all over, such as relationships or proprietary reporting systems. Seeing the distributor make these investments leads you to believe the organization really means to build a future with you and sacrifice on your behalf. If it doesn't, it imposes a penalty on itself.

Actions That Bind Distributors to Suppliers

So far, we have focused on the necessity of exhibiting commitment in order to inspire commitment. But what makes downstream channel members, such as distributors, commit to a supplier? Part of the story is calculation: The distributor enters relationships when it believes the payoffs will justify the cost. This means the downstream channel member expects results that it cannot get with a more conventional relationship.

To get these results, the distributor dedicates resources to a supplier. The supplier-specific investments mentioned above (dedicated personnel, joint marketing, and so forth) are made by the distributor to "expand the pie," that is, generate exceptional results for the entire marketing channel.[23] If these investments are well considered, if the supplier works with the distributor, and if the distributor collects an equitable share of the pie, then the distributor is motivated to invest more. *Over time, the accumulated investments themselves become a motive to commit.* The distributor works to keep an alliance going in order to protect these investments.

Thus, supplier-specific investments serve three purposes: (1) They expand the channel pie, (2) they keep the distributor motivated to stay in the alliance, and (3) they are a convincing signal to the supplier that the distributor really is committed—which invites the supplier to reciprocate with its own commitment.

Other elements also build the distributor's commitment, particularly two-way communication. This means freely exchanging information (even though sensitive), getting involved in the supplier's marketing efforts, allowing the supplier to see weaknesses as well as strength, and giving advice to the supplier. Of course, no distributor will do this if the supplier is not open to it: Two-way communication is a mutual effort.

Another important element is reputation. Downstream channel members hold back from allying with suppliers thought to look out for their own interests at the expense of fair treatment of channel members. Manufacturers have an image to uphold not only among end-customers but also among channel members, current and prospective. Those who wish to forge channel alliances must manage the impression they create in their channel dealings.

Actions That Bind Suppliers to Distributors

Turning the lens around, what makes suppliers commit to a downstream channel member? They too, calculate the payoffs and don't commit unless they forecast returns they could not get otherwise. Before making investments, many of them will rigorously verify the downstream channel member's ability and motivation.[24] They make investments that are idiosyncratic to selected distributors in order to expand the channel pie. They serve not only to grow the pie but also to strengthen the relationship. Suppliers that make distributor-specific investments increase their commitment, because they know the assets will lose value if the distributor is replaced.

Two-way communication also plays a very substantial role in assuring supplier commitment. Such communication allows the producer to look over the wall and see the market the distributor serves. Of course, this is dangerous for the distributor: The supplier could use the information against the downstream channel member. Communication increases vulnerability.

Summary: Creating Alliances via Ties That Bind

To put this section in a nutshell, the formula for building a channel alliance is this: To get commitment, give commitment. But don't give commitment in a one-sided manner. Commit to those who commit to you. Observe their daily behavior and go by the image they present every day, not the professed intentions of top management. Judge their commitment by their actions. Be wary of an acrimonious trading partner that claims to have positive intentions and to be ready to forget the past. Take seriously the commitment of those that limit dealings with your competitors, as well as those that make investments tailored to you—and difficult to redeploy to another organization.

Given the other party's commitment, don't hesitate to make these investments yourself. They generate value, inspire your counterpart, and oblige you to work to keep the alliance growing. Invest, as well, in two-way communication. Particularly if you are a supplier, manage the image of fair dealings you present to the channel. This reputation spreads quickly and influences the downstream channel member considerably.

Channel Sketch 11.2 is a comprehensive example of these principles. It details how Caterpillar, a leading maker of earthmoving equipment, has spent decades cultivating alliances with independent equipment dealers to create exceptional results through its marketing channels.

CHANNEL SKETCH 11.2

Caterpillar Makes Its Dealers into Partners[25]

Caterpillar is a leading manufacturer of construction and mining equipment. Its CEO, Donald Fites, publicly proclaims that the single biggest reason for Caterpillar's considerable success is its marketing channel. Fites's reasoning is tied to the nature of the product category ("the machines that make the world work"). Earthmoving equipment is highly expensive, so industry unit volume is low. Thus, there are few points of sale. The products are complex, but fairly standard: The same machine, with minor customization, can be sold to mining operations, farms, and construction projects throughout the world. Although machines have a working life of up to 30 years, they break down frequently, due to heavy use in difficult and often remote environments. Breakdowns literally stop all operations. Minimizing the frequency and duration of breakdowns is therefore critical.

Caterpillar's strategy in this market is to charge a premium price, justified by differentiation on the basis of postsales service. Product service is critical to avoid breakdowns and to minimize downtime once they occur. To ensure superior service, Caterpillar sells most of its product worldwide through a close network of alliances with only 186 dealers, all of them independently owned, two-thirds of them outside the company's North American home market.

Caterpillar sells through independent dealers because it believes no one else can provide the market intelligence and customer service that are essential to the company's marketing strategy. According to Fites, local dealers are long-standing members of their communities. They understand customers and can relate to them better than a global company can. For their customers, they serve as trusted sources of advice (Which product? How to use it? When to trade it in?), financing, insurance, operator training, maintenance, and repair. Repair is critical: Repairing or rebuilding a part must be done on the spot. Caterpillar commands a price premium by convincing customers they will have a higher percentage of uptime than they will with less expensive competing products.

To do this, Caterpillar forges alliances with dealers, who in turn are the face of the company to its customers. This may seem out of place for a company whose motto is "Buy the Iron, Get the Company." But Caterpillar considers that its dealers are a critical part of the company.

This does not mean dealers are solely responsible for all channel flows. Caterpillar maintains an extensive (and expensive) inventory of parts, with guaranteed delivery anywhere within 48 hours. And Caterpillar makes idiosyncratic investments in its dealers, including:

- Territory exclusivity
- Strong working relations with dealer personnel, resulting in dealer-specific learning
- Assistance in inventory management, logistics, equipment management, and maintenance
- Generalized business training (forecasting, advertising, etc.)

- Joint marketing campaigns
- Technical training of dealer personnel

The accumulated value of these investments cannot be transferred to another dealer.

Dealers, in turn, make heavy Caterpillar-specific investments, including:

- The time they put into their interactions with company personnel
- Exclusive dealing (no competing brands)
- Multimillion-dollar inventories of parts
- Heavy fixed investments in Caterpillar-specific service equipment and information technology
- Joint marketing
- Training their customers in the use of Caterpillar equipment

Of course, these are not the only investments dealers make. But they are the investments that would make it difficult to become a dealer for Komatsu, Hitachi, Kobelco, and Caterpillar's other competitors.

Caterpillar and dealers communicate frequently, giving them a common understanding of how to execute a strategy of superior customer service. Dealer input is used heavily in product design, and products are developed in consideration of what would fit the dealer network. Dealer and factory personnel work together to resolve product problems. Dealer and marketing personnel work together to keep massive data-bases on customer experiences with the products. Virtually every Caterpillar employee has contact with dealer personnel. Perhaps most extraordinary, Caterpillar holds the financial statements of each dealer and even reviews them in annual meetings with dealer management. Caterpillar acts as a sort of benchmarking organization, using pooled data to tell dealers how their results fit with those of comparable dealers. The manufacturer is open as well: Virtually any of thousands of dealer personnel can access huge corporate databases.

Those 186 dealers combined are bigger than Caterpillar in employment and in financial worth. Like many strong relationships, Caterpillar and its dealers have many stories to tell of crises that were overcome by "sharing the pain and spreading the gain." In these stories, both sides take turns: The dealers save the situation on one occasion, Caterpillar steps in and loses money to protect dealers on another occasion. Caterpillar goes to lengths to project honesty, consistency, benevolence ("don't gouge your dealers"), and continuity.

In this regard, Caterpillar refuses to do direct selling around its dealers. Even when customers insist, the company refers the business to dealers. The Alaska Pipeline was one such project: The contract ultimately went to a partnership of two of the 186 dealers of Caterpillars. Some markets in their entirety are served directly by the company: newly opened, formerly socialist countries, the U.S. government, and original equipment manufacturers (OEMs). Most of this business, however, gets its after-sales service and support from the dealer network.

Over time, a large stock of trust has accumulated. But there is also a reasonable level of conflict—functional conflict. Much of it is over perennial channel issues for any company: the limits of service territories, product and pricing policies, the dealer's desire to diversify into other product categories Caterpillar does not serve. Although personal relationships are good and mutual respect is high, neither side misses an opportunity to criticize the other: Both are interventionist. Both sides are frankly interested in accumulating wealth, in making an attractive return on the very considerable investments that are required to manufacture and distribute earth-moving equipment.

Each dealer, with its stock of trust and idiosyncratic assets, is extremely valuable. Therefore, Caterpillar prefers to work with privately held companies, believing they have greater management continuity than publicly held companies. Indeed, Caterpillar is so interested in continuity that it runs programs for the teenage children of dealership owners to interest them in Caterpillar and in working in the family business.

What are the performance implications of these 186 alliances? Competitors have a substantial cost advantage, which Caterpillar counters by the premium pricing its dealers are able to uphold. Dealer input is essential in designing, manufacturing, and troubleshooting the products, which benefits the supplier considerably. Caterpillar dealers pioneer new products for the company, enter new markets, and offer extraordinary cooperation, even helping the producer to sell products the dealers do not carry. For example, Caterpillar sells engines directly to original equipment manufacturers. Dealers offer indirect assistance with these engine sales, and in return, it is the dealers who get the subsequent service contracts on the engines.

Ultimately, Caterpillar credits its dealers with the manufacturer's very survival, and with its recovery from a very difficult period to restore its profitability and leading position as a global supplier.

Fundamentally, this is a recipe for mutual vulnerability, mutual exposure. The principle is that if both sides depend on each other, both sides will make the alliance strong. If one side tries to reduce its vulnerablity, the other side will sense withdrawal and will match it. And indeed it should—high and one-sided vulnerability is dangerous (Chapter 9 explores some ways of dealing with it). One entrepreneur describes an alliance like this:

> It's like a balance, a scale—in return for commitment on their part we say we are committed to you and we prove it. So it's a quid pro quo. It's a balanced relationship that says you make investments, we make investments; you take risks, we take risks; you perform, we perform. That's the basis on which you build trust and everything that I would consider to be a strong successful relationship.[26]

Many managements find this recipe unappealing. Commitment is costly. Alliances take time, risk, resources, and determination—from both sides. To justify these costs, alliances must generate exceptional returns. When they do, it is because they have made relationship-specific investments and have driven their organizations to communicate frequently, intensely, and thoroughly.

Trust is also essential to alliances. To some extent, it is created in the course of making relationship-specific investments and communicating. But trust is far more complex. It is a function of daily interactions, many of which are beyond top management's control.

BUILDING COMMITMENT BY THE MANAGEMENT OF DAILY INTERACTIONS

What goes on "in the trenches" (i.e., in the conduct of daily business) has an enormous impact on relationship formation, far more than do pronouncements from corporate headquarters. Daily interactions between individuals in the channel drive the "channel culture" to improve, degrade, or stay stable. This creates a very complex picture. The cumulative effect of daily interactions conditions the relationship heavily. In particular, the daily detail of events and one-on-one interactions determine how much trust exists, which is essential for an alliance to function.

How Can Channel Members Manufacture Trust?

Trust, although easy to recognize, is difficult to define.[27] In channels, your trust in a channel member is usefully conceptualized as your confidence that the other party is honest (stands by its word, fulfills obligations, is sincere). This is also associated with benevolence, which is your confidence that the other party is genuinely interested in your welfare and your interests, and will seek mutual gains, rather than manipulate you to appropriate all the gains for itself. Overwhelming field evidence indicates that in channel relationships, honesty and benevolence go together: Where one is missing, so is the other. *To trust a channel member is to believe in that party's integrity and concern for mutual well-being.* To distrust is to fear deception and exploitation.

An alliance needs mutual commitment, and commitment cannot occur without a high level of trust. This is rational behavior: It is obviously a mistake to invest resources, sacrifice opportunities, and build a future with a party bent on exploitation and deception. A reasonable level of trust is necessary for *any* channel relationship to function. Distrust does not characterize channel relationships for long: It is either resolved, or the channel dissolves. But committed relationships exhibit higher-than-usual trust levels.

If building commitment requires building trust, then how can channel members increase their stock of trust?

The Fundamental Role of Economic Satisfaction

Channel members commit in the rational expectation of financial rewards. They will not commit without the prospect of financial returns, and they will not wait indefinitely for those rewards to materialize. Economic satisfaction plays a fundamental role in building and maintaining the trust that is necessary for committed relationships.[28]

Economic satisfaction is a positive, affective (emotional) response to the economic rewards generated by a channel relationship. Economic rewards are ultimately financial. Why cast this as an emotional state, rather than as, say, utility? Why not speak in terms of money rather than affect?

The reason is that the players don't count and compare money directly. It is difficult to put an accounting valuation with confidence on many of these outcomes (such as higher market share or greater store traffic). And even if a valuation were to be made, it cannot be compared directly across organizations. One hundred thousand euros' worth of economic returns will satisfy one channel member but disappoint another.

Channel members do not react to results. They react to how the results compare with several baselines, such as what they consider possible, equitable, what they had expected, or what they expect to gain from their next best alternative use of the resources. Therefore, economic satisfaction, rather than economic outcomes, is a major factor that increases trust.

The reader may detect circular logic here. Organizations build alliances in order to produce outcomes and therefore to increase economic satisfaction. Now we learn that economic satisfaction increases trust, and therefore builds alliances. Is economic performance a cause or an effect of committed relationships?

It is both. The better the alliance is doing financially, the more satisfied are the parties (at least, roughly), and the more they place their trust in the relationship. This builds commitment, which helps the parties expand their pie, increases satisfaction (unless the baseline went up more than the results did), enhances trust, and so forth.

Now we are in a difficult situation. We need results to build an alliance, but we need an alliance to generate results. This process must start somewhere. How do you build an alliance before having economic performance results to show?

Noneconomic Satisfaction Also Matters

A very substantial body of evidence indicates that trust is associated with a set of other properties, many of which have to do with the psychological state of noneconomic satisfaction. This is a positive, affective (i.e., emotional) response to the psychosocial aspects of the relationship.[29] A satisfied channel member finds interactions with the channel partner fulfilling, gratifying, and easy. Contacts with the other party are appreciated. It likes working with its partner and perceives the partner to be concerned, respectful, and willing to exchange ideas (one foundation of two-way communication).

Noneconomic satisfaction sounds interpersonal. It can also be an interorganizational property, one that reproduces itself over and over at the level of daily interactions among people working for channel organizations. In some circles, these positive sentiments are dismissed as being "nice but not necessary." These sentiments are even ridiculed as being irrelevant, or not "businesslike." Yet, study after study demonstrates that noneconomic satisfaction is tightly bound up with trust, which in turn is critical to building financially desirable alliances.

What produces noneconomic satisfaction? Two drivers stand out by their absence. One is the absence of dysfunctional conflict, which is lingering, unresolved intense disputes over major issues. The other is the absence of coercion by the other side. A party that sees its counterpart employing pressure, punishment, threats, and retribution experiences a rapid decline of positive sentiment, even if the relationship moves in a direction that the channel member favors.

In contrast, liberal use of noncoercive influence strategies, such as exchanging information, offering high-quality assistance, and making requests, effectively raises noneconomic satisfaction. These methods help to resolve conflict without appearing blunt or intrusive. By trying to influence partners in a noncoercive way, organizations create the impression of being accommodating, responsive problem solvers. Chapter 8 on power covers this issue in depth.

Noneconomic satisfaction is also bound up in perceptions of fairness on two fronts.[30] One is procedural fairness, the sense that one is treated equitably on a day-to-day basis, regardless of the rewards derived from the relationship. The other is distributive fairness, the sense that one gains equitable rewards from the relationship, regardless of daily interaction patterns. Distributive and procedural equity (discussed at length in Chapter 9) reinforce noneconomic satisfaction.

Picking the Partner and the Setting

At minimum, organizations are not good candidates for forging a committed relationship unless they possess *complementary capabilities*, which they could exploit to create competitive advantage. Given complementarity, organizations can attempt to ally by declaration: Each corporate headquarters can issue instructions that bonding will commence, effective immediately. Of course, this doesn't work, as has been demonstrated by many channel members! Trust is never awarded. It is earned. This takes time and effort, and may not work anyway.

This is why many organizations build on what they already have. When the parties have prior social and economic ties, they possess an asset (social capital). Frequently, they seek to leverage it by developing their ties further. In foreign markets, for example, firms that have a marketing arrangement with a distributor tend to add their new products to the existing arrangement, even if it is not the best channel for the product in isolation. Familiarity causes termination if organizations don't like what they find. Otherwise, familiarity breeds trust. Firms do business with firms they know, and they extend their network by working with firms that are known by the firms they know (referral).[31] Personal relationships and reputations between people in the channel organizations play an important role in making existing relationships deeper, increasing the social capital that is already embedded in them.[32]

Of course, organizations do not always work with organizations they know. In building trust with another organization, it is useful to select one with similar goals. Goal congruence is effective in dampening conflict (see Chapter 9 for further discussion). Channel Sketch 11.3 explains how a supplier, Fujitsu, swiftly built an alliance with a logistics provider, FedEx, from the ground up, beginning with congruent business objectives.

It has been demonstrated that some people are trusting as a personality trait. (Similarly, some people are given to cynicism and unlikely to trust under any circumstances.) There is evidence that the same is true for organizations. It is part of the culture of some companies to be trustworthy and to cultivate a reputation as such. (Others

CHANNEL SKETCH 11.3

Fujitsu and FedEx Build a Close Relationship[33]

This is a story of building an alliance from nothing in very little time.

In 1996, Fujitsu's PC division did 70 percent of its business in Japan. Fleeing fierce competition, Fujitsu entered the U.S. laptop market, only to discover the competitive situation was just as bad there. Disappointed with its performance, Fujitsu did a thorough review that pinpointed logistics as a major problem. Laptops were manufactured in Tokyo, then shipped by sea in large batches to two warehouses on the West Coast. The result was that channel partners were served too slowly.

In recognition that logistics is a channel competence, Fujitsu transferred all warehousing and distribution functions to a third party, FedEx. In October 1997, Fujitsu also made a FedEx-specific investment by opening a customer support center near Memphis, Tennessee, the FedEx superhub, but poorly served by other carriers. Fujitsu further increased its reliance on FedEx by closing one of its West Coast warehouses.

Fujitsu's site-specific asset in Memphis created close physical proximity, which fueled communication. FedEx then came up with a radical idea: Why bring finished laptops from Tokyo? Why not instead expand the Memphis facility to create *customized* laptops? One hurdle was how to do the final assembly: FedEx suggested CTI, a company that did such work for many other FedEx customers. (In turn, FedEx got the entire idea by working with another of its customers, Dell Computer. This is an excellent example of channel members offering economies of scope.)

Fujitsu implemented the idea. Subassemblies are flown from Osaka to Memphis and turned over to FedEx and to CTI. FedEx takes operational responsibility for the entire subassembly and customization process, and delivers the final product to the retailer or end-user.

Within a year, Fujitsu was no longer taking a month to supply mass-produced products to its channel. Instead, it transformed its business into customized production, with delivery guaranteed within *four days* of the placement of the order. The effect on Fujitsu's competitive advantage and profit is spectacular.

One analyst summarizes the alliance like this:

> Fujitsu entered the relationship with a spirit of true strategic alliance. The company didn't choose FedEx because it was the cheapest provider. Nor did it reward its purchasing managers for jerking around and lying to FedEx to save a few yen. Nor did it enter the "partnership" with an arm's-length, quasi-adversarial, hyper-legalistic, super-secretive, no-trust, lowest-cost-at-all-cost, dump-them-tomorrow-if-we-get-a-better-deal mind-set.
>
> Instead, it enlisted FedEx as a full, active, intimate partner. Fujitsu and FedEx people tackled Fujitsu's operational problems together—openly and cooperatively—and developed a revamped logistics package.

seek to disguise a culture of exploitation and dishonesty vis-à-vis trading partners.) To some extent, an organization's trustworthiness is a part of its culture.[34]

Some environments are conducive to building trust. Trust goes up in generous ("munificent") environments, ones that offer resources, growth, and ample opportunity. These environments provide every incentive to work together, with rewards to be had by everyone. Conversely, trust goes down in volatile, complex, unpredictable environments. These are risky, treacherous, and difficult, requiring constant monitoring and fast adaptation. Conditions like this strain any relationship and create many opportunities for misunderstanding and dispute.

Decision Structures That Enhance Trust

The decision making that goes on inside a marketing channel has a structure. One very important element of that structure is how much it is centralized in the upper reaches of an organization's hierarchy. This may be upstream or downstream. Whatever its source, *centralization* hurts trust.[35] Concentrating decision power in the upper echelons of one organization (as opposed to delegating decision making to the field level, preferably in both organizations) undermines the participation, cooperation, and daily interaction that help trust grow. Note, however, that centralization *is* a way for an organization to marshal its own resources to get things done. Centralized decision making should not be condemned, but one must acknowledge its cost in terms of building trust.

Another aspect of a channel's decision-making structure is *formalization*, the degree to which decision making is reduced to rules and explicit procedures. Formalization is widely considered to hurt trust. The reasoning is that this mechanistic approach to interactions robs the players of autonomy and thereby increases resentment. Formalization is also thought to be a signal that one party mistrusts the other, which invites reciprocity. However, recent evidence suggests that it is its *nature* that matters. Formalization can actually enhance positive attitudes and trust if it helps to clarify how tasks are to be done and who is responsible for doing them.[36] If it focuses on clarifying roles, it can be helpful rather than constraining. In this vein, the more that channel members agree about who is responsible for what (domain consensus), the higher their level of trust.

In general, the more channel members communicate, they more they also cooperate with each other on a daily basis. And the more they cooperate, the more they come to trust each other. Working together on issues of mutual relevance, such as on market plans, serves to build a basis for trust.

We are back to circular logic: Working together is both a cause (immediately) and an effect (later) of trust. This circularity—that actions that enhance trust and commitment create further trust and commitment—is why alliances take time to build.

So How Do You Manufacture Trust in a Channel?

Consider that you are the top management of a downstream channel member desirous of building an upstream alliance with one of your suppliers. Your channel's trust level is low, and you intend to improve it. What should you do? Increase communication? Seek greater cooperation? Reduce conflict? Make conflict more functional? Align your organization's goals? Reduce your efforts to influence the other party coercively, substituting reasoned arguments and greater accommodation instead? Pay more attention to issues of fairness?

All these actions are designed to create properties of your relationship that match properties of trusting relationships. Here is the paradox: Even though you, as top management, are dedicated to building trust, neither your employees, nor the employees of your counterpart organization, will be inclined to implement your plans. Why? Because they don't trust each other. And even if you can induce your own employees to make the effort, your channel counterpart may block their implementation and ignore your best efforts.

The top management of organizations can attempt to create a *structure* conducive to building trust and hope that employees will alter their everyday behavior accordingly. For example, organizations can balance each other's dependence by such actions as granting selectivity and creating idiosyncratic investments. Doing so in forgiving environments with little uncertainty or volatility makes it more likely that trust will take root. And organizations can eschew centralized decision making and can use their influence over their own personnel to elicit desired behavior, hoping for reciprocity.

Ultimately, however, structures and policies to implement them only create a foundation for trust. From there, it is the daily interactions between people and the accumulation of experience that turn a structural opportunity into an operating reality. The bad news is that this is a slow, expensive, and uncertain process. The good news is that trust encourages the behaviors that maintain trust. Further, *a marketing channel with high levels of trust is difficult for competition to imitate.*

MOVING A TRANSACTION THROUGH STAGES OF DEVELOPMENT TO REACH ALLIANCE STATUS

From the Cradle to the Grave: The "Life" of a Marketing Channel Partnership

An appealing way to think about a close marketing channel relationship is to use the metaphor of a living creature, which moves through a life cycle marked by stages of development. An alliance represents the peak, the best and most intense part, of the close channel relationship's existence. Let us take a hypothetical supplier, Omega Industries, and a hypothetical distributor, Annecy Ltd. These two organizations could form a marketing channel that is a series of ongoing transactions, each evaluated on its own merits, with each side ready to terminate or reduce business dealings easily. This series of discrete transactions *is* a marketing channel, but is not a close relationship. This channel could develop into an ongoing committed relationship by passing through up to five phases, in this order.[37] Figure 11.3 gives background on the phases. Here is a brief sketch, with representative quotations from managers engaged in the phases.

Phase 1: Awareness. Omega is aware that Annecy is a feasible exchange partner but has not made contact to explore doing business or upgrading their one-by-one business dealings into a stronger, more continuous relationship. (We could also turn the scenario around, making Annecy the focal party, aware that Omega is a feasible supplier to upgrade to a preferred partnership level.) This phase can last a very long time, with no

Relationship Stage 1: Awareness	Relationship Stage 2: Exploration	Relationship Stage 3: Expansion	Relationship Stage 4: Commitment	Relationship Stage 5: Decline and Dissolution
• One organization sees another as a feasible exchange partner • Little interaction • Networks are critical: One player recommends another • Physical proximity matters: Parties more likely to be aware of each other • Experience with transactions in other domains (other products, markets, functions) can be used to identify parties	• Testing, probing by both sides • Investigation of each other's natures and motives • Interdependence grows • Bargaining is intensive • Selective revealing of information is initiated and must be reciprocated • Great sensitivity to issues of power and justice • Norms begin to emerge • Role definitions become more elaborated • Key feature: Each side draws inferences and tests them • This phase is easily terminated by either side	• Benefits expand for both sides • Interdependence expands • Risk taking increases • Satisfaction with results leads to greater motivation and deepening commitment • Goal congruence increases • Cooperation increases • Communication increases • Alternative partners look less attractive • Key feature: Momentum must be maintained. To progress, each party must seek new areas of activity and maintain consistent efforts to create mutual payoffs	• Each party invests to build and maintain the relationship • Long-time horizon • Parties may be aware of alternatives but do not court them • High expectations on both sides • High mutual dependence • High trust • Partners resolve conflict and adapt to each other and to their changing environment • Shared values or contractual mechanisms (such as shared risk) reinforce mutual dependence • Key features: Loyalty, adaptability, continuity, high mutual dependence set these relationships apart	• One side tends to spark it • Mounting dissatisfaction leads one side to hold back investment • Lack of investment provokes the other side to reciprocate • Dissolution may be abrupt but is usually gradual • Key feature: It takes two to build but only one to undermine. Decline often sets in without the two parties' realization
1	2	3	4	5

FIGURE 11.3 **Phases of Relationships in Marketing Channels**

real progress. Or it can disappear: Either firm could discard the other from its partnership consideration set. Or the arrangement can move to:

Phase 2: Exploration. Omega and Annecy investigate forging a stable relationship together. They may test each other during a trial and evaluation period (which can be lengthy, especially for important, risky, or complex channel flows). Each side forecasts and weighs the costs and benefits of creating a close marketing channel together.

> You can't start out with a full-blown relationship. It's got to be incremental. You get closer as each side takes small steps.
> If it's going to be long-lasting, it doesn't happen overnight.[38]

If the players judge the calculation promising, they engage in communication and negotiation. Norms (expected patterns of behavior) may begin to form in the process. Mutual trust and joint satisfaction should start to grow. This delicate phase resembles two people in a dating relationship: These early behaviors have a great impact because each side is drawing inferences about the other, but without much history to use as a basis. How each partner uses its power is important here in determining whether both sides want to move on to:

Phase 3: Expansion. Omega and Annecy grow their relationship considerably. Each is deriving greater benefits, developing greater motivation, and elaborating their relationship. Trust is spiraling; interdependence is increasing. Annecy and Omega cooperate and feel they are pursuing common goals. Interaction becomes much greater than strictly necessary, in part because each side's personnel likes the communication.

> When I first started, I didn't know whether I could believe what they told me, but experience, facts you collect, the transactions, build trust.
>
> We went through a period of trial and error. We learned from mistakes and incrementally became part of their operation. Every relationship is unique, so it takes time.
>
> Over time, you build a history of situations, compromises, and solutions. You learn the unwritten rules and how they want to play the game, which makes it increasingly easier to do business.
>
> The supplier kept pushing us, saying, if you do this, I'll do that. We did, and he did. He would suggest that if we would work with this particular program then he felt sure it would result in X amount of additional business. And it did. He always did what he said he would do. We needed to be encouraged because we had been operating in a slow-moving industry and were cautious about trying something different. This was how it grew from a very small beginning to a very significant relationship today.[39]

After this has gone on for some time, the relationship passes to:

Phase 4: Commitment. The alliance is now easily recognizable by the stability both Annecy and Omega believe to exist in their relationship. Further, both sides invest heavily to maintain the strong partnership they have achieved. Neither side is very open to overtures by other firms: They prefer doing business with each other.

> It takes a lot of work to maintain the relationship, including day-to-day communications across all levels of both organizations to constantly improve service. You need a breadth of relationships to catch problems immediately.
>
> We look at them as if they were another division, an extension of us. When I talk to them, it is like calling someone who works for us directly.
>
> Here there is serious involvement together which differentiates us from more typical customer relations. Honesty and understanding makes the relationship different. We're in this together and the attitude is, here's what I need, what's that going to do to you?
>
> We want continuity. We're interested in his being a successful business so that we are successful together. . . . It takes a lot of communication and trust.
>
> We are constantly changing things to try and improve the way we do business together. We will experiment with new ideas, test new processes, try something different. Costs are incurred on both sides but we are willing to pay them. We have learned a lot from them. They have made us a better printing company because they are demanding, innovative, and willing to try things.
>
> If they ask for some cooperation we will do all we possibly can to accommodate their requests—and vice versa. But if we can't do something, then we say so, and that's OK. It's not as comfortable, but you do what you can.
>
> Am I going to react any differently, represent [their] interests in this business any differently than I am other important customers, some of whom do more business with us? Yes, there will be better service, extra effort, a sense of urgency difference. There's no doubt about it. Somehow they are always first to get the creative programs, the first with whom we had long-term development discussions. It's because they work very, very hard

at developing the relationship that says we are still human beings, and straightforward as mature businesses can be, we are still driven by subjective things even though we may not want to admit it. The businesses are still run by people.[40]

But strains occur, even in committed relationships. Sometimes they move to:

Phase 5: Decline and Dissolution.   The Omega–Annecy relationship declines to the point that they cease to have a close partnership. They may resume their old one-deal-at-a-time transactions, but are more likely to cease doing business at all. Dissolutions are usually accompanied by acrimony. Frequently, they are initiated by one side, which has grown dissatisfied with the arrangement. This side begins to withdraw and to behave in a manner inconsistent with commitment. This annoys the other party, which often reciprocates with neglectful, damaging, even destructive behavior. Decline rapidly takes on a momentum of its own.

Decline and dissolution often happen because one party takes the relationship for granted and doesn't work to keep it going. Sometimes, one party sabotages the relationship, perhaps to free itself to move on to other opportunities. Usually, decline is a lingering process. It may not be apparent that decline has set in until it is too far advanced to be repaired.

Managing the Phases

One implication of the phases-of-development idea is that relationships are difficult to build quickly and difficult to build from the ground up. Development takes time, particularly if the targeted partner firms do no business with each other as yet. Every existing channel member is a potential asset in this respect, because extant business, even if minor, means the awareness and exploration phases can proceed much faster and the relationship can be upgraded more swiftly and surely.

The exploration phase is particularly sensitive. Intangible perceptions (such as goal congruence) play a major role, partly because the parties know each other poorly and have little shared history. Early interactions and outcomes are also crucial: They weigh heavily in the projections and calculations each side makes. The expectations developed during the exploration phase determine whether partnership becomes achievable.

In the expansion phase, management must ensure that each side perceives that the benefits are being shared equitably. This is an exciting stage, when morale is high and sentiments are positive. Managements of both sides can use this stage to deepen the interdependence of the marketing channel members, setting the stage for commitment to stabilize.

In the commitment stage, the relationship has a substantial history, marked by investments, interdependence, and strong norms. Here, intangible factors (such as the perception of goal congruence) are less important than they were in exploration, simply because the partnership has a rich infrastructure to make it robust. In the commitment stage, management must be attentive to maintaining the relationship, lest it slip into decline and dissolution. If the relationship moves to the last stage, it is not easy to salvage.

A caveat is in order here. The phases-of-development idea is an appealing way to think about creating an alliance and keeping it going. However, relationship development is frequently not as linear, orderly, and sequential as the five stages would seem.[41] On a daily basis, relationships may be experienced as a series of episodes, or critical incidents. These events help the players define their common purpose, set boundaries to their relationship, create value (and claim their share of it), and evaluate what they are getting from the relationship. By repeated interaction, firms develop enough of these critical incidents to move their relationship from a series of transactions to a real partnership. And when they go back over their history, managers may tend to *remember* their experiences as corresponding to stages—which they can *recognize* only after considerable development has occurred.

In other words, relationships do not develop in an orderly way. The bad news is that it is difficult to say with confidence what stage a relationship is in during much of its history. The good news is that if a relationship seems to be regressing (e.g., moving backward from expansion to exploration), in all likelihood, there is no real cause for alarm. This regression will appear in retrospect as a blip or a minor disturbance: The relationship is not doomed to deteriorate.

PUTTING IT ALL TOGETHER: WHAT IT TAKES AND WHEN IT PAYS TO CREATE A MARKETING CHANNEL ALLIANCE

We have arrived at the point of taking stock. We know that marketing channel alliances, *once achieved*, function admirably. They generate competitive advantage, with attendant financial rewards. When they work, they are capable of outperforming a channel owned by one organization. They function so well that the customer cannot see where one company stops and another begins. Shouldn't every marketing channel aim to become an alliance?

Yet, we know that an alliance is more akin to truffles than to wheat. A truffle is a type of mushroom prized by gourmet cooks. Wheat can be grown commercially to order, according to a known formula. Truffles cannot be produced to order. No one knows how to grow them. They appear randomly in nature, given certain conditions. This is why there are truffle hunters but not truffle farmers so far.

Similarly, the conditions that favor an alliance can be created, but an alliance may or may not grow up in them. Unlike wheat, alliances cannot be produced at will. Like truffles, alliances are often discovered by looking where the right conditions hold. Management's ability to create the right conditions is limited, and truffles don't always appear where they should be expected. In other words, many firms have tried unsuccessfully to build a channel alliance. They often discover that they *have* an alliance, which they may have failed to appreciate. These alliances occur seemingly spontaneously, without top management direction, due to the (often unsuspected) efforts of field personnel.

What are the right conditions? This depends on the firm's strategy, industry, and market. *For most circumstances, an alliance may not be necessary.* Building one may even be counterproductive, because the costs of alliance building are so substantial that they may outweigh the benefits. A more typical marketing channel may not only be perfectly adequate but may generate better net results. In particular, there is a substantial opportunity cost to an alliance because few firms have the resources to develop intense relationships with all the organizations necessary to cover their markets. A firm must select its alliances and invest in them. The risk is real that the firm has picked the wrong partner, or that it would be better off with several more mundane but less demanding channel relationships.

This said, an alliance is appropriate when three conditions hold simultaneously.[42] Let us return to Omega (upstream) and Annecy (downstream). Their alliance is more likely to hold together and to meet their expectations when:

1. One side has special needs.
2. The other side has the capability to meet these needs.
3. Each side faces barriers to exiting the relationship.

Conditions one and two create the basis for distinctive value added, which is the foundation of a strategic alliance. Special needs means that most parties with these needs will not find satisfaction in the marketplace. They will be poorly served by using a mundane transaction and by using most of the available channel members. The channel member's ability to meet those out-of-the-ordinary needs is the basis for exchange between these two parties, *to the exclusion of most other possible pairings.*

Condition three, exit barriers, is necessary to prevent one side from exploiting the other. For example, if Omega has special needs (say, for product handling and customization) and Annecy can meet them, fruitful exchange goes on—but not indefinitely. Annecy may make investments specific to Omega, creating a vulnerability. Or Annecy might train customers to value Omega's brands—only to have Omega appoint a new distributor to "harvest" this loyal customer base. Annecy can be exploited by Omega. But if Omega builds barriers to exiting its relationship, the situation stabilizes, as Omega now values Annecy more highly. Ideally, both Omega and Annecy will develop enduring reasons to stay in their relationship.

What kinds of barriers to exit exist? In general, relationships with strong norms, or with mutual dependence, are so difficult to disentangle that the parties prefer to invest to keep them going.

The Caterpillar situation (Channel Sketch 11.2) illustrates these three conditions well. (1) Caterpillar has special needs for postsales support and market feedback. (2) Its small set of dealers is well able to meet these needs. They choose to do so, creating exceptional value. Neither side uses its valued position against the other, decade after decade. This situation seems utopian: How could it be duplicated 186 times and last so long? Put differently, why doesn't the relationships degenerate at some point, due to perceived exploitation by one side or the other? It is because (3) strong relationship norms of solidarity and fairness, combined with heavy and nonredeployable investments *by both sides*, have created a relationship neither side wishes to leave—or can afford to abandon. These relationships are full of conflict—but the conflict stays functional and serves to motivate each partner to do better.

If these conditions do exist (special needs, the ability to meet them, and mutual barriers to exit), an alliance is viable and valuable. Although we do not know how to "manufacture" commitment with certainty, we do know that alliances need mutual dependence and the perception of mutual commitment. Asymmetric commitment doesn't last long. And to convince the other side of false commitment is difficult: Organizations involved in marketing channel flows judge each other's intentions with reasonable accuracy. In doing so, they rely more heavily on actions, particularly by people at the field level, than on what top management announces. And they pay attention to history, both their own and the history that underlies a firm's reputation for fair business dealings with channel members.

The foundation of alliance is trust, a combination of confidence in the other party's honesty and in its genuine interest in your welfare. Trust, in turn, flourishes under conditions of satisfaction with noneconomic outcomes, associated with the absence of coercion and of dysfunctional conflict. (Functional conflict and trust *do* coexist easily.) Perceptions of procedural and distributive fairness (equity in daily functioning and in the split of rewards) also support trust. They do so by enhancing noneconomic satisfaction.

Economic satisfaction is both a driver of alliances and a result of an alliance. This is because as a party derives more financial rewards from the relationship, its trust increases. This strengthens the alliance, which then works together more effectively, generating even more rewards and accelerating an upward spiral of commitment.

Who might be a good partner? The best place to look is in the set of channel members one already knows where some social capital can be enhanced. Particularly good candidates are firms with strengths and weaknesses that offset yours: Together, you have complementary capabilities.

When is alliance building more likely to work? Favorable settings are environments that offer resources, growth, and opportunity, whereas less favorable settings are compex, volatile, unpredictable. Working with firms that decentralize decision making and that have a culture of cultivating trust raises the odds of success. So, too, does agreement about who is responsible for what.

Finally, two fundamental factors are crucial to all efforts to build trust and create alliances. The first is candid, mutual, frequent communication. The second is the passage of time. Alliances must be nurtured—must mature, grow and develop into a valuable asset. They cannot be built quickly (although they can be destroyed rather rapidly). A strategy of building and maintaining channel alliances requires persistence, resources, and patience.

Discussion Questions

1. You are manager of a manufacturer. You are highly committed to a distributor. You suspect your distributor is committed to you, but you are unsure. Should you try to project that you are not as highly committed as you are? Why or why not? How would you go about projecting lower commitment than is true? How well would you expect your efforts to work? Why?

2. A powerful idiosyncratic investment is mingling your identity with that of your channel member. Why? If you are the manufacturer, how could you do this mingling, and how could you induce your downstream channel member to cooperate? Now try the same exercise in reverse: How would you, the downstream channel member, mingle your identity with the upstream channel member's image, and how would you induce the upstream partner to cooperate?

3. What are upstream and downstream motives to ally? What are motives not to ally? Are upstream and downstream motives congruent?

4. Marketing channel alliances are capable of extraordinary results. Should every management focus on alliances? If not, why? Are there other ways of generating exceptional results?

5. As a supplier, what sort of program could you devise to build trust with a distributor? What distributor types would you target? How well would you expect your program to work? Now try the same exercise in reverse: What program can a distributor devise to build trust with a manufacturer, how well should it work, and what manufacturers would you target?

6. Channel Sketch 11.1 covers the private-label industry in France. France supermarket chains have a history of bargaining extremely hard with downstream channel members. If you were management of a successful small firm and you were approached to become a private-label supplier to a giant such as Carrefour, would you agree? Why, and under what conditions?

7. The idea of phases of a relationship has been described as being a good idea in theory but a difficult idea to put into practice. Do you agree? Why? How would you know what phase you were in? And how would you, as a manager, try to drive your firm to progress from an early phase to a later phase?

Notes

1. Thomas L. Doorley, "Corporate Strategies: Building Successful Alliances," *Crossborder Monitor*, 5, no. 10 (1997), pp. 1, 9.

2. Gary L. Frazier, "Organizing and Managing Channels of Distribution," *Journal of the Academy of Marketing Sciences*, 27, no. 2 (1999), pp. 226–40.

3. Ibid., p. 238.

4. Adam J. Fein and Sandy D. Jap, "Manage Consolidation in the Distribution Channel," *Sloan Management Review*, 41 (fall 1999), pp. 61–72.

5. Nirmalya Kumar, "The Power of Trust in Manufacturer–Retailer Relationships," *Harvard Business Review*, 60 (November–December), pp. 92–106.

6. Keysuk Kim, "On Determinants of Joint Action in Industrial Distributor–Supplier Relationships: Beyond Economic Efficiency," *International Journal of Research in Marketing*, 16 (September 1999), pp. 217–36.

7. Robert M. Morgan and Shelby D. Hunt, "The Commitment-Trust Theory of Relationship Marketing," *Journal of Marketing*, 58 (July 1994), pp. 20–38.

8. Roderick M. Kramer, "Trust and Distrust in Organizations: Emerging Perspectives, Enduring Questions," *Annual Review of Psychology*, 50 (1999), pp. 569–98.

9. Zhan G. Li and Rajiv P. Dant, "Effects of Manufacturers' Strategies on Channel Relationships," *Industrial Marketing Management*, 28, no. 1 (1999), pp. 131–43.

10. Judy A. Siguaw, Penny M. Simpson, and Thomas L. Baker, "Effects of Supplier Orientation on Distributor Market Orientation and the Channel Relationship: The Distributor Perspective," *Journal of Marketing*, 62 (July 1998), pp. 99–111; Rajagopalan Sethuraman, James C. Anderson, and James A. Narus, "Partnership Advantage and Its Determinants in Distributor and Manufacturer Working Relationships," *Journal of Business Research*, 17 (December 1988), pp. 327–47.

11. Dawn Iacobucci and Jonathan D. Hibbard, "Toward an Encompassing Theory of Business Marketing Relationships (BMRs) and Interpersonal Commercial Relationships (ICRs): An Empirical Examination," *Journal of Interactive Marketing* (2000).

12. Erin Anderson, William T. Ross, and Barton Weitz, "Commitment and Its Consequences in the American Agency System of Selling Insurance," *Journal of Risk and Insurance*, 65, no. 4 (1998), pp. 637–69.

13. Sandy D. Jap, "Pie-Expansion Efforts: Collaboration Processes in Buyer–Supplier Relationships," *Journal of Marketing Research*, 36, no. 4, (1999); Manohar Kalwani and Narakesari Narayandas, "Long-Term Manufacturer–Supplier Relationships: Do They Pay Off for Supplier Firms?" *Journal of Marketing*, 59 (January 1995), pp. 1–16.

14. Barbara Bund Jackson, "Build Customer Relationships That Last," *Harvard Business Review*, 63 (November–December 1985), pp. 120–28.

15. Jan B. Heide and Anne S. Miner, "The Shadow of the Future: Effects of Anticipated Interaction and Frequency of Contact on Buyer–Seller Cooperation," *Academy of Management Journal*, 35 (June 1992), pp. 265–91.

16. Allen M. Weiss, Erin Anderson, and Deborah J. MacInnis, "Reputation Management as a Motive for Sales Structure Decisions," *Journal of Marketing*, 63 (October 1999), pp. 74–89.

17. Erin Anderson and Barton Weitz, "Determinants of Continuity in Conventional Channel Dyads," *Marketing Science*, 8 (fall 1989), pp. 310–23.

18. Jakki Mohr and John R. Nevin, "Communication Strategies in Marketing Channels: A Theoretical Perspective," *Journal of Marketing*, October 1990, pp. 36–51.

19. Much of this section draws on Erin Anderson and Barton Weitz, "The Use of Pledges to Build and Sustain Commitment in Distribution Channels," *Journal of Marketing Research*, 24 (February 1992), pp. 18–34.

20. Akbar Zaheer, Bill McEvily, and Vincenzo Perrone, "Does Trust Matter? Exploring the Effects of Interorganizational and Interpersonal Trust on Performance," *Organization Science*, 9 (March–April 1998), pp. 141–59.

21. William T. Ross, Erin Anderson, and Barton Weitz, "Performance in Principal–Agent Dyads: The Causes and Consequences of Perceived Asymmetry of Commitment to the Relationship," *Management Science*, 43 (May 1997), pp. 680–704.

22. Adeline Trégouët, "Alimentaire: La Nouvelle Offensive des Marques Distributeurs," *Capital*, 10 (November 1999), pp. 92–94.

23. Jap, Sandy D., "'Pie-Expansion' Efforts: Collaboration Processes in Buyer–Supplier Relationships," *Journal of Marketing Research*, 36 (November 1999), pp. 461–75.

24. Rodney L. Stump and Jan B. Heide, "Controlling Supplier Opportunism in Industrial Relations," *Journal of Marketing Research*, 33 (November 1996), pp. 431–41.

25. Donald V. Fites, "Make Your Dealers Your Partners," *Harvard Business Review*, 74 (March–April 1996), pp. 84–95.

26. Andrea Larson, "Network Dyads in Entrepreneurial Settings: A Study of the Governance of Exchange Relationships," *Administrative Science Quarterly*, 37 (March 1992), pp. 76–104. Quotation from p. 89.

27. Inge Geyskens, Jan-Benedict E. M. Steenkamp, and Nirmalya Kumar, "Generalizations About Trust in Marketing Channel Relationships Using Meta Analysis," *International Journal of Research in Marketing*, 15, no. 1 (1998), pp. 223–48.

28. Shankar Ganesan, "Determinants of Long-Term Orientation in Buyer–Seller Relationships," *Journal of Marketing*, 58 (April 1994), pp. 1–19.

29. Inge Geyskens, Jan-Benedict E. M. Steenkamp, and Nirmalya Kumar, "A Meta-Analysis of Satisfaction in Marketing Channel Relationships," *Journal of Marketing Research*, 36 (May 1999), pp. 223–38.

30. Nirmalya Kumar, Lisa K. Scheer, and Jan-Benedict E. M. Steenkamp, "The Effects of Supplier Fairness on Vulnerable Resellers," *Journal of Marketing Research*, 32 (February 1995), pp. 54–65.

31. Ranjay Gulati, "Alliances and Networks," *Strategic Management Journal*, 19, no. 1 (1998), pp. 293–317.

32. Barton A. Weitz and Sandy D. Jap, "Relationship Marketing and Distribution Channels," *Journal of the Academy of Marketing Science*, 23, no. 4 (1995), pp. 305–20.

33. Oren Harari, "The Logistics of Success," *Management Review*, 88, no. 6 (1999), pp. 24–26. Quotation from p. 25.

34. Jeffery H. Dyer and Harbir Singh, "The Relational View: Cooperative Strategy and Sources of Interorganizational Competitive Advantage," *Academy of Management Review*, 23, no. 4 (1998), pp. 660–79.

35. Frazier, "Organizing and Managing Channels of Distribution," *Journal of Marketing Sciences*, 27 (1999), pp. 226–40.

36. Robert Dahlstrom and Arne Nygaard, "An Empirical Investigation of Ex Post Transaction Costs in Franchised Distribution Channels," *Journal of Marketing Research*, 36 (May 1999), pp. 160–70.

37. Dwyer, F. Robert, Paul H. Schurr, and Sejo Oh, "Developing Buyer–Seller Relationships," *Journal of Marketing*, 51 (April 1987), pp. 11–27.

38. Larson, "Network Dyads in Entrepreneurial Settings." Quotations from p. 88.

39. Ibid. First three quotations from p. 88, and fourth quotation from pp. 89–90.

40. Ibid. Quotations 1, 2, 3 taken from p. 91, 4 from p. 92, 5 from p. 94, 6 from p. 96, and 7 from p. 97.

41. James C. Anderson, "Relationships in Business Markets: Exchange Episodes, Value Creation, and Their Empirical Assessment," *Journal of the Academy of Marketing Science*, 23, no. 4 (1995), pp. 346–50.

42. Barbara Bund Jackson, "Build Customer Relationships That Last," *Harvard Business Review*, 63 (November–December 1985), pp. 120–28.

12

Legal Constraints on Marketing Channel Policies

LEARNING OBJECTIVES

After reading this chapter, you will:

- Understand the array of channel policies that are available for channel management
- Know the types of channel activities that are subject to governmental scrutiny
- Understand the difference between per se and rule-of-reason criteria
- Be familiar with the major U.S. legal cases that shape channel practices

Channel managers can use many policies to administer distribution systems. However, some of these policies restrain or redirect the activities of the various members of channels, and may affect the competitiveness of the overall market. As such, they can fall under legal antitrust scrutiny.

The purpose of this chapter is twofold. First, is to catalog a variety of policies that are available for managing channels and explain the reasons why they might be adopted. Second, it lays out when and how such policies might run afoul of U.S. federal antitrust laws. The chapter focuses primarily on legal stances on these policies in the United States, although the discussion of each policy's *business* purpose is useful regardless of the market in which the channel manager operates.

The policies addressed below are as follows:

- Market coverage policies
- Customer coverage policies
- Pricing policies

- Product line policies
- Selection and termination policies
- Ownership policies

The principal federal antitrust laws affecting the setting of these policies are listed in Table 12.1.

MARKET COVERAGE POLICIES

One of the key elements of channel management is deciding how many sales outlets should be established in a given geographic area and what kind of participation in the marketing flows should be required from each of the outlets so that the needs of existing

TABLE 12.1

Principal U.S. Federal Laws Affecting Marketing Channel Management

Act	Key Provisions
Sherman Antitrust Act, 1890	1. Prohibits contracts, combinations, or conspiracies in restraint of interstate or foreign commerce.
Clayton Antitrust Act, 1914	Where competition is, or may be, substantially lessened, it prohibits: 1. Price discrimination in sales or leasing of goods 2. Exclusive dealing 3. Tying contracts 4. Interlocking directorates among competitors 5. Mergers and acquisitions
Federal Trade Commission (FTC) Act, 1914	1. Prohibits unfair or deceptive trade practices injurious to competition or a competitor. 2. Sets up FTC to determine unfairness.
Robinson-Patman Act, 1936	1. Discriminatory prices for goods are prohibited if they reduce competition at any point in the channel. 2. Discriminatory prices can be given in good faith to meet competition. 3. Brokerage allowances are allowed only if earned by an independent broker. 4. Sellers must give all services and promotional allowances to all buyers on a proportionately equal basis if the buyers are in competition. The offering of alternatives may be necessary. 5. Buyers are prohibited from knowingly inducing price or promotional discrimination. 6. Price discrimination can be legal if it results from real cost differences in serving different customers.
FTC Trade Practice Rules	1. Enforced by FTC. Defines unfair competition for individual industries. These practices are prohibited by the FTC. 2. Defines rules of sound practice. These rules are not enforced by the FTC, but are recommended.

and potential customers may be adequately served. Chapter 10 discusses in depth the channel design and management issues concerning channel intensity. From a legal perspective, channel intensity is linked to the concept of market coverage, about which there is significant legal concern.

Implicit in the term *market coverage* are issues concerned with geography or territory. The more a channel structure moves away from intensive to selective coverage, the fewer resellers of a particular brand there will be in any given area. Selective and exclusive coverage policies have been called "territorial restrictions" by antitrust enforcement agencies, because they are used by suppliers to limit the number of resellers in a defined territory. In reality, territorial assignments are rewards or spatial allocations given by suppliers adopting selective or exclusive market coverage policies in return for distributors' promises to cultivate the geography they have been given.

The supplier's objective in instituting territorial and a number of other kinds of so-called "vertical restraints" is to limit the extent of *intrabrand competition*. A critical issue that has evolved in antitrust cases is whether such policies actually promote (or at least do not substantially lessen) *interbrand competition*. Intrabrand competition is competition among wholesalers or retailers of the same brand (e.g., Coca-Cola or Chevrolet). Interbrand competition is competition among all the suppliers of different brands of the same generic product (e.g., brands of soft drinks or automobiles). The rationale behind restricting intrabrand competition is that by protecting resellers of its brand from competition among themselves, a supplier will supposedly improve their effectiveness against resellers of other brands. From an interorganization management perspective, the attempt to dampen intrabrand competition in order to strengthen interbrand competition is very sensible. A manufacturer would often rather have the channel members handling its brand compete with those of other brands than compete among themselves.

In the language of antitrust enforcement, territorial restrictions range from absolute confinement of reseller sales, which is intended to completely foreclose or eliminate intrabrand competition, to lesser territorial restrictions, designed to inhibit such competition. These lesser restrictions include areas of primary responsibility, profit pass-over arrangements, and location clauses. For example, a manufacturer may prohibit its bricks-and-mortar resellers from engaging in Internet selling, which is essentially without geographic boundaries.

Absolute confinement involves a promise by a channel member that it will not sell outside its assigned territory. Often combined with such a promise is a pledge by the supplier not to sell to anyone else in that territory, an arrangement known as an exclusive distributorship. On the other hand, an *airtight* territory exists when absolute confinement is combined with an exclusive distributorship. On the other hand, an *area of primary responsibility* requires the channel member to use its best efforts—or to attain a quantified performance level—to maintain effective distribution of the supplier's goods in the territory specifically assigned to it. Failure to meet performance targets may result in termination, but the channel member is free to sell outside its area, and other wholesalers or retailers may sell in its territory.

Profit pass-over arrangements require that a channel member who sells to a customer located outside its assigned territory compensate the distributor in whose territory the customer is located. Such compensation is ostensibly to reimburse the distributor for its efforts to stimulate demand in its territory and for the cost of providing services on which the channel member might have capitalized.

Finally, a *location clause* specifies the site of a channel member's place of business. Such clauses are used to "space" resellers in a given territory so that each has a "natural" market comprising those customers who are closest to the reseller's location. However, the reseller may sell to any customer walking through its door. Furthermore, the customers located closest to it may decide to purchase at more distant locations.

Any attempt to confine wholesalers' or retailers' selling activities to one area may be viewed either as a restraint of trade or as an unfair method of competition and therefore may be challenged under the Sherman Act or Section 5 of the FTC Act. The dominant antitrust perspective relative to territorial restrictions (market coverage policies) was established on June 23, 1977, when the Supreme Court handed down a decision in the *Sylvania* case.[1] Because of the significance of the *Sylvania* case, we devote some time to understanding it.

Prior to 1962, Sylvania, a manufacturer of television sets, sold its sets through both independent and company-owned distributors to a large number of independent retailers. RCA dominated the market at the time, holding 60 to 70 percent of national sales, with Zenith and Magnavox as major rivals. Sylvania had only 1 to 2 percent of the market. In 1962, Sylvania decided to abandon efforts at saturation distribution and chose instead to phase out its wholesalers and sell directly to a smaller group of franchised retailers. Sylvania retained sole discretion to determine how many retailers would operate in any geographic area, and, in fact, at least two retailers were franchised in every metropolitan center of more than 100,000 people. Dealers were free to sell anywhere and to any class of customers, but agreed to operate only from locations approved by Sylvania. A critical factor in the decision was Sylvania's desire to decrease the likelihood of one retailer free riding on the efforts of another retailer's marketing activities in the area.

Continental TV was one of Sylvania's most successful retailers in northern California. After a series of disagreements arising from Sylvania's authorizing a new outlet near one of Continental's best locations, Continental opened a new outlet in Sacramento, although its earlier request for approval for that location had been denied. Sylvania then terminated Continental's franchise. In resulting litigation, Continental counterclaimed against Sylvania. The Court sided with Sylvania, which had argued that the use of its territorial allocation policy permitted its marketing channels to compete more successfully against those established by its large competitors.

In its decision, the Court favored the promotion of interbrand competition even if intrabrand competition were restricted. It indicated that territorial restrictions encourage interbrand competition by allowing the manufacturer to achieve certain efficiencies in the distribution of its products. And, in a footnote, the Court recognized that the imposition of such restrictions is consistent with increased societal demands that manufacturers directly assume responsibility for the safety and quality of their products. As a result of the Court's decision, territorial restrictions, when challenged, are to be evaluated under a "rule of reason" doctrine in which proof must be established that the restrictions substantially lessen interbrand competition. Furthermore, the burden is on the plaintiff to prove that the restraints are unreasonable. (For definitions of the various legal rules applied in vertical restraint antitrust cases, see Table 12.2.)

TABLE 12.2
Legal Rules Used in Antitrust Enforcement

Per se illegality	The marketing policy is automatically unlawful regardless of the reasons for the practice and without extended inquiry into its effects. It is only necessary for the complainant to prove the occurrence of the conduct and antitrust injury.
Modified rule of reason (also called "quick look")	The marketing policy is presumed to be anticompetitive if evidence of the existence and use of significant market power is found, subject to rebuttal by the defendant.
Rule of reason	Before a decision is made about the legality of a marketing policy, it is necessary to undertake a broad inquiry into the nature, purpose, and effect of the policy. This requires an examination of the facts peculiar to the contested policy, its history, the reasons why it was implemented, and its competitive significance.
Per se legality	The marketing policy is presumed legal.

Empirical research suggests that manufacturers in fact do use a wide array of efficiency-related reasons to justify territorial restrictions in their channels.[2] Free-riding concerns, such as those operative in Sylvania's decision to impose restrictions, have been shown to be important. But beyond this, vertical restrictions have been shown to be more likely when (1) distributors have superior market information to that of the manufacturer; (2) detecting distributor violations of the restrictions is easier; (3) distributors invest more in manufacturer-specific assets; (4) competition at the manufacturer level is more intense; and (5) distributors are willing to limit their sales to this manufacturer's product. Of these reasons, the last two could be anticompetitive, but the first three are efficiency motivated and support a rule-of-reason legal stance.

Although the use of territorial restrictions in the United States is widespread and, for the most part, legal, treatment of territorial restrictions varies elsewhere in the world. For example, until 2000, European Union Law (first established in the Treaty of Rome) held to the premise that all territorial restriction agreements were distortions of free trade, whether vertical (i.e., between channel members at different levels of distribution) or horizontal (i.e., among competitors). The EC competition rules essentially required manufacturers to supply goods to anyone who wanted to sell them. The only way in which manufacturers could employ policies such as selective distribution was for them to secure "exemption" from the rules from the EC headquarters in Brussels.[3] Exemptions were granted in three industries: cars, consumer electronics, and perfume. In the case of cars and electronics, selective distribution was permitted on the grounds that the products were complex and needed after-sales service. For perfume, the justification was that the products were luxury goods, which depended for their appeal on an aura of exclusivity maintained by high price, large investments in marketing, and a sophisticated sales environment.[4]

In 1999, the European Commission worked on relaxing the rules on vertical restraints so as to impose a "single block exemption" rule instead, to take effect in early

2000. Under this exemption, in any case where the firm in question has less than 30 percent market share, it can engage in distribution agreements with its distributors or retailers without explicit permission. Any restrictive business agreement involving firms with more than 30 percent market share is still prohibited without an individual exemption from the Commission.[5] Clearly, it is wise to check carefully into specific regulations pertaining in each region of the world in which one's products are sold, because regulations vary.

CUSTOMER COVERAGE POLICIES

Suppliers may wish to set policies regarding to whom wholesalers or retailers may resell their goods and services. For a variety of reasons, suppliers may wish to reserve certain customers as "house accounts." It includes the desire to maintain close relationships with highly valuable customers, their requirements for technical assistance, the efficiency associated with serving accounts on a direct basis, the expected profits on the sale, the need for price concessions to win certain accounts, and, in the case of some retailers, such as Home Depot and Wal-Mart, the insistence of accounts to be sold on a direct basis. In other cases, suppliers may set customer coverage policies that have the goal of assuring that their goods and services will be sold by intermediaries capable of providing specific service outputs to their customers. This way, suppliers can be confident that their products are handled only by competent resellers.

Many manufacturers have used such policies in their attempts to prevent the emergence of "gray markets," which appear when their brands are sold by unauthorized resellers. Clauses in contracts written by manufacturers often stipulate that authorized dealers are prohibited from selling their brands to anyone but bona fide end-users. Authorized dealers are often tempted to sell off their excess inventories to unauthorized dealers, such as 47th Street Photo, Kmart, Syms, and other well-known discounters.

In addition, suppliers might wish to allocate different accounts to different intermediaries.[6] This limits intrabrand competition; the customer sees only one seller of the firm's product, not multiples. This policy can also facilitate segmented pricing, charging higher prices to segments of buyers with a higher willingness to pay for the firm's product. Or, the different service output demands of different segments may suggest that they be served by different intermediaries, each with the necessary skills to provide the demanded service outputs. Customer coverage policies could also be used for safety reasons; certain specialized dealers may be willing to screen potential customers or provide information required in a product's use (e.g., herbicides).

Such policies have an economic as well as a service rationale. As mentioned in the context of market coverage policies, permitting multiple channels to compete for the same customer makes it possible that one channel will bear the cost of providing valued service outputs to the customer, whereas another channel closes the sale. The free-riding channel does not bear the costs of channel flows necessary to provide the demanded service outputs, but does get the sale and the profit from the customer. In the long run, profits and economic viability will suffer in the cost-bearing channel. This is not in the manufacturer's best interest, because the failure of the cost-bearing channel will hurt the manufacturer as well as the free-riding channel.[7]

Indeed, many of the reasons for adopting customer coverage policies are the same as those for the adoption of market coverage policies. Customer coverage restrictions are basically exercises of coercive power (e.g., prohibitions on distributors reselling to discount houses) whereas territorial restrictions are basically exercises of reward power (e.g., the granting of a monopoly on the sale of a brand within a defined territory). For this reason, the antitrust concerns are handled similarly. The antitrust enforcement agencies and the courts refer to customer coverage policies as "customer" or "resale restrictions." Policies of this type become illegal when it can be shown that their effects tend to reduce competition substantially.

Despite their different characters, territorial and resale restrictions are treated identically under the law. Both are viewed as restraints of trade and, therefore, can be directly challenged under the Sherman Act. But, given the *Sylvania* decision, their legality is to be judged under a rule-of-reason approach. That is, they will be considered legal if they have not substantially lessened interbrand competition.

Although the presence of gray markets is not necessarily an antitrust concern, it may be useful for channel managers to note that, in 1988, the U.S. Supreme Court upheld a Customs Service regulation permitting gray market imports (although it did not endorse the entire concept of gray markets under all conditions). Gray markets into the United States are specifically permitted when the U.S. trademark is owned by a U.S. company with its own manufacturing facility abroad. Or when the U.S. trademark owner has established a subsidiary or affiliate abroad that is under the U.S. company's "common control."[8] Duracell batteries fit this description, for example, because they are manufactured abroad in plants owned by the company, as well as in U.S. plants under its control. Gray market importers in the United States generally obtain their goods from foreign distributors who buy the products overseas.[9] As a result of the lack of protection against gray market imports from the U.S. Customs Service, some manufacturers have used other laws to challenge gray market imports to the United States, such as the Lanham Act, which governs trademark use. Chapter 9 further discusses gray marketing as an international channel management issue.

PRICING POLICIES

Prices and price levels can be influenced in many ways throughout marketing channels. In fact, we have just finished discussing two of them—market coverage and customer coverage. Because these policies are both aimed at reducing or restraining the amount of intrabrand competition, the indirect effect of the reduction is, in theory, supposed to be an increase in the price of the brand from its level in the absence of the policies. If the price is at a "reasonable" level, this means gross margins available to resellers may be sufficient to pay for the provision of service outputs desired by end-users, as assessed by the supplier setting the policy. In other words, restrictions on intrabrand competition are indirectly supposed to result in higher prices and, thus, higher gross margins. Obviously, price competition induced by interbrand competitors can upset this arrangement.

Two policies that have a direct effect on price—price maintenance and price discrimination. We separate the discussion of the two because they have very different motivation, implementation, and antitrust concerns.

Price Maintenance

Price maintenance in marketing channels is the specification by suppliers, typically manufacturers, of the prices below or above which other channel members, typically wholesalers and retailers, may not resell their products. Thus, the policy is frequently called resale price maintenance (RPM). Minimum RPM means the manufacturer's specification of a downstream price below which the product cannot be sold. Maximum RPM means the manufacturer's specification of a downstream price above which the product cannot be sold. It is also possible to specify an *exact* price at which the product should be sold downstream, as Saturn automobiles are sold.

The main argument in favor of maximum RPM is related to the use of selective or exclusive distribution. Manufacturers who grant exclusivity to their dealers endow them with a local monopoly for the sale of their products. With local monopoly power, dealers have a strong incentive to raise prices above competitive levels, contrary to the interests of manufacturers and consumers. But through the use of maximum RPM, price can be maintained at a competitive level even if limited numbers of intermediaries are used.

Several arguments favor minimum RPM. The main thrust of the arguments follows from an understanding of the service outputs consumers get from a channel, in addition to the products they buy. Shoppers can choose to gain information and services at full-price dealers and then purchase through price discounters who do not offer service, but do offer lower prices. By not offering the same level of presale and postsale service as do full-price dealers—such as extensive product information and demonstrations, and postsale installation, maintenance, and repair—discounters free ride on the services offered elsewhere. Full-service dealers will then have provided costly service without the compensating revenue from the sale of the product. Their natural reaction will be to reduce service levels. But if service is really a necessary part of buying the product, this in turn will lead to a reduction in demand, to the detriment of all parties. Minimum resale price maintenance prevents discounting, reducing the extent of rival dealers free riding on services. In these types of markets, then, it can be argued that minimum resale price maintenance is actually a procompetitive policy.

Variants on the argument in favor of minimum RPM include the following:

- Manufacturers must gain entry to dealers faced with limited shelf and floor space. For many goods, dealer networks compatible with a product's quality and image are required. Manufacturers purchase such access through higher markups, advertising and brand-name drawing power, advertising allowances to dealers, and other expenditures in competition with rival brands. Minimum RPM provides a means for new manufacturers to gain dealer access by assuring dealers a given retail markup and ensuring against loss-leader pricing.[10]
- If dealers can earn a "reasonable" retail markup through minimum RPM, channel intermediaries may engage in quality certification for end-users so that the normal risks associated with purchasing a good or service are minimized.
- Minimum RPM may provide a high enough margin to the intermediary to induce it to push the firm's product over others carried by the intermediary, thus increasing the brand's visibility in the market.

- For products for which spatial convenience demands are high, minimum RPM helps assure widespread and immediate availability of the brand.
- Because minimum RPM guarantees a reasonably high profit margin to the intermediary, termination (causing the loss of these profits) would be very costly to the intermediary. Such powerful incentives are likely to discourage price maintainers from becoming price discounters.[11]

Despite all of these reasons supporting an RPM policy, the legal status of minimum and maximum RPM has varied over time. Minimum RPM has been considered per se illegal since the *Dr. Miles Medical Co. v. John D. Park & Sons Co.* decision in 1911. The illegality of minimum RPM was weakened, however, by two legal decisions in 1984 and 1988.

The first of these was the *Monsanto Company v. Spray-Rite Service Corporation* case.[12] Spray-Rite (now defunct) sued Monsanto after Monsanto cut off Spray-Rite's distributorship of herbicides in northern Illinois in 1968. Spray-Rite claimed that Monsanto did this because Spray-Rite would not join in an effort to fix prices at which herbicides were sold. Spray-Rite alleged a conspiracy between Monsanto and some of its distributors to set resale prices. The U.S. Supreme Court found in Spray-Rite's favor, but made it clear that the presence of concerted action between Monsanto and its distributors was critical to its per se ruling. In fact, the court explicitly stated that "a manufacturer . . . generally has a right to deal, or refuse to deal, with whomever it likes, as long as it does so independently." Citing the *Colgate* doctrine (discussed later in this chapter), the court went on to say that "the manufacturer can announce its resale prices in advance and refuse to deal with those who fail to comply." In other words, manufacturers may stipulate resale prices to their distributors as long as the stipulations are made on a unilateral basis. Where concerted conspiratorial action is found, a per se illegal ruling can be expected.

Reliance on the *Colgate* doctrine was the main reason why in 1983 Russell Stover, a major manufacturer of boxed chocolates, was not found guilty of unlawfully fixing retail candy prices. Russell Stover had announced in advance that it would refuse to deal with retailers who resold below the prices designated on lists, invoices, and order forms and the boxed candy itself. Stover wouldn't sell initially to stores that it believed would sell its products at less than designated prices, and it stopped dealing with established retailers that actually did so.[13]

The *Monsanto* decision may be viewed as a chink in the armor of the per se illegal status of resale price maintenance. The problem that Monsanto has created is how the term *agreement* ought to be defined and what evidence is sufficient to support a jury verdict that there was a price-fixing conspiracy. The Supreme Court ruled that evidence must be presented both that the distributor communicated its acquiescence regarding the manufacturer's resale pricing policy and that the acquiescence was sought by the manufacturer. It added that the mere fact that other distributors complained about a price cutter prior to termination wasn't sufficient to support a finding of agreement.

The second major case weakening the per se illegality of maximum RPM was *Business Electronics Corp. v. Sharp Electronics*, decided in 1988. In this case, the Supreme Court ruled in a vote of 6 to 2 that a manufacturer's agreement with one dealer to stop supplying a price-cutting dealer would not necessarily violate the Sherman Act.[14]

The plaintiff, Business Electronics, was the exclusive retailer of Sharp calculators in Houston from 1968 to 1972. During that period, Sharp became dissatisfied with Business Electronics' policy of selling calculators at prices lower than those suggested by Sharp. In 1972 Sharp appointed Hartwell's Office World as a second retailer of its calculators in Houston. Subsequently, Hartwell's told Sharp that it would quit distributing its products unless Sharp ended its relationship with Business Electronics, and, in 1973, Sharp terminated its dealership. The company then sued Sharp.

The U.S. Supreme Court upheld an appeals court ruling that the agreement to terminate Business Electronics was not a per se violation of antitrust law. It stated that such an agreement would be illegal per se only if it had been part of an agreement by the manufacturer and one or more retailers to fix prices at some level. There was no proof in the case of such a specific price-fixing agreement between Sharp and Hartwell's. Writing for the Court, Justice Antonin Scalia observed that it is sometimes legitimate and competitively useful for manufacturers to curb price competition among their dealers, and he referred to the free-rider problem mentioned earlier as a reason for manufacturers' actions. Thus, if there is no specific agreement as to price between the complaining dealers and the manufacturer, the reasonableness of an agreement to terminate will be determined by the rule of reason; that is, by balancing the anticompetitive intrabrand effects against any procompetitive interbrand effects.[15]

The *Monsanto* and *Business Electronics* decisions appear to have stimulated a number of manufacturers of upscale consumer goods, such as Prince Manufacturing Inc. (makers of Prince tennis racquets) and Specialized Bicycle Components (makers of mountain bikes), to use unilaterally implemented minimum resale price maintenance as one of their major distribution policies.[16] In fact, it is claimed that resale prices have been set for certain brands of televisions, athletic shoes, cameras, china, furniture, cosmetics, golf clubs, VCRs, women's sportswear, men's suits, stereos, toys, ceiling fans, watches, appliances, skis, cookware, perfume, chocolates, luggage, and video games, among others.

Some of the arguments that have been raised in opposition to the increasing minimum price maintenance activity are:

- Minimum RPM does not ensure that retailers will use their larger gross margins to provide service; they may simply pocket the extra money.
- Although interbrand competition may be fostered, minimum RPM inhibits competition between stores carrying the same brand.
- If a manufacturer deems service to be essential, it can be required of all retailers through dealership contracts, rather than through minimum RPM.
- Higher prices deny goods to consumers with less money.[17]

Despite these arguments, setting minimum resale prices remains a legal activity as long as it is not done as part of a concerted effort among multiple parties.

The status of maximum RPM has followed a somewhat different route.[18] The *Albrecht* decision in 1968 was a major case in the area, making maximum resale price maintenance per se illegal.[19] Albrecht, a newspaper carrier for the Herald Company, granted exclusive territories to its carriers. The Herald Company advertised a subscription price for home newspaper delivery and required its carriers to charge that price.

Albrecht charged a higher price to its customers, leading to his termination by the Herald Company. Albrecht sued and won in the Supreme Court, which argued that when maximum RPM sets prices too low, it prevents a dealer from offering services that customers need and value. Although this argument was challenged in the academic literature, the per se illegality of maximum RPM was maintained until 1997.

The 1997 *State Oil Co. v. Khan* decision by the U.S. Supreme Court overturned the *Albrecht* decision, ruling that henceforth maximum RPM agreements would be decided on a rule-of-reason basis (i.e., being viewed as legal unless they harm competition) rather than being viewed as per se illegal.[20] In this case, Khan was a dealer of Union 76–brand gasoline. The supply contract he had with State Oil in essence was a maximum RPM contract, although this was somewhat veiled by the specific pricing stipulations in the agreement. Khan sued, seeking to be able to charge higher prices for his gasoline and pocket the increased revenue from doing so.

In a unanimous ruling, the U.S. Supreme Court found in favor of State Oil. It found that the benefit to consumers in the form of lower prices outweighed the possible harm that could be caused by the practices, and pointed out that in the previous 30 years, firms had found many ways around the *Albrecht* ruling against maximum RPM in any event. These actions, it argued, had not had a serious negative impact on competitiveness or welfare and hence suggested the appropriateness of returning to a rule-of-reason criterion for determining the legality of maximum RPM when engaged in through concerted action.

In sum, minimum, maximum, or exact RPM can be implemented if not done so in the context of an agreement to restrain trade. That is, if RPM is a policy of the manufacturer, enacted unilaterally, there is by definition no agreement that could be construed as an antitrust violation. Maximum RPM agreements can be used as long as they do not harm competition. But minimum or exact RPM arrangements, when arrived at through a legal contract or agreement, are per se illegal. These criteria suggest that legal control over resale prices by manufacturers is possible under various conditions:[21]

- Act unilaterally; statements and actions should come only from the manufacturer.
- Avoid coercion; don't use annually renewable contracts conditioned on dealer adherence to manufacturer's specified resale price.
- Vertically integrate; form a corporate vertical marketing system.
- Avoid known discounters; establish screening and performance criteria difficult for discounters to meet.
- Announce resale price policy up front; the policy should be established when arrangements are first made with channel members and should specify that the manufacturer will refuse to deal with any dealer not willing to adhere to the announced terms.

The Supreme Court noted in *Business Electronics*, however, that the per se prohibitions on resale price maintenance do not apply "to restrictions on price to be charged by one who is in reality an agent of, not a buyer from, the manufacturer."[22] For example, where the restrictions would apply in the case of a distributor (who takes title to the goods it sells for a manufacturer), they would not apply in the case of an independent sales representative (who does not take title to the manufacturer's goods). The Court was quoting from *U.S. v. General Electric Co.* where it was stated that "The owner of an article . . . is not violating the common law, or the Anti-Trust Law, by seeking to dispose of his article directly to the consumer and fixing the price by which his agents transfer the title from him directly to the consumer."[23] This stance is echoed in the words of a lower court in a more recent case: ". . . where the manufacturer bears the financial risks of transactions with the customers and continues to retain 'title, dominion and control over its goods,' then it is likely that the distributor is merely an agent for the manufacturer."[24]

Price Discrimination

When a seller offers or grants a buyer a lower price than another on the exact same product, the seller is discriminating between the buyers by giving one of them a monetary reward. In actuality, discriminating among buyers, whether via prices, service outputs, or product features, makes abundant sense. From a managerial perspective, it would be foolish not to approach buyers typified by high demand elasticities differently from those with low demand elasticities. At the core of well-conceived market segmentation schemes are discriminatory tactics, because segments are supposed to be solicited dissimilarly. In fact, optimal profits can be achieved only if sellers discriminate among buyers. Not only price sensitivity but also cost to serve and intensity of competition vary across market segments. Charging different, or segmented, prices is the right economic decision.[25]

Although channel members can discriminate among their customers and suppliers in many ways, the focus here is mainly on price. The major segmented pricing policies that are enacted by channel managers tend to revolve around reductions from list price, promotional allowances and services, and functional discounts. The rationale for each of these is straightforward—the object is to increase demand, fight off competitors, reward customers, or compensate channel partners for services rendered. Although price discrimination can certainly be profitable, it can also be illegal. Instances of illegal price discrimination are covered under the Robinson-Patman Act. In what follows, we summarize the legal stance on price discrimination by sellers and by buyers, as well as promotional allowances and functional discounts.

Price Discrimination by Sellers. When sellers offer different prices to different buyers, the most directly relevant part of the Robinson-Patman Act is Section 2(a), which states:

> It shall be unlawful for any person engaged in commerce, . . . either directly or indirectly, to discriminate in price between different purchasers of commodities of like grade and quality, where either or any of the purchases involved in such discrimination are in commerce, where such commodities are sold for use, consumption, or resale within [any area] under the jurisdiction of the United States, and where the effect of such discrimination may be to substantially lessen competition or tend to create a monopoly in any line of commerce, or to injure, destroy or prevent competition with any person who either grants or knowingly receives the benefit of such discrimination, or with customers of either of them.

We can clarify three of the more significant phrases as follows:

- *Commodities*. The Robinson-Patman Act applies to goods and to goods bundled with services where the value of the goods predominates. It does not cover the sale of services. Some excluded categories therefore are printing, advertising space, and even real estate.

- *Like grade and quality*. Where products are of different materials or workmanship level, they are not ordinarily considered to be of "like grade and quality," but where differences are small and do not affect the basic use of the goods, then selling at price-differentials has been attacked. For example, there have been challenges to price differences involving private-label versus branded goods whereby the product was identical in both instances (i.e., evaporated milk made by Borden).[26]

- *Substantially lessen competition*. This factor is a critical issue in all antitrust cases, including those filed under Section 2(a) of the Robinson-Patman Act, which are tried under the rule-of-reason doctrine. It has become increasingly difficult for plaintiffs to prove, because an important difference exists between injury to competitors and injury to competition. A loss of sales by one firm and their gain by another is the essence of competition, and the object of each competitor is to outsell rivals. Evidence of intent to destroy a competitor, however, may indicate an injury to competition.

Price discrimination between customers who are not competing is not illegal. Retailers charge consumers different prices for identical goods and services (e.g., airline tickets or automobiles)—consumers are not "in competition" with one another. Also, if one retailer does business only on the East Coast of the United States and another does business only on the West Coast, a vendor may charge them different prices, as long as they do not compete for the same end-users.

Price discrimination that injures any of three levels of competition may end up being prohibited by the Robinson-Patman Act:

- *Primary level*. Competition between two sellers may be injured when one of them gives discriminatory prices to some customers.

- *Secondary level*. Competition between two customers of a seller may be affected if the seller differentiates between them in price. In effect the seller is aiding one customer and harming the other in their mutual competition, and this is illegal if it is sufficient to cause substantial lessening of competition.

- *Tertiary level*. If a manufacturer discriminates in prices between two wholesalers such that the customers of one wholesaler are favored over those of the other, competition is being injured by the price discrimination.

Perhaps one of the most important Robinson-Patman Act cases in decades was decided in 1993. It involved primary-level discrimination in which Liggett & Myers, formerly the Brooke Group, charged Brown & Williamson (B&W) with predatory pricing.[27] In 1980, Liggett, which had a 2.3 percent market share, introduced a generic, unadvertised cigarette that sold for 30 percent less than the branded price. Eventually, B&W entered with a generic product packaged in an identical box to Liggett's and began to undercut Liggett's price. B&W had a market share of around 12 percent at the time.

During the 18-month price war that ensued, B&W allegedly cut its prices substantially below average variable cost. Liggett could not sustain the below-cost pricing, and the price of generic cigarettes rose.

Liggett sued under the Robinson-Patman Act, because B&W's predatory price cuts were implemented via discounts that were given to different distributors in varying degrees—hence, the price discrimination. Although many aspects of this case make for interesting reading and analysis from a marketing management perspective, the most important is the decision itself. The Court's decision rested on its assessment of whether B&W could earn back, via monopoly pricing, the costs of its predatory actions after Liggett was quieted. The Court stated that, in addition to showing below-cost prices, the plaintiff (Liggett) must also demonstrate "that the competitor had a reasonable prospect . . . of recouping its investment in below-cost prices."[28] As the Court noted, "Recoupment is the ultimate object of an unlawful predatory scheme; it is the means by which a predator profits from predation."[29]

Through an analysis of competition in the cigarette industry, the Court came to the conclusion that B&W, despite the fact that it had quieted Liggett, didn't have the power to quiet R.J. Reynolds, Philip Morris, and the rest of its competitors and, therefore, would not be able to retrieve its investment. It found in favor of B&W, stating that, without recoupment, predatory pricing produces lower aggregate prices in the market, and consumer welfare is enhanced. A federal court in Texas followed the same line of reasoning shortly after the Brooke Group decision when it cleared American Airlines of predatory pricing against Northwest and Continental Airlines.[30]

Defenses to Price Discrimination Charges. Price discrimination is not a per se violation of the antitrust laws. Three potential escape routes exist, beyond the fact that the discrimination may have an insignificant impact on competition. Discrimination may be justified through proof that (1) it was carried out to dispose of perishable or obsolete goods, or under a closeout or bankruptcy sale; (2) it merely made due allowance for differences in "the cost of manufacture, sale, or delivery resulting from the differing methods or quantities" in which the commodity was sold or delivered; or (3) it was effected "in good faith to meet an equally low price of a competitor." The first defense poses few problems, but the second and third are more complex.

Cost Justification Defense. Companies attempting to sustain a Robinson-Patman Act cost justification defense have seldom been successful because of the stringent standards set by the U.S. Federal Trade Commission and the courts; that is, requiring detailed documentation of full (not marginal) costs and causing the defense to fail if less than 100 percent of the price differential is shown to result from cost differences.[31] The burden of proof is on the seller, because quantity discounts are permitted under Section 2(a) only to the extent that they are justified by cost savings.

For example, the U.S. Supreme Court has ruled that quantity discounts must reflect cost savings in deliveries made to one place at one time. This places limitations on the use of cumulative quantity discounts. In 1988 the Federal Trade Commission charged six of the nation's largest book publishers with illegally discriminating against independent bookstores by selling books at lower prices to major bookstore chains, such as Waldenbooks, B. Dalton, and Crown Books. The FTC said the publishers treated orders placed by the chains as a single order, even if the books were separately packed, itemized, and shipped to individual chain outlets. As a result, the chain stores were able to pay lower prices than independent bookstores "that receive shipments as large or larger than shipments to individual chain outlets."[32]

Pricing policies in the health care industry have attracted considerable litigious attention over the past decade. Late in 1994, 1,346 independent pharmacies in 15 states sued the largest drug manufacturers and mail-order distributors, charging them with price discrimination. Early in 1994, four major grocery chains (Kroger, Albertson's, Safeway, and Vons) filed a suit in Cincinnati federal court charging 16 pharmaceutical firms and a mail-order prescription company with discriminatory and "pernicious" pricing. The suit claims the firms' pricing policies favor institutional pharmacies, health-maintenance organizations, and mail-order prescription ("pharmacy benefit management") companies with lower prices, while charging supermarket chains more. And late in 1993, similar charges were levied by 20 chain and independent drugstores in yet another suit.[33] The suits were settled in 1996 and in mid-1998, with pharmaceutical companies paying about $350 million in each settlement to independent pharmacies and agreeing not to charge two-tier prices to the market.[34] However, the nonsettling defendants succeeded in having the case dismissed when it went to trial, and this ruling was upheld on appeal.

Meeting Competition Defense. The meeting competition defense (found in Section 2[b] of the act) has proven as difficult to apply as the cost justification defense, yet is even more complex. The defense is valid even if there is substantial injury to competition, but the burden of proving good faith falls on the defendant:[35]

- The price being met must be lawful and not a price produced by collusion. A seller does not have to prove the price that it is meeting is lawful, but it must make some effort to find out if it is.
- The price being met must really exist, and must not be undercut.[36] Price reductions on a "premium" product to the level of "standard" products can be a form of illegal price discrimination. If the public is willing to pay a higher price for the premium product, the equal prices may be considered beating and not meeting competition.
- The competition being met may have to be at the primary level. Granting a discriminatory price to some customers to enable them to meet their own competition may not be protected.[37]

According to a 1983 Supreme Court ruling, the good-faith defense is applicable to gaining new customers as well as retaining old ones. But firms practicing discrimination are permitted only to match rival prices exactly; they cannot undercut or "beat" them.[38]

Availability Defense. Pricing differences for different customers can be defended if the reason was the offering of a pricing policy available equally to all customers, but not chosen by all customers. For example, a manufacturer may offer a discount for early payment of invoices. Even though all customers do not take advantage of the discount, all have equal opportunity to do so, and there is no violation.

Price Discrimination by Buyers. *Price discrimination* by a seller between two competing channel members can be viewed as an attempt to exercise reward power relative to the channel member receiving the lower price. However, forcing a discriminatory price from an upstream seller in a channel may be viewed as coercion by the buyer.

Section 2(f) of the Robinson-Patman Act makes it unlawful for a person in commerce knowingly to induce or receive a discrimination in price. To violate this section, buyers must be reasonably aware of the illegality of the prices they have received. This section prevents large, powerful channel members from compelling sellers to give them discriminatory lower prices. It is enforced by means of Section 5 of the Federal Trade Commission Act on the grounds that this use of coercive power is an unfair method of competition.

It is also illegal for buyers to coerce favors from suppliers in the form of special promotional allowances and services. This stipulation raises the possibility that slotting allowances could be illegal. Slotting allowances are fixed payments made by a manufacturer to a retailer for access to the retailer's shelf space. They are used predominantly in grocery retailing, but have also been observed in the software, music, pharmaceutical, and bookselling industries.[39] Retailers claim that slotting allowances are necessary to defray the costs of stocking a new product in the store, including one-time costs of including the new product in the store's computer system, warehouse management, and shelf placement. They argue that these costs have risen with the increase in new-product introductions in recent years.[40] Slotting allowances have also been argued to perform a beneficial signaling role. Only if its product has high market potential would a manufacturer be willing to offer an up-front fixed payment to the retailer to stock the product, so retailers could use slotting allowances to screen out potentially poor products from the store shelf.[41]

Slotting allowances are very commonly used and can involve very substantial fees, particularly in grocery retailing. In a study done by A. C. Nielsen in 1997, manufacturers reported on those of their most recent national product introduction. One-third of respondents in the food category spent between $500,000 and $1 million on slotting allowances alone, and 14 percent spent more than $3 million. Only 6 percent of respondents reported paying none.[42]

Manufacturers complain that they are nothing more than price discrimination or even extortion. Particular complaints have been raised by small manufacturers, who say that slotting allowances prevent their very access to store shelves. Indeed, in the 1997 A. C. Nielsen study, 83 percent of manufacturers selling through retailers paid some slotting allowances, but that the percentage was higher for companies with sales under $1 billion (86 percent) than for larger ones (75 percent).[43]

Slotting allowances are not illegal in and of themselves. However, they could be construed as illegal under certain conditions. A panel session on this issue at an annual meeting of the American Bar Association Section of Antitrust Law in 1997 noted that slotting allowances could be challenged under the Sherman Act and the FTC Act if competing retailers agreed on the amount of slotting allowances or the allocation of shelf space to manufacturers. The practice could also be challenged if used as part of a conspiracy to monopolize trade or if used to exclude certain manufacturers from retail shelf space. In a merger of two retailers, slotting allowances could be prohibited if they could prevent some manufacturers' market entry. Finally, they could violate the Robinson-Patman Act if it were possible to prove their use as price discrimination mechanisms.[44]

Despite all of these possibilities, the use of slotting allowances continues and has yet to be ruled illegal. The assistant director of the FTC's Bureau of Competition noted that although manufacturers commonly "grumble" about them, no formal complaint has been made in recent history. It is also hard to prove that retailers' increased "power" gives them the ability to extract profits from manufacturers through slotting allowances, because, as a result, retailers' profits have not risen appreciably.[45] Both the academic research evidence and real-world examples suggest that a successful lawsuit involving slotting allowance violations is unlikely.[46]

In a different context, large buyers such as A&P have been known to set up dummy brokerage firms as part of their businesses in order to obtain a brokerage allowance from sellers, which in effect permits them to receive lower prices than their competitors. This form of coercive power is deemed illegal under Section 2(c) of the Robinson-Patman Act, which makes it unlawful to pay brokerage fees or discounts or to accept them except for services rendered in connection with sales or purchases. It also prohibits brokerage fees or discounts paid to any broker who is not independent of both buyer and seller.

However, as is the case with slotting allowances, the reality is that buyer-induced price discrimination is extremely difficult to prove and therefore seems to be widely practiced. For example, in 1991, Coca-Cola allegedly lost a major contract to Pepsi-Cola to provide soda fountain service to Marriott Corporation after Coke refused to lend Marriott $50 million to $100 million at less than prevailing interest rates. The Marriott hotel and food-service chain provides food services for its own 600 hotels and about 2,300 restaurants and kitchens at schools, businesses, hospitals, and other institutions. Apparently, Pepsi was willing to lend Marriott the money. The Marriott business meant about $2 million in annual profit to Coke.[47]

Promotional Allowances and Services. In order to entice channel members to advertise, display, promote, or demonstrate their wares, suppliers use all sorts of monetary inducements. These rewards are circumscribed by Sections 2(d) and 2(e) of the Robinson-Patman Act, which prohibit a seller from granting advertising allowances, offering other types of promotional assistance, or providing services, display facilities, or equipment to any buyer unless similar allowances and assistance are made available to all purchasers. Section 2(d) applies to payments by a seller to a buyer for the performance of promotional services; Section 2(e) applies to the actual provision of such services (e.g., display racks or signs). Because buyers differ in size of physical establishment and volume of sales, allowances obviously cannot be made available to all customers on the same absolute basis. Therefore, the law stipulates that the allowances be made available to buyers on "proportionately equal terms."

The prohibitions of these sections of the Robinson-Patman Act are absolute and are not dependent on injury to competition. Although meeting competition is a defense, cost justification of the discrimination is not. If it can be shown that discriminatory allowances exist and that the victims are firms in competition with each other, then the violation is deemed to be illegal per se, unless the pricing action was taken to meet the competition. However, for firms to be "in competition," they must be in sufficient geographical proximity to compete for the same customer groups. For example, if retailers are involved, only those retailers in a limited market territory need be included when granting allowances. On the other hand, the market might be construed as national if mail-order or e-commerce companies are involved. In the latter situation, a manufacturer (or wholesaler) would have to grant allowances or services to all national sellers if it were to grant them to one, unless the meeting competition defense is available. In addition, a time dimension is important in defining the domain of the allowance. For example, if advertising allowances are granted in one month, they do not have to be granted to another buyer five months later. Otherwise, the initial allowance would determine all future allowances.[48]

According to the U.S. Federal Trade Commission's guidelines, certain stipulations have been made regarding adherence to Sections 2(d) and 2(e).[49] Among them are the following:

- Allowances may be made only for services actually rendered, and they must not substantially exceed the cost of these services to the buyer or their value to the seller.
- The seller must design a promotional program in such a way that all competing buyers can realistically implement it.
- The seller should take action designed to inform all competing customers of the existence and essential features of the promotional program in ample time for them to take full advantage of it.
- If a program is not functionally available to (i.e., suitable for and usable by) some of the seller's competing customers, the seller must make certain that suitable alternatives are offered to such customers.
- The seller should provide its customers with sufficient information to permit a clear understanding of the exact terms of the offer, including all alternatives, and the conditions on which payment will be made or services furnished.

The FTC has stipulated that when promotional allowances or merchandising services are provided, they should be furnished in accordance with a written plan that meets the listed requirements.[50] In the case of sellers who market their products directly to retailers as well as sell through wholesalers, any promotional allowance offered to the retailers must also be offered to the wholesalers on a proportionately equal basis. The wholesalers would then be expected to pass along the allowance to their retail customers, who are in competition with the direct-buying retailers.[51]

In a 1990 revision of the Guides for Advertising Allowances and Other Merchandising Payments and Services, the FTC recognized two ways of measuring proportional equality: either based on purchase or based on the customer's cost. Offering an equal amount of allowances or services per unit of sales is a permissible example of the purchase-based measurement method. Placing newspaper advertisements in connection with the resale of products for which advertising allowances are provided is an example of the customer cost basis. In addition, the FTC reiterated its previous position that a company that grants a discriminatory promotional allowance may argue that the allowance was given in "good faith" to meet the promotional program of a competitor.[52]

Functional Discounts. In the discussion of channel flows in Chapter 4, the Equity Principle was introduced. That principle involves the use of reward power in granting discounts to individual channel members based on the functions, or marketing flows, they perform as they divide distribution labor. A *functional discount* is a means of implementing the Equity Principle directly. It provides for a set of list prices at which products are transferred from the manufacturer to a downstream channel member, plus a list of discounts off list price to be offered in return for the performance of certain channel flows or functions.

Functional discounts are directly tied to the performance of actual channel flows, and therefore payment is made differentially to channel members who perform valued channel flows to different degrees. For example, a discount of 3 percent off list price might be offered for payment in 10 days after purchase rather than the usual 30 days. The discount is directly tied to the distributor's bearing of the financing flow through early payment. Or, a discount of 2 percent might be offered to the distributor in return for a promise to maintain a certain level of safety stocks of inventory in the distributor's warehouses, including permission for the manufacturer to inspect the warehouses periodically. In this case, compensation is given directly for bearing the physical possession and ownership flows.

In theory, functional discounts should be allotted to each channel member on the basis of the degree of its participation in the marketing flows (e.g., physical possession, ownership, promotion, etc.) associated with making a product or service available to end-users. In reality, the legality of functional discounts, which are a form of price discrimination, has been shrouded in controversy and confusion for decades. One of the major reasons for the confusion is the fact that, historically, the discounts were primarily based on the level of distribution (e.g., wholesale versus retail) in which a recipient resided and not strictly on the functions the company performed. Hence, they are frequently called "trade" as opposed to "functional" discounts.

When independent wholesalers sold to numerous, relatively small retail outlets, each level in the channel was distinct and could be rewarded differently (e.g., the wholesaler got a larger price discount from the manufacturer than the retailer). In addition, each level in the channel dealt with a specific class of customer (e.g., the wholesaler sold only to retailers, and retailers only to consumers). Wholesalers and retailers normally performed different functions in different markets and, thus, did not compete against each other.

Now, however, the commercial world is much more complex. Distinctions in distribution systems have blurred as wholesalers have formed voluntary chains and as retailers have vertically integrated backward, assuming numerous wholesaling functions. Kmart, a major discount store chain, performs many of its own wholesaling operations. It receives merchandise in large lots from manufacturers, breaks bulk, assorts, and reships it from its warehouses to its retail stores. However, it is generally classified as a "retailer" and, therefore, is supposedly entitled only to the functional (trade) discounts given to retailers. (It can, of course, avail itself of whatever quantity discounts are offered by its suppliers.)

The dilemma is as follows. If Kmart cannot receive a wholesaler's functional discount when it does, in fact, perform wholesaling functions, then it is the victim of discrimination. But if Kmart were to be given both a wholesaler's and a retailer's trade discount, then independent wholesalers who resell to independent retailers would argue that their customers (small retailers) are not able to compete with Kmart on an equal footing. Further, suppose it did not receive the wholesale discount, and a wholesaler decided to open up a warehouse club such as Price Club or Sam's to sell to small businesses and consumers. The warehouse club could then use the wholesale discount to cut prices below those at Kmart. Kmart would then be able to argue that it was at a disadvantage relative to the warehouse club.[53]

The problem underlying this whole controversy is one of classification. Because of it, the Food Marketing Institute (whose members are primarily supermarket chains), the Grocery Manufacturers of America, the National Association of Chain Drug Stores, and a number of other wholesale and retail trade associations issued a statement in 1989 urging manufacturers not to make distinctions among competing distributor customers in a market area based on their class of trade. Instead it urged manufacturers to offer equally to all downstream members all prices and terms of sale that were offered to one. Such exhortations are of course only necessary when the manufacturer uses dual distribution to reach the market (see Chapter 5) and when functional discounts are offered differentially to the different channels used.

Functional discounts are not specifically referred to in the Robinson-Patman Act, but, via a number of court decisions, it has been established that the stipulations of the act (including the defenses mentioned above) apply to them. A 1990 Supreme Court decision is relevant in this regard: *Texaco Inc. v. Hasbrouck*.[54]

In *Hasbrouck*, Texaco had sold gasoline directly to a number of independent retailers in Spokane, Washington, at its "retail tank wagon" prices, while it granted more substantial discounts to two distributors. Those two distributors sold to service stations that the distributors owned and operated, passing on nearly the whole discount from Texaco. The distributor-controlled retailers thereby were able to sell well below the price charged by the competing independent retailers. Between 1972 and 1981, sales at the stations supplied by the two wholesaler-distributors increased dramatically, whereas sales at the competing independents declined.

Texaco argued that its discriminatory pricing was justified by cost savings, by a good-faith attempt to meet competition, and as lawful functional discounts. The Ninth Circuit Court of Appeals and the Supreme Court did not accept Texaco's arguments in defense of its actions, even though they validated the use of the cost-based and good-faith defenses in lawsuits challenging functional discounts.

The Supreme Court's affirmation of the cost justification defense is very significant for channel management, because this means that functional discounts are no longer merely tied to classification schemes. The Court stated that:

> In general, a supplier's functional discount is said to be given to a purchaser based on the purchaser's role in the supplier's distributive system, reflecting, at least in a generalized sense, the services performed by the purchaser for the supplier.[55]
>
> A legitimate functional discount constituting a reasonable reimbursement for a purchaser's actual marketing functions does not violate Section 2(a).[56]

This case leaves the door open to manufacturers to use functional discounts to compensate channel members for their participation in specific marketing flows. Furthermore, it also suggests that such discounts bearing a reasonable relationship to the supplier's savings or the channel member's costs are legal, refuting the need for precise measurement. There is still a problem about which cost base to use—the supplier's or the reseller's. In the latter case, setting discounts based on the reseller's costs may grant different discounts to competing resellers and possibly larger discounts to less efficient buyers, a strange outcome indeed. In the former case, the discounts based on the seller's savings would not necessarily be adequate or fair compensation to the reseller for performing the function.[57] The sentiment seems to be in favor of using seller's savings, although both approaches have imperfections.

PRODUCT LINE POLICIES

For a wide variety of logical reasons, channel managers may wish to restrict the breadth or depth of the product lines that their channel partners sell. Here, we look at the rationale for four policies—exclusive dealing, tying, full-line forcing, and designated product policies—as well as the antitrust concerns surrounding them.

Exclusive Dealing

Exclusive dealing is the requirement by a seller or lessor that its channel intermediaries sell or lease only its products or brands, or at least no products or brands in direct competition with the seller's products. If intermediaries do not comply, the seller may invoke negative sanctions by refusing to deal with them. Such arrangements clearly reduce the freedom of choice of the intermediaries (resellers). Some of the managerial benefits of exclusive dealing follow:

- Resellers become more dependent on the supplier, enabling it to secure exclusive benefit of the reseller's energies. If the supplier has devoted considerable effort to develop a brand image, it may fear that the resellers will use the brand as a loss leader and that suppliers of other, directly competing brands stocked by the reseller will free ride off of the demand stimulated by the supplier's heavily promoted, well-known brand. The supplier may be concerned about free riding with regard to other services as well, such as the use of specialized display cases, the provision of technical training or financing, and assistance in the operations of the business.
- Competitors are foreclosed from selling through valuable resellers.
- With a long-term exclusive relationship, sales forecasting may be easier, permitting the supplier to achieve more precise and efficient production and logistics.
- Resellers may obtain more stable prices and may gain more regular and frequent deliveries of the supplier's products.
- Transactions between resellers and the supplier may be fewer in number and larger in volume.
- Resellers and the supplier may be able to reduce administrative costs.
- Both may be able to secure specialized assets and long-term financing from each other.
- Resellers generally receive added promotional and other support as well as avoid the added inventory costs that go with carrying multiple brands.[58]

The example of Kodak and Fuji in the photofinishing business is illustrative. From 1954 until 1995, Kodak was prevented from linking sales of film to photofinishing (e.g., by offering coupons in photofinishing envelopes good for Kodak film). When the consent decree was lifted, Kodak started making deals with U.S. retailers to be their exclusive provider of photofinishing business. By the end of 1996, Kodak had deals in place giving it exclusive rights at Kmart, Walgreen (a nationwide pharmacy chain), CVS (another national pharmacy chain), Eckerd (also a pharmacy chain), Price–Costco, and American Stores (the parent company of several U.S. grocery retailers). Meanwhile, Kodak's main rival, Fuji, signed a contract with Wal-Mart to be its exclusive supplier of photofinishing services. Despite Fuji's signing on with a retail giant like Wal-Mart, Kodak still controlled about 75 percent of the wholesale photofinishing market by the end of 1996. Retailers supported the exclusive agreements, citing the expense of upgrading photofinishing equipment and training staff.[59]

Requirements contracts are variants of exclusive dealing. Under these, buyers agree to purchase all or a part of their requirements of a product from one seller, usually for a specified period and price. Such arrangements clearly reduce the freedom of choice of the buyer, but guarantee the buyer a source of supply at a known cost, often over a very long period of time (e.g., 10 years).

Exclusive dealing lessens interbrand competition directly, because competing brands available from other suppliers are excluded from outlets. Exclusive dealing and requirements contracts are circumscribed mainly by Section 3 of the Clayton Act, which stipulates that

> it shall be unlawful for any person . . . to lease or make a sale or contract for sale of goods, wares, merchandise, machinery, supplies or other commodities, whether patented or unpatented, . . . on the condition, agreement, or understanding that the lessee or purchaser thereof shall not use or deal in the goods, . . . of a competitor or competitors of the lessor or seller, where the effect of such lease, sale, or contract for sale or such condition, agreement or understanding may be to substantially lessen competition or tend to create a monopoly in any line of commerce.

However, these policies may also violate Section 1 of the Sherman Act and Section 5 of the FTC Act. Under the Sherman Act, various types of exclusive contracts may be deemed unlawful restraints of trade when a dominant firm is involved and when the contracts go so far beyond reasonable business needs as to have the necessary effect, or disclose a clear intention, of suppressing competition.[60]

A case decided in 1961 established the modern guidelines for assessing exclusive dealing policies from an antitrust perspective. The case, *Tampa Electric Co. v. Nashville Coal Co.*,[61] involved a contract between Nashville Coal and Tampa Electric, a Florida public utility producing electricity, covering Tampa's expected requirements of coal (i.e., not less than 500,000 tons per year) for a period of 20 years. Before any coal was delivered, Nashville declined to perform the contract on the ground that it was illegal under the antitrust laws because it amounted to an exclusive dealing arrangement, which foreclosed other suppliers from serving Tampa Electric. (In actuality, the price of coal had jumped, making the arrangement less profitable for the Nashville Coal Company.) Tampa brought suit, arguing that the contract was both valid and enforceable.

To be illegal, the court explained, such arrangements must have a tendency to work a substantial, not merely remote, lessening of competition in the relevant competitive market. Justice Clark, speaking for the majority, indicated that "substantiality" was to be determined by taking into account the following factors:

- The relative strength of the parties involved
- The proportionate volume of commerce involved in relation to the total volume of commerce in the relevant market area
- The probable immediate and future effects that preemption of that share of the market might have on effective competition within it

The district court and the court of appeals had accepted the argument that the contract foreclosed a substantial share of the market, because Tampa's requirements equaled the total volume of coal purchased in the state of Florida before the contract's inception. The Supreme Court, in an interesting piece of economic reasoning, defined the relevant market as the *supply* market in an eight-state area, noting that mines in that coal-producing region were eager to sell more coal in Florida. When the market was defined as the entire multistate Appalachian coal region, the foreclosure amounted to less than 1 percent of the tonnage produced each year. The Court concluded that given the nature of the market (i.e., the needs of a utility for a stable supply at reasonable prices over a long period as well as the level of concentration), the small percentage of foreclosure did not actually or potentially cause a substantial reduction of competition, nor did it tend toward a monopoly.

The decision in this case indicates that the type of goods or merchandise, the geographic area of effective competition, and the substantiality of the competition foreclosed must all be assessed in determining illegality or legality. It also indicates that exclusive dealing arrangements or requirements contracts that are negotiated by sellers possessing a very small share of the relevant market have a good chance of standing up in court.[62] The critical issue may involve the definition of the relevant market; firms with large shares may still be circumscribed. And, when shares are sufficiently high (e.g., 30 to 40 percent), the so-called "modified" rule of reason standard established in *Tampa Electric* requires courts to examine the following factors:

- The duration of the contracts
- The likelihood of collusion in the industry and the degree to which other firms in the market also employ exclusive dealing
- The height of entry barriers
- The nature of the distribution system and distribution alternatives remaining available after exclusive dealing is taken into account
- Other obvious anti- or procompetitive effects, such as the prevention of free riding and the encouragement of the reseller to promote the supplier's product more heavily.[63]

Even though the *Tampa Electric* case was decided almost 40 years ago, legal battles surrounding exclusive dealing are very much alive. For example, the U.S. cigarette maker Philip Morris, which had a 53 percent market share for cigarettes, initiated a "Retail Leaders" program in the fall of 1998. This incentive program for retailers granted them significant benefits (including rebates of $5.50 or more per cigarette carton, as well as merchandising aid) in return for 100 percent of the visible display rights in the retail outlet and the exclusive right to offer consumer discounts for three months of each year. As a result, the company placed about 80,000 cigarette displays in retail outlets.

In March 1999, competitor R.J. Reynolds filed a lawsuit against Philip Morris (later joined by two other major competitors, Loew's Corporation's Lorillard unit and Brown & Williamson Tobacco Corporation), charging that Philip Morris was attempting to monopolize the U.S. cigarette market by making exclusive dealing arrangements with retailers.[64] The plaintiffs showed evidence that 14 percent of the smoking population (six million adult smokers) had switched brands in the prior two years, and that store displays are important tools in competing for these sales. Hence, they argued, Philip Morris's campaign would prevent them from fair competition for these sales and could increase Philip Morris's market share significantly. On June 29, 1999, a federal judge granted the plaintiffs' request for a preliminary injunction against Philip Morris, requiring it to dismantle the program completely pending the conclusion of the lawsuit filed by the three rivals. The judge found that the program irreparably damaged Philip Morris's competitors and further, that the company would suffer no substantial hardship due to the injunction. This interim ruling illustrates how exclusive dealing by a dominant market share firm, when combined with a harm to competition, is looked upon dimly by the courts.[65]

Tying

Tying exists when a seller of a product or service that buyers want (the "tying product") refuses to sell it unless a second ("tied") product or service is also purchased, or at least is not purchased from anyone other than the seller of the tying product. Thus, a manufacturer of motion picture projectors (the tying product) might insist that only its film (the tied product) be used with the projectors, or a manufacturer of shoe machinery (the tying product) might insist that lessees of the machinery purchase service contracts (tied service) from it for the proper maintenance of the machinery.

Many of the business reasons for using tying policies are similar to those for using exclusive dealing. Both policies are similar—their immediate aim is to lock in the purchase of a supplier-specific brand and lock out the purchase of directly competing brands. Additional reasons for tying, beyond those that apply from the discussion of exclusive dealing, are:

- Transferring the market demand already established for the tying product (e.g., can closing machines) to the tied product (e.g., cans).
- Using the tied product (paper) to meter usage of the tying product (copying machines).
- Using a low-margin tying product (razors) to sell a high-margin tied product (blades).
- Achieving cost savings via package sales. For example, the costs of supplying and servicing channel members might be lower, the greater the number of products included in the "package."

- Assuring the successful operation of the tying product (an automobile) by obliging dealers to purchase tied products (repair parts) from the supplier.[66]

A tying agreement in effect forecloses competing sellers from the opportunity of selling the tied commodity or service to the purchaser. Indeed, like exclusive dealing policies, the critical issue in the condemnation of tying is the foreclosing of interbrand competition from a marketplace. But tying contracts are viewed much more negatively by the courts than are exclusive dealing arrangements or requirements contracts. For example, in distinguishing between a requirements contract and a tying contract in the *Standard Stations* case, Justice Frankfurter stated that tying arrangements "serve hardly any purpose beyond the suppression of competition."[67] Like exclusive dealing, tying is circumscribed by the Sherman Act, the Clayton Act, and the FTC Act. Given the overwhelmingly negative attitude of the courts toward tying, it is little wonder that its use would rarely be approved.

However, certain types of tying contracts are legal. The courts have ruled that if two products are made to be used jointly and one will not function properly without the other, a tying agreement is within the law. (Shoes are sold in pairs, and automobiles are sold with tires.) In other cases, if a company's goodwill depends on proper operation of equipment, a service contract may be tied to the sale or lease of the machine.[68] The practicality of alternatives to the tying arrangement appears to be crucial. If a firm will suffer injury unless it can protect its product, and there is no feasible alternative, the courts permit tying agreements. Despite these exceptions, the general rule is that tying agreements are presumptively anticompetitive, although defenses are still available.

Serious legal questions regarding tying agreements have been raised relative to the franchising of restaurants and other eating places, motels, and movie theaters, among others. As detailed in Chapter 17, an individual or group of individuals (franchisees) are usually permitted to set up outlets of a national chain in return for a capital investment and a periodic fee to the parent company (the franchisor). In some cases, the parent company also requires the franchise holders to buy various supplies, such as meat, baked goods, and paper cups in the case of restaurants, either from the corporation or an approved supplier.

In franchising, the tying product is the franchise itself and the tied products are the supplies that the franchisee must purchase to operate his business. Companies with such requirements have argued that they are necessary in order to maintain the quality of their services and reputation. However, critics of such agreements assert that franchisors often require franchisees to purchase supplies and raw materials at prices far above those of the competitive market. The potential for a conflict of interest on the part of the franchisors is high.

In franchising, the primary tying product is the trademark itself (e.g., "McDonald's," "Budget" Rent-A-Car, "Sheraton" Hotels). Therefore, the courts have sustained agreements that link the trademark to supplies only when franchisors have been able to prove that their trademarks are inseparable from their supplies and that the tied product (the supplies) are, in fact, essential to the maintenance of quality control. For example, in a lawsuit involving Baskin-Robbins, a chain of franchised ice cream stores, certain franchisees contended the Baskin-Robbins ice cream products were unlawfully tied to the license of the trademark.[69] However, the tie-in claim was disallowed because the franchisees did not establish that the trademark was a product separate from the ice cream; in tying cases, two distinct products must be involved in order for tying to be present.

In a decision involving the Chock Full O'Nuts Corporation, it was held that the franchisor "successfully proved its affirmative defense [to tying charges] of maintaining quality control with regard to its coffee and baked goods."[70] On the other hand, Chock Full O'Nuts was unsuccessful in defending its tying practices with respect to a number of other products (e.g., french fries, soft drink syrups, napkins, and glasses). These products were viewed as illegally tied to the franchise because they were easily reproducible.

A major antitrust case with tying at its core, but stretching to other antitrust issues as well, is the U.S. government suit against Microsoft Corporation. In 1991, the Department of Justice began investigating Microsoft's actions and found that it illegally exploited its monopoly over personal computer (PC) operating systems. Microsoft and the government signed a consent decree in 1995 under which Microsoft agreed not to impose anticompetitive licensing terms on PC makers. However, Microsoft retained the right to develop integrated products.

In October 1997, the Department of Justice filed a complaint in a federal court that Microsoft had violated the terms of the 1995 consent decree. In particular, it said that Microsoft forced PC makers to install Microsoft's Web browser, Internet Explorer (the tied good in this case), in every PC in which Windows 95 (Microsoft's operating system, the tying good in this case) was installed. Thus, an argument of illegal tying was brought: The government claimed that Windows 95 and Internet Explorer were two distinct products and did not need to be sold together. Further, the government argued that bundling Internet Explorer with Windows 95 caused competitive damage to Microsoft's main competitor, Netscape. The Netscape Navigator program had dominated the market, but Microsoft's share was rising to close to 50 percent of the market.

In a subsequent lawsuit brought by the government against Microsoft (and joined by 19 states), further evidence against Microsoft was offered. IBM and Gateway, two PC makers, testified that they were forced to pay higher prices for Microsoft software licenses when they refused to stop offering competitive Internet browsers. Thus, elements of exclusive dealing were introduced into the case as well.

On November 5, 1999, a U.S. District Court judge issued his finding of facts in the case and ruled squarely against Microsoft. He said that Microsoft used its monopoly power to harm competition through its bundling of products and its threats leveled against its business customers (PC makers) who refused to comply with its demands. On November 19, a mediator was appointed to work with the parties to achieve a settlement. If no settlement is reached, a final ruling in the case will determine whether Microsoft is judged to have illegally used monopoly power in the software marketplace. The penalties for losing the case are potentially very severe. The judge could force the breakup of Microsoft or, at a lesser level, could force Microsoft to open up its software codes so that rivals could viably compete. Further, if Microsoft is deemed legally to be a monopoly, competitors can file civil suits to collect damages as well. The message is that tying is clearly frowned upon when the company in question has a very strong market position and when its actions hamper the ability of competitors to access the market.[71]

Full-Line Forcing

One special form of product policy is called *full-line forcing*. Here a seller's leverage with a product is used to force a buyer to purchase its whole line of goods. This policy is illegal if competitive sellers are unreasonably prevented from market access. In the case of a farm machinery manufacturer, a court held that the practice was within the law, but implied that full-line forcing that caused the exclusion of competitors from this part of the market might be illegal if a substantial share of business was affected.[72]

Block booking imposed by motion picture distributors and producers on independent theater owners can also be viewed as full-line forcing or tying. This practice compels theaters to take many pictures they do not want in order to obtain the ones they do. Independent producers have consequently been unable to rent their films to theaters whose programs were thus crowded with the products of the major firms. Similar arrangements have been found in the sale of motion picture "packages" to television. Such practices have typically been held to be illegal, especially when copyrighted films have been used as tying mechanisms.[73]

Other instances of prohibition of full-line forcing have occurred. For example, E&J Gallo Winery, the largest seller of wine in the United States, consented to a Federal Trade Commission order prohibiting it, among other things, from requiring its wholesalers to distribute any Gallo wines in order to obtain other kinds.[74] And Union Carbide Corporation agreed to a consent order prohibiting the company from requiring its dealers to purchase from it their total requirements of six industrial gases (acetylene, argon, helium, hydrogen, nitrogen, and oxygen) and from making the purchase of the six gases a prerequisite for dealers buying other gases or welding products.[75]

Even though tying has been labeled as per se illegal, courts have sought answers to a number of critical questions before condemning these policies. For example, it is necessary to determine when conditions of economic power exist. In theory, where no leverage exists in a product, there can be no tying arrangement by coercion; the buyer can always go elsewhere to purchase. Thus, plaintiffs must prove more than the existence of a tie. As Sullivan points out, they must also show that the tying product is successfully differentiated and that the commerce affected by the tie is significant.[76] Therefore, the presumption against tying arrangements is not quite as strong as the per se rule against horizontal price-fixing conspiracies.

Evidence of this comes from a 1984 Supreme Court case involving hospital services.[77] In *Jefferson Parish*, anesthesiologist Edwin Hyde, who had been denied admission to the staff of East Jefferson Hospital, sued the governance board of the hospital. It had an exclusive contract with a firm of anesthesiologists requiring that all anesthesiological services for the hospital's patients be performed by that firm. The Supreme Court agreed with the district court that the relevant geographic market was Jefferson Parish (i.e., metropolitan New Orleans) and not the neighborhood immediately surrounding East Jefferson Hospital. The Court reasoned that "70 of the patients residing in Jefferson Parish enter hospitals other than East Jefferson. . . . Thus, East Jefferson's 'dominance' over persons residing in Jefferson Parish is far from overwhelming."

The Court further explained that "the fact that the exclusive contract requires purchase of two services that would otherwise be purchased separately does not make the contract illegal. Only if patients are forced to purchase the contracting firm's services as a result of the hospital's market power would the arrangement have anticompetitive consequences." East Jefferson's market power was not significant enough to make the contract illegal.

The most important dictum in the *Jefferson Parish* decision was the following sentence, which provides the foundation on which other tying cases are to be analyzed:

> The essential characteristic of an invalid tying arrangement lies in the seller's exploitation of its control over the tying product to force the buyer into the purchase of a tied product that the buyer either did not want at all, or might have preferred to purchase elsewhere on different terms.[78]

The issues on which courts are most likely to focus are whether (1) there are two distinct products; (2) the seller has required the buyer to purchase the tied product in order to obtain the tying product; (3) the seller has sufficient market power to force a tie-in; (4) the tying arrangement affects a substantial amount of commerce in the market for the tied product; and (5) whether the tie is necessary to fulfill a legitimate business purpose. However, these structural per se criteria are not likely to be satisfied for sellers with relatively small market shares, especially when the tying product is unpatented.[79]

The criteria are more likely to be satisfied in situations typified by the FTC's 1991 investigation of Sandoz Pharmaceuticals Corporation, which was accused of violating antitrust laws by requiring buyers of Clorazil, a drug for schizophrenia, also to purchase a weekly blood test from a company under contract with Sandoz.[80] Sandoz's dominant position relative to the specific drug category under investigation was, at the time, obvious. The company agreed to settle the charges by promising not to require Clorazil purchasers to buy the blood monitoring service from Sandoz or anyone designated by Sandoz.[81]

In Europe, reactions similar to those in the Sandoz situation are evident. For example, in 1994, Tetra-Pak, the Swedish packaging group, lost an appeal case. The Court found, among other things, that customer contracts that tied Tetra-Pak machine users to using Tetra-Pak cartons were not objectively justified and were intended to strengthen the company's dominant position in such packaging by reinforcing its customers' economic dependence on it.[82]

One of the most remarkable and significant cases involving tying was decided by the U.S. Supreme Court on June 8, 1992. At that time, the Court ruled that Eastman Kodak Company would have to stand trial on a tying claim brought against it by 18 independent service organizations (ISOs).[83] The case arose out of Kodak's efforts to keep to itself the business of servicing Kodak-brand copiers. Kodak had refused to sell replacement parts to the ISOs that wanted to service its copiers. The Court alleged that Kodak's conduct amounted to an illegal monopolization of the business of servicing Kodak-brand copiers and an illegal tying of the sale of servicing copiers to the sale of replacement parts.

To succeed on the tying claim, the ISOs had to prove that Kodak had "appreciable market power" in the business of selling replacement parts for Kodak-brand copiers. To succeed on the monopolization claim, the ISOs had to prove that Kodak had "monopoly power" in the sale of the replacement parts. Kodak argued that sales of its copiers represented, at most, 23 percent of the sale of copiers for all manufacturers, and the Supreme Court agreed that the 23 percent share did not amount to appreciable power in the copier sales business. But the Court found that Kodak controlled nearly 100 percent of the market for its replacement parts—which are not interchangeable with the parts of other manufacturer's machines—and between 80 percent and 95 percent of the service market.

The Court reasoned that the relevant market for antitrust purposes is determined by the choices available to Kodak equipment owners who must use Kodak parts. Thus, the company's motion for summary judgment (i.e., it wanted the Supreme Court to dismiss the case because of its lack of market power in the copier market) was rejected by a vote of 6 to 3, and the case was sent back to the Federal District Court in San Francisco for trial. Kodak lost verdicts both in that trial and in an appeal to the Ninth U.S. Circuit Court of Appeals in August 1997, and was ordered to pay $35 million to the 11 plaintiffs in the case.[84]

Designated Product Policies

A manufacturer may want to sell some portion of its product line only through a limited number of resellers, whereas its other resellers may sell a different subset of the company's products. For instance, very sophisticated Toro brand lawn mowers may sell only through its authorized service-providing dealers, whereas less exclusive products (such as lawn edging tools) can sell through mass-merchandisers as well. Such a policy can help preserve the manufacturer's exclusive brand name and prevent its erosion through overly broad distribution through outlets with an insufficiently high-quality image or service provision capabilities. Further, this effectively gives resellers reasonable profit-making opportunities. If the reseller has at least some products for which there is little or no competition, it can confidently invest in customer service and promotional activities, secure in the knowledge that its efforts will not fall victim to free riding by other resellers.

In the United States, a manufacturer has no legal obligation to sell all of its products to all resellers who wish to do so, under most circumstances. Two exceptions apply. One is the situation in which the manufacturer is a monopolist with excess capacity. Then, because there is no other source for the product, the manufacturer is required to supply it to requesting resellers. This was the case when AT&T was forced to open its exchanges to the independent long-distance phone companies, MCI and Sprint, in the United States; AT&T was the only holder of these exchanges and thus was required to grant access to its competitors.

The other exception is the case in which the manufacturer has signed a contract with its reseller promising to supply all of its products. In this case, the manufacturer is required to honor the contract. Beyond these two exceptions, however, there is still the usual antitrust restriction that a refusal to deal with a reseller is not the result of a conspiracy or other agreement in restraint of trade.

An interesting instance of a case in this area involved the toy retailer Toys "R" Us. The situation is somewhat unusual because it was Toys "R" Us, the *retailer*, rather than a manufacturer, who was accused of instigating limited access to various manufacturers' products at competing retailers.[85] In May 1996, the Federal Trade Commission filed charges against Toys "R" Us, alleging that the retailer threatened not to buy any toy whose manufacturer also sold the toy through a warehouse club store chain. It thus effectively forced the suppliers into exclusive dealing with Toys "R" Us of the most popular toys in the market. In particular, the charges alleged that the company did this to prevent warehouse clubs such as Sam's Club, Price Club, and Costco from competing with it. The threat was real, because the warehouse clubs had a much lower cost structure than Toys "R" Us and therefore could effectively price compete, given product supply. For example, Toys "R" Us offered Mattel's Hollywood Hair Barbie at a retail price of $10.99, but the produce was sold to warehouse clubs only packaged with an extra dress, forcing the retail price up to $15.99 and preventing direct price comparisons between Toys "R" Us and other retailers. Hasbro, another toy manufacturer, refused to supply Hall of Fame G.I. Joe dolls directly to warehouse clubs; Mattel also declined to offer Fisher-Price brand pool tables to warehouse clubs; and Toys "R" Us allegedly blocked sales of Disney's *Toy Story* movie figures to the discount chains as well. The FTC argued that the anticompetitive threat was great, because Toys "R" Us had an approximate 20 percent market share of all U.S. retail toy sales. Although this figure was seen as somewhat low overall, the relevant manufacturers sold as much as 30 percent of their total volume through Toys "R" Us, thus creating a significant degree of dependence on the retailer and allowing it to force them into anticompetitive actions. Further, after Toys "R" Us started this enforced boycott in 1993, Costco Company's toy sales dropped by 1.6 percent, even while its overall sales grew by 19.5 percent. And Mattel's sales to warehouse clubs fell from over $23 million in 1991 to only $7.5 million in 1993.

On October 1, 1997, an FTC administrative judge ruled against Toys "R" Us, and while awaiting review by the full Commission, New York's attorney general filed a lawsuit against the toy company and three of its largest suppliers (Mattel, Hasbro, and Rubbermaid Inc.'s Little Tikes Co.), alleging an illegal conspiracy to raise prices and stifle competition. On November 17, the suit was amended to add 37 additional states, Puerto Rico, and Washington, DC to the lawsuit. Eventually 44 of the 50 states joined the lawsuit. On October 15, 1998, the FTC upheld the administrative law judge's 1997 ruling, issuing a cease and desist order to Toys "R" Us. FTC chairman Robert Pitofsky wrote that it had "used its dominant position as toy distributor to extract agreements from and among toy manufacturers to stop selling to warehouse clubs the same toys that they had sold to other toy distributors." Again the retailer appealed the decision to the U.S. Circuit Court of Appeals.

In December 1998, Hasbro settled in the suit filed by the states, agreeing to pay $6 million in donations and other payments to the states and charities. In May 1999, Toys "R" Us and the other suppliers also settled in that lawsuit. Toys "R" Us agreed to pay a total of $40.5 million in cash and toy donations in the settlement. Mattel agreed to pay $8.2 million in cash and toy donations, and Little Tikes agreed to pay $1.3 million in cash and toys. None of the parties admitted wrongdoing in agreeing to the settlement. The key to the case was both the degree of harm to competition and the concerted effort made to influence multiple manufacturers, who all agreed to the restrictive dealing practices.

SELECTION AND TERMINATION POLICIES

A central theme throughout this text is that organizations must devote a great deal of time, attention, effort, and monetary resources to the design and management of their distribution systems. In order to achieve success with their marketing channels, channel managers must set up selection criteria with regard to potential channel partners and must monitor the performance of anyone admitted to the distribution system. Even with intensive distribution systems, selection procedures are necessary, because it is unlikely that every conceivable outlet will be asked to sell every intensively distributed product. (Department stores are not typically asked to sell milk, for example.) Anytime anyone establishes selection criteria, there is an extremely high likelihood that someone will not make the cutoff, no matter how low the admission standards are set. Therefore, refusing to deal with certain channel members is a key element of channel policy. The same rationale applies to performance criteria, which means that another key element of channel policy is termination.

Sellers can select their own distributors according to their own criteria and judgment. They may also announce in advance the circumstances under which they would refuse to sell to certain intermediaries. These two commercial "freedoms" were granted in *U.S. v. Colgate & Co.* in 1919 and are referred to as the *Colgate doctrine*.[86] The doctrine was formally recognized by Congress in Section 2(a) of the Robinson-Patman Act, which reads that "nothing herein contained shall prevent persons engaged in selling goods, wares, or merchandise in commerce from selecting their own customers in bona fide transactions and not in restraint of trade." Implicit in a seller's general right to select its preferred distribution system is the right to deal with certain channel members on a limited basis. General Motors, for example, is not obligated to sell Chevrolets to a Buick dealer.

The *Colgate* doctrine contains two explicit exceptions. First, the decision not to deal must be "independent" or unilateral (i.e., it cannot be part of a concerted action). This was one of the problems faced by the toy manufacturers named in the Toys "R" Us example: It would not have been illegal for any of the manufacturers named in the case *unilaterally* to refuse to sell a particular product to warehouse club stores. It was rather the concerted effort, led by the toy company that made the action illegal. Second, the refusal must occur in the absence of any intent to create or maintain a monopoly. If a unilateral refusal to deal is ever illegal, it is when the refusal is undertaken by a monopolist or by someone who hopes by the refusal to become one.[87]

Clearly, refusal to deal is a major "punishment" underlying a channel member's coercive power. After a number of court decisions dealing with the right of refusal to deal, the "right" has been narrowly confined. Suppliers may formally cut off dealers for valid business reasons, such as failure to pay or poor performance in sales or service. But where the suppliers have set up restrictive, regulated, or programmed distribution systems and there are complaints that the dealers who are being cut off have somehow stepped out of line with the edicts of the programmed system, refusal to deal becomes harder to defend. Losing such a lawsuit imposes treble damages on the defendant, so the stakes are high. The courts generally ask two important questions in determining whether a refusal to deal violates the law:

- Was the decision to delete certain channel members a unilateral decision on the part of the manufacturer?
- Was there a legitimate business reason for the change in channel membership?[88]

Many cases continue to be brought under Sections 1 and 2 of the Sherman Act involving decisions by suppliers or franchisors to terminate an existing dealer, to substitute a new for an old dealer, or to vertically integrate. Although it appears the original selection of distributors or dealers for a new product poses no legal problems, it is increasingly clear that the termination of existing distributors and dealers can cause difficulties, even in the absence of group boycotts or conspiracies. It is risky to drop a distributor or dealer who refuses to do as the manufacturer asks.[89] Thus, when exclusive dealing, customer or territorial restrictions, or other types of vertical restraints have been applied by a supplier within its distribution network and when a dealer is cut off from that network, the dealer may take the supplier to court. It can charge that the refusal to deal was based on the supplier's desire to maintain an unlawful practice.

The orientation toward litigation in these cases has been furthered by particularistic legislation, such as the Automobile Dealers Franchise Act of 1956, which entitles a car dealer to sue any car manufacturer who fails to act in good faith in connection with the termination, cancellation, or nonrenewal of the dealer's franchise. However, the manufacturer is open to produce evidence that the dealer has not acted in good faith and that its own action was thereby justified. In nearly all the cases to date, this defense has been successful.[90] Nevertheless, many lawsuits are filed every year by franchisees who claim to be wrongly terminated by franchisors. Most of these cases are fought over contract and property rights; few of them involve antitrust.

A manufacturer's right to terminate resellers outside the United States varies widely from country to country. In many countries, it is very difficult to terminate a distributor, particularly if the distributor has been the exclusive representative of the manufacturer's product. Given the wide variation in the laws on termination in various areas, a manufacturer seeking to expand distribution transnationally must check local regulations carefully.

OWNERSHIP POLICIES

The make-versus-buy (vertical integration) question is another central concern in this text (see Chapter 7). Here, we focus on the antitrust concerns surrounding vertical integration. Frequently, the decision to vertically integrate puts a company in competition with independent channel intermediaries that are already carrying, or being asked to carry, the company's brands. We have already argued that most suppliers, for example, will have a number of different channels so that the needs of various market segments can be addressed. In most cases, one of those channels is a direct channel comprised of salespeople employed by the company. Clearly, dual distribution is the rule rather than the exception.

Vertical integration may come about through forward integration by a producer, backward integration by a retailer, or integration in either direction by a wholesaler or a logistics firm, such as a common carrier. Integration may be brought about by the creation of a new business function by existing firms (internal expansion) or by acquisition of the stock or the assets of other firms (mergers).

The two methods of creating integration are fundamentally different in their relationship to the law. Internal expansion is regulated by Section 2 of the Sherman Act, which prohibits monopoly or attempts to monopolize any part of the interstate or foreign commerce of the United States. External expansion is regulated by Section 7 of the Clayton Act, which prohibits the purchase of stock or assets of other firms if the effects may be to substantially lessen competition or tend to create a monopoly in any line of commerce in any part of the country.[91] Internal expansion is given favored treatment under the law, under the theory that internal expansion expands investment and production and thus increases competition, whereas growth by merger removes an entity from the market.

Integration, whether by merger or internal expansion, may result in the lowering of costs and make possible more effective interorganizational management of the channel. It may also be a means of avoiding many of the legal problems previously discussed, because an integrated firm is free to control prices and allocate products to its integrated outlets without conflict with the laws governing restrictive distribution policies.

Vertical Integration by Merger

The danger posed by vertical mergers from an antitrust perspective is the same as that posed by many of the policies already discussed in this chapter—the possibility that vertical integration will foreclose competitors by limiting their access to sources of supply or to customers. Thus, prior to the purchase of McCaw Cellular by AT&T in 1994, the U.S. Justice Department focused attention on the fact that AT&T makes equipment, such as radio towers, that some of McCaw's competitors, including several regional Bell operating companies, use in their cellular-phone operations. Officials were concerned that the merger would give AT&T an incentive to charge McCaw's competitors more while providing poor service.[92]

Similarly, in 1993, when Merck, the world's largest drug company, bought Medco Containment Services, the largest U.S. distributor of discount prescription medicines, for $6.6 billion, competitors raised antitrust concerns about foreclosure from Medco. Indeed, when, in 1994, Eli Lilly, another major pharmaceutical manufacturer, indicated that it wanted to purchase PCS Health Systems, another enormous managed care drug distributor, for $4 billion, it agreed to restrictions imposed by the Federal Trade Commission preventing Lilly from unfairly pushing sales of its own brands through PCS or gaining information about prices at which competing drugs sell.[93] In a statement announcing its decision to reexamine the Merck–Medco merger and another one involving SmithKline Beechham (SKB) and Diversified Pharmaceutical Services (DPS), the FTC said, "We remain concerned about the overall competitive impact of vertical integration by drug companies into the pharmacy benefits management market."[94] Although all of these mergers (including AT&T–McCaw) were eventually approved, the questions raised indicate that, from time to time, vertical mergers will draw the attention of the antitrust enforcement agencies.

The most significant vertical merger case in the United States over the last 45 years was decided in 1962 when the merger of the Brown Shoe Company and the G. R. Kinney Company, the largest independent chain of shoe stores, was declared illegal by the U.S. Supreme Court because it was believed that the merger would foreclose other manufacturers from selling through Kinney.[95] However, between the 1970s and 1990s, the government has refrained from challenging vertical mergers by and large. The interest shown by the Federal Trade Commission in the Lilly–PCS, Merck–Medco, and SKB–DPS mergers in the 1990s could be a signal of reignited governmental interest in vertical mergers.

In its 1982 *Merger Guidelines*, the Justice Department announced that it would challenge vertical mergers only when they facilitated collusion or significantly raised barriers to new entry.[96] Nevertheless, this should not be intepreted to mean that the issue is dead and gone. In addition to the drug mergers mentioned above, the Federal Trade Commission became active in 1994 when TCI and Comcast, the largest and third-largest cable-TV companies in the United States, agreed to form a joint venture to take ownership of QVC. At the time, QVC was one of two cable-shopping ventures that controlled 98 percent of sales made via TV. The other was Home Shopping Network, which was 79 percent controlled by TCI. The vertical issue investigated by the Federal Trade Commission was whether existing and potential competitors to QVC and Home Shopping Network would have trouble selling on cable TV, because TCI and Comcast together controlled access to about 30 percent of cable-wired homes.[97] The merger was finally approved because the relevant market was defined as all of retailing, not just home shopping via television.

Vertical mergers also have attracted attention outside the United States. For example, in 1990, Grand Metropolitan, the U.K. food, beverage, and retailing conglomerate, and Elders IXL, the Australian brewer, agreed to a $5 billion pubs-for-breweries swap. Grand Met was to transfer its four breweries and the Ruddles, Watneys, Truman, and Webster's beer brands to Courage, owned by Elder, whereas Courage was to combine its 4,900 pubs with GrandMet's 3,570 pubs. A major challenge to the merger arose when the United Kingdom's Monopolies and Mergers Commission issued a 500-page report concluding that United Kingdom's large breweries were operating a "complex monopoly"—a series of practices that restrict competition. These were said to be centered on the long-established tied-house system, which ensures that most of Britain's 80,000 pubs stock the products of only one supplier—the company that owns them.[98] The merger was allowed, but only after the British government put into effect "guest beer orders" allowing pubs to stock beers from suppliers other than the ones that own them.[99]

Vertical Integration by Internal Expansion

This form of integration is limited only by the laws preventing monopoly or attempts to monopolize. A firm is ordinarily free to set up its own supply, distribution, or retailing system unless this would overconcentrate the market for its product.[100] Section 7 of the Clayton Act specifically permits a firm to set up subsidiary corporations to carry on business or extensions thereof if competition is not substantially reduced.

Dual Distribution

The term *dual distribution* describes a wide variety of marketing arrangements by which a manufacturer or a wholesaler reaches its final markets by employing two or more different types of channels for the same basic product. However, the dual arrangement (whereby manufacturers market their products through competing vertically integrated and independently owned outlets on either the wholesale or retail level) often creates controversy. This practice is customary in many lines of trade, such as the automotive passenger tire, personal computer, paint, and petroleum industries. Dual distribution also takes place when a manufacturer sells similar products under different brand names for distribution through different channels. This latter kind of dual distribution comes about because of market segmentation or because of sales to distributors under private labels.

In all dual distribution situations, conflict among channel members is likely to be relatively high. But serious legal questions arise mainly in two situations: (1) when price "squeezing" is suspected or (2) when horizontal combinations or conspiracies are possible among competitors. The first situation brings about issues comparable to those found when examining the use of functional discounts. The second relates to potential restraints of trade arrived at in concert by vertically integrated firms and their customers.

Price Squeezes. A seller operating at only one market level in competition with a powerful vertically integrated firm might be subject to a *price squeeze* at its particular level. For example, a manufacturer of fabricated aluminum might be under pressure from its raw material (ingot) supplier to increase prices. If the supplier were also a fabricator, it could take its gain from the price increase, which represents higher costs to the customer-competitor, and use all or a portion of the increased returns for marketing activities at the fabricating level. This was exactly the scenario in the *Alcoa* case.[101] A number of lower court decisions have declared unlawful an integrated supplier's attempt to eliminate a customer as a competitor by undercutting the customer's prices and placing the customer in a price squeeze.[102]

The same kind of competitive inequality arises from the granting of functional discounts when different functional categories may be represented by buyers that, at least in part of their trade, are in competition with each other. As was the situation in the previously mentioned *Hasbrouck* case, oil jobbers, for example, sometimes sell at retail, and they may use their functional discounts received as jobbers to advantage in competition with retailers. Such pricing raises the possibility of Robinson-Patman Act as well as Sherman Act violations.

Horizontal Combinations or Conspiracies. In dual distribution situations, the distinction between purely vertical restraints and horizontal restraints may be critical in determining the legality of a marketing activity. Section 1 of the Sherman Act is not violated by the purely unilateral action of a supplier; at least one additional party must be present whom the court may find contracted, combined, or conspired with the supplier. Dominant manufacturers may replace distributors, but they may not enter into competition with them and destroy them.

In sum, each challenge to dual distribution is generally appraised in terms of its special circumstance. However, whenever a supplier competes directly with its customers, any of its actions that threaten the customers are likely to be subject to antitrust scrutiny. The question of intent will be crucial. The decision may rest on the issues raised in the *Sylvania* case discussed earlier in this chapter. There, the Supreme Court mandated a balancing of the effects of a marketing policy on intrabrand and interbrand competition in situations involving vertical restraints.

SUMMARY

The setting of channel policies is at the center of distribution strategy. Policies are rules to guide the functioning of channels. They are the means by which channel managers can achieve effective integration, coordination, and role performance throughout the channel in the absence of outright ownership. However, whenever policies are set, there is the potential for conflict, because policies tend to be exclusionary, elitist, or restrictive. That is, they are used to focus or redirect efforts of channel members and to assure that behavior within channels is not random. These limits on behavior have evoked a series of antitrust concerns.

We have addressed six different, but frequently interrelated, channel policy areas in this chapter. They deal with market coverage, customer coverage, pricing, product lines, selection and termination, and ownership. Regarding market coverage, the major focus is on the geographic spacing of channel members. Attention in this policy area is given to intensive versus selective versus exclusive distribution. The more intensive distribution becomes, the greater the sales a company can expect in the short run. However, over time, channel members will be less and less willing to provide costly service outputs because of the price competition that is likely to ensue from the presence of many intra-brand competitors in the same territory. This fact compels suppliers to consider selective and exclusive distribution policies, thereby dampening the amount of intrabrand competition. Following the *Sylvania* case, the legality of these policies is determined under the rule-of-reason doctrine.

Marketing managers may also wish to assure that only the "right" channel members service specific kinds of customers. They may want company-employed salespeople to call on technically sophisticated heavy users and distributor salespeople to call on other kinds of accounts. Or they may want authorized dealers to sell the company's brand only to end-users and to prevent them from acting like master distributors, making sales to other, unauthorized dealers. Antitrust enforcement agencies often categorize these and other customer coverage policies as customer or resale restrictions. They are governed by the same line of reasoning applied to market coverage policies.

Both market and customer coverage policies have an indirect effect on prices. Direct effects are achieved via price-setting procedures. Although a host of pricing policies can be adopted in marketing channels, two of particular interest here are price maintenance and price discrimination. The former deals with the setting of specific resale prices throughout a marketing channel. The latter deals with setting different prices to different buyers. Minimum resale price maintenance is per se illegal if there is some form of agreement or concerted action between or among channel members involved in setting or policing the policy. Otherwise, it can be adopted unilaterally. Maximum resale price maintenance (when arrived at by agreement) is now subject to a rule of reason and hence may be implemented as long as there are no anticompetitive effects. Price discrimination is at the heart of market segmentation strategies, but can run afoul of the law if it substantially lessens competition. It covers such significant activities as the granting of promotional allowances and services and the offering of quantity and functional discounts.

The product line policies addressed in this chapter—exclusive dealing, tying, and full-line forcing—are all adopted with the aim of gaining the undivided attention of channel members on suppliers' products. They restrict interbrand competition directly, whereas market and customer coverage policies restrict intrabrand competition. Because of this potential for foreclosing competitors, sometimes more concern is shown about them by antitrust agencies than about the coverage policies. Exclusive dealing is the supplier's requirement that its distributor sell or lease only its products or at least no products in direct competition with the supplier's products. Tying is the requirement that customers purchase other products in order to obtain a product they desire. Full-line forcing is a variant of tying, under which the buyer must buy the entire line of items to obtain one item.

Finally, the vertical integration question is addressed by ownership policies. If the decision has been made to "make" (own one's own distribution system or source of supply) rather than to "buy" (deal with independently owned channel intermediaries or suppliers), then the choice remaining is either acquisition (or merger) or internal expansion. Internal expansion seems to pose very little problem from an antitrust perspective. Until recently, the same was true for vertical mergers, but in the wake of acquisition and merger activity in the pharmaceutical and entertainment distribution channels, the issue has been brought back to life. In any case, when vertical integration takes place and the company continues to employ other, nonintegrated channels as well, conflicts often arise with regard to the common dual distribution problem.

This chapter has addressed only federal antitrust law, with a predominantly U.S. focus. The states of the United States have become much more active in the antitrust arena, and therefore marketing executives would make a serious mistake to ignore the vast outpouring of legislation and court case precedents regulating distribution practices in each of the states in which the products of their companies are sold. In addition, antitrust and competitive laws vary widely throughout different countries of the world. It behooves the international channel manager to become familiar with local variations.

Discussion Questions

1. Debate the pros and cons of the following policies for the products listed below. (Do not be concerned about the antitrust issues; just ask yourself whether you would adopt them from a managerial point of view.)

Policies	Products–Brands
Exclusive distribution	Ping brand golf clubs
Price maintenance	General Electric washing machines
Tying	DeWalt power tools
Exclusive dealing	Copeland compressors
Price discrimination	Wrigley chewing gum
	Mead notepads
	Liz Claiborne skirts

2. Which is preferable—intrabrand or interbrand competition? Can there be one without the other? Where do you stand on the issue of intrabrand competition: Is it necessary in order for there to be viable general competition from a macro perspective? Discuss these questions in the context of resale restrictions and the granting of exclusive territories.

3. Which of the policies discussed in this chapter are governed by the following legal rules and why: (a) rule of reason, (b) per se illegal, (c) modified rule of reason, and (d) per se legal?

4. Do you believe that the Robinson-Patman Act should be stricken from the laws of the United States? Debate the pros and cons of this question and come out with a position on it.

5. The president of an automobile accessory manufacturing business wants to purchase a chain of automotive retail stores. What managerial questions might you raise about the decision? What legal issues might this raise?

6. Name five uses of coercive power that would be legal in interorganizational management. Name five uses of reward power that would be legal.

7. From a strictly managerial perspective, what are the differences between market coverage and customer coverage policies? Do they accomplish the same or different ends in the same or different ways? If different, why do you think they were coupled together in the *Sylvania* case by the Supreme Court justices? Was this a mistake?

8. Which conflict management strategies suggested in Chapter 9 might be questionable from a legal perspective? Why?

Notes

1. *Continental T.V., Inc. v. GTE Sylvania Inc.*, 433 U.S. 36 (1977).

2. Shantanu Dutta, Jan B. Heide, and Mark Bergen, "Vertical Territorial Restrictions and Public Policy: Theories and Industry Evidence," *Journal of Marketing*, 63 (October 1999), pp. 121–34.

3. David Thunder, "Key Considerations in European Distribution," *Client Communique*, 3 (April 1991), p. 1.

4. See John Griffiths, "Commission Plans Will Loosen Carmakers' Grip on Dealers," *Financial Times*, October 6, 1994, p. 6; "Carved Up," *The Economist*, October 31, 1992, p. 73; Guy de Jonquieres, "Electric Suppliers Blames for EC Price Variations," *Financial Times*, August 3, 1992, p.1; Robert Rice, "Whiff of Controversy Hangs in the Air," *Financial Times*, November 16, 1993, p. 10; and Emma Tucker and Haig Simonian, "Brussels Plans to Give More Freedom to Car Dealers," *Financial Times*, May 26, 1995, p. 1.

5. Emma Tucker, "Easing the Pain of 'Vertical Restraints,'" *Financial Times*, January 22, 1997, p. 2; "'Vertical Restraints' Eased," *Financial Times*, October 1, 1998, p. 2; "Competition: Industry Council Gives Green Light for Changes to Vertical Restraints Rules," *European Report*, May 1, 1999; "Council Formally Adopts Two Competition Regulations," *European Report*, June 16, 1999; and "Competition: Commission Firms Up Single Block Exemption Rule," *European Report*, July 17, 1999.

6. Phillip Areeda and Louis Kaplow, *Antitrust Analysis: Problems, Text, Cases*, 4th ed. (Boston: Little, Brown, 1988), p. 659.

7. Richard A. Posner, *Antitrust Law: An Economic Perspective* (Chicago: University of Chicago Press, 1976), p. 162.

8. *Kmart Corporation v. Cartier, Inc.*, 56 LW 4480 (1988).

9. Ibid. Also, see Stephen Wermiel, "Justices Uphold Customs Rules on Gray Market," *Wall Street Journal*, June 1, 1988, p. 2; and "A Red-Letter Day for Gray Marketeers," *BusinessWeek*, June 13, 1988, p. 30.

10. These and other reasons can be found in Stanley I. Ornstein, "Exclusive Dealing and Antitrust," *The Antitrust Bulletin*, spring 1989, pp. 71–74.

11. See Areeda and Kaplow, *Antitrust Analysis*, pp. 630–35; and Paul H. Rubin, *Managing Business Transactions* (New York: Free Press, 1990), pp. 126–27.

12. *Monsanto Co. v. Spray-Rite Service Corp.*, 104 U.S. 1464 (1984).

13. *Russell Stover Candies, Inc. v. Federal Trade Commission*, 718 F. 2d 256 (1983).

14. *Business Electronics Corp. v. Sharp Electronics Corp.*, 99 S. Ct. 808 (1988).

15. Patrick J. Kaufmann, "Dealer Termination Agreements and Resale Price Maintenance: Implications of the Business Electronics Case and the Proposed Amendment to the Sherman Act," *Journal of Retailing*, 64 (summer 1988), p. 120.

16. Paul M. Barrett, "Anti-Discount Policies of Manufacturers Are Penalizing Certain Cut-Price Stores," *Wall Street Journal*, February 27, 1991, p. B1.

17. Michael Arndt, "Consumers Pay More as Price-Fixing Spreads," *Chicago Tribune*, August 18, 1991, sec. 7, p. 5.

18. See, for example, Roger D. Blair and Francine Lafontaine, "Will *Khan* Foster or Hinder Franchising? An Economic Analysis of Maximum Resale Price Maintenance," *Journal of Public Policy & Marketing*, 18, no. 1 (spring 1999), pp. 25–36.

19. *Albrecht v. Herald Co.*, 390 U.S. 145 (1968).

20. Blair and Lafontaine, "Will *Khan* Foster or Hinder Franchising?"; Edward Felsenthal, "Manufacturers Allowed to Cap Retail Prices," *Wall Street Journal*, November 5, 1997, p. A3; and Susan B. Garland and Mike France, "You'll Charge What I Tell You to Charge," *BusinessWeek*, October 6, 1997, pp. 118–20.

21. Mary Jane Sheffet and Debra L. Scammon, "Resale Price Maintenance: Is It Safe to Suggest Retail Prices?" *Journal of Marketing*, 49 (fall 1985), pp. 89–90.

22. *Business Electronics Corp.*, 485 U.S. at 733.

23. 272 U.S. 476, 486–488 (1926).

24. *Ryko Manufacturing Co. v. Eden Services*, 823 F.2d 1215 at 1223 (8th Cir. 1987).

25. See Thomas T. Nagle and Reed K. Holden, *The Strategy and Tactics of Pricing*, 2nd ed. (Upper Saddle River, NJ: Prentice Hall, 1995), p. 210, for a discussion of segmented pricing.

26. *U.S. v. Borden Co.*, 383 U.S. 637 (1966).

27. *Brooke Group Ltd. v. Brown & Williamson Tobacco Corp.*, U.S. 114 S.Ct. 13 (1993).

28. Ibid. at 25.

29. Ibid.

30. See Bridget O'Brian, "Verdict Clears AMR on Illegal Pricing Charges," *Wall Street Journal*, August 11, 1993, p. A3.

31. F. M. Scherer and David Ross, *Industrial Market Structure and Economic Performance*, 3rd ed. (Boston, MA: Houghton Mifflin, 1990), p. 514.

32. *FTC News Notes*, 89 (December 26, 1988), p. 1.

33. Anita Sharpe, "Pharmacies Sue Drug Manufacturers and Distributors over Pricing Policies," *Wall Street Journal*, October 18, 1994, p. B9; Dave Kansas, "Four Grocery Chains Sue 16 Drug Firms, Mail-Order Concern in Pricing Debate," *Wall Street Journal*, March 7, 1994, p. B5; and Steven Morris, "Independent Phamacies Face Bitter Pill," *Chicago Tribune*, November 6, 1994, business section, p. 1.

34. Robert Langreth, "Settlement Cleared in Pharmacies' Suit over Price Fixing, but Debate Lingers," *Wall Street Journal*, June 24, 1996, p. B5; Elyse Tanouye and Thomas M. Burton, "Drug Makers Agree to Offer Discounts for Pharmacies," *Wall Street Journal*, July 15, 1998, p. B4.

35. See *Fall City Industries, Inc. v. Vanco Beverage, Inc.*, 460 U.S. 428 (1983).

36. *Standard Oil Co. v. FTC*, 340 U.S. 231 (1951).

37. *Federal Trade Commission v. Sun Oil Co.*, 371 U.S. 505 (1963).

38. *Fall City Industries v. Vanco Beverage*.

39. Gregory T. Gundlach and Paul N. Bloom, "Slotting Allowances and the Retail Sale of Alcohol Beverages," *Journal of Public Policy & Marketing*, 17, no. 2 (fall 1998), pp. 173–84.

40. Mary W. Sullivan, "Slotting Allowances and the Market for New Products," *Journal of Law and Economics*, 40 (October 1997), pp. 461–93.

41. Wujin Chu, "Demand Signalling and Screening in Channels of Distribution," *Marketing Science*, 11 (1992), pp. 327–47; and Martin A. Lariviere and V. Padmanabhan, "Slotting Allowances and New Product Introductions," *Marketing Science*, 16, no. 2 (1997), pp. 112–28.

42. "More Facts and Figures on Slotting," *Supermarket Business*, July 1997, p. 19. The percentages were lower for health and beauty products and for general merchandise–nonfood products, with 14 and 15 percent, respectively, paying between $500,000 and $1 million, and close to 30 percent of respondents reporting no payment of slotting allowances.

43. Ibid.

44. Neal R. Stoll and Shepard Goldfein, "The Spring Trade Show: Explaining the Guidelines," *New York Law Journal*, Antitrust and Trade Practice Section, May 20, 1997, p. 3.

45. Sang-Yong Kim and Richard Staelin, "Manufacturer Allowances and Retailer Pass-Through Rates in a Competitive Environment," *Marketing Science*, 18, no. 1 (1999), pp. 59–76.

46. Leslie Hansen Harps and Warren Thayer, "FTC Is Investigating 'Exclusive Dealing,'" *Frozen Food Age*, May 1997, p. 78; Sullivan, "Slotting Allowances"; Joseph P. Cannon and Paul N. Bloom, "Are Slotting Allowances Legal Under the Antitrust Laws?" *Journal of Public Policy and Marketing*, 10 (spring 1991), pp. 167–86. Note, however, that slotting allowances are prohibited for alcoholic beverages, as discussed by Gundlach and Bloom, "Slotting Allowances and the Retail Sale of Alcohol Beverages." Nevertheless, Gundlach and Bloom also stress that the logic for slotting allowances varies from market to market and thus a general rule for its use should not be inferred.

47. Martha Brannigan, "Coke Is Victim of Hardball on Soft Drinks," *Wall Street Journal*, March 15, 1991, p. B1.

48. See *Atlantic Trading Corp. v. FTC*, 258 F.2d 375 (2d Cir. 1958).

49. Federal Trade Commission, *Guides for Advertising Allowances and Other Merchandising Payments and Services*, 16 C.F.R. part 240 (1983).

50. Ibid., 240.6.

51. *FTC v. Fred Meyer Company, Inc.*, 390 U.S. 341 (1968).

52. "Federal Trade Commission Adopts Changes in Robinson-Patman Act Guides," *FTC News*, August 7, 1990, pp. 1–2.

53. See Fred Pfaff, "The Club Store Ruckus," *Food and Beverage Marketing,* May 1, 1989, p. 53.

54. 496 U.S. 492 (1990).

55. Ibid.

56. Ibid.

57. For an excellent discussion of this problem, see Mark T. Spriggs and John R. Nevin, "The Legal Status of Trade and Functional Price Discounts," *Journal of Public Policy and Marketing*, 13 (spring 1994), p. 63.

58. See Stanley I. Ornstein, "Exclusive Dealing and Antitrust," *The Antitrust Bulletin*, spring 1989, pp. 71–79; and Areeda and Kaplow, *Antitrust Analysis*, pp. 773–76.

59. Wendy Bounds, "Kodak Signs Pact to Take Control of Eckerd's Regional Photo Labs," *Wall Street Journal*, February 6 (1996), p. B4; Wendy Bounds, "Kodak Rebuilds Photofinishing Empire, Quietly Buying Labs, Wooing Retailers," *Wall Street Journal*, June 4, 1996, p. B1; Wendy Bounds, "Fuji Will Buy Wal-Mart's Photo Business," *Wall Street Journal*, July 9, 1996, p. A3; Ronald E. Yates, "Fuji Knocks Kodak Out of Focus," *Chicago Tribune*, July 12, 1996, sec. 3, p. 1; Emily Nelson, "Kodak to Supply Photofinishing to American Stores," *Wall Street Journal*, July 30, 1996, p. A10; Emily Nelson, "Kodak Signs Pact with Price/Costco, Dealing Fuji Blow," *Wall Street Journal*, December 5, 1996, p. B13.

60. A. D. Neale and D. G. Goyder, *The Antitrust Laws of the U.S.A.*, 3rd ed. (New York: Cambridge University Press, 1980), p. 266.

61. 365 U.S. 320 (1961).

62. F. M. Scherer and David Ross, *Industrial Market Structure and Economic Performance* (Boston: Houghton Mifflin 1990).

63. Herbert Hovenkamp, *Federal Antitrust Policy* (St. Paul, MN: West Publishing, 1994), p. 390.

64. *R.J. Reynolds Tobacco Co. v. Philip Morris*, No. 1:99cv00185; the lawsuits by the two other competitors that were merged into this case were *Lorillard Tobacco Co. v. Philip Morris Inc.*, No. 1:99cv00207, and *Brown & Williamson v. Philip Morris Inc.*, No. 1:99cv00232, M.D. N.C. See "Court Tells Philip Morris to Halt Contracts For Prime Retail Space," *Mealey's Litigation Report: Tobacco*, 13, no. 5 (July 1, 1999).

65. See Suein L. Hwang, "Philip Morris Is Investigated on Marketing," *Wall Street Journal*, May 15, 1997, p. A3; Yumiko Ono, "For Philip Morris, Every Store Is a Battlefield," *Wall Street Journal*, June 29, 1998, p. B1;

Richard Turcsik, "Philip Morris Fires Up New Program," *Brandmarketing*, 7, no. 2 (February 1999), p. 50; Paul Nowell, "Philip Morris Exec Says Program Wasn't Intended to Coerce Retailers," *The Associated Press State & Local Wire*, June 10, 1999; Paul Nowell, "Judge Issues Preliminary Injunction in Cigarette Display Case," *The Associated Press State & Local Wire*, June 30, 1999; "Philip Morris Enjoined on Store Displays," *New York Times*, June 30, 1999, p. C2; Bloomberg News, "Rivals Win Temporary Ban on Philip Morris Ad Strategy," *The Plain Dealer*, 1999, business section, p. 2C; "Court Tells Philip Morris to Halt Contracts for Prime Retail Space"; and John Willman and Emma Tucker, "Space Invaders," *Financial Times*, October 21, 1999, p. 16.

66. See Areeda and Kaplow, *Antitrust Analysis,* pp. 705–10.

67. *Standard Oil Company of California v. U.S.*, 337 U.S. 293 (1949) at 305.

68. *U.S. v. Jerrold Electronics Corp.*, 187 F. Supp. 545 (1960), affirmed per curian at 363 U.S. 567 (1961).

69. *Norman E. Krehl, et. al. v. Baskin-Robbins Ice Cream Company, et. al.*, 42 F. 2d 115 (8th Cir. 1982).

70. In re: *Chock Full O'Nuts Corp. Inc.*, 3 Trade Reg. Rep. 20, 441 (Oct. 1973).

71. See, for example, Bryan Gruley et al. "U.S. Sues Microsoft Over PC Browser," *Wall Street Journal*, October 21, 1997, p. A3; David Bank, "Why Software and Antitrust Law Make an Uneasy Mix," *Wall Street Journal*, October 22, 1997, p. B1; Susan B. Garland, "Justice vs. Microsoft: Why It Has a Case," *BusinessWeek*, November 17, 1997, p. 147; Steve Hamm and Susan B. Garland, "Just vs. Microsoft: What's the Big Deal?" *BusinessWeek*, December 1, 1997, pp. 159–64; Louise Kehoe, "Hard Case for Software," *Financial Times*, January 22, 1998, p. 13; Steve Lohr, "Just What Constitutes a Consumer Stranglehold?" *New York Times*, January 18, 1998; "Now Bust Microsoft's Trust," *The Economist*, November 13, 1999, pp. 15–16; "Busted," *The Economist*, November 13, 1999, pp. 21–23; Mike France et al., "Does a Breakup Make Sense?" *BusinessWeek*, November 22, 1999, pp. 37–41; "The Go-Between," *The Economist*, November 17, 1999, pp. 69–70; John R. Wilke and David Bank, "Signals in the Microsoft Case: The Judge Hints at Ideas for a Remedy," *Wall Street Journal*, December 2, 1999, pp. B1, B4; and Mike France, "A Microsoft Settlement? Don't Bet On It," *BusinessWeek*, December 6, 1999, p. 50.

72. *U.S. v. J. I. Case Co.*, 101 F. Supp. 856 (1951).

73. *U.S. v. Paramount Pictures*, 334 U.S. 131 (1948); U.S. v. Loew's Inc., 371 U.S. 45 (1962).

74. "Consent Agreement Cites E&J Gallo Winery," *FTC News Summary*, May 21, 1976, p. 1. See also "Gallo Winery

Consents to FTC Rule Covering Wholesaler Dealings," *Wall Street Journal*, May 20, 1976, p. 15.

75. "Union Carbide Settles Complaint by FTC on Industrial-Gas Sales; Airco to Fight," *Wall Street Journal*, May 20, 1977, p. 8.

76. Sullivan, "Slotting Allowances," p. 439.

77. *Jefferson Parish Hospital District No. 2 v. Hyde*, 104 LW 1551 (1984). See also Robert E. Taylor and Stephen Wermiel, "High Court Eases Antitrust Restrictions on Accords Linking Sales of Goods, Services," *Wall Street Journal*, March 28, 1984, p. 6.

78. *Jefferson Parish Hospital District No. 2 v. Hyde*.

79. Scherer and Ross, *Industrial Market Structure*, p. 568.

80. See Paul M. Barrett, "FTC's Hard Line on Price Fixing May Foster Discounts," *Wall Street Journal*, January 11, 1991, p. B1.

81. *FTC News Notes*, 91 (June 17, 1991), p. 1; Paul M. Barrett, "Sandoz Settles FTC Charges over Clorazil," *Wall Street Journal*, June 21, 1991, p. B3.

82. "Tetra Pak Appeal," *Financial Times*, October 18, 1994, p. 10.

83. *Eastman Kodak Co. v. Image Technical Service Inc.*, U.S. 112 S.Ct. 2072 (1992).

84. Wendy Bounds, "Jury Finds Kodak Monopolized Markets in Services and Parts for Its Machines," *Wall Street Journal*, September 19, 1995, p. A4; and "Court Upholds Jury Verdict Against Kodak, Cuts Damages," *The Buffalo News*, August 27, 1997, business section, p. 6B.

85. See Bryan Gruley and Joseph Pereira, "FTC Is to Vote Soon on Staff's Request for Antitrust Action Against Toys 'R' Us," *Wall Street Journal*, May 21, 1996, p. A3; Joseph Pereira and Bryan Gruley, "Toys 'R' Us Vows It Will Challenge Any Antitrust Charges Brought by FTC," *Wall Street Journal*, May 22, 1996, p. A3; Joseph Pereira and Bryan Gruley, "Relative Power of Toys 'R' Us Is Central to Suit," *Wall Street Journal*, May 24, 1996, p. B1; William M. Bulkeley and John R. Wilke, "Toys Loses a Warehouse-Club Ruling with Broad Marketing Implications," *Wall Street Journal*, October 1, 1997, p. A10; "Judge Faults Toys 'R' Us," *International Herald Tribune*, October 1, 1997, p. 13; John M. Broder, "Toys 'R' Us Led Price Collusion, U.S. Judge Says," *New York Times*, October 1, 1997, p. A1; David Segal, "Judge Rules Toys 'R' Us Wasn't Playing Fair; Product Agreements Found Anti-Competitive," *Washington Post*, October 1, 1997, financial section, p. D10; "Action Against Toymakers Grows," *Arizona Republic*, November 18, 1997, business section, p. E4; Jerri Stroud, "Missouri and Illinois Join Suit over Toys; The FCC Concluded the Retailer Bullied Toymakers," *St. Louis Post-Dispatch*, November 19, 1997, business section, p. C1; Norman D. Williams, "California, 37 Other States

Claim Toys 'R' Us Fixed Prices," *Sacramento Bee*, November 19, 1997; David Segal, "Toys 'R' Us Told to Change Its Tactics; FTC Says Methods Limited Manufacturers' Sales to Discounters," *Washington Post*, October 15, 1998, financial section, p. C12; Joel Brinkley, "F.T.C. Tells Toys 'R' Us to End Anticompetitive Measures," *New York Times*, October 15, 1998, p. C22; Gina Chon, "Hasbro Agrees to Pay $6 Million in Antitrust Settlement," *The Associated Press State & Local Wire*, December 11, 1998; David Segal, "Toys 'R' Us to Settle Suit for $40.5 Million; Discount Clubs Squeezed Out, States Allege," *Washington Post*, financial section, p. E3; and Amy Westfeldt, "Toy Makers to Pay $50 Million in Cash and Toys to Settle Antitrust Suit," *The Associated Press State & Local Wire*, May 26, 1999.

86. *U.S. v. Colgate & Co.*, 250 U.S. 300 (1919).

87. See Hovenkamp, *Federal Antitrust Policy*, p. 263.

88. Debra L. Scammon and Mary Jane Sheffet, "Legal Issues in Channels Modification Decisions: The Question of Refusals to Deal," *Journal of Public Policy & Marketing*, 5 (1986), p. 82.

89. Neale and Goyder, *The Antitrust Laws of the U.S.A.*, p. 282.

90. Ibid., p. 282.

91. Under the wording of Section 7 of the Clayton Act, it is unnecessary to prove that the restraint involved has actually restrained competition. It is enough that it "may" tend to substantially lessen competition.

92. Edward Felsenthal and Joe Davidson, "Two Big Deals Spur Concerns About Antitrust," *Wall Street Journal*, December 9, 1993, p. B1.

93. Thomas M. Burton, "Eli Lilly Agrees to Restrictions on Buying PCs," *Wall Street Journal*, October 26, 1994, p. A3.

94. Viveca Novak and Elyse Tanouye, "FTC Restudies 2 Acquisitions by Drug Firms," *Wall Street Journal*, November 15, 1994, p. A16.

95. *Brown Shoe Co. v. U.S.*, 370 U.S. 294, Vertical Aspects, 370 U.S. 323 (1962).

96. U.S. Department of Justice, *Merger Guidelines* (Washington, DC: June 14, 1982), pp. 22–26.

97. Viveca Novak, "TCI–Comcast Agreement to Buy QVC May Face an FTC Antitrust Challenge," *Wall Street Journal*, September 15, 1994, p. B3.

98. Tom Maddocks, "Brewers Play the Tie-Break," *Business*, August 1990, p. 76; Philip Rawstorne, "A Change of Pace to Restructuring," *Financial Times*, September 19, 1990, p. 17; and Philip Rawstorne, "GrandMet Backed on $2.6bn Deal," *Financial Times*, November 21, 1990, p. 34.

99. Philip Rawstorne, "Reduced Importance of the Brewer's Tie," *Financial Times*, February 25, 1991, p. 20.

100. *FTC v. Consolidated Foods Corp.*, 380 U.S. 592 (1965).

101. *U.S. v. Aluminum Co. of America*, 148 F. 2d 416 (2nd Cir. 1945).

102. See, for example, *Columbia, Metal Culvert Co., Inc. v. Kaiser Aluminum & Chemical Corp.*, 579 F. 2d 20 (3d Cir. 1978); *Coleman Motor Co. v. Chrysler Corp.*, 525 F. 2d 1338 (3d Cir. 1975); and *Industrial Building Materials, Inc. v. Inter-Chemical Corp.* 437 F. 2d 1336 (19th Cir. 1970).

PART FOUR

CHANNEL INSTITUTIONS

13

Retailing

LEARNING OBJECTIVES

After reading this chapter, you will:

- Be familiar with the types of retail structures that exist worldwide
- Understand how a retail positioning strategy flows from both cost-side and demand-side factors
- Understand that the retailer's positioning strategy implies a set of service outputs delivered to the market, and helps differentiate a retailer from its competitors, even if the products sold are identical
- Be aware of important trends and developments on the consumer and channel side that affect retail management
- Understand the power and coordination issues facing retailers and their suppliers, and how suppliers respond to retailers' use of power to influence channel behavior
- Be aware of the increasing globalization of retailing and how it affects not only the retailers, who themselves are selling outside their national borders, but also their suppliers and local competitors

Modern retailing is fiercely competitive and innovation oriented. It is populated by an ever-growing variety of institutions and constantly buffeted by a highly fluid environment. The purpose of this chapter is to describe how retailers position themselves in this environment and to discuss some of the more significant competitive developments that have made retailing so volatile. An understanding of the chapter's material will help channel managers more fully account for "bottom-up" pressures when forming strategies and designing distribution systems.[1]

The chapter proceeds by first defining the distinction between retail and wholesale sales. Then, we explain the operational characteristics that define retail position and the nature of retailing competition. Finally, we consider some of the strategic issues currently facing retailers.

RETAILING DEFINED

> *Retailing consists of the activities involved in selling goods and services to ultimate consumers for personal consumption.*

Thus, a retail sale is one in which the buyer is an ultimate consumer, as opposed to a business or institutional purchaser. In contrast to wholesale sales (i.e., purchases for resale or for business, industrial, or institutional use), the buying motive for a retail sale is always personal or family satisfaction stemming from the final consumption of the item being purchased.[2]

Although the distinction between retail and wholesale sales may seem trite, it is really very important, because buying motives are critical in segmenting markets. Companies that sell personal computers to high school students for use in doing their homework (or playing computer games) are engaged in making retail sales. Companies that sell personal computers to their parents for use in a family business run out of a home office are engaged in making wholesale sales. CompUSA or Office Depot in the United States make both retail and wholesale sales. They need to understand the differences in serving these different market segments, even though they are served out of the same retail establishments.

Table 13.1 profiles the world's 100 leading retailers in 1998 sales. The table shows a wide variety of retail types (supermarkets, hypermarkets, department stores, etc.) and of countries of origin, suggesting that retail success comes in many shapes, sizes, and cultural origins. Many of these top retailers are also transnational, crossing country borders to expand their businesses. The challenges of transnational and global retailing are therefore an important focus for leading retailers today.

Chapter 15 focuses on wholesale sales. More and more businesses sell to other businesses out of what look and feel like retail stores. Here, though, the focus is on businesses engaged in making retail sales. The discussion includes both store and nonstore (e.g., mail-order or direct-selling) retailing. We defer a discussion of electronic retailing channels to Chapter 14.

CHOOSING A RETAIL POSITIONING STRATEGY

How a retailer chooses to position itself in the marketplace significantly affects its competitiveness and performance. Retailers make choices about cost-side and demand-side characteristics of their businesses. On the cost side, they commonly focus on margin and inventory turnover goals. On the demand side, the retailers choose what service outputs

TABLE 13.1
The World's Top 100 Retailers, 1998

Retailer (by rank; home country; primary line of trade)	1998 Sales (US $ million)	Compound Annual Growth Rate, 1996–1998	Number of Stores (owned + networked)	Number of Countries	% of Sales Outside Home Country
1. Wal-Mart Stores, Inc. (USA; discount stores)	130,523	14.5%	3,599	9	9.4%
2. Metro AG (Germany; diversified)	52,110	21.6	2,085	20	35.0
3. The Kroger Co. (USA; supermarkets)	43,082	30.8	3,370	1	0.0
4. ITM Enterprises SA (France; supermarkets)	38,986	30.2	3,148	7	18.8
5. Royal Ahold (Netherlands; supermarkets)	37,070	41.9	3,927	16	70.9
6. Sears, Roebuck & Co. (USA; department stores)	36,704	4.2	5,132	2	8.6
7. Promodès Group (France; diversified)	36,204	12.7	5,978	16	38.1
8. Carrefour SA (France; hypermarkets, supercenters)	36,020	17.1	1,661	20	43.6
9. Albertson's, Inc. (USA; supermarkets)	35,872	61.4	2,563	1	0.0
10. Kmart Corp. (USA; discount stores)	33,674	3.5	2,161	1	0.0
11. Edeka Gruppe (Germany; diversified)	32,553	0.6	11,183	6	2.4
12. Rewe-Gruppe (Germany; supermarkets)	32,221	0.3	11,509	9	18.5
13. Tengelmann Warenhandelsgesellschaft (Germany; supermarkets)	31,009	6.2	7,853	11	49.0
14. Dayton Hudson Corp. (USA; discount stores, department stores)	30,951	10.5	1,182	1	0.0
15. JCPenney Company, Inc. (USA; department stores)	30,456	16.0	4,578	4	N/A
16. The Home Depot (USA; hardlines, specialty stores)	30,219	24.4	761	3	N/A
17. Aldi Group (Germany; supermarkets)	29,000	1.7	3,100	8	30.8
18. Tesco PLC (United Kingdom; supermarkets)	28,436	11.2	821	8	7.8
19. Safeway Inc. (USA; supermarkets)	27,090	25.2	1,623	3	12.9
20. J. Sainsbury PLC (United Kingdom; supermarkets)	25,184	6.5	833	2	18.4
21. Auchan Groupe (France; hypermarkets, supercenters)	25,087	11.1	1,269	11	38.1
22. Centres E. Leclerc (France; diversified)	24,832	6.6	823	4	N/A
23. Ito-Yokado Co., Ltd. (Japan; general merchandise superstores with food)	24,068	4.1	18,494	19	29.9
24. Costco Companies, Inc. (USA; warehouse clubs)	23,830	11.4	294	6	19.1
25. Daiei, Inc. (Japan; diversified)	22,063	−1.2	8,871*	2	N/A
26. Otto Versand Gmbh & Co. (Germany; nonstore catalog)	19,684	18.2	603	19	49.2

(continued)

TABLE 13.1

The World's Top 100 Retailers, 1998 *(continued)*

Retailer (by rank; home country; primary line of trade)	1998 Sales (US $ million)	Compound Annual Growth Rate, 1996–1998	Number of Stores (owned + networked)	Number of Countries	% of Sales Outside Home Country
27. Jusco Co., Ltd. (Japan; general merchandise superstores with food)	18,825	7.5	2,355	9	8.4
28. IGA Inc (Independent Grocers Alliance) (USA; supermarkets)	18,000	3.5	3,400	23	N/A
29. Federated Department Stores, Inc. (USA; department stores)	17,428	7.0	401	1	0.0
30. Kingfisher PLC (United Kingdom; diversified)	15,579	27.1	2,919	13	40.0
31. Walgreen Co. (USA; drugstores)	15,307	14.0	2,549	1	0.0
32. CVS Corporation (USA; drugstores)	15,274	66.2	4,122	1	0.0
33. Casino Groupe (France; hypermarkets, supercenters)	15,130	13.9	4,799	7	17.7
34. Delhaize "Le Lion" Group (Belgium; supermarkets)	14,346	12.4	1,926	10	77.5
35. MYCAL Corporation (Japan; department stores)	14,142	1.4	419*	1	0.0
36. Lidl & Schwarz Stiftung & Co. KG (Germany; supermarkets)	14,123	8.4	3,000	10	20.6
37. Winn-Dixie Stores, Inc. (USA; supermarkets)	13,909	2.9	1,182	2	N/A
38. Marks & Spencer PLC (United Kingdom; general merchandise superstores with food)	13,630	3.8	683	36	19.7
39. Asda (United Kingdom; supermarkets)	13,553	9.8	227	1	0.0
40. Lowe's Companies, Inc. (USA; hardlines specialty stores)	13,331	24.5	522	1	0.0
41. The May Department Stores Company (USA; department stores)	13,072	5.9	393	1	0.0
42. Seibu Saison Group (Japan; supermarkets)	13,026	2.2	279*	6	N/A
43. Coles Myer Ltd. (Australia; diversified)	12,952	6.4	1,772	2	0.9
44. Rite Aid Corporation (USA; drugstores)	12,732	35.2	3,821	1	0.0
45. Safeway PLC (United Kingdom; supermarkets)	12,448	6.8	476	2	1.8
46. Publix Super Markets, Inc. (USA; supermarkets)	12,067	7.6	591	1	0.0
47. Karstadt AG (Germany; department stores)	11,917	−1.0	455	11	20.0
48. Woolworths Ltd. (Australia; supermarkets)	11,416	10.7	1,296	2	N/A
49. Toys "R" Us, Inc. (USA; hardlines specialty stores)	11,170	6.0	1,481	26	26.8
50. Migros—Genossenschaftsbund (Switzerland; supermarkets)	10,444	9.2	578*	6	1.3

TABLE 13.1
The World's Top 100 Retailers, 1998 (*continued*)

Retailer (by rank; home country; primary line of trade)	1998 Sales (US $ million)	Compound Annual Growth Rate, 1996–1998	Number of Stores (owned + networked)	Number of Countries	% of Sales Outside Home Country
51. Best Buy Co., Inc. (USA; hardlines specialty stores)	10,078	13.9	311	1	0.0
52. Pinault-Printemps-Redoute SA (France; diversified)	9,899	−14.8	275	20	29.5
53. Circuit City Stores, Inc. (USA; hardlines specialty stores)	9,388	14.3	587	1	0.0
54. Systeme U. Centrale Nationale SA (France; supermarkets)	9,289	7.3	776	1	0.0
55. The Limited, Inc. (USA; apparel specialty stores)	9,191	3.1	5,382	1	0.0
56. Takashimaya Company, Limited (Japan; department stores)	9,079	−2.2	19*	6	1.9
57. Gap, Inc. (USA; apparel specialty stores)	9,055	30.9	2,428	6	10.1
58. The Office Depot (USA; hardlines specialty stores)	8,998	21.8	789	19	11.6
59. Dillards, Inc. (USA; department stores)	8,937	19.8	335	1	0.0
60. Meijer, Inc. (USA; hypermarkets, supercenters)	8,500	8.6	115	1	0.0
61. Coop Schweiz (Switzerland; supermarkets)	8,472	2.4	1,691	1	0.0
62. Uny Co., Ltd. (Japan; general merchandise superstores with food)	8,427	9.0	5,144*	2	1.4
63. Loblaw Companies Limited (Canada; supermarkets)	8,423	12.7	1,993	1	0.0
64. COOP Italia scarl (Italy; supermarkets)	8,383	5.2	1,240	1	0.0
65. Somerfield PLC (United Kingdom; supermarkets)	8,234	35.2	1,423	1	0.0
66. Euromadis SpA (Italy; supermarkets)	8,217	16.7	4,000	1	0.0
67. Mitsukoshi Ltd. (Japan; department stores)	8,113	0.9	N/A	11	N/A
68. The TJX Companies, Inc. (USA; apparel specialty stores)	7,949	9.0	1,246	5	7.8
69. Cora Group (France; supermarkets)	7,878	35.3	530	5	26.1
70. El Corte Ingles (Spain; department stores)	7,472	−8.8	733**	3	N/A
71. The Boots Company, PLC (United Kingdom; drugstores)	7,442	−1.0	2,018	4	4.9
72. Empire Company Limited (Canada; supermarkets)	7,414	86.9	700	1	0.0
73. The Great Universal Stores, PLC (United Kingdom; nonstore)	7,180	33.8	959	15	14.3
74. Staples, Inc. (USA; hardlines specialty stores)	7,123	34.0	913	4	N/A
75. IKEA AB (Sweden; hardlines specialty stores)	7,016	20.5	143	29	89.3
76. ICA AB (Sweden; supermarkets)	6,967	17.0	3,300	3	N/A

(*continued*)

TABLE 13.1
The World's Top 100 Retailers, 1998 *(continued)*

Retailer (by rank; home country; primary line of trade)	1998 Sales (US $ million)	Compound Annual Growth Rate, 1996–1998	Number of Stores (owned + networked)	Number of Countries	% of Sales Outside Home Country
77. H. E. Butt Grocery Company (USA; supermarkets)	6,900	18.1	260	2	N/A
78. Quelle Aktiengesellschaft (Germany; non-store)	6,876	−7.7	492	26	17.7
79. Army and Air Force Exchange Service (USA; diversified)	6,494	1.6	1,423	N/A	N/A
80. Saks Incorporated (USA; department stores)	6,220	81.4	349	1	0.0
81. Laurus NV (Netherlands; supermarkets)	6,136	N/A	2,480	3	24.3
82. CompUSA (USA; hardlines specialty stores)	6,046	29.8	209	1	0.0
83. des Galeries Lafayette, SA (France; department stores)	5,979	10.8	484*	2	N/A
84. S Group (Finland; diversified)	5,880	9.2	1,203	1	0.0
85. GIB Group, S.A. (Belgium; diversified)	5,621	−2.9	1,070	6	18.8
86. Dairy Farm International Holdings Limited (Hong Kong; supermarkets)	5,594	−10.4	1,572	9	N/A
87. Faellesforeningen Danmarks Brugser Group (FDB Group) (Denmark; diversified)	5,484	−0.6	1,205	1	0.0
88. John Lewis Partnership PLC (United Kingdom; department stores)	5,250	5.4	140	1	0.0
89. SuperValu Inc. (USA; supermarkets)	5,091	4.1	1,027	1	0.0
90. Nordstrom, Inc. (USA; department stores)	5,028	10.6	98	1	0.0
91. La Rinascente (Italy; department stores)	5,023	16.9	883	1	0.0
92. Tandy Corporation (USA; hardlines specialty stores)	4,788	−12.7	7,030	1	0.0
93. Hudson's Bay Company (Canada; department stores)	4,769	8.5	546	1	0.0
94. Mdo SpA (Italy; supermarkets)	4,692	1.8	3,548	1	0.0
95. Vendex NV (Netherlands; diversified)	4,688	−12.5	2,436*	6	15.0
96. Anton Schlecker (Germany; drugstores)	4,603	12.0	8,110	5	15.0
97. Venator Group, Inc. (USA; diversified)	4,555	−25.0	6,002	14	16.3
98. Dixons Group (United Kingdom; hardlines specialty stores)	4,515	7.6	959	2	N/A
99. Pepkor Ltd. (South Africa; diversified)	4,385	37.7	2,409	13	18.0
100. Kesko Ltd. (Finland; supermarkets)	4,368	−11.1	2,184	3	1.1

*1997 results, latest data available.
**1996 results, latest data available.
Source: PricewaterhouseCoopers Global Retail Intelligence System, 1998 data.

to provide to their shoppers. Here, we discuss each of these issues in turn and then summarize by showing how choices on each of these dimensions help shape the retailers' overall strategy.

Financial and Cost-Side Positioning: Margin and Inventory Turnover Goals

"Traditional" retailing systems have been categorized as high-margin–low-turnover operations offering numerous personal services. (Turnover refers to the number of times per year inventory turns on the retail shelf.) In contrast, "modern" retailing systems are characterized by low margins, high inventory turnover, and minimal service levels. Both sets of institutions continue to exist, but in recent years, the spotlight has focused on the revolutionary volume efficiencies flowing out of modern retailing systems. The most advanced retailers, such as Home Depot, are able to combine low margin and high turnover with excellent personal service. They generate high rates of return on the capital employed in their businesses by continuous improvements in asset management made possible by using sophisticated information systems. Service attracts consumers, but it can be provided only if it can be paid for.

Historically, the low-margin–high-turnover model has been oriented toward generating high operational efficiency with the savings generated passed on to the customer. However, many of these savings must be seen as involving a *transfer* of cost (opportunity cost as well as actual "effort" cost) rather than a clear elimination of it. Thus, reductions in service output levels—such as those associated with product selection opportunity, convenience in location, "atmosphere" of the retail environment, personal services, financial and delivery accommodations, and the like—accompany the typical retail package offered by the low-margin–high-turnover operation. Table 13.2 describes the major economic and operating factors driving performance in different types of retail chains. The economic drivers of gross margin,

TABLE 13.2
Economic and Operating Drivers of Various Retail Chain Types

Chains	Economic Drivers	Operating Drivers
Apparel specialty (e.g., The Limited)	High gross margin	Merchandise management; markdown control
	High inventory turns	Merchandise management
Discount (e.g., Wal-Mart)	Low operating expense	Low cost; high sales productivity
	High fixed-asset productivity	Low investment; high sales productivity
Category killer (e.g., Home Depot)	Low operating expense	Low cost; high sales productivity
Department store (e.g., Federated)	High gross margin	Merchandise mangement
National chain (e.g., JCPenney)	High gross margin	Merchandise management

Source: Nancy Karch, director, McKinsey & Company, presentation at Northwestern University, April 3, 1995.

expense control, and merchandise productivity imply methods of operation that focus differentially on picking the right merchandise for the market (to avoid markdowns) and controlling investment levels in retail assets.

Note that an operational philosophy trading off margin and turnover is based on a recognition of the costs (represented by marketing flows) that certain segments of consumers are willing to absorb in certain classes of purchasing behavior. The retailer should pursue this strategy only if consumers are willing to make a trade-off of lower service levels for the lower price that can accompany low-margin retail operations.

Of critical importance in determining which path to follow—low margin–high turnover or high margin–low turnover—are management's perceptions of the organization's best chance for achieving its financial target. The appropriate pathway can be highlighted using the *strategic profit model (SPM)*. A brief description of the SPM is introduced here so that the reader can gain some appreciation of its influence on the margin and turnover dimensions of retail strategy.[3] The SPM can be stated as follows:

$$\frac{\text{Net Profit}}{\text{Net Sales}} \leftrightarrow \frac{\text{Net Sales}}{\text{Total Assets}} = \frac{\text{Net Profit}}{\text{Total Assets}}$$

and

$$\frac{\text{Net Profit}}{\text{Total Assets}} \leftrightarrow \frac{\text{Total Assets}}{\text{Net Worth}} = \frac{\text{Net Profit}}{\text{Net Worth}}$$

Thus:

$$\frac{\text{Net Profit}}{\text{Net Sales}} \leftrightarrow \frac{\text{Net Sales}}{\text{Total Assets}} \leftrightarrow \frac{\text{Total Assets}}{\text{Net Worth}} = \frac{\text{Net Profit}}{\text{Net Worth}}$$

Management can pursue margin management (net profit–net sales), asset turnover (net sales–total assets), or financial management via financial leverage (total assets–net worth) in order to secure a target return on net worth (net profit–net worth). (Net sales are gross sales less customer returns and allowances.) If there is strong downward pressure on margins, because of competitive forces and economic conditions, then management is likely to pursue asset turnover. These sets of conditions have led management to emphasize such criteria as sales per square foot (which reflects space and location productivity), sales per employee (which reflects labor productivity), and sales per transaction (which reflects merchandising program productivity).

More specific to the retail context are three interrelated measures of performance that help retailers improve profitability (see also Appendix 13.1):[4]

- *Gross margin return on inventory investment (GMROI)*. GMROI is equal to the gross margin percentage times the ratio of sales to inventory (at cost). It combines margin management and inventory management and can be calculated for companies, markets, stores, departments, classes of products, and stockkeeping units (SKUs). GMROI allows the retailer to evaluate inventory on the return on investment it produces and not just on the gross margin percentage. Efficient consumer response (ECR) initiatives in the grocery industry have been aimed at reducing average inventory levels while maintaining sales, through the use of just-in-time shipments, electronic data interchange (EDI) linkages between manufacturers and retailers, and the like. Such actions reduce the denominator of GMROI without reducing the numerator, thus increasing retailing returns. GMROI often considers items with widely varying gross margin percentages as equally profitable, as in the following example:

$$Gross\ Margin \times Sales\text{-}to\text{-}Inventory\ Ratio\ =\ GMROI$$

	Gross Margin		Sales-to-Inventory Ratio		GMROI
A	50%	×	3	=	150%
B	30%	×	5	=	150%
C	25%	×	6	=	150%

- *Gross margin per full-time equivalent employee (GMROL).* Retailers should *optimize,* not maximize, GMROL. As sales rise per square foot, not all fixed costs (e.g., rent, utilities, and advertising) rise in proportion. In fact, they decline as a percentage of sales as sales increase. Having more salespersons may actually lower average sales per full-time equivalent (FTE) employee, but nevertheless increase profitability, because they leverage the other fixed assets in the store.

- *Gross margin per square foot (GMROS).* Such a measure permits an assessment of how well retailers are using their unique asset—the shelf or floor space they can allocate to suppliers' products.

A problem with GMROI, however, is that gross margin accounts for the cost of goods sold and not for differences in variable costs associated with selling different kinds of merchandise. Other measures, such as contribution dollars per square foot of selling space or direct product profit (DPP), are more comprehensive, but more difficult to derive. In any case, retailers' use of measures such as GMROI or DPP places pressure on suppliers. They must attend to: (1) the gross margins their brands permit retailers to earn, (2) the sales volume (in units) their brands generate, (3) the amount of shelf or floor space consumed by their brands, and (4) the costs incurred in storing, handling, and selling their brands. There is increasing emphasis on systems designed by suppliers to speed up the replenishment of inventory, because faster replenishment rates mean less need for shelf space and less inventory replenishment, and therefore a reduction in the denominators of these formulae.

Fixed costs of retailing are also a key focus in some retailing situations. The plans of Kingfisher and Asda, two British food and general merchandise retailers, to merge in April 1999 were based in large part on the synergies in fixed costs the merger could bring. Combining their distribution networks and headquarters operations alone was forecast to save £10 million per year, in addition to millions of pounds of savings in joint purchasing economies and the ability to cross-sell each retailer's products in the other retailer's stores.[5] Ultimately, Wal-Mart bought Asda to expand its entry into the European market. Undoubtedly this move will also reduce Asda's retailing costs, because Wal-Mart is the expert on cost-cutting in retailing.

One significant element of retailing cost—the rent paid to landlords for bricks-and-mortar stores—ideally should be charged based on the return the specific retailer generates for the mall developer, who is the retailer's landlord. In shopping malls in particular, the largest stores, or "anchor" stores as they are known, generate disproportionate benefits for the developer, because they attract shoppers who then also patronize other stores in the mall—that is, they generate "positive externalities." One research study documented differences in rents charged to various retailers at shopping malls, and, consistent with this notion, found that anchor stores pay a significantly lower rental rate (72 percent lower per square foot!) than nonanchor stores. One could state that bargaining power on the part of large, desirable retailers is the sole reason for this. But the research also found that anchor stores pay a lower rent per square foot in larger super-regional malls than in smaller regional malls. It suggests that the mall developers recognize the differentially larger positive externality endowed upon the larger mall. These subsidies persist despite the generally lower sales per square foot that anchor stores generate versus specialty and other smaller stores. Thus, the economics of the retail store depend not only on internal cost factors but also on cost factors determined by the retail environment in which the store is found.[6]

More generally, the product-by-product profitability calculations mentioned earlier are done not only by grocery retailers (where direct product profitability originated; see Chapter 16 for more information) but also in department and specialty stores. Table 13.3 details the product categories, their floor locations, and the percentage of total store profits earned by each, at Saks Fifth Avenue's flagship store on Fifth Avenue in New York City in 1996. Total revenue for the store was $420 million, and operating profits for this store alone were about $36 million, one-third of the company's total operating profit. The table shows a standard retailing strategy of a multifloor department store or specialty store: to put the highest profit-margin items on the easily accessible main floor, while locating more specialized merchandise or merchandise that the shopper is willing to search for on higher floors. Each of the lower floors has at least one important department to attract shoppers. The image of a high-end department store is that of a retailer that makes high profits from the sale of designer clothing. But the profitability data suggest otherwise. Saks compensates for the low-volume designer label business with its own attractive (and profitable) private-label clothes, and seeks to target a younger customer than its traditional target.

Demand-Side Positioning

Clearly, higher retail profits through higher margins, higher merchandise turnover, and lower retailing costs are all desirable. From the previous discussion, it should be clear that the same financial outcome is possible with many combinations of these variables. Thus, the stance the retailer chooses on the supply side constitutes part of its positioning strategy in the retail landscape. The demand side, too, is important. The retailer's choice of service outputs to provide makes any given product purchase more or less attractive to the chosen target market.

Bulk-Breaking. One of the classic functions of a retail intermediary is the breaking of bulk. Manufacturers make their products in large batch lot sizes, but consumers may want to consume just one unit of the product. Higher-service retailers may buy in large quantities from their suppliers, but offer the consumer the opportunity to purchase in small quantities.

Some retailers, such as warehouse stores (e.g., Sam's Club or Aldi), offer consumers a lower price, but require them to buy in larger lot sizes than at traditional grocery retailers. Consumers who do not have a high cost of transportation or storage and who have

TABLE 13.3

Profit Percentages at Saks Fifth Avenue's Flagship Store, 1996

Floor	Department	Percent of Total Store Profit Generated by This Department
Main floor (39% of total profit)	Cosmetics	18%
	Accessories (belts, handbags, sunglasses)	10
	Costume jewelry	3
	Fine jewelry	4
	Hosiery	0.5
	Men's shirts, ties, accessories	3
	Penhaligon's (British shop)	0.5
Second floor (12% of total profit)	Designer sportswear	8
	Men's sportswear	4
Third floor (6% of total profit)	High-end designer collections	4.5
	Furs	1
	Bridal boutique	0.5
Fourth floor (9% of total profit)	Career wear	8
	Designer shoes	1
Fifth floor (7% of total profit)	Women's contemporary designers	6
	Shoes	1
Sixth floor (10% of total profit)	Men's suits	8
	Men's designer clothing	2
Seventh floor (9% of total profit)	Women's coats	3
	Women's petite sizes	4
	Women's dresses	2
Eighth floor (5.5% of total profit)	Lingerie	3
	Children's clothes	2
	Restaurant and candy shop	0.5
Ninth floor (2.5% of total profit)	Salon Z (large sizes)	2
	Beauty salon	0.5

Source: Adapted from Jennifer Steinhauer, "The Money Department," *New York Times,* April 6, 1997, magazine section, pp. 62–64.

adequate disposable income can choose to buy a case of paper towels or 10-pound bags of frozen vegetables at lower unit prices. Clearly, only those who can afford to buy in such quantities, transport their purchases home, and store unused product until it is needed, choose to buy from these retailers. More traditional grocery retailers may encourage, but not force, large-lot-size purchases through special pricing, such as "buy one get one free" (BOGO) deals or pricing products in multiple units (e.g., "three for $1.00").

Spatial Convenience. In a general sense, products can be classified as convenience, shopping, or specialty goods. Implicit in this understanding is the extent of *search–shopping* activity the consumer is willing to undertake. For example, convenience goods should require little effort to obtain, whereas considerable effort may be required to secure highly regarded, relatively scarce specialty goods. Consequently, retail location decisions receive a great deal of attention.

Consumer search–shopping behavior varies between consumer segments as well as between product categories. It also varies over time as demographic and lifestyle changes occur across market segments. As women enter the labor force in increasing numbers and the opportunity cost of time increases, the effective cost of search and shopping increases. For these consumers, time saved is becoming as important as money saved. This factor, along with widespread access and exposure to multiple media, reduces both shopping frequency and the necessity of searching for information for these consumer segments.

These observations have profound implications. They mean that although location decisions remain critical, the dominant consideration in many consumers' choices is convenience, usually defined in terms of ease and speed of access. The tremendous increase in the use of various home shopping technologies (catalogs or on-line retailing, the topic of Chapter 14) is a testimony to the importance of spatial convenience. Shopping from home essentially makes physical outlet location a nonissue. These issues led Levi-Strauss to drop 20,000 catalogs for Dockers brand men's pants each in France and the United Kingdom in 1997, in an effort to increase sales in Europe. Levi's management says that shopping is not a pleasant experience for young men. Its strategy was to create a purchase experience for its target market of men aged 25 to 35 that would require only one trip to a store, to establish the shopper's preferred size and style of pants. Thereafter, the shopper could make repeat purchases from the catalog from home.[7]

Waiting and Delivery Time. Consumers differ in their willingness to tolerate out-of-stock products when they shop. This variation occurs not only between different consumers but also for the same consumer across different purchase occasions. An intense demand for this service output translates to a demand that the product be in stock at all times. Retailers can respond to a demand for low waiting time by holding extra safety stocks in their stores, but this is expensive. As with the other consumer service output demands, the retailer must gauge how damaging to its business an out-of-stock occurrence would be. For example, most grocery retailers make it a high priority to avoid out-of-stocks on basic products such as milk or bread, which are frequently purchased and important items in many families' shopping baskets. But a family purchasing a piece of furniture such as a sofa, on the other hand, is typically willing to wait a long time (e.g., 8 to 12 weeks) to get delivery of the product and virtually never expects the product to be in stock in the store. (Chapter 6 discusses the principle of postponement and speculation as a response to differing levels of demand for waiting and delivery time.)

Despite these norms of consumer expectation, retailers do create positions in the market by deviating from standard practice on the waiting–delivery time dimension. Discount grocery retailers do not routinely stock a given brand of product, and therefore the shopper visiting a Sam's Club, for example, might or might not find a favorite brand of laundry detergent. The consumer could wait a long (and more importantly, an *unpredictable*) amount of time before finding the product in the store again. A very brand-loyal consumer would find this intolerable, because it might involve purchasing a non-favored brand until the favorite brand once again appears on the store shelf, and would also involve revisiting the store (possibly multiple times) until the brand is once again found on the shelf.

Even the elapsed time in the store can be viewed as an element of total waiting and delivery time, and is the subject of retail attention. The "portable shopper," a handheld scanning device that grocery shoppers can use to self-scan their purchases while they travel up and down the aisles of the grocery store, reduces checkout times at the cash register, and hence total elapsed shopping time. Shoppers using the device have access to a special express checkout line that does not scan all their purchases, but shoppers are subjected to random scan checks to make sure they have not "forgotten" to scan some items. The Symbol company, a bar-code technology firm, invented the device at the request of Dutch grocery retailer Albert Heijn. In Europe, where the device was first introduced, about half of shoppers who are given the opportunity to use the portable shopper do so.[8]

The classic no-waiting retail outlet is the vending machine. In the past, vending machines generally sold only products like cigarettes, soft drinks, candy, or snacks. Cigarettes are now outlawed from the vending outlet in the United States; although the other categories continue to be sold this way, there is an interesting trend toward new products sold through vending machines as well. Some movie theater lobbies now sport vending machines to sell movie soundtracks for $15, payable with either cash or a credit card. This allows the movie patron to immediately purchase the soundtrack to a movie he or she has just viewed and liked, rather than having to wait to find it in a store. Other products being incorporated into the vending machine business include office supplies sold at supermarkets; live fishing bait near fishing holes; and fresh flowers at hospitals. Sophisticated technology lets the vending machine operators track what is sold and when the machines are out of stock, thus maximizing sales potential, given the inherent impulse nature of vending purchases.[9]

Product Variety. In the retailing world, the service output of product variety is represented by two dimensions. *Variety* describes generically different classes of goods making up the product offering, that is, the *breadth* of product lines. The term *assortment*, on the other hand, refers to the *depth* of product brands or models offered within each generic product category. Discount department stores such as Kmart, Target, and Wal-Mart have limited assortments of fast-moving, low-priced items across a wide variety of household goods, ready-to-wear, cosmetics, sporting goods, electric appliances, auto accessories, and the like. In contrast, a specialty store dealing only, or primarily, in home audiovisual electronic goods, such as Audio Warehouse, would have a very large and complete line of radios, tape recorders, and high-fidelity equipment, offering the deepest assortment of models, styles, sizes, prices, and so on.

One of the more interesting additions to the variety offered in retail stores is that of banking services in British and U.S. retail stores. In Britain, the trend began in 1996 when Tesco, a leading British grocery chain, extended its ClubCard loyalty-card program to include debit and savings options. The ClubCard Plus account pays 5 percent interest on cash balances. Consumers can transfer money into their accounts and then debit the accounts whenever they shop at Tesco. The ClubCard attracted over 100,000 customers in its first six months of operation. Other British retailers, such as Safeway and Marks & Spencer, have also participated in the trend. These services are not only a profitable addition to variety in and of themselves but also a means of increasing store loyalty and purchases in the store and of offering one-stop shopping to consumers.[10]

In the United States, retailers have begun to enter the banking arena as a result of a change in regulatory restrictions on opening financial institutions. In 1996, the unitary thrift charter was changed. Previously, it had required savings and loan institutions to devote at least 65 percent of their assets to home lending. The rules were changed to require 65 percent of assets to be devoted to any consumer loans. This gave retailers such as Nordstrom, Ford Motor Company, and Ukrops Super Markets Inc. of Richmond, Virginia, the incentive to open their own savings and loan institutions. They can offer only those financial services that are the most profitable and focus their offerings on those services that are complementary to the ones shoppers value in their stores. (Ford, for example, plans simply to help car buyers pay for their vehicles over the Internet.)[11]

The variety and assortment dimension of retailing operations demands the attention of top management, because decisions in this area color the entire character of the enterprise. Once the basic strategy is established for the organization, however, the task of choosing specific products or brands usually falls to functionaries called *buyers*, who play a central role in retailing. Unlike their counterparts in manufacturing concerns, their status within their home organizations is very high. Some retailers generate more profits via negotiations for trade deals and allowances than they do through merchandising efforts. Because buying is such a critical aspect of retailing, it is important to understand the evaluative processes and procedures that take place in merchandise and supplier selection. The appendices to this chapter are geared to that end. Appendix 13.1 is a glossary of pricing and buying terms commonly used by retailers, and Appendix 13.2 briefly describes some of retailers' merchandise planning and control procedures.

Customer Service Possibilities. Virtually all major retail innovations of the twentieth century have relied, to greater or lesser degrees, on manipulating the customer service variable. The principle is easy to appreciate when we consider such services as in-store sales help. When retailers drop the "friendly" behind-the-counter sales assistant who helps customers locate and compare merchandise and is available for "expert" advice, the whole locate–compare–select process is shifted to the consumer. For suppliers, the change from in-store assistance to self-service on the part of retailers is a major reason for shifting from a "push" strategy to a "pull" strategy.

Retailing is one of the few remaining industries that is highly labor intensive, even though it is becoming less so. Payroll expenses are in the neighborhood of 30 percent of sales for the higher-priced–higher-service department stores, such as Bloomingdale's. For specialty stores, they are even higher—approximately 35 percent of sales.[12] Contrast these numbers to Wal-Mart and Home Depot; their operating expenses (which include *all* expenses to operate their companies, not just payroll) are 20 percent or less. Hence, the savings that can be passed on to the consumer by eliminating certain kinds of in-store assistance or improving the productivity of a downsized workforce are usually substantial.

Even in Japan, once a bastion of high store service demands, a new willingness on the part of consumers to trade off customer service for lower prices is visible. When the Japanese economy was booming in the late 1980s, Japanese consumers demanded both exclusive branded goods and very high levels of service. Prestigious department stores such as Takashimaya and Mitsukoshi still pride themselves on top-notch personal sales service and extras such as gift wrapping in the valued store wrapping paper (a gift wrapped in Mitsukoshi wrapping paper carries a cachet that cannot be matched by giving the same gift bought at a lesser store). But increasingly, consumers who are less sure of keeping their jobs, are better traveled to foreign countries with more competitive pricing at retail, and are more willing to buy products without service, are moving away from the traditional department stores. Department store shares of total retail sales in Japan plateaued and fell throughout the late 1980s and early 1990s, while sales at convenience and discount stores grew. Discounters account for about 14 percent of total sales of men's clothing in Japan, with liquor (7 to 8 percent) and shoes (8 to 9 percent) being other successful discount categories.

Customer service is a costly benefit to provide, but retailers continue to invest in customer service because it can bring substantial benefits. One humble example is the provision of shopping carts in retail stores. Carts are of course common in grocery stores, as well as in mass-merchandisers such as Carrefour or Wal-Mart, but soft goods (apparel) retailers have resisted them as inconsistent with the stores' images. It is hard to imagine a shopper at a department store like Nordstrom or Dayton Hudson using a shopping cart. Nevertheless, shoppers in mass-market retail outlets have been shown to buy 7.2 items when using a cart, but only 6.1 items without a cart. One relieved Montgomery Ward department store shopper with one child in the cart's seat, one child at her side, and several items of children's clothing remarked that she would be likely to shop at the store more often since it started offering carts. It is easy to see why such a relatively small investment (each cart costs about $100) generates such large consumer service benefits to certain segments of shoppers.[13] This investment, like others that can be made in customer service, implies an expenditure on channel functions that takes a cost from the consumer's shoulders. As with the other demand-based dimensions of retailing strategy, a successful operation is dependent on being able to identify the functions that consumers are or are not willing to assume and the cost in time, money, effort, and convenience at which taking them on becomes attractive.

Implications for a Taxonomy of Retail Types

Given the cost-side and demand-side dimensions just discussed, retailers have a wide variety of possibilities open to them when positioning their retail operation in the marketplace. The positioning strategy chosen should always be driven by the demands of the target market segment for service outputs. Thus, a high-cost, high-service retail strategy, which might work perfectly well in an affluent neighborhood, is a mistake in an area populated by less wealthy consumers who cannot afford to consume high service levels at high prices. Further, the decision is not just to offer generically "high service output levels." Within a certain intensity of demand for service outputs, there are almost always variations in the importance given to one or another specific service output. Thus, in furniture purchasing, there is room both for retailers that offer broader variety and assortment, at the cost of longer waiting and delivery times. And for those that offer a somewhat curtailed product line, in a shorter delivery time. Finally, price is the arbiter of the system. Higher service output levels can only be offered at higher price levels when all is said and done, because of the cost to produce these service outputs. Thus, in deciding which services to offer and which to drop, retailers are always constrained by the target consumer's total willingness to pay.

Table 13.4 shows how different classes of retailers can be characterized by their cost-side and demand-side positioning strategies. The differences across these different retailer types permit the survival of multiple types of retail outlets selling the same physical merchandise. For example, consider two toy stores, FAO Schwarz and Toys "R"

Us. FAO Schwarz is a toy *specialty store*, whereas Toys "R" Us is a *category killer*. Although both break bulk, offer a low waiting time to consumers (i.e., few out-of-stocks), and carry a narrow variety (toys) along with a deep assortment (many makes and types of toys), few consumers would confuse the two stores. FAO Schwarz differs from Toys "R" Us in its focus on high margin rather than high turnover as a key to retail profitability,

TABLE 13.4
A Taxonomy of Retailer Types

Retailer Type	Main Focus on Margin or Turnover?	Bulk-Breaking	Spatial Convenience	Waiting and Delivery Time	Variety (Breadth)	Assortment (Depth)
Department store (e.g., May Co.)	Margin	Yes	Moderate	Low waiting time	Broad	Moderate–shallow
Specialty store (e.g., Gap)	Margin	Yes	Moderate	Low waiting time	Narrow	Deep
Mail Order–Catalog (e.g., Lands' End)	Margin	Yes	Extremely high	Moderate–high waiting time	Narrow	Moderate
Convenience store (e.g., 7-Eleven)	Both	Yes	Very high	Low waiting time	Broad	Shallow
Category killer (e.g., Toys "R" Us)	Turnover	Yes	Low	Low waiting time	Narrow	Deep
Mass-Merchandiser (e.g., Wal-Mart)	Turnover	Yes	Low	Moderate waiting time (may be out of stock)	Broad	Shallow
Hypermarket (e.g., Carrefour)	Turnover	Yes	Low	Moderate waiting time	Broad	Moderate
Warehouse Club (e.g., Sam's Club)	Turnover	No	Low	Moderate–high waiting time (may be out of stock)	Broad	Shallow

along with slightly lower spatial convenience on average, due to the smaller number of stores FAO Schwarz has as compared to Toys "R" Us. Similar comparisons among the rows of the table suggest that it is through its choices on these dimensions that a store creates its position in the marketplace and can survive even in the face of competition offering a seemingly similar set of products to consumers.

STRATEGIC ISSUES IN RETAILING

From a marketing channel design and management perspective, suppliers attempting to sell their products to ultimate consumers for personal consumption must understand the major strategic issues facing retailers. We first discuss an important consumer trend: the increasing importance of convenience. We then treat a variety of issues pertaining to increased levels of retailer power; including retailers' capitalization on the scarcity of shelf space, their increasing reliance on private-label brands, and manufacturers' responses to these moves. We also discuss some of the developments in types of retail outlets that suggest ever finer targeting of consumers, through the creation of power retailers, also known as category killers, and through the polarity of retailing. We finally discuss the increasing internationalization of retailing and its implications for retail competition within a single country or market.

Importance of Convenience to Consumers

Convenience is measured by the time required to make a purchase, including getting to and from the store, getting in and out of the store, and, where applicable, getting delivery of the purchased product. The consumer trends that have defined changing shopping patterns in the 1990s—a poverty of time and increasing numbers of working women (in the United States in 1995, 75 percent of women worked outside the home)—have fueled an increasingly intense demand for convenience. Between 1980 and 1995, the average number of monthly visits to a mall in the United States dropped from 3 to 1.6, and the number of stores shopped per trip dropped from 7 to just 3.[14] In survey after survey, consumers have indicated that speed and convenience are more important to them than price. In order to assure themselves of achieving speed and convenience, they frequently prefer to wait on themselves.[15] In fact, many consumers are so convinced that self-service is the height of good service that they are willing to pay extra for the privilege (e.g., to tap their own computers for desired databases). Consumers are often far more comfortable wrestling with electronic aids (e.g., touch-screen kiosks) than they are with inattentive, surly, or hard-to-find salespeople.[16]

On the other hand, when companies can really provide first-rate service—bold, fast, unexpected, innovative, and customized—they can achieve a remarkable differential advantage. Outstanding retailing examples are Lexus in automobiles, Nordstrom in apparel, Home Depot in home improvement products, and Taco Bell in fast food.

Even in the absence of technological assistance, the drive to make life simpler (spurred by dual-income families; time-poor, increasingly wealthy singles; or households with no children) has spawned all sorts of convenience marketers, from child-care centers to maid services. The quest for convenience on the part of consumers is shown by:

(1) the almost frantic growth of the convenience store sector, fueled by the entry of petroleum marketers such as Arco (with its AM/PM Stores); (2) the exploding popularity of on-line shopping and home banking; (3) the diversification of vending machine operators into food, clothing and videotapes; and (4) the increased share of the retailing market being taken by direct-response marketing (e.g., telephone selling and direct-mail advertising). Contrast this with the fate of minimalls in the United States, which once were destination shopping locations for consumers, populated with small specialty and variety stores. Now they are dying a slow death, as consumers no longer have time to browse these smaller, regional, enclosed malls. The time-starved shopper prefers outdoor shopping centers anchored by superstores such as Wal-Mart or Sam's Club. Retail developers are responding by converting their increasingly unprofitable indoor malls in accordance with consumers' wishes.[17] To make it even more difficult, consumers are unwilling to trade quality for convenience, which means that delivering customer satisfaction at a profit—the main goal of marketers—is becoming more difficult to achieve.

Increased Power of Retailers

Packaged-goods manufacturers (makers of branded health and beauty aids, and packaged foods and beverages) are, arguably, the smartest marketing people in the world. At one time, companies such as Procter & Gamble, Colgate, Kraft, and Clorox dominated retailers; now the retailers tend to dominate them. How could such a thing happen?

The reasons for this reversal are many and diverse. First, the sales of most items normally sold through grocery, drug, and mass-merchandising chains have not been increasing at rapid rates in the aggregate. If these retailers are to grow, they must take sales away from their competitors rather than waiting for overall demand to expand. Competition has, therefore, evolved into a market share game. This has created enormous pressure on retailers to perform, and given that most chains tend to carry the same products, the type of competition that has consumed them has tended to be price oriented. In other words, better prices—coupled with excellent locations, appealing stores, and reasonable service—have been the major routes to survival and success in this arena. It is little wonder, then, that the chain retailers have increasingly begun to pressure suppliers for price concessions.

Food stores, in particular supermarket chains, still remain the major outlets for packaged goods. Over the past decade, however, warehouse clubs, deep-discount drugstores, and mass-merchandisers have been growing more rapidly than food stores. Although none of these so-called "alternative formats" to the supermarket can match the supermarket in terms of variety and assortment of grocery items, they have been able to expand at the expense of the supermarket. Each of them offers a unique combination of benefits that appeals to a particular niche market of consumers, including not only a "value price" but also a selected set of valued services.[18]

Given the fact that supermarket profit ratios (net profits–to–sales) are only about one percent, any loss of sales to alternative formats, especially from heavy buyers (such as household heads of large families), could be disastrous. The investments made by retailers such as Wal-Mart, Kmart, and Target in supercenter retailing outlets pressure standard retailers even further. Although the power of these traditional retailers has been diminished by the new entrants, the pressure they feel is being immediately transmitted back up the channel to suppliers. Of course, the long-term solution for super-markets does not come via squeezing suppliers, but from meeting the needs of consumers.

Second, retailers are continuously concerned with improving their productivity. Given the competitive environment, it is virtually impossible for grocery retailers to raise prices, but it is not impossible to find ways to lower costs. They are always trying to achieve economies of scale while simultaneously providing consumers with the convenience of one-stop shopping. Consequently, they have built larger and larger stores, thereby elevating their fixed costs. This has created higher break-even points, forcing supermarkets and mass-merchandisers (such as discount stores) to place even greater emphasis on the need to generate enormous sales volumes.

The resulting competition for store traffic has led to consolidation. For example, in a 1993 study, the three leading grocery chains in 26 out of 50 major markets controlled at least 50 percent of "all commodity volume" (ACV).[19] Loblaw's, Canada's largest grocer, purchased Provigo, the dominant grocery chain in Quebec, in December 1998, increasing its national market share from 19 percent to 26.2 percent. In the Atlantic provinces of Canada, Loblaw's commands a 32.9 percent market share. But it is not alone: Table 13.5 summarizes acquisitions in the United States and Canada. This list does not include acquisitions elsewhere in the world, which have also been progressing (see the discussion of international retailing later). To put these changes in perspective, consider that Kroger's purchase of Fred Meyer gives it annual sales of $43 billion, which is five times the sales of Nestlé USA. Such statistics indicate that the nature of supplier–retailer relations in the grocery arena have changed significantly.[20]

Third, there is more and more pressure on retail buyers as a result of the increased pressures on the companies in which they are employed. At one time, they focused primarily on purchasing and maintaining balanced inventories. Now, they are profit centers that are also responsible for capital management, service levels, turnover, retail margins and pricing, quality control, competitiveness and variety, operating costs, shelf

TABLE 13.5

Major Grocery Acquisitions in the United States and Canada, 1995–1998

Acquiring Company	Acquired Company	Date	Value (US $ billions*)
Kroger	Fred Meyer	1998	12.9
Albertsons	American Stores	1998	11.8
Ahold NV	Stop N Shop	1996	2.9
Ahold USA	Giant Food	1998	2.7
Safeway	Vons	1996	2.3
Fred Meyer	QFC	1997	1.7
Yucaipa	Ralph's	1997	1.5
KKR	Bruno's	1995	1.2
Loblaws	Provigo	1998	1.1
Empire	Oshawa	1998	1.1
Tosco	Circle K	1996	1.0

*Canadian acquisitions converted at US $1.00 = CDN $1.5.
Source: Company statements, as reported in Nora Aufreiter and Tim McGuire, "Walking down the Aisles," *Ivey Business Journal*, 63, no. 3 (March/April 1999), pp. 49–54.

space and position, and vendor float and terms.[21] In order to help their companies make money, they look for suppliers to give them price breaks and merchandising support, and they become very upset when those price breaks and support are not forthcoming.[22]

Fourth, retailers have many new products from which to choose when deciding what to stock on their shelves. Industry estimates in the grocery business are that they are offered over 20,000 new stockkeeping units (SKUs) each year, although there has been a 26 percent decline in new food offerings in grocery stores between 1995 and 1997.[23] One study agreed with the estimate of new SKUs per year, but broke new products into several categories: (1) classically innovative products, (2) equity transfer products, (3) line extensions, (4) competitive clone products, (5) seasonal or temporary items, and (6) items substituted for other products in a manufacturer's line (e.g., new sizes). Only the first three categories were identified as truly new products. By that criterion, only 1,100 to 1,200 new products are introduced each year.[24]

But this distinction obscures the fundamental issue for grocery product manufacturers. Retailers have an abundance of new products from which to choose, and store sizes have not increased significantly (median grocery store size in the United States in 1996 was 38,600 square feet). Retailers are therefore likely to choose products to stock on their shelves with a goal of making themselves (not the manufacturers!) better off. The manufacturers' bargaining position is weakened further because most new products do not succeed, by any reasonable definition of success (whether one measures increases in sales over time, survival of the product on the store shelf, or percent of all commodity volume [ACV], a measure of penetration at retail).[25] Procter & Gamble has responded to this challenge by *decreasing* the number of product offerings it sells to retailers. For instance, instead of 30 SKUs of shampoos, it offers only 15.[26]

Fifth, information technology has diffused throughout retailing to such an extent that virtually all of the major retailers can capture item-by-item data, via scanning devices, at their electronic point-of-sale terminals. Figure 13.1 profiles how the universal product code (or UPC) is used to help track the movement of product at retail and reduce both stockouts and supply cycle time.

The knowledge gained from this information has permitted retailers to calculate the *direct product profitability (DPP)* of individual items, track what moves and what does not move well in their stores, engage in forward investment buying, and leverage suppliers. The evidence suggests that retailers use these data for their own benefit more than to coordinate the channel. For example, supermarket retailers can now tailor promotional offers to their loyalty card shoppers that link directly to their past buying behavior, rather than needing to offer the same deal to all consumers. In one instance, retailers American Stores and Grand Union installed kiosks inside their stores, accessible with a consumer's loyalty card, that distribute coupons related to the shopper's prior purchases. About 35 percent of coupons generated by the kiosks are redeemed (versus an industry average of only about 1 or 2 percent), and kiosk users spend about $71 per store visit, versus shopping baskets of $48 per visit for loyalty cardholders who do not use the kiosk and only $33 per visit for non–loyalty cardholders. One retailer claims that these kiosks can replace as much as $1 million in advertising expenditures per 12 stores per year.[27]

The stated intent of such technology-based programs is of course to better match promotional offerings to consumers' actual purchase preferences. Theoretically, these

1. **The UPC is scanned.**
   The SKU of the product is registered into Wal-Mart's database, along with a description of the product.

2. **Item locator program.**
   If a store runs out of this UPC, Wal-Mart's item locator program can find the closest store with that SKU in stock. Stock transfers can then be ordered by phone.

3. **Data transmission.**
   Data is also shared multiple times per day with Wal-Mart headquarters in Bentonville, Arkansas, via satellite.

4. **Retail link.**
   This is Wal-Mart's database, shared with 2,500 of its 10,000 suppliers. Sales history of this UPC is available to the manufacturer to help in production scheduling.

5. **Forecasting.**
   Collaborative forecasting and replenishment programs can be carried out. Supply cycles can be cut significantly, even in half, from production to presence on the store shelf.

0 50000 10152 8

UPC Code for Carnation Nonfat Dry Milk, 25.6 oz. size

37000 41100 0

UPC Code for Duncan Hines Moist Deluxe Lemon Supreme Flavor Cake Mix, 18.25 oz. size

ISBN 0-13-205865-0

9 780132 058650

UPC Code for *Marketing Channels,* 5th edition

FIGURE 13.1 **Use of the UPC Code in Retail Product Replenishment: Wal-Mart Example**

Source: Text is adapted from Linda F. Magyar, "A Turn of the SKU," *New York Times,* April 6, 1997, section 6, p. 55. UPCs are scanned from real products.

programs can benefit both the retailer and its suppliers. But one study conducted by Arthur Andersen found that the majority of supermarket retailers (57 percent) did not intend to increase their sharing of data with suppliers. Only 33 percent of those currently sharing data share their sales forecasts with suppliers, lessening the ability to coordinate operations.[28] And manufacturers of consumer packaged goods frequently complain that "efficient consumer response" (ECR) translates into the need for the manufacturers to hold greater inventories in their own warehouses to prevent stock outages at retail, rather than helping them also control their inventory investments.

Although other events have contributed to the influence of retail buyers, suppliers themselves are partly to blame. We have already mentioned the thousands of new products introduced every year. In addition, manufacturers have engaged in many new-product price and promotional allowances as a way of "bribing" their way onto retailers' shelves. These activities play into the hands of already powerful buyers. Figure 13.2 and Table 13.6 describe the types and objectives of various trade deals.

1. *Off invoice.* An off-invoice promotion discounts the product to the dealer for a fixed period of time. It consists of a temporary price cut, and when the time period elapses, the price goes back to its normal level. The specific terms of the discount usually require performance, and the discount lasts for a specified period (e.g., one month). Sometimes the trade can buy multiple times and sometimes only once.

2. *Bill-back.* Bill-backs are similar to off invoice except that the retailer computes the discount per unit for all units bought during the promotional period and then bills the manufacturer for the units sold and any other promotional allowances that are owed after the promotional period is complete. The advantage from the manufacturer's position is the control it gives and guarantees that the retailer performs as the contract indicates before payment is issued. Generally, retailers do not like bill-backs because of the time and effort required.

3. *Free goods.* Usually free goods take the form of extra cases at the same price. For example, buy three get one free is a free-goods offer.

4. *Cooperative advertising allowances.* Paying for part of the dealers' advertising is called cooperative advertising, which is often abbreviated as co-op advertising. The manufacturer either offers the dealer a fixed dollar amount per unit sold or offers to pay a percentage of the advertising costs. The percentage varies depending on the type of advertising run. If the dealer is prominent in the advertisement, then the manufacturer often pays less, but if the manufacturer is prominent, then it pays more.

5. *Display allowance.* It is similar to a cooperative advertising allowance. The manufacturer wants the retailer to display a given item when a price promotion is being run. To induce the retailer to do this and to help defray the costs, a display allowance is offered. It is usually a fixed amount per case, such as 50 cents per case.

6. *Sales drives.* For manufacturers selling through brokers or wholesalers, it is necessary to offer incentives. Sales drives are intended to offer the brokers and wholesalers incentives to push the trade deal to the retailer. For every unit sold during the promotional period, the broker and wholesaler receive a percentage or fixed payment per case sold to the retailer. It works as an additional commission for an independent sales organization or additional margin for a wholesaler.

7. *Terms or inventory financing.* The manufacturer may not require payment for 90 days, thus increasing the profitability to the retailer who does not need to borrow to finance inventories.

8. *Count–recount.* Rather than paying retailers on the number of units ordered, the manufacturer does it on the number of units sold. This is accomplished by determining the number of units on hand at the beginning of the promotional period (count) and then determining the number of units on hand at the end of the period (recount). Then, by tracking orders, the manufacturers know the quantity sold during the promotional period. (This differs from a bill-back because the manufacturer verifies the actual sales in count–recount.)

9. *Slotting allowances.* Manufacturers have been paying retailers funds known as slotting allowances to receive space for new products. When a new product is introduced, the manufacturer pays the retailer X dollars for a "slot" for the new product. Slotting allowances offer a fixed payment to the retailer for accepting and testing a new product.

10. *Street money.* Manufacturers have begun to pay retailers lump sums to run promotions. The lump sum, not per case sold, is based on the amount of support (feature advertising, price reduction, and display space) offered by the retailer. The name comes from the manufacturer's need to offer independent retailers a fixed fund to promote the product because the trade deal goes to the wholesaler.

FIGURE 13.2 **Description of Trade Deals for Consumer Nondurable Goods**

Source: Robert C. Blattberg and Scott A. Neslin, *Sales Promotion: Concepts, Methods, and Strategies* (Upper Saddle River, NJ: Prentice Hall, 1990), pp. 318-19.

TABLE 13.6

Objectives of Trade Deals for Nondurable Goods

	Objectives*					
Tactics	1	2	3	4	5	6
Off invoice	x	x	x	x	x	
Bill-back	x	x	x	x	x	
Free goods	x		x			
Cooperative advertising	x				x	x
Display allowances	x				x	
Sales drives	x	x				
Slotting allowances		x	x			
Street money	x				x	

*Objectives:

1. Retailer merchandising activities

2. Loading the retailer

3. Gaining or maintaining distribution

4. Obtain price reduction

5. Competitive tool

6. Retailer "goodwill"

Source: Robert C. Blattberg and Scott A. Neslin, *Sales Promotion: Concepts, Methods, and Strategies* (Upper Saddle River, NJ: Prentice Hall, 1990), p. 321.

In 1998, about $203 billion was spent in the United States on consumer promotions, with an additional $85 billion spent on trade promotions (promotions to retailers rather than to final consumers). This represented an 8.6 percent growth rate over 1997. Over the prior decade, promotional spending also gained in relation to advertising spending, rising from 67 percent of all marketing dollars (promotional plus advertising spending) to 74 percent. Trade promotions have increased their share as well, rising from 41 percent of all marketing dollars in 1987 to 50 percent in 1997.[29] Buyers who receive these "deals" grow to expect and insist on them as a price of doing business. Some of the types of deals offered by manufacturers to retailers include:

- Forward buying on deals
- Slotting allowances
- Failure fees
- Payment for participation in newspaper inserts
- Deepest case allowances possible
- Highest possible payments for displays and even shelf placements
- No-cost new item introductions
- Guaranteed returns at full retail
- Invoice deductions for late coupon redemption reimbursements
- Manufacturer-supplied labor for shelf sets[30]

To illustrate the array of offers, we describe the first three deal types in more detail below.

Forward Buying on Deals. Consumer packaged-goods manufacturers can experience wide swings in demand for their products from retailers when they use trade promotions heavily. Temporary wholesale price cuts of one sort or another cause the retailer to engage in *forward buying*—buying significantly more product than the retailer needs and stockpiling it until stocks run down again. In the past, companies such as Campbell Soup Company sometimes sold as much as 40 percent of annual chicken noodle soup production to wholesalers and retailers in just 6 weeks because of trade dealing practices. Although this strategy clearly increases quantity sold to the retail trade, particularly during the promotional period, it plays havoc with the manufacturers' costs and marketing plans. When a manufacturer marks down a product by 10 percent, for example, it has become common practice for the trade to stock up with a 10- to 12-week supply. That means fewer products are purchased at list price after the promotion ends, and manufacturer profitability is not guaranteed to increase.

The increasing use of EDI technologies in the grocery channel has decreased the forward buying problem somewhat. *Continuous replenishment programs (CRP)* have been particularly helpful in changing buying practices. Under CRP, a manufacturer and retailer maintain an electronic linkage that informs the manufacturer when the retailer's stocks are running low, triggering a reorder. If manufacturers and retailers have this level of cooperation, forward buying is much less likely to be a problem. However, the pricing practices of manufacturers are the clear drivers of forward buying behavior. These practices induce periodic heavy buying by retailers, and as long as these pricing practices remain in vogue, forward buying is likely to result.[31]

A related problem is *diverting*. When manufacturers offer a regional trade promotion, for example, on the West Coast of the United States, some retailers and wholesalers will buy large volumes and then distribute some cases to stores in the Midwest where the discount is not available. This practice upsets manufacturers' efforts to tailor marketing efforts to regions or neighborhoods. It is the domestic counterpart to *gray marketing*, the distribution of authorized, branded goods through unauthorized channels overseas. Gray marketing is discussed in more detail in Chapter 9 as a channel conflict problem.

Slotting Allowances. Slotting allowances originated in the 1970s as a way to compensate the grocery trade for all the costs of working a new product into their systems: creating a space or slot in the warehouse, revising computerized inventory systems, resetting the shelves to make a place in the store, and helping to defray the cost of stocking and restocking the item.[32] (See Chapter 12 for a discussion of the legal status of slotting allowances.) Because of the scarcity of shelf space, slotting allowances have grown significantly. Suppliers paid $300 to $1,500 per new item in 1982 in slotting allowances. In a study done by A. C. Nielsen in 1997, one-third of respondents in the food category spent between $500,000 and $1 million on slotting allowances, and 14 percent spent more than $3 million. Only 6 percent of respondents reported paying no slotting allowances.[33] Slotting allowances reportedly cost manufacturers up to $9 billion in 1999.[34]

In September 1999, the U.S. Senate held hearings on slotting allowances and began an investigation of them. Some manufacturers even testified anonymously, for fear of retailer reprisals. Whereas small manufacturers argue that slotting allowances are so high as to prevent their access to store shelf space, retailers counter that manufacturers should share in the risk of failure of new products. Up to this point, the Federal Trade Commission had reviewed the practice and failed to find it a violation of antitrust law, but the continued complaints from manufacturers illustrate the continued use of retail power.[35]

Failure Fees. Starting in April 1989, J. M. Jones Company, a wholesaling unit of Super Valu Stores Inc. began imposing a fee when it had to pull a failing product from its warehouses. If a new product failed to reach a minimum sales target within three months, Jones withdrew it and charged $2,000 for the effort.[36] Although the practice of charging failure fees is not widespread, it has been connected with the other fees, such as slotting allowances, that are under scrutiny in the United States.[37] As an additional retailer tool along with slotting fees, failure fees are simply another indication of the degree of retailer control in the channel for consumer packaged goods.

Broadened Role and Impact of Private Branding

There is some debate as to whether private branding by retailers is increasing or not. Private labels (also known as "store brands") have been, and continue to be, very popular in the United Kingdom. Their sales account for about 36 percent of all grocery sales in Britain. Sainsbury, a leading British grocery chain, launches 1,400 to 1,500 new private-label items per year; private labels account for about half of the products in its stores, and 54 percent of its sales.[38] And Marks & Spencer, a British retailing legend, has always relied upon its own St. Michael's brand label to carry its product lines.

Years ago, some American retailers—notably Sears, JCPenney, Montgomery Ward, and A&P—also committed themselves to private labels. It was a way of generating loyalty to their stores, rather than to the manufacturers' brands they carried, and of earning extra profits, because private-label merchandise generally affords retailers higher gross margins than comparable branded merchandise. Private labels have always been used to provide consumers with extra value, but at these retailers, they have also usually come in generic wrappings and varieties. In other words, they were money-saving but unexciting alternatives relative to national, heavily advertised brands.

Now, however, a number of retailers are upgrading their private-label programs in order to offer an even closer substitute to branded products. A private brand (or private label) is one that is owned or controlled through contract rights by a retailing company, an affiliated group of retailers, or a buying organization (e.g., Federated-Allied Merchandising Services and Frederick Atkins, Inc.). There are five basic categories of private brands: (1) store-name identification programs (products bear the retailer's store name or logo, e.g., Gap, Kroger, Ace, NAPA, Benetton); (2) retailer's own brand-name identity programs (a brand image independent of the store name that is available in only that company's stores, e.g., Forenza [The Limited], Boundary Waters Marketplace [Dayton Hudson], Kenmore and Craftsman [Sears], True-Value and Tru-Test [Cotter & Co.], Valu-Rite [McKesson]); (3) designer-exclusive programs (merchandise designed and sold under a designer's name in an exclusive arrangement with the retailer, e.g., Halston III [JCPenney]); (4) other exclusive licensed-name programs (celebrity-endorsed lines or other signature or character label lines developed under exclusive arrangements with the retailer, e.g., Allen Solly [Federated Department Stores], Cheryl Tiegs and McKids [Sears], Jaclyn Smith [Kmart]); and (5) generic programs (goods that are essentially unbranded, e.g., Yellow pack no name [Loblaw's], Cost Cutter [Kroger]).[39]

Increasingly, private brands of large retailing companies are being positioned as the "leading brand" in their assortment. Loblaw's, the Canadian grocery chain, pioneered the store brand President's Choice, an upscale offering in everything from chocolate chip cookies to olive oil. The brand has been so successful that it sells it through several chains in the United States as well, where it is also positioned as a very credible alternative to the national brands.

In general, private brands are a route to gaining exclusivity, thereby permitting their purveyors to avoid direct price competition. In contrast, designer and other popular brands of clothes have become so widely distributed that every store in the mall seems to carry the same lines. Retailers of private-label jeans have followed this route, increasing their share of the total U.S. jeans market from 16 percent in 1990 to 25 percent in 1997, largely due to the success of Gap, an entirely private-label retailer. But even such jeans labels as Arizona (JCPenney), Canyon River Blues (Sears, Roebuck), and Badge (Federated Department Stores) have become not only acceptable, but even trendy to the consumers buying them, thanks to clever image advertising that develops the product image separately from the store image. These private labels pose a significant and increasing threat to the branded-goods manufacturers.[40]

On first glance, supermarkets and discount stores have a clear incentive for pushing their own offerings: Private-label goods typically cost consumers 10 to 20 percent less than other brands, but their gross margins are as much as twice as high as those for non-store brands.[41] U.S. supermarkets get 15 percent of their sales from private labels and make an average pretax profit of 2 percent on sales. In contrast, European grocery chains, which focus much more heavily on store brands, average 7 percent pretax profits. Clearly, private labels are not the only reason for higher profits in European grocery chains; the industry is also much more concentrated in Europe than in the United States, leading to less price competition (the top five supermarket chains in the United States in 1996 accounted for 21 percent of grocery sales, whereas the top five in the United Kingdom accounted for 62 percent of national grocery sales). Nevertheless, European chains' success with private labels makes their competitors in the United States consider them more seriously.[42]

Although a great deal of media attention has been given to the use of private brands by supermarkets, they have in fact accounted for an average of only 14 percent of total dollar supermarket sales in the United States in the 1980s and 1990s. In comparison, approximately 20 percent of U.S. apparel purchases are private-label clothes. For specific product classes, however, there are large deviations from the mean. Research shows that private labels tend to do well in grocery categories where they offer quality comparable to national brands. Surprisingly, high quality is much more important than lower price. They also perform better in large dollar-volume categories offering high margins (e.g., paper goods, bleach). They do much worse in categories in which there are multiple national manufacturers investing heavily in national advertising.[43]

The use of private branding has resulted in even greater power for the retailer in the channel of distribution. It has changed the character of manufacturer–retailer relationships in that there is more (1) retailer initiative or responsibility for fashion direction, trend setting, innovation, and the like; (2) retailer responsibility for marketing to consumers, as opposed to an orientation as a distributing agent for suppliers; and (3) strategic concern on the part of many suppliers with marketing to important retailers as opposed to direct concern with the consumer market.[44]

On the other hand, private-label management is not trivial for retailers. For apparel in particular, developing and marketing a distinctive private label can be difficult, costly, and risky, especially if a store does not have a high level of prestige. But even for upscale merchants, many private labels are uninspired in design, mainly because retailers generally have little talent in that part of the marketing process. Nevertheless, many of the larger apparel chains are putting their own labels on their best clothes.[45]

In addition, private-label programs can go too far. They often must rely on a strong national-brand program in order for the value comparison to come alive to consumers.[46] When store brands soared to 35 percent of A&P's sales mix in the 1960s, shoppers, perceiving a lack of choice, defected to competitors. In the late 1980s, Sears began to add more brand-name goods so that it could begin to appeal to a broader base of customers. And competition from competent and stylish specialty retailers has weakened the position of some formerly strong private-goods retailers such as Marks & Spencer in the late 1990s, whose management admits that it "lost touch with our customers."[47]

On balance, the retailer can clearly use private-label products to effectively target its consumers who seek value for the money they spend in the store. When done well, these private labels are formidable competitors to national (or international) brands. However, if not executed properly, or if the environment changes to make the private-label program obsolete in its product design, the retailer may suffer. Thus, the threat to branded-goods manufacturers lies not with private labels *in general,* but with the more upscale private labels that are well managed by their retailers.

Strategic Responses by Suppliers to Growing Power in the Retail Sector

This discussion implies that there has been a shift in power to the retail level in virtually all lines of trade (e.g., food, apparel, electronics, etc.). It is useful to consider some examples of concrete steps that suppliers have taken to confront the situation facing them.

One manufacturer response is to *take on more channel flows or develop new channel technologies* that help rebalance some channel power. VF Corporation manufactures jeans in the United States under such brand names as Lee, Wrangler, Brittania, Rustler, Riders, and Maverick. It commands more than 30 percent of the U.S. jeans market. It has been a pioneer in the implementation of EDI and VMI (vendor-managed inventory) technologies with its retailers throughout the 1990s—in effect managing both the physical possession and the ordering flows in the channel. It calls its activities "micromerchandising," meaning that today VF is capable of monitoring inventory and sales levels, not just at the level of the corporate retail account (e.g., ShopKo's corporate level) but also at the individual store and stockkeeping unit (SKU) level. Its latest technological innovation has been the creation of a retail floor-space management program that helps retailers plan the contents and organization of their retail space devoted to jeans sales. Using historical sales data, the program creates a "planogram," a geographic plan for the retail space showing how many racks of various stockkeeping units of jeans to install in the store. Combined with VF's other EDI technologies that link retailers directly with the manufacturer, this brings the channel even closer to true just-in-time delivery of product. In a beta test of the technology at ShopKo, a discount retailer, the VF program suggested a 12 percent *decrease* in floor space allocated to men's denim products from both VF and other manufacturers. But even with the smaller amount of space, sales *increased* by 20 percent due to the efficiencies in VF's floor-space planning system. The freed-up space could then be allocated to other merchandise at an additional profit to the retailer. This sort of innovation in the bearing of channel flow costs earns VF a valued role in its relationship with retailers because it benefits both channel members; a manager at ShopKo says, "No other company has come as far with VMI as VF; going ahead with retail floorspace management will keep us competitive, too."[48]

Another manufacturer strategy is to *change the role of price promotions in the total marketing mix* to retailers and consumers. Procter & Gamble, the U.S. consumer packaged-goods company that makes such brands as Crest toothpaste and Tide detergent, led a movement in 1992 to abandon trade promotions and seek "value pricing" for its products to the trade. It recognized that with fewer trade promotions, the wide swings in sales to retailers would diminish and permit the company to reduce the costs of production and inventorying in the channel system. These savings, combined with some of the money that would otherwise have been used for trade promotions, could then be allocated toward the reduction of wholesale and retail prices. Although some retailers reduced the number of P&G products they carried, the strategy as a whole has worked, partly due to the preexisting strength of P&G brands.[49]

Procter & Gamble went further in 1996, when it decided to cut its use of direct-to-consumer coupons. It ran an experiment in upstate New York in which it banned couponing completely and cut its use of coupons by half in the rest of the United States. Other manufacturers, such as Clorox, Kimberly-Clark, and Lever Brothers, also tried coupon cutbacks in the region. P&G viewed this as another in a series of cost-cutting measures aimed at freeing up funds to further build brand equity for its products. But the experiment backfired when, in 1997, P&G, nine other manufacturers, and the Wegman's grocery chain in upstate New York agreed to pay $4.2 million to New York shoppers to settle an investigation by New York State's attorney general into possible collusive pricing practices.[50] Despite this setback, the strategy for many well-known brands remains to build and maintain brand equity through pricing and marketing practices in order to counteract increasing retailer power.

A third strategy is to *expand the product line* to counteract the popularity of ever more upscale store brands. Quaker Oats Company turned to this strategy in 1998, allocating more funds to its set of inexpensive imitations of major cereal brands. Alternatively, a fourth strategy is to *divest nonmarketing functions and redirect spending* toward new-product development and marketing. Campbell Soup Company has followed this path by selling its can-making operations in order to spend more on marketing its soup, sauce, and biscuit brands. Similarly, Sara Lee Corporation has outsourced production of meat products and allocated the savings to new-product development.[51]

Finally, a fifth strategy to counteract increasing retailer power is to *expand the number of channels used* to distribute product (i.e., to practice dual distribution), in order to reduce dependence on one or just a few retailers. American consumers now spend less than half of their food dollars inside grocery stores, with the remainder being spent at prepared-food outlets such as fast-food or full-service restaurants. Thus, the operative principle may well become consumer management, not category management in the standard grocery context. As an example, consider that General Foods (now part of Kraft) identified flavored coffees as an important growth area around 1990, focusing its marketing efforts on selling through standard grocery stores. Meanwhile, Starbucks, the coffee retailer, built its business through an entirely different channel, in the process becoming a completely new type of competitor to standard coffee manufacturers and increasing the coffee market by more than 25 percent. Although Starbucks began as a freestanding chain of stores, it is now a brand that sells in supermarkets and is offered in restaurants and on airlines, in direct competition with brands like General Foods International Coffees.[52] The relevant competition for General Foods clearly did not lie only on the grocery store shelves it shared with other coffee brands!

This strategy is not limited to grocery products. Toy manufacturers who had a difficult time earning shelf space in the major toy retailers such as Toys "R" Us turned to specialty toy stores to stock their products. This turned out to be more than just a desperation move. The placement of such toys as Playmobil construction toys or "Shining Time Station" train toys in these stores can add a certain cachet to products that would otherwise look like just another mass-marketed product. Meanwhile, specialty toy retailers are delighted to have "exclusive" rights to distribute products that will not have to price compete with the offerings at larger discount toy stores. Some toy manufacturers, such as Oddzon Products Inc., makers of Koosh Balls, which sells through both specialty stores and mass-merchandisers, limit the distribution of new products to specialty stores initially.[53] Even major toy retailers use dual distribution strategies. Mattel Inc., owner of the Barbie doll brand as well as the American Girl doll brand and many other toy lines, publicly announced its intention in early 1999 to reduce its dependence on large retailers such as Toys "R" Us and Wal-Mart. Its plans have included selling directly to consumers through Internet sales, direct-sales companies such as Avon Products Inc., and catalog and own-store selling like that used for American Girl dolls.[54] Such strategies protect the exclusive brand image of the products, while giving manufacturers a chance to sell established favorites in higher-volume stores.

It has been argued that using manufacturers' outlet stores as an additional channel to reach the market, most prevalent in general merchandise categories such as apparel, is a reaction to the power of primary retailers as well.[55] Decades ago, manufacturers opened outlet stores near their factories and used them to sell second-quality merchandise, as well as overstocked merchandise and merchandise that had been sent back by retailers. Today, this pattern is very different. Most outlet stores carry at least some current-season merchandise (sometimes with some delay in availability), and some (such as Jones New York) carry entirely current-season merchandise. This merchandise is not just made for the outlet stores; rather, it is the same as that available in standard department stores. There were 325 outlet malls in the United States in the late 1990s, and many manufacturers run dozens of outlet stores (e.g., Polo Ralph Lauren operates 73 outlet stores!). These patterns of manufacturer behavior suggest strongly that outlet store retailing is not just for the disposal of overstocked or second-quality merchandise. Indeed, if that were the case, the manufacturers could significantly increase their profitability merely by improving their sales forecasting alone.

Outlet store retailing angers some standard retailers, who believe their business is cannibalized by the lower-priced, low-service outlets. A few groups, such as the National Sporting Goods Association and the National Shoe Association, have urged members to reduce or eliminate purchases from manufacturers establishing outlet stores. Not all retailers complain, however; some view the outlet stores as a means of focusing sales to price-sensitive, service-insensitive customers, permitting them in turn to focus their own retailing efforts on the more lucrative high-end segment of the market. Further, to appease retailers, outlet mall developers locate their malls outside major cities, at an average travel distance of about an hour from major shopping areas. Only consumers with a relatively low cost of time, who are also of course likely to be the most price-sensitive, are thus willing to travel the distance to the outlet mall.

In sum, manufacturers' most effective responses to increased retailer power have been to take action to build and maintain the value of their core brands. They used innovations within the channel, new-product development, increased investments in brand equity rather than in consumer promotions, and a judicious use of multiple channels to balance their reach in the market.

"Power Retailing" and Category Killers

Power retailing is not restricted to one type of format, even though the term is most frequently applied to retailers of general merchandise (soft goods [e.g., apparel, linens] and hard goods [e.g., appliances, hardware] as opposed to food). It is populated by specialty stores (e.g., Borders bookstores, Toys "R" Us); discount stores (e.g., Wal-Mart, Target); and electronics superstores (e.g., Best Buy, Circuit City). Apart from the most significant factor—a sharp definition of their customers and of their needs—the attributes that make power retailers so successful are (1) a willingness to take risks via market testing and trend forecasting; (2) ordering early and selling merchandise in high volume, with a consistent emphasis on generating high gross margin returns on inventory investment (GMROI); (3) investing large sums in information systems that can deliver to an executive's desk instant sales-trend data from across a large geographic area and multiple locations; (4) a commitment to delivering value so that the price a customer pays is always perceived as fair and commensurate with the promise of the store; and (5) an old-fashioned emphasis on customer service so that shopping is made easier for generally time-impoverished customers.

These retailers generate superior financial performance, high productivity, strong consumer franchises, and sustained competitive advantage. Above-median performance on several measures of retail performance are common, as shown in Table 13.7.

A number of these retailers concentrate on building dominant or so-called "power" assortments of merchandise so that consumers know that they will almost always find what they need at the outlets of the retail chain. Sometimes these assortments are broad and deep (such as those provided by IKEA in furniture and Toys "R" Us in toys); at other times, they are focused, such as those provided by Victoria's Secret (women's lingerie), Gap (jeans and other casual apparel), or Crate & Barrel (modern furniture and home accessories). Frequently, the focused assortment programs of power retailers are supported by strong private-label programs, which give added value to their merchandise while making them appear unique.

TABLE 13.7

Financial Performance of Selected Power Retailers*

Store (Category)	Five-Year Cumulative Average Growth Rate (CAGR) in Profits, 1992–1997**	Return on Net Worth**	GMROI**	Inventory Turnover**
Best Buy Co., Inc. (consumer electronics, computer and appliance stores)	36.6% (−1.1%)	16.9% (0.7%)	121.5% (145.8%)	6.4 (4.3)
Borders Group, Inc. (bookstores)	28.3% (20.9%)	13.4% (8.4%)	78.2% (68.6%)	2.0 (2.3)
The Home Depot, Inc. (home improvement centers)	26.2% (27.8%)	16.3% (4.9%)	214.9% (155.8%)	5.5 (4.6)
The Sports Authority, Inc. (sporting goods stores)	31.1% (19.7%)	6.7% (10.2%)	138.2% (117.2%)	3.4 (2.3)
Wal-Mart Stores, Inc. (discount department stores)	12.1% (5.9%)	19.1% (3.9%)	151.4% (153.6%)	5.8 (4.0)
Williams-Sonoma, Inc. (home furnishings and accessories stores)	87.2% (35.6%)	21.4% (7.4%)	309.7% (169.0%)	4.6 (2.8)

* Data are from 1997 except for the five-year CAGR in profits, which is from 1992–1997.
** First number is the performance for this company. Number in parentheses is the median performance for stores of this category.
Source: PricewaterhouseCoopers LLP, *1998 Retail Yearbook*. Reprinted by permission.

The assortments of some of the power retailers are so deep and attractive that the stores stocking them have become known as *category killers*. Often, these retailers are discounters that specialize in one product area, such as toys, electronics, or books, offering wider selections and steeper price cuts. They include such companies as Barnes & Noble and Borders, Inc., two book superstore chains; The Sports Authority, a sporting goods chain; Best Buy, a consumer electronics and appliance discounter; Home Depot, a home center chain focused mainly on home improvement products and services; F&M, a health and beauty aids discounter; and Toys "R" Us. The assortments of the category killers are so deep and so low-priced relative to those of other, more traditional retailers that consumers willingly make special trips to purchase individual items there. In fact, consumers forego the low-price, one-stop shopping convenience of Wal-Mart and Target (whose assortments are generally broad but not deep) in favor of the category killlers.

Retailing Polarity: Price Sensitivity or the Flight to Quality

Two major trends in retailing have typified the increasing polarity of retail trade (see Figure 13.3). First, the growth of tightly managed, limited line, highly focused specialty store chains, such as Gap, The Body Shop, Eddie Bauer, and Ann Taylor. Many of these

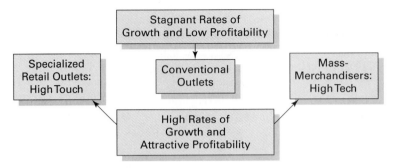

FIGURE 13.3 **The Polarity of Retail Trade**

chains can be categorized as power retailers because they feature deep assortments. They also meet the service needs of customers on a personalized basis, the so-called "high-touch" retailers.

The second trend is the growth of very large stores (in terms of square footage), which often rely on warehouse technology and self-service to move massive amounts of merchandise at very low margins. Although discount stores such as Kmart, Wal-Mart, and Target have traditionally been viewed as "high-tech" retailers, other, more extreme high-turnover–low-margin–massive-volume retailers have come along in the form of home centers (e.g., Home Depot), warehouse clubs (e.g., Price–Costco stores, Sam's Wholesale Clubs [owned by Wal-Mart]), and office supply superstores (Staples, Office Club, and Office Depot).

Although warehouse clubs and office supply superstores were basically established to serve small business customers (thereby making them wholesalers, not retailers), a significant portion of their trade comes from consumers buying for personal consumption. By carrying only the most popular item in a merchandise category, warehouse clubs strive to achieve high turnover (18 to 20 turns per year) with gross margins as low as 8 to 10 percent. Unlike normal discount retailers, which might carry 80,000 items, a warehouse club's range is usually limited to about 4,000. Its retail and wholesale customers must be so price sensitive that they are willing to sacrifice convenience, brand loyalty, merchandise consistency, and individual packaging for lower prices.

On the high-touch side, several specialty store chains have been very successful. They identify a narrow niche as their target market and do not try to be everything to everyone. They sell assortments of goods that meet the lifestyle needs and fashion attitudes of their customers. They put these goods into a retail environment that is compelling and fits the merchandise being sold. Many sell their own private-label merchandise or refuse to sell mass-marketed brands. In short, they tightly define the desires of their target consumers and seek to meet them through both product and service choice.

Specialty toy stores are a good example of high-touch marketing. One such store, No Kidding, outside of Boston, Massachusetts, is staffed by preschool teachers who can explain what toys a child of a particular age would like. The store wraps gifts at no charge and accepts returns without receipts. It routinely brings in outside speakers on topics of interest to the families who shop there. And it sells toys not found at mass-merchandisers such as Toys "R" Us. Rather than selling heavily advertised toys, No Kidding substitutes personal selling to educate its shoppers about the toys for sale.[56]

A successful example on the high-tech, warehouse-technology side of the retail spectrum is IKEA, the Swedish retailer that operates one of the world's largest volume furniture chains. Its worldwide sales in 1998 were $7 billion, operating almost 150 stores in 28 different countries and sourcing its 12,000 different products from 2,400 suppliers in 65 countries. Almost 200 million people visited an IKEA store in its 1998–1999 fiscal year alone. How did the company grow to this size in its 50-year history? The key lies in its stated business vision: "We shall offer a wide range of home furnishings items of good design and function, at prices so low, that the majority of people can afford to buy them." The company's founder, Ingvar Kamprad, has made IKEA stores easy to shop in and the furniture they offer easy to buy. Stores offer child-care playrooms for busy parents, baby changing rooms, and restaurants offering Swedish food. Furniture is sold unassembled in "flat packs," which reduces the retailer's transport volume by close to 70 percent on bulky furniture items (relative to the volume necessary to ship preassembled pieces).

With minimal sales staff, IKEA consumers select furniture in the retail warehouse and wheel their choices on a heavy cart to a checkout hall. They can take purchases home immediately after buying them, rather than having to endure long waiting times for deliveries through a standard channel. Because of this lower cost structure, consumers are able to buy products less expensively than they would in a standard furniture store that must cover the costs of assembly, breakage in transit, and delivery. In return, they take the flat packs home and assemble furniture themselves—in essence, trading a lower price for the performance of more channel flows. Even with prices 20 to 30 percent lower than those of their rivals', IKEA sales per square foot are estimated to be three times the industry average, and its pretax margins of 8 to 10 percent are twice as high as those of rival furniture retailers. Although IKEA has been operating in the United States only since 1985, it has earned a place among the top 10 sellers in the fragmented U.S. furniture market.[57]

Caught in the middle, between specialty stores and price-oriented, volume-driven outlets, are the "all things to all people" department stores, variety stores, "conventional" supermarkets, traditional drugstores, and hardware stores. Only a few department store chains have escaped the competitive squeeze. Midscale American department stores are not helped by the lack of variation in their product lines. Designers such as Liz Claiborne, Jones New York, DKNY, and Anne Klein in women's clothes, and Tommy Hilfiger, Nautica, Ralph Lauren, and Dockers (made by Levi's) in men's clothes, are found at every department store. One story recounts how a shopper "momentarily forgets which downtown Chicago department store she's shopping in. 'These stores all look exactly alike,' she says later."[58]

This sameness in inventory is in large part the retailers' own faults. Department stores now make heavy logistical demands of their suppliers, such as requiring them to pack hanging garments, fill out extensive paperwork, and deliver only on certain days of the week. When a supplier fails to meet retailers' standards, the retailer punishes it with a "chargeback," or deduction from payment of the merchandise invoice. As a result of all of these demands, only the most successful and largest garment designers can afford to do business with mainstream department stores. As a result, the available pool of product lines from which to choose is small and does not vary from store to store. Meanwhile, smaller designers (with potentially attractive and differentiated merchandise) cannot gain access to the retail stores.[59] In short, in the quest for logistical efficiencies, mainstream department stores have hobbled themselves in the competitive positioning realm, whereas rivals at either end of the price–service spectrum take sales from them.

Those retailers "in the middle" who have survived and succeeded (the top three U.S. department store retail companies are Federated Department Stores, May Company, and Dillard's) have also changed dramatically over time. First, they have centralized many management functions and maintained close control over expenses. Second, they have all downsized departments in which they no longer can deliver a differential advantage to their customers. Very few department store chains devote enormous amounts of floor space to toys, sporting goods, or major appliances, for example. Third, because of the more focused nature of their assortments and the way in which they have remodeled their stores, they resemble a series of specialty stores under one roof rather than a "traditional" department stores. In fact, many of the stores that are usually put into the "department store" category are, in actuality, departmentalized specialty stores, and a number of them do exceedingly well (e.g., Nordstrom, Lord & Taylor [part of the May Company stores chain], and Burdine's [part of Federated Department Stores]).

The Emergence of Global Retailing

Retailing has lagged behind other industries in the race to globalize. In 1996, for example, the top five retailers in the world had only 12 percent of their sales outside their home markets. This percentage was far higher for other industries (e.g., entertainment, 34 percent; aerospace, 35 percent; banking, 48 percent; and petroleum refining, 66 percent).[60] Several sources of difficulty exist in expanding a retail operation across national boundaries:

- The need for quality real estate locations on which to site stores
- The need to develop physical logistics operations comparable to those in the home country to source and distribute product
- The need to develop supplier relationships in new markets or to internationalize one's home-market suppliers
- The differences in zoning, pricing, taxation, hours of operation, labor and hiring, and other regulations in each market
- the need to offer locally attractive products, packaged and positioned in a culturally sensitive manner

As a result of these difficulties, even well-known retailers such as Marks & Spencer, Tiffany's, and Price–Costco failed to generate a return on invested capital in international retail operations exceeding their average corporate cost of capital.[61] The difficulties are particularly troublesome in emerging-market economies, where in addition to the problems listed, the necessary infrastructure to support a retail effort may be lacking.

Despite these difficulties, retailers increasingly are choosing to globalize (or at least internationalize) their operations. They are driven by many factors, including slowing growth in their home markets and the overwhelming attractiveness of overseas markets that offer less intense competition and weakening barriers to foreign market entry. Developing markets offer quickly improving environments. By 1994, free currency convertibility was offered in Indonesia, Poland, Argentina, Mexico, Hungary, Russia, India, China, and Brazil; free majority ownership by a foreign business was permitted in Indonesia, Poland, Argentina, Mexico, Russia, India, and Brazil; and free repatriation of capital and earnings was permitted from Poland, Argentina, Mexico, Hungary, India, China, and Brazil.[62] Such liberalizations have made expansion into developing as well as developed nations much more attractive.

Not only can the legal and governmental environment be more inviting, but the retail opportunities have grown in many emerging markets. Consider Southeast Asian markets. Retail business in India is forecast to be $350 billion by the year 2005, with a cumulative average growth rate of over 7 percent. Meanwhile, retailing is very fragmented, with 500,000 retail outlets for 950 million people. Food and drug retailing have yet to establish a set of national chains. Yet the economic promise of such a market is great, so that foreign manufacturers from Reebok to Tommy Hilfiger are entering the market with an array of retailing strategies including licensing, franchising, and sales through incumbent retailers.[63]

There is a similarly strong market potential in countries such as China, Thailand, and Indonesia, although the current retailing infrastructure is not nearly as sophisticated as it is in North America, Europe, or Japan. China, with retail sales of $250 billion in 1995 and about $500 billion in 2000, is forecast to grow to $900 billion in retail sales by 2005. Retail sales are forecast to grow in Thailand from $40 billion in 1995 to $120 billion in 2005, and other "Asian tigers" will grow as well.[64] Retailers such as Carrefour and Continental of France (owned by Promodès) and Makro (the company's site in Indonesia) and Ahold of the Netherlands have built significant presences in Thailand and Indonesia in particular in response to the nascent opportunities for large-scale, low-cost retail outlets. Indeed, while total retail sales in Thailand in 1999 were down 20 to 30 percent over the precrash period of the mid-1990s, sales at hypermarkets dropped only 10 to 15 percent, and the hypermarket–superstore category rose in number of stores from 9 to 48 in Thailand.[65] If one considers the percentage of "unstaked" grocery purchases—that is, those not made through organized retailer groups or chains—these and other developing markets leave ample opportunity for entrants. For example, in 1994 the unstaked market potential in Argentina was 60 percent of the grocery market; in Taiwan and South Korea it was 45 percent; in Brazil it was 55 percent; and in Poland it was 80 percent.[66] A well-organized retail chain will find such markets ripe for development.

The result has been a flurry of expansionary activity by major world retailers, some of it greenfield investment and some of it fueled by acquisitions. Of the top 20 world retailers listed in Table 13.1, only 4 operate in just one country (and for all 4, that country is the United States). Carrefour operates stores in 8 European countries, 8 Asian countries, and 5 countries in the Americas.[67] Wal-Mart operates stores only in Germany, in 3 Asian countries, and in 6 countries in the Americas.[68]

Not only has there been expansion, but consolidation has also been the order of the day among the biggest retailers, particularly in Europe. Karstadt, a German department store operator, and Quelle, the German (and world's second largest) mail-order group, announced a merger of their mail-order businesses in 1999.[69] Wal-Mart acquired two German retail chains, Wertkauf in 1997 and Interspar in 1998, and Asda of the United Kingdom in 1999, giving it a beachhead in Europe from which to expand. Wal-Mart is already the largest retailer in Mexico and Canada, through both greenfield expansion and through acquisition of the Woolco chain in Canada.[70] And two of the largest chains in France, Carrefour and Promodès, announced plans to merge in late 1999. If approved by antitrust authorities, the merged firm would be the second-largest retailer in the world, after Wal-Mart.[71] The move to consolidate in Europe is driven in large part by the unification of Europe, creating a single market larger in size than the United States. With a common currency, the euro, and cross-border barriers eliminated, it is possible to rationalize supply arrangements and benefit from some of the economies of scale that large U.S. retailers have been able to enjoy.

What makes for a successful entry into a foreign retail market? There have certainly been failures. The French department store Galeries Lafayette was forced to withdraw from the U.S. market after an abortive attempt at operating a store in Manhattan; Carrefour pulled out of the United States after attempting to enter; and Wal-Mart sold out to its Hong Kong partner after trying to set up a warehouse club there. The key is a sensible balance between exporting the distinctive retail competencies that make the retailer strong in the home market and being sensitive to local preferences for products and retail services. Wal-Mart's initial entry into Argentina in 1995 showed a lack on these dimensions; it tried to import its American style of retailing with no adaptations at first. The merchandise mix included appliances wired for 110-volt electric power (Argentina operates on 220 volts) and American cuts of beef, and the stores themselves had too-narrow aisles and carpeting that quickly looked faded and dirty. Meanwhile, French competitor Carrefour had been operating hypermarkets in Argentina for some time, very successfully. Not surprisingly, Wal-Mart made large losses in its first two years in Argentina, which it only began to turn around in 1998 when it revised its local strategy to be more in keeping with local norms.[72]

The retailers that successfully expand outside their local borders can benefit from what is known as a "virtuous cycle." As they grow in scale, they gain ever more from economies of scale in purchasing and sourcing as well as in advertising and information technology management. Successful products from one market can be easily exported into another. Large scale also permits efficient investment in common assets such as marketing research expertise and financing. With successful expansion, profits can be funneled into the enhancement of brand equity in worldwide markets. Thus, the "big" can get "bigger," and this is part of what motivates the worldwide expansion characterizing retailing today.[73]

Faced with increasingly strong transnational competitors, what can a local incumbent retailer do? Some have sold out, as Woolco did to Wal-Mart in Canada. But others have found the ability to sell to niche segments in their home markets, offering superior service, products, and location, tailored to local tastes. Brazil's grocery chain Pao de Azucar followed this strategy following the entry of Carrefour and then Wal-Mart into the country. Rather than try to beat these retail behemoths at their own game, Pao de Azucar instead refocused its business to emphasize the convenient locations its stores enjoyed and to provide credit to its customers, a popular local service that the entrants did not provide. Because the entrants could not match the locations of the incumbent retailer, Pao de Azucar had a basis for viable competition even in the face of higher costs.[74] There is likely to remain a market for high-service, conveniently located retail outlets in these markets, just as there is in Wal-Mart's or Carrefour's home markets. But only those local competitors who are excellent at providing the extra service that these segments demand will survive the onslaught of multinational retailers like these.

An important insight to take away from this description of the globalization of retailing is that international competition is now a given, rather than an exception, as it was until recently. This is not just an item of curiosity, even for local retailers who themselves do not cross national borders to do business. Given the entry of multinational retailers into many markets, and not just the major developed ones, even local retailers need to consider how international retail competition is likely to affect them, and how to protect their businesses (or profitably harvest them) in the face of potential and actual competition from outside entrants.

SUMMARY

Retailing is an enormously complex and varied enterprise the world over. As the key channel member in direct contact with the consumer end-user, the retailer's actions are critical to the success of the marketing channel. A retailer's position is defined by the demand-side and cost-side characteristics of its operation. These characteristics map into the service outputs provided to consumers who shop with the retailer. Because markets are made up of distinct consumer segments, each of which demands different levels of service outputs, a retailer can successfully differentiate itself from the competition on the demand and cost sides, even if it sells comparable or identical products to those of its competitors. Indeed, without a distinct offering on the service output side, or a distinct cost advantage, a retailer of competitive products risks failure in the marketplace. Different types of retailers can be categorized by the levels of service outputs they provide and by their cost positions.

One of the most important developments on the consumer side has been the increasing importance of convenience in retail shopping. Consumers in many countries suffer from time poverty, and when this is combined with growing purchasing power, they demand a broader array of channel services that lower their time cost of shopping. Conversely, if they choose to buy at a lower-service retail outlet, they demand a lower price to compensate for the full cost of shopping there. This places increasing pressure on retailers both to control costs and to enhance the value they add to the products sold in their stores.

Power and coordination issues still affect retail channel management. Retailers use their leverage to engage in forward buying on deals, and to demand concessions from their suppliers such as slotting allowances and failure fees. In grocery and apparel industries, they have also developed strong private branding programs that pose a competitive threat to the nationally branded goods supplied by manufacturers. Manufacturers respond by building and maintaining strong brands and by bearing the cost of more channel flows. They also seek to change the basis for pricing to their retailers, and use multiple channel strategies to limit their dependence on any one retailer.

The globalization of retailing is an emerging phenomenon that will affect consumers and competing retailers very significantly. Hypermarkets have been very active in global expansion, although some specialty retailers have also moved overseas. Globalization and consolidation have been facilitated by the formalization of regional blocs, such as the European Union. The increasing level of concentration on a transnational level suggests that suppliers will sell to fewer retail corporations in the future, and that these global retailers in turn will seek more and more favorable terms from their suppliers, who will be expected to serve them on a worldwide basis. International product sourcing of the most popular products, combined with greater cost controls, is likely to mean greater choice at lower prices for many consumers. Even local retailers who themselves do not intend to sell in overseas markets cannot escape the competitive effects of global retailers entering their home markets.

Discussion Questions

1. Think of a product you have recently purchased at retail. Evaluate (a) what service outputs you expected to get from the retail experience, (b) how you chose the retailer to visit based on your service output demands, and (c) how well the retailer met those service output demands. Would you buy the same product at a different type of retailer in a different purchase occasion (e.g., when shopping for home use versus at work; when shopping at home versus on vacation)?

2. Why are a low average retail margin and a high turnover rate in a retail outlet a viable combination for retail financial success? What would happen if margin and turnover were both low? Both high? Can you think of retailer examples that fit (a) a low-margin–high-turnover strategy; (b) a high-margin–low-turnover strategy; or (c) a high-margin–high-turnover strategy?

3. What type(s) of power are represented by retailers demanding slotting allowances or failure fees from their suppliers? Why do suppliers comply? Is conflict generated by the use of this power, and if so, of what sort?

4. You are an apparel manufacturer, selling to major department stores in the United States. Each retailer makes different demands of you. One requires that you ship garments to each store, rather than to one central warehouse, and that each garment already be tagged and ready to hang on the retailer's store racks. Another requires you to adopt its electronic data interchange (EDI) system to implement continuous replenishment, meaning that you will have to ship frequent replacements for garments that sell throughout the season. Your cost structure is increasing significantly as a result. What can you do to protect your profit margins?

5. Describe the demand and supply conditions that support polarity in retailing. In such a system, what happens to middle-of-the-road retailers?

6. Why do retailers sometimes choose to acquire overseas retailers or build their own overseas retail outlets, and sometimes choose to partner with a local licensee or retailer (without completely acquiring it)? Benetton, for example, chooses to license its retailers and not control their activities, but it controls the creation of the merchandise and how it is promoted. But Wal-Mart chooses to acquire or build outlets rather than franchise or license them. In your answer, consider the strategic competencies of a retailer, the local market conditions, and costs.

A Glossary of Pricing and Buying Terms Commonly Used by Retailers

Original Retail: The first price at which the merchandise is offered for sale.

Sale Retail: The final selling price.

Merchandise Cost: The billed cost of merchandise less any applicable trade or quantity discounts plus inbound transportation costs, if paid by the buyer. Cash discounts are not deducted to arrive at merchandise cost. Usually, they are either deducted from "aggregate cost of goods sold" at the end of an accounting period or added to net operating profits. If cash discounts are added to net operating profit, the amount added is treated as financial income with no effect on gross margins.

Markup: The difference between merchandise cost and the retail price.

Initial Markup or Mark-on: The difference between merchandise cost and the original retail value.

Maintained Markup or Margin: The difference between the *gross* cost of goods sold and net sales.

Gross Margin of Profit: The dollar difference between the *total* cost of goods and net sales.

Gross Margin Return on Inventory (GMROI): Total gross margin dollars divided by average inventory (at cost). GMROI is used most appropriately in measuring the performance of products within a single merchandise category. The measure permits the buyer to look at products with different gross margin percentages and different rates of inventory turnover and make a relatively quick evaluation as to which are the best performers. The components of GMROI are

Gross Margin Percentage		**Sales-to-Inventory Ratio**		**GMROI**
(gross margin)/(net sales)	×	(net sales)/(average inventory) (at cost)	=	(gross margin)/ (average inventory) (at cost)

Total Cost: Total cost of goods sold—gross cost of goods sold + workroom costs − cash discounts.

Markdown: A reduction in the original or previous retail price of merchandise. The *markdown percentage* is the ratio of the dollar markdown during a period to the net sales for the same period.

Off-Retail: Designates specific reductions off the original retail price. Retailers can express markup in terms of retail price or cost. Large retailers and progressive small retailers express markups in terms of retail for several reasons. First, other operating ratios are expressed in terms of percentage net sales. Second, net sales figures are available more often than cost figures. Finally, most trade statistics are expressed in terms of sales.

Markup on retail can be converted to cost base by using the following formula:

Markup % on Cost = (Markup % on Retail)/(100% − Markup % on Retail)

On the other hand,

Markup % on Retail = (Markup % on Cost)/(100% + Markup % on Cost).

F.O.B.: The seller places the merchandise "free on board" the carrier at the point of shipment or other predesignated place. The buyer assumes title to the merchandise and pays all freight charges from this point.

Delivered Sale: The seller pays all freight charges to the buyer's destination and retains title to the goods until they are received by the buyer.

Freight Allowances: F.O.B. terms can be used with freight allowances to transfer the title to the buyer at the point of shipping, whereas the seller absorbs the transportation cost. The seller ships F.O.B. and the buyer deducts freight costs from the invoice payment.

Trade Discount: Vendors usually quote a list price and offer a trade discount to provide the purchaser a reasonable margin to cover its operating expenses and provide for net profit margin. Trade discounts are sometimes labeled *functional discounts*. They are usually quoted in a series of percentages, such as list price less 33 percent, 15 percent, 5 percent, for different channel functions performed by different intermediaries. Therefore, if a list price of $100 is assumed, the discount applies as follows for the different channel members:

List Price	$100.00	
Less 33%	$ 33.00	(retailer-performed flow)
	$ 67.00	
Less 15%	$ 10.05	(wholesaler-performed flow)
	$ 56.95	
Less 5%	$ 2.85	(manufacturers' representative–performed flow)
	$ 54.10	

Quantity Discounts: Vendors offer two types of quantity discounts: noncumulative and cumulative. Although noncumulative discounts are offered on volume of each order, cumulative discounts are offered on total volume for a specified period. Quantity discounts are offered to encourage volume buying. Legally, they should not exceed production and distribution cost savings to the seller because of volume buying.

Seasonal Discounts: Discounts offered to buyers of seasonal products who place their order before the season's buying period. This enables the manufacturer to use its equipment more efficiently by spreading production throughout the year.

Cash Discount: Vendors selling on credit offer a cash discount for payment within a specified period. The cash discount is usually expressed in the following format: "2/10, net 30." This means that the seller extends credit for 30 days. If payment is made within 10 days, a 2% discount is offered to the buyer. The 2% interest rate for 10 days is equivalent to a 36% effective interest rate per year. Therefore, passing up cash discounts can be very costly. Some middlemen who operate on slim margins simply cannot realize a profit on a merchandise shipment unless they take advantage of the cash discount. Channel intermediaries usually maintain a line of credit at low interest rates to pay their bills within the cash discount period.

Cash Datings: Cash datings include C.O.D. (cash on delivery), C.W.O. (cash with order), R.O.G. (receipt of goods), S.D.–B.L. (sight draft–bill of lading). S.D.–B.L. means that a sight draft is attached to the bill of lading and must be honored before the buyer takes possession of the shipment.

Future Datings: Future datings include

1. Ordinary dating, such as "2/10, net 30."

2. End-of-month dating, such as "2/10, net 30, E.O.M.," wherein the cash discount and the net credit periods begin on the first day of the following month rather than on the invoice date.

3. Proximo dating, such as "2%, 10th proximo, net 60," which specifies a date in the following month on which payment must be made in order to take the cash discount.

4. Extra dating, such as "2/10—30 days extra," which means that the buyer has 70 days from the invoice date to pay its bill and benefit from the discount.

5. Advance or season dating, such as "2/10, net 30 as of May 1," which means that the discount and net periods are calculated from May 1. Sometimes extra dating is accompanied by an anticipation allowance. For example, if the buyer is quoted "2/10, 60 days extra," and he pays in 10 days, or 60 days ahead, an additional discount is made available to him.

13.2 Merchandise Planning and Control

Merchandise planning and control start with decisions about merchandise variety and assortment. Variety decisions involve determining the different kinds of goods to be carried or services offered. For example, a department store carries a wide variety of merchandise ranging from men's clothing and women's fashions to sports equipment and appliances. On the other hand, assortment decisions involve determination of the range of choice (e.g., brands, styles or models, colors, sizes, prices) offered to the customer within a variety classification. The more carefully and wisely decisions on variety and assortment are made, the more likely the retailer is to achieve a satisfactory rate of *stockturn*.

The rate of stockturn (stock turnover) is the number of times during a given period in which the average amount of stock on hand is sold. It is most commonly determined by dividing the average inventory at cost into the cost of the merchandise sold. It is also computed by dividing average inventory at retail into the net sales figure or by dividing average inventory in physical units into sales in physical units. To achieve a high rate of stockturn, retailers frequently attempt to limit their investment in inventory, which, in turn, reduces storage space as well as such expenses as interest, taxes, and insurance on merchandise. "Fresher" merchandise will be on hand, thereby generating more sales. Thus, a rapid stockturn can lead to greater returns on invested capital.[75]

Although the retailing firms with the highest rates of turnover tend to realize the greatest profit-to-sales ratios, significant problems may be encountered by adopting high-turnover goals.[76] For example, higher sales volume can be generated through lower margins, which in turn reduce profitability; lower inventory levels may result in additional ordering (clerical) costs and the loss of quantity discounts; and greater expense may be involved in receiving, checking, and marking merchandise. Merchandise budget planning provides the means by which the appropriate balance can be achieved between retail stock and sales volume.

MERCHANDISE BUDGETING

The merchandise budget plan is a forecast of specified merchandise-related activities for a definite period. Although the usual period is one season of six months, in practice it is often broken down into monthly or even shorter periods. Merchandise budgeting requires the retail decision maker to make forecasts and plans relative to five basic vari-ables: sales, stock levels, reductions, purchases, and gross margin and operating profit.[77] Each of these variables will be addressed briefly.

Planned Sales and Stock Levels

The *first step* in budget determination is the preparation of the *sales forecast* for the sea-son and for each month in the season for which the budget is being prepared. The sec-ond step involves the determination of the *beginning-of-the-month* (B.O.M.) *inventory* (stock on hand), which necessitates specification of a desired rate of stockturn for each month of the season. If, for example, the desired stock-sales ratio for the month of June is four and forecasted (planned) sales during June are $10,000, then the planned B.O.M. stock would be $40,000.[78] It is also important, for budgeting purposes, to calculate stock available at the *end of the month* (E.O.M. stock). This figure is identical to the B.O.M. stock for the following month. Thus, in our example, May's E.O.M. stock is $40,000 (or June's B.O.M. stock).

PLANNED REDUCTIONS

This third step in budget preparation involves accounting for markdowns, shortages, and employee discounts. Reduction planning is critical because any amount of reductions has exactly the same effect on the value of stock as an equal amount of sales. Markdowns vary from month to month, depending on special and sales events. In addition, shortages are becoming an increasing problem for retailers. Shortages result from shoplifting, employee pilferage, miscounting, and pricing and checkout mistakes. Generally, mer-chandise managers can rely on past data in forecasting both shortages and employee dis-counts.

Planned Purchases

When figures for sales, opening (B.O.M.) and closing (E.O.M.) stocks, and reductions have been forecast, the fourth step, the *planning of purchases* in dollars, becomes merely a mechanical mathematical operation. Thus, planned purchases are equal to planned stock at the end of the month (E.O.M.) + planned sales + planned reductions – stock at the beginning of the month (B.O.M.). Suppose, for example, that the planned E.O.M. stock for June was $67,500 and that reductions for June were forecast to be $2,500.[79] Then,

Planned E.O.M. stock (June 30)	$67,500
Planned sales (June 1–June 30)	10,000
Planned reductions	2,500
Total:	$80,000
Less	
Planned B.O.M. stock (June 1)	40,000
Planned purchases	$40,000

The planned-purchases figure is, however, based on *retail prices*. To determine the financial resources needed to acquire the merchandise, it is necessary to determine planned purchases at *cost*. The difference between planned purchases at retail and at cost represents the initial markup goal for the merchandise in question. This goal is established by determining the amount of operating expenses necessary to achieve the forecasted sales volume, as well as the profits desired from the specific operation, and combining this information with the data on reductions. Thus,

$$\text{Initial Markup Goal} = (\text{Expenses} + \text{Profit} + \text{Reductions})/(\text{Net Sales} + \text{Reductions})$$

A term frequently used in retailing is *open-to-buy*. It refers to the amount, in terms of retail prices or at cost, that a buyer can receive into stock during a certain period on the basis of the plans formulated.[80] Thus, planned purchases and open-to-buy may be synonymous where forecasts coincide with actual results. However, adjustments in inventories, fluctuations in sales volume, unplanned markdowns, and goods ordered but not received all serve to complicate the determination of the amount that a buyer may spend.[81]

Planned Gross Margin and Operating Profit

The *gross margin* is the initial markup adjusted for price changes, stock shortages, and other reductions. The difference between gross margin and expenses required to generate sales will yield either a contribution to profit or a *net operating profit* (before taxes), depending, of course, on the sophistication of a retailer's accounting system and the narrowness of its merchandise budgeting.

Notes

1. For a more comprehensive and in-depth discussion of retailing structure, competition, and management than space allows here, the reader is urged to consult Michael Levy and Barton A. Weitz, *Retailing Management,* 3rd ed. (Boston: Irwin/McGraw-Hill, 1998); and Barry Berman and Joel R. Evans, *Retail Management: A Strategic Approach,* 7th ed. (Upper Saddle River, NJ: Prentice Hall, 1997).

2. William R. Davidson, Daniel J. Sweeney, and Ronald W. Stampfl, *Retailing Management,* 5th ed. (New York: John Wiley, 1984), p. 14.

3. For a detailed discussion of financial strategies adopted by retailers, including the strategic profit model, see Levy and Weitz, *Retailing Management.*

4. Robert F. Lusch, Patrick Dunne, and Randall Gebhardt, *Retail Marketing,* 2nd ed. (Cincinnati, OH: South-Western Publishing, 1993).

5. Peggy Hollinger, "Angling to Build a Retailing Behemoth," *Financial Times,* April 20, 1999, p. 24. In June 1999, these motives became moot when Wal-Mart bought Asda.

6. B. Peter Pashigian and Eric D. Gould, "Internalizing Externalities: The Pricing of Space in Shopping Malls," *Journal of Law and Economics,* 41, no. 1 (April 1998), pp. 115–42.

7. "Dockers Drops 40,000 Catalogs in UK, France Test," *DM News International,* August 18, 1997, p. 7.

8. "Zipping Down the Aisles," *New York Times,* April 6, 1997, magazine section, p. 36.

9. Rodney Ho, "Vending Machines Make Change," *Wall Street Journal,* July 7, 1999, pp. B1, B4.

10. "Checkout Accounts," *The Economist,* January 4, 1997.

11. Matt Murray, "Retailers Use Legal Wrinkle to Link Sales, Bank Services," *Wall Street Journal,* February 8, 1999, pp. B1, B4.

12. Data on payroll expenses compiled from the National Retail Federation, *Financial and Operating Results of Retail Stores in 1992* (Washington, DC: National Retail Federation, 1993), pp. 46–56, 124–34.

13. Joseph B. Cahill, "The Secret Weapon of Big Discounters: Lowly Shopping Cart," *Wall Street Journal,* November 24, 1999, pp. A1, A10.

14. Mary Kuntz et al., "Reinventing the Store," *Business Week,* November 27, 1995, pp. 84–96.

15. Claudia H. Deutsch, "The Powerful Push for Self-Service," *New York Times,* section 3, April 9, 1989, p. 1.

16. Neil Buckley, "Reality Catches Up with Vision," *Financial Times,* July 22, 1994, p. 10.

17. Lola Smallwood, "Era of Openness Hits Malls," *Chicago Tribune,* February 18, 1999, section 2, p. 10.

18. McKinsey & Company, Inc., *Evaluating the Impact of Alternative Store Formats, Final Report* (Chicago: McKinsey & Company, Inc., May 1992), p. 2.

19. A. C. Nielsen Company, *1992–1993 Profiles of Nielsen SCANTRACK Marketing,* December 1993.

20. Nora Aufreiter and Tim McGuire, "Walking Down the Aisles," *Ivey Business Journal,* 63, no. 3 (March–April, 1999), pp. 49–54; James F. Peltz, "Food Companies' Fight Spills into Aisles," *Los Angeles Times,* October 28, 1998, business section, p. 1; "Loblaw's Continues to Strengthen Position," *MMR/Business and Industry,* 16, no. 21 (October 18, 1999), p. 20.

21. Christopher W. Hoyt, "Key Account Manager Fills Hot Seat in Food Business," *Marketing News,* November 6, 1987, p. 22.

22. See Christina Duff, "Nation's Retailers Ask Vendors to Help Share Expenses," *Wall Street Journal,* August 4, 1993, p. B3.

23. Marcia Mogelonsky, "Product Overload?" *American Demographics,* 20, no. 8 (August 1998), pp. 64–69.

24. Ryan Matthews, "Efficient New Product Introduction: Shattering the Myths," *Progressive Grocer,* July 1997, pp. 8–12.

25. To be fair, it should be noted that not all consumer product categories are like groceries. Apparel markets, for example, are characterized by a strong preference for new products each season, leading to virtual total turnover of SKUs from season to season. However, the fundamental issue of number of products chasing after a fixed amount of shelf space persists in any bricks-and-mortar retail context. Chapter 14 expands on this theme in discussing the limitations (or lacks thereof) in "shelf space" availability in on-line emporiums.

26. Mogelonsky, "Product Overload?"

27. Laurie Freeman, "Retailers Seek to Add Value to Loyalty Card Programs," *Card Marketing,* 2, no. 5 (May 1998), p. 16.

28. "Supermarkets," *Chain Store Age Inventory Management Policies and Practices,* December 1998, pp. 18A–19A.

29. Claire Rosenzweig, "PMA Releases State of Industry Report," *Brandmarketing,* 6, no. 9 (September 1999), p. 29.

30. Hoyt, "Key Account Manager Fills Hot Seat," p. 22.

31. See, for example, "Distribution Discourse," *Supermarket News,* October 14, 1996, pp. 17, 20, 22.

32. Joann Muller, "Rent Goes Up on Grocery Shelf," *Chicago Tribune,* April 16, 1989, section 7, p. 14D.

33. "More Facts and Figures on Slotting," *Supermarket Business,* July 1997, p. 19. The percentages were lower for health and beauty products and for general merchandise–nonfood products, with 14 and 15 percent, respectively, paying between $500,000 and $1 million, and close to 30 percent of respondents reporting no payment of slotting allowances.

34. Nahal Toosi, "Congress Looks at the Selling of Shelf Space," *St. Louis Post-Dispatch,* September 15, 1999, business section, p. C1; Darlene Superville, "Are 'Slotting Fees' Fair? Senate Panel Investigates; Practice Involves Paying Grocers for Shelf Space," *San Diego Union-Tribune,* September 15, 1999, business section, p. C1.

35. Ibid.

36. Elliott Zwiebach, "Super Value Division Imposes Failure Fee," *Supermarket News,* May 8, 1989, p. 1.

37. Roger K. Lowe, "Stores Demanding Pay to Display Products on Shelves, Panel Told," *Columbus Dispatch,* September 15, 1999, business section, p. 1H.

38. Eleena deLisser and Kevin Helliker, "Private Labels Reign in British Groceries," *Wall Street Journal,* March 3, 1994, pp. B1, B9; John A. Quelch and David Harding, "Brands versus Private Labels: Fighting to Win," *Harvard Business Review,* January–February 1996, pp. 99–109.

39. Daniel J. Sweeney, *Product Development and Branding* (Dublin, OH: Management Horizons, 1987).

40. Ellen Neuborne and Stephanie Anderson, "Look Who's Picking Levi's Pocket," *Business Week,* September 8, 1997, pp. 68, 72.

41. deLisser and Helliker, "Private Labels Reign in British Groceries."

42. Quelch and Harding, "Brands versus Private Labels."

43. Raj Sethuraman, "The Effect of Marketplace Factors on Private Label Penetration in Grocery Products," University of Iowa Working Paper, December 1991; Stephen J. Hoch and Shumeet Banerji, "When Do Private Labels Succeed?" *Sloan Management Review,* summer 1993, pp. 57–67.

44. Sweeney, *Product Development and Branding.*

45. Tri Agins, "Big Stores Put Own Labels on Best Clothes," *Wall Street Journal,* September 26, 1994, p. B1.

46. For example, Perrigo Company supplies no fewer than 857 imitations of major health and beauty aid brands to chains such as Wal-Mart, Kmart, and Rite Aid. See Gabriella Stern, "Perrigo's Knockoffs of Name-Brand Drugs Turn into Big Sellers," *Wall Street Journal*, July 15, 1993, p. A1.

47. Ernest Beck, "Britain's Marks & Spencer Struggles to Revive Its Old Luster in Retailing," *Wall Street Journal*, November 8, 1999, p. A34.

48. Isabelle Sender, "Microplanning Jeanswear for the Masses," *Chain Store Age Executive*, 74, no. 1 (January 1998), pp. 60–62; "VF Corp. Wields VMI Power," *Discount Store News*, 37, no. 22 (November 23, 1998), pp. S8–S9.

49. Edwin L. Artzt, "Redefining Quality," a speech delivered at the Quality Forum VIII, New York City, October 1, 1992, p. 3; Valerie Reitman, "Eliminated Discounts on P&G Goods Annoy Many Who Sell Them," *Wall Street Journal*, August 11, 1992, p. A1; "Ed Artzt's Elbow Grease Has P&G Shining," *BusinessWeek*, October 10, 1994, p. 84.

50. Richard Tomkins, "P&G in $4.2m Payout to Settle Coupons Dispute," *Financial Times*, September 11, 1997, p. 17.

51. James F. Peltz, "Food Companies' Fight Spills into Aisles," *Los Angeles Times*, October 28, 1998, business section, p. C1.

52. Monica Torrence, "Goodby Category Management," *Food & Beverage Marketing*, 17, no. 5 (May 1998), pp. 18–20.

53. Joseph Pereira, "Toys 'R' Them: Mom-and-Pop Stores Put Playthings Like Thomas on Fast Track," *Wall Street Journal*, January 14, 1993, p. B1.

54. Stacy Kravetz, "Mattel Revamps Retail Plan to Reduce Dependence on Traditional Outlets," *Wall Street Journal*, February 17, 1999, p. B8.

55. This discussion is based on Anne T. Coughlan and David Soberman, "Good Marketing to 'Bad' Consumers: Outlet Malls, Gray Markets, and Warehouse Sales," working paper, INSEAD, July 1999.

56. Joseph Pereira, "A Small Toy Store Manages to Level the Playing Field," *Wall Street Journal*, December 20, 1996, pp. A1, A8.

57. See, for example, the IKEA corporate Web site at www.ikea.com; Sharen Kindel, "IKEA: Furnishing a Big World," *Hemispheres*, February 1997, pp. 31–34; Julia Flynn and Lori Bongiorno, "IKEA's New Game Plan," *BusinessWeek*, October 6, 1997, pp. 99–102; Gregory Shoro, "With 'Flat Packaging,' IKEA Sells a Business Philosophy," *BrandPackaging*, 3, no. 4 (July 1999), p. 32; Meghan Cath, "IKEA Founder Ingvar Kamprad," *Investor's Business Daily*, October 8, 1999, p. A4; "IKEA International A/S," *Hoover's Company Profile Database—World Companies*, 1999.

58. Christina Duff, "Big Stores' Outlandish Demands Alienate Small Suppliers," *Wall Street Journal*, October 27, 1995, p. B1.

59. Ibid.

60. Denise Incandela, Kathleen L. McLaughlin, and Christiana Smith Shi, "Retailers to the World," *McKinsey Quarterly*, 3 (1999), pp. 84–97.

61. Karen Barth, Nancy J. Karch, Kathleen McLaughlin, and Christiana Smith Shi, "Global Retailing: Tempting Trouble?" *McKinsey Quarterly*, 1 (1996), pp. 116–25.

62. Ibid.

63. Neelam Mathews, "India's Retail Rush," *Chain Store Age*, August 1, 1999, p. 52.

64. Wing-Kwong Chan, Javier Perez, Anthony Perkins, and Miranda Shu, "Current Research: China's Retail Markets Are Evolving More Quickly than Companies Anticipate," *McKinsey Quarterly*, 2 (1997), pp. 206–11.

65. "Megastores Transforming Retail Sector in Thailand, Indonesia," *Asia Today*, June 1999.

66. Barth et al., "Global Retailing."

67. Carrefour Web site at www.stores.carrefour.com.

68. Ira Kalish, "Insights on Wal-Mart in Europe," White Paper, PricewaterhouseCoopers, 1999.

69. Tony Barber and David Owen, "Schickedanz, Karstadt in Mail-Order Deal," *Financial Times*, April 20, 1999, p. 18.

70. Richard Tomkins and Graham Bowley, "Wal-Mart to Double European Sales with $660m German Deal," *Financial Times*, December 10, 1998, p. 16.

71. "French Fusion," *The Economist*, September 4, 1999.

72. Clifford Krauss, "Selling to Argentina (as Translated from the French)," *New York Times on the Web* (www.nyt.com), December 5, 1999, business world section.

73. Incandela, McLaughlin, and Shi, "Retailers to the World."

74. "Retailing in South America: Survival Skills," *The Economist*, July 12, 1997, pp. 57–58.

75. Delbert J. Duncan, Stanley C. Hollander, and Ronald Savitt, *Modern Retailing Management*, 10th ed. (Homewood, IL: Richard D. Irwin, 1983), p. 266.

76. Ibid., pp. 266–67.

77. All of these variables have been treated more completely elsewhere, should the reader desire more detail. See Duncan, Hollander, and Savitt, *Modern Retailing Management;* see also Michael Levy and Barton A. Weitz, *Retailing Management*, 2nd ed. (Chicago: Richard D. Irwin, 1995), pp. 303–24.

78. There are numerous variations used to determine B.O.M. stock. See Ibid., p. 229.

79. Derived from a desired stock–sales ratio for July of 4.5 and projected sales for July of $15,000. Remember, June's E.O.M. is the same as July's B.O.M.

80. Duncan, Hollander, and Savitt, *Modern Retailing Management*, p. 234.

81. Ibid.

14

Nonstore Retailing and Electronic Channels

LEARNING OBJECTIVES

After reading this chapter, you will:

- Know how significant catalog retailing is in world retail markets
- Understand the differences in service output provision between catalog and standard retail markets
- Understand the differences in channel structure among standard retail, catalog, and direct-selling organization channels
- Know how compensation affects growth patterns in direct channels
- Be familiar with the on-line marketplace for consumer and business-to-business sales
- Be able to identify how on-line selling changes the service output mix available to end-users
- Understand how flow performance and channel structure can both change when a manufacturer adds an on-line presence to its overall channel structure
- Be able to analyze the sources of conflict in on-line channels and suggest means to deflect that conflict

The classic study of retailing has always centered on an understanding of bricks-and-mortar stores, as discussed in Chapter 13. However, we discuss some other alternatives to standard store-based retailing in this chapter. We first summarize the catalog and direct-selling channel strategies for reaching the market. Both have been established for some time as "shorter" channels for selling to the consumer end-user. We then discuss electronic channels for both consumer and business-to-business markets, from a channel-analytic point of view. E-commerce has provided a different set of service outputs to end-users as well as implying a different split of flow performance among channel members. It also has been the source of several types of channel conflict, which have been dealt with in varying ways. Channel partners are learning to add this new channel alternative into their arsenal of ways to reach the market, with increasing success.

NONSTORE RETAILING

Retailing does not have to take place through bricks-and-mortar stores. We discuss two major forms of nonstore retailing in this section: catalog retailing and direct selling. Each produces service outputs in its own way and has its own supply-side issues.

Catalog Retailing

Consumer retail sales through catalogs have a long history. A hundred years ago in the United States, Richard Warren Sears and Alvah Curtis Roebuck partnered to start selling first watches, and then many other consumer products, in the Sears, Roebuck catalog.[1] Since then, other American and European companies have offered "big books" (as the broad general-merchandise catalogs like the Sears catalog are known), including JCPenney and Montgomery Ward in the United States; GUS in the United Kingdom; and Otto Versand, Quelle, and Neckermann of Germany, among others. This section discusses the size of the catalog retailing channel, the service outputs provided in catalog retailing, supply- and cost-side issues in catalog retailing, and strategic issues facing catalog retailers today, including integration of catalog and noncatalog channels, and the rush to on-line retailing by catalog companies.

The U.S. retail (i.e., excluding business-to-business catalog sales) catalog market grew from $85 billion in 1997 to $93 billion in 1998, and accounts for over half of all worldwide mail-order retail sales.[2] This rate of increase was double that of the nation's bricks-and-mortar retailers. This total is still less than 4 percent of the total U.S. retail sales, even though nearly 60 percent of Americans buy something from a catalog each year.[3] Outside the United States, catalog retailing is also a viable retailing channel, with Germany, Japan, France, and the United Kingdom the next largest mail-order countries in order. The top five countries account for 87 percent of worldwide mail-order sales in value.[4] European mail-order volumes vary from country to country, but in Germany, for example, they have approached 5 percent of all retail sales. Japanese mail-order sales represented just 1.3 percent of total retail sales in 1992; sales by foreign mail-order companies in Japan were reported to be US $1 billion in the mid-1990s. The South Korean mail-order market is growing very fast, with an estimated US $1.25 billion in sales in 2000; and the Australian mail-order market is US $1.2 billion in size.[5] Table 14.1 reports on the 30 largest U.S. catalog retailers in 1998 sales. As the list shows, computer sellers are most numerous (9 entries), followed by apparel (8 entries), and general merchandise (6 entries).

TABLE 14.1

Top 30 U.S. Catalog Retailers, 1998

Company	1998 Sales ($ million)	Market Segment
Dell Computer Corp.	$18,243	Computer hardware, software, and peripherals
IBM Corp.	5,500 (est.)	Computer hardware, software, and peripherals
JCPenney Co.	3,929	General merchandise
Micro Warehouse	2,200	Computer hardware, software, and peripherals
CDW Computer Centers	1,734	Computer hardware, software, and peripherals
Fingerhut Cos.	1,609	General merchandise
Spiegel	1,394	General merchandise
Lands' End	1,371	Apparel and home goods
Brylane	1,328	Apparel and home goods
Micron Electronics	1,300 (est.)	Computer hardware, software, and peripherals
L.L. Bean	1,030	Outdoor gear, apparel, and home goods
Intimate Brands	759	Women's apparel
PC Connection	732	Computer hardware, software, and peripherals
Creative Computers	690	Computer hardware, software, and peripherals
CompUSA	646 (est.)	Computer hardware, software, and peripherals
Hanover Direct	546	General merchandise
Blair Corp.	507	Apparel and home goods
Multiple Zones International	501	Computer hardware, software, and peripherals
Cabela's	500 (est.)	Outdoor sporting goods
Oriental Trading Co.	487	Gifts and novelties
Damark International	484	General merchandise
Foster & Gallagher	480	Gardening, gifts, food, and children's products
Williams-Sonoma	384	Home and garden goods
J. Crew Group	347 (est.)	Apparel
Coldwater Creek	320	Apparel, gifts, and home goods
Cornerstone Brands	320	Home goods and apparel
Mattel	300 (est.)	Toys and collectibles
American Express	300	General merchandise
Bass Pro Shops	300 (est.)	Outdoor sporting goods
Neiman Marcus Group	285 (est.)	Women's apparel and home decor

Source: Adapted from Sherry Chiger, "The Catalog Age 100: The High & the Mighty," *Catalog Age*, 16, no. 9 (August 1999), pp. 1, 68–80. For companies that also operate retail stores, the figures are for catalog sales only. The notation "(est.)" indicates an estimate.

Retail catalogs offer a particular set of service outputs to their buyers. Like a typical retail store, a catalog breaks bulk. Assortment and variety vary widely from catalog to catalog, but the historical trend (particularly in the United States, but more recently elsewhere as well) is away from general-merchandise, broad variety catalogs, toward more focused, specialty ones with an in-depth assortment in a narrower range of goods. Even catalogers like JCPenney or Spiegel, owned by Otto Versand, offer their big book about twice a year, but augment this with several smaller, much more specialized, catalogs sent out throughout the year. The smaller catalogs also permit more targeted mailings than a general merchandise catalog does, and can be produced and mailed at much lower cost.[6] But most importantly, they offer the ultimate in spatial convenience to the consumer: the ability to shop from home, without ever visiting a retail store. This benefit is counterbalanced by the delay in getting the product(s) one has just bought. Typical delivery delays range from four days to two weeks, and overnight delivery generally carries a significant price premium.

This set of service outputs holds great appeal for a certain segment of retail buyers. For example, a time-starved working mother may be perfectly willing to wait a week for delivery, given that she is unlikely to be able to visit a bricks-and-mortar store in that time period in any event. Thus, the total effective delivery time from shopping through a catalog may actually be shorter for some shoppers than would be shopping at a regular retail store. Further, paying for delivery may seem reasonable to a shopper whose time and travel costs to get to a retail store are high. This has long been a source of success for mail-order retailers selling in rural areas where retail store selection is limited. One limitation of mail-order shopping, however, remains the buyer's inability to touch, feel, and (in the case of clothing) try on the merchandise before buying it. Some mail-order companies try to reduce the severity of this problem by offering to send fabric swatches, offering precise measurements for clothing, and sometimes offering free returns on merchandise that does not fit.

One survey of catalog shoppers in the United States in 1999 reveals interesting patterns of mail-order buyer demographics, purchase behavior, and attitudes.[7] Figure 14.1 summarizes some of the findings of the survey. Women are more likely than men to shop by catalog. About half of married respondents, and half of those with children in the home, shop by catalog, more than the percentage of respondents who either are single or do not have children. This is consistent with the notion of catalog shopping as an antidote to time poverty. Also consistent is the effect of income on catalog shopping behavior: The affluent are much more likely to shop by catalog than are lower-income shoppers, with almost two-thirds of those in the $80,000-plus income category doing so, but less than 30 percent of those with incomes under $25,000 shopping by catalog.

Of those buying from catalogs, almost 65 percent buy women's apparel and about 45 percent buy mens' apparel. Only 16 percent buy food, with gifts, home products, children's clothing, books, music, and computers in between these figures. Most important to all shoppers is the convenience of catalog shopping, followed by the availability of unique merchandise and a perception of fair prices. The first two factors are increasingly important to higher-income catalog shoppers, whereas a fair price is most appreciated by lower-income buyers. Interestingly, just over 90 percent of respondents said catalog shopping was either as satisfying as, or more satisfying than, regular retail shopping, suggesting that catalogers offer a very viable alternative to standard retail stores. The most commonly cited reason for *not* using catalog shopping was the desire to see the product before buying, mentioned by 44 percent of noncatalog shoppers. In sum, whereas catalog buying may not be for everyone, it does appeal to a broad spectrum of shoppers and particularly to those who are sensitive to the value of spatial convenience.

But providing this spatial convenience, while running a successful catalog operation, carries some specific costs and risks. A catalog company must manage the following:

● *The procurement of product from suppliers if it does not produce itself.* For example, Lands' End relies on any one supplier for no more than 10 percent of its product; this reduces the chance of poor product quality or availability across a broad portion of the product line.

Percentage buying from a catalog in the past year:	46.3%
Percentage of women:	53
Percentage of men:	35.4
Percentage buying from a catalog:	
Married:	47.8%
Children in home:	49.1
Single:	37.3
No children in home:	43.6
Percentage of various income groups buying from a catalog:	
$0–$25,000:	29.3%
$25,001–$40,000:	40.9
$40,001–$80,000:	57.7
Over $80,000:	64.8
Top reasons for shopping by catalog (percent of respondents mentioning):	
Convenience:	60.0%
Unique merchandise:	52.3
Price is right:	49.6
Past experience with catalog company:	42.7
Want product delivered to home:	35.5
Have no time to go to store:	28.4
Recommendation from a friend:	13.5
Impulse:	12.4

FIGURE 14.1 **Retail Catalog Shopper Characteristics**

Source: Adapted from Laura M. Beaudry, "The Catalog Age 1999 Consumer Catalog Shopping Survey," *Catalog Age,* 16, no. 6 (May 1999), pp. A5–A18. Survey was done on a sample of 1,047 consumers in the United States.

• *The creation of the catalog itself.* The company must decide how large it will be, what each page's layout will be, and what array of catalogs to create. Many catalogers send out an array of specific catalogs, none of which represents the full product line available, but which are designed to appeal to a targeted subset of their mailing list or focus on a particular set of product categories (e.g., home furnishings versus apparel).

• *The mailing list.* A catalog company constantly monitors the productivity of its mailing list. A common measurement is the *lifetime value of a customer.* This measure calculates or forecasts how much revenue a catalog shopper can be expected to generate for the catalog company before ceasing to buy from the company. In general, catalog companies seek to maintain their relationships with their best buyers, who are relatively less expensive to target than are new prospects. Catalog companies also treat their mailing lists as direct revenue sources, renting them out to other direct sellers for their use. Costs can also be controlled by reducing duplicate catalog mailings that can result from poor management of the mailing list. A study of customer data at a number of catalog retailers done by Pitney Bowes Software Systems found that 37 percent of customer records were incorrect in a severe enough way to affect deliverability of catalogs and sales. The same study found that 10 percent of a typical catalog mailing database consists of duplicate customer records. Reducing these errors can save significantly on the costs of catalog mailings, as well as reduce the incidence of lost sales opportunities.[8]

- *Order fulfillment and shipping.* These tasks comprise the physical logistics of picking and packing an order to be delivered to the buyer. Very sophisticated warehouse management technologies are now available to minimize the costs of fulfillment inside the warehouse. Larger catalog companies now also have long-term arrangements with particular shippers (e.g., UPS or FedEx) to provide low-cost, timely, and reliable shipment of merchandise to buyers.[9]

- *Out-of-stocks.* Catalog companies try to balance the benefit of having desired products in stock at the time of order against the cost of holding high inventory levels (the classic trade-off between postponement and speculation). Consumers are unwilling to wait to get many categories of products and have learned that when a product is out of stock, it is likely not to be restocked for a considerable time, if ever. Thus, if a company does run out of stock, it is important to let the consumer know at the time of ordering, so that the consumer can revise the basket of products purchased.

- *Merchandise returns.* Returns are a very expensive part of the cost structure of a catalog business. Although returns are estimated to be between 6 percent and 15 percent of sales in mass-merchandise retail stores, they increase up to 35 percent for catalog retailers.[10] Returns must be handled one by one and do not benefit from economies of scale the way initial shipments do. Returned products must be individually inspected to see if they can be resold (and if so, what must be done to them before resale can occur). Because of the differences between handling initial shipments and returns, the distribution center is typically not well equipped to process returns. This issue in catalog retailing is a specific example of the more general problem of *reverse logistics,* which can plague any retailer, but which appears to carry a higher cost in catalog sales.

The most successful catalog companies have expanded overseas from their home bases, through either greenfield expansion (building up the businesses themselves) or acquisition of existing businesses in overseas markets. Such expansion is a tricky business for a catalog company. The company must decide how to fulfill orders: Although it is expensive to ship from the home market to the foreign buyer, it is even more expensive and risky to build and manage a warehouse and a separate supply of inventory in the foreign market. Catalogers typically respond to this by first shipping from the home market, and only when a solid base of business is established do they set up warehouses overseas. Hanna Andersson, a children's clothing cataloger, and L.L. Bean both ship from one centralized location in the United States to foreign addresses. Lands' End, with $40 million in sales in the United Kingdom and $80 million in Japan in 1997, has invested in warehouses in both of these countries as well as in Germany, but did not build its first overseas warehouse, in England, until it had two years' worth of sales to support it.[11]

Another challenge in internationalizing the catalog business is the internationalization of the catalog itself and the prices within it. Catalog companies that fail to translate their catalogs to local languages suffer in sales, so the trend typically is to translate the catalog relatively soon after entry into the foreign market. The issue of pricing is less clear. Pricing in local currencies appears to make the most sense, but opens up the catalog company to currency risk. In 1992, Lands' End issued a catalog in the United Kingdom priced in British pounds. The prices at the time the catalog was printed were somewhat, but not significantly higher than, comparable U.S. prices. But in the ensuing months, the dollar weakened significantly against the pound, until British prices were so much higher than U.S. prices that some British Lands' End customers were telephoning the United States to order their clothes. Even with the higher shipping rates for overseas delivery, the total price was lower this way than through local buying. Such developments do not serve the catalog well; they give the impression that the international cataloger is trying to charge an unfairly higher price in the overseas market relative to the home-country price.

The catalog retail channel is frequently used in tandem with other channels in a dual distribution channel strategy. It was once feared that a cataloger that opened a standard retail store would suffer cannibalization of its catalog sales in the store area, and conversely, that standard store sales would suffer with the issuance of a catalog. In fact, it is now known that the two tend to be complementary strategies, rather than competing. For instance, Bloomingdale's operates a mail-order business, Bloomingdale's by Mail, separately from its retail stores, but issues sales catalogs to build store traffic. Some retailers use catalogs in new markets to establish the sales potential in the area, prior to establishing bricks-and-mortar stores. Catalogs also allow a standard retailer to build a database of loyal customers, to whom it can market on a more targeted basis. And some retailers issue "magalogs," hybrids between catalogs and magazines, to build brand image as well as sales: The U.S. specialty retailer Abercrombie & Fitch issues "A&F Quarterly," a publication that not only offers the retailer's merchandise for sale but also contains lifestyle articles on topics such as what beer brands, accessories, and even transportation modes are the most trendy and stylish.[12]

Direct-Selling Organizations (DSOs)

Direct selling is defined as "the sale of a consumer product or service in a face to face manner away from a fixed retail location."[13] Direct-selling organizations, or DSOs, are companies that use direct-selling techniques to reach final consumers. They are distinguished from catalog sales operations by their reliance on personal selling, which is the key to both the DSO's channel structure and its positioning as a retail option. Some of the best-known DSOs worldwide include Amway (household cleaning products, personal care products, appliances, etc.), Mary Kay (cosmetics), Herbalife (nutritional supplements and vitamins), Avon (cosmetics), and Tupperware (household storage containers), although there were 150 companies listed as members of the U.S. Direct Selling Organization as of December 1999.

Global retail sales through direct-selling organizations were almost $80 billion in 1998, employing 34 million salespeople worldwide. The top 20 countries by DSO retail sales are listed in Table 14.2, along with the number of salespeople in that country and the average sales per DSO salesperson.

As the data show, significant sales are made in many countries. However, in many countries, the typical DSO distributor does not make his or her living. The typical DSO

TABLE 14.2
Direct Sales by Country

Country	Year	Retail Sales (in US $)	Number of Salespeople	Average Sales per Salesperson	Per Capita Income (1998)
1. Japan	1998	$26.2 billion	2,500,000	$10,480	$32,380
2. United States	1997	22.2 billion	9,300,000	2,387	29,340
3. Brazil	1997	4.045 billion	1,839,044	2,200	4,570
4. Germany	1997	3.6 billion	335,000	10,746	25,850
5. Korea	1997	2.1 billion	909,000	2,310	7,970
6. Italy	1997	2.1 billion	340,000	6,176	20,250
7. Mexico	1998	1.95 billion	1,320,000	1,477	3,970
8. United Kingdom	1997	1.767 billion	470,000	3,760	21,400
9. Taiwan	1996	1.74 billion	2,360,000	737	16,500*
10. Canada	1997	1.6 billion	1,300,000	1,231	20,020
11. Australia	1997	1.2 billion	650,000	1,846	20,300
12. France	1997	1.16 billion	163,468	7,096	24,940
13. Argentina	1998	1.101 billion	394,000	2,794	8,970
14. Malaysia	1997	658 million	1,800,000	366	3,600
15. Spain	1995	652 million	123,656	5,273	14,080
16. Thailand	1998	541 million	2,500,000	216	2,200
17. Venezuela	1997	450 million	200,000	2,250	3,500
18. South Africa	1997	400 million	200,000	2,000	2,880
19. Switzerland	1997	362 million	5,438	66,569	40,080
20. Austria	1997	357 million	42,000	8,500	26,850

Top 10 Direct-Selling Countries by Ratio of (Average Sales per Salesperson) to (Per Capita Income)

Country	Ratio of (Average Sales per Salesperson) to (Per Capita Income)
1. Costa Rica	2.88
2. Switzerland	1.66
3. Panama	.97
4. Guatemala	.73
5. South Africa	.69
6. Peru	.68
7. India	.65
8. Venezuela	.64
9. Brazil	.48
10. Germany	.42

Note: The top table lists the top 20 countries by level of direct sales. The second table lists the top 10 countries ranked by the ratio of sales per direct-selling salesperson to per capita income (a value of .97, for example, means that the average direct salesperson makes 97 percent of the average per capita income in that country).
* Taiwan per capita income is reported as gross domestic product (GDP) per capita, purchasing power parity (PPP), for 1998, in *The World Factbook 1999*, published by the U.S. Central Intelligence Agency.
Source: Adapted from World Federation of Direct Selling Associations Web site (www.wfdsa.com), December 1999. Average sales per salesperson are calculated. Per capita income is from the World Development Indicators database of the World Bank.

distributor in the United States is female, married, between the ages of 25 and 44, Caucasian, and likely to have a high school diploma but not a graduate school degree. Similar profiles were found in Eastern European countries as well, although comparable studies have not been mounted in other countries. A 1992 study also found that 56 percent of DSO distributors work at one or more other jobs.[14] Clearly, some of them make very large amounts of money, but much more common are earning levels that supplement the family's main source of income.

The channel structure of a DSO can have many or few levels. The DSO company itself may manufacture the goods it sells or may contract it out the manufacture of the goods. The DSO contracts with intermediaries, variously called "distributors," "consultants," or "salespeople" (we will call them "distributors" for convenience). In almost all cases, these distributors are independent contractors rather than employees of the companies whose products they sell. Further, in many cases, they truly do act as distributors, in the sense of buying inventory and reselling it at a markup to downstream buyers. They thus bear physical possession and ownership costs, as well as risking, ordering and payment flow costs. Perhaps their most important flow performed is the promotion flow, because it is usually the only promotional tool the DSO uses (standard advertising is very rare among DSOs).

In a "multilevel" DSO, or MLDSO, distributors are compensated in three different ways. First, they make the distributor-to-retail markup on the goods they buy wholesale from the DSO itself. Second, a commission is paid to the distributor by the DSO on every sale made. Third (and specific to the multilevel DSO), a distributor makes commissions on the sales made by distributors that he or she recruits. Compensation plans differ widely in MLDSOs, but for illustration, consider the following example.[15]

Catherine has been recruited directly by Janet. Janet is known as Catherine's "upline," and Catherine, Susan, Kent, and all their recruits collectively are known as Janet's "downline." Janet herself sells $200 worth of product in the month in question, while Catherine, Susan, and Kent each sell $100 and Catherine's three recruits each sell $50 of product. Thus, it is said that Janet's "personal volume" is $200, but her "group volume" is $650 (the sum of her volume and the volumes of every distributor in her downline).

Given the commission schedule in Figure 14.2, Janet's group volume commission rate is 7 percent. She earns $45.50 on her group volume. But from this $45.50 is deducted the net commissions earned by her downlines. Susan, Kent, and Catherine are each in the 5 percent category, because the group volume for each one of them is between $100 and $275. Thus, on the $450 that they collectively sell, they get $22.50 (or 5 percent of $450). Janet's net *commission* earnings are therefore $23.00 ($45.50 minus $22.50). Janet, of course, also earns money on the wholesale-to-retail markup she garners on her own personal sales, and suggested markups generally range from 40 to 50 percent. The commission earnings of the other distributors in Janet's downline can be calculated similarly (i.e., Catherine does not keep all of the gross commissions her group volume earns; she gives some of it up to *her* downline distributors).

Clearly, depending on the structure of the compensation system (the relative rewards gotten from personal selling versus from override commissions on the sales of downline distributors), different incentives are created for direct-selling of product versus building of the direct-selling network. There is a delicate balance here. On the one

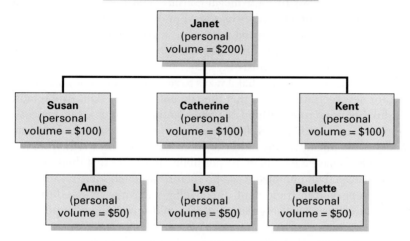

COMMISSION SCHEDULE

Volume	Commission Rate
$0 – $99	3%
$100 – $275	5%
> $275	7%

Janet
(personal
volume = $200)

Susan
(personal
volume = $100)

Catherine
(personal
volume = $100)

Kent
(personal
volume = $100)

Anne
(personal
volume = $50)

Lysa
(personal
volume = $50)

Paulette
(personal
volume = $50)

FIGURE 14.2 **A Sample Multilevel Direct-Selling Organization: Structure and Compensation**

Source: Anne T. Coughlan and Kent Grayson, "Network Marketing Organizations: Compensation Plans, Retail Network Growth, and Profitability," *International Journal of Research in Marketing,* 15 (1998), p. 403.

hand, the more time one's current distributors spend in recruiting new distributors, the bigger the DSO's network gets. On the other hand, recruiting new distributors without spending sufficient time selling product does not generate revenues and profits for the DSO.[16] Indeed, a clear distinction is drawn between legitimate direct-selling organizations and illegitimate "pyramid schemes."[17] A *pyramid scheme* is a fraudulent mechanism whereby new recruits are required to pay a nonrefundable fee for becoming a distributor. Furthermore, distributors are rewarded simply for getting new recruits to sign on and pay this fee. Thus, both the company and the distributor earn money without selling a product or service. Because companies can succeed only to the extent that they provide value and benefits in exchange for customer payments, this reward system is economically unstable. Many pyramid-scheme victims do not appreciate the risk of this instability, although even those who do realize this will participate in the hope that the system will not collapse before they benefit from it.

To guard against illegal pyramid schemes, legitimate DSOs have created a code of ethics that every member must follow. Legitimate DSOs are characterized by the low expense of joining the organization (e.g., a reasonable fee for a "starter kit" may be charged); by the ability to return unsold merchandise for a 90 percent or better refund;

and by the provision of rewards based on product sales, rather than on the recruiting of downline members of the network. The sample compensation scheme described above fits these criteria, because Janet's commissions are all based on someone's actual product sales, *not* on the mere fact that Janet recruited Catherine, Susan, and Kent into her downline.

However, the distinction between a legitimate DSO and an illegal pyramid scheme is not usually obvious to the casual observer. This means that the former can sometimes be blamed for the excesses of their illegal cousins. DSOs have also historically come under fire from time to time for other reasons. For example, DSO distributors often are encouraged to use their existing social network as a potential customer base, and some view this as an inappropriate use of friends and relatives for commercial gain.

Furthermore, because it is relatively easy to sign on as a distributor, many do so without serious consideration for what it takes to run a part-time sales business. It can be frustrating for new recruits to learn that they do not have the skills or the motivation to be successful. Some recruits without the right business acumen can make costly mistakes before they quit, such as spending too much of their revenue on training materials.

Although no company of any kind can protect its associates fully from making bad decisions, DSOs do have a legitimate responsibility to ensure that their new recruits are selected and managed to minimize these problems. Although some unscrupulous entrepreneurs have engaged in fraudulent direct-selling activities, the industry as a whole makes a strong effort to self-regulate and to avoid government imposition of DSO restrictions.

Table 14.2 illustrates that, although average incomes from direct selling may not be high in some absolute sense, they do compare favorably with annual per capita income in emerging-market economies. Direct selling is growing in emerging markets faster than in developed economies. One possible reason for this is the personal selling aspect of this mode of retailing, which can be very effective in a market lacking the infrastructure for standard retailing. Another reason is the economic opportunity available to direct sellers: For a very small initial investment, a person can become an entrepreneur with his or her own business and earning capability. Thus, although worldwide direct-selling revenues are less today than the annual sales of Wal-Mart, the importance of direct selling (particularly in emerging markets) is greater than the sales numbers imply.[18]

Direct-selling organizations sell almost every type of good and service that consumers can buy.[19] Most popular, however, are consumable products that can be purchased repeatedly or the sale of broad product lines. Both lead to the possibility of repeat purchases by a distributor's customers, which is eminently sensible, given the emphasis placed on personal networking and personal selling abilities of DSO salespeople. Direct selling is a very old method of distribution. It remains a viable channel because of consumers' interest in personal interactions in the selling process, and because of the low cost of forming and running these channels.

Nonstore Retailing: Summary

Catalog selling and direct selling both offer viable alternatives to standard store-based retailing. The former offers superior spatial convenience, but falls short of store-based retailing on the waiting and delivery time dimension. For the time-pressed consumer, however, catalogs are an attractive alternative because they remove the need to travel to a store to shop. The latter also offers a high level of spatial convenience, because the distributor comes to the consumer. More distinctively, it relies on personal selling skills and relationships to survive.

Both catalogers and direct sellers are responding to the changing demographics of time-starved consumers, who increasingly have Internet access, by forming dual distribution systems, including on-line selling in tandem with their traditional sales methods. When a consumer can inspect a Lands' End catalog at home and then shop on-line to place her merchandise order, should that be counted as a catalog sale or an on-line sale? When a Mary Kay consumer looks for an on-line purchase, then is served by a Mary Kay consultant, is that an on-line sale or a standard DSO sale? The lines between these alternative nonstore retailing options are blurring.

In developed markets, as direct sales growth has slowed, DSOs are also starting to recognize that consumers' poverty of time makes them less interested in buying in a personal selling atmosphere. The days of the "Tupperware party" in a private home, although not gone, may well be fading. To counteract this trend, many direct-selling companies are augmenting their channels by adding on-line presences of one sort or another. Different companies use different tactics to try to attract buyers, while not alienating their core channel—the direct sales force. These combination channel strategies are sometimes called "clicks-and-mortar" strategies, to exemplify the combined use of on-line click buying technology with more standard personal selling and product stocking mortar selling processes.

The main direct-selling companies all have on-line presences of one sort or another. Mary Kay is developing such a system; Amway launched its on-line channel, called Quixtar.com, in September 1999; and Avon and Tupperware opened on-line outlets in late 1999 as well.[20] In some cases, the companies have provided for their distributors to have their own Web sites to facilitate routine reordering by their customers, and to provide for Internet communication between the distributors and the DSO itself.

The DSOs have thus far arranged for compensation to be awarded to their distributors for sales made on-line, either by assigning these sales to distributors in the buyer's area, as Mary Kay does, or by randomly assigning on-line profits among distributors, as Amway does. Some companies provide incentives for customers to order through a distributor, thus seeking to preserve the distributor direct-selling channel; Avon, for example, waives shipping charges on Internet orders placed through its distributors. The issues of domain and goal conflicts still arise, however, as distributors fear that they may become expendable.

ELECTRONIC CHANNELS

By *electronic channels*, we mean any channel that involves using the Internet as a means of reaching the end-user or any channel for which the consumer literally buys on-line. They are used both for sales to consumers (sometimes called B2C channels) and in business-to-business (B2B) selling. We focus mainly on consumer sales in this discussion, with comments about business-to-business e-commerce where appropriate.

Market Potential for Electronic Channels

The market potential for consumer electronic channels is bounded by the number of consumers who are *able* to shop on-line. Table 14.3 reports on the number of households in the United States who have access to on-line Internet sites, and Table 14.4 reports current and projected numbers of Internet users in the top 10 Internet countries. The forecasts show that the United States will remain the most Internet-connected country in the world, but that several other countries will approach it in terms of percent of population who use the Internet. The Netherlands, Canada, Germany, the United Kingdom, and France will follow the United States in percent access on-line. Despite its high rankings in absolute numbers of Internet users, Japan is forecast to be a much smaller percentage user of the Internet, probably because of language issues: English is still (and will probably remain) the dominant language of the Internet, and the Japanese language is very different from English, hampering the spread of on-line usage there.

One of the key conclusions from data like these is that the majority of consumers in industrialized countries *will not be connected to the Internet* in the near future. Thus, although Internet channels remain attractive, marketing channel strategies revolving around the Internet as a purchasing enabler need to recognize that the entire market is *not* the relevant market potential on which to base sales forecasts.

Internet users also have a particular demographic profile. As Table 14.5 shows, the Internet user population in the United States is only slightly skewed toward males versus females; tends to be made up predominantly of adults aged 18 to 54; is skewed toward professional and executive occupations; and is disproportionately represented by more highly educated and more wealthy individuals. This population has a higher-than-average opportunity cost of time. This suggests that Internet selling is likely to be more successful when it offers time savings, high-quality service, and products that appeal to a more affluent audience. It would be less attractive in purchase occasions requiring a "high-touch" selling experience with extensive personal service.

On-line *access* is not the only important indicator of market potential for on-line sellers. The time spent on-line is also crucial, because in such conditions shopping is still not an instantaneous affair. Indeed, much of the time a consumer spends on-line may

TABLE 14.3

U.S. Households On-line

Year	Total U.S. Households (millions)	Total U.S. Households On-line (millions)	Percentage of U.S. Households On-line
1998	101.0	33.3	33.0%
1999	102.1	38.8	38.0
2000(e)	103.2	44.4	43.0
2001(e)	104.6	51.3	49.0
2002(e)	106.7	56.0	52.5
2003(e)	106.8	59.8	56.0

(e): estimated

Source: Adapted from iconocast.com, "Internet at a Glance," data from June 1999 Jupiter Communications.

TABLE 14.4
Top 10 Internet Countries

1998			2002 (est.)		
Country	Users (millions)	Percentage of Population[*]	Country	Users (millions)	Percentage of Population[*]
U.S.	70.1	26.3%	U.S.	154.6	57.9%
Germany	10.3	12.6	Germany	32.9	40.1
U.K.	8.9	15.3	Japan	23.3	18.5
Japan	8.8	7.0	U.K.	23.0	39.6
France	4.0	6.8	France	23.0	39.2
Canada	4.0	13.2	Italy	13.2	23.2
Australia	3.4	18.3	Canada	12.3	40.6
Italy	3.1	5.5	China[**]	9.4	0.8
Sweden	2.5	28.3	Netherlands	7.6	49.7
Netherlands	2.5	16.4	Australia	5.8	31.3

[*] Population data are from 1997. *Source:* OECD Web site at (see glossary).
[**] Chinese population (1998) is from U.S. Department of State background notes, August 1999.
Source: Adapted from iconocast.com, "Internet at a Glance," data from April 1999 IDC.

TABLE 14.5
U.S. On-line Demographics

		(A) Percentage of Internet Users Who Are:	(B) Percentage of Total U.S. Population Who Are:	Intensity Index (A) ÷ (B)
Gender	Men	51%	48%	106
	Women	49	52	94
Age	18–34	40	33	121
	35–54	48	40	120
	55 plus	12	27	43
Education	Graduated college plus	40	22	182
	Attended college	36	27	133
	Did not attend college	25	51	49
Occupation	Professional	20	10	200
	Executive–manager–administrative	18	10	180
	Clerical–sales–technical	26	19	139
	Precision–crafts–repair	6	7	86
Household Income	$150,000 plus	7	4	195
	$75,000–$149,999	33	19	173
	$50,000–$74,900	26	20	128
	Below $50,000	33	56	59

Source: Adapted from iconocast.com, "Internet at a Glance," data from fall 1999 MRI Cyberstats.

not be aimed at a purchase at all, but rather at gathering information or communicating with other users. The average Web surfer had only 16 sessions on the Internet per month in late 1999, visiting 10 unique sites and spending only a little over 8 hours in the entire month on-line. Thus, each session lasted about half an hour. The average viewing time per Web page was less than one minute. And the average "clickthrough rate"—the percentage of times a viewed advertisement was clicked on to move to the advertiser's Web site—was less than one-half of one percent.[21] Finally, shopping was only the third most popular activity to engage in when on-line, according to a 1999 PricewaterhouseCoopers survey. Ninety-six percent of respondents said they access the Internet to send and receive e-mail; 91 percent research or get information from the Internet; and only 48 percent shop on-line.[22] These data make clear that the Internet is still very far from being the shopping venue of choice, even for those who do use it.

Compounding the lack of intensity of usage is the fact that in 1999, 41.5 million of the 43.9 million U.S. households using the Internet did so with a dial-up modem, the slowest way of accessing sites on the Internet (faster mechanisms include ISDN lines, DSL lines, and cable modems).[23] Downloading a page from a Web site when one uses a modem can be so long that it becomes practically impossible to comparison shop for an item effectively, or even to do a thorough job of searching for one item at one Web site. This, too, currently hampers the market potential of Internet selling.

Despite this, consumer-based Internet commerce is growing by leaps and bounds, albeit from a small base. On-line holiday shopping orders in the United States (occurring between November 20 and December 24) grew by 270 percent, and sales quadrupled between 1998 and 1999, with 1999 holiday sales weighing in at approximately $10 billion, and total on-line consumer sales for the year of about $35 billion (compared to about $20 billion in calendar year 1998). This is still only about 1 percent of U.S. retail sales (considerably smaller than catalog sales in the United States for example), but promises to continue to grow.[24] An Ernst & Young study found that 39 million Americans shopped on-line in 1999, with nearly half spending $500 or more on-line during the year. And Forrester Research forecasts business-to-consumer (or B2C) sales of $184 billion by 2004.[25] Figure 14.3 summarizes Forrester's estimates of category-specific e-commerce sales in 1999 and forecast for 2004. As the figure notes, the proportion of a given category's sales that can be expected to shift to the Internet varies considerably, with 40 percent of computer hardware expected to be bought on-line in 2004, versus only 3 percent of food and beverages.

Business-to-business (B2B) e-commerce sales are much larger in volume than are B2C sales. Forrester Research estimates that 80 percent of the $150 billion of e-commerce in 1999 was B2B in nature.[26] By 2003, Forrester predicts that B2B electronic commerce will amount to $1.3 trillion, with B2C electronic commerce at $144 billion in volume.[27] Even this estimate may be low: A joint electronic purchasing exchange announced in February 2000 by Ford, General Motors, and DaimlerChrysler is expected to handle $240 billion in annual spending by the three car companies alone, plus a substantial part of the $500 billion that auto suppliers themselves spend. Meanwhile, the joint on-line purchasing venture of America's Sears and France's Carrefour, also announced in February 2000, will handle the $80 billion in these two retailers' orders, as well as those of other retail partners that might join the exchange.[28]

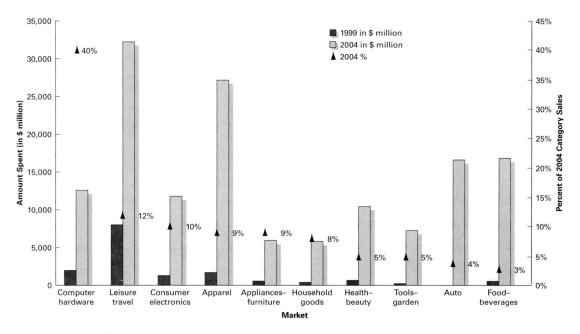

FIGURE 14.3 **Commerce Sales and Projections**

Key: Computer hardware generated $1,964 million in sales in 1999; is forecast to generate $12,541 million in 2004; and on-line computer hardware sales are forecast to be 40 percent of all computer hardware sales in 2004.

Source: Adapted from iconocast.com, "Internet at a Glance," data from September 1999 Forrester Research.

These and other buying exchanges are beginning to replace the earlier-generation electronic data interchange (EDI) relationships that business buyers and sellers have become familiar with.

In some markets, Internet sales do not have to grow much to significantly affect commerce. In the travel business, for instance, it is estimated that if 3 to 5 percent of the market is sold through Internet sites rather than through traditional travel agents, many agents will be driven out of business because of the very thin margins they face already. In 1999, on-line purchases of travel services had already reached 2 percent of sales in this sector, suggesting impending upheaval in this industry. More generally, Goldman Sachs analysts suggest that e-commerce sales will cause off-line retail sales growth to slow from a 5 percent per-year growth rate to a 3 percent per-year growth rate.[29]

If the data presented above appear to be United States–focused, it is because e-commerce is still highly concentrated in the United States, as of this writing. A full 98 percent of intercontinental Internet bandwidth starts or ends in the United States or Canada; 78 percent of Web sites are written in English; 70 percent of secure Web servers used in e-commerce are located in the United States; and 65 percent of e-commerce users are in North America.[30] About 75 percent of all e-commerce sales occur in the United States.[31] European retail Internet sales amounted to $3.6 billion in 1999, although the forecast is for this to increase to $9 billion in 2000. Asian retail Internet sales are forecast to reach $6 billion in 2000, with Japan, Australia, and Korea the biggest markets.

The spread of American e-commerce to other countries is not trivial, because of the challenges of fulfillment and delivery, which many on-line retailers do not do well even inside the U.S. borders. Environmental bounds of tax and regulatory restraints in some European countries constrain the expansion of U.S. Web retailers to the European market. For example, value-added taxes (VAT) are charged in European countries; it is not clear how they will be collected for on-line commerce. In another example, Lands' End, the American-based clothing catalog and on-line retailer, was found to be violating German law by offering its usual 100 percent replacement guarantee for clothing that wore out, leading it to drop that guarantee in Germany. Beyond governmentally based environmental bounds, on-line payment is not as straightforward outside the United States, because credit cards are not as commonly used in Europe and Asia. Telephone services are also significantly more expensive than in the United States; in Europe, they can be as much as five times as high, making Web surfing on average twice as expensive as in the United States.

As a result, the on-line share of various markets tends to be higher in the United States than overseas. One comparison of the United States and Europe in 1999 shows over 15 percent of financial brokerage sales in the United States occurring on-line, but less than 6 percent in Europe. Similarly, about 9 percent of U.S. computer hardware and software sales occurred on-line in 1999, but less than 4 percent of European sales in this category. The differences are similar for books (about 5 percent versus less than 2 percent), event tickets (about 5 percent versus a fraction of 1 percent), consumer electronics (slightly more than 2 percent versus a fraction of 1 percent), and several other categories.

Despite all this, the potential for on-line retail commerce in overseas markets in Europe and Asia is still very strong. Constraints on bricks-and-mortar expansion imposed governmentally (in several European countries in particular) make it relatively more attractive for retailers to seek on-line expansion, to avoid high property prices, planning restrictions, and constraints on hours of operation. Indeed, in select instances, non-U.S. firms already exceed the on-line penetration of their U.S. counterparts. A Finnish–Swedish bank, MeritaNordbanken, claims that 50 percent of its retail customers bank on-line, whereas Sweden's SE bank reports a figure of 25 percent. Both are significantly higher than similar percentages in the United States. In airline ticket sales, Easyjet and Go, two British discount carriers, say they are selling 60 and 50 percent, respectively, of tickets on-line. And 40 percent of Dell Computer's Chinese orders are now placed on-line, rather than by phone.

Thus, although worldwide on-line sales may appear small, it seems clear that they are here to stay, and further, that they will continue to grow rapidly, at least in the short term. Particular sectors may disproportionately feel the effect of the growth of e-channels. What are the key determinants of how fast on-line B2C sales can grow? For this, we turn first to a discussion of service output provision through on-line sellers—a look at the demand side—and then to a discussion of channel flow performance in on-line channels—a look at the supply and the cost side. This will help us to determine what channel gaps exist today, and which need to be closed, for on-line retailing to achieve its full potential.

Service Output Provision and Demand-Side Gaps in Electronic Channels

On either the consumer side or the business buyer side, end-users have demands for the same service outputs on-line that have been discussed earlier in general (see Chapter 3): bulk-breaking, spatial convenience, quick delivery, assortment and variety, and various aspects of pre- and postsale customer service. Consider the implications behind the data in Table 14.6, which summarizes the top reasons consumers gave for *not* making an on-line purchase in the 1999 holiday season, as well as the top reasons for *spending a larger share* of holiday expenditures on-line in the 1999 holiday season. On-line purchasing at the consumer level is seen as attractive because it can be done at any time of the day or night and can save time relative to shopping at bricks-and-mortar stores. It is viewed as more pleasant than fighting the holiday crowds at stores. Some retailers offered special

TABLE 14.6

Consumer Reasons Against and for On-line Shopping, Holiday 1999

Top Reasons for Not Making an On-line Purchase (among those not doing so) and Service Output(s) Affected	Percent of Respondents (multiple responses possible)
Product returns might be difficult (customer service)	39%
Desired product not available or in stock on-line (assortment–variety)	32
Worried about timely delivery of gifts for holidays (wait–delivery time)	31
Privacy concerns (customer service)	26
Don't want to pay shipping–handling costs (spatial convenience)	20
Enjoy holiday shopping at malls/stores (general; all service outputs)	17
Total cost of buying on-line is higher than at stores (all service outputs; signifies intensity of demand for on-line service outputs is too low to merit price)	16

Top Reasons for Spending a Larger Share of Holiday Gift Spending On-line in Holiday 1999 versus Holiday 1998	Percent of Respondents (multiple responses possible)
Can shop anytime (waiting–delivery time)	76%
Takes less time than shopping at stores (waiting–delivery time)	70
Dislike holiday crowds at stores (waiting–delivery time, spatial convenience)	65
Received special promotion to shop on-line (all service outputs; improves price–value offering of on-line product + service output bundle)	47
Easier to shop compared to catalogs (waiting–delivery time)	46
Enjoy shopping on-line (general; all service outputs)	45
Lower prices (all service outputs; improves price–value offering of on-line product + service output bundle)	41
Access to products/brands not available where I live/work (assortment–variety)	38

Source: Adapted from Catherine Finamore, "The Connected Consumer," *E-Retail Intelligence Update,* PricewaterhouseCoopers, January 2000, pp. 5–8.

inducements to shop on-line but on-line shopping had its negatives as well. Difficulty in returning products, out-of-stock issues, and delivery time uncertainties kept many away from on-line shopping. Information security and price also mattered to some. Some consumers found the total cost of buying on-line to be too high relative to the benefits it offers, whereas others found prices to be actually lower on-line than at standard stores. On net, it appears that on-line retailing offers some improvements over standard store retailing, but is not unambiguously better.

Thinking more specifically about each of the major service outputs, we can make some observations about how well on-line retailers are providing service outputs to shoppers.

Bulk-breaking. One of the biggest distinctions between selling through a bricks-and-mortar retailer and selling on-line is the need to master the art of bulk-breaking. Manufacturers who choose to open their own Web sites find that they now must be able to ship *few* units at a time to *many* addresses, versus the standard in retailer-based channels of shipping *many* units at a time to *few* addresses (the retailers). Amazon.com used intermediaries for some time to perform fulfillment and shipping functions, but now operates its own warehouses to generate bulk-breaking benefits directly for its consumers. In general, on-line sellers do quite a good job of meeting this fairly standard service output demand, with the help of third-party shippers.

Spatial convenience is a two-edged sword for on-line retailers. On the *shopping* dimension, the spatial convenience of shopping at home simply cannot be beat by any bricks-and-mortar retailer, and this is one of the strongest draws of on-line shopping, both for consumer and business-to-business buyers. But (particularly for consumer goods) if the product is not what the consumer wanted (e.g., a garment does not fit right), *returns* can be spatially quite inconvenient. If the item was bought from a "pure-play" on-line retailer (i.e., one that does not operate any bricks-and-mortar stores), the buyer must rewrap the item, take it to a post office or other shipping site, and pay to send it back. Some on-line sellers mitigate this irritation by contracting with shippers to pick up the items from the consumer's home, although this can raise other service output problems if the consumer has to wait for the shipper to arrive to pick up the package. On-line sellers who also operate retail stores (e.g., Williams-Sonoma, Lands' End, Eddie Bauer, Victoria's Secret, and many more) sometimes choose to allow the on-line shopper to return items to the bricks-and-mortar store, which gives the buyer some choice when a return is necessary.

Waiting and delivery time is not a major strength of on-line sellers in many categories. Waiting time can be perceived to be too long in at least two dimensions. First, particularly on the consumer side, the delay time to load and view screens on the Internet can be frustrating, particularly at heavy traffic times, as was experienced by consumers trying to do holiday shopping during the weekend after Thanksgiving in November 1999 in the United States. Recall from the earlier discussion that the vast majority of Internet users connect to the Internet via a modem, which is the slowest technology available. Thus, consumers often find on-line shopping too slow merely from the point of view of discovering and viewing their purchase choices. Interestingly, this service output problem is not within the control of the on-line seller itself, because it is a function of the Internet connect speed the consumer chooses. However, as the cost of faster connections falls, a greater number of on-line shoppers can be expected to use high-speed connections and thus minimize the inconvenience of waiting to view on-line shopping venues.

   The second dimension of waiting and delivery time that hampers the attractiveness of on-line shopping is literally the time to delivery after purchase. True, one can now buy and immediately download products like music and computer software, and on-line banking or stock trading can be accomplished instantly. But other physical products have to be shipped after the order is received, and the elapsed time from order to receipt can vary enormously. This is fundamentally the same problem in service output delivery faced by catalog sellers for many years. The classic response is to offer a variety of different delivery times, with quicker delivery (e.g., overnight express) carrying a higher delivery charge than standard (say, five business days' delay) delivery. However, some on-line sellers offer almost "instant gratification" upon purchase. PC Connection, a seller of computer hardware and software, offers delivery by 10:00 A.M. in the United States if the purchaser orders by 2:00 A.M. that day, for example. This delivery speed comes at only a slight price premium over standard (three to five business-day delivery lag) shipping. Thus, a buyer can shop on-line in the evening and receive his or her shipment the next morning. Although this is not always as quick an option as traveling to a local computer or office supplies store, it can be quicker—if the buyer discovers a purchase need after the bricks-and-mortar store has closed for the night.[32]

   The time to delivery is of course also a function of the on-line seller's stock. In the holiday shopping seasons of 1998 and 1999, many on-line retailers promised, but did not produce, on-time delivery of goods ordered as gifts. The on-line arm of Toys "R" Us realized in December 1999 that some customers who ordered after December 10 would not receive their shipments before Christmas and offered them the option of canceling their orders as well as sending them a $100 Toys "R" Us voucher good in its bricks-and-mortar stores. Some customers who ordered early also did not receive their packages on time; some of these were so angry that they filed a class-action lawsuit against the retailer.[33] Timely delivery is thus clearly a must for on-line retail success, and forecasts are that in future holiday seasons, those on-line sellers who have not already proven themselves capable of accurately estimating time to delivery will fail to grow. This is one demand-side gap that must be closed for an on-line seller to succeed.

   Assortment and variety can be vastly increased (theoretically at least) with on-line shopping over what is available at standard bricks-and-mortar stores. Specific on-line retailers seek to offer a very broad assortment of products in order to attract on-line shoppers looking for choice. For example, Amazon.com markets itself as having the "Earth's biggest selection," offering over 5 million book titles (not to mention its increasing business in music, electronics and software, toys and videos, etc.).

   Beyond single-outlet on-line retailers, many on-line malls and search engines (or "bots") exist today that effectively increase the assortment and variety available at one destination. For example, www.shoesonthenet.com offers one-click access to dozens of Web sites selling shoes for men, women, and children. Another search engine, www.mysimon.com, is the largest comparison shopping site on the Web, with access to over 2,000 merchants in categories such as computers, books and music, electronics, fashion, flowers, sporting goods, and toys. This Web site markets itself as offering unbiased information on products and merchants, including price comparisons, availability, and other merchant information. Mysimon.com provides access to charts detailing product price histories at all merchants and lets users register to receive personalized e-mail alerts when products they are looking for become available or drop below a specified price (effectively reducing total search costs while offering broad assortment and variety). These and other similar portals offer the consumer a way to both expand their scope of search and have retailers find them when they can offer products and prices that meet the consumer's needs. Thus, both an "outbound" and an "inbound" search service is provided to the on-line shopper through these search engines.

On the B2B side, many initiatives have been undertaken to expand assortment and variety available to business buyers in various industries. Grainger's orderzone.com business (profiled in Channel Sketches in Chapters 3 and 4) brings together the assortments of six business-to-business sellers to offer a much fuller array of products to the MRO buyer than would be possible through any one alone. General Motors, Ford, and DaimlerChrysler announced the formation of a joint Internet-based automotive-parts buying exchange (to be run as an independent company) in February 2000. GM and Ford gave up their individual Internet purchasing sites (called GM TradeXchange and auto-xchange, respectively) to form the new joint exchange. They plan to run $240 billion in annual spending through the site worldwide.[34] The auto companies are not alone in their initiative to increase assortment available to them on one site. In January 2000, Matsushita Electric Industrial group of Japan announced the intention to set up an Internet site to purchase materials and parts, with the goal of 100 percent of its manufacturing-related purchases to flow through the site by March 2001. Rival steelmakers Bethlehem Steel Corporation, LTV Corporation, Weirton Steel Corporation, and Steel Dynamics Inc. in the United States formed a single buying exchange, MetalSite, in early 1999 as well. Consolidating buying power is viewed as beneficial to these buyers because of both the assortment benefits it creates and the competitive prices it can generate.[35]

The *customer service* dimension of service output provision is actually a multidimensional offering. It includes *presales service* such as educational information, specification of a system of components (such as a computer system), or provision of a pleasant in-store shopping ambiance. It also includes *postsale service* dimensions such as home delivery, assembly (e.g., for furniture, electronics), troubleshooting, and repair. From a consumer shopping perspective, neither bricks-and-mortar retailers nor on-line retailers hold a clear lead in the provision of pre- or postsale service. Some bricks-and-mortar retailers, particularly more upscale ones, invest very heavily in in-store service, with many clerks on the store floor ready to help a shopper find the right product. But, as Chapter 13 discusses, many other bricks-and-mortar retailers now purposefully position themselves as low-touch rather than high-touch retailers, emphasizing self-service in their stores rather than a personal shopping experience. In these situations, it is possible for an on-line retailer to exceed the presales service offerings of a standard retail establishment.

On-line women's clothing retailer Coldwater Creek, which also sells through a catalog, excels in the provision of presales service. It offers its shoppers detailed information on the dimensions of its clothing. Beyond this, it offers on-line access to a Personal Shopper that sorts through its inventory to match the shopper's need (e.g., for casual clothing, in a particular size range, and in a particular color). If the shopper is uncertain about the item she is choosing, she can choose an "Instant Help" function that connects her with a customer service representative (by name) to whom she can direct on-line questions in real time about fabric, size, or care. Other on-line apparel merchants, such as Lands' End, can create a virtual model on-line with the shopper's physical dimensions, so that clothing is "modeled" in three dimensions before the purchase is made.

Note that offering such service generates multiple benefits to the seller. First, it increases the shopper's comfort level with buying on-line, because it helps to resolve any uncertainty she may have about the product she is contemplating buying. This increases the probability of a sale. Second, because her choice is likely to be better informed, post-sale returns will be a lower fraction of sales, saving significant costs for the on-line retailer.[36]

Sometimes, presale education and information is offered by having *other buyers* act as experts. Amazon.com pioneered this practice, offering on-line reviews of books so that prospective purchasers could see what other actual consumers thought of a book before buying. This clearly does not substitute for the in-store experience of browsing through a book, but can help compensate, especially given the superior spatial convenience and assortment and variety offered on-line.

Elements of postsale service can also be offered on-line, to both consumer and business buyers. Hewlett-Packard has moved 80 percent of its postsale customer support activities to the Internet in the wake of expanding its on-line presence in the late 1990s. This can make customer support both more spatially convenient for the consumer and less expensive for HP to provide. Many other sellers contract with state-of-the-art shippers, such as FedEx, UPS, or Schneider trucking company, who can offer postsale (but predelivery) information on the whereabouts and status of a shipped order. This service is of particular importance to business buyers, who may need to plan for personnel to be available to unload a shipment in a timely fashion after receipt.

Although these examples illustrate the efforts that the best on-line sellers are making to mimic good in-store service, many on-line sellers do not live up to this standard, creating demand-side gaps in on-line channels. On-line retailing is often a virtual analog of buying through a catalog, without the ability to talk to a real person about any questions one might have about the products purchased, thus compromising customer service. The failure of Toys "R" Us to ship many packages on time for holiday delivery in the 1999 holiday season seriously compromised consumers' perceptions of the ability of the on-line channel to offer quick (enough) delivery. Consumers' own use of slower Internet connect technologies also means that the shopping process itself can be time-consuming and arduous—not at all the quick experience that many consumers expected on-line shopping to be. And the lack of ease of returns compromises the spatial convenience of on-line shopping.

Finally, for the trade-offs in service outputs that consumers in particular make when shopping on-line, they expect a lower purchase price. Yet the data in Table 14.6 suggest that at least some consumers find on-line shopping to be too expensive for the product-plus-service-output bundle available there. One survey shows that on-line shoppers' price perceptions are strongly affected by shipping and handling charges: Among Internet users, almost half saw on-line prices as lower than store prices, ignoring shipping and handling. But only 25 percent perceived on-line prices to be lower than bricks-and-mortar store prices once shipping and handling are considered as part of the total price.[37] Given the demand-side gaps and price issues, it is perhaps no wonder that on-line buying has not taken the retail market by storm. But as these gaps close through technological advances, on-line purchasing will continue to expand, and as business buyers have found, not only will help to improve service output levels but also will reduce the cost of running the channel in many ways. We turn to this issue next, in our discussion of supply-side channel flow issues and gaps in on-line channels.

Channel Flow Performance and Supply-Side Gaps in Electronic Channels

Selling on-line changes the structure and cost of running a marketing channel. New fixed costs may be added to channel operating costs, such as the cost of warehouse creation (e.g., Pets.com, a pet supplies on-line retailer, estimates that a new distribution center will cost between $7 million and $9 million to build) or of Web site creation and maintenance.[38] Completely new intermediaries may be added: The success of Internet portal businesses such as Yahoo! are based at least in part on their "market-making" ability to offer a large number of consumers to sellers desiring to reach them, on the one hand, and a large number of potentially attractive Web sites for those consumers to visit, on the other hand.

In some cases, injecting an on-line element to the channel is a purposeful move to reduce the cost of performing certain channel flows. Business-to-business commerce has benefited from various forms of electronic commerce for several years, which position the users of these services to adopt more purely Internet-based versions of their buying systems in the near future. Initiatives of note in this vein include all the technologies involved in *electronic data interchange,* or EDI; as well as *vendor-managed inventory,* or VMI; and *continuous replenishment* systems, or CRP.

Electronic data interchange refers to the use of any or all of a variety of electronic technologies to share data on shipments, sales, orders, and the like. It usually rests on a computer platform that is proprietary to the buyer, implying that sellers serving multiple EDI-ready retailers have had to adopt multiple computer systems to communicate with them all. EDI is widely used in the business supply chains of leading retailers the world over, as well as by many business-to-business firms in their channels. West Bend, an American manufacturer of small electrical appliances, is just one example of a supplier who routinely uses EDI linkages with major mass-merchandise retailers. When it first adopted EDI technologies, retailers such as Kmart shared sales data from the previous two years with West Bend, so that West Bend could improve its sales forecasting and hence reduce its costs of *physical possession* (of both raw materials and finished product) and *risking* (with better forecasts, it could minimize the chance of lost sales opportunities due to underpredicting the size of the market). Because better historical and seasonal sales data reduce the need to hold safety stocks of product, *ownership* costs also fall for the supplier benefiting from EDI linkages, as do the costs of *financing* inventory. West Bend, for example, was able to reduce its holding of sheet metal—a raw material input to the production of its appliances—from 26 weeks to just a fraction of that as a result of the EDI sales information now available to it.[39]

In vendor-managed inventory, a supplier has electronic access to its customer's inventory and literally manages that inventory for the customer. VF Corporation, maker of many brands of jeans and other casual wear, has pioneered the use of this technology with mass-market retailers over the years (see the discussion of VF's use of VMI in

Chapter 13). When the supplier, not the retailer, manages the inventory for a brand electronically, costs of physical possession, ownership, financing, and risking are reduced in much the same way as with EDI, because of the much improved information flow about what specific items are selling at retail and hence what must be replenished when.

Continuous replenishment programs are often used in VMI systems. CRP means that the vendor, which is electronically linked to the buyer's warehouse or retail point-of-sale computer systems, has instantaneous information about the movement of inventory out of the buyer's hands. For example, when a consumer buys a certain size of a certain style of pants at retail, the sales clerk records the precise item that has been sold by running the item's tag across the point-of-sale scanner at the checkout counter. The scanner reads the precise information about what has been sold (not just that a pair of pants has been sold, but what color, size, and style), and this information flows immediately back to the supplier. The supplier can then tell accurately what needs to be restocked at each of the retailer's locations.

Typically, under a CRP program, the supplier and retailer (or other channel buyer) have an agreement specifying trigger points: minimum stock levels at each retail store below which restocking automatically occurs. Through this system, again physical possession, ownership, financing, and risking flow costs are minimized as with the use of EDI and VMI. Here, too, the costs of negotiation and ordering are minimized, because a blanket agreement is signed (perhaps once a year) specifying reordering policies, so that reordering does not have to involve a person-to-person interaction each time stock runs low in the store.

Using some subset of this "alphabet soup" of electronic channel technologies thus reduces the cost of performing many of the "back-room" flows necessary to the smooth working of a marketing channel. A report from Goldman Sachs & Company estimates that the efficiencies produced by B2B e-commerce will add about 0.25 percent to the annual growth of major industrialized countries during the period 2000 to 2010. Although this may not seem like a large amount, in the United States alone, it would amount to $23 billion more annually in goods and services. The report predicts that business-to-business on-line transactions, which now account for only 0.5 percent of all B2B transactions, will rise to 10 percent by 2004.[40]

Some other instances of specific channel flows whose costs are notably affected by the use of electronic channels include the following.

- *Physical possession.* As mentioned in the discussion of the bulk-breaking service output, on-line retailing to individual consumers requires small lot sizes to be efficiently picked, packed, and shipped to many different addresses. Inventory can no longer be shipped in large (efficient, low shipping cost) lot sizes to a few bricks-and-mortar retail locations. The costs of physical possession, including the costs of building and maintaining warehouses, picking and packing operations, and operating truck fleets (or other physical transportation operations), all increase as a result. Third-party experts in handling many small shipments (such as UPS, national postal services, FedEx, Airborne, and other shippers) have seen extremely healthy increases in their businesses as a result: They are becoming an important new channel member to complete the marketing channel in an e-commerce world. Typically, the consumer pays the freight, which is a fair trade for the increased spatial convenience of shopping from home. In an ideal world, then, increased physical possession costs would be shifted entirely to the consumer, who would be willing to pay them if the compensating differential benefits of increased spatial convenience and assortment and variety are high enough. However, in a bid to build business, many on-line retailers waived shipping fees in late 1999 and early 2000, bearing this cost themselves.

- *Promotion.* In the consumer e-commerce world, personal in-store shopping help and interactivity disappear. These are important promotional inputs to the sale of many products in the bricks-and-mortar retailing world. But overall, promotional expenses on-line are higher currently than in bricks-and-mortar retailers: When building up a new e-commerce site, it is necessary to invest in promotional expenditures to generate sales and customers at the site. These are nontrivial. In the four business quarters of 1999, Buy.com reported spending 12 percent of revenue on sales and marketing expenses, but Drugstore.com spent 176.5 percent of revenue on sales and marketing! Many other pure-play on-line retailers spent large amounts on promotion as well, with eToys.com weighing in at 77.5 percent and CDnow, Inc. spending 59.9 percent. A comparable sample of bricks-and-mortar retailers spent from a fraction of 1 percent to about 5 percent of revenues on sales and marketing, significantly smaller proportions.[41]

- *Promotion.* Promotional efforts also occur in an effort to provide information to the on-line buyer, either about the company and its offerings (i.e., education about the business), or about the products themselves. For example, Hewlett-Packard's Web site offers extensive product information about all of its products (printers, computers, handheld devices, calculators, etc.) as well as about supplies and accessories. The on-line site also gives customers the opportunity to design a system or to customize their search for accessories. For example, the owner of a laser-jet printer is not interested in viewing screens with color cartridges for ink-jet printers. HP offers not only information but also the ability to buy from its Web site, but it sets regular list prices to avoid alienating its other retail outlets.[42]

- *Negotiation.* The advent of electronic commerce has in some cases reduced the intensity of negotiation activities, and in other situations has actually increased them. The use of technologies such as continuous replenishment, discussed earlier, routinizes replenishment and reduces the need to negotiate purchases on a deal-by-deal basis, thus economizing on negotiation flow costs. On the consumer side, however, the rise of on-line auction businesses such as e-Bay makes negotiation the heart of the on-line experience. Every purchase is individualized and prices are not fixed beforehand. Other on-line buying options, such as Priceline.com, let the shopper set the price he or she is willing to pay for hotel rooms, airline tickets, rental cars, groceries, and home financing, among other categories of purchases. The consumer must provide credit card information prior to learning what option has been chosen (e.g., which hotel will be booked), and reservations cannot be changed. Thus, although there is some uncertainty about the final purchase, the consumer does get a chance to purchase at a price significantly lower than the street price.

- *Negotiation.* In the B2B arena, new buying exchanges are emerging in many industries. They are typically set up by manufacturers (sometimes competing manufacturers) and post the purchase needs the manufacturers have for supplies and raw materials. Vendors can log on to the site and bid on the manufacturers' business, thus increasing the intensity of negotiation in the channel for these vendors. One example is

MyAircraft.com, a Web site for aerospace parts and services launched jointly by United Technologies Corporation and Honeywell International Inc. that will include original equipment manufacturers and airlines as partners.[43] In all cases, the buyers organizing these exchanges predict significant cost savings in supplies or upstream product purchases, and the vendors fear much stiffer price competition, leading to lower vendor margins through auction-like transactions. In most of these cases, the ventures are to be set up as independent companies with their own management, employees, and financing, although the founding partners take equity stakes in the ventures.

- *Risking.* Many risks inherent in product distribution decrease with effective use of electronic commerce, because of the reduction in the need to hold speculative inventory (see the earlier discussion of EDI, VMI, and CRP). From a consumer retailing perspective, however, the issue of on-line security is still worrisome. Many are reluctant to give credit card numbers to Web retailers, fearing that a computer hacker will break into their systems and use the information to charge expenses without the consumer's knowledge. The true risk of this is relatively low, particularly because credit card companies themselves offer to cover that risk above a certain limit. Encryption technologies increase in sophistication month by month as well, making on-line shopping more secure. This issue is likely to fade over time as consumers become more comfortable with on-line shopping.

- *Ordering.* The alliances formed by automakers and retailers to buy supplies described above, as well as unilateral initiatives by companies such as Wal-Mart to make buying an electronic process, facilitates the ordering flow significantly. The Goldman Sachs report mentioned earlier forecasts that 10 percent of business-to-business purchases will be made on-line by 2004, implying significant efficiencies in the ordering process.

- *Payment.* Electronic banking technologies lower the cost of making payment on bills and invoices because they allow transfers of funds from one account to another with a minimum of paper handling (and hence a minimum of errors). Although these technologies did not come into existence only in the era of electronic commerce, their existence helps encourage the spread of e-commerce. Indeed, without electronic means of secure payment, electronic channels and electronic sales would not have progressed as far as they have today.

Whereas electronic commerce can cut total channel costs significantly, pure-play on-line retailing remains an unprofitable venture. Amazon.com passed the $1 billion revenue mark in 1999, in its fifth year in business, but posted a net loss of $720 million, for a net profit margin of −43.9 percent. Amazon.com is not alone, however; eToys.com lost $154 million, Buy.com lost $130 million, CDnow lost $119 million, Drugstore.com lost $116 million, and barnesandnoble.com lost $102 million in 1999. Not only are the costs of building and maintaining their Web businesses extraordinary relative to the ongoing costs of running an established bricks-and-mortar operation, but their gross margins were deflated in 1999 by extensive promotional discounting, aimed at building a buyer base that (one hopes) would translate to long-run consumer loyalty. For example, eToys' gross margin ratio for 1999 was 18.8 percent, whereas Toys "R" Us enjoyed a gross margin ratio of 29.6 percent. Barnes & Noble's bricks-and-mortar business had a gross margin ratio in 1999 of 28.8 percent, but barnesandnoble.com's gross margin ratio was only 21.0 percent. As the number of new U.S. households shopping on-line is expected to peak in the year 2000, on-line retailers are likely to shift their focus from *acquiring* customers to making more money from their existing customer base, which may help some to move toward positive net profitability.[44]

In sum, electronic channels increase the efficiency of channel operation in several flows, although the move to bulk-breaking for consumer e-commerce can increase the cost of physical possession. Interestingly, efficiency is frequently increased through the alteration of the channel structure itself, rather than through mere reallocation of flows among preexisting channel members. Specialized intermediaries focus on Web site design (a promotional function), and shippers such as FedEx or UPS take over the physical movement of inventory in place of large-lot-size movements of product from manufacturers' to retailers' warehouses. These fundamental changes can also threaten the viability of existing nonelectronic channels. We turn next to a discussion of the challenges to channel coordination raised by the use of electronic channels to reach the market.

Coordination Challenges in Electronic Channels

Channel conflicts can and do arise when an on-line channel is created alongside a more traditional channel, be it a business-to-business distributor-driven channel or a bricks-and-mortar retail channel. Goal, domain, and perception-of-reality conflicts can all arise. It is up to the manufacturers involved to evaluate the severity of these conflicts and decide what, if anything, to do about them.

It is useful to differentiate the situations in which conflicts due to on-line sales can play a part. Figure 14.4 depicts the possibilities schematically. In case (a) of Figure 14.4, the manufacturer itself creates an owned on-line presence, in direct competition with its standard channel(s). For example, Mattel sells its toys and software both through bricks-and-mortar toy stores and through its own Web site, and Tupperware sells its kitchen storage containers both through its independent direct sales force and over the Internet. In this case, *disintermediation* is said to occur: That is, an intermediary is being cut out of the channel when the manufacturer sells direct.

In case (b) of Figure 14.4, the manufacturer contracts to sell through third-party pure-play on-line resellers (i.e., on-line resellers who themselves do not own purely bricks-and-mortar distribution). Callaway golf clubs, for example, can be bought on-line at Buy.com, which does not operate bricks-and-mortar stores.

Finally, as in case (c) Figure 14.4, the manufacturer may find itself in a situation where its products are sold on-line because some of its bricks-and-mortar resellers themselves are starting up on-line operations. A manufacturer selling through Wal-Mart, Nordstrom, Barnes & Noble bookstores, and a host of other bricks-and-mortar retailers that have opened an on-line emporia is in this situation. Of course, any combination of these on-line strategies may be used; they do not have to be used in isolation. Barbie computer software, for example, is available not only at Mattel's own on-line Web site but also at both www.buy.com (a pure-play Internet retailer) and www.toysrus.com, the on-line shopping outlet of the bricks-and-mortar Toys "R" Us.

Case (a), where the manufacturer itself mounts an on-line marketing and selling effort, carries the potential for goal, domain, and perception-of-reality conflicts. *Goal*

(a) Manufacturer has own on-line presence (e.g., Tupperware; dotted line indicates common ownership)

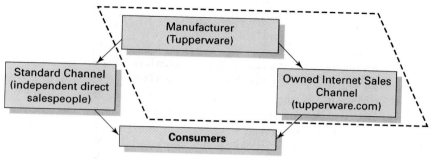

(b) Manufacturer sells through third-party pure-play on-line reseller (e.g., Callaway Golf selling through buy.com)

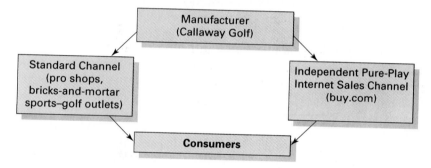

(c) Manufacturer sells through some standard channels that do operate their own on-line stores and some that do not (e.g., books sold through bricks-and-mortar retailers and Barnes & Noble's on-line site, bn.com)

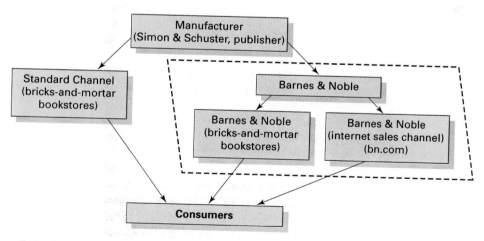

FIGURE 14.4 **Dual Distribution with On-line Selling: Channel Structure Options**

conflict can arise because the manufacturer now wants to maximize its profit over its totality of sales channels, one of which is the on-line channel. This channel may offer the manufacturer a higher margin on sales than does the standard bricks-and-mortar channel. In addition, it needs to make enough sales on-line to cover the significant fixed costs of establishing and maintaining its Web site. It may thus push consumers to buy directly from it, rather than from its standard bricks-and-mortar channel partners.

Domain conflict is also a problem in case (a). The manufacturer who sells on-line may directly cannibalize the consumers of the bricks-and-mortar channel, causing conflict over the population to be served. The bricks-and-mortar channel of course will believe that these consumers who now choose to shop on-line at the manufacturer's site *would have* purchased from the bricks-and-mortar channel if the on-line channel did not exist. Further, the manufacturer's on-line site reaches far and wide, and can take away sales from anywhere in the market area served by the bricks-and-mortar channel, thus causing domain conflict over the territorial rights. This is particularly a problem for direct-marketing organizations such as Amway or Mary Kay, whose businesses have been built on the premise that a distributor of their products "owns" his or her customers.

Domain conflict over the functions and duties to be performed by channel members can also arise in case (a), where the manufacturer sells through an owned on-line channel. Here the problem is the classic free-riding opportunity. A consumer may go to a bricks-and-mortar store, for example, a specialty toy retailer, inspect a collector's Barbie doll, ask the retail clerk some questions about the product, check the price, and then buy the product on-line (sometimes for a lower price). When this sequence of events occurs, the bricks-and-mortar retailer has borne the costs of the promotional flow, but has received no compensation for it, because it does not get the sale on the product. This conflict implies a violation of the Equity Principle.

Yet another domain conflict possibility exists if a consumer who has bought from the on-line outlet of the manufacturer decides to return the product, and tries to do so at a bricks-and-mortar retailer. Generally, bricks-and-mortar retailers will not accept a return of this sort, again because it results in the retailer bearing a cost without compensation.

As the earlier discussion suggests, the possibility of conflict over *perceptions of reality* also exists in case (a). The manufacturer often believes that it is merely expanding its reach in the market, generating sales from consumers who cannot buy its products in any other way or are not inclined to do so. Indeed, Table 14.6 reports that 38 percent of survey respondents who spent a larger share of holiday gift spending on-line in holiday 1999 versus holiday 1998 said that they were able to buy products on-line that were not accessible to them near where they live or work. Nevertheless, bricks-and-mortar resellers are likely to perceive that the manufacturer who disintermediates and goes on-line is stealing sales that are rightfully theirs.

In sum, the manufacturer that opens its own on-line store, as case (a) depicts, faces the possibility of conflict generation on several fronts. Is the nature of conflict the same in cases (b) and (c)?

In case (b) of Figure 14.4, the manufacturer does not itself open an on-line outlet, but sells through on-line resellers who are pure-play companies—that is, they do not operate their own bricks-and-mortar channels, but rely solely on the Internet for sales opportunities. Meanwhile, the manufacturer continues to use its standard pure bricks-and-mortar resellers as well. This overall channel structure creates the classic dual distribution conflicts that any manufacturer faces when it uses multiple channel types to reach the market. The on-line reseller offers a different bundle of service outputs than does the bricks-and-mortar reseller, possibly at a different price, and competition is created for sales in the market.

In this case, the same types of conflict—goal, domain, and perceptual—can exist as in case (a). However, the conflict can now exist between the bricks-and-mortar retailer and its on-line counterpart directly. The two competing resellers generally have very different goals: The on-line retailer in the current Internet marketplace often has a strong need to generate sales volume and market share in order to maintain its flow of venture capital as it seeks to grow and dominate the on-line channel for its product type. This can lead to significant price-cutting, offers of free delivery, and other inducements to sell. In contrast, standard bricks-and-mortar resellers focus on a shorter-term horizon for profit and cost covering, charge higher prices, and find it hard to compete.

This problem is exacerbated by the fact that free riding is possible in this channel structure, just as it was in case (a). The bricks-and-mortar retailer offers presales education and service to the prospective buyer, who then goes to the on-line emporium to buy his or her preferred product at a discounted price. Over time, the bricks-and-mortar retailer continues to face the higher cost structure arising from its provision of presales service, further limiting its ability to price-compete with the on-line retailer, who enjoys a lower marginal cost of sales.

Note that in case (b), unlike in case (a), the manufacturer does not have direct pricing or service control over the on-line channel. This limits somewhat its ability to prevent conflict between its different reseller channels.

The conflict issues that arise in case (b) of Figure 14.4 seem to come in new guises because they are part of the new Internet economy. But in actuality, they are just new examples of the type of dual distribution conflict that has plagued manufacturers for a long time. Left untreated, they can have the same negative outcomes as those arising from the use of multiple non-Internet channels.

Case (c) in Figure 14.4 puts yet another twist on the situation. Here, on-line sales occur—but they are made by one of the manufacturer's resellers that itself also operates bricks-and-mortar outlets. This would initially appear to be a situation with the same conflict potential as in case (b), accompanied by the same inability of the manufacturer to control pricing, merchandising, and other marketing activities of the on-line reseller. But there is a crucial difference: The on-line reseller *internalizes*, at least in part, the negative effects of aggressive on-line competition on the bricks-and-mortar channel, because *it too will suffer from cannibalization of in-store sales by the on-line channel.*

Beyond this, the combination reseller, who operates both bricks-and-mortar outlets and an on-line sales operation, risks confusing and alienating its own customers if it offers terms that are wildly different through the two different types of outlets. For example, suppose it charges a much lower price for on-line purchases. Suppose the difference between on-line and in-store purchase prices is greater than the value of the difference in service outputs. Then even consumers who do not free ride on the bricks-and-mortar outlet before buying on-line will still choose the on-line purchasing option. In this case, the combination reseller cannibalizes itself. It suffers more if consumers free ride on its bricks-and-mortar outlets and then buy at the lower price on-line. A combination reseller is thus more likely to charge a "fair" price for its on-line wares, in comparison to the offering it gives in its bricks-and-mortar stores.

Thus, a purely bricks-and-mortar reseller apparently faces less potential conflict with a combination bricks-and-mortar and on-line competitor than it does with a pure-play on-line reseller. But the competitive strength of the combination reseller may prove to be greater in the long run, because of its ability to offer a fuller array of service outputs than either a purely bricks-and-mortar player or a pure-play on-line reseller, and because of its generally stronger negotiating position vis-à-vis suppliers. Almost 50 percent of the most visited Web sites in the 1999 holiday shopping season were associated with either a bricks-and-mortar retailer or an established catalog business. This suggests the likelihood of consolidation of Internet retail businesses with standard retailers in coming years.[45]

Yet another form of conflict can arise in case (c), not directly affecting the manufacturer. In the holiday 1999 shopping season, some shopping mall owners prohibited their retail tenants from advertising their on-line retail outlets inside the mall. This reflected the goal and domain conflicts between the mall owners and the retailers. The retailer, who would like to maximize its profits across the combination of its on-line and bricks-and-mortar stores, naturally wants to cross-promote one type of outlet in the other, to maximize its sales potential. But the mall owner faces the prospect of lower sales through its retail stores if more and more shoppers go on-line. This would lessen the overall attractiveness of any bricks-and-mortar store rental. Further, many retail mall rental agreements specify payments as a function of the sales of the retail store in the mall. If retailers send their shoppers on-line, they gain not only in total sales but also in reduced rents—precisely the opposite outcome from that preferred by the mall owner.

Conflict potential seems to be very high when manufacturers embark on electronic commerce, whether through owned, third-party pure-play, or combination on-line resellers. What can be done to manage the conflict so that it does not become pathological? Is it always optimal to seek to reduce these conflicts? Channel Sketch 14.1 profiles several manufacturers' strategies to manage channel conflict when the manufacturer itself chooses to operate an on-line buying site as part of the channel mix. Among the actions being taken at the manufacturer level are:

- Going on-line, but offering benefits to standard retailers not available on the company Web site—case (a), Nike
- Product line differentiation to preserve the bricks-and-mortar retailer's market position—case (b), Procter & Gamble and Tupperware
- Using reward power to share sales credit with bricks-and-mortar retailers—case (c), Ethan Allen
- Avoiding selling on a manufacturer-operated Web site—case (d), Levi-Strauss

In case (b) or (c) of Figure 14.4, it becomes more difficult for the manufacturer to control channel conflict because it does not fully control the on-line part of its channel. However, the computer industry uses one interesting mechanism to increase control. A *minimum advertised price*, or *MAP*, policy determines whether a reseller earns the right

CHANNEL SKETCH 14.1

Conflict Reduction Strategies for Electronic Channels

Case (a) Managing Conflict from Owned On-line Channels: Nike[46]

Nike is a good example of a manufacturer that has taken several steps to minimize the conflicts inherent in case (a), where the manufacturer goes on-line itself. The athletic shoe and apparel manufacturer communicated with its retailers both before and after the company went on-line in February 1999 to explain how its site would not undermine the sales efforts and performance of its off-line retailers. It promised that Nike.com would sell its products at list price, not at a discount. Its site helps shoppers find a bricks-and-mortar store near them where they can shop for Nike products. And it offers special benefits to its largest retailers that it does not even take advantage of on its own Web site: Venator Group, which owns such retail sporting goods chains as Foot Locker and Champs Sports, had the exclusive right to sell Nike's Air2 Max shoe in 1999 in its retail stores and on-line. Through these actions, Nike first stemmed any potential perception-of-reality conflicts that retailers might have about Nike's intentions to continue valuing its bricks-and-mortar retailers. It also minimized domain conflict by offering its largest retailers "private goods" like the Air2 Max shoe, which even an on-line store could not do. And it exhibited its common goals with retailers by referring shoppers to bricks-and-mortar sites from the Nike.com Web site.

Case (b) Electronic Channel Conflict Management Through Product Line Differentiation: Procter & Gamble and Tupperware

Some manufacturers choose to manage channel conflicts due to on-line retailing by offering a different on-line product line from that sold through the bricks-and-mortar channel. Procter & Gamble is one such example: It chooses not to sell its standard line of beauty products on-line, but instead has created a completely different line of products that are sold only on-line but not in bricks-and-mortar retailers, called Reflect.com. This type of action reduces domain conflict (1) by failing to offer the consumer the chance to buy the same product in the two different channels; and (2) by naming the on-line product line by a completely different name to minimize price, feature, and brand-equity comparisons. This strategy is very similar to that followed by some clothing designers that sell through both bricks-and-mortar retailers and through their own outlet stores: For example, Ann Taylor sells its line through exclusive Ann Taylor stores. It also operates outlet stores called Ann Taylor Loft, where only "Ann Taylor Loft" label clothes can be found. These clothes are made from the designs that were current in the previous year's season, to avoid direct competition with the full-price stores. Yet another policy is to sell only a portion of the company's full line through the on-line store; Tupperware does this to protect its direct-selling distributors, who have access to the full line of products to sell to their customers.

Case (c) Sharing Credit for an On-line Sale with Bricks-and-Mortar Retailers: Ethan Allen[47]

An alternative for some manufacturers is to sell on-line, but to credit (in full or in part) their off-line channel partners who perform promotional or fulfillment flows to support the sale. Ethan Allen, a U.S. maker of a full line of premium, upscale furniture, has historically served the market through a network of over 300 quasi-independent dedicated stores. These stores sell only Ethan Allen product, but are operated by independent licensees who not only sell product but also provide significant levels of pre- and postsales service (interior decorating, delivery and assembly, etc.). When Ethan Allen's chairman and CEO, Faroq Kathwari, decided to launch an on-line sales channel, he partnered with the stores to retain their services for performing certain flows, even when product was sold on-line. The Web site is used to make sales of any item to any customers who wish to shop on-line. If Ethan Allen ships directly, the store in the customer's territory receives a 10 percent commission on the purchase (a means of reducing territorial domain conflict). If the store assists (e.g., by delivering, making minor repairs, setting up, or handling returns), it receives a 25 percent sales commission. These commissions maintain the Equity Principle, compensating retailers more for a greater degree of participation in channel flows. In addition, the Web site asks customers if they would like decorating help and refers those interested to the nearest bricks-and-mortar store. In essence, the Ethan Allen Web site supplants only those flows that can be best done on-line, leaving others to the licensed retailers in local areas. It further supports its retailers through lead generation, feeding customers to them for follow-on sales or services. This investment on the company's part in turn obliges the stores to invest in personnel and software to track and follow up on Web site inquiries. The net result is a much higher likelihood that the stores will see the Web site as a complement, not a substitute, to their sales efforts.

Case (d) Conflict Reduction Through Avoidance of Owned On-line Selling: Levi-Strauss[48]

Yet other manufacturers take the strategy one step further and completely avoid selling on-line. Levi-Strauss, the jeans maker, sold its clothing on-line through the 1999 holiday season, but has since then closed its on-line operation completely, announcing that it would sell on-line exclusively through the Web sites of combination retailers JCPenney and Macy's. It claimed that on-line selling was just too expensive to maintain, and beyond this, sales volumes were disappointing from its own on-line site. It continues to operate a Web site, but its main purpose is promotional rather than to close the sale. Its Web site states: "Levi.com has transitioned all on-line sales to select retailer web sites. Levi.com will still be the ultimate hot spot to check out hip new styles, plus product news, TV commercials, and special promotions you won't want to miss. We'll also help you with the where-to-buy option that's best for you! If you would like to purchase Levi's® products on-line, stop by www.jcpenney.com and www.macys.com." Although in general it might be a good strategy for a company like Levi's to sell on-line, if the economic benefits are not strong enough, and other on-line sellers can do as good a job, the manufacturer can be just as well served (and preserve greater channel harmony) by shutting down direct on-line sales operations.

to cooperative advertising money. Only if the reseller advertises a product price at least as high as the MAP, does it qualify for cooperative advertising dollars. This does not restrict the reseller from price promoting the manufacturer's product, but it does punish the reseller for doing so by withholding a payment. This policy can be equally well used either in standard reseller channels or on-line, as a means of reducing the goal conflict under which on-line resellers tend to underprice their bricks-and-mortar counterparts.[49]

In some cases, the move to on-line selling is accompanied by minimal efforts to control resulting conflict. In Channel Sketch 6.4 about airline travel agents, the reductions in commissions paid to travel agents was accompanied by an increasing ability to sell on-line or through other more direct channels. The changes in commissions were tied to the diminished value added by the agents relative to the service travelers could get from other channels, thus reflecting the Equity Principle once again (when an intermediary begins to add *less* value, it should be paid *less*). Part of the reason these lower commissions could stick is precisely that other means of selling, relying on e-commerce technologies, were emerging as viable alternatives to the standard agency channel. Although agents complained and voiced their discontent with every decline in commission fees, they have had little choice but to go along with the changes. In short, the spread of less costly on-line selling capabilities has made it worthwhile to endure some channel conflict with intermediaries in the pursuit of increased channel efficiencies.

In sum, conflict can be generated from any of the major ways in which a manufacturer can choose to sell on-line. In many cases, these conflicts resemble those that are encountered in any dual distribution situation. Various means of controlling the conflicts are used, from avoiding them altogether (by avoiding on-line selling) to investing in other ways in one's bricks-and-mortar reseller channels or using the on-line presence to enhance the marketability of the standard channel. In some cases, it may be worthwhile to let the conflict exist, when on-line selling shows unambiguous benefits on the supply and demand sides. Hybrid channels, with some flows performed on-line by the manufacturer (or third parties) and others performed in bricks-and-mortar outlets, are an emerging solution to the problem of channel conflict due to on-line selling. Such solutions take the best from both the on-line and off-line worlds to offer the consumer the broadest array of service outputs at the minimum cost.

SUMMARY

This chapter discusses how selling through other than standard bricks-and-mortar channels—in particular, catalog selling, direct selling, and electronic channels—can take place.

Catalog retailing remains an important method of selling to consumer end-users. It offers superior spatial convenience to bricks-and-mortar retail stores, although it falls short on the delivery and waiting time service output dimension. Prices at catalog retail outlets may be higher or lower than in standard stores; the price charged must reflect both the convenience offered to the consumer and the consumer's reduced ability to search if not faced with several retail opportunities simultaneously. The growth of catalog retailing is slowing, reflecting a move by catalogers to the on-line selling world. Indeed, one report notes that 1999 will be the last year in which we can easily report separate statistics for catalog and on-line retailing, because so many catalogers have now created on-line presences to augment their catalogs. It is simply no longer possible to distinguish on-line from catalog sales in such sellers' operations.[50]

Direct selling, like catalog selling, avoids the use of bricks-and-mortar stores to distribute product to final consumers. Here, however, the emphasis is on personal selling and relationship marketing. Direct-sales organizations have relatively low costs because they rely on the personal sales effort of their distributors to sell product, rather than on expensive advertising and promotional campaigns. Further, distributors are not employees, so that salary costs are not an issue. Distributors make money through: (1) commissions on the products they sell; (2) markups from wholesale to retail price; and (3) override commissions on the sales of the downline distributors that they recruit. Direct selling is a successful channel in many developing countries, because it does not rely on an established infrastructure of stores or delivery systems. Like catalog retailing, direct selling is slowly moving to the Internet as the largest direct sellers create on-line sales presences alongside their traditional distributor channel.

Electronic commerce has grown by leaps and bounds in recent years, albeit from a very small base. Retail e-channel sales to consumers in 1999 reached only about one percent of all retail sales in the United States, the leading e-commerce country. The Internet is still not the preferred retail outlet for most shoppers. However, the data suggest that in particular categories, such as computer hardware and software, electronic channels will contribute a very significant proportion of all retail sales in coming years. Meanwhile, in B2B markets, various means of electronic commerce (including electronic data interchange, vendor-managed inventory, and continuous replenishment programs) have been in place for several years in many markets, paving the way for a larger presence of electronic commerce than in the consumer arena.

Buying on-line offers superior spatial convenience to buying through a standard store, at least for the initial purchase. It can also offer extensive assortment and variety, thanks to the development of shopping "bots" that act as search engines for many categories of goods. Waiting and delivery time is still an issue with on-line sales of most products, similar to the situation in catalog retailing; except in certain categories, such as downloading software or music, or in financial services or stock trading. Pre- and post-sale customer service varies widely from site to site, with some sites providing copious amounts of information about their products and others acting mostly as a purchasing portal. Prices are generally perceived to be competitive with bricks-and-mortar outlets, although consumers resent the shipping and handling charges that are tacked on to on-line product purchases. In sum, although on-line retailing is not a completely dominant method of buying most consumer products, it offers an attractive alternative for consumers who highly value its spatial convenience and search capabilities.

On-line retailing also provides a great opportunity for free riding, however. Consumers learn to consume presales service at standard stores, then buy on-line, particularly when price differences are significant (as they are for many electronics-related products, for instance). The challenge to many retailers is to retain the sale in the store, after the consumer has benefited from in-store displays and help from store clerks.

Free riding is just one source of conflict that arises when a manufacturer adds an on-line channel to the existing total channel structure. Goal, domain, and perception-of-reality conflicts can all plague these channels. In many cases the conflicts are no different in nature than those found in any dual distribution channel structure, and the techniques used to manage conflict parallel those in standard channel contexts.

E-commerce is here to stay, both for consumer retailing and business-to-business selling. However, it behooves channel managers to think not just about "how to sell on-line" but rather *what flows and functions make the most sense to move on-line*. Just as a distributor is not a channel, nor is a Web site a channel. It relies on the inputs of many other channel members (credit card companies, shippers, etc.) to make the whole e-commerce concept work for the consumer. In the future, varying hybrid channel forms will likely emerge and persist that combine electronic interfaces with the consumer with bricks-and-mortar fulfillment operations and showrooms, to optimize the service output offering to consumers. Pure bricks-and-mortar retailers are likely to survive, but only if they offer a superior combination of service outputs compared to their hybrid counterparts.

Discussion Questions

1. What are the key service outputs offered by a catalog retailer, as opposed to a standard bricks-and-mortar retailer?

2. What are the key service outputs offered by a direct-selling organization channel, as opposed to a standard bricks-and-mortar retailer?

3. If you were a distributor selling in a direct-selling organization, how would you change the way you choose to allocate your time between (a) selling product and (b) recruiting new distributors, if the compensation plan in Figure 14.2 were altered to increase the difference in commission levels between sales categories? For instance, suppose the percentages were not 3 percent, 5 percent, and 7 percent, but 3 percent, 6 percent, and 10 percent?

4. Why do most catalog retailers and many direct-selling organizations believe they need to set up an on-line selling presence? Will an on-line channel (a) increase valued service output provision; (b) reduce the costs of running the channel; (c) increase conflict?

5. Why is business-to-business e-commerce greater in financial value than business-to-consumer electronic commerce?

6. Suppose you need to buy some flowers for your mother for Mother's Day. Consider two possibilities: (a) You live near by and will see her on Mother's Day; (b) you live far away from your mother and won't see her on Mother's Day. You are evaluating how to buy flowers for her—whether through your local florist (who can get an order out either locally or to faraway cities) or on-line through a provider such as ftd.com or flowers.com. Describe the differences in your decision process depending on whether you are in situation (a) or (b), and how you would end up buying the flowers.

7. Is on-line retailing cheaper than operating a bricks-and-mortar chain of stores? What factors would you have to measure to answer this question if (a) you were starting a retail operation from scratch, or (b) you had a preexisting bricks-and-mortar chain in place?

8. In what ways is an on-line retail operation (a) substitutable for and (b) complementary to a bricks-and-mortar operation?

9. Some manufacturers choose not to sell directly on-line because of threats from their retailers that, if they do, the retailers will drop these suppliers' lines from their stores. This is an example of those exerting coercive power over the suppliers. Under what conditions (market, competitive, demand side) should a supplier accommodate this demand of the retailer?

Notes

1. Donald R. Katz, *The Big Store: Inside the Crisis and Revolution at Sears* (New York: Viking, 1987) p. 9.

2. Michelle A. Morganosky, "Mail Order Direct Marketing in the United States and the United Kingdom; Responses to Changing Market Conditions," *Journal of Business Research*, 45, no. 3 (July 1999); Michael D. Devine and Faye Musselman, "E-tailing Gaining Steam, but Print Catalogs Still Tops," *HFN*, 73, no. 49 (November 29, 1999), p. 6. However, "State of the Industry: Nonstore Retailing," *Chain Store Age State of the Industry Supplement*, August 1999, p. 29A, reports U.S. retail catalog sales increasing to $98 billion in 1998, with computer retailers accounting for over $27 billion of the total.

3. Laura M. Beaudry, "Old Worlds Still to Conquer," *Catalog Age*, 15, no. 2 (February 1998), p. 21.

4. Morganosky, "Mail Order Direct Marketing."

5. Helen Allen, "Taming the Wild Frontiers Overseas," *Catalog Age*, 14, no. 7 (July 1997), pp. 219–20.

6. Paul Miller, "Big Books, Redefined," *Catalog Age*, 16, no. 12 (November 1999), p. 5.

7. Laura M. Beaudry, "The Catalog Age 1999 Consumer Catalog Shopping Survey," *Catalog Age*, 16, no. 6 (May 1999), pp. A5–A18.

8. Eric Malmborg, "Improve Customer Information—A Key to Catalog Success," *Direct Marketing*, 62, no. 2 (June 1999), pp. 64–66.

9. See, for example, Curt Barry, "The 10 Best Operations Innovations," *Catalog Age*, 16, no. 7 (June 1999), pp. 165–68.

10. Connie Robbins Gentry, "Reducing the Cost of Returns," *Chain Store Age*, 75, no. 10 (October 1999), pp. 124–26.

11. Mark Del Franco, "Here, or Over There?" *Catalog Age*, 16, no. 3 (March 1, 1999), p. 43.

12. Kelly Shermach, "Retail Catalogs Designed to Boost In-Store Sales," *Marketing News*, July 3, 1995, p. 1; Laura Bird, "Beyond Mail Order: Catalogs Now Sell Image, Advice," *Wall Street Journal*, July 29, 1997, pp. B1, B5.

13. This definition is taken from the Direct Selling Association's Web site (www.wfdsa.org); it is very similar to a definition provided in Robert A. Peterson and Thomas R. Wotruba, "What Is Direct Selling?—Definition, Perspectives, and Research Agenda," *Journal of Personal Selling & Sales Management*, 16, no. 4 (fall 1996), pp. 1–16. The Direct Selling Association (DSA) is a U.S. trade association of direct-selling organizations, including such well-known multilevel marketing organizations as Amway (soaps, detergents, and many other home products) and Mary Kay (cosmetics), and party-plan organizations such as Tupperware (home storage) and Discovery Toys (children's educational toys). The DSA serves as the Secretariat for the World Federation of Direct Selling Organizations (WFDSA), which is the superorganization of all national DSAs around the world. The WFDSA has over 50 national DSAs as members.

14. Peterson and Wotruba, "What Is Direct Selling?"

15. The example is drawn from Anne T. Coughlan and Kent Grayson, "Network Marketing Organizations: Compensation Plans, Retail Network Growth, and Profitability," *International Journal of Research in Marketing*, 15 (1998), pp. 401–26.

16. See Coughlan and Grayson, ibid., for a model showing these effects.

17. Other names for pyramid schemes include Ponzi schemes, chain letters, chain selling, money games, referral selling, and investment lotteries. See, for example, the World Federation of Direct Selling Associations Web site (www.wfdsa.org), and a consumer alert on the U.S. Federal Trade Commission's Web site (www.ftc.gov/bcp/conline/pubs/alerts/pyrdairt.htm) entitled "Profits in Pyramid Schemes? Don't Bank on It."

18. Personal communication with Richard Bartlett, vice chairman, Mary Kay Corporation, December 1999. See also Richard C. Bartlett, *The Direct Option* (College Station, TX: Texas A&M University Press, 1994), chap. 12.

19. For a fascinating set of profiles of successful direct selling companies, see Bartlett, *The Direct Option*.

20. Rachel Beck, "Amway Brings Its Direct-Selling Model On-line," *The Associated Press State & Local Wire*, March 3, 1999; Dennis Berman, "Is the Bell Tolling for Door-to-Door Selling?" *BusinessWeek E.BIZ*, November 1, 1999, pp. EB58–EB60; and personal communication with Richard Bartlett, vice chairman, Mary Kay Corporation, December 1999.

21. Iconocast.com, "Internet at a Glance," data from November 1999 Nielsen Netratings.

22. Catherine Finamore, "The Connected Consumer," *E-Retail Intelligence Update*, PricewaterhouseCoopers, November 1999, p. 7.

23. Iconocast.com, "Internet at a Glance," data from October 1999 IDC. The forecast for the year 2002 is not much more rosy: Of a forecasted 61.3 million on-line households, a predicted 49.6 million will still be using a modem to dial up to the Internet.

24. In a press conference on March 2, 2000, U.S. Secretary of Commerce William M. Daley announced the first U.S. government measurement of on-line retail sales. Its figure was $5.3 billion in the United States between October and December 1999 (0.64 percent of all retail sales), considerably less than the $10 billion figure that many consulting firms have publicized. Daley emphasized in his comments, however, that the U.S. Department of Commerce numbers are based on *nonservice* retail sales, and hence exclude sales of travel, financial, or other services. This measure is based on the same set of businesses that the Department of Commerce uses to measure regular retail sales, and hence has more comparability with other U.S. government numbers. The U.S. Department of Commerce will continue to issue quarterly reports on consumer e-retail spending and also plans a business-to-business accounting starting in early 2001. The full text of Daley's press release is available at the Web site of the U.S. Department of Commerce (www.doc.gov).

25. "Year-End Results of Shop.org/BCG Tracking Study Shows 300% Surge in U.S. Internet Sales During Holiday Shopping Season," shop.org Research, December 29, 1999 press release; "Shopping Around the Web," *The Economist*, Febuary 26, 2000, pp. 5–6, E-commerce Survey; and Kristin Allstadt, "Spinning the Web," *E-Retail Intelligence Update*, PricewaterhouseCoopers, January 2000, pp. 9–12.

26. "Shopping Around the Web."

27. Iconocast.com, "Internet at a Glance," data from November 1999 Forrester Research.

28. Robert L. Simison, Fara Warner, and Gregory L. White, "GM, Ford, DaimlerChrysler to Create a Single Firm to Supply Auto Parts," *Wall Street Journal*, February 28, 2000, on-line edition; and Calmetta Y. Coleman, "Sears, Carrefour Plan Web Supply Exchange," *Wall Street Journal*, February 29, 2000, p. A4.

29. "Shopping Around the Web."

30. Kristin Allstadt, "Spinning the Web," *E-Retail Intelligence Update*, PriceWaterhouseCoopers, February 2000, pp. 11–14.

31. The following discussion of retail e-commerce outside the United States is based on "First America, then the World," *The Economist*, February 26, 2000, pp. 49–53, E-commerce Survey.

32. For example, a $27.95 computer software program could be shipped for delivery via Airborne Express the next day within the continental United States for a $9.95 delivery charge. Or, the shopper could choose UPS ground service, with a three to five business-day delivery lag, for a $6.70 delivery charge, only slightly lower. By contrast, the same item shipped from Amazon.com would not be delivered the next day, even if overnight delivery were chosen—but rather overnight, once the order was packed (thus, delivery would take two to three days). This service, through UPS next-day air, would cost $11.00 plus $2.99 per item; or, standard shipping (three to five business-day delivery lag after the order is packed) would cost $4.00 plus $0.99 per item.

33. Allstadt, "Spinning the Web," *E-Retail Intelligence Update*, PricewaterhouseCoopers, January 2000, pp. 9–12.

34. Simison, Warner, and White, "GM, Ford, DaimlerChrysler to Create a Single Firm to Supply Auto Parts."

35. Robert Guy Matthews, Karen Jacobs, Susan Warren, and Dean Starkman, "Industries, from Steel to Chemicals, Say One Internet Site May Not Meet Needs," *Wall Street Journal*, February 28, 2000, on-line edition.

36. Joseph Alba, John Lynch, Barton Weitz, et al., "Interactive Home Shopping: Consumer, Retailer, and Manufacturer Incentives to Participate in Electronic Marketplaces," *Journal of Marketing*, 61 (July 1997), pp. 38–53.

37. Catherine Finamore, "The Connected Consumer," *E-Retail Intelligence Update*, PricewaterhouseCoopers, February 2000, pp. 7–10.

38. Arlene Weintraub and Robert D. Hof, "For on-line Pet Stores, It's Dog-Eat-Dog," *BusinessWeek*, March 6, 2000, pp. 78–80.

39. Anne T. Coughlan, Jonathan D. Hibbard, and Kent Grayson, "The West Bend Company Case," J. L. Kellogg Graduate School of Management, Northwestern University, 1991.

40. Simison, Warner, and White, "GM, Ford, DaimlerChrysler to Create a Single Firm."

41. Geoff Wissman, "E-Retail Economics," *Hot Topics*, PricewaterhouseCoopers, February 2000, pp. 4–5.

42. For an excellent treatment of the decision to go online, see Kirthi Kalyanam and Shelby McIntyre, "Hewlett-Packard Consumer Products Business Organization: Distribution Through E*Commerce Channels" case, Leavey School of Business, Santa Clara University, 1999.

43. Simison, Warner, and White, "GM, Ford, DaimlerChrysler to Create a Single Firm"; Matthews, Jacobs, Warren, and Starkman, "Industries, from Steel to Chemicals"; Jeffrey Ball, Gregory L. White, and Mark Yost, "Parts Suppliers Worry About Effect of Centralized System on Profits," *Wall Street Journal,* February 28, 2000, on-line edition; Coleman, "Sears, Carrefour Plan Web Supply Exchange"; and Susan Chandler, "Sears Is on E-supply Bandwagon," *Chicago Tribune,* February 29, 2000, sec. 3, pp. 1, 5.

44. Geoff Wissman, "E-Retail Economics," *Hot Topics,* PricewaterhouseCoopers, February 2000.

45. See Allstadt, "Spinning the Web," *E-Retail Intelligence Update,* PricewaterhouseCoopers, January 2000, pp. 9–12.

46. Bob Tedeschi, "Web Sales Can Hurt Brick-and-Mortar Profits," *Chicago Tribune,* January 10, 2000, sec. 4, p. 6.

47. James R. Hagerty, "Ethan Allen's Revolutionary Path to the Web," *Wall Street Journal,* July 29, 2000, pp. B1, B11.

48. An interesting analysis of Levi's decision can be found in Anne Standley, "What Went Wrong with Levi's Web Strategy," November 3, 1999, on the Web site of Mainspring Communications, Inc. (an Internet consultancy) (www.mainspring.com/analysis). See also the Levi-Strauss Web site, which has a window explaining the services that will be available on-line and offers one-click access to on-line Levi's sales at either JCPenney or Macy's. See www.levi.com Web site for the quote.

49. A discussion of the MAP policy can be found in the Kalyanam and McIntyre, "Hewlett-Packard Consumer Products Business Organization: Distribution Through E*Commerce Channels" case.

50. Karl Haller, "The End of E-Retailing," *E-Retail Intelligence Update,* PriceWaterhouseCoopers, February 2000, pp. 1–3.

15 Wholesaling

LEARNING OBJECTIVES

After reading this chapter, you will:

- Distinguish three broad categories of institutions that constitute the wholesaling sector
- Describe the nature of an independent wholesaler-distributor's value added and explain why this sector is growing
- Sketch mechanisms by which channel members become a federation to offer exceptional services while cutting their costs
- Pinpoint the major distinctions between a wholesaler voluntary group and a dealer cooperative, and relate this to the value they provide their members
- Explain why consolidation is common in wholesaling, and sketch the manufacturer's possible responses to a consolidation wave
- Sketch the ways in which wholesaling is being altered by electronic commerce
- Contrast sales agents and wholesaler-distributors in the ways that matter to a manufacturer
- Explain why the future for wholesaler-distributors is optimistic

Wholesaling (wholesale trade, wholesale distribution) refers to business establishments that do *not* sell products to a significant degree to *ultimate household consumers*. Instead, these businesses sell products primarily to *other businesses:*

retailers, merchants, contractors, industrial users, institutional users, and commercial users. Wholesale businesses sell physical inputs and products to other businesses. Wholesaling is closely associated with tangible goods. However, these entities create their value added through providing services, that is, channel flows. Although that value added is quite real, very little is tangible about wholesaling: It is the epitome of a service industry. In a channel stretching from the manufacturer to the final household user, wholesaling is an intermediate step.

This chapter is about the institutions that wholesale; that is, provide physical goods as inputs to other businesses. The rest of this book covers in depth what they do and how to deal with them. This chapter is about the *nature of these institutions* and the unique *challenges* they face.[1] What is behind such an important sector of the world's largest economy?

This chapter focuses on wholesaler-distributors, the largest and most prevalent companies in business-to-business channels. First we explore the nature of the wholesaler-distributor sector, with descriptions of how it creates value added. Then we describe innovative ways of banding together to provide exceptional services *and* lower channel costs. Although these methods (called adaptive channels) are novel, there is every reason to believe they will become more widespread. Next, we examine contractual arrangements to achieve economies of scale (voluntary groups and cooperatives). This leads to a discussion of the wave of consolidation that is altering wholesaling in many industries. Then we explore causes and effects of wholesale consolidation and the possible responses of manufacturers. The chapter then turns to informed speculation on the future of the wholesaling sector, and closes by returning to that part of the wholesaling sector that is not covered by independent wholesaler-distributors. These are the options of vertical integration and outside sales agents.

This chapter will refer heavily to statistics from the United States. These are not unrepresentative of other developed economies. In emerging economies, the size and activity of the wholesale sector is more difficult to document, but it is surely substantial and varied.

AN OVERVIEW OF THE WHOLESALING SECTOR

Wholesaler-Distributors

Many different institutions perform the channel flows in business-to-business marketing channels. Wholesaler-distributors are the largest and most significant participants.

They are independently owned and operated firms that buy and sell products to which they have taken ownership. Generally, wholesaler-distributors operate one or more warehouses in which they receive and inventory goods for later reshipping. In aggregate, wholesale distribution contributed 5.8 percent of U.S. national income in 1997. Independent wholesaler-distributors have consistently accounted for roughly 1 in every 20 jobs in the United States throughout the past century. The industry is represented by the National Association of Wholesaler-Distributors (NAW), a federation of 112 national wholesale distribution line-of-trade associations and 45 state, local, and regional associations. Table 15.1 lists some sources of information on wholesaler-distributors and on the wholesaling industry in general.

TABLE 15.1
Some Sources of Information About the Wholesaling Sector

General Industry Information

- http://wholesaledistribution.services.ibm.com (a general information site sponsored by IBM Corporation)
- http://ww3.knowledgespace.com/Wholesale (a general information site sponsored by Arthur Andersen)
- The National Association of Wholesaler-Distributors (NAW) operates two Web sites:
  www.NAWpubs.org (on-line bookstore of NAW reports)
  www.NAWmeetings.org (upcoming NAW-sponsored events)

Industry Consultants
The Web sites of all of these companies have current information and articles about wholesale distribution.

- Pembroke Consulting, Inc.
- Merrifield Consulting Group, Inc.
- Indian River Consulting Group
- Frank Lynn & Associates
- Michael E. Workman & Associates

Total U.S. sales of wholesaler-distributors in 1998 were approximately $2.6 trillion. As a result, they are the largest and most important of the organizations counted in wholesale trade. As this is the largest and best-documented category, it is the focus of this chapter.

There is a distinction between wholesalers and distributors, which we shall ignore. However, it is worth noting that the terms have different roots and at one time represented distinct sectors in themselves. Typically, the term *wholesaler* usually refers to a company that resells products to *another intermediary*, whereas the term *distributor* refers to a company that resells product to the customer *that will use the product*. Thus, a pharmaceutical wholesaler resells prescription drugs to a retail pharmacy, which then resells the product to a household consumer. An industrial maintenance, repair, and operating (MRO) distributor sells products such as cutting tools to an industrial customer that may use the tools in its manufacturing facilities.

The reader is warned that terminology varies from industry to industry. For example, distributors of printing paper are called "merchants" and distributors of automotive after-market products are called "jobbers." Further, the terminology can vary from market to market within an industry. Regardless of terminology, the critical point is that wholesaler-distributors have the title to the goods they resell, the authority to set price. They know the identity of the next buyer in the channel, which they may or may not share with the manufacturer. Wholesaler-distributors are defined by their performance of the channel flow of ownership.[2]

The Wholesaler-Distributor's Role in the Supply Chain

Supply chains can be complex, involving many participants, intermediaries, and service providers to facilitate the movement of goods and services from sourcing to consumption. Thus, the channel functions and activities of wholesaler-distributors can, and often are, performed by other supply chain participants. For example, *manufacturers' sales branches* are captive wholesaling operations that are owned and operated by manufacturers.[3] Many also have sales offices to perform certain selling and marketing functions. These locations do not take physical possession of inventory and may work with independent wholesaler-distributors. Customers, particularly larger multi-establishment retail firms, often perform the functions of wholesale distribution. These represent the vertical integration mode of governing the channel. Unfortunately, limited comparable data exist about the overall magnitude or importance of these other activities.

Agents, brokers, and *commission agents* buy or sell products for commissions or fees, but do not take ownership to the products they represent. These are important channels, particularly for service industries, where there is nothing to inventory, therefore nothing to own. By convention, agents in service industries are not considered as part of the wholesale trade because no goods are involved. Wholesaling is historically related to tangibles.

Many other types of companies perform supply chain activities in a marketing channel. For example, the transportation and warehousing industry has almost $350 billion in annual sales.

Third-party logistics providers and value-added warehousing companies are also vying to perform the functions of wholesaler-distributors. Consider Ryder Integrated Logistics, Inc. (RIL), a subsidiary of Ryder Systems. The RIL division provides integrated logistics support of its clients' entire supply chains, from inbound raw materials supply through finished goods distribution. Its services include the following activities:

- Logistics system design
- Provision of vehicles and equipment maintenance
- Provision of drivers
- Warehouse management (including cross-docking and flow-through distribution)
- Transportation management
- Vehicle dispatch
- Inbound and outbound just-in-time and merge-in-transit delivery[4]

Unlike wholesaler-distributors, third-party logistics providers do not take title (legal possession) for the products that they handle. These supply chain companies charge their customers on an activity-based, fee-for-service basis in place of the traditional sell-side markup pricing model of wholesaler-distributors. See Chapter 16 (logistics and supply chain management) for more on these topics.

The Growth and Influence of Wholesaler-Distributors

In the United States, wholesaler-distributors' sales have been growing faster than overall economic growth during the recent economic expansion. The actual share of channel volume handled by wholesaler-distributors varies substantially by industry.

Consider the $450 billion industrial distribution channel. We can distinguish between OEM (original equipment manufacture) products and MRO products.

Although the two sets of products are complementary in usage, the distribution channels and product makeups are distinct. OEM products are the capital investments in machinery and supplies used to produce the customers' end product. This includes such items as transmission belts, control computers, and hydraulic pumps. MRO products are those needed to keep the OEM machinery functional and productive, and are short-term expenses, rather than long-term investments. This includes such items as adhesives, abrasives, gaskets, seals, and power tools. Approximately 80 percent of MRO products as compared with less than 50 percent of OEM products are sold through wholesaler-distributors.

The importance of wholesaler-distributors is striking, partly in and of itself and partly because it is not apparent from the business press. Reports commonly offer pessimistic predictions of the sector's future, based on a gloomy reading of its past. To some extent, this pessimism prevails because the sector in the United States is well organized into active trade associations. These bodies commission regular reports focusing the membership on how it can improve operations and cautioning against complacency.

But a more fundamental reason for misplaced pessimism is that the wholesale sector has been subject to a massive wave of consolidation, industry by industry, for several decades. We examine some of the reasons in a later section. For now, suffice it to say that the rapid disappearance of two-thirds of the companies in an industry creates an atmosphere of panic and dread. Yet this is unfounded because most firms in a consolidation wave in the wholesale sector exit by being acquired, *not* by going bankrupt or being shut down. The acquirers are large, healthy businesses that help account for the steady progression of the wholesale sector's share of business over the decades.[5] Consolidation strengthens wholesaler-distributors even while reducing their number.

This said, there were 341,376 wholesale distribution firms operating 414,836 establishments in 1992 in the United States. Only 301,167 of those firms were operating during the entire Census year. This demonstrates a feature of wholesaling: When an industry is fragmented, mobility barriers in wholesaling are low. Firms enter and exit easily. As will be seen, this situation reverses after wholesale consolidation.

In 1997, preliminary estimates indicate 440,211 establishments, an increase of 29 percent over 1992. The majority of wholesaler-distributors are very small companies operating in a single location (establishment). *Ninety-two percent of wholesaler-distributors* had annual sales of less than $10 million in 1992, the most recent year for which complete data are available. These companies *represented 25 percent of total wholesaler-distributor sales*. In contrast, the largest companies with sales greater than $250 million represented *0.2 percent of total firms but 37 percent of sales*. (It is estimated that these large firms represented 40 percent of sales in 1998.)

The polarity between the smallest and largest firms has been growing over time. In 1982, wholesaler-distributors with sales of less than $10 million represented a slightly higher proportion of total wholesale distribution firms (94 percent), but a much greater percentage of sales (31 percent).

Another important disparity between the large and small firms derives from their geographic scope of operation. In 1992, those with sales less than $10 million operate in one or two locations, whereas the largest operate at an average of 29 locations.

The disparity in establishment size is even greater. Wholesaler-distributors with total firm sales greater than $250 million operated establishments that average $38.5

million in sales, roughly 10 times as large as the establishments operated by firms with sales below $10 million. More current data are not yet available.

Despite these consolidation trends, traditional measures of industry concentration are low relative to most manufacturing sectors. To some extent, this low level of concentration reflects the fact that *competition among wholesaler-distributors traditionally occurs in geographically distinct markets*. A wholesaler-distributor can dominate one region of a country, yet account for a very small proportion of national sales. Thus, the apparent fragmentation of this distribution channel may not accurately reflect the true nature of concentration in any single region.

This sets up an issue discussed in Chapter 8: Power is a property of a relationship, not of a business. Paradoxically, this means a very large and reputable manufacturer, such as Monsanto or DuPont, may not be more powerful than a single wholesaler-distributor *in a given market*. Indeed, such a supplier may be less powerful: Customer loyalty may mean that the supplier cannot go around a downstream channel member to reach a territory effectively. For example, some distributors of pesticides, herbicides, and farm equipment enjoy excellent relations with the farmers in their markets, many of whom will not do business without going through the distributor.

A Sketch by Industry

Sales growth for wholesaler-distributors in the United States has been very strong in recent years, exceeding overall economic growth. The *compound annual growth rate (CAGR)* for durable good wholesale distribution from 1993 to 1998 was 6.6 percent. For nondurable wholesale distribution during the same period it was 4.5 percent.

These strong aggregate growth rates indicate clearly that wholesaler-distributors have been an attractive channel for manufacturers and customers during the economic expansion of the 1990s. *And they have been willing to pay for the value added they receive*. According to the Department of Commerce, gross profit margins have been remarkably steady for wholesaler-distributors at approximately 21 percent of sales in each of the past 10 years. The partition of their activities by industry is shown in Figures 15.1 and 15.2.

WHAT THE INDEPENDENT WHOLESALE SECTOR OFFERS: THE ESSENTIAL TASKS

What is this value added by the wholesale sector? Wholesalers perform each of the eight generic channel flows (Chapter 4, Figure 4.5). They take physical possession of the goods, take title (ownership), promote the product to prospective customers, negotiate transactions, finance their operations, risk their capital (often in giving credit to both suppliers and customers), process orders, and handle payments. In general, they manage the flow of information both ways: upstream to the supplier and downstream to other channel members and to prospective customers. And in so doing, they provide utility upstream and downstream in a variety of ways. One reason that wholesaler-distributors have increased their share of total wholesale sales is that they can perform these functions more effectively and efficiently than can either manufacturers or customers.

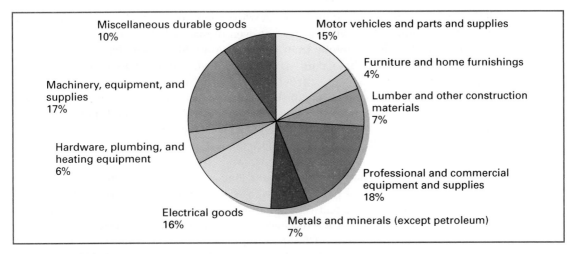

Miscellaneous durable goods
10%

Motor vehicles and parts and supplies
15%

Furniture and home furnishings
4%

Machinery, equipment, and supplies
17%

Lumber and other construction materials
7%

Hardware, plumbing, and heating equipment
6%

Professional and commercial equipment and supplies
18%

Electrical goods
16%

Metals and minerals (except petroleum)
7%

FIGURE 15.1 **Durable Goods: U.S. Industry Shares or Wholesaler-Distribution Activity**

Source: U.S. Department of Commerce, Bureau of the Census, from Adam J. Fein, "Wholesaling," in *U.S. Industry and Trade Outlook 2000* (New York: DRI/McGraw-Hill, p. 5).

This generalization, of course, varies from one economy to another. Japan is noted for very long channels, with multiple wholesalers passing goods several times between manufacturers and the final point of consumption. Many of these wholesalers add margin but little value. Beginning in the 1990s, the wholesale sector in Japan is steadily

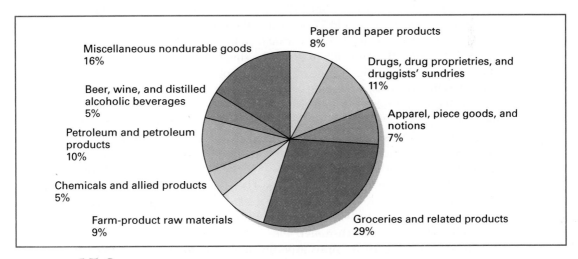

Miscellaneous nondurable goods
16%

Paper and paper products
8%

Drugs, drug proprietries, and druggists' sundries
11%

Beer, wine, and distilled alcoholic beverages
5%

Apparel, piece goods, and notions
7%

Petroleum and petroleum products
10%

Chemicals and allied products
5%

Farm-product raw materials
9%

Groceries and related products
29%

FIGURE 15.2 **Nondurable Goods: U.S. Industry Share or Wholesaler-Distribution Activity**

Source: U.S. Department of Commerce, Bureau of the Census, from Adam J. Fein, "Wholesaling," in *U.S. Industry and Trade Outlook 2000* (New York: DRI/McGraw-Hill, p. 6).

shrinking. Channels are getting shorter and wholesalers are being cut out. The first to go are secondary and tertiary wholesalers, but even primary wholesalers are giving way as more retailers purchase directly from manufacturers. Shortening channels—and the subsequent squeeze on wholesalers—is a response to increasing price consciousness by Japanese consumers.[6]

The size and economic vitality of the wholesale sector belies the fact that many of these functions are invisible to the buyer, who takes them for granted. Both manufacturer and customer often understate three great challenges of wholesaling: doing the job *correctly* (no errors), doing the job *effectively* (a maximum of service) and doing the job *efficiently* (low costs).

The history of the pharmaceutical wholesaling industry in the United States offers a good example of these three points.[7] The wholesale drug trade can be traced back to the mid-1700s. Europe already had retail pharmacies, but the colonies did not. Medical practitioners both prescribed and dispensed medicine. Wholesalers arose to meet their demand for medicines imported from Europe. They were also integrated forward— some of them held a few retail apothecaries—and backward—manufacturing drugs from indigenous plants.

In the nineteenth century, pharmacies arose that were independent of physicians. These, in turn, grew with an increase in hospitals. The wholesaling industry grew to serve this burgeoning retail industry. Drug wholesalers were local and numerous. They stayed in the sector, no longer integrating forward or backward.

From 1929 to 1977, the industry entered a phase in which larger wholesalers arose to offer regional, even national coverage, not only of pharmaceuticals but also of health and beauty aids. But apart from two large national firms, most were smaller, regional firms operated by the original founding family out of one location.

From 1978 to 1996, this old industry went through a period of dramatic consolidation. Drug wholesalers went from 147 firms down to 53, mostly by acquisition. At the end of this period, 6 firms held 77 percent of the national market.

Why did it take so long to discover such enormous economies of scale in this industry? The answer is the difficulty of doing the simple job of wholesaling drugs correctly, effectively, and efficiently. The heart of drug wholesaling, and much of wholesaling in general, is the banal task of *picking*.

Picking means taking from a shelf the items the customer needs and assembling them for shipment. Pharmacies typically order frequently, in a pattern of a few units of many different items. The variety of the units is substantial, with many stockkeeping units (SKUs). Because the products are medical, doing the job correctly—picking exactly the right item in the right quantity—is critical. For generations, this job was done by people, picking from warehouse shelves. There are few economies of scale in picking millions of items to move from a pallet to a warehouse loading dock to a storage shelf (taking inventory from the supplier), then picking those items from the shelves to put into a box for an individual customer.

Beginning in the 1950s, firms experimented with different ways to do the picking better and did find some. But the potential of massively restructuring the task via information technology (IT) and automation is what really changed the fundamentals of the industry. In the 1977 to 1996 period, firms experimented furiously with IT and automation. Which approach was best was not all clear (to this day, multiple methods are in use—there is no standard). A number of firms bet all their resources on one approach or another and went out of business when their bets turned out to be wrong.

The winners changed so many aspects of their operations that they became unrecognizable. On the operations side, they changed not only their picking technology but also order processing, billing, inventory control, delivery route scheduling, and tracking huge inventory movement through warehouses. They developed electronic links with suppliers, replacing hundreds of clerks with their ordering innovations.

On the demand side, wholesalers also made massive changes, profiting from IT. For their customers, they developed bar coding, scanning, and electronic order systems with direct data entry, replacing the salesperson who wrote down the pharmacist's order and the clerk who entered it. Wholesalers created systems that allowed their customers, the pharmacies, to offer computerized accounts receivable and credit (charge accounts) to *their* customers, services the pharmacies could never have been able to afford otherwise. Using the information thus obtained, wholesalers also offered detailed advice about what inventory to hold and how to display it (planograms), and updated prices quickly.

In short, technology made it possible to change *everything* and very rapidly. Acquiring firms were rushing to achieve the size needed to amortize their huge investments. Firms that sold out were seeking to avoid making those same investments. And the freedom of action that mergers and acquisitions create allowed a few big firms to create an astonishing degree of organizational change. The winners used technology to do the job right (fewer errors in picking, the key task), do it effectively (with swift and complete service to pharmacies), and do it efficiently (at lower cost). This is how an industry took 200 years to grow large—and then only 20 years to consolidate.

INNOVATIVE WAYS TO DELIVER VALUE IN WHOLESALING

Wholesaler-distributors keep goods on hand that customers need and have them accessible instantly. That availability very often makes the wholesaler-distributor a backup for, and an extension of, the customer's own inventory system. In breakdown emergencies and in cases of other unplanned repairs or maintenance, distributors are an invaluable resource for supplying products that minimize downtime. A trend in wholesaling is to find innovative ways to respond to such emergencies *while cutting costs!* This section covers some ways to accomplish this extraordinary feat.

The key is for one business to take the lead to organize *federations* of businesses. These federations are based on making progressive, cooperative arrangements with other channel members, with all elements—the nature of assistance, the procedures for providing it, and the appropriate compensation—all defined *in advance*.[8] Such arrangements have the potential to cut costs, often by 15 percent to 20 percent, while improving service and opening new business opportunities. The common feature of these arrangements is that, by cooperating, the players reduce *redundant* pools of inventory and duplicate service operations. These adaptive practices are being developed by Japanese, European, and U.S. corporations, among others. They are not common, as yet. We now detail some of the prototypes led by wholesalers or by manufacturers.

Wholesaler-Led Initiatives

An example of these *new adaptive channels* is the growth of alliance (or consortium) relationships—wholesaler-distributors pooling resources to create a new, separate organization for joint action.[9] These alliances now exist in almost every industry and can become very large. For example, Affiliated Distributors is one of the largest distribution alliances in North America, comprised of 283 independent wholesaler-distributors with over $12 billion in aggregate sales.

One such alliance is led by four wholesalers. The consortium, the Intercore group, sells machine tools. Each of the four distributors who formed it has difficulty providing timely, high-quality service to large customers on large contracts—those most likely to have an emergency and to demand exceptional service. Each distributor in the consortium refers business it has trouble handling to Intercore, which is largely an administrative operation staffed by personnel sent by each distributor. Intercore draws on the resources of all four distributors (including their inventories, engineers, and other service personnel) to service these customers, and has the ability to call on each distributor to demand the help it needs. Intercore sends invoices and collects payments in its own name. Its profits are then distributed to the owners (the four distributors) via dividends.

Alliances and consortiums represent an intermediate form of organization that lies somewhere between two extremes of operational integration. At one extreme, wholesaler-distributors in an industry can interact through loosely knit alliances, such as a trade association. These groups do not link their members together in any formal manner except for collective actions that benefit the entire group. A wholesaler-distributor can fairly easily reverse commitment and participation in such a group. At the other extreme, a group of distributors can come together through mergers and acquisitions—the "visible hand" of equity ownership and control that meshes the operations, organization, and culture of multiple wholesaler-distributors.

Another way for downstream channel members to create their organizer is through a *holding company*. For example, Otra is a Dutch company holding 70 wholesalers of electrical products. One of these firms, BLE, excels in service and training. Otra uses BLE to provide training programs and materials for all the other wholesalers in the group. It has become so proficient that it also offers training to some of the group's suppliers! And due to BLE's focus on the market, not on the producer, these programs are more thorough and less biased than the programs suppliers put on themselves.

Integrated Supply

Integrated supply, a more sophisticated type of customer–distributor relationship, is changing wholesale distribution in industrial markets.[10] In an integrated supply arrangement, a customer gives a single wholesaler-distributor (or a selected group of wholesaler-distributors) *all* of its business in a particular product category or categories. In exchange, the distributor agrees to provide a high level of service on the entire product mix at set prices. Alternatively, it may agree to cost-plus product pricing in combination with a service management fee. In 1997, 12 percent of large-plant procurement of industrial products in the United States went through integrated supply arrangements.[11]

Unlike supply chain solutions that are imposed from above, such as the efficient consumer response movement in the grocery industry, these new relationship arrangements have sprung up organically by channel partners acting in their own best interests. Large customers face enormous organizational costs for purchasing the lowest cost, most frequently used items. They essentially look for a complete outsourcing of the procurement function to the merchant wholesale distribution channel. Larger customers attempt to minimize their total acquisition costs by reducing the supplier base, shrinking internal purchasing staffs, and applying supply chain management technologies, such as electronic data interchange (EDI), to reduce inventory.

Integrated supply can be carried out by a single distributor. But the customer's demands are so great that it is not unusual to combine to create some sort of federation of firms led by a wholesaler. An example is Grainger Integrated Supply Operations (GISO), a division of W. W. Grainger, a large broad-line industrial distributor, is complex: It draws on its own internal sourcing group, plus a set of specialty suppliers with which it has strategic relationships, plus Grainger's traditional distribution business.

GISO meets the obligations of its integrated service contracts in a stylized way. When it receives an order, it goes on-line to fill it from Grainger. Failing that, GISO turns to its suppliers. These suppliers operate from contracts that make them participants in GISO. They pay an annual fee, a fee per transaction, and logistics costs. Their contracts specify which products they will provide, and they set the price. GISO pays them immediately, then invoices and collects payment itself.

Failing Grainger, then failing the participating suppliers, GISO turns to its own internal sourcing group. This group specializes in concocting, then implementing, innovative solutions to bizarre problems, such as how to protect the builders of the Alaska Oil Pipeline from attacks by bears.

Manufacturer-Led Initiatives

Adaptive channels need one party to take the initiative, to act as organizer. We have focused so far on wholesalers, who create such mechanisms as a consortium, a holding company, or a division. Manufacturers also take the initiative to organize distributors to pool their abilities.

An example is Volvo GM Heavy Truck Corporation, which sells commercial trucks and repair parts in the United States via truck dealers and its own regional warehouses. Dealers reported they were losing lucrative repair business because they couldn't provide consistent, timely repairs. The problem was stockouts of the right parts. Yet, the channel collectively carried huge inventories. Via market research, Volvo GM learned that dealers couldn't predict the nature of demand for emergency roadside repairs and didn't know what to stock. Truck downtime is so expensive that truck owners would shop competing dealers to find substitute parts, rather than wait for an authorized Volvo GM dealer to get the right part.

Volvo GM addressed the problem by assuming more of the inventory flow itself and by setting up a delivery service, for which it bills its dealers. The supplier closed three warehouses, then built a massive new warehouse, stocking every part, located near the FedEx hub in Memphis, Tennessee. This is a rather obscure airport, but Volvo GM made a FedEx-specific investment, thereby taking on risk. The supplier set up a mechanism for dealers to call for the precise part they need and get it by FedEx the same day. Dealers are billed for the service, but pass it on to customers, who are price insensitive in the face of roadside emergencies.

The result is more business for the supplier and its dealers, and a sharp drop in inventory costs, more than offsetting the sharp rise in express delivery charges.

This solution is centralized: It all passes through Volvo GM. A decentralized solution is demonstrated by Okuma, a Japanese machine tool manufacturer. Okuma operates two of its own warehouses, electronically linked to 46 distributors. In addition, Okuma links the distributors to each other and facilitates drawing on each other's inventories. The company's electronic system creates 48 sources (2 warehouses, 46 distributors) for any tool.

The Requirements for Innovative Wholesale Service

These success stories, whether led by wholesalers or by manufacturers, all draw on the idea of *pooling resources to improve service and cut costs simultaneously.* This is done by eliminating redundancies, particularly in inventory and in expertise (technical support). These federations simulate the advantages of one firm (coordination, scale) while preserving the advantages of separate firms (manageable size, entrepreneurial motivation, specialization, independence). This is a very difficult feat to achieve. The players are required to make considerable changes in their operating methods and to reveal a good deal of privileged information (such as opening electronic access to their inventories). Most of all, they must rely on each other. How is this achieved?

The leaders of this initiative must build trust and gain commitment by pledging essential resources and guarantee performance (see Chapter 11 on building strategic alliances). This means assuming considerable risk. For example, Okuma backs its distributors by guaranteeing 24-hour delivery of parts ordered by the distributor to the customer's site from its warehouse. The part is free if the deadline is missed. This encourages the 46 distributors to rely on Okuma, rather than duplicating its inventories.

Another critical property of these federations is equitable compensation, specified in advance. This requires channel members to experiment with more complex pay mechanisms than the traditional trade discount. Typically, the investments each party must make are the basis for setting compensation, *some of which is fixed.*

For example, LeBlonde Makino, a Japanese machine-tool maker, has a limited presence in Europe, too small to justify a full-scale service facility. The supplier has an arrangement with its distributors to call on them for service engineers. Distributors invest in the supplier by training their own engineers to support the brand, then guaranteeing a number of hours of availability. The supplier compensates them for this investment by paying for the hours whether or not they are used, as well as paying for any additional hours. This is effectively a fee (retainer, salary, fixed pay). Such take-or-pay contracts (either take the services at the agreed price or don't take them—but pay for them anyway) are not unusual in manufacturing. They are excellent ways to induce the other party in a wholesale arrangement to make specialized investments.[12]

Other unusual ways to compensate the parties to such arrangements include liberal functional discounts, bonuses for sales growth, outright fees, guaranteed functional allowances, and future considerations (such as the right to private label or to manufacture derivative products). This latter point illustrates that wholesaling is difficult to bound neatly. Many wholesalers do some manufacturing as well.

Despite these control mechanisms, alliances have important limitations. Many channels are filled with small, independent wholesaler-distributors. Alliances attempt to maintain this density, often at the expense of creating a low-cost distribution channel. By sharing resources, hard decisions are postponed into the future, even when circumstances require proactive channel change.[13]

Thus, the consolidation trend that we discuss later is another manifestation of wholesaler-distributors creating structures for joint action. However, crucial differences exist between consolidations and alliances. Most importantly, wholesaler-distributors that come together through a consolidation formally and legally combine their ownership structure. The newly created company has the authority to eliminate redundant activities and assets among its member companies. This can be a crucial source of competitive advantage in the face of margin pressure and other challenges. Alliance relationships rarely involve rationalization or reduction of assets among the members.

VOLUNTARY AND COOPERATIVE GROUPS

Often organizations desire to formalize the division of marketing "labor" within their channels so that they can assure themselves that the responsibility for performing specific distribution tasks is clearly placed. In these situations, vertical coordination is frequently accomplished through the use of contractual agreements. We concentrate here on one way to do this: wholesaler-sponsored voluntary and cooperative groups.

Wholesaler Voluntary Groups

A wholesaler, by banding together a number of independently owned retailers in a voluntary group, can provide goods and support services far more economically than these same retailers could secure solely as individuals. A well-known wholesaler-sponsored voluntary is the Independent Grocers Alliance (IGA). Such groups are particularly popular in the hardware industry. The principal services provided by a number of major hardware voluntaries are listed in Table 15.2. Underlying this list is the principle of economies of scale. This is important in the hardware industry, where a huge assortment of low-value items makes stockkeeping particularly difficult, and where the presence of large chains make retailing very competitive.

Wholesaler voluntary groups enlist a number of independently owned dealers. The wholesaler acts as a leader, and the members agree to purchase a substantial portion of their merchandise from the organization. They also agree to standardize some operating procedures and present a common logo to consumers via signage and promotion. The wholesaler is a locus of expertise and a source of leadership. Member retailers give up some of their autonomy to the wholesaler. Net, wholesaler voluntary groups are intended to simulate vertical integration to some degree.

In practice, the simulation turns out to be a poor one. The wholesaler cannot and does not exercise the authority of a chain organization, because the dealers can and will walk away from the voluntary group. Although the voluntary group does offer cost sav-

TABLE 15.2

Principal Services Provided by Major Hardware Wholesaler-Sponsored Voluntary Groups and Wholesaler Buying Groups in the United States

- Store identification
- Telephone ordering
- Microfiche or computerized records of prices and compatible parts numbers
- Catalog service
- Private-label merchandise
- Merchandising aid
- Basic stock lists
- Direct-drop ship programs
- Pool orders
- Consumer advertising
- Co-op advertising programs
- Advertising planning, aid
- Preprinted order forms
- Data-processing programs
- Inventory control systems
- Accounting services
- Management consultation services
- Employee training
- Dealer meetings
- Volume rebates and dividends
- Store planning, layout
- Financing
- Insurance programs
- Field supervisors and salespeople
- Dealer shows

ings to its members due to bulk purchasing, the dealers themselves compete via niche strategies in their neighborhoods: They leave price competition to the chains. These groups function rather loosely.[14] As such, they do not achieve the same operating efficiencies as does a well-run vertically integrated firm.[15]

Alternative Federations of Downstream Channel Members

A fascinating alternative to wholesaler voluntary groups is superficially similar. This alternative is the retailer-sponsored cooperative (often simply called "co-op"). On paper, it is the same idea but initiated by the retailers, not by a wholesaler. In practice, there is a substantial difference.

In order to coordinate among themselves, dealers are obliged to create an organization, like a consortium. They then join this organization and agree to do a certain amount of business with it and to follow some of its procedures. So far, this looks like a wholesaler voluntary group. What differs is that the members also buy shares in the co-op: *They are owners as well as members*. And as owners, they receive shares of the profits generated by their co-op (as stock dividends) and end-of-year rebates on their purchases. *This creates a powerful congruence between the goals of the co-op and of its members.*

As a result, retailer co-ops differ from wholesaler voluntary groups in two important respects.[16] First, they have a more formalized structure, run by dedicated professional managers whose jobs have fairly elaborate role descriptions. Second, they are better able to influence the marketing efforts of their owner-members. The dealers more aggressively adhere to the co-op's advertising, signage, and use of the co-op's brands. In short, marketing coordination is stronger. Channel Sketch 15.1 profiles Ace Hardware, the largest retailer co-op in the U.S. hardware industry.

CHANNEL SKETCH 15.1

Ace Hardware Corporation[17]

The roots of Ace Hardware go back to 1924, when Richard Hesse, owner of a Chicago hardware store, decided to circumvent wholesalers to reduce costs. Hesse formed a partnership with other small retailers to buy in bulk. The idea worked so well that Ace Hardware Stores incorporated in 1928. Today, Ace is a very profitable *Fortune* 500 firm (in size), counting its sales in billions of dollars. Yet, its stock is not traded: It is owned by over 5,000 dealers—only.

To become an Ace dealer requires an initial membership fee of $400, an initial purchase of $5,400 in voting stock, and the real commitment—a minimum of $100,000 per year of merchandise purchased from the company. Much of this is private-label merchandise, brightly trademarked in red, difficult to sell if one is no longer an Ace dealer. These sums are a substantial commitment because most members are small family-owned operations ("mom and pop" stores). At the end of each year, dealer-owners receive a cash rebate and more stock, based on how much they bought from Ace. This incentive draws members further into this profitable system and gives them a reason not to leave it. Should they decide to leave, Ace will buy back their stock immediately—unless they join a competing co-op, such as Cotter (now merged with True Value) or ServiStar (now merged with Coast Corporation). If a dealer leaves Ace for another co-op, Ace will still buy back its stock—very slowly. Defection is one thing, whereas joining the enemy is another.

The real enemy, however, has ceased to be other dealer cooperatives but has become the vertically integrated retail chain store, such as Home Depot. The business of independent hardware stores is growing, but the chains' business is growing faster. These chain retailers operate enormous, impersonal stores ("big boxes") featuring selection and price. Their soaring popularity has driven more small hardware independents to join co-ops such as Ace.

Over time, Ace has changed its focus from signing up new outlets (for purposes of blocking other co-ops) to helping its existing members compete against the big boxes. How does it do it?

By managing the wholesale side of its business carefully, Ace uses its buying power to get low prices from suppliers. It achieves high inventory turns, even though there are many thousands of SKUs. This keeps procurement costs down for its members, while providing them with an appealing assortment.

A major problem for independent hardware dealers is consumer perception. Shoppers tend to view Ace stores as "little corner stores with great service" but without competitive pricing. To counter this view, the company mounts advertising campaigns to project the image that the local "helpful hardware people" are part of a larger organization, with buying power and expertise.

Another problem is that Ace's members are heterogeneous. They serve local communities, adapting to local tastes. As a result their offerings vary so much that it is difficult to figure out how to help them. To overcome this problem, Ace has studied its members' businesses intensively, using point-of-sale (POS) data from those dealers with scanners in order to search for the best assortments. Ace also sends over 100 "retail consultants" to work closely with dealers to develop and implement new business plans, store by store.

Through this learning, Ace has come to categorize its members' businesses five ways: (1) home centers, (2) lumber, (3) farm, (4) general store, and (5) hardware. Hardware is further subdivided into three formats: convenience, neighborhood focus, and superstore. By studying its members, Ace has been able to distinguish best practices and to turn that knowledge into elaborate format manuals for different store types. Thus, it offers detailed, proven operational recommendations for each category of its membership. The retail consultants customize these recommendations to each of the members and help them in implementation.

To further its learning, Ace operates some of its own stores. It then appreciates the dealers' daily management problems and devises solutions by experimenting at its own risk. This covers issues beyond the traditional inventory questions, such as how to recruit, motivate, and retain good retail personnel. The stores also provide a good place for Ace to experiment with items its dealers usually won't carry, such as water heaters and lawn tractors (Ace dealers tend to specialize in small, inexpensive items). Ace demonstrates that certain of its owner-member's stores can step up to these complex, high-margin items.

In short, Ace binds its members to the system, but delivers them value in return for their compliance and participation. Members make commitments to the system, erecting barriers to their own exit. Thus motivated, they are more willing to work with Ace, to accept its suggestions, and to funnel their purchases. The system is surprisingly close to a franchise, whereby Ace acts as a franchisor. The difference is that the profits go not to the franchisor (because Ace is the "franchisor" in role) but to the dealers (as *they* are the owners of Ace). Should the company be called a model of "self-franchising"?

It is worth noting that co-op doesn't refer just to dealers. There can be many types of co-ops. The principal is that the members set up an organization to serve them and own shares in it. Cooperatives are becoming better known in Japan in response to the pressures that are shortening marketing channels. Small and medium-size wholesalers, seeing their roles being taken over by large wholesalers or manufacturers, have reacted by creating their own cooperatives to gain economies of scale.

An example is the Cooperative Association Yokohama Merchandising Center (MDC), set up and owned by 75 wholesalers. These wholesalers use MDC to pool their activities to gain scale. They supply MDC, which warehouses the goods in a huge distribution center. By serving from this center, MDC minimizes separate deliveries. This cuts transportation costs, a major item in Japan. Its wholesalers, via their co-op, now have the scale to serve major retailers and to build a modern, on-line information center to manage orders. In a similar fashion, small and medium-size wholesalers have also banded together to create co-op import companies, for the purpose of increasing their flexibility and cutting their inventories.

One other type of cooperative has played a major role in distribution in the United States—the *farm cooperative*. The emergence and growth of farm cooperatives could fill an entire textbook. Suffice it to say here that organizations such as Farmland Industries, Associated Milk Producers, Agway, Sunkist, Ocean Spray, and Land O'Lakes have become extremely powerful forces on behalf of their memberships in organizing both the farm equipment and supply markets, as well as the markets into which farmers sell their produce. Although some farm co-ops have vertically integrated both backward and forward within their marketing channels, they are primarily wholesalers of goods and services, and they administer the channels that they control with the approval of the farmers who own them.

Another type of cooperative—the *consumer cooperative*—has also had an impact on distribution. The most famous is Switzerland's Migros, which is organized as a federation of 12 cooperative societies. As much as three-quarters of the country's two million households are owners of the cooperative or so-called "co-operators" (i.e., members of one of the 12 societies).

In the United States, an example is Recreational Equipment, Inc. (REI), a marketer of climbing equipment, with over 900,000 active member-owners. Consumer co-ops are not common in the United States and tend to flourish in small, homogeneous, closed communities, such as college towns or rural communities.[18]

Consumer cooperatives, their properties, and the reasons for their success or lack of it, are not well understood at this time. They deserve further study, because they have great potential to improve consumer welfare.[19]

CONSOLIDATION

The popular image of wholesaling as small business contrasts with today's reality, in many industries, of a wholesaler as a large, sophisticated, capital-intensive corporation. This transformation is due to *consolidation,* a phenomenon that has swept through many industries along with improvements in information technology and changes in the wholesaler's customer base. In the United States, wholesaling is a very active area for merger and acquisition, often funded by private buyout capital.

Consolidation Pressures in Wholesaling

In wholesaling, the pressure to consolidate often comes from a wholesaler-distributor's larger downstream customers, including large manufacturers, multi-unit retailers, and sizable purchasing groups.[20] Such buyers value being able to access multiple suppliers over a large geography, all the while passing through a single source. This creates a demand for huge wholesalers.

Typically, distribution consolidators grow rapidly by acquisition, as noted earlier. They use their newfound scale to form partnerships with customers. This cuts down the ability of manufacturers to access these same customers. Indeed, newly large wholesalers often prune their supplier list, using their bargaining leverage to wring concessions from their shorter list of vendors. This, in turn, sets off a wave of consolidation upstream.

Net, large customers provoke wholesaler consolidation, which stimulates manufacturer consolidation. The pace of consolidation can be startlingly fast. For example, periodical and magazine wholesalers in the United States dropped from over 180 firms to under 50 firms in only nine years: The five largest wholesalers controlled 65 percent of the national market by the end of the 1990s.

The Manufacturer's Response to Wholesale Consolidation

What can manufacturers do when a wholesale consolidation wave starts? There are four solutions. The first is to *predict winning wholesalers and build a partnership with them* (see Chapter 11 on strategic alliances). This has been going on in Europe at a feverish pace, as economic union lessens the relevance of national boundaries.

Who are likely to be winners? There are four basic types:

1. The "catalyst firms" that trigger consolidation by moving rapidly to acquire.
2. Wholesalers that enter late, after consolidation is well along: These firms do not enter unless they have found defensible niches.
3. Extreme specialists, already attuned to the conditions that are likely to prevail after consolidation.
4. Extreme generalists: Large full-line firms can serve many environments well. Their versatility is valuable once the market has consolidated.

The second strategy for manufacturers facing wholesale consolidation is to *invest in fragmentation*. This strategy bets on and works with smaller independents trying to survive the wave of consolidation. This is the opposite of the strategy of betting on a few winners.

One way to invest in fragmentation is to capitalize on a wholesaling trend: Smaller wholesaler-distributors are banding together into alliances. Members can bid for national or multiregional contracts, offering the same geographic reach as a larger, multi-establishment company. The groups can also take advantage of volume purchasing opportunities from suppliers. At the same time, the alliance members retain operational autonomy, enabling them to maintain high levels of service for local customers.

The manufacturer can deal with these alliances. Or it can help independents to create an alliance that is a credible alternative to consolidators. For example, Parker Hannifin, an industrial products manufacturer, encouraged its distributors to form cooperatives and favored the co-ops in its dealings.

The third strategy for the manufacturer facing wholesale consolidation is to build an alternative route to market by *vertically integrating forward*. This is the topic of Chapter 7.

The fourth strategy for a manufacturer is to *increase its own attractiveness* to the remaining channels. In general, this involves increasing the manufacturer's ability to offer benefits to the channel (e.g., the benefit of a strong brand name). In fact, this strategy is a theme that permeates this book. Chapter 8, in particular, focuses on ways to gain the potential to influence channel members.

Once wholesale consolidation has occurred, the balance of power in the channel changes. The majority of industry sales at wholesale now goes through a handful of large, publicly traded, professionally managed companies. Entry barriers are high, and entrants must seek niche markets. These large wholesalers have lower gross margins than in the days when the industry's wholesalers were fragmented, local, and privately held. However, the large firms have a higher total business and operate so efficiently that their net margins are healthy, even though their gross margins are lower. These wholesalers put great pressures on their suppliers, particularly in terms of pricing. And they offer their customers increased service. The large surviving wholesalers redesign supply chain management processes in their industry, often revolutionizing current operating methods.

Wholesaler consolidation is a sea of change in an industry. Once it begins, it tends to progress quite rapidly. Manufacturers must react rapidly and be ready to change their marketing channels and methods. Wholesale consolidation is a force that cannot be overlooked.

THE FUTURE OF WHOLESALER-DISTRIBUTORS

International Expansion

A striking feature of wholesaler-distributors is that, although they can become quite large, they seldom become global. Is this a historical artifact of the days of family-owned businesses? Will the large firms that survive an industry consolidation go global?

Many U.S. domestic wholesaler-distributors are expanding internationally, often by acquiring foreign wholesaler-distributors, in order to meet the needs of both customers and suppliers. Global manufacturers and customers are asking that their distribution partners have a presence in all major markets. The reduced costs of cross-border shipping and falling trade barriers also encourage expansion. For the same reasons, foreign wholesaler-distributors are making inroads into the domestic U.S. market. This trend of cross-border growth and acquisitions is also occurring in Europe.

In 1999, for example, Netherlands-based N. V. Hagemeyer scooped up Vallen Corporation and Tri-State Electrical & Electronics Supply Company. Two of the largest electric products distributors in France, Sonepar and Rexal, have been aggressively acquiring U.S.-based electrical wholesaler-distributors to expand their core business internationally.

Yet, the nature of the business suggests that most actors will never be truly global. Fundamentally, wholesaling means meeting the needs of a local market, and these needs are so varied that it is exceedingly difficult to standardize marketing channels. This makes it very difficult for suppliers, customers, or wholesaler-distributors to pursue a truly global supply chain strategy. The few successful examples come from industries in which many participants in the channel are global, such as the electronic components and computer industries.

Electronic Commerce

Debate rages about the impact of electronic commerce on wholesalers. On the one hand, doomsday predictions abound to the effect that intermediaries will be eliminated by the ruthless efficiency of an Internet search engine. On the other hand, wholesaling has genuine value added. Eliminating wholesalers will not eliminate their functions. And the Internet cannot provide all channel flows.

A more likely scenario is that e-commerce will change but not replace wholesalers. Indeed, early indicators show that wholesalers are actually *benefiting* from e-commerce! They are co-opting the Internet, finding ways to use it to bring in new business and to improve how they go about their work.

To date, the Internet poses four important challenges for wholesaler-distributors:

1. Companies can aggregate markets across broader geography.
2. Comparative price information is more easily accessible and widely available.
3. It may separate physical distribution from functions of customer service and account management.
4. Information-focused functions can migrate to Web-based third-party institutions.

E-business Models and Wholesaler-Distributors

Two types of e-businesses seem particularly likely to impact wholesaler-distributors.[21] *Independent exchanges* operate as on-line brokers within a given industry. These companies aggregate supplier catalogs on the Internet, enabling buyers of like products to source and purchase items from multiple suppliers in a single location. Examples of independent exchanges include Chemdex (scientific supplies) and Neoforma (medical supplies). Literally hundreds of these companies have already been formed as of this writing.

Although these businesses are largely independent entities, many have formed partnerships with wholesaler-distributors in their industry to gain presence in the market and tap into existing product flows and customer relationships. Sources of revenue for these exchanges include transaction fees (charged primarily to sellers), Web site advertising, and consulting services centered on creating and managing electronic catalogs.

In contrast, *supply chain networks* facilitate transactions between current supply chain partners (manufacturers, distributors, and customers). To a large extent, supply chain networks are a kind of Internet-based integrated supply. Large buyers set up purchasing infrastructures to enable them to manage high volumes of purchasing activities with multiple suppliers through a single, standardized point of integration. The majority of revenues for start-ups in this part of the market come from software licensing fees. Over time, they hope to generate substantial revenue through transaction fees. They also earn revenues through consulting fees for Web site development, hosting services, and fees for building catalogs. Prevalent examples of these businesses are Commerce One, Ariba, and MRO.com. Supply chain networks are actively trying to incorporate wholesaler-distributors.

Neither exchanges nor supply chain networks take away the logistic and physical distribution functions of wholesaler-distributors. However, they insert themselves at the point when customers decide whom to buy from, how much to buy, and how much they will spend. These supply chain options are shown in Figure 15.3.

Wholesaler-distributors are at risk if customers attach loyalty to the exchange that is providing the mechanism to find suppliers and order product, rather than to the distributor that is doing the actual warehousing and order fulfillment. Exchanges will then siphon off the information and order processing functions, and the associated profits, from distributors.

As customers begin using exchanges to search, check inventory, order, and track purchases from distributors, exchanges will attempt to control the customer relationship. The customer could view the exchange as the entity that solves problems and view the local or even national distributor as just an interchangeable logistics operation.

As a central connection point, an exchange will know more about an individual customer's overall purchases and buying habits than any other member—buyer or sup-

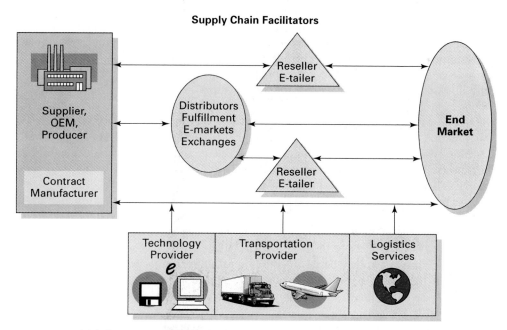

FIGURE 15.3 **The Supply Chain Options for E-Merchants**
Source: Robert W. Baird Incorporated, *Distribution, Fulfillment, E-Markets, and Exchanges,* January 2000.

plier—in the exchange. On-line exchanges also gain the first opportunity to sell value-added services that distributors otherwise might deliver.

Exchanges also allow the customer to search and scan multiple supplier catalogs or inventory stocks and compare prices side by side. As exchanges grow, a customer will no longer have to trade off a large number of suppliers (to ensure a fair price) with limiting the amount of time (and money) spent by the purchasing department on each order.

Although independent exchanges appear to pose the most direct threat to wholesaler-distributors, they have been forced to partner with wholesaler-distributors to ensure basic customer service. For example, Chemdex is linked to VWR Scientific Products, the largest distributor of scientific supplies (and a member of OrderZone), through an alliance relationship and an equity investment by VWR. Similarly, the "virtual intermediary" e-chemicals recently entered into a similar agreement with Ashland Distribution.

On-line Retailing and Wholesaler-Distributors

On the retail side, as of this writing Internet retailing is thriving in areas in which the wholesale distribution is already highly consolidated—such as books, music, video, and pharmaceuticals. On-line retailing is actually leading to growth at the larger consolidated distributors because these Internet companies have a "virtual" drop-ship model. They rely on large wholesaler-distributors for fulfillment, returns, and service. Thus, such channels provide an infrastructure for virtual companies. In a very real sense, wholesaler-distributors are "making the Web happen."

Elsewhere, the effect of the Internet should vary. In theory, logistics and manufacturing firms that specialize in delivery of small-package orders could eliminate wholesale distribution in many industries. Further, to the extent that a product—such as books, films, or music—can be digitized, then recreated elsewhere, the industry may be radically altered, as there is no more tangible product to handle.

Nonetheless, as of this writing, wholesaler-distributors have not been replaced by electronic commerce solutions because it is extremely complex to replace *all* of the valuable functions performed *as a package* by wholesale distribution intermediaries.

Many members are seeking to build their own e-commerce hubs aimed at corporate purchasers. These Web sites are essentially on-line storefronts for an established company. For instance, Grainger.com allows W. W. Grainger customers to access their standard accounts and price discounts and company catalog on-line. These sites could have the effect of allowing individual distributors to reach much larger, potentially global, marketplaces that were previously unavailable due to advertising and servicing costs. Niche market distributors or distributors with specialized processing skills may find a previously limited customer base expanded significantly. Larger wholesaler-distributors may be able to channel significant portions of their overall customer base through an in-house Web site, thereby lowering the costs of customer ordering and gaining greater control in the customer relationship.

Over the centuries, the industry has proven adept at reinventing itself to cope with changes in markets and technology. There is every reason to expect that the industry as a whole will find ways to create value added via e-commerce, even if some sectors are greatly diminished or altered by its possibilities.

A SKETCH OF VERTICAL INTEGRATION AND OF AGENTS IN WHOLESALING

This chapter has focused heavily on wholesaler-distributors because this is the largest and best-documented sector of wholesaling. Let us return to the other two broad categories of the activity and sketch them briefly.

Vertical Integration Forward into Wholesaling by Manufacturers

When manufacturers perform wholesaling activities themselves, they are operating manufacturer's sales branches and offices. The merits and demerits of this approach are analyzed in Chapter 7 on vertical integration. Here we address a trend at the retail level for huge "power retailers" to bypass independent wholesaler-distributors by setting up their own branches to perform channel flows. This trend is gathering momentum in Europe—fueled by economic union—and in Japan—fueled by rising price elasticity among consumers and a trend in industry to question the length and operating methods of Japanese channels. Let us examine the U.S. case, where the trend is already well advanced.

Wholesaler-distributors are a small part of many traditional (physical) retail channels in the United States due to the influence of power retailers. An industry report describes two different types of power retailers:[22]

1. General-merchandise power retailers that sell a broad variety of product lines, either discount broad-line stores (such as Carrefour, Wal-Mart, and Kmart) or membership warehouse clubs (such as Price–Costco and Sam's Club).

2. Category-dominant power retailers (category killers) that concentrate on one or more closely related merchandise lines. Examples include Toys "R" Us (toys), Petco (pet supplies), Staples (office supplies), and Home Depot (home improvement).

Because direct purchases by retailers are not included in the Census of Wholesale Trade, it is hard to determine the aggregate sales impact of such retailers in the United States.

Power retailers typically buy in large quantities in select product categories, giving them a very prominent position in the channel. This purchase volume has caused many power retailers to adopt a "buy direct" approach. Retailers such as Wal-Mart have squeezed costs out of the channel by creating in-house distribution systems in which wholesaler-distributors play a small role. Manufacturers have been forced to respond to the demands of dominant buyers, often at the expense of wholesaler-distributors. In addition, power retailers have triggered industry consolidation among the small- and medium-size retailers that were traditional wholesale distribution customers.

These retailers have reduced or eliminated the role of wholesaler-distributors in retail channels during the past 20 years, leaving fewer, but larger, wholesaler-distributors among the survivors. This is one reason why e-commerce should not have a devastating effect on independent wholesalers in many retail sectors. The devastation has already occurred. Due to power retailers, there are few wholesaler-distributors for the Internet to effect.

At the same time, the hyperefficient retail distribution systems used by power retailers are ill-suited for the "unit of one" shipping required for on-line buying and shipping to a consumer's home. Currently, many retailers are partnering with either wholesaler-distributors or third-party fulfillment companies such as Fingerhut as they enter e-commerce. The Internet, curiously, may prove to be a way to bring independent wholesalers back into retail channels.

Set the Price and See the Buyer: Agents, Brokers, and Commission Agents

Agents, brokers, and commission agents buy or sell products for commissions or fees. They focus on the flows of promotion and negotiation, and are critical players in the transmission of information up and down the marketing channel. They do not take ownership to the products they represent.

This distinction has critical ramifications. Essentially, agents are pure specialists in selling. They leave the ownership, handling, and financing of the goods to other players. Manufacturers using agents are free to unbundle other channel flows and to assign them to other channel members. It gives them freedom to fashion channels with multiple players.

Further, the manufacturer has much greater control over the channel in going through an agent than in going through a wholesaler-distributor. The agent sells but does not set the price unless the manufacturer delegates pricing authority. Thus, the manufacturer has more pricing discretion. And it has much better information. Via the agent, the manufacturer knows who bought what and at what price. Thus, the supplier can see the customer. In contrast, wholesaler-distributors own the goods and can do with them as they see fit. The manufacturer knows as much or as little as the wholesaler divulges.

Sales agents are typically called *manufacturers' representatives (MR)*, the terminology we shall adopt here. Like wholesalers, MRs (or simply "reps") go by different names in different sectors, and their properties vary. The defining characteristic is that they are an independent firm acting as an agent for a manufacturer (the principal) to sell products. They are almost always paid by a commission on their sales. Reps can also sell services: For example, much radio advertising time is sold by "radio reps" in the United States. As this chapter focuses on wholesaling, we set aside services of MRs to concentrate on MRs selling tangibles.

The fundamental issues around MRs are the domain of sales force management, a topic separate from the management of marketing channels. For our purposes, a key question is what role an MR fills. A rep is a downstream channel member, functioning as an equivalent to a company sales force. Like the "direct" sales force (i.e., employed directly and solely by the manufacturer), an MR sells to other channel members, such as wholesaler-distributors, OEMs, and retailers.

Conventions for MRs vary widely. In the United States, reps traditionally but not always sell a portfolio of complementary products, but give each manufacturer exclusive representation in its own product class. In this manner, a rep offers assortment to the customer while offering exclusive dealing to each manufacturer. This is an appealing combination for the customer, who enjoys one-stop shopping, and the manufacturer, who faces no interbrand competition. In Europe, reps are not used as extensively, perhaps due to more restrictive labor laws. And in Asia, they have traditionally been captive agencies, serving one manufacturer on an exclusive basis. This is changing, with more manufacturers experimenting with allowing their reps more autonomy.[23]

Whether to use a rep or a company sales force is a vertical integration issue (Chapter 7). For many companies, the question is not whether to go "rep or direct" but *how* to go rep *and* direct. The decision to use an MR depends on the nature of the market and the brand–product class.[24] For many brand–markets, an MR is a compelling choice. For others, a direct sales force is preferable. Net, it is common for a manufacturer, especially a large one—with a broad product line and multiple markets to cover—to use an MR to take some products to market and a direct sales force or forces for other products in other markets.

How much are MRs used? It is somewhat difficult to say, given the variety of forms and titles that fit this channel institution. Rep usage in the United States has been increasing since the 1970s, particularly in business-to-business transactions. Estimates of the MRs' share of industrial selling in the United States go up to 50 percent, although some observers put the figure closer to one third.[25] The MRs' share of sales varies considerably by industry and by market. For example, MRs may account for over half the sales in the electrical products and food service industries, while accounting for much less than half in health and beauty items (dominated by chain stores). And these figures can vary by market: For example, MRs appear to have a much bigger share of the market in HVAC (heating, ventilation, and air conditioning) in Canada than in the United States.[26]

Manufacturers' representatives can be difficult to recognize. To their customers, they may appear to be employees of the manufacturers they represent, much as a franchisee may be indistinguishable from a company-owned outlet. To their manufacturers, they can form a strategic partnership so close that the lines between firms are not sharp. And to the observer, the only indicator of their status may be the many product lines listed on their business cards.[27]

An MR provides professional services on an outsourced basis. In this respect, the institution resembles a law office, an accounting firm, or an advertising agency. And like these service providers, a rep can be quite large, employing hundreds of people and supporting heavy fixed investments in buildings, IT facilities, even private airplanes. (Reps are often used in large geographies with low customer density.) However, the economies of scale in this business are not great, with the result that most MRs cover a restricted territory.

The same issues that arise with any downstream channel member arise with an MR. The principles described in this book—such as how to gain and use power—apply to this channel institution as to any other.

SUMMARY

The wholesaling sector covers the sale of product between businesses, as opposed to ultimate household consumers. The sector creates value added by providing channel flows. Just as the value of these flows is often underappreciated, so is the value added and economic importance of the wholesaling sector. The essential tasks the industry performs are mundane, but it is no simple matter to carry them out with few errors, bundled with valued services, and at low cost.

Players in the wholesale sector are experimenting with innovative ways to deliver value to the customer base while simultaneously cutting costs. By assembling federations of channel members to share resources, redundancies in inventories and in processes are cut down. These efforts may be led by wholesalers or by manufacturers, and can be organized in multiple ways. Channel members further downstream, such as dealers, can also organize to capitalize on economies of scale. The cooperative is an effective vehicle for so doing.

One way to achieve such economies is consolidation. In wholesaling, consolidation is endemic and is usually achieved by a wave of mergers and acquisitions by a handful of players. The causes and consequences of consolidation are explored in this chapter, and four generic manufacturer responses are outlined.

The future of wholesaler-distributors will be one of changes. This is due to the pressures and opportunities of international expansion, as well as the new possibilities opened up by electronic commerce. The idea that it will eliminate wholesaler-distributors is simplistic: Indeed, these institutions are finding ways to benefit from the Internet. But change is certain and will affect various wholesaling sectors in different ways.

No discussion of wholesaling is complete without examining the role of manufacturers' representatives (more generally, sales agents and brokers). These institutions are professional services firms. They do not take title and do not offer inventory. By specializing in a subset of channel flows, they provide the manufacturer the ability to fashion a variety of channels. Via agents, suppliers have a better view of the market and more control over price than they typically do when title changes hands.

Wholesaling is a vibrant, economically important sector of most economies. The players continually reinvent themselves to provide new value added. More on the functions they provide is available in Chapter 16 on logistics.

Discussion Questions

1. What are the essential distinctions among the three categories of wholesale trade?

2. Consider the following statement: "A wholesaling operation can be eliminated as an entity, but someone must perform the wholesaling tasks and absorb the costs sustained by the wholesaler if it is assumed that those tasks are necessary." Take a position on this statement, pro or con, and offer support for your reasoning.

3. Inventories and accounts receivable represent 65 percent to 85 percent of the total assets of a wholesaler. Many bankers consider that these are the only assets worth considering when deciding whether to lend to a wholesaler. What are the bankers overlooking? What determines the true value of a wholesaler?

4. Wholesaling is often thought of as a less glamorous intermediary venture when compared with other channel intermediary operations, such as retailing. In your opinion, which of these two would be the more difficult to manage—a wholesaling or a retailing operation? Which would seem to have the best chance, on the average, of achieving a high ROI (return on investment) today? Which would you say has had to face more challenges to its survival in the last 50 years?

5. When facing consolidation at the wholesale level, what is the manufacturer's best reaction?

Notes

1. Adam J. Fein, "Wholesaling," in *U.S. Industry and Trade Outlook 2000* (New York: DRI/McGraw-Hill, 2000). Sections of this chapter are adapted or excerpted from this source with permission.

2. R. L. Lusch and D. Zizzo, *Foundations of Wholesaling: A Strategic and Financial Chart Book* (Washington, DC: Distribution Research and Education Foundation, 1996).

3. The U.S. Census Bureau has historically measured manufacturers' forward integration into sales and distribution as part of the Census of Wholesalers. At the time of writing, the Bureau has proposed that these establishments be excluded from wholesale trade.

4. *Cross-docking* is a term used to describe the movement of freight from one truck to a loading dock, then reloaded into another truck. This is done so the trucking company does not have to use the same truck and drivers to cover the full length of the transit. This term is discussed in Chapter 16 (logistics). *Merge-in-transit* operations work as follows: A carrier picks up separate loads from two or more different origins, transports the loads to a location near their final destination, and then performs a "merge" operation. At the simplest, the merge operation comprises consolidating the loads in a cross-dock operation. In more complex examples, the merge operation comprises consolidation and a value-added process, such as assembly. *Flow-through distribution* is essentially another type of combination of cross-docking and consolidation. Products from multiple locations are brought into a central facility, consolidated by delivery destination and shipped, minimizing facility investment and material handling. This differs from merge-in-transit in that it tends to serve multiple customers and customer locations instead of being focused at just one location or customer.

5. The U.S. Census Bureau is changing from the Standard Industrial Classification system (SIC) to a new North American Industry Classification System (NAICS). Substantial differences in the old and new reporting systems make comparisons over time somewhat problematic. Here, we will rely on estimations contained in Fein, "Wholesaling," an excellent and detailed guide to the industry as a whole.

6. "Ever-Shorter Channels—Wholesale Industry Restructures," *Focus Japan,* 24 (July–August, 1997), 3–4.

7. Adam J. Fein, "Understanding Evolutionary Processes in Non-Manufacturing Industries: Empirical Insights from the Shakeout in Pharmaceutical Wholesaling," *Journal of Evolutionary Economics,* 8, no. 1 (1998), pp. 231–70.

8. James A. Narus and James C. Anderson, "Rethinking Distribution," *Harvard Business Review,* 96 (July–August 1996), pp. 112–20. The section on adaptive contracts and the examples are drawn from this article, which goes into much greater depth on the specifics of such arrangements.

9. Adam J. Fein, "The Future of Distributor Alliances," *Modern Distribution Management,* September 1998.

10. F. Lynn and J. Baden, *Integrated Supply 2: Shaping the Future of the Industrial Marketplace* (Chicago: Frank Lynn & Associates, 1998).

11. Adam J. Fein and Sandy D. Jap, "Manage Consolidation in the Distribution Channel," *Sloan Management Review,* 41 (fall 1999), pp. 61–72.

12. Oliver E. Williamson, *The Mechanisms of Governance* (New York: Oxford University Press, 1996).

13. Adam J. Fein, "How Good Is Your Consolidation Survival Strategy?" *Modern Distribution Management,* November 1997.

14. F. Robert Dwyer and Sejo Oh, "A Transaction Cost Perspective on Vertical Contractual Structure and Interchannel Competitive Strategies," *Journal of Marketing,* 52, no. 2 (April 1988), pp. 21–34.

15. Philip K. Porter and Gerald W. Scully, "Economic Efficiency in Cooperatives," *Journal of Law & Economics,* 30, no. 2 (October 1987), pp. 489–512.

16. Dwyer and Oh, "A Transaction Cost Perspective."

17. Debby Garbato Stankevich, "Ace of Diamonds," *Discount Merchandiser,* 36 (August 1996), pp. 28–37; Susan Jackson and Tim Smart, "Mom and Pop Fight Back," *BusinessWeek,* April 14, 1997, p. 46.

18. Steven Weinstein, "A Consuming Interest," *Progressive Grocer,* 75 (May 1996), pp. 161–63.

19. Richard J. Sexton and Terri A. Sexton, "Cooperatives as Entrants," *Rand Journal of Economics,* 18, no. 4 (winter 1987), pp. 581–95.

20. For a more complete discussion of the forces triggering consolidation, see Adam J. Fein, *Consolidation in Wholesale Distribution: Understanding Industry Change* (Washington, DC: Distribution Research and Education Foundation, 1997).

21. Adam J. Fein, Michael J. Skinner, and James Solodar, "The Promise and Perils of On-Line Exchanges," *Modern Distribution Management,* December 1999.

22. R. F. Lusch and D. Zizzo, *Competing for Customers: How Wholesaler-Distributors Can Meet the Power Retailer Challenge* (Washington, DC: Distribution Research and Education Foundation, 1995).

23. Gary L. Frazier, "Organizing and Managing Channels of Distribution," *Journal of the Academy of Marketing Sciences,* 27, no. 2 (1999), pp. 226–40.

24. Erin Anderson, "The Salesperson as Outside Agent or Employee: A Transaction-Cost Analysis," *Marketing Science,* 4 (summer 1985), pp. 234–54.

25. Paul Dishman, "Exploring Strategies for Companies That Use Manufacturers' Representatives," *Industrial*

Marketing Management, 25, no. 1 (1996), pp. 453–61; Gilbert A. Churchill, Neil M. Ford, and Orville C. Walker Jr., *Sales Force Management,* 5th ed. (Chicago: Irwin Publishing, 1997).

26. Estimates supplied by the Manufacturers' Representative Educational and Research Foundation (MRERF).

27. One of the authors was describing the rep function in class. A student sat up abruptly and gasped, "Now I know what my father does for a living! I always wondered why he talked about so many different brands."

16

Logistics and Supply Chain Management

LEARNING OBJECTIVES

After reading this chapter, you will:

- State why logistics has become a critical topic in the management of marketing channels
- Distinguish good and bad reasons to hold inventory, and productive versus dysfunctional ways to cut inventory holding costs
- Trace the shift from push to pull systems of managing inventory
- Sketch why contract logistics is growing explosively
- Define supply chain management and state its boundaries
- Describe the critical elements of efficient consumer response and quick response
- Relate a brand's characteristics to the need for its supply chain to be market responsive versus physically efficient
- List the forces needed to implement the supply chain management paradigm in an organization

*L*ogistics is the management of the flow of physical materials. In the context of marketing channels, *physical distribution* and *logistics* have traditionally been used interchangeably, with the understanding that only finished goods are part of distribution and the proper concern of a marketing channel manager. This, and many other ideas about channel logistics, has changed radically since the mid-1980s.[1]

Logistics has metamorphosed into the concept of *supply chain management (SCM),* which in turn has come to implicate *every* element of the value-added chain. Going backward, or upstream, this means channel logistics encompasses not only inventories of finished goods but also work in process (WIP) and raw materials. Indeed, SCM at its fullest goes back not only to the factory floor but also to the *suppliers of the suppliers of the suppliers.* At the extreme, SCM means signaling the very beginning of the value-added chain what to do and when to do it, as a function of what is happening at the very end of the value chain. Thus, transactions at the grocery checkout counter could pass through multiple steps, ultimately to be used to suggest to a farmer what to plant—and to the farmer's suppliers what to fabricate. This is the extreme (some would say utopian, or even ludicrous) version of SCM.

The implications also go downstream. Every player in a channel sends information or places orders that triggers behavior by any and every other player, including those downstream. This is not just a matter of stockpiling or moving inventories, it may be marketing behavior. For example, what is going in the warehouse may signal a supplier not to offer a promotion this month, or to offer one price instead of another price. Inventory management may result in a change of assortment, with some SKUs being eliminated and others being added, to be produced to the express specifications of a single customer.

These are marketing decisions. The idea that logistics should influence marketing—which is one premise of SCM—is revolutionary to many managers. Some would consider it retrograde, a return to the past, when cost-based thinking overrode the marketing orientation.

What is this revolution called SCM? The idea of a channel becoming more effective (better meeting the buyer's service output demands) while simultaneously cutting costs is the promise of SCM. Is it merely fanciful? Is it the latest slogan, the most recent buzzword or fad? Will it be outmoded in a matter of years?

This chapter addresses these questions. We begin with the building blocks of logistics: *inventory* (which involves storage and warehouses), *fulfillment* (picking and packing), *transportation,* and *payment* (the flow of orders and invoices, which used to be called paperwork).

This chapter covers the building blocks of logistics, one by one, laying the groundwork for supply chain management. It overviews SCM, first in general terms, and then in two formulations: efficient consumer response (ECR) and quick response (QR). Although these two models of SCM are often confused, they are in fact extremely different. After contrasting them, the chapter covers when each is appropriate and then closes on a critical question: If SCM is such a good idea, why hasn't it been popular before? In other words, why only now?

The reader is warned that logisticians are fond of acronyms (preferably three characters) and that there is a very large number of these, far more than will be covered here. This chapter, unlike many of the abundant industry readings on the topic, will refrain from acronyms as much as possible. Table 16.1 provides a glossary of the best-known and most critical acronyms, in their order of appearance in this chapter.

Logistics is often treated as a highly technical field, amenable to the methods of operations research. This should not deter managers from using their judgment and from relying on simple tools, such as graphs and spreadsheets, to make logistical deci-

TABLE 16.1

A Glossary of Acronyms Commonly Used in Channel Logistics

These acronyms are listed in the order of appearance in this chapter.
- SCM (supply chain management)
- WIP (work in process inventory)
- 3PL (third-party logistics providers)
- ECR (efficient consumer response)
- QR (quick response)
- SKU (stockkeeping unit)
- ABC (activity-based costing)
- EOQ (economic order quantity)
- MRP (material requirements planning)
- JIT (just-in-time)
- VAN (value-added network)
- EDI (electronic data interchange)
- CRP (continuous replenishment program)
- CAD–CAM (computer-aided design and computer-aided manufacturing)
- POS (point of sale)

sions. Nonetheless, formal methods are often a powerful aid to the manager. These are covered in a number of texts and articles on logistics. This chapter focuses on the role of the logistics manager in the management of marketing channels.

THE BUILDING BLOCKS OF LOGISTICS IN MARKETING CHANNELS

The Newfound Importance of Logistics in Channels

Logistics involves the processing and tracking of factory goods during warehousing, inventory control, transport, customs documentation (a small issue or a nonissue inside trading zones), and delivery to customers. Channel logistics is now a less obscure function in some firms, due to the new options available and to the realization that enormous gains in effectiveness and efficiency can be had from better logistical management.

The effectiveness gains come in providing the right product at the right time in the right place. This is an issue in fast-changing industries, such as personal computers, wherein a product can easily become obsolete in one order cycle (the time it takes from receipt of an order to delivery of the goods). Thus, a laptop computer may become worthless in midshipment. The losses here are enormous: Not only the accounting loss of the value of the inventory but also the opportunity loss of the order that might have been (i.e., what the buyer wants instead of the abruptly obsolete laptop).

The personal computer industry is unstable and unpredictable. At the opposite end of the spectrum is food retailing. Yet here, too, logistics increases effectiveness. Consumers are increasingly demanding and increasingly diverse in what they demand. It is difficult to have the right flavors, sizes, variety, packages—every consumer insists on some combinations in some categories that other consumers value little. To have the right SKU (stockkeeping unit) at the right time and place makes a difference in sales and in store loyalty.

Industries sometimes overlook that logistics can improve effectiveness. They more often see primarily its role in increasing efficiency by cost cutting. And indeed, the potential for cost cutting in channels is enormous. But how to do it, and how to do it *without reducing buyer appeal?* The answers to this question are many. Let us start with what is to be sold: the inventory.

Inventory Management in Marketing Channels

Inventories are stocks of goods or the components of goods. It has become fashionable to think of them as somehow bad. In fact, they exist for four good reasons.[2]

Reasons for Holding Inventory. First, *demand surges* outstrip production capacity. To smooth production, factories anticipate the surge, producing to forecast. Inventory results. The demand surge may be natural (e.g., ice cream demand rises in summer), or it may be due to marketers' actions. Supply chain management developed in the grocery industry mainly because retailers stockpile goods to take advantage of manufacturer promotions. The result is high inventory carrying costs, including the cost of obsolescence.

Second, *economies of scale* are to be had in production or in transportation. Inventory is a result of batch-processing orders to make a long production run, or stockpiling goods to fill containers, trucks, ships, and planes.

Third, distance between the point of production and the point of consumption means that *transportation takes time*. Customers keep inventories (pipeline stock) to hold them over until a shipment arrives and can be unpacked and put out to use.

Fourth, both supply and demand are *uncertain*. Buyers are uncertain how long it will take for them to be resupplied (lead time)—if they can get the stock at all. Thus, they acquire safety stock (the excess of inventory over the best estimate of what is needed during an order cycle) as a hedge against uncertainty. That uncertainty is often in the form of ignorance as to what will sell (demand uncertainty).

Inventory Holding Costs. Holding inventory, then, saves money, but also holds costs in:

1. *Capital:* the internal cost of funds multiplied by the value of inventory.
2. *Storage:* climate control, security, insurance, and the like.
3. *Obsolescence:* loss of value due to the product's decay. This can be due to changes in tastes (think of fashion).
4. *Quality:* or rather, the deterioration of quality (think of food).

These costs are customarily estimated roughly as a percentage of inventory value, then rolled into an aggregate *inventory holding cost rate*. This rate is multiplied by the total cost of the inventory to determine *inventory carrying cost*.

Activity-Based Costing (ABC), wherein costs are assigned in the function of the activities needed to support them, has been slow to come to marketing channels. But it is now widespread and has enabled channel members to get a better idea what their inventory holding costs are, and how they vary by product, even by customer.[3] They are often shockingly high. This has been an impetus for considerable change in logistical practice in marketing channels.[4]

How much inventory should a channel member hold is a very difficult question.[5] A large number of operations research models have been developed to solve this problem: They vary in what assumptions they make in order to render the inventory problem mathematically tractable. The choice of model among the six major families of inventory models depends on circumstances. The EOQ (economic order quantity) model is the oldest and best known.[6]

Reducing Inventory. How can inventory be reduced? Some obvious methods are to avoid items that turn slowly ("sit in inventory"), lengthen the life of the goods (e.g., fill foods with preservatives), find a vendor who resupplies faster, locate a cheaper warehouse (perhaps a more modern one), and so forth. Some less obvious methods are to develop better ways to forecast demand, or to alter factory processes to attain scale economies at lower levels of production. Advances in manufacturing practice have done a great deal to achieve this latter goal.

Some companies are astute at finding ways to hold inventories of only what is necessary. For example, Surcouf, a computer retailer in Paris, is famous for low prices and high customer service in every possible aspect of information technology. Customer loyalty is enhanced by Surcouf's ability to offer a tremendous assortment.[7] Yet, it somehow evades the usual problem of accumulating items that turn slowly. Surcouf's secret is that its salespeople are well-paid computer professionals specializing in only one aspect of computer technology (e.g., only flight simulation software). Surcouf gives its salespeople the task that most stores give a purchasing agent (store buyer)—it is the retail (floor) salespeople who specify what will be carried in inventory. Their closeness to customers allows them to know which items to avoid.

A powerful way to cut inventory is to simplify, that is, to *cut variety*. Of course, this can be a powerful way to cut sales as well! The key is to find those offerings no one will really miss. These can be items—or merely things to track. For example, France has a very low rate of obesity, so low that larger customers (most of whom are still within sizes that would be considered ordinary in most countries) are ill served by clothing stores.[8] These stores simply do not stock much in the way of larger sizes, even though most factories make them. This may be why mail-order catalogs have a disproportionate number of larger-size customers. All French catalogs historically charge one price for the most common sizes and another (higher) price for larger sizes. Because this doubles the number of price references for clothes—the differential is not simply a fixed surcharge—it complicates logistics considerably.

In a bid for logistic simplification, La Redoute abruptly announced a one-price-per-article policy. In so doing, La Redoute is taking a substantial commercial risk: Eighty-four percent of clothing revenue in France comes from the smaller (i.e., "normal") sizes, and the new unitary prices are intermediate between the former price points. Effectively, most customers will see a price increase, even though it is estimated that, all told, La Redoute is dropping its aggregate margins. That a major catalog would take such a risk attests to the cost savings available from reduction of variety of any sort.

One method of reducing variety is to design products to be modular, and then design manufacturing processes to fit the principle of postponing as late as possible the point of differentiating a product for a customer or customer base. For example, Hewlett-Packard redesigned a line of laser printers so as to make a standard subassembly. This subassembly (only) is shipped to a European distribution center in Germany. The center procures, then adds in, those elements needed to tailor the printer to its destination market: power supplies, packaging, and manuals, all of which are tailored to the language and infrastructure of each national market. This involves assembly and light manufacturing, thereby expanding the role of the marketing channel. As a result, manufacturing costs are slightly higher, in part because this sort of redesign often obliges upgrades in the materials used. But total costs (manufacturing, shipping, and inventory) are 25 percent lower.[9]

One of the biggest reasons inventory accumulates is demand uncertainty. And one of the major causes of demand uncertainty is poor communication between members of marketing channels. Even a simple product, such as beer, can serve as a good example of the *bullwhip effect*.[10] Imagine a supply chain ending with a beer drinker, going back through the retailer who sells the beer, the wholesaler who supplies the retailer, and the brewer who makes the beer. Each party must forecast end-user demand, then take production, shipping, and stocking delays into account to plan (1) how much to order to serve its own level of demand (the retailer, hence the wholesaler); and (2) how much to brew, and therefore what ingredients to order (the brewer). Because each player sees only its link in the supply chain, there is demand uncertainty, obliging each party to guess. The result is that inventories of beer and ingredients oscillate, going up and down in dramatic surges, then plunges. The graph of inventories resembles the path a bullwhip cuts through the air—see Figure 16.1. In particular, small changes in end-user demand magnify into ever-larger changes upstream. This is costly, in terms of both stockouts (unfilled orders, or back orders) and excessive inventory holding costs. Reducing the bullwhip effect is a major theme of supply chain management.

Pseudo Inventory Reduction. Inventory in and of itself is *not* a negative, contrary to much current thinking. An unfortunate side effect of the movement to minimize inventory is that many costs have simply been shifted elsewhere. For example, in one firm, warehouse managers (given incentives to keep low inventories) regularly sent their inventory to a distribution center for shipping just before inventory was counted. They then arranged for the inventory to be returned after the audit. These sorts of issues can be corrected by changing incentives or by improving measurement systems (in this case, random audits were the solution). Different incentives get in the way of good logistics, and this is one of the greatest obstacles to streamlining supply chains.

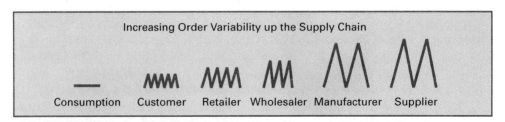

FIGURE 16.1 **The Bullwhip Effect**
Source: Based on the lecture notes of Enver Yücesan at INSEAD.

The drive to minimize inventory can have two pernicious effects. The first, noted above, is that managers simply shift the costs elsewhere. The second is that managers can eliminate opportunities by eliminating inventory. Consider the consequences for automobile makers of their obsession with minimizing stocks of raw materials and finished goods at the factory. Customers are interested in customizing their cars by specifying a personal choice of options. Although the possible combinations run into the millions, a few combinations are quite popular. Yet, many car makers keep such low factory stocks that they cannot quickly respond to a customer's request. Some customers are willing to wait, but these are fewer and fewer. They are therefore obliged to settle for what a dealer has in inventory or can get from another dealer. But inventory holding costs in the auto channel are high, so dealers keep very low stocks themselves. Thus, the customer wanting fast delivery is badly served. Yet, holding higher WIP and finished goods inventories at the factory level is cheaper than holding finished goods in the channel. By counting on dealers to stock a range of models, rather than assuming the inventory holding costs themselves, automakers deny themselves sales and customer satisfaction.[11] We shall return to this theme later in this chapter.

Real Inventory Reduction. Historically, most products have been produced to fit a demand forecast.[12] By necessity, factories have produced on speculation that demand would appear. Similarly, marketing channels have ordered and stocked on speculation that demand would appear. The idea here is produce to forecast or stock to forecast. Players try to make their forecasts come out by pushing their products into the system, planning activities so as to make the next level of the system agree to purchase output. These *push systems* (based on forecasted demand) have dominated for many years and are the basis of much of manufacturing theory and practice, especially in Western economies.

In the 1980s, many firms discovered that certain Japanese firms, notably Toyota, operated their factories with a very different philosophy. Typical car factories produce inventories of raw materials and work in progress, getting ready to push them onto the factory floor according to an activity plan. These push systems (such as MRP, material requirements planning) are based on anticipation that a workstation would need a component eventually. Toyota reversed the process. Rather than pushing components onto the factory floor in anticipation of demand farther down the assembly line, Toyota practiced a *pull system*. When demand for a component (say, a gray bucket seat) materialized (construction of the car began), Toyota called for the component. An intricate *just-in-time* system (JIT) enabled it to commandeer the gray bucket seat—often not from its own warehouse but from outside suppliers—and have it placed at the workstation just before it was needed.

JIT is a philosophy supported by a variety of techniques (such as kanban and quality circles) and management motivational methods. Initial disbelief about its efficacy and robustness (the ability to transplant it) gave way to an intense zeal for JIT in manufacturing practice and theory. It gave rise to new interest in pull methods, whereby actual (not anticipated) demand triggers supply in a synchronized manner. This interest has revolutionized manufacturing.

What does this have to do with marketing channels? It matters because the idea of pull systems (make to order) has achieved great credibility. The objection that only push systems (make to forecast) are "practical" has been discredited. This idea (pull systems to supplant push systems) has gained currency far outside its origin of manufacturing. *The success of pull systems in manufacturing has inspired channel players to transplant many of the underlying principles and values to marketing channels.* In particular, the success of JIT has muted critics who argue that pull systems are impractical when they cross organizational boundaries. This has been the inspiration of prominent supply chain management initiatives, such as efficient consumer response (ECR) and quick response (QR). These will be covered in a later section.

Fulfillment and Transportation

To fulfill an order in a marketing channel is to obtain the items and prepare them to ship, otherwise known as picking and packing. Chapter 15 on wholesaling discusses how difficult it is to do this humble task without errors, to do it cheaply, and to meet the customer's service requirements (e.g., a requirement for *fast* delivery of *small lots* of an *assortment* of items to a given *location*). Catalog companies master the art of shipping small lots directly to individuals, or quite often they contract with an organization that *has* mastered the art, that is, a fulfillment house. This is one reason why many pundits think catalog marketers will adapt to the Internet better than mass-merchants, who specialize in shipping large lots to a few locations (see Chapter 14 on e-commerce and non-store retailing).

The Essentials. Transportation, of course, is a complex and expensive endeavor. In a simpler time, shippers often thought in terms of a single type of carrier, such as a railcar, a truck, a ship, or a plane. Carriers encouraged this single-mode mentality, often creating barriers to mixing shipping modalities. Competition and deregulation has obliged the readjustment of attitudes and methods. Mixing modalities is common in many economies and the carriers themselves make it even easier. For example, some maritime shippers use containers that can be affixed directly to a truck bed by a crane, then moved directly to a railroad flatcar, sized to seat the container securely. Postal carriers routinely connect with private truck depots. Airfreight operators freely cooperate with truckers. The list of coordinating mechanisms available in many economies is long.

Transportation is not just the routing of shipments. It is closely linked to the location and operation of some number of warehouses. This determines the routing possibilities and is therefore a critical decision. Hence, an increased interest in contract warehousing, that is, outsourcing the warehousing function.[13] By abandoning their own warehouses (whose configuration, emplacement, and number they may have come to regret), shippers create great transportation flexibility.

Increasingly, they are making a distinction between a warehouse and a distribution center. Warehouses are intended to hold inventory for some time. Distribution centers are meant to hold inventory only for the short time necessary to send it somewhere else. They are central points to accumulate large lots, break and sort them into smaller lots and mixed lots, and reroute inventory. They are not intended to hold large lots for long periods. As such, distribution centers are like central dispatches.

The ultimate in dispatching quickly is a fairly new system called *cross-docking*. The key to cross-docking is that the end-user's site (say, a retail store) places an order for an assortment of items (say, a selection of sweaters of various colors, sizes, and styles). Ordinarily, the order would be composed from pallets of merchandise (conceivably one pallet per style-color-size combination) at the distribution center, then sent to the store. In cross-docking, the store's assortment is composed *at the factory or at a holding ware-house* and labeled for the store. It goes to the distribution center, where it is merely loaded with a variety of other orders onto a truck bound for the store. The merchandise crosses the asphalt from one loading dock to another, never entering a warehouse.

The efficient and effective use of cross-docking requires considerable know-how. This know-how is one reason why the Netherlands, renowned for logistical expertise, is emerging as a leader in pan-European physical distribution in the new Europe, in spite of the drawback of the country's small size. Indeed, these are exciting times for logisticians in Europe. Economic union is reducing barriers to pan-European commerce at the same time that a common currency, the euro, is enlarging markets. These new opportunities inspire channel managers to rethink every aspect of their nationally based logistics systems, and to assess warehousing and transportation decisions by a new set of criteria.[14]

Third-Party Logistics Providers. There is a general theme in the business press: Logistics is more and more being reconsidered, rebundled, and outsourced—not just to a single party. In this vein, a striking phenomenon has been the explosive growth of *third-party logistics providers* (3PL), otherwise known as contract logistics providers (mercifully, this has not been made into an acronym). Unitary examples (i.e., one company) are FedEx (the pioneer of many transportation innovations) and UPS. Many alliances (multiple companies) also exist, for example, between freight forwarders (companies that arrange transportation) and companies that actually do the transportation (such as airlines). In an interesting twist, some 3PL firms (e.g., FedEx) are also forming working partnerships with freight forwarders and air carriers.[15] On paper, this looks like duplication of service. In reality, it represents an effort by FedEx to expand its in-house ability to offer service to various locations and industry sectors.

A critical determinant of the popularity of 3PL is the providers' willingness to give fast, reliable transportation at what were once considered absurdly low prices. But what has caught managers' imaginations, and fueled the interest of the business press, is these providers' willingness to *bundle fulfillment and transportation*. In so doing, they have become generalized logistics problem solvers, not only freight carriers. An example is presented in Chapter 11 as Channel Sketch 11.3: Fujitsu and FedEx Build a Close Relationship. The key to these arrangements is that 3PL firms provide *contract logistics,* meaning up to and including . . . everything.

For example, Hewlett-Packard needs to get parts from Panang, Malaysia, directly to the factories of multiple end-customers (mostly telecommunications and automotive manufacturers) in Europe.[16] HP's model for this business is that customer demand pulls components through the system: The components arrive at the customer's site on a just-in-time basis. It is easy for something to go wrong here, causing the customer to halt production. HP has been operating with a two-week lead time to go from Malaysia to the customer's site.

To cut that time to four days and increase reliability, HP has contracted with a subsidiary of UPS. Called UPS Worldwide Logistics (WWL), this contract logistics provider will reengineer the entire HP supply chain. It will begin by staffing HP's Panang manufacturing site with five WWL employees. They will do the fulfillment (put together the shipments). A freight forwarder, Expeditors International, will pick up the packages and handle the routing and export documentation. Then an independent carrier (Lufthansa) will fly the packages to Cologne or to Frankfurt. There, UPS will pick up the packages and put them into its own combination air–ground delivery systems to go to the end-user. Figure 16.2 sketches the new logistics system. What inspires HP's faith that all of these transfers will work is, in part, WWL's EventTracker, a Web-based system for looking up the location of any package at any time.

HP may be unusual in its willingness to trust its businesses to contract logistics providers—it does so with several companies other than WWL. This is not common practice. But it is growing rapidly and inspiring other firms to consider outsourcing not just fulfillment, and not just transportation, but both in a bundle.

Orders, Invoices, and Payments (the Documentation)

A major facilitator of logistical change is reduction in the exchange of documents and in the amount of human processing they require. Handling the documentation consumes large amounts of clerical time and opens the door to errors of transcription. Document handling has been greatly reduced due to the growth of electronic data interchange, or EDI. This means direct, company-to-company communication strictly via computer,

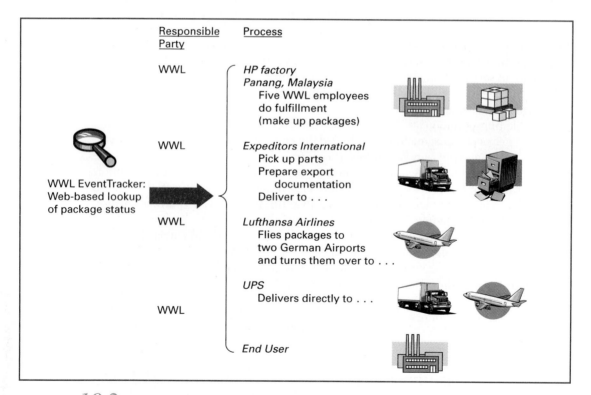

FIGURE 16.2 **Outsourcing Logistics**

with no human intervention. This computer-to-computer exchange can be of anything: queries about the status of inventories, orders, reports of receipt of goods, invoices, and even automatic money transfers to pay the invoices. In theory, the idea is simple.

In practice, it is difficult to implement. Bypassing people means not only powerful computer hardware and software but also good communication transmission and perfect standardization of the information flow. This is easier said than done. It has been done largely via proprietary software purchased from third parties, software called VAN (value-added network). In some industries, the pressure to adopt EDI has been so great that some firms have felt it necessary to pretend to do so. They claim to be on EDI, but they hide their real practice of receiving the EDI information, printing it off, and having a clerk key it into their computers manually.[17]

Why this reluctance to actually adopt EDI? Unfortunately, no single standard exists, which makes it difficult to have EDI with multiple channel members. Furthermore, the technology is new, expensive, cumbersome, and proprietary. Channel members have been (rightly) afraid to lock themselves in by making investments to fit themselves to closed-system architecture.

You may wonder why they don't just move it all to the Internet. And you are right. EDI via the Internet is becoming a reality.[18] It is rapidly putting it within reach of smaller and medium-size firms, which have held back. Their reluctance now looks like good forecasting, because the Internet offers the possibility of leapfrogging proprietary EDI. This, in turn, offers new possibilities for improving logistics management.

Inventory, fulfillment, transportation, and documentation—these are the building blocks of channel logistics. The supply chain management movement is an effort to put these elements together in new ways to add value to marketing channels. We now turn to SCM.

SUPPLY CHAIN MANAGEMENT: ORIGINS AND PRACTICES

What Is Supply Chain Management?

A *supply chain* is the set of entities that *collectively* manufactures a product and sells it to an endpoint (the ultimate customer).[19] In this sense, supply chains are like value-added chains: However, they include only players that add value in production and distribution. The concept of a supply chain is narrower than that of a value-added chain, but it is broader than the idea of marketing channels. These go from factory to buyer. A supply chain goes back to a more distant starting point—the suppliers of the factory that makes whatever is being sold—and the suppliers of the suppliers. Indeed, the beginning point of a supply chain is somewhat arbitrary, although it usually is considered to include only the immediate suppliers of the factory that produces finished goods. A supply chain is also distinctive in that it ends with the ultimate buyer, the customer of someone's customer. The end of the supply chain is the last invoice.

In practice, much of what is called SCM does not go all the way forward to the last invoice, nor backward to the suppliers of suppliers of manufacturers. The general understanding of a supply chain is shown in Figure 16.3.

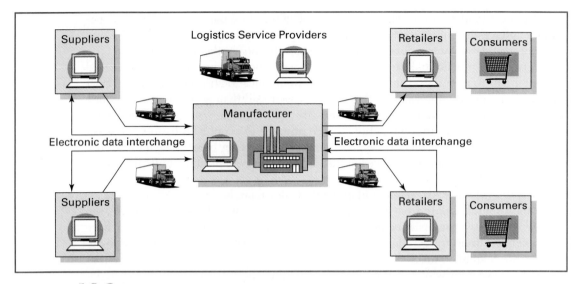

FIGURE 16.3 **Critical Supply Chain Elements**
Source: Adapted from Valérie Guez, "La Technique Pour Etre Près Du Client," *Management*, 10 (May 1999), pp. 118–20.

A good working definition of SCM is that it is an organizing concept that starts with customer service and argues that this results from the cumulative efforts of the entire channel.[21] Customer service cannot be interpreted as the sole responsibility of any single channel member. The guiding principle is to unify product flows and information flows up and down the production and distribution chain. Doing this requires (1) a market orientation, focused on the last customer; (2) effective channel management, to enable smooth transfers of product and information; and (3) effective logistics.

An organizing concept, a statement of principles, a focus on end-customers, channel management, and logistics—critics charge, with some fairness, that SCM needs a more precise definition. Yet, SCM is not really a package of techniques. It is akin to a paradigm; that is, a set of common values, beliefs, and tools that unites a group of people engaged in related tasks. Any paradigm has subfields, and SCM is no exception. A number of concepts and techniques can be folded into SCM, and we will treat these as we encounter them.[22] Let us begin with the roots of SCM in the grocery industry.

Efficient Consumer Response

Efficient consumer response (ECR) is a landmark in marketing channels. As a movement it has wrought radical change in the U.S. grocery industry, and that change is spreading to other sectors and other countries. Its success is surprising, given how different it is from the usual operating methods of most channels. Indeed, ECR is so successful that some critics are now declaring it outdated and looking for a new movement to replace it.

The source of ECR is fear. In 1992, the U.S. grocery store industry was feeling threatened by the rapid growth of nongrocery outlets, such as drugstores.[23] These "alternative format" (alternative to a supermarket) stores were aggressively adding food to their assortments, and the consumer was responding positively. A principal threat was seen to be Wal-Mart, which was moving from mass-merchandising to a hypermarket concept (merchandise and groceries). This is why, in 1992, two grocery trade associations commissioned a study of grocery methods. The report strongly criticized existing grocery channels and proposed a radical and complex series of changes to these channels. This program of change was named according to its objective: to achieve *efficient* (as opposed to wasteful) *consumer* (the final buyer) *response* (supplying only what is desired).

As initially proposed, the idea is to focus on four areas where the industry as a whole had and still has great potential for improvement. How great? The United States grocery industry converged on an estimate of $30 billion annually, or 5 percent of retail sales. Interestingly, a similar figure (£21 billion, 5.7 percent of retail sales) is being suggested for European grocers.[24] The four areas are

1. *A continuous replenishment program (CRP).* The goal is to end the bullwhip effect. The method is to use purchase data captured via scanners from the final buyer to inform all upstream supply chain members of demand, right back to the suppliers of suppliers. This requires massive standardization of codes and methods, and implementation of EDI.

2. *Efficient pricing and promotions.* A scourge of the industry is poorly calibrated promotions that wreak havoc with pricing and buyer behavior. At the consumer level, excessively generous promotions (such as one free for one purchased) create demand spikes and degrade brand equity. Nontargeted promotions encourage price comparisons and brand switching purely for temporary price cuts. At the wholesale level, manufacturer promotions lead to huge demand spikes. These push factory production up too high, then down too low. This, in turn, pushes inventory up too high (resulting in spoiled food) or down too low (running out of stock).

3. *Changes in product introduction.* Thousands of new-product introductions, most of which fail, are endemic to grocery retailing. ECR calls for combining market research commissioned by channel members in order to forecast new-product success better on a store-by-store basis, or based on reasonable store groupings (store clusters).

4. *Changes in merchandising.* This is the same idea (combine research) for the purpose of finding better ways to merchandise brands and their associated categories (e.g., snack foods, pet food, soups) store by store, or cluster by cluster.

Over time, these ideas have been developed and expanded. ECR has become an umbrella term that now encompasses a variety of means by which pure grocers combat alternative format stores. Some major operational features of ECR follow.

Category Management and Efficient Promotions. Historically, grocers think of what they sell in terms of how they buy: one brand of one type of item (e.g., Frito-Lay Taco Chips). *Category management* is the principle that a higher level of aggregation is called for. A consumer's shopping list is composed of product categories ("remember to buy two bags of salty snacks"). Therefore, a grocer should think in terms of a product category, and manage it as a whole, rather than managing each product–brand and letting the collection of items amount to a category. Further, in the spirit of ECR, retailers and suppliers should work together to understand each category's dynamics as perceived by the consumer.[25]

The rationale is that any item competes with any other item for shelf space. Consumers think in categories, and some as a whole merit more space than do others. Depending on the store, the diaper *category,* for example, may merit (on a contribution-per-space basis) more space than it is getting, whereas the laundry detergent category might merit less. This conclusion may not emerge from analyzing items one by one. And what should be in a category? The principle is to look for groupings that seem natural to a consumer. Thinking in category terms is made easier by advances in activity-based costing (ABC). The cost of slow-moving items is often surprisingly high, and ABC helps point out these items.

The category management focus is related to the idea of an efficient assortment: Having what the customer wants and skipping the rest. For groceries, skipping the rest is of great importance. It is widely believed that brand managers have proliferated SKUs to lock up shelf space and brand share, with the result that consumers are overwhelmed with unsought variety. For example, P&G claims that in the laundry category 40 percent of SKUs could be eliminated, yet 95 percent of consumer needs would still be met. Some manufacturers believe that having fewer SKUs actually *increases* overall sales.[26] This paradoxical observation might be explained by the idea that buyers aren't motivated to sift through multiple options in low-involvement product categories. Bewildered by more variety than they want, consumers depart with fewer purchases. A simplified display enables faster information processing, thereby increasing consumer confidence and motivation to purchase.[27]

Category management sparks thinking about *efficient promotions*. These can be defined as limited-time offers that are win–win for all parties. This means that they (1) move product (the manufacturer's concern), (2) drive store traffic and category sales (the retailer's concern), and (3) provide added value (to the *targeted* consumer). This third objective masks the real concern of many manufacturers: that their promotions do not offer value to their brand-loyal shoppers, nor do they build brand loyalty within the segment of consumers who rely solely on promotions to decide what to buy.

Efficient promotions use data about consumer behavior to discover what is selling, at what price, and to whom. Retailers, wholesalers, and manufacturers work together (often by commissioning a market research firm) to make sense of reams of transaction data or market research data. The purpose is to discover win–win promotional opportunities for a store or a cluster of stores.[28] For example, in Italy, manufacturer Kraft Jacobs Suchard and retailer Groppo GS have jointly analyzed loyalty card data to target consumers in a single attitude-based segment labeled "seeking healthy relaxation." As the label implies, it is no easy matter to identify these people. Similarly, in Spain, manufacturer Elida Fabergé and retailer Auchan have jointly analyzed panel data to identify a mutually interesting growth opportunity: susceptible consumers who are secondary customers of Fabergé and who are secondary shoppers at Auchan.[29]

Continuous Replenishment. *Continuous replenishment planning (CRP)* is the practice of replacing stock based on speedy knowledge of consumer "withdrawals" (i.e., sales). More precisely, in SCM the term means partnering between distribution channel members in order to replace the traditional practices (push systems, stocking to fore-cast) with a pull system. In this pull system, a retailer's stock is replenished based largely on actual sales data from the end of the supplier chain (the consumer).

The goal is to automate the process related to warehouse fulfillment and shipping, using consumer demand (captured by scanners) to trigger just-in-time restocking. By automating, ECR practitioners seek to cut errors and processing costs, which are sub-stantial. For example, British grocer Sainsbury's estimates that one-quarter of the chain's supply chain management budget is spent confirming the location and movement of inventory.[30]

Continuous replenishment is an arduous task. In CRP, a supplier (perhaps a distrib-utor, perhaps the manufacturer directly) takes complete responsibility for monitoring and refilling the retailer's inventory. In the grocery industry, CRP is often accomplished by charging the manufacturer with managing the downstream channel member's inven-tory. In most of these cases, powerful retailers have obliged manufacturers to make the significant expenditures necessary to perform continuous replenishment. Intriguing, albeit preliminary evidence suggests the biggest winners of this exercise are consumers (lower prices, fewer stockouts) and retailers (higher profits). The profit benefits for manufacturers are somewhat difficult to document. Although many report sales increases, they also find that significant logistical complexities and costs have been moved back to their level. As one industry analyst notes, just-in-time (JIT) often becomes just inventory shift (JIS). Perhaps the biggest benefit of CRP for manufactur-ers is that they remain suppliers to large retailers. CRP keeps them in the game. It may or may not yield increased profits.[31]

Obstacles to ECR. The list of obstacles to ECR is formidable.[32] At a physical level, ECR requires agreement on codes and on a huge number of EDI choices. In gen-eral, it requires standardization of methods. For example, the delicate exercise of cross-docking is difficult to pull off if channel members cannot agree on a number of issues. ECR implementation is a long and expensive affair.

One of the greatest barriers to ECR is the necessity of trusting other channel mem-bers. Trust and good working relationships are necessary for the information exchange, joint planning, and joint actions that underpin efforts to make the entire grocery channel respond to consumers while cutting waste. And trust is essential for continuous replen-ishment. The idea of making another party responsible for one's own stock, and doing so without an abundant safety stock, is a very difficult one for many industries to accept.

Trust is based on equity. The fundament of ECR is not that channel members share risk and information to produce gains for the channel as a whole, but that they then *share the gains equitably*. Opportunism (reneging on a promise to compensate all play-ers fairly) is fatal to ECR.

And yet, ECR exists. Although not the norm in grocery retailing in the United States, it has made great progress. If imitation is the most sincere form of flattery, sin-cere compliments of ECR abound. Trade publications of many industries overflow with discussions of how to create ECR in their sectors. For many, ECR has become synony-mous with supply chain management, which is attracting considerable attention in Europe.

Demanding customers seem to create excellent supply chain operations—albeit painfully. The auto giants and the major retail chains not only know what they want, they are determined to get it: delivery to a tightly specified time slot, in exactly specified quantities, at near-faultless quality; and "faultless" is extended to cover not only the products themselves but also the associated planning, delivery, and invoicing systems. In these industries, that is now the entry ticket to the game, not a differentiator. And the word is spreading.[33]

That ECR began in the grocery industry is miraculous. When the initiative was unveiled at a trade conference in 1993, few in the audience were confident that the traditionally adversarial relations in these marketing channels could be set aside. The cooperation and transparency that ECR requires had to be brought into being. The power of example is critical, and here the example used is the now-legendary arrangement between Wal-Mart and P&G (Chapter 11 on strategic alliances). Ironically, Wal-Mart's entry into the food business drove the grocery industry to devise ECR in the first place.

ECR also requires considerable change in the internal operations of a channel member. Jobs are lost and roles are redefined when EDI rationalizes supply chains. People representing many different functions in the organization (sales, marketing, purchasing, production, shipping, warehousing, accounting) must work together in project teams to create tremendous organizational change. And teamwork becomes permanent. Salespeople and purchasing agents, for example, are replaced by multifunctional teams on the buyer's side and the seller's side. And each side is expected to understand the other's business. These are wrenching changes.

RAPID RESPONSE

Rapid response, or what logisticians prefer to call quick response (QR), is another approach to supply chain management.[34] It appears similar to, and is often compared with, ECR, but is really quite different. QR originated in the early 1980s in the fashion industry, in which it has seen its greatest development. Many of the original developments are attributed to Benetton, the knitwear retailer. Many of the later ones are due to Giordano, a retailer that perfected QR from the late 1980s to the early 1990s. Since 1993, Giordano's methods have diffused considerably in the industry and are now practiced by retailers such as Gap and The Limited.

In some ways, QR is like ECR. The fundamental pull system idea—let the consumer tell the entire channel what to make and what to ship, then do it quickly—is the same. And the emphasis on interfirm cooperation, data analysis, data transmission, inventory management, and waste reduction is the same. The fundamental difference is in the volatile, unpredictable nature of what is being sold. For FMCG (fast-moving consumer goods) categories, such as toothpaste, *consumers know well in advance what they want* and what they don't want. ECR enables them to tell the retailer and the suppliers readily.

In fashion, *consumers don't know what they want until the moment they are ready to buy it*. They don't know what will be fashionable and whether the next fashion will appeal to them. In fashion retailing, consumers see and try an item, then form an opinion. And they change their minds readily. Benchmarks are difficult to find, in part because of lack of standardization (e.g., of sizes) in the industry. Routinely, retailers *put out* a line of clothing, *then discover* consumer reaction. If the sizes tend to run bigger or smaller than normal, the retailer will have the wrong size assortment. If one fabric or color or variation pleases more than another, retailers will find themselves with too much of one item and not enough of another. And fashion is perishable: Consumers won't wait months for restock of a desirable item, and items that sell poorly must be marked down quickly in order to get rid of them at all.

Historically, store buyers forecasted fashion demand well in advance and committed to orders, sometimes six seasons before the items would be sold. This is a push system (make to forecast). Over time, consumer fashion tastes have become so difficult to forecast that many fashion retailers have adopted the opposite strategy: Try something in a small way and see if it works. If it sells, stock more and quickly. But stock how? Manufacturers need lead time. By the time fashion is discovered, it's too late to order up more.

Here is the impetus for quick response. The essence of QR is in manufacturing. QR involves keeping manufacturing flexible as to what to make and how much to make. In contrast, ECR is more focused on how much to make and when to put it into a warehouse. There is no need to keep manufacturing flexible to produce variations of toothpaste, and there is little harm in stockpiling it for a while. Demand can be steadied (e.g., by restraining promotions), heading off production surges. But it is critical to keep clothing fabrication flexible to produce more of the latest hot dress or jacket, in this season's hit colors and fabrics, in the sizes that have proven popular. Production volume needs to be scaled up or down dramatically, and setups from one item to another should be quick. The items produced should be out the factory's door and to the customer rapidly.

Thus, whereas ECR focuses on shipments and promotions, QR focuses more on manufacturing. QR firms are heavy users of flexible manufacturing techniques. Computer-aided design and computer-aided manufacturing (CAD–CAM) occupy center stage in quick response programs. And a good deal of emphasis goes into keeping the components flexible. Benetton, for example, is famous for waiting until the last minute to dye its wools, after receiving early information from POS (point-of-sale) cash registers about what colors are selling.

Much of ECR is about pricing and promotion. This does not figure at all in QR. The objective is always the same: Catch the fashion and charge highly for it. When mistakes are made, which should be a frequent event, catch the mistake soon and mark it down quickly—but modestly. Then mark down again what is left—quickly. In this way, drastic markdowns are reduced: These become necessary to move out merchandise that has been around well after people realized they didn't want it.

In short, QR is not about merchandising and inventory. It is about manufacturing and timing. Another difference is that ECR always seeks to minimize transportation costs. This is fitting in FMCG: Toothpaste and foodstuffs are low-margin items that don't pass out of style while in transit. Fashion goods are the reverse. Hence, many channel members in the fashion industry willingly airfreight the hot sellers—as soon as they know what those are. And to save time, suppliers locate near designers and final points of assembly for the most fashion-sensitive categories.

Net, ECR is about demand that consumers know they will have. QR is about demand that consumers don't sense themselves until they're at the point of purchase. Both are pull systems that respond to a consumer. But ECR focuses on being efficient (holding down physical costs), whereas QR focuses on being quick; that is, fast to produce what the market has just decided it wants.

Quick response is an objective. In general, the key is to have access to POS data, then to use the information to cue an array of shippers to pick up and deliver within a network of flexible factories. These factories can be individuals working at home. The transportation network shunts raw materials, work in process, and finished goods around through various steps: design, pretreatment of fabrics, cutting, sewing, labeling, quality control, fulfillment of orders, shipment of packages. Firms have multiple suppliers, some of which act as backup systems, and others of which check on work in process.

These intricate arrangements drive off of POS data. Those with access to the data are in position to trigger frantic waves of manufacturing once a "winner" has been noticed.

The speed required to respond to fashion puts a premium on EDI (for fast transfers), CAD–CAM (for changing what is being manufactured), excellent POS systems, standing arrangements with members of the supply chain, and standardized identification. One of the most difficult challenges to QR has been implementing a standard system of universal product code (UPC) and scanning.[35] In contrast, the grocery industry had already made great progress on this problem in the 1970s, making ECR easier in the 1990s.

Given the intricacy of the production process, QR puts a very great strain on the myriad fashion channel members, particularly the subcontractors in manufacturing. Trusting relationships and open information transmission are difficult to keep up among so many players. The uncertainty of the demand environment also puts a strain on the system, making it hard to issue guarantees.

Hence, some vertical integration is commonly used to achieve QR in fashion. It occurs in two functions: design of the merchandise and retailing. Design is wholly owned because it is the key to manufacturing. Retailing is wholly owned in order to have stores to serve as test sites, observatories, and transmitters of fast, thorough information. Benetton, for example, is largely franchised but keeps some stores under company ownership. And with their stores, integrated providers such as Gap can quickly alter prices, raising them to stave off stockouts on surprise winners (while rushing more into production), or lower prices early, before it is obvious to consumers which items are losers. This is quick response indeed.

How quick it has to be depends on how fashionable the goods are. The less demand is influenced by fashion trends, the more the supply chain looks conventional. For moderately priced staple clothing, for example, a hyperresponsive supply chain is neither necessary nor profitable. A good system of regional warehouses will suffice to fill in surprise inventory gaps, and long lead times for production and transportation are employed to cut costs without penalty.[36]

PUTTING IT ALL TOGETHER: WHAT IS THE RIGHT SUPPLY CHAIN?

To this point, we have discussed building blocks of supply chain management and have seen them put together in different ways to serve different environments. Which model is better: the QR philosophy (keep manufacturing design flexible, don't focus on minimizing transportation costs) or the ECR philosophy (fix design, control costs tightly)? Both are pull systems, but differ in how and when they react.

Physical Efficiency versus Market Responsiveness

A good starting point is the nature of demand for a brand.[37] A *functional* brand is of a product that is a staple, which people buy in many outlets and which serves basic, stable needs. Thus, the brands have stable, predictable demand and long life cycles. This invites competition, which creates low margins. In contrast, an innovative brand of a product is new and different. This enables it to earn higher margins. But the sales cycle of the product–brand is short and unpredictable, in part, because such brands are quickly imitated, and their advantage dissipated. Fundamentally, an innovative product faces unpredictable demand, has a short product life cycle, and is hard to forecast. It has high margins but also higher markdowns and stockouts (due to changing tastes and forecast errors). And, because these products are differentiated, they often exist in many variations. Functional products have the reverse profile. Figure 16.4 summarizes the contrasts between these two endpoints of a spectrum.

The key to supplying functional goods is to hold down three types of costs: (1) manufacturing, (2) holding inventory, and (3) transportation. These observable physical costs all involve handling a good and accountants to track them. Efficient manufacturing and logistics are crucial. They matter first because low margins make cost consciousness important and second because predictable demand simplifies decision making. ECR fits in this spirit, as do many manufacturing methods based on tight planning and management of supplies. Here, the most important information flow occurs inside the chain from retailers back to suppliers of manufacturers.

Supply chains for these products need to be *physically efficient*. At the factory, this means running at high capacity; in the warehouse, fast-turning inventory. Products are

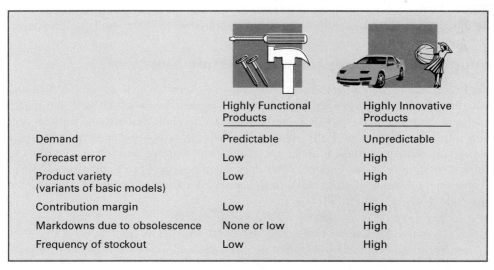

	Highly Functional Products	Highly Innovative Products
Demand	Predictable	Unpredictable
Forecast error	Low	High
Product variety (variants of basic models)	Low	High
Contribution margin	Low	High
Markdowns due to obsolescence	None or low	High
Frequency of stockout	Low	High

FIGURE 16.4 **Types of Goods for Supply Chain Management**

Source: Adapted from Marshall Fisher, "What Is the Right Supply Chain for Your Product?" *Harvard Business Review,* 78 (March–April 1997), pp. 105–16.

designed once and for all to make them easy to manufacture and to maximize their performance. Cost and quality are the criteria used to select suppliers.

Innovative goods demand the opposite. The greatest risk with these products is to miss the market by having the wrong item at the wrong time at the wrong price. The key to innovative goods is speed: Demand can't be estimated, only noted as it begins to surge. Hence, the point of sale is a critical information flow. For innovative goods, the opportunity cost of a stockout is very high, given the high margins. And by the time the stockout is rectified, the item may have lost favor, leaving the supplier with drastically devalued stocks.

Supply chains for innovative products need to be *market responsive*. To do this, product design must be modular to postpone final assembly as long as possible. Performance and cost are less critical here and can be sacrificed somewhat to achieve modularity. Suppliers are selected for quality and flexibility, not lowest cost. The manufacturing system keeps buffer stocks of supplies, just in case. An obsession exists with reducing the lead time needed to fill an order, even though this raises transportation and fulfillment costs.

These differences are summarized in Table 16.2. Market responsiveness and physically efficiency are two endpoints on a continuum, along which a supply chain philosophy can be fitted.

An intriguing element here is that where a brand falls on the spectrum from highly functional to highly responsive depends on the brand's marketing strategy. Thus, the same product category can have more innovative or more functional *brands,* each calling for a different supply chain. For example, in cars, some brands are very conservative and stable, often appealing to a buyer who resists change (Cadillac Seville, Ford Fairmount). Others have an ephemeral, faddish appeal (the BMW Z3 roadster, the Mazda Miata). The more functional brand needs a more physically efficient supply chain and doesn't need to be so market responsive. The more innovative one needs somewhat more market responsiveness and can afford somewhat less physical efficiency in its supply chain.

Supply Chain Management: Why Only Now?

On paper, supply chain management is an eminently sensible idea, so sensible that one wonders why it is having its heyday only now. Even now, SCM is more a slogan than a reality at many companies, and the methods needed to make pull systems work are still very difficult to implement. Pull systems in channels are so different from push ones that it is a very challenging task to make the changeover. Internal and external barriers to implementation exist everywhere. What does a company need to build a supply chain management mentality into its marketing channels? Experience from data suggests that these elements are critical:

1. Pressure. A common threat is a marvelous impetus. A huge opportunity (e.g., European economic union) can be phrased as a threat (develop pan-European logistics or be shut out of the game).
2. Industry agreement on standards (preferably regional, even global) for EDI. This means agreement on coding of goods and the definition of templates (e.g., for invoices) as well as on software.

TABLE 16.2
Two Kinds of Supply Chains

	Physically Efficient Supply Chain (Functional Goods) ⟶	Market-Responsive Supply Chain (Innovative Goods)
Objective	Cut costs of manufacturing, holding inventory, transportation	Respond quickly as demand materializes
Consequences of Failure	Low prices and higher costs create margin squeeze	Stockouts of high-margin goods Heavy markdowns of unwanted goods
Manufacturing Goods	Run at high capacity utilization rate	Be ready to alter production (quantity and type) swiftly Keep excess production capacity
Inventory	Minimize everywhere	Keep buffer stocks of parts and finished goods
Lead Times	Can be long, because demand is predictable	Must be short
Suppliers Should Be	Low cost Adequate quality	Fast, flexible Adequate quality
Product Design	Design for ease of manufacture and to meet performance standards	Design in modules to delay final production

Source: Adapted from Martin Fisher, "What Is the Right Supply Chain for Your Product?" *Harvard Business Review*, 78 (March–April 1997), pp. 105–16.

3. Heavy EDI investment, or more generally, heavy IT (information technology) investment.

4. Excellent cost accounting (speedy, accurate, detailed, activity based).

5. Internal incentive systems that focus on system gains and reward managers for making local sacrifices (i.e., in their own functions) for system gains.

6. Internal culture of cross-functional integration (as opposed to functional silos). Task forces and team incentives are valuable tools here. Participative management and flattened hierarchies are also conducive to devising and implementing the dramatic changes that SCM thinking demands.

7. Effective channel management, i.e., trust, good working relations, good design, the judicious exercise of power—in short, the implementation of the principles described in this book.

SUMMARY

Logistics involves the processing and tracking of factory goods during warehousing, inventory control, transport, customs documentation (a small issue or a nonissue inside trading zones), and delivery to customers. Business is renewing its focus on logistics (considered a backwater in some companies until recently). Changes in logistics can create astonishing increases in effectiveness and in efficiency. Many companies have dramatically altered their manufacturing processes and have reaped great rewards from so doing. Now they are turning to their marketing channels and applying the same principles, such as pull systems and electronic information sharing, looking to achieve another wave of gains. Most businesses need an example to follow: Good examples of better logistics are becoming abundant. And changes in logistics are becoming more and more feasible.

The building blocks of logistics are inventory (which involves storage and warehouses), fulfillment (picking and packing), transportation, and payment (the flow of orders and invoices, which used to be called paperwork). Logistics is a fertile area for improving operating results because there are (1) many ways to perform these functions, (2) many ways to bundle them, and (3) many parties to whom one could outsource some or all of the bundles.

Inventory performs valuable functions in reducing some costs (such as factory overtime) and increasing effectiveness (encouraging sales). These benefits must be weighed against the substantial costs of holding inventory, costs due to the commitment of capital, the expense of storage, and the risks of obsolescence and degradation. These costs are high, a fact that has become more evident with the development of sophisticated activity-based cost systems. There are a number of ways to reduce inventory holding costs, many of which have nothing to do with reducing inventory. Nonetheless, high inventory holding costs have led some firms to exert inordinate pressure to reduce inventories. The results are stockouts, insufficient variety, and efforts to shift costs elsewhere, rather than eliminate them.

Genuine reductions in inventory (rather than displacing costs elsewhere) at little cost in terms of consumer appeal are possible. Manufacturing has demonstrated that push systems (make to forecast) can often be replaced by sophisticated pull systems (make to demand, or make to order). This demonstrated success has helped inspire marketing channel members to devise pull systems for their channels.

This leads to the idea of supply chain management, a paradigm that starts with customer service and argues that this results from the cumulative efforts of the entire channel. Customer service cannot be interpreted as the sole responsibility of any single channel member. The guiding principle is to unify product flows and information flows up and down the production and distribution chain. Doing this requires (1) a market orientation, focused on the last customer; (2) effective channel management, to enable smooth transfers of product and information; and (3) effective logistics.

To many people, the principles of supply chain management are epitomized in efficient consumer response. As initially proposed, the idea is to focus on four areas where the industry as a whole had and still has great potential for improvement. These are continuous replenishment, efficient pricing and promotions, changes in product introduction, and changes in merchandising. Improvements in each of these areas are based on the entire channel sharing information and working together to devise ways to (1) cut needless and baffling variety, (2) redirect promotions to build brand equity, (3) balance stocks, and (4) eliminate the bullwhip effect (oscillating inventories, with a tendency to accumulate upstream). In the process of elaborating the principles of ECR, channel managers come to focus on changing the unit of what they track. Instead of managing SKUs, managers under ECR focus on managing product categories, as defined by the consumer.

Another kind of pull system is quick response. The objective here is to manage the supply chain for products whose demand is difficult to predict. QR puts the emphasis on flexible manufacturing to react to trends detected in point-of-sale data. To gain the information and flexibility, many channel members choose to own some stores (for the demand information) and to employ designers (for the ability to reset a production process quickly).

A spectrum from more functional to more innovative products can be used to determine which supply chain philosophy is most appropriate for a given brand. Innovative brands (whose demand is fundamentally volatile) need supply chains that respond quickly to market signals. Functional products (whose demand is stable) need supply chains that hold down physical costs. Both types of supply chains have become more feasible with the development of new technologies and with changes in management practice. And one of the cornerstones of good supply chain management is effective marketing channel management.

Discussion Questions

1. What are the most important components of inventory holding costs rates for each of these categories: fresh fruit, breakfast cereal, personal computers, evening dresses, jewelry? How would these costs vary for a large versus a small firm, and for a firm in a high-growth industry versus a low-growth industry?

2. Assume you are a logistics manager for a firm operating in Europe. Your logistics decisions have been made country by country, with the result that you have multiple national systems. Now you are designing a pan-European system, on the assumption that frontiers will have little impact on your decisions and all your bills and receivables will be in Euros, regardless of the country of operation. What factors would you take into consideration in designing your new system? What information would you be seeking, and how would you be evaluating your options?

3. "The goal is zero inventory." Debate the merits and demerits of this slogan for marketing channels.

4. Give three examples of more innovative products (for SCM purposes) and three examples of more functional products. Give at least one example of two brands (one more innovative, one more functional) in the same product category (e.g., automobiles). What is the right supply chain for the more innovative products, and why? How does this differ from the more functional products?

5. In your opinion, what is the greatest obstacle to implementing the principles and practices of supply chain management?

Notes

1. The authors are grateful to Frédéric Dalsace, Enver Yücesan, and the late Xavier de Groote. Over the years, they have been a source of instruction, guidance, and inspiration in the domain of logistics and supply chain management. Errors and omissions remain the responsibility of the authors.

2. Garett van Ryzin, "Analyzing Inventory Cost and Service in Supply Chains," *Technical Note,* Columbia Business School, New York, 1997.

3. Stephen L. Pearce, "Activity-Based Costing: A Practical Approach," *Industrial Distribution,* 86 (May 1997), pp. 82–90.

4. Michael Garry, "ABC in Action," *Progressive Grocer,* 75 (February 1996), pp. 71–72.

5. A thorough treatment of inventory models is Paul Zipkin, *Foundations of Inventory Management* (New York: McGraw-Hill, 2000).

6. This section is based on Wallace J. Hopp and Mark L. Spearman, *Factory Physics.* Chicago: Irwin Publishing, 1996.

7. Alexandre Phalippou, "Chez Surcouf, C'est le Bazar . . . et ça Marche!" *Management,* 10 (December 1999), pp. 34–35.

8. Alexandre Phalippou, "La Redoute Révolutionne la VPC," *Management,* 10 (December 1999), p. 36.

9. Edward Feitzinger and Hau L. Lee, "Mass Customization at Hewlett-Packard: The Power of Postponement," *Harvard Business Review,* 75 (January–February 1997), pp. 116–21.

10. Hau L. Lee, V. Padmanabhan, and Seungjin Whang, "The Bullwhip Effect in Supply Chains," *Sloan Management Review,* 38 (spring 1997), pp. 93–102.

11. Marshall L. Fisher, "What Is the Right Supply Chain for Your Product?" *Harvard Business Review,* 78 (March–April 1997), pp. 105–16.

12. This section is based on Hopp and Spearman, *Factory Physics.*

13. Clyde E. Witt, "Distribution: Let Someone Else Do It," *Material Handling Engineering,* 52, no. 2 (1997), pp. 38–45.

14. Yves Puget, "L'Europe Logistique se Construit," *LSA,* March 9, 2000, pp. 48–54.

15. Michael D. White, "Air Cargo Takes Wing," *World Trade,* 12, no. 6 (1999), pp. 60–62.

16. Jennifer L. Baljko, "HP Forges Tighter Supply Chain," *Electronic Buyers' News,* June 7, 1999, p. 1.

17. Bernie Knill, "The Straight Line of Supply Chain Flow," *Transportation and Distribution,* 39 (February 1998), pp. SCF16–SCF22.

18. Angel Abcede, "EDI, Internet Connect as Data Go Electronic," *National Petroleum News,* 89 (October 1997), pp. 110–14.

19. Tom Davis, "Effective Supply Chain Management," *Sloan Management Review,* 34 (summer 1993), pp. 35–46.

20. Valérie Guez, "La Technique Pour Etre Prés Du Client," *Management,* 10 (May 1999), pp. 118–20.

21. Elise Truly Sautter, Arnold Maltz, and Kevin Boberg, "A Customer Service Course: Bringing Marketing and Logistics Together," *Journal of Marketing Education,* 21 (August 1999), pp. 138–45.

22. SCM is a rapidly advancing field. A good site to keep up with these changes (www.ascet.com) is offered by the ASCET Project: Achieving Supply Chain Excellence Through Technology.

23. Tim Triplett, "More U.S. Grocers Turning to ECR to Cut Waste," *Marketing News,* 3 (September 12, 1994), pp. 12–13; "Lessons Learned from the Grocery Industry," *Oil and Gas Investor* (second quarter 1998), p. 23.

24. Malory Davies, "Shifting into High Gear," *Director,* 50 (February 1997), pp. 46–51.

25. Bob Qureshi and Jenny Baker, "Category Management and Effective Consumer Response: The Role of Market Research," *Marketing and Research Today,* 26, no. 1 (1998), pp. 23–31.

26. Alan Mitchell, "P&G Slams Inefficient Marketing," *Marketing Week,* November 8, 1996, pp. 26–27.

27. Pierre Chandon, Gilles Laurent, and Brian Wansink, "When and Why Does Consumer Stockpiling Accelerate Consumption Volume?" *Journal of Marketing,* 64 (2000).

28. "It's a Brand New Deal Out There," *Progressive Grocer,* 74 (February 1995), pp. SS2–SS3.

29. Alan Mitchell, "ECR's Big Idea Requires Sharing of Information," *Marketing Week,* April 16, 1998, pp. 22–23.

30. Malcolm Wheatley, "Pile It Low, Sell It Fast," *Management Today,* February 1998, pp. 68–70.

31. Roger C. Vergin and Kevin Barr, "Building Competitiveness in Grocery Supply Through Continuous Replenishment Planning: Insights from the Field," *Industrial Marketing Management,* 28, no. 1 (1999), pp. 145–53.

32. Denis O'Sullivan, "ECR: Will It End in Tears?" *Logistics Focus,* 5 (September 1997), pp. 2–5; Yves Puget, "Les Quatre Niveaux de la 'Supply Chain,'" *LSA,* October 1999, p. 71.

33. The Economist Intelligence Unit, "Delivering the Goods," *Business Europe,* February 9, 2000, pp. 1–2. Quotation from p. 1.

34. James Richardson, "Vertical Integration and Rapid Response in Fashion Apparel," *Organization Science,* 7 (July–August 1996), pp. 400–12. This article is the basis for the section on rapid response.

35. Bernie Knill, "How Efficient Is Efficient Consumer Response?" *Material Handling Engineering,* July 1997, pp. 13–15.

36. Garrett van Ryzin and Siddarth Mahajan, "On the Relationship Between Inventory Costs and Variety Benefits in Retail Assortments," *Management Science,* 45 (November 1999), pp. 1496–1509; Robert E. Dvorak and Frits van Paasschen, "Retail Logistics: One Size Doesn't Fit All," *The McKinsey Quarterly,* 2, no. 2 (1996), pp. 120–29.

37. This section is based on Fisher, "What Is the Right Supply Chain for Your Product?"

17 Franchising

LEARNING OBJECTIVES

After reading this chapter, you will:

- Define franchising and distinguish the two major forms, business format franchising and the authorized franchise system
- Describe why an entrepreneurial individual would become a franchisee rather than founding a new business—and what would make a candidate hesitate to join a franchise system
- Explain why a firm with a business model would opt for franchising rather than expanding by setting up its own branches run by employee managers
- Sketch the features of businesses that are not well suited to franchising
- Describe the essential elements of a franchise contract—and why contracts are so important when franchising
- Weigh the positive and negative features of a business that mixes some franchisees with company-owned outlets—and describe why most franchising systems evolve to this mixed form
- Evaluate the biggest problems the franchisor faces once the business becomes clearly viable—if it survives the founding stage

ranchising is a marketing channel structure intended to convince end-users that they are buying from a vertically integrated manufacturer, when in fact they may be buying from a separately owned company. As such, franchise systems masquerade as company subsidiaries. In reality, they are a category within the classic marketing channel structure of two firms, one supplying, the other performing downstream marketing channel flows. Franchisors are upstream manufacturers of a product or originators of a service.[1] They write contracts with franchisees—separate companies that are downstream providers of marketing channel flows. But there are several crucial distinctions to a franchise system.

End-users (customers of the franchisee) should believe they are dealing with the franchisor's subsidiary. Therefore, the franchisee *assumes the identity* of the franchisor, projecting itself *as though it were the franchisor's operation*. This deliberate loss of separate identity is a hallmark of franchising.

To do so, the franchisee awards the franchisor category exclusivity (no competing brands in the product category). Usually, the masquerade is completed by carrying no other product categories, either. Thus, franchising goes beyond granting a producer favored status in one of the reseller's product categories.

To further the projection of the franchisor's identity, the franchisee purchases, via contract and by the payment of fees, the right to market the franchisor's brand, using the methods, trademarks, names, products, know-how, production techniques, and marketing techniques developed by the franchisor. Effectively, the franchisor develops an entire business system, a *business format,* and licenses it to the franchisee to use in a given market area.

By paying fees and signing a contract, the franchisee assumes more than the right to exploit a broad license. It also assumes the obligation to follow the franchisor's methods. By contract, the franchisee cedes a great deal of legitimate power to the franchisor.

And yet, the franchisee *is* a separate business, with its own balance sheet and income statement. From the standpoint of an accountant or tax authority, a franchise is a business like any other. Franchisees invest their own capital, run the business, and keep the profits or assume the losses. They own the business: It is theirs to alter, sell, or terminate, although even this fundamental property right can be circumscribed by the franchise contract!

Franchising is an inherently contradictory marketing channel. It is technically two independent businesses joining forces to perform marketing flows to mutual benefit. It is actually an attempt to project something else entirely: one company, owned and operated by the owner of the brand name. In order to convince the final customer that the channel and the brand name have only one owner, franchisees compromise their independence. They voluntarily cede an almost astonishing degree of power to the franchisor—*and* pay him for the privilege of doing so!

Why would any downstream entrepreneur accept—indeed, seek out and pay for—a franchise? For that matter, why would any manufacturer go to market through independent companies when its real intention is to control the channel so tightly that the final customer doesn't know the difference? Why not give customers what they think they are getting: company-owned and managed outlets?

On the face of it, franchising might seem like such a flawed concept that it should be rare. But it is the fastest-growing form of retailing and has been for some time. Chain organizations using franchising, in whole or in part, account for over 40 percent of retail sales in the United States, a figure that is expected to pass 50 percent rapidly.[2] In Europe, franchising was once dismissed in some circles as an aberrant form of organization, suitable only in North America. This viewpoint has been discredited: Franchising has taken off in Europe, having appeared in the 1970s.

Indeed, it has become a global phenomenon, so well established that it has come full circle. Countries that first experienced franchising as a U.S. import have spawned their own firms, which have developed a business format and exported franchising to other countries—including "back" to the United States![3] A small indication of the global pervasiveness of franchising is that the largest private employer in Brazil is . . . McDonald's, via its franchised network.[4]

Clearly, franchising has advantages that are not evident at first glance. Its meteoric rise has attracted considerable research attention in many fields, provoking a great deal of recent theorizing and empirical study in marketing, as well as in finance, economics, and management. This chapter brings the principal arguments together, frames them in a common terminology, and organizes them around the managerial issue of whether, when, and how to enter a franchise agreement, as either the franchisor or the franchisee. The references in the endnotes go further into the rich and puzzling institution that is franchising.

This chapter begins by asking why either side, franchisee or franchisor, would enter into such an arrangement. Business format franchising is then contrasted with an earlier-generation form, product or trade name franchising. Next, the broad outlines of the contract are discussed. This is critical, because it determines who will enter the agreement and why, as well as setting the balance of power. The chapter then turns to a curious fact: Most franchisors also own some outlets. The motives for this, and the way it is implemented, are discussed at length. Finally, the daily issues of surviving and gaining cooperation from established franchisees are examined. Channel Sketch 17.1 describes the world's most admired franchisor, McDonald's, whose operations touch on every aspect of the franchising system.

CHANNEL SKETCH 17.1

McDonald's[5]

McDonald's is the world's largest and most admired franchisor. It is also the world's largest retail chain organization in number of outlets—25,000 units in 115 countries representing 95 percent of the world's wealth. Franchising is the backbone of this highly profitable system, the scale of which is difficult to grasp. Here are a few indicators:

- On average, a new outlet opens somewhere in the world every five hours.
- Fourteen billion client transactions occurred in 1998, the equivalent of serving two meals to each person on the planet.
- With 1.5 million employees, McDonald's is the world's largest private employer.
- McDonald's is also the world's largest holder of real estate.

Of the 25,000 outlets, McDonald's owns 5,500, generating a quarter of its worldwide sales. Four thousand outlets, mostly in Asia and the Middle East, are joint ventures with local shareholders. The remaining 15,500 outlets are owned by 5,300 franchisees. These franchisees invest heavily to build an outlet, often selling all their possessions to raise the capital. Then they pay McDonald's up to 25 percent of their revenue in fees and in rent, as McDonald's is usually their landlord. In return, they share in the system. Let us examine the critical elements.

Method: The operating manual weighs two kilograms (over four pounds) and specifies how operations are to be performed, down to tiny details. For example, all servers wear a uniform that has no pockets. This is thought to discourage both accepting tips and putting one's hands in the pockets. Hands free in turn encourages constant action ("if you've got time to lean, you've got time to clean"). Other details include cooking and serving specifications down to the second, as well as detailed role descriptions for personnel.

Setup assistance: Months of on-site training terminate at Hamburger University, which teaches 7,000 people a year how to run the business. McDonald's also undertakes to secure the site and build the restaurant, which it then rents back.

Enforcement of norms: Once in operation, a franchisee is assisted by an army of "regional consultants," who run frequent and detailed checks on operations. McDonald's insists that franchisees abide by its intricate system. The first franchisee in France lost his 12 units when he was terminated in 1982 for noncompliance.

Worldwide supply: McDonald's has a network of favored suppliers, who function almost as subsidiaries. When entering a new market, McDonald's begins with local suppliers, then asks them to adapt to its methods. Often, the franchisor finds them inadequate and induces its own suppliers to enter the market as replacements. These key suppliers process astonishing quantities of food and supplies to McDonald's exacting specifications. The result is uniformity of product, as well as economies of scale that allow the franchisor to operate profitably, yet charge low prices.

Marketing strategy: McDonald's positions itself to families (the target segment) as fast and inexpensive. To draw in the family, the strategy focuses on pleasing children by in-store events (e.g., birthday parties), Happy Meals, and the Ronald McDonald clown mascot. The menu is extremely similar worldwide, with limited adaptation to local tastes. This standardization enhances the capture of economies of scale, and not just in food: McDonald's is one of the world's leading distributors of toys, via the Happy Meal.

Marketing communication: Massive advertising budgets go to campaigns, particularly the backing of sporting events. For example, McDonald's spent roughly $40 million on advertising the World Soccer Cup in 1998. Unlike the rest of the strategy, advertising is not standardized: Countries and regions have their own slogans and campaigns. Communication is partly financed by franchisees, who pay 4.5 percent of revenue as an advertising fee. They may also run their own local campaigns: They are aided by ready-to-use kits provided by the franchisor.

To enter this system, a prospective franchisee must pass a number of tests of motivation and capability. Doctors, lawyers, and executives are among the applicants. They are frequently screened out for inadequate motivation and lack of a customer service orientation. In France, successful candidates invest 500,000 FF (roughly $80,000) in up-front fees. They add six times this figure to outfit the interior and the kitchen although the franchisor pays the bulk of the costs of building the restaurant and is the landlord.

In spite of these costs, McDonald's locations break even after several years and become quite profitable. In France, for example, a franchisee draws a salary comparable to an executive paycheck, as well as collecting substantial dividends and building wealth through the location. Resale values typically run upward of several million French francs. Satisfactory performance means a franchisee can open more stores. However, McDonald's discourages building large operations, fearing the owner will become too removed from operations.

Of course, McDonald's draws criticism as well as admiration. Social critics charge that the franchisor's personnel practices are heavy-handed and anti-union. Some suppliers feel exploited. The chain is often accused of being secretive and portrayed as a heartless multinational. And many a critic charges that McDonald's creates an unhealthy "fast-food culture" wherever it goes, suppressing local businesses and displacing local customs. On the other hand, McDonald's is praised for offering employment (and ultimately franchising opportunities) to young people and to people who face discrimination in their job market (e.g., Latinos and African Americans in the United States, youths of North African descent in France). McDonald's franchisees operate in blighted neighborhoods, creating jobs and businesses that benefit residents. And the popularity of the product suggests that fast-food culture is not unwelcome!

McDonald's acknowledges it has made errors along the way. The format was developed by a family business in California after World War II. Ray Kroc, a salesman of milk-shake machines, realized its potential and licensed the concept from its developers. In 1955, Kroc opened his own McDonald's and began to build his empire. Growth was steady until 1996, when franchisee profitability began to fall. A major reason was that the U.S. market was becoming saturated, yet McDonald's continued to add units at a pace that cannibalized existing franchises. This led to an in-house revolt and a change of management. Subsequently, the chain slowed its growth (in part by closing one unit for every two it opened) and invested heavily to modernize kitchens in order to improve both product and profitability. McDonald's has also purchased small chains selling a variety of foods outside of the usual menu. The motive? To have a laboratory in which to test ways to diversify beyond hamburgers.

WHY BECOME A FRANCHISEE?

You are a private individual with a certain amount of capital, perhaps due to an inheritance, severance pay, accumulated savings, or liquidating your equity in a previous business. You could invest the money and collect the earnings, but you are more interested in starting a business, say, a fast-food restaurant. You find the idea of owning your own business attractive for psychological reasons. You feel that other opportunities in society are closed to you, perhaps because of your gender, race, or background. Or perhaps you simply value independence from an employer, and you are willing to assume some risk to get it. You are confident that you can get better returns in the long run from your own company than from investing in someone else's. You see a variety of advantages in being the owner of a business. For example, you may be a recent immigrant looking to bring family members to join you by offering them employment.

What would divert you from starting a fast-food restaurant from the ground up? Failure rates for new businesses are high. It takes time and resources to build a clientele. And there are literally thousands of decisions, big and small, to be made: Where should the restaurant be located? Should it have a theme? What size should it be? What kind of food should it serve, and how to prepare it—economically? Any entrepreneur can be overwhelmed by the many legal, financial, marketing, managerial, and operating decisions to be made. Setting up a business takes months, even years. And it may well fail, wiping out your capital.

Contemplating this prospect may extinguish your entrepreneurial ambition and send you to the job market. If you remain interested in owning your own business, it is little wonder that you would be attracted to a franchising arrangement. In effect, you sell a piece of your independence to the franchisor. In return, you purchase the services of a corporate backer, a coach, a problem solver—and, curiously, another role, to be discussed in a later section. Franchisor personnel step in to assist you. They train you, work with you, share with you the franchisor's formula, its business format. The business format should be a prepackaged solution to all your start-up problems. By paying a fee (usually in several parts, fixed and variable—discussed further later in this chapter), you buy a license to exploit the format in a market area.

The Start-up Package

When you buy this license for a business format, that is, a franchise, you acquire a brand name and an explanation from the franchisor of all the marketing decisions that have been made for the business. You also acquire all the decisions you need to make initially as well as training and assistance to implement them. This includes:

- Market survey and site selection
- Facility design and layout (architectural and building services)
- Lease negotiation advice
- Financing advice
- Operating manuals
- Management training programs
- Training the franchisee's employees

All of these *initial* services are valuable. But *site selection* is particularly important to a retail operation because market potential is a critical determinant of a store's sales and productivity.[6] Exactly how much help the franchisor will give you will vary. For example, McDonald's typically does all site analysis and most land acquisition and development.

In contrast, Budget Rent-A-Car merely assigns a territory and allows the franchisee to build where he or she pleases, subject to franchisor review and advice.

Another critical piece of the start-up is usually the *brand name* itself. The franchisee uses the brand equity of the name to build a clientele quickly.

These initial services are all subject to *economies of scale*, which the franchisor can capture and share with the franchisee. By providing these services over and over, the franchisor acquires a deep knowledge of the nuances of each activity. The franchisor also pools demand for these services. This makes it economical to dedicate personnel to the setup job (e.g., statistical specialists to do site analyses; company lawyers to help deal with zoning authorities and draft documents; architects to draw plans and supervise construction; technicians to train, install, and test equipment). The franchisor's scale also makes it possible to have preferred-customer status with service providers such as contractors and bankers. All of this means better results and at lower cost.

Ongoing Benefits

Were this the end of the story, franchising would be a system only for *launching* a business. But it is primarily a system for *running* a business. Once you have started your franchised fast-food restaurant, what services could you expect your franchisor to provide continuously? These include:

- Field supervision of your operation, including quality inspection
- Management reports
- Merchandising and promotional materials
- Management and employee retraining
- National advertising
- Centralized planning
- Market data and guidance
- Auditing and record keeping
- Group insurance plans

Of this list, the first two items stand out for their potential for conflict. Almost all franchisors have a continuous program of *field supervision*, including monitoring and correcting quality problems. Field representatives (with titles such as "franchise consultant") visit the franchise outlet. Their purpose is to aid the franchisee in everyday operations, check the quality of product and service, and monitor performance. They should play the roles of coach and consultant, inspector, evaluator, and reporter to the franchisor. The policing role conflicts with the coach and consultant roles. It requires diplomacy and skill to balance them.

Many franchisees are required to make monthly or semimonthly *management reports*, on key elements of their operations—weekly sales, local advertising, employee turnover, profits, and other financial and marketing information. This reflects the almost-a-subsidiary nature of franchising and is highly unusual in other contractual channels. Reporting on operations is intended to facilitate the various financial, operating, and marketing control procedures. It is the basis of franchisor feedback intended to assist the franchisee. But this confidential information goes to the heart of the business. To oblige feedback, many systems require franchisees to buy special electronic invoicing and reporting systems. The franchisor's review of the books can create resentment. After all, isn't part of the idea of franchising to run your own business so as to escape having a boss?

Why Ask a Franchisor to Provide These Services?

We now have a list of services that you are willing to use your capital to pay someone to provide. Now the question is: Who should be the provider? Put another way, *Why should the provider be a franchisor?* These services are available from others. One could contract with an architect, an accountant, a consultant, and so forth. What advantage does a franchisor have?

First, franchisors act as consolidators: They bring all the necessary services, no more, no less, together under one roof and consolidate them, achieving economies of scale (size) and of scope (synergy). But others could do that, too.

Second, franchisors focus on one product line (fast-food restaurants, car repair, etc.). They develop benefits from this specialization. But others could do that, too.

The critical and distinguishing benefit of a franchisor is to bring everything together to focus it on *a branded concept*. Everything is dedicated to the needs of the brand and to the implementation of the concept. The franchisor develops specialization benefits that are tied to brand equity. This, in turn cannot be built unless there are many units. A major reason to go to a franchisor is to rent brand equity, to become part of a large network, not just to contract for business services.

This brings us to a crucial and often-misunderstood reason why you would pay for a franchise. *You are hiring an enforcement agency.* The franchisor acts as a police officer, judge, and jury. The business format is a system, and the franchisor makes sure that all players (franchisees) observe its rules. You, the franchisee, hire the franchisor to police the system, to make sure that *everyone else* implements the concept. It is in your interest to have a police officer to protect brand equity—and it is the basis of the franchising concept.

This idea is often labeled the *prevention of free riding*. Free riding is when one party reaps benefits ("gets a ride") while another party bears the costs. Thus, the ride is free to the one who benefits. For example, Dunkin' Donuts positions itself as a producer of premium fresh bakery goods. To sustain the positioning, franchisees agree to throw out unsold product after a few hours and to replace it with freshly produced goods. This is costly. It is tempting to keep selling the doughnuts for a few more hours, hoping that no one will notice they are a bit stale. The franchisee that sells stale doughnuts benefits from the Dunkin' Donuts image. But this practice hurts the brand's image, which hurts all franchisees.

If franchisees didn't have a franchisor, they would invent one, *for the purpose of policing each other*. Brand equity is so critical to the franchising proposition. Safeguarding brand equity is one reason why franchising has become associated with the production of services of all kinds: document handling, building, business aids and services, child care, hospitality, tourism, travel, weight control—even the conduct of autopsies! One of the most important problems of a services business is ensuring consistency of the result. By branding a service business, a producer guarantees consistency, which attracts customers. By franchising, the producer of a service implements the guarantee it gives its customers, thereby enhancing its brand equity.

WHY BECOME A FRANCHISOR?

Let us turn the lens around, changing your perspective. Now you head a company with a concept and a brand. You have a business format. You desire tight control over the implementation of your concept. You want that control to uphold the brand's image and to ensure the proper sale and servicing of your product. Given your focus on directing how your brand is presented, sold, and serviced, the logical thing for you to do is to set up a network of outlets that you own and operate. This means hiring managers, who in turn hire a staff for each outlet. The outlet needs to be set up and the manager and staff hired and trained. Once past these initial actions, your company will run the outlet. With this, you have control.

Why would you instead rent your brand name and format to a person who has a fierce drive for independence, a desire to be an entrepreneur? Why would you reveal your business secrets to this entrepreneur and then entrust the business to him or her? Why would you encumber yourself with a contract and take on the responsibility of coaching, consulting, and policing a group of entrepreneurs? Inexperienced franchisors imagine that guiding a group of entrepreneurs is like herding a flock of sheep. It is more like herding cats. So if you really want control, why not own the channel?

Raising Financial and Managerial Capital to Grow Fast

You want to grow fast. You are not just motivated by entrepreneurial ego and impatience. Perhaps you have a unique idea, and you want to exploit it before others copy it. Or you are entering a business in which there is fragmented competition, with no strong brands, and you want to build a brand name before someone else does. Conversely, there may be a strong competitor, and you wish to grow large before the competitor notices you and tries to block you. You may want to get to minimum efficient scale quickly, so that you can amortize costs over a large operation, and it may be very large: To justify national advertising in the United States, for example, requires national coverage of a market almost as large as the European Economic Community. Or you might want to exploit a developing trend (such as American-style fast food in Southeast Asia) rapidly, before the market becomes saturated.

Immediately, you will need a high level of financial capital. You could go public, selling shares in your company. Early explanations of franchising focused on the idea that franchisees are a cheaper source of capital or even the only source of capital. Franchisees would invest for a lower rate of return than would a passive investor because franchisees understand the business in their location better. This idea, while appealing, was discredited for some time because it appears to run counter to financial portfolio theory. Investors should prefer less risk. The risk of any single location is likely to be greater than the risk of the entire chain. Therefore, prospective franchisees should prefer to buy a share of the entire chain, rather than buying the rights to one location.

The idea that entrepreneurs franchise to get access to capital has come back, in part because there is evidence that it is true in practice.[7] Perhaps capital markets are not so efficient that a prospective franchisor can access them readily. Or perhaps franchisees are not just financial investors, indifferent between owning their own business and owning a piece of a company.[8] Let us explore this idea further.

A franchisee is the manager of her outlet and so influences the risk–return ratio of her operation. She won't invest unless she is confident that she can run it well. She reasons that if she buys the franchise rights to a location of her choice, she can drive her unit to high profit at low risk. But if she buys a piece of a company, her influence on operations will be miniscule. Further, if her expectation is correct, she may become wealthy, as she is the "residual claimant." After paying suppliers and the franchisor, she owns all the profits. She would not expect the returns to her share of a company, run by other people over many locations, to be as great. Thus, she is *not* indifferent between owning a franchise and owning a piece of the franchisor.

The key to this argument is that anyone who can find franchisees has passed a screen, a sort of examination of his or her investment idea. (Many would-be franchisors never find any franchisees—and can't find buyers for their stock, either.) With their investment, *franchisees endorse their own operation*. They may not value the entire chain as highly as they value their location. This makes it easier for you, the franchisor, to persuade the franchisee to invest. You don't need to present the entire operation as being as interesting as any single location.

By finding franchisees, you have done more than alleviate your financial problem. You have also addressed another pressing issue—a shortage of good managers. Once you have capital, you need to find managers for your outlets. Once you have enough managers, you need to build layers of management. Having solved the capital scarcity problem, you, the entrepreneur, will quickly find yourself spending inordinate time trying to solve your *managerial scarcity problem*.[9]

As you are racing to grow your business and have plenty of other issues to occupy your attention, you will want to build your management team fast. You could spend your resources looking at employment applications from people whose motivation and qualifications are very difficult to assess. Are they misrepresenting themselves? Are they adept at projecting capability and drive, or are they really what they say they are? One way to tell is to *"screen" applicants by asking them to become franchisees*. The unmotivated, uninterested, or incapable are less likely to pay your lump-sum entry fee and put up the initial investment. Nor will they accept to pay an ongoing royalty and live off leftover profits.

These arguments for starting up by franchising are defensible on rational grounds. Do franchisors reason this way? Some do. But the reality is not always so rational. Many founders of franchise organizations take the franchising route because their overriding objective is to control the enterprise as it grows. They believe that it is easier to influence (really, dominate) each franchisee (hence, the entire operation) than it is to influence a board of directors. Their decision is driven by fear of losing control if they sell shares, rather than by the desire to raise financial capital or solve a shortage of human capital. Ironically, these founders often find they underestimated the independent spirit of their franchisees.[10] Even more ironically, many founders lose control anyway: They give way to professional managers as their organization grows.

Harnessing the Entrepreneurial Spirit

Raising capital and finding management—quickly—are reasons to start out by franchising. Once launched, there are reasons to continue to franchise. They revolve around *harnessing the drive and capabilities of an entrepreneur*. We are talking about businesses that can be encapsulated in a formula, a transferable business format. If you could transfer it to a franchisee, you could also transfer it to a manager you employ (the company-owned outlet). Why choose a franchisee?

To simplify reality, a firm can motivate people in two major ways. One is by monitoring them—making them employees, so as to be able to supervise them and apply sanctions and rewards. The other is to make them residual claimants—profit sharing who doesn't need as much monitoring. He or she will work anyway, out of desire for profit and fear of loss. *Franchising is a way to cut down monitoring costs by making people into residual claimants.*

Thus, the franchisee will be more motivated to exert sheer effort than will an employee manager. This explains why many franchises exist in businesses, such as many retailing sectors, where the jobs are relatively programmable but the hours are long and the margins are too low to pay supervisors well. Effort matters, and the business can't pay someone enough to make sure effort is continuously put forth, while maintaining minimum standards of behavior (accuracy, cleanliness, friendliness to customers, etc.). This is critical for service businesses, where production and distribution occur simultaneously, making it impossible to inspect goods before the customer sees them. A motivated person needs to be monitoring closely at all times.

A distinction exists between lack of effort and misdirected effort. The franchising contract is a good way to combat lack of effort. But it is often unsuccessful in solving the problem of misdirected effort. Franchisees often battle their franchisors because they have different ideas of how things should be done. Franchising cannot solve this problem—but it does create a mechanism that encourages the franchisor to take the franchisee seriously and to consider whether he might, after all, be right.

There is more to franchising than inducing managers to keep managing, even in the middle of the night on a holiday. A major reason to franchise is to *use the franchisee as a consultant*. Your "consultant" works out implementation problems and generates new ideas for you. This argument holds that a franchisor has a general vision. To be implemented on a large scale, this vision will *need adaptation to local circumstances*. The franchisor doesn't have the know-how to adapt locally and doesn't have the willingness to change the vision over time. Franchisees do.

An example occurs in Southeast Asia, where U.S.-style fast food has become quite popular. William Heinecke, an American raised in Thailand, approached Pizza Hut with the idea of opening a franchise outlet in Bangkok. Citing Asian's well-known dislike of cheese, Pizza Hut was skeptical, but allowed Heinecke to go ahead. The franchisee's judgment proved to be stunningly good, with the result that Pizza Hut now had a very substantial business in Thailand, and Heinecke owns dozens of outlets. This illustrates the insight of one person. Franchisees often collectively find solutions, one by one, to a franchisor's challenges. This is how A&W, another American fast-food chain, has been able to adapt its menus in Malaysia to offer meals that can be certified as meeting the Muslim requirements of *halal* (proper methods of slaughtering and the complete absence of pork).[11]

This is an inversion of the usual notion of an all-knowing franchisor consenting to uplift the unsophisticated franchisee, in return for fees and royalties. Instead, we have the image of some franchisees who are very sophisticated: They solve problems the national office doesn't even notice and come up with better ideas than does corporate. The job of corporate is to collect these ideas—screening out the lesser ones—adapt them to the entire chain, then spread them to other franchisees. We can extend the idea of the sophisticated franchisee even further: Some may have a much better idea of the value of a prospective site than would a franchisor.

If this idea sounds unlikely, consider this: Most of the best-known images and product ideas of today's McDonald's were generated by franchisees.[12] For example, the fish burger was invented by a franchisee in a Catholic neighborhood as a way to bring customers in on Friday, when eating meat is discouraged. Although the franchisor has the original vision of the business format, over time franchisees further develop the vision *collectively*. In general, no single franchisee has a better format. *The franchisor gathers, adapts, and diffuses the best ideas of the set of franchisees.*

Harnessing the motivation of a capable person, then, is a major reason to franchise. Franchising is a means not only of finding motivated, capable managers but also of keeping them. For example, many large French retailers face slow growth in their home market. This has forced them to consider secondary locations, such as small towns that cannot support a large store and an employee manager. Seeking to find franchisees for these locations, many chains have rediscovered an excellent source of talent: their existing managers.

The result has been a boom in converting French employees to franchisees. They see the move to owning their own businesses as intrinsically satisfying. Franchisors see the move as a way to reduce risk and investment: Both parties know each other. The one drawback is that employees usually lack the necessary capital. Most of them also lack some aspect of know-how; for example, the manager of the produce section of a hypermarket will need training in finance.

Franchisors are willing to "bet" on people they know, in order to preserve their loyalty and know-how. Hence, French franchisors often favor their employees, giving them financial backing, unusual assistance to make the transition, and training. This can be overdone: Many employee managers are unable to make the shift to doing all the tasks themselves, without staff, and cannot adopt an entrepreneurial attitude toward risk. By assisting them too much, franchisors may inadvertently shift them to a role they are ill suited to undertake.[13]

Here, we have come full circle. We began with franchising as a way to find good managers (without having to hire them) quickly and to induce them to supply you with capital. Now we see it as a way to keep the managers you hired years ago, which necessitates that you give *them* the necessary capital. Franchising is more than a way to grow fast, to get capital, or to avoid overhead. *It is a versatile and generalized system of management motivation in marketing channels.*

When Is Franchising Inappropriate?

Franchising is using a marketing channel that is almost a subsidiary. When is a subsidiary more appropriate? Chapter 7 on vertical integration covers this issue in detail. Generally, a subsidiary is more appropriate when the business format is highly unusual and rather difficult to codify, and when it is difficult to ascertain whether the store is achieving the best possible results. As examples, Channel Sketch 17.2 profiles Truffaut, a garden supply center, and Buffalo Grill, a restaurant chain. Both chains vertically integrate much more than does their more conventional competition.

CHANNEL SKETCH 17.2

Vertically Integrating Instead of Franchising: Truffaut Garden Centers and Buffalo Grill Restaurants

Truffaut Garden Centers[14]

Truffaut Garden Centers is a French retail chain. Founded in 1824 as a producer and wholesale grower by Charles Truffaut, the chain was still family-owned when the founder's great grandson paid a visit to the United States in the 1960s. Impressed by the large, full-line garden centers there, Georges Truffaut refocused his family firm. Abandoning production, Truffaut became a retail chain imitating the U.S. idea of offering all garden-related products, from plants to fertilizer to lawn mowers, under one roof. The novel concept pleased French consumers—which meant it was soon imitated.

Truffaut fell on hard times, was sold several times, and lost money. Early in the 1990s, the chain's new owners changed management, invested heavily, restructured, and reinvented the all-under-one-roof concept. Reasoning that gardening is fundamentally an emotional affair, Truffaut Garden Centers set out to "seduce" customers, to make them experience a thunderclap of emotional longing for a beautiful garden on their apartment window, balcony, terrace, or in their yard.

To seduce prospective customers, Truffaut's massive stores resemble greenhouses. Truffaut lavishes millions of francs annually on each store to create and re-create elaborate walks along garden paths throughout the greenhouse. These stores resemble a tourist destination: Only the price tags remind visitors that they are allowed to purchase. Visitors are drawn to the greenhouse and store to browse. For this purpose, Truffaut wins zoning variances permitting it to open when other stores are legally obliged to close, for example, on Sundays.

Visitors stroll along the long paths (some stores go up to 13,000 square meters, over 100,000 square feet, twice the size of competing stores). They encounter thousands of plant varieties, appealingly displayed, come across ponds, pergolas, fountains, benches, and the like. These items exist in kits: Competing stores display only the boxes. Truffaut displays the result. Knowledgeable, helpful, low-pressure salespeople appear and explain that technology has made affordable ponds easy to install and maintain. Visitors become customers. And they come back, over and over. In less than a decade, Truffaut, with only 31 stores in France, has become *the* reference for seven million customers.

To create and build the habit of visiting, which almost invariably leads to purchasing, Truffaut mounts expensive marketing campaigns. An elaborate fidelity card rewards regular customers for purchases. Stores open their doors and invite their best customers to evening theme parties, such as Halloween (a new concept in

France) and back-to-school. For the public, in-store events abound: all about rabbits, get to know the Newfoundland breed of dog, learn to do arts and crafts
projects, and so forth. Why rabbits, dogs, and arts and crafts? People who like to
garden are home oriented. They frequently have pets and in-home hobbies. To
amortize its high fixed costs, Truffaut includes a pet center and devotes greenhouse
space to crafts in the winter. Thus, visitors keep visiting year round, ready to fall in
love with a new display and make an unplanned purchase.

The elements of this formula are unusual in France. In particular, high labor
costs and inflexible labor laws lead French companies to minimize sales help. Yet,
Truffaut spends heavily on a large, well-trained sales force. Truffaut is also willing to
incur the high fixed costs needed to build and maintain the greenhouses, set up and
rotate the displays, keep the stores open long and unusual hours, hold an immense
and varied inventory of perishables, and run recurring marketing campaigns.

This is why Truffaut prefers to own every store, even though this means slower
growth. In contrast, its largest competitor, Jardiland, is a franchisor. Jardiland's operations are more conventional; the formula is easier to transmit, and franchisees are
less tempted to deviate from it. It is easier for the franchisor to tell if a store is not
realizing its potential. In contrast, Truffaut creates potential: It has enlarged the size
of the French garden market by its presence.

Buffalo Grill Restaurants[15]

Buffalo Grill Restaurants shows how the same situation can evolve into a franchis-
able concept. Buffalo Grill is a much-talked-about personal success story in France.
It begins in the 1960s, when Christian Picart, a young man who had grown up in
France under difficult circumstances, decided to seek his fortune in the United
States. Working several hotel service and restaurant jobs simultaneously, Picart
observed firsthand the U.S. concept of a Wild West steak house. Returning to
France, Picart adapted the concept and opened his first Buffalo Grill in 1980.
Today, Picart owns the largest chain of theme restaurants in France. His rags-to-
riches story rests on a formula that is highly unusual for France.

Picart took his Wild-West-in-France concept to an extreme, even by U.S. standards. A Buffalo Grill restaurant is instantly recognizable by its distinctive architecture: a large building, resembling a saloon and covered by an enormous garish roof,
bright red emblazoned with the name in white. French zoning discourages such
flamboyant, nontraditional architecture. But Picart will not open a restaurant unless
he can get a zoning variance, no matter how desirable the site. He is helped by his
insistence on locating where there is little competition: remote highways, industrial
zones, and other underserved locations.

Inside each restaurant, the black-and-red decor is almost painfully Wild Western
(e.g., carved cowboy and Indian statues indicate the toilets). The result is a fun,
informal, inviting atmosphere, supported by large numbers of friendly personnel.
Theme restaurants typically start well, then fade as the novelty of the theme wears
off. But the real appeal of Buffalo Grill's limited menu is a combination of high-
quality steaks and very low prices. This brings repeat customers: Proprietary
processes (particularly for treating meat) and extremely rigorous cost control con-

vert this formula into profits. Buffalo Grill's business format is elaborate, unusual, and precise. Low margins leave no room for deviation.

Having opened 175 restaurants in 20 years, Christian Picart has perfected his formula. One key to the formula is the architecture. The roof, for example, substitutes for advertising, of which the chain does virtually none. Building these large, customized restaurants costs millions of francs. Buffalo Grill guards the knowledge of the idiosyncracies of these buildings by vertically integrating backward into architectural services. Similarly, the way Buffalo Grill cuts its meat is proprietary, so the chain is vertically integrated backward into meatcutting. This proved to be essential during the scandal of Mad Cow disease, when infected beef was discovered in the European food supply. Overnight, frightened customers decided to boycott beef. Buffalo Grill responded by offering unusual meats (bison, ostrich, and so forth). Competitors could not copy its action because Buffalo Grill's meatcutters used their unique experience to devise their own ways to cut these little-known meats. Customers reacted so well that these items became standard on the menu after beef returned to favor.

The formula is unusual, but it is well elucidated and thoroughly demonstrated by now. The essential parts (meatcutting, architecture) are owned by the firm. To date, most of the restaurants are owned by the parent corporation, rather than a franchisee, and run by employee managers. To continue his expansion, Christian Picart has started moving toward franchising. Many of his franchisees are drawn from the ranks of his managers. The best managers are rewarded for years of excellent service by being offered a franchise. They are required to put up as much capital as they can, but the initial investment of 10 million francs is excessive. Therefore, Buffalo Grill cosigns bank loans for the difference, assuming responsibility in case of default. Because the restaurants are highly profitable, there is no shortage of interested managers or willing banks.

To date, among the 175 restaurants, Buffalo Grill counts some 50 franchisees, about half of whom are ex-managers of company-owned restaurants. A proprietary, unusual, and specialized concept has matured to become franchisable. With it, Christian Picart hopes to bring the Wild West á la française to Europe. Now that his concept is demonstrated to work well, he is poised to use franchising as his means to keep ownership of the idea. Bison and ostrich, priced for a family budget, in Prague? Why not?

Frequently, franchising affords more control than is really necessary. As a business becomes more conventional and free riding on the brand becomes a less important issue, franchising may involve more responsibility than the company needs to assume. There are alternatives. One can step down from franchising to a preferred supplier status. For example, Elf, an oil company (now part of Total), has done this with gasoline stations in Italy, downgrading them from franchises, with satisfactory results.[16] Along these lines, a franchise can be downgraded to a conventional channel and then treated using the many influence techniques described throughout this book.

Alternatively, some variations afford a substantial degree of control, athough not as much as franchising. These include forms such as strategic alliances (Chapter 11), licensing, joint ventures, and cooperative networks.

THE HISTORICAL ROOTS OF FRANCHISING

Franchising is often considered a post–World War II phenomenon. But its roots go back much farther, to ancient times in practice and to the Middle Ages in law. Franchising as we know it today can be readily traced to the late nineteenth-century United States, when it was identified with soft drink bottling and with the retailing of gasoline, automobiles, and sewing machines. In business-to-business applications, the concept was developed by the McCormick Harvesting Machine Company to sell directly to farmers, bypassing wholesalers.

Autos, sewing machines, and harvesters were relatively new, complex, mass-produced products, which needed to be sold in huge volumes to gain economies of scale in manufacturing. Selling these machines at that scale required specialized marketing services that were unusual for their time: The extension of credit, plus demonstration and postsale repair. Firms in these industries could not hire and train their own dealers fast enough. They turned to near-subsidiaries as a way to grow quickly. Once growth was achieved, firms often turned away from their franchising operations and went into company-owned and managed outlets.[17] This trend then repeats itself.

The Authorized Franchise System: Moving the Product

What these sellers did was to induce dealers to acquire some of the identity of the producer and to concentrate on one product line. Fundamentally, dedicated dealers stocked a product and resold it, adhering to certain guidelines about what to offer the market. This stops somewhat short of licensing an entire business format. In particular, the producer's aim is to sell its product. The manufacturer seeks to maintain some semblance of control over how the brand name is presented *for the purpose of increasing profits from the product directly*. Producers make money on the margins they obtain by selling to their dealers, rather than on fees and royalties.

This form of franchising has come to be called *product and trade name franchising*, or *authorized franchise systems*. Authorized dealers, distributors, resellers, agents—all these terms apply—meet minimum criteria the manufacturer establishes regarding the outlet's degree of participation in marketing flows. In these situations, a franchisor authorizes distributors—wholesalers or retailers or both—to sell a product or product line using its trade name for promotional purposes. Examples at the retail level are authorized tire, auto, computer, major appliance, television, and household furniture dealers whose suppliers have established strong brand names. Such authorization can also be granted at the wholesale level—for example, to soft drink bottlers and to distributors or dealers by manufacturers of electrical and electronics equipment. Channel Sketch 17.3 shows an example of this system.

What is usually referred to as franchising today is *business format franchising*. This is the licensing of an entire way of doing business under a brand name. For a franchisor, the reward for this activity is the generation of ongoing fees.

The term *authorized franchise* can be extended considerably. For example, suppliers can also include, as part of their "authorized franchise network," outlets that are already part of another franchisor–franchisee relationship. Thus, MicroAge is the name of a franchisee–franchisor system of computer stores. IBM has authorized MicroAge to

CHANNEL SKETCH 17.3

Goodyear Tire & Rubber Company[18]

A good example of how product and trade name franchising works is Goodyear Tire & Rubber Company. This producer distributes its Goodyear-brand automotive replacement tires through its own and outside-owned channels: Selected mass-merchants (e.g., Sears), company-owned outlets, independent authorized franchise dealers, and franchised dealers. The company has the least control over how its name is used and its tires are sold in the mass-merchant outlets, because these are thoroughly diversified in brand and in product category. Goodyear has the greatest control in its company stores. In between are the "independent authorized franchised dealers" and the "franchised dealers." What's the difference?

For the independent authorized franchise dealers, Goodyear provides a variety of services, including the following:

- Expertise and training on issues such as financing, architecture, wholesaling, operations, and merchandising
- Certified Auto Service, which allows dealers to attend training classes and become certified in auto services
- The Goodyear Business Management System, a computer system to help dealers with inventory and accounting
- National and regional advertising to support dealer sales
- Research on market trends, such as information on the popularity of each tire, by size, in a given market
- Assistance in outlet location, either in selling company-owned outlets to independent dealers or in avoiding locations for company-owned outlets that would compete with dealers

This is classic product and trade name franchising, designed to ensure that customers don't know whether they are in one of the company-owned stores or a franchised outlet. Approximately 50 percent of its sales come from these independent dealers. So what's a "franchised dealer"? It is the same idea, taken to an extreme (covering more domains of the business) and applied in a unique way to dealers who are new to Goodyear.

For three years, Goodyear provides the new entrant with training in operations, finance, and other aspects of the business. As explained by a Goodyear executive:

> Goodyear's franchises are designed somewhat differently from those of other companies who have become franchisors. Rather than trying to earn money from franchising per se, Goodyear simply wants to use the channel to move tires, and its fee structures are set up to facilitate this objective. Goodyear requires no franchise fee and has only two requirements of the prospective franchisee: (1) an unencumbered $50,000 for working capital and (2) a good track record in business (it does not want these outlets to fail).

> As for continuing fees, there is only a small fee on sales, to cover the cost to Goodyear of the data processing, accounting, and counseling services for the franchisees.
>
> After three years, these dealers then become "normal" independent dealers. The number of so-called franchised dealers is kept small, that is, less than 10 percent of the total dealer base. What is the point of the exercise? It is to acculturate dealers to identify completely with Goodyear and its methods. As such, it is more like licensing a business format than it is a system of authorizing dealers. The differences are (1) it is a launch vehicle, not a means of running a business permanently; and (2) more importantly, Goodyear wants to "move tires" rather than make money on fees. This difference in objective, and therefore the scope and direction of the franchisor's involvement, is critical.

sell its personal computers. Therefore, IBM must work closely with each MicroAge store to make certain that the appropriate service outputs are being delivered to end-users, and it must work with the franchisor, who plays a critical role in the performance of the franchisees via the various programs the franchisor administers and the incentives it establishes. To make certain it can control its own destiny, IBM has developed contracts specifying role relationships with the individual stores in franchising systems such as MicroAge's. It has also retained the right not to authorize individual stores within a franchising system if the stores do not meet IBM's own criteria for admission to its authorized dealer network.

The Dividing Line: When Does Franchising Stop?

Establishing an authorized franchise system is a means for suppliers, without assuming financial ownership, to raise the probability that channel members will provide the appropriate type and level of service outputs to end-users. A major way in which organizers of authorized franchise systems have achieved this end is to specify or impose restrictions on how channel members can operate. As such, this system is a way to exercise power.

But there are others. How do we know when franchising stops and other channels begin? In some jurisdictions, the line is clear because legal requirements oblige any so-called franchisor to follow disclosure and reporting rules. These impose a significant legal cost on the franchisor.

But outside these jurisdictions, there is no sharp dividing line. Once vertical integration is eliminated, there is a gray area between franchising and many other forms of distribution. A franchisee, as imagined by Henry McCormack, was almost a company subsidiary. Logically, there are other ways to deal with an independent company, yet simulate a company subsidiary. Therefore, it is sometimes difficult to say whether a channel is franchised or whether it is technically separable, but led or dominated by an influential upstream channel member.

For example, a retailer cooperative or a wholesaler-sponsored voluntary group resembles franchising. Regulators have intervened in such disputes to ascertain whether franchising laws apply to these groups.[19] A key criterion is whether joining these groups is voluntary and whether the use of their services is optional. In franchising, these are not choices but are mandatory.

So just what is a franchise? The linguistic roots of the term *franchise* reflect McCormack's conceptualization of a dealer selling his harvesting machines. In both English and French, the term goes back to the Middle Ages, from which it draws two facets: freedom and privilege. A franchise formally contractually limited a sovereign's authority in some way (e.g., tax exemption or in the guarantee of certain rights). Thus, a franchise enlarged the freedom of the franchisee from the sovereign, just as dealers enjoyed more freedom from the McCormack Harvesting Machine Company than would a corporate division. The aspect of privilege comes from the benefits that should accrue from the granting of such an advantage.

What "franchising" is usually taken to mean today is the licensing of an entire business format. The European Union provides a good definition: A franchise is a *package of industrial or intellectual property rights*. The package relates to trade names, trademarks, shop signs, utility models, designs, copyrights, know-how, or patents. It is to be exploited for the resale of goods or the provision of services to end-users. The EU points out that this definition uses three features to distinguish franchising:

1. Use of a common name or sign, with a uniform presentation of the premises
2. Communication of know-how from franchisor to franchisee
3. Continuing provision of commercial or technical assistance by the franchisor to the franchisee

The EU exempts franchising from many of the regulations designed to encourage intra- and intercountry competition within its boundaries. This exemption is made in recognition that it is critical to project a common identity in franchising, and that doing so involves writing contracts that do restrict competition. It is justified from a consumer welfare standpoint because franchising should "combine the advantages of a uniform and homogeneous network, which ensures a constant quality of the products and services, with the existence of traders personally interested in the efficient operation of their business."[20]

We now return to this system, business format franchising, and examine how it operates.

THE FRANCHISE CONTRACT

Giving and Taking Hostages, or Why You Shouldn't Leave It to Lawyers

Unlike many business arrangements, franchising is tightly governed by elaborate and formal contracts. Many of these contracts run on for pages of intricate legal language. It is tempting for both franchisor and franchisee to leave the contract to the lawyers and simply presume that working arrangements will arise that will govern the relationship anyway. This is a dangerous error. In franchising, the contract really matters. In particular, three sections of a franchise contract determine who will enter the arrangement and how it will function.[21] These are:

1. The payment system, particularly the lump-sum fee to enter the system, the royalty fee, and the initial investment. How these are calculated and how they may be adjusted over the contract life are critical.
2. The real estate: who holds the lease and how it may be transferred. This looks like a financing detail but is actually far more important.
3. Termination. Franchise arrangements are like a prenuptial contract: They anticipate a possible divorce and spell out how it would be conducted.

We will examine these three issues in detail.

In the United States, where franchising has its fullest history, regulators and courts are concerned about whether it is socially beneficial. In particular, they are worried that franchisors (typically seen as large, powerful, and sophisticated) exploit franchisees (typically seen as small, weak, and naive). A major reason for this concern is that franchise contracts typically contain clauses that, on the face of it, are outrageously favorable to the franchisor. This implies that franchisors have better lawyers and more bargaining power.

But are these contracts actually unfair? Are franchisees really so weak and naive? Do they hire inferior lawyers? Or is there something else going on?

In political affairs, two parties often safeguard an agreement by exchanging hostages. *The party that is in a better position to break its promises offers a hostage to the other side.* If it (the poster of the hostage) reneges, the other party keeps the hostage. If both sides are tempted to break their promises, they exchange hostages; each side posts a hostage, to be kept by the other in case of breach of promise.

Franchise contracts can be understood as attempts by each side to make sure the other side will live up to its promises.[22] *Contract clauses are used to post hostages.* Because both franchisor and franchisee are tempted to renege, each side will post some hostages. But the franchisee is in a better position to renege, so it posts more hostages (accepts contracts that give great power to the franchisor). This is curious: The usual presumption is that the franchisee is in an excellent position to cheat the franchisor and must be stopped from so doing. To make sense of this, read on.

The Payment System

The franchisee usually pays a fixed fee, or lump-sum payment, to start up. If this were all, the franchisee would be in danger. The franchisor would be inclined to abscond; that is, collect the fee and then do nothing to help the franchisee.

The franchisee also makes an initial investment, which covers acquiring inventory, obtaining and adapting the facility, purchasing tools and equipment, and advertising the opening of the outlet. If the store closed quickly, a good part of that investment would be lost. Fixtures and equipment, for example, might sell secondhand for half what the franchisee paid for them. Even worse, if they are specialized to the franchisor's decor (distinctive colors, patterns, emblazoned logos and slogans, and so forth), they might resell for a quarter of their acquisition cost. That part of the initial investment that the franchisee can't recover is a sunk cost.

The up-front fee and the unrecoverable part of the initial investment are at risk for the franchisee. They are hostages. If the franchisee doesn't carry out its promises and the business fails, it loses the hostages.

Once it has posted these hostages, the franchisor must post some of its own. An excellent hostage is a royalty on sales (a variable fee). If the franchisor doesn't help the franchisee, sales suffer, and it shares the suffering by collecting less royalty income. Therefore, royalties motivate the franchisor to pay attention to the franchisee.[23]

Why a royalty on sales rather than on profit? After all, the franchisor's real function is to help the franchisee make money. The answer is that, in most cases, sales can be readily observed and verified. In contrast, profit is easy to manipulate and difficult to check.

What do you do if sales are not easy to observe? Here, you have a real problem, without a good solution. An example occurs with Nationwide, a British franchisor of private investigation services (detective work).[24] The clients of a franchisee (a local detective) frequently pay in cash and don't want the detective to keep any records of their transaction. This customer-driven feature of the business makes it very difficult for Nationwide to tell how much revenue the franchisee is booking! Nationwide's solution is to charge a flat fee, but to collect it in small amounts weekly. This gives dissatisfied franchisees the ability to stop payment at will. Some franchisees do complain that Nationwide doesn't help them enough. To be fair, most franchisees feel entitled to more help from any franchisor. But this curious means of payment would be consistent with not giving the local detective enough help: If a franchisee's sales go down, Nationwide doesn't suffer. The franchisees may have a point. Yet, Nationwide is under pressure to use this second-best system because revenue is difficult to audit.

By getting payments from franchisees, franchisors make money. *What is the best way to get money out of them?* Put differently, if fixed fees and sales royalties are common, what should be their ratio? It can be argued that fixed and variable payments to the franchisor should be negatively correlated.[25] The rationale is that a franchisor charging a high fixed fee is sending two signals. The first one is positive: My franchise is valuable. The second signal is negative: I am extracting as much as I can from you up front so that I can exploit you later (abscond, or "take the money and run"). To avoid sending this negative signal, franchisors can cut their up-front fee (sometimes to zero, even for well-known franchises) and seek to make their money later, by raising their royalty rates.[26] In so doing, they are sharing risk with their franchisees.

They may be sharing too much risk! By eschewing up-front money now in favor of potential royalty payments later, franchisors take on a risk. This is the risk that franchisees will accept their assistance to set up the business (because this is a large part of the franchisor's role), and later try to renegotiate the contract to their advantage. This "opportunistic holdup" of the franchisor by the franchisee could take many forms, including deferment or reduction of royalties, extra assistance, rent relief, and other considerations. Franchisors might renegotiate in order to avoid losing the money they invested to set the franchisee up in business.

In short, fear of holdup by the franchisee (renegotiating the deal once the business is running) drives the franchisor to ask for more up-front money in lieu of royalties. Its fear of neglect drives the franchisee to demand the opposite.

How does it settle out? There is some indication that the franchisor concedes. It takes less up-front money than it would like and might reasonably demand. In return, the franchisee makes concessions on other aspects of the contract. In addition, the franchisee makes heavy initial investments, much of which it cannot recover, *especially if the investments are in franchise-specific decor and equipment or in merchandise that is difficult to return or resell*. These initial investments are often much higher than the franchisor's fixed fee.[27] By incurring this investment, the franchisee offers a hostage to assure the franchisor that it will exert its best efforts and stay in the business. This is a deterrent to mistreating the franchisor by renegotiating the contract at every opportunity.

The observation that franchisors could ask for higher fixed fees up front than they do is intriguing. They may restrain themselves to reassure franchisees. The temptation to cheat franchisees by taking a high fixed fee and doing little is so great that franchisors may fear that courts, arbitrators, and regulators will look unfavorably on those who charge high fixed fees and then terminate franchisees.

Franchisors and franchisees often explain the amount of the lump sum as a rough approximation of the costs incurred by the franchisor to set up a franchisee in business. This claim, while difficult to verify, serves to hold the sum demanded well below the level that many franchises would fetch on the open market. It has the important advantage of appearing to be equitable to both franchisors and franchisees.[28]

A major reason to reduce up-front fixed fees is to *enlarge the pool of applicants*. A good candidate to be a franchisee possesses a certain profile (personality, background, management ability, and local knowledge) sought by the franchisor. If to this list one must add substantial personal wealth, the pool of qualified candidates shrinks dramatically.

Indeed, there is strong indication that many franchisors could ask for much higher *total* income than they do. This means they are also asking a lower royalty rate than they could. One estimate holds that McDonald's leaves several hundred thousand dollars "on the table" (i.e., in the franchisee's bank account) each time this organization grants a franchise.[29] Why would it do this? The answer is to *make the business precious to each franchisee*. By being generous, McDonald's gives the franchisee a great deal to lose. This greatly enhances the franchisee's desire to live up to its promises, which is exactly what franchising is designed to do.

In this vein, consider tied sales. This is a clause obliging franchisees to buy their inputs (products, supplies, etc.) from the supplier. (See Chapter 12 for a discussion of the legal status of tied sales.) For example, Avis and Budget in the United Kingdom require their franchisees to purchase from the franchisor the cars they rent out. Why not let them buy a car anywhere, and see if they can make better deals on their own? After all, a Ford is a Ford. This issue is important to regulators, who see tie-ins as a hidden way to exploit franchisees by overcharging them for products and services they could buy elsewhere. If so, tie-ins are a disguised way to collect more fees on an ongoing basis.

On the other hand, overcharging franchisees for what they buy can go against the franchisor's interest if the franchisee can compensate by cheating in some other way. For example, a restaurant forced to buy overpriced ingredients from the franchisor might cut portion size or save food too long. So who uses tied-sales clauses?

Evidence indicates that many franchisors elect tied sales only when they need to *facilitate quality control*. Avis and Budget, for example, want to ensure that the cars being rented are fully equipped as promised. When the quality of inputs is difficult to measure on an ongoing basis, franchisors are more likely to use tied-sales clauses—and to price them fairly, so as to avoid resentment and allegations of profiteering. But where any other product would do as an input, franchisors are less likely to write tied-sales clauses. And when many, but not any, other products would do, franchisors oblige franchisees to buy from sources they approve, but not from the franchisor alone.

Product franchising is an interesting case. Many product franchisers don't bother with tied-sales clauses. They don't need to. Ford and Rover in the United Kingdom don't write such clauses: Physically, you can only buy a Rover from Rover, *and* the customer would object to a substitution. What if it might not object? For example, Bally Shoes doesn't write tied-sales clauses for its British franchises, even though they are expected to be dedicated, exclusive outlets. The customer might not object or even notice if a Bally store also sold other brands. But Bally would notice that a store wasn't doing the volume it should and could take countermeasures. A tied-sales clause is not needed when the franchisor could detect and deter excessive substitution: Why bother to negotiate the clause?

Who Will Be the Landlord?

An issue of particular interest to regulators is *who collects the rent* on the franchisee's premises. Many franchisors take pains to ensure that they are the landlord. Failing that, they want to hold the right to lease the property to the franchisee. Therefore, they negotiate a lease with the property owner, then sublet to the franchisee. Their leases are frequently quite protective of the franchisor's rights, at the expense of the franchisee's rights. Owning the land is a capital-intensive practice that absorbs much management attention and leads to frequent disputes. Why do it?

A common explanation is that retailing depends on location, and the best locations are difficult to secure. According to this reasoning, owners of prime commercial locations would rather deal with franchisors than with a franchisee. And the franchisor may negotiate better than can a franchisee.

This would not explain why some franchisors insist on holding the lease for *all* their sites, even the lesser ones. Insistence on controlling the lease is best explained as a way to *make termination of the franchisee a credible threat*.[30] A noncompliant franchisee who is your tenant is easier to eject from your system if you can terminate the lease at the same time you terminate the franchisee. A franchisee who agrees to be a tenant and who, in addition, agrees to a lease that favors the landlord is a franchisee who is offering a hostage to the franchisor. This is particularly potent if the franchisee makes improvements to the property, because these improvements usually can be appropriated by the landlord.

Contract clauses can be coupled to multiply the desired compliance effect. For example, a franchisor may offer a generous contract (lower royalties and fixed fee than the market would bear) and add in a mandatory lease. The franchisee who accepts this arrangement will be very motivated to comply with the franchisor's guidelines. Noncompliance means the sure and speedy loss of a lucrative business.

Leasing arrangements favoring the franchisor are so powerful that they have inspired some U.S. states to regulate its ability to terminate a franchise at will. In the United Kingdom, which is less regulated, franchisors are quite free to choose contract terms. Many do not oblige the franchisee to lease from them. Often, those who do so soften the contract. They may couple the contract with an arbitration clause in case of dispute. Or they may build in terms under which they would buy back the unexpired lease and improvements, sometimes at preset prices. This careful anticipation of termination, with some concession to the franchisee, underscores how powerful a lease can be for the franchisor.

Leasing is not always a control device. Being the landlord or the lessor can be a vehicle that franchisors use to assist franchisees by reducing their capital requirements or rents. Indeed, franchisors often defer rents on franchises that are in trouble. But by design or by accident, franchisors who are landlords have a potent way to enforce termination of a franchisee. They can evict the franchisee while keeping the site for their operations. This ability to keep the site is very important for some businesses. In the United Kingdom, businesses that require special zoning (such as auto repairs) or scarce locations (such as prime High Street frontage—the major shopping districts) are the most likely to demand that franchisees lease from them. Businesses that can readily find new locations, or find candidates holding suitable locations, don't bother requiring leases.[31]

Termination

Losing a franchisee is difficult and costly. For the franchisor, it is necessary to replace the franchisee and, in the absence of leasing clauses, perhaps replace the location as well. The new franchisee must be brought up to norms, which takes time and creates the opportunity cost of lost business. Knowing this, it might be tempted to hold up the franchisor (threaten to quit while negotiating a better deal). To a point, the franchisor will concede, just to avoid having to replace the franchisee.

Not surprisingly, many make it expensive and difficult for the franchisee to leave them. As already noted, franchisees are less willing to walk away from a lucrative business (low royalties on a good business) and from other investments they have made (such as franchise-specific decor). Other contract devices make it even more difficult to quit.

In the United Kingdom, many contracts require the franchisee to find his own replacement! It must find an acceptable candidate to the franchisor quickly. Otherwise, the franchisor can impose a candidate. The franchisee must pay a "transfer fee," a sum that is lower if he finds his own replacement (saving the franchisor the trouble). Franchisors often insert a clause ("right of first refusal") giving them the right to take the franchisee's contract if they match any offer the franchisee can find.

This protects the franchisor against a franchisee who threatens to sell to an unsuitable buyer. But it also gives the former some ability to abuse the latter by denying him the right to liquidate his business at a fair value in a timely way. In the United States, a number of states regulate termination precisely to prevent such abuse. In the United Kingdom, where regulation is less pervasive in franchising, another safeguard is needed. The parties find it in arbitration: Arbitration clauses are very common.

Why Contracts Don't Vary Within a System

Franchise contracts have surprisingly *little variance*. One would expect that every contract would quote different terms of trade, because no two franchisees face the same situation. Yet, franchisors tend to have a single contract, with only minor variations, and a single price. They offer their contracts on a take-it-or-leave-it basis.

Contracts also don't vary much over time. Adjustments occur occasionally, particularly in the price (royalties or fixed fees): The price rises as the franchisor gets better established. But contracts are surprisingly stable.[32] Part of the reason is that contracts tend to be for fairly long periods, 15 years being common in the United States. Moreover, tailoring contracts incurs high legal fees, especially in jurisdictions with high disclosure requirements. And part of it is the importance to franchisors of being perceived as fair, as treating franchisees equitably. By offering the same contract to all, the franchisor avoids appearing to practice discrimination. This threat seems to loom larger than the possible loss of flexibility or the appearance of arbitrariness.

Safeguards Outside the Contract

Ultimately, *the contract is a delicate balancing act*. Each side has incentives to cheat the other. Franchisors can take the money and do nothing to help (abscond). Franchisees operate their own businesses and are difficult to monitor and direct. This means they can dishonor their promises to comply with the franchisor's rules, abuse the brand name, and fail to offer their best efforts (noncompliance, free riding, shirking). In writing a contract, the objective is to create a "self-enforcing agreement," an arrangement that neither side wants to violate. They comply without being monitored or threatened, because the contract rearranges their incentives so that cheating is not in their *own* interest.

The trouble is that every clause that stops one side from cheating creates a new way for the other side to cheat. *Every effort to balance up the power creates a new possibility for imbalance.*

This is true of most business arrangements between independents. Often, businesses don't try to solve the problem by writing elaborate contracts. But franchisors and franchisees take a great risk if they permit themselves to operate in this way. The two parties are agreeing to tie their fates together for years. The former is sacrificing its secrets and its trademarks. The latter is sacrificing its autonomy. Their arrangement is elaborate and forward looking. Their contracts must be as well.

Franchise contracts can be understood as an effort to balance out, roughly, the interests of both sides. Where one side is tempted to cheat, a clause is created to block cheating. Often, that same clause gives too much power to the other side, creating the need for another clause to rectify the excesses of the first one, and so on.

Contracts become complex fast. And they are probably not correctly calibrated at the end of the process anyway. No contract can specify all contingencies and craft the proper solution for all problems. Nonetheless, a franchise contract should be thorough and forward looking. Table 17.1 suggests what should be covered in some form in a franchise contract.

What else is there besides contracts to safeguard the relationship? The answer that comes up over and over is *reputation*. Franchisors who take a long-term view of their

TABLE 17.1
The Franchise Contract

The *International Franchise Guide* of the International Herald Tribune suggests that any franchise contract should address these subjects.

- Definition of terms
- Organizational structure
- Term of initial agreement
- Term of renewal
- Causes for termination or nonrenewal
- Territorial exclusivity
- Intellectual property protection
- Assignment of responsibilities
- Ability to subfranchise
- Mutual agreement of pro forma cash flows
- Development schedule and associated penalties
- Fees: front end, ongoing
- Currency and remittance restrictions
- Remedies in case of disagreement

Source: Susan L. Moulton (ed.), *International Franchise Guide* (Oakland, CA: Source Books Publications, 1996).

businesses worry, and rightly so, about creating a bully-boy image, of being seen as harsh, oppressive, or greedy. They worry for fear of losing current franchisees, of losing their cooperation, and of being unable to attract new franchisees. Most of all, they worry about being classed as a fly-by-night, a franchisor who is out to make money quickly through fees and lucrative tie-in sales and then abandon the franchisees. Such franchisors are swindlers. The others, those who wish to build a business, make it a point to treat franchisees correctly and to project that they do so. Their reputation is worth more to franchisors than the short-term gains they might extract by invoking harsh contract terms to "win" disputes with their franchisees.

WHY FRANCHISE SYSTEMS INCLUDE COMPANY OUTLETS

Franchisee-owned and company-owned outlets are usually considered as substitutes. The reasoning is that one or the other fits the situation, but not both. Why, then, do so many franchisors also have company-owned stores, often doing exactly the *same thing* in exactly the *same markets?* A franchising system without any company-owned stores is somewhat unusual.[33] Among U.S. firms that franchise, on average 30 percent of their outlets are company owned.[34] What is the explanation?

Variation in Situations

The obvious explanation is that some markets are different from others. If so, company outlets and franchisee outlets should serve different types of markets. But different in what respect?

A popular supposition is that some markets require monitoring from the franchisor.[35] According to this reasoning, the franchisee is tempted to cheat when repeat business is low (i.e., when business is transient). For example, a fast-food restaurant on a superhighway should draw heavily on people passing through only once. If this location were franchised, the franchisee would be tempted to cheat (e.g., cutting costs by serving stale food). Travelers would be drawn to the restaurant by the franchisor's brand name. The franchisee would damage brand equity but would not suffer the usual consequences (lost future sales) because the customer wouldn't return anyway. To protect its brand equity from such free riding, the franchisor should own the outlet. (As noted earlier, the other franchisees should welcome this decision.)

However, apart from the restaurant on a highway, it is difficult to think of situations that demand the company substitute monitoring for the motivation of an entrepreneur. This leads us to another explanation.

Temporary Franchises and Temporary Company Stores

One explanation for the simultaneous existence of franchise and company-owned stores is that some of the stores are temporary. This reasoning has it that circumstances at one point in time create a need for one form or the other.

Franchisors usually start out with some outlets of their own, where they formulate the business format and develop the brand name. This gives them something to sell to franchisees. If they skirt this step and start franchising early, they cannot attract many franchisees and must write generous contracts. So franchisors start out with company stores. Then they add franchisees, usually at a high rate. The company stores are a necessity at the founding of the franchisor.

The general question is this: Once the business is underway, why add *any* company stores? Sometimes the cause is accidental or transient: A franchisee has a problem, and the franchisor buys out the location. This can cover up franchisee problems for purposes of system morale (or, in the United States, to avoid a lawsuit). Or it can be to help a profitable franchisee who needs to exit quickly (say, for health reasons). Or it may be to hold the location. For all these motives, the company outlet is temporary. It is sold as soon as a new franchisee can be found.

In Italy, opening a retail store in a particular sector (say, food retailing) requires a sector-specific license from the local authorities. They are limited in supply, hence valuable, and an obstacle for Italian franchisors. If they wish to expand quickly, they may be obliged to accept an undesirable franchisee simply because the individual holds one of the licenses to sell that product category in an area. Forecasting conflict with the license holder, the franchisor declines to franchise. Instead, it elects to use its corporate influence to get a license for itself, which means running a company outlet for some time. This leads to a pattern in Italian franchising *of system growth by divesting corporate assets*. The franchisor operates the outlet, learns from the experience, then divests the outlet by selling out to a suitable franchisee. There is some indication that divestment costs the franchisor little: The newly franchised store cooperates with management, much as the company store did, but often with better operating results.[36]

Ultimately, the idea of temporary franchisees or company stores does not go very far in explaining why many franchisors have both systems. Most franchisors, as they grow, add new company outlets, albeit at a lower rate than they add franchisees.[37] Those systems that grow the fastest do so by favoring franchisees over company units. (These systems in turn have lower failure rates, to be discussed).[38] So there must be permanent reasons for having both types—the *plural form*.

The Plural Form: Exploiting the Synergy of Having Both Company and Franchisee Outlets

Simultaneously and deliberately maintaining both company and franchised outlets to do the same thing is the strategy of using the plural form.[39] The principle is that franchisors can manage the duality of their organization (simultaneously vertically integrated and outsourced) by drawing on the strengths of each system to offset the weaknesses of the other.

The plural form in franchising enables franchisors to build a control system that creates functional rivalry between the two forms. This works because they monitor their own units very heavily. They do so with:

1. Elaborate management information systems that generate detailed daily reports on every aspect of the outlets' operations
2. Frequent, elaborate, unannounced field audits, covering hundreds of items and requiring hours to complete
3. Mystery shoppers (paid professional auditors, posing as customers)

This heavy, invasive control mechanism is tolerated by company managers of the outlets because they are paid a salary for observing the rules. Top management tells them what to do, and they do it. They are not held accountable for making profit.

In contrast, these practices are less invasively implemented, less frequent, less thorough, and less often used *at all* with franchisees. Rather than telling franchisees what to do, franchisor managers attempt to persuade them. Titles and terms are telling here: Company-stores managers report to district managers, whereas franchisees work with (do not report to) franchise consultants. The information and experience gained from this heavy control mechanism in company stores *help the franchisor to stay in touch with the business* it purports to master.

Another feature of plural systems is that *each form benchmarks the other*. Franchisors encourage competition, comparing the performance of company and franchisee outlets and encouraging each type to do better than the other type. As company and franchisee outlets do exactly the same thing (which is seemingly senseless), direct comparisons are possible, which *heightens the competition*.

Another advantage of the plural form is that the franchisor can create *career paths* for personnel to go back and forth between the company side and the franchisee side of the house. In so doing, the franchisor can accommodate its personnel while at the same time creating a means of socializing everyone on both sides of the house. One career path is up through the company side only, by dealing with company outlets as a manager, then a supervisor, then a corporate executive. Another path is up through the franchise side only, by starting a unit, adding new ones, and growing into a minihierarchy. (Some are not so mini: One major U.S. restaurant chain has a franchisee who owns over 400 units, which is bigger than many other restaurant chains in their entirety.)

Three other career paths are noteworthy because they connect the franchisee and company-owned sides of the franchisor:

1. Company people become franchisees: This is a surprisingly common path. Company people like it because they can develop into entrepreneurs, often with less capital than an outsider would need. Franchisors like it because their franchisee community is seeded with people they know they can work with.
2. Company-unit managers become franchise consultants: This is a shift from running a company store (being on salary, following the rules) to working with franchisees to persuade them. The jobs are very different (like a promotion from a factory supervisor to a diplomatic post). The transition can be difficult, but the ex-company-store-manager has credibility with franchisees because of his or her hands-on experience.
3. Company managers become franchisee managers: This is a move from the franchisor's hierarchy to managing in a multi-unit franchisor. This move from one organization to another, still in a management position, is an important way in which minihierarchies mimic the franchisor's organization.

The beauty of these three border-crossing career paths is that they solidly unite the franchisor and franchisee. They do it by creating a *means of exchanging personnel* regularly on a large scale. By this vehicle, franchisees and franchisors socialize with each other and develop bonds.

Another advantage of the plural form is that *each side engages in teaching the other side,* which helps create a mutual strategy. It is commonly believed that franchisors set the strategy, then convince franchisees to adhere to it. In plural forms, each side (company and franchisee) tries out ideas, then tries to persuade the other side. In the process, strategy is formed by rigorous debate. Plural forms create more options and debate them more candidly and thoroughly than do unitary forms. In the process of debate, the ideas are refined, each side becomes committed to them, and may allow new initiatives.

Why not have only franchisees, then simply give franchisees a free hand to try things out and then transmit best practices across franchisees? Company stores are good laboratories: The company can test rigorously, absorbing the risk of failure itself. For example, Dunkin' Donuts (DD) experiments with new products and processes in its own stores. This is a sort of test market: DD can assure that the test is conducted properly and that feedback is entirely candid. The franchisor can also experiment at its own expense, without putting a franchisee at risk if the chain experiments with a bad idea. Once the new product or process has been perfected, DD can point to its own success to encourage franchisees to adopt the change themselves.

Why not have only company stores, then use the stores to generate ideas? One answer is that store managers don't generate ideas: They follow rules. Ideas come from the franchisor's central database of store operations. To figure out how to refine and implement them requires the active involvement of motivated entrepreneurs. Further, as noted earlier, many ideas come from entrepreneurs as they cope with local circumstances: competition, labor force, and customers. For example, the popularity of Indian food in London has led McDonald's to add curry and spice to its British menus.[40] Ideas like this can come from corporate, but are more likely to come from local owners adapting to local competition and tastes.

In short, plural forms complement each other in ways that make the chain stronger, and both franchisors and franchisees better off. Of course, this depends on active management. Having company and franchisee units simultaneously is beneficial *if both sides work to make it so* and appreciate the benefits of a "dual personality." Absent this, simultaneously entertaining both forms can actually be destructive.

Exploiting Franchisees: Redirection of Ownership

To this point, explanations for a dual system are benevolent. However, a malevolent explanation exists that has attracted substantial attention from regulators and from scholars.[41] The premise is that franchisors would rather have company outlets than franchisees, in order to control the operation closely and to appropriate all the profits generated by the marketing channel. (This, of course, assumes a company system would be as profitable. This is a heroic assumption, given the franchisee's entrepreneurial motivation, but it is an assumption the franchisor might be tempted to make.) Given this premise, the owner of a trademark might franchise anyway, *but only to build the business*. Once established, the franchisor would be tempted to use its profits to buy back franchises. In case the franchisees don't agree, the franchisor might attempt to appropriate their property (e.g., by fabricating a reason to invoke a termination clause, end a lease, etc.).

This sinister scenario projects that over time, franchisors will build up the fraction of its units that are company owned, especially in the most lucrative locations, such as urban commercial districts. The logic here is that franchisors use franchisees to build the system, then expropriate them. The idea is euphemistically labeled the "redirection of ownership hypothesis." *Fortunately, the evidence does not suggest that this happens systematically*. However, anecdotal evidence and court cases suggest that it does happen occasionally.

Buying back a franchise need not be sinister. It is malevolent when the buyback is below market prices or when termination is based on a pretext. Otherwise, ownership redirection is a calibration, which need not be motivated in a negative manner.

Multi-Unit Franchising: Handicap or Advantage?

Thus far, we have asked whether a franchisor would deal with a manager (company owned) or an individual owner-manager (franchisee). Curiously, many franchisors do neither.[42] Rather than dealing with a different individual for each location, they deal with the same individual or a company for multiple locations. This is *multi-unit franchising*. A number of variations of the idea exist, but the principle is that the manager of a unit is not the owner but an employee of the owner. The franchisee owns more than one unit and must hire its own employees to run the locations.

On the face of it, this system is difficult to rationalize. If the purpose of franchising is to replace lackluster employee managers of an outlet with motivated owner-managers, multi-unit franchising is nonsensical. All it does is put a layer of franchisee management between the franchisor and the person running the outlet. Why would the franchisee do a better job of managing the store manager than would the franchisor?

This issue is little understood at present. Some evidence indicates that franchisors resort to multi-unit franchising to grow faster and to deal with markets they know very little. For example, U.S. franchisors heavily favor multi-unit operators to open opera-tions in Africa and the Middle East.[43] Doing so may simply postpone problems, which is why there is some indication that franchisors that use multi-units fail more frequently than those which insist that franchisees own and manage their stores.[44] This slows growth, but may make the system healthier. In this regard, McDonald's prefers (but does not require) single-unit franchising. Perhaps as a result, it has virtually no presence in Africa.[45]

Before dismissing multi-unit franchising, however, we should examine its positive side.

A multi-unit franchisee commonly creates an organization structure that mimics the franchisor's structure. The multi-unit franchisee also imitates the franchisor's practices. These "mini-hierarchies" simplify things enormously for the franchisor. They allow the franchisor to deal with one organization, the multi-unit franchisee. At the same time, the multi-unit operators replicate the franchisor's management practices and policies in their own organizations. In so doing, multi-unit franchisees reduce the enormous job of managing hundreds of relationships into a more tractable management problem.

An example is Kentucky Fried Chicken (KFC). The franchisor has more than 3,500 U.S. restaurants. Over half of them are owned by . . . 17 people. If KFC can convince only 17 franchisees of the merits of an idea, it influences almost 1,800 restaurants! And if these 17 franchisees accept an idea, they exert a powerful influence on the opinions of the remaining franchisees.

Of course, if mini-hierarchies are to be helpful to the franchisor, it is critical to have their cooperation, to have them be replicates of the franchisor. Many large restaurant chains appeared to have mastered this process, demonstrating that multi-unit franchis-ing can be a viable and valuable strategy. One important feature is that prospective fran-chisees are carefully screened, given a trial period, and observed. If they do not satisfy the franchisor, they are not allowed to open more units.

ONGOING CHALLENGES FACING THE FRANCHISOR

Most of this chapter focuses on the decision to franchise and the strategic choices that follow: the form of the contract, the balancing of company and franchisee units, and the use of multi-unit franchisees. These are policy issues at the corporate level. But what really makes franchising work is the daily behavior of people at the field level. Once a franchisor gets past its founding stages, it often finds that these operating issues over-whelm all others. In this section, we look at some of the challenges a franchisor faces once the system is launched.

Survival

This presumes that franchisors *do* survive past launch! If you are a prospective fran-chisee and you have done your research, you will be acutely aware that this is not so common. Franchisors have very high failure rates. Various estimates have it that some three quarters of the hundreds of franchisors launched in the 1980s in the United States survived fewer than 10 years.[46] For every high-profile franchisor like McDonald's, which makes franchisees wealthy, several business formats and brand names went out of business, stripping franchisees of their wealth. Many of these build up to a substantial size over a number of years before collapsing.

Which franchisors are most likely to survive? Evidence indicates that *success forecasts success*.[47] The older the system and the more units it has, the greater its odds of continuing to age (not going out of business). For a prospective franchisee, these established franchisors may offer the most expensive franchises, but they also carry lower risk of system failure.

Survival is also more likely if the franchisor can attract a *favorable rating from a third party*. For example, in the United States, the magazine *Entrepreneur* surveys franchisors, collecting information from them. The magazine insists on verifying some of the information, then adds in subjective judgment to compile proprietary ratings of hundreds of franchisors. This rating is a good predictor of franchisor survival many years later. Perhaps the magazine's staff is especially prescient. But a more likely explanation is that the ranking acts like a third-party certification, which helps the franchisor be seen as a legitimate player in its operating environment. This, in turn, helps the franchisor acquire the resources needed to survive. This is worth considering: Many entrepreneurs attach a low priority to certification and will not cooperate with certifying bodies.

Gaining and Keeping a Cooperative Atmosphere

A critical issue in franchising is that franchisees see the benefits they derive when the outlet is new. Once it is underway, they may question whether they are receiving continuing value in return for their royalties. Franchising's inherent conflict between being one's own boss and being almost a subsidiary becomes prominent. Franchisors must respond by earning the franchisee's continuing cooperation and goodwill. How can they do so?

Franchisees are more cooperative when they sense there is a solid relationship between them and their franchisor. Strong relationships with franchisors can thrive, even in high-pressure environments, such as many intensely competitive retail industries. Several conditions encourage franchisees to hold feelings of solidarity for the franchisor.[48] Stronger bonds exist when franchisees feel:

1. Their franchisor encourages them to innovate (try new methods, develop ideas, solve problems).
2. A team spirit among themselves, getting on well internally and taking an interest in each other.
3. That good performance is recognized by the franchisor.
4. The franchisor is fair, setting reasonable objectives and not terminating franchisees without good reason.
5. They control their own business, setting standards and making decisions as they see fit.

This last point is paradoxical. By definition, franchisees do *not* control their own businesses. They have sold a substantial amount of autonomy in return for the franchise package. Franchising is inherently asymmetric, with franchisees being highly dependent on the franchisor. Yet, franchisees *are* entrepreneurs and feel the entrepreneur's need to be the boss.[49]

The job of a franchisor's manager is to exert influence without appearing to threaten the franchisee's autonomy. This difficult balancing act requires diplomacy and persuasive skills. Hence, franchisors tend to resolve serious conflicts by searching for integrative, win–win solutions, in which franchisee and franchisor collectively craft a mutually acceptable solution.[50]

A structural source of conflict, built into every franchising system, is that there is a clash of goals between franchisee and franchisor. This clash is due to the difference between what each side puts into the business and what each side gets out of it. For the franchisor, higher sales are always better. Higher sales mean higher variable fees, therefore more income. This in turn enables more promotion, which raises brand equity. More brand equity increases the fixed and variable fees that can be charged and enlarges the pool of prospective store managers and franchisees.

For a franchisee in a given trading area, more sales means more profit—up to a point (see Figure 17.1).[51] The franchisee breaks even at sales of B^*. After B^*, profits rise with sales. But gaining higher sales necessitates adding costs (new units, longer hours,

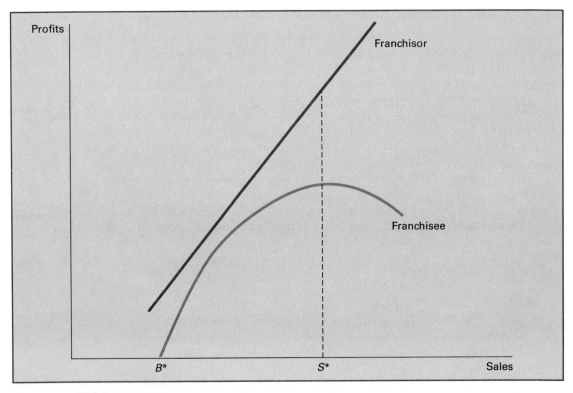

FIGURE 17.1 **Typical Sales-to-Profit Relationships for Franchisors and Franchisees**
Source: Adapted from Carmen and Klein (1986).

and so forth) that are subject to diminishing returns. After the point S^* in sales, profits turn down. Past this point, franchisees and franchisors have incongruent goals, which will create intense conflict.

In short, franchisors seek to maximize sales, whereas franchisees seek to maximize profits. This *incongruity of goals* shows up vividly as chains expand. Seeking to maximize system sales, franchisors are motivated to saturate a market area by authorizing new outlets. In the process, they often cannibalize their own franchisees. This hurts the franchisor's reputation reducing morale. But the financial gains from authorizing new outlets tempt the franchisor to cannibalize anyway.[52] One solution is to offer new sites to existing nearby franchisees or to give them right of first refusal to a new location near them. If there are economies of scale in operating multiple sites, the franchisee is in position to gain them.

On a daily basis, what can franchisors do to gain cooperation? An important tool is to offer genuine assistance—and remind the franchisee of it. Franchisees are more cooperative when they attribute their successes to the aid of the franchisor—and attribute their failures to themselves.[53]

Another factor that helps makes franchising run smoothly is formalization. Being explicit about who is responsible for doing what greatly improves the functioning of a franchise system. This increases coordination and reduces resentment.[54]

SUMMARY

Franchising a business format is a way to grow quickly while investing in building brand equity. For the franchisee, it is a system for gaining assistance and reducing risk. By paying fees, entrepreneurs purchase the services of a corporate backer, a coach, a problem solver, and an enforcement agency, who polices the way the brand is presented. For the franchisor, the system is a way to acquire capital and management quickly, and to harness the motivation and capability of an entrepreneur.[55] For businesses that can be put into a format and transmitted, franchising is an excellent solution to the problems of monitoring employee managers.

But part of the codification of the formula is writing a complex contract specifying rights and duties. It is crafted to give both sides good reason to abide by their agreement. Many franchisors price their franchises lower than the market will bear. In so doing, they increase the applicant pool and give their franchisees a reason—the profit motive—to stay in the business. They also signal, via lower lump-sum entry fees, that they do not intend to take the franchisees' money and fail to provide promised services. But franchisors frequently bind their franchisees with clauses that award control of the property to the franchisor. And they limit their ability to terminate their business easily. These contracts vary surprisingly little over franchisees and over time in a franchise system. They serve to give the franchisor a means to punish noncompliance, which not only allows the protection of brand equity but also reinforces the franchisee's dependence on the franchisor. Part of that dependence rests on the franchisee's heavy investment in franchise-specific assets, which have a low resale value outside the business. Franchisors cannot rely entirely on their contracts to run the system. They must also develop a reputation for fair dealings with their franchised channel. This requires the franchisor not to exploit the franchisees' dependence opportunistically.

Franchise systems typically mix company-owned and franchised outlets. This gives the franchisor a laboratory and a classroom to train personnel, try out ideas, and refine the business format. Dual or plural systems also permit the franchisor to achieve synergies between the two sides of its business. This can be achieved by permitting multi-unit franchising but encouraging the owners to build minihierarchies to mimic the franchisor. Plural forms permit the franchisor to collect, adapt, and spread new products and practices. Plural forms can ensure vigorous debate and build commitment to new initiatives. And some degree of rivalry motivates both sides of the operation to improve.

Failure rates of franchisors are very high. Survival becomes more likely as a system grows, ages, and acquires certification by third parties. Part of the challenge of aging is retaining the franchisees' cooperation. This is enhanced by building a sense of solidarity, seeking win–win solutions to major conflicts, offering genuine assistance, and formalizing roles and duties. But conflict is inevitable, in part because of a built-in clash of goals. Franchisees pursue profit, franchisors pursue sales, and the two goals collide as operations become large. In particular, franchisors are tempted to saturate markets and cannibalize their own franchisees.

The complexity and risk of franchising should lead channel managers to consider other solutions. Frequently, the level of control afforded by franchising is simply not necessary. Other means are available to achieve cooperation. Nonetheless, franchising affords a very high level of control. It is an effective way to create incentives to perform tasks according to a standard, without needing to monitor operations constantly.

By the 1970s, it was clear that franchising had become a permanent force, not just a fad, in structuring distribution channels in the United States. Today, it is clear that the same is true worldwide. Franchising has become an institution so stable and so pervasive that franchising is the single most common way to become an entrepreneur in North America, Europe, and Asia.[56] The dynamism of this channel institution is remarkable. Franchising is an institution that deserves serious consideration by any manager in any marketing channel.

Discussion Questions

1. Write a plan for starting your own franchising operation. What would be the essential elements of the plan? What specific points would you include in the contractual arrangement you establish with your franchisees?

2. In 1988, Vidal Herrera founded a U.S. company, Autopsy/Post Services, to perform autopsies in Los Angeles.[57] An autopsy is a medical examination of a corpse, including dissection and tests of tissue and body fluids. The purpose is to ascertain the cause of death. Autopsy/Post Services will autopsy a body for a flat $2,000, more if a body has been exhumed (removed from burial) or if extra tests are ordered. Since 1988, Herrera's business has grown larger than he can handle.

   Clients include insurance companies, government bodies (who have the right to demand autopsies when the cause of death is unknown or may be criminal), family members, and medical providers such as hospitals. An autopsy is requested to discover or to verify a cause of death, and is considered good medical practice. Autopsies contribute to medical research. Many medical conditions (such as toxic shock syndrome and congenital heart disease) were discovered by autopsy, permitting researchers to develop treatments.

Unfortunately, they can be expensive, from several hundred to several thousand dollars. And the logical party to suggest an autopsy is the provider of medical care. But the autopsy's results may disagree with the provider's estimation of the cause of death. (One study shows autopsies disagree with the attending physician almost half the time.) Thus, the provider may hesitate to suggest an autopsy. Autopsies are frequently requested by someone who suspects negligence or other malpractice or who wishes to have tests performed (such as genetic tests) to answer a troubling question.

They are being performed at a declining rate in the United States (and in the world), but Vidal Herrera nonetheless believes the market potential is considerable. Herrera plans to franchise Autopsy/Post Services to achieve rapid growth. If you were medically qualified, would you buy a franchise from him? What factors would you consider? How would you evaluate his offer? What would make you inclined to sign onto his franchise system? What would cause you to refuse?

3. In what ways does a franchise contract motivate a franchisee to cooperate with the franchisor? What are the positive and negative aspects of these contracts from the franchisee's viewpoint? From the franchisor's viewpoint? Now turn the question around. In what ways does a franchise contract motivate a franchisor to treat franchisees fairly?

4. In the McDonald's example, trace the ways in which franchisee and franchisor influence each other. Who has the greater power and why?

5. "The franchisor wants to own the very best locations. These are money makers, and their prime locations make them an advertisement for the brand. They have to be just perfect." Debate this statement.

Notes

1. Spelling note: *Franchisor* is U.S. English, whereas *franchiser* is British English. This textbook adopts the U.S. convention, but many documents, particularly in Europe, specify "franchiser."

2. Jeffrey L. Bradach, *Franchise Organisations* (Boston: Harvard Business School Press, 1998).

3. Lawrence S. Welch, "Diffusion of Franchise System Use in International Operations," *International Marketing Review*, 6, no. 5 (1989), pp. 7–19.

4. Reported as an interesting factoid in the "Numbers" regular feature of *Time*, August 16, 1999, p. 8.

5. This information is drawn from multiple sources: Patrick J. Kaufmann and Francine Lafontaine, "Costs of Control: The Source of Economic Rents for McDonald's Franchisees," *Journal of Law and Economics,* 36 (October 1994), pp. 417–53; John F. Love, *McDonald's: Behind the Golden Arches* (New York: Bantam Books, 1986); Eric Wattenz, "La Machine McDonald's," *Capital,* 96 (September 1999), pp. 48–69.

6. Werner J. Reinartz and V. Kumar, "Store-, Market-, and Consumer-Characteristics: The Drivers of Store Performance," *Marketing Letters*, 10, no. 1 (1999), pp. 5–22.

7. James G. Combs and David J. Ketchen, "Can Capital Scarcity Help Agency Theory Explain Franchising? Revisiting the Capital Scarcity Hypothesis," *Academy of Management Journal*, 42, no. 2 (1999), pp. 198–207.

8. Seth W. Norton, "An Empirical Look at Franchising as an Organizational Form," *Journal of Business,* 61, no. 2 (1988), pp. 197–218.

9. Scott A. Shane, "Hybrid Organizational Arrangements and Their Implications for Firm Growth and Survival: A Study of New Franchisors," *Academy of Management Journal*, 39, no. 1 (1996), pp. 216–34.

10. Rajiv P. Dant, "Motivation for Franchising: Rhetoric versus Reality," *International Small Business Journal*, 14 (winter 1995), pp. 10–32.

11. Richard Martin, "East Eats West: Southeast Asian Nations Embrace American Restaurant Brands," *Nation's Restaurant News*, June 3, 1996, pp. 1–3.

12. Alanson P. Minkler, "Why Firms Franchise: A Search Cost Theory," *Journal of Institutional and Theoretical Economics*, 148, no. 1 (1992), pp. 240–49.

13. Yves Aoulou and Olivia Bassi, "Une Opportunité de Cassière à Saisir," *LSA* (1999), pp. 42–47.

14. "Le Jardinier Truffaut a la Main Verte," *Capital,* July 1999, pp. 44–45.

15. "Buffalo Grill: Le Cow-Boy Est Un Radin," *L'Essential du Management,* July 1999, pp. 20–24.

16. Alessandro Baroncelli and Angelo Manaresi, "Franchising as a Form of Divestiture: An Italian Study," *Industrial Marketing Management,* 26, no. 1 (1997), pp. 223–35.

17. Alfred D. Chandler, *The Visible Hand: The Managerial Revolution in American Business* (Cambridge, MA: Belknap Press, 1977).

18. *Goodyear: The Aquatred Launch,* Harvard Business School, Case No. 9-594-106, Rev. December 2, 1993, p. 11; quote from William T. Ross, "Managing Marketing Channel Relationships," Marketing Science Institute Working Paper Series, Report No. 85–105 (Cambridge, MA: Marketing Science Institute, 1985), p. 8.

19. "Franchise Rule Exemption for Wholesale Grocers Announced by Federal Trade Commission," *FTC News Note,* 25, no. 83 (March 18, 1983), p. 3.

20. European Commission, *Green Paper on Vertical Restraints in EU Competition Policy,* Brussels, Directorate General for Competition, 1997, p. 44. Available at http://europa.eu.int/en/comm/dg04/dg04home.htm.

21. Anthony W. Dnes, "A Case-Study Analysis of Franchise Contracts," *Journal of Legal Studies,* 22 (June 1993), pp. 367–93. This reference is the basis for much of this section and the source of comparative statements about franchising in the United Kingdom.

22. Benjamin Klein, "The Economics of Franchise Contracts," *Journal of Corporate Finance,* 2, no. 1 (1995), pp. 9–37.

23. Deepak Agrawal and Rajiv Lal, "Contractual Arrangements in Franchising: An Empirical Investigation," *Journal of Marketing Research,* 32 (May 1995), pp. 213–21.

24. Dnes, "A Case-Study Analysis of Franchise Contracts."

25. Rajiv Lal, "Improving Channel Coordination through Franchising," *Marketing Science,* 9, no. 4 (1990), pp. 299–318.

26. The Economist Intelligence Unit, "Retail Franchising in France," *EIU Marketing in Europe,* December 1995, pp. 86–104.

27. Little if anything indicates that royalty rates and fixed fees really are negatively correlated in practice. This may be because the nonrecoverable part of the initial investment complements the fixed fee and is usually overlooked.

28. Dnes ("A Case-Study Analysis of Franchise Contracts") arrived at this conclusion by detailed examination of franchise contracts and by interviewing both franchisors and their franchisees. His description of contracts is particularly interesting because franchise contracts in the United Kingdom (and in Europe) are much less regulated

than in the United States. This gives Dnes the ability to observe what both sides do under free choice.

29. Patrick J. Kaufmann and Francine Lafontaine, "Costs of Control: The Source of Economic Rents for McDonald's Franchisees," *Journal of Law and Economics,* 36 (October 1994), pp. 417–53.

30. Benjamin Klein, "Transaction Cost Determinants of "Unfair" Contractual Arrangements," *Borderlines of Law and Economic Theory,* 70, no. 2 (1980), pp. 356–62.

31. Dnes ("A Case-Study Analysis of Franchise Contracts") gives the example of Ford, which sells cars through repair garages (a common practice in Europe). Ford has a long queue of garages ready to take up a franchise and does not find it necessary to lock up any given location. Mobiletuning also eschews leasing. This is a van-based car tuning franchise: Because the van comes to the client, the location of the franchisee is of little relevance.

32. Francine Lafontaine and Kathryn L. Shaw, "Franchising Growth and Franchisor Entry and Exit in the U.S. Market: Myth and Reality," *Journal of Business Venturing,* 13, no. 1 (1998), pp. 95–112.

33. Ibid.

34. Mick Carney and Eric Gedajlovic, "Vertical Integration in Franchise Systems: Agency Theory and Resource Explanations," *Strategic Management Journal,* 12, no. 1 (1991), pp. 607–29.

35. James A. Brickley and Frederick H. Dark, "The Choice of Organisational Form: The Case of Franchising," *Journal of Financial Economics,* 18 (1987), pp. 401–20.

36. Baroncelli and Manaresi, "Franchising as a Form of Divestiture."

37. Francine Lafontaine and Patrick J. Kaufman, "The Evolution of Ownership Patterns in Franchise Systems," *Journal of Retailing,* 70, no. 2 (1994), pp. 97–113.

38. Shane, "Hybrid Organizational Arrangements."

39. Jeffrey L. Bradach, "Using the Plural Form in the Management of Restaurant Chains," *Administrative Science Quarterly,* 42 (June 1997), pp. 276–303. This source is the basis for this section and is an excellent guide to the working operations of large chain franchisors.

40. "In the Pink," *The Economist,* 351 (August 7, 1999), pp. 30–31.

41. This discussion is based on Rajiv P. Dant, Audehesh K. Paswan, and Patrick J. Kaufman, "What We Know About Ownership Redirection in Franchising: A Meta-Analysis," *Journal of Retailing,* 72, no. 4 (1996), pp. 429–44.

42. Patrick J. Kaufmann and Rajiv Dant, "Multi-Unit Franchising: Growth and Management Issues," *Journal of Business Venturing,* 11, no. 1 (1996), pp. 343–58.

43. Rajiv P. Dant and Nada I. Nasr, "Control Techniques and Upward Flow of Information in Franchising in Distant

Markets: Conceptualisation and Preliminary Evidence," *Journal of Business Venturing,* 13, no. 1 (1998), pp. 3–28.

44. Scott A. Shane, "Making New Franchise Systems Work," *Strategic Management Journal,* 19, no. 1 (1998), pp. 697–707.

45. "Through a Glass, Drunkenly," *The Economist,* May 8, 1999, p. 90.

46. Shane, "Hybrid Organizational Arrangements"; Lafontaine (1992).

47. Scott Shane and Maw-Der Foo, "New Firm Survival: Institutional Explanations for New Franchisor Mortality," *Management Science,* 45 (February 1999), pp. 142–59.

48. David Strutton, Lou E. Pelton, and James R. Lumpkin, "Psychological Climate in Franchising System Channels and Franchisor–Franchisee Solidarity," *Journal of Business Research,* 34, no. 1 (1995), pp. 81–91.

49. Rajiv P. Dant and Gregory T. Gundlach, "The Challenge of Autonomy and Dependence in Franchised Channels of Distribution," *Journal of Business Venturing,* 14, no. 1 (1998), pp. 35–67.

50. Rajiv P. Dant and Patrick L. Schul, "Conflict Resolution Processes in Contractual Channels of Distribution," *Journal of Marketing,* 56 (January 1992), pp. 38–54.

51. James M. Carmen and Thomas A. Klein, "Power, Property, and Performance in Franchising," *Research in Marketing,* 8 (1986), pp. 71–130.

52. Patrick J. Kaufmann and V. Kasturi Rangan, "A Model for Managing System Conflict During Franchise Expansion," *Journal of Retailing,* 66, no. 2 (1990), pp. 155–73.

53. Punam Anand and Louis W. Stern, "A Sociopsychological Explanation for Why Marketing Channel Members Relinquish Control," *Journal of Marketing Research,* 22 (November 1985), pp. 365–76.

54. Robert Dahlstrom and Arne Nygaard, "An Empirical Investigation of Ex Post Transaction Costs in Franchised Distribution Channels," *Journal of Marketing Research,* 36 (May 1999), pp. 160–70.

55. Paul H. Rubin, *Managing Business Transactions* (New York: Free Press, 1990).

56. "The Tiger and the Tech," *The Economist,* February 5, 2000, pp. 70–72.

57. "Autopsies—Dial One Yourself," *The Economist,* 351 (1999), p. 45.

Company Index

Note: Locators in *italics* indicate display additional display material; "n" indicates note

Name Index

"n" indicates note

A

Abcede, Angel, 526n18
Abelson, Reed, 76n3, 108n5
Achrol, Ravi S., 156n3–4, 156n8
Agrawal, Deepak, 564n23
Alden, Edward, 127n6
Alderson, Wroe, 4, 18n6, 27n3
Allen, Helen, 472n5
Allstadt, Kristin, 473n25, 473n30, 473n33, 474n45
Alvarado, Ursula Y., 128n8, 156n5
Anand, Punam, 565n53
Anderson, Erin, 197n11, 197n21, 197n24, 197n35, 197n39,198n40, 233n22, 233n25, 234n39, 275n45, 275n50, 276n72, 312n6, 313n14, 313n16, 345n12, 346n16–17, 346n19, 346n21, 501n24
Anderson, James C., 75n2, 107n4, 234n49, 274n11, 345n10, 346n41, 501n8
Angelmar, Reinhard, 234n52
Aoulou, Yves, 563n13
Areeda, Phillip, 384n6, 384n11, 386n66
Ariano, Alexis, 157n14
Armour, Philip, 182
Arndt, Michael, 385n17
Assmus, Gert, 275n40
Atkinson, Helen, 157n13
Avery, Susan, 75n2, 107n4

B

Baden, J., 501n10
Baker, Jenny, 526n25
Baker, Thomas L., 345n10
Balachandran, Bala, 40n5
Baljko, Jennifer L., 526n16
Ball, Jeffrey, 474n43
Bank, David, 386n71
Barney, Jay B., 198n44
Baron, David P., 158n19
Baroncelli, Alessandro, 564n16, 564n36

Barr, Kevin, 526n31
Barrett, Paul M., 384n16, 387n80
Barrett, William P., 75n3, 108n5
Barry, Curt, 472n9
Bartlett, Richard, 472n18, 473n20
Bassi, Olivia, 563n13
Baumgartner, Peter, 196n4
Beam, Chris, 234n47
Beaudry, Laura M, 472n3, 472n7
Beck, Ernest, 40n6
Beck, Richard, 473n20
Bedi, Subjash, 40n4
Berg, Eric, 28n14
Bergen, Mark, 197n18, 197n38, 274n13, 275n30, 275n44, 313n33, 313n40, 314n45, 384n2
Berman, Dennis, 473n20
Bernstein, Andy, 28n12
Betts, Paul, 76n8
Bialobos, Chantal, 275n27, 312n7, 312n11
Bielinski, Donald, 51, 75n2
Bird, Laura, 472n12
Biscard, Daniel, 234n44
Blair, Roger D., 385n18, 385n20
Block, Sandra, 76n3, 108n5
Bloom, Paul N., 385n39, 385n46
Boberg, Kevin, 526n21
Boisseau, Charles, 157n14
Bolton, Patrick, 312n2
Bonanno, Giacomo, 312n2
Bonazza, Patrick, 198n41–42
Bongiorno, Lori, 276n62
Bounds, Wendy, 386n59, 387n84
Boyle, Brett F., 235n56
Bradach, Jeffrey L., 276n69, 563n2, 564n39
Brannigan, Martha, 385n46
Breit, William, 312n12
Brickleu, James A., 564n35
Brinkley, Joel, 387n85
Briody, Dan, 128n13
Broder, John M., 387n85
Brooker, Katrina, 275n37
Brown, Doreen L., 76n8

Brown, Eryn, 233n19
Brown, James R., 233n10, 234n33, 274n5, 274n18
Bryant, Adam, 157n14
Bryceland, Kristen, 157n11
Buchanan, Lauranne, 234n35, 313n28
Bucklin, Christine B., 275n29
Bucklin, Louis P., 40n1, 40n3, 58, 59, 76n4, 148, 158n15–17
Bulkeley, William M., 387n85
Bumstead, Jon, 27n8
Bunn, Dina, 157n14
Burrows, Peter, 128n13
Burton, Thomas M., 385n34, 387n93
Busch, August, 266
Butaney, Gul, 313n34
Buzzell, Robert D., 275n53

C

Cadotte, Ernest R., 41n8
Calvert, Jacques, 299
Cannon, Joseph P., 385n46
Cantin, Anne, 313n17
Carmen, James M., 565n51
Carmichael, Trent, 75n3, 107n5
Carne, Simon, 276n60
Carney, Mick, 564n34
Carver, Todd B., 276n58
Celly, Kirti Sawhney, 313n23
Cespedes, Frank V., 196n10, 274n25, 275n43, 313n14
Champion, David, 275n39
Chandler, Alfred D., 197n34, 474n43, 564n17
Chandon, Pierre, 526n27
Chapdelaine, Sophie, 275n26, 312n10
Charron, Heather, 27n8
Chatterjee, Sharmila C., 313n14
Chen, Xiao-Ping, 274n4
Choi, Audrey, 313n32
Christian, Nichole M., 313n32
Chu, Woosik, 234n28, 312n8
Chu, Wujin, 234n28, 312n8, 385n41

Subject Index

Note: locators in *italics* indicate additional display material; "n" indicates note